Burial and social change in first-millennium BC Italy: approaching social agents

Gender, personhood and marginality

edited by

Elisa Perego and Rafael Scopacasa

OXBOW | books

Oxford & Philadelphia

Published in the United Kingdom in 2016 by
OXBOW BOOKS
The Old Music Hall, 106–108 Cowley Road, Oxford OX4 1JE

and in the United States by
OXBOW BOOKS
1950 Lawrence Road, Havertown, PA 19083

© Oxbow Books and the individual contributors 2016

Paperback Edition: ISBN 978-1-78570-184-9
Digital Edition: ISBN 978-1-78570-185-6 (epub)

A CIP record for this book is available from the British Library

Library of Congress Cataloging-in-Publication Data

Names: Perego, Elisa, 1978- editor of compilation. | Scopacasa, Rafael,
    editor of compilation.
Title: Burial and social change in first-millennium BC Italy : approaching
    social agents : gender, personhood and marginality / edited by Elisa
    Perego and Rafael Scopacasa.
Description: Oxford ; Philadelphia : Oxbow Books, 2016. | Includes
    bibliographical references and index.
Identifiers: LCCN 2016022503 (print) | LCCN 2016028999 (ebook) | ISBN
    9781785701849 (paperback) | ISBN 9781785701856 (ePub) | ISBN 9781785701856
    (epub) | ISBN 9781785701863 (mobi) | ISBN 9781785701870 (pdf)
Subjects: LCSH: Italy--History--To 476--Congresses. |
    Italy--Antiquities--Congresses. | Burial--Italy--History--To
    1500--Congresses. | Funeral rites and ceremonies,
    Ancient--Italy--History--Congresses. | Tombs--Italy--History--To
    1500--Congresses. | Social change--Italy--History--To 1500--Congresses. |
    Sex role--Italy--History--To 1500--Congresses. |
    Individuality--Italy--History--To 1500--Congresses. | Marginality,
    Social--Italy--History--To 1500--Congresses. | Social
    archaeology--Italy--Congresses.
Classification: LCC DG221.5 .B87 2016 (print) | LCC DG221.5 (ebook) | DDC
    363/.93093709014--dc23
LC record available at https://lccn.loc.gov/2016022503

Printed in Malta by Gutenberg Press

For a complete list of Oxbow titles, please contact:

UNITED KINGDOM
Oxbow Books
Telephone (01865) 241249, Fax (01865) 794449
Email: oxbow@oxbowbooks.com
www.oxbowbooks.com

UNITED STATES OF AMERICA
Oxbow Books
Telephone (800) 791-9354, Fax (610) 853-9146
Email: queries@casemateacademic.com
www.casemateacademic.com/oxbow

Oxbow Books is part of the Casemate Group

Contents

Section 2: Identities on the fringe

Finale

Preface and acknowledgements

This book has its origins in the international workshop 'Burial and Social Change in Ancient Italy, ninth–fifth century BC: Approaching Social Agents', held at the British School at Rome on 7–8 June 2011. The aim of the workshop was to bring together a range of both early career and more senior scholars working on ancient Italy to discuss new approaches to archaeological mortuary evidence, and construct innovative frameworks for investigating social complexity. Another aim was to gather speakers working on pre-Roman Italy either in Italy itself or in Anglophone countries in order to foster collaborations and dialogue between researchers educated in different scholarly traditions. After reviewing the developments of our work after a few years, in the wake of the publication of this volume, we believe that we were able to fulfil these aims, as the workshop contributed to cement research collaborations that continue to this day, and to promote the spread of new research topics in Italian archaeology, such as that of social marginality. A follow-up of the 'Burial and Social Change' workshop, the international symposium 'Collapse or Survival? Micro-dynamics of Crisis, Change and Socio-political Endurance in the First-millennium BC Central Mediterranean', was co-organized by the editors of this volume, in collaboration with Silvia Amicone (UCL), at the British School at Rome in June 2014. Among other topics, the 'Collapse or Survival' workshop addressed the consequences of micro-scale phenomena of crisis and collapse on marginal social agents and peripheral sub-regions of the ancient Mediterranean basin.

Hence, the editors wish to warmly thank the British School at Rome and its Director, Prof. Christopher Smith, for hosting and supporting both symposia. We also acknowledge the staff at the British School at Rome for their wonderful assistance in the practical organization of the workshops, as well as the participants in both events for the lively and challenging discussion promoted by everyone. Our gratitude also goes to: the anonymous peer-reviewers who greatly helped us to improve this volume; Owain Morris and Peter Fane-Saunders for their careful proof-reading of the book proposal that was originally submitted to the publisher; the staff at Oxbow Books for their support throughout the publication process; and Veronica Tamorri for revising some chapters. The revision of chapters written by scholars whose first language is not English was carried out by Elisa Perego, Rafael Scopacasa and some anonymous reviewers, whom the editors acknowledge for their helpfulness. Elisa Perego worked with Rafael Scopacasa on the final proof-reading and copy-editing of the volume while holding a Ralegh Radford Rome Fellowship at the British School at Rome in 2013–2014 and an Honorary Research Associate position at the Institute of Archaeology, University College London, in 2013–2016; Rafael Scopacasa held an honorary fellowship at the University of Exeter: all these institutions are acknowledged for their support, which included admission to their libraries and IT facilities.

While not all the participants in the 'Burial and Social Change' workshop published their original paper in this volume, other contributions were specifically commissioned to complement the original line-up of contributors. We wish to thank both these authors and the original speakers in the symposium – as well Oxbow Books – for their interest in this initiative.

Despite our primary focus on Italian material culture, we see this volume as a contribution towards strengthening the interdisciplinary dialogues with cognate disciplines such as anthropology and ancient history. We hope that our investigation of specific social phenomena and ritual practices underlying change in increasingly complex communities will attract the attention of scholars studying the development of social complexity in any time-span and region. We have also made an effort to ensure that this book is accessible to undergraduate students and non-academic practitioners in archaeology, who are searching for an articulated but easily understandable analysis of mortuary behaviour and aspects of archaeological theory.

List of contributors

MARIASSUNTA CUOZZO
is Associate Professor at the Università degli Studi del Molise, Dipartimento di Scienze Umanistiche Sociali e della Formazione. She is the author of several publications on burial practice in Iron Age, Orientalizing and Archaic Campania, including the monograph *Reinventando la Tradizione: Immaginario Sociale, Ideologie, e Rappresentazione nelle Necropoli Orientalizzanti di Pontecagnano* (Paestum 2003).

GIORGIA DI LORENZO
obtained her first degree in Archaeology (Etruscology and Italic Archaeology) from the Università degli Studi di Napoli L'Orientale and her *Diploma di Specializzazione* in Greek Archaeology from the Università degli Studi di Pisa. Giorgia undertook her PhD in Archaeology jointly at the Universitad Autonoma de Madrid and the Università degli Studi di Napoli L'Orientale. She has been involved in the study of Iron Age Verucchio (RN) since 2008 and is the author or co-author of several publications on the funerary ritual at this key archaeological site.

AMALIA FAUSTOFERRI
is an archaeologist based at the *Soprintendenza per i Beni Archeologici dell'Abruzzo* (Chieti). She studied at the Università degli Studi di Perugia, where she graduated with a dissertation on the Throne of Bathykles at Amyklai. She then obtained a degree in Archaeological Disciplines at the Università degli Studi di Urbino. Having held several scholarships (including the DAAD and the Fulbright), she developed research projects on iconography, iconology and artefacts from Archaic Greece. Since 1992 she has been working at the *Soprintendenza per i Beni Archeologici dell'Abruzzo*, where she has developed several research projects, including the Sangro Valley Project, begun in 1994 with John Lloyd and Gary Lock of the University of Oxford. More recently her research interests have included cult and funerary practice in Iron Age Abruzzo; she co-edited the volume *I Luoghi degli Dei: Sacro e Natura nell'Abruzzo Italico* (Chieti 1997).

CRISTIANO IAIA
is an Italian archaeologist whose main area of specialization is the later prehistory of Europe. Currently a Marie Skłodowska-Curie Fellow at the University of Newcastle Upon Tyne, Cristiano has also been a Temporary Research Fellow at the Antiquity Science Department of the Sapienza Università di Roma and taught Prehistory and Protohistory at the Università degli Studi di Modena e Reggio Emilia (2008–2011) and the Università degli Studi della Tuscia, Viterbo (2011–2012). Cristiano is the author of two monographs and about 50 papers that address a wide range of topics related to the Italian Bronze and Iron Ages. His current research project focuses on craft production, with particular regard to copper-based metallurgy and its social implications.

LISA MANZOLI
is an Italian archaeologist who graduated in Ancient History at the Università degli Studi di Bologna in 2005, with a dissertation on the Etruscan settlement of Marzabotto (BO). In 2009 she obtained her *Diploma di Specializzazione* in Archaeology from the same university with a thesis on Verucchio (RN). Lisa has worked as a museum operator, guide and field archaeologist under the scientific direction of the *Soprintendenza per i Beni Archeologici dell'Emilia Romagna*; furthermore, she contributes to projects

aiming at the study and publication of Iron Age archaeological contexts. Lisa is the co-author of several publications and international presentations focusing on the cemeteries of Verucchio and their funerary rite.

OWAIN MORRIS
is currently completing his PhD on Iron Age Campania at Birkbeck, the University of London. He has worked within the Departments of Greece and Rome and Coins and Medals at the British Museum, and taught Greek Archaeology at Birkbeck. His research interests include Greek Archaeology from the Iron Age to Hellenistic periods. He has a particular interest in colonization, mobility and networks in the western Mediterranean.

CLAUDIO NEGRINI
is an Italian archaeologist based at the Institut für Alte Geschichte und Altertumskunde, Payirologie und Epigraphik, Universität Wien. He obtained his first degree in Classics and Archaeology from the Università degli Studi di Bologna, where he also completed his *Diploma di Specializzazione* in Etruscan and Italic Archaeology in 2005. Claudio has also worked as an archaeologist, field archaeologist, trench supervisor and field director since the 1990s. He is also the author or co-author of several articles focusing on Iron Age Italy and Verucchio.

EÓIN O'DONOGHUE
is a University Fellow in Classics at the National University of Ireland, Galway. His research focuses on gender and social identities in pre-Roman Italy. Current writing projects include a monograph on Etruscan gender identity, the subject of his doctoral dissertation. He works on the excavation project of the Etruscan site of Poggio Civitate (Murlo).

ELISA PEREGO
is an Honorary Research Associate at the Institute of Archaeology, University College London, where she completed her PhD in 2012. In 2013–2014 she was the Ralegh Radford Rome Fellow at the British School at Rome, where she researched the construction of social marginality and inequality in late prehistoric Italy. Her main research interests include Italy and the central Mediterranean between the Bronze Age and the early Roman period, the rise of social complexity, collapse and crisis in the ancient world and archaeological theory. Her publications include the volume *Food and Drink in Archaeology 3* (Totnes 2012, co-edited with D. Collard and J. Morris) and several articles focusing on the Veneto region, food consumption, gender, personhood, social exclusion, ritual and the socio-political development of Italy in late prehistory.

PAOLA POLI
is an Italian archaeologist who graduated in Classics and Archaeology at the Università degli Studi di Bologna, with a dissertation focusing on the Etruscan settlement of Marzabotto (BO). The thesis deriving from her *Diploma di Specializzazione* in Archaeology – obtained from the same university – was on Verucchio (RN). As a freelance archaeologist, museum operator and tutor, Paola has joined and coordinated numerous excavation campaigns held under the scientific direction of the *Soprintendenza per i Beni Archeologici dell'Emilia Romagna* and has been involved in the organization of different museum activities and the teaching of archaeology at different levels; she also contributes to projects aiming at the study and publication of Early Iron Age archaeological contexts. Paola is the author or co-author of over 20 publications and international presentations in Italic Archaeology. Presently, she is also museum conservator at MUV, *Museo della Civiltà Villanoviana*, Castenaso (BO).

ULLA RAJALA

is an archaeologist specialized in landscape archaeology, settlement patterns, funerary customs and GIS in central Italy. She did her *Magister Philosophiciae* Degree in Finland, M.A. in Landscape Archaeology at Bristol and PhD at Cambridge. She participated in the Tiber Valley Project of the British School at Rome and has published a series of articles on the Nepi Survey Project and "Remembering the Dead" excavations at Crustumerium. Ulla is a docent at the University of Oulu in Finland, is affiliated with the McDonald Institute for Archaeological Research at Cambridge and currently works as a researcher at the Department of Archaeology and Classical Studies at the Stockholm University in Sweden.

ELENA RODRIGUEZ

graduated in Classics and Archaeology at the Università degli Studi di Bologna in 2000. In 2010, she was awarded her *Diploma di Specializzazione* in Archaeology by the Università Cattolica del Sacro Cuore di Milano, while in 2011 she undertook an M.A. in Museum Studies at the Università di Roma Tre. Elena has been working as a field archaeologist, curator, research archaeologist and consultant since 1997; her main publications focus on pre-Roman and Roman Italy.

RAFAEL SCOPACASA

teaches Ancient History at the University of Minas Gerais (UFMG), and is an Honorary Research Fellow at the University of Exeter, where he got his PhD in 2010. He was the Ralegh Radford Rome Scholar at the British School at Rome in 2010–2011. Among his most recent publications is a book on *Ancient Samnium: Settlement, Culture and Identity between History and Archaeology* (Oxford, 2015). He is interested in bringing together historical, epigraphic and archaeological evidence as a means of constructing alternative histories of pre-Imperial Italy.

LUCY SHIPLEY

completed her doctorate at the University of Southampton. She is primarily interested in the social archaeology of Etruria, a subject she pursued through an analysis of Archaic period ceramic morphology and decoration in her doctoral thesis. Lucy is also interested in the use of ceramics in Etruscan funerary practice, and exploring relationships between the changing function of ceramics in burials and long-term social change. Her monograph *Experiencing Etruscan Pots: Ceramics, Bodies and Images in Etruria* has been published in 2015 by Archaeopress.

PATRIZIA VON ELES

graduated in Classics and Archaeology at the Sapienza Università di Roma in 1969. In 1970 and 1971, she attended postgraduate courses at the *Scuola Nazionale di Archeologia* in Rome. Patrizia has worked as a research archaeologist, field archaeologist and field director since 1971, initially as an external collaborator at the Pigorini Museum of Rome, then as a prehistoric archaeologist at the *Soprintendenza per i Beni Archeologici dell'Emilia Romagna*. In 1992 Patrizia was appointed as the Scientific Director of the Archaeological Museum in Verucchio and since then has been Manager and Coordinator of the International Project for the study and publication of the Villanovan finds from the Verucchio cemeteries. Patrizia's publications include the *Praehistorische Bronzefunde* volume on northern Italian Fibulae (München 1984) as well as numerous books and articles on the Italian Iron Age, with a focus on Emilia Romagna. Her edited volumes include *Guerriero e Sacerdote. Autorità e Comunità nell'Età del Ferro a Verucchio. La Tomba del Trono* (Firenze 2002), *La Ritualità Funeraria nell'Età del Ferro Italiana* (Pisa 2006) and *Le Ore e i Giorni delle Donne. Dalla Quotidianità alla Sacralità* (Verucchio 2007).

LORENZO ZAMBONI

is a post-doctoral researcher in Archaeology at the Università degli Studi di Pavia, where he also completed his doctoral degree in 2013. His PhD dissertation, entitled *Spina. Gli Scavi in Abitato 1977-1981 e i Materiali di Età Arcaica e Classica*, investigates the excavations and finds from the ancient Greek and Etruscan Adriatic hub of Spina (RO). His monograph *Spina Città Liquida* has been recently published in the Zürcher Archäologische Forschungen (Verlag Marie Leidorf). For his *Diploma di Specializzazione* in Archaeology at the Università degli Studi di Milano (2007–2010), Lorenzo studied all the sixth-century BC funerary contexts of western Emilia. Previously, his B.A. and M.A. dissertations focused on the Etruscan rural settlements and material culture of the Po Plain. Another research topic concerns deviant burials in northern Italy during the Bronze and Iron Age.

VERA ZANONI
received her first degree in Classics and Etruscan Archaeology by the Università degli Studi di Milano (2003), where she also completed her *Diploma di Specializzazione* in Classical Archaeology in 2006 and a course in Palaepathology in 2009. In 2010 she was awarded a PhD in Mediterranean Archaeology by the Università degli Studi di Pavia. Vera has collaborated with the Università degli Studi di Pavia and is the author of several articles focusing on the funerary ritual of late prehistoric Italy. Her monograph *Out of Place. Human Skeletal Remains from Non-Funerary Contexts: Northern Italy during the 1st Millennium BC* was published by Archaeopress in 2011.

Introduction

Burial and social change in first-millennium BC Italy: an agent-focused approach

Elisa Perego and Rafael Scopacasa

Peopling social transformation

In the first millennium BC, communities in Italy underwent crucial transformations which scholars have often subsumed under the heading of 'state formation', namely increased social stratification, the centralization of political power and in some cases urbanization (e.g. Balista and Ruta Serafini 2004; Bartoloni 2006; Bradley 2000; Capuis 1998–1999; 2009; Carandini 2006; 2007; Guidi 2006; 2010; Herring and Lomas 2000; Iaia 1999; Mandolesi 1999; Pacciarelli 1991; 2001; Riva 2010; Scopacasa 2015; Smith 1996; 2005; Terrenato and Haggis 2011; *cf.* also Ampolo 2013 for a review of the Roman case). Most of the research developed on this topic, and especially the studies produced by scholars working in Italy, tend to approach the phenomenon of state formation and social change in view of its relation to specific territorial dynamics of growth and expansion, changing modes of exploitation of food and other resources over time, and the adoption of selected socio-ritual practices by the ruling élites in order to construct and negotiate authority (e.g. Bianchin Citton *et al.* 1998; Boaro 2001; Cifani 2003; De Min *et al.* 2005; Fulminante 2003; 2012; 2014; Menichetti 1994; Paoletti 2000; Smith 2006; Trentacoste 2013). Within this framework, scholars have also been interested in large-scale processes such as the formation of ethnic groups (*cf.* for example Bellelli 2012; Bourdin 2012; Cerchiai 2010; Cifani and Stoddart 2012; below) and increase in settlement size as an indicator of urbanization (e.g. Guidi 2006; 2010, with bibliography; but *cf.* Smith 2012, 22).[1] Other recurrent topics include the identification of socio-economic and socio-ritual indicators of social complexity (including formal cult) (e.g. Balista and Ruta Serafini 2008; Ruta Serafini 2002; Sassatelli and Govi 2005; Zifferero 1995); the role of inter-regional commerce, international trade, colonization and foreign contacts in driving socio-political evolution (e.g. *Confini* 1999; Delpino 1986; 1997; d'Agostino and Cerchiai 2004; Luni 2004); the impact of warfare, military activity and their ideological value on social organization (e.g. Iaia 2013a; Rawlings 1999; Rich 2007); the identification of markers of (high) social rank and status in graves; and supposedly 'aristocratic' social practices such as the symposium and gift-giving (e.g. Bartoloni 1984; 1987; Cuozzo 2007; Delpino 2000; Iaia 2005; 2006; 2007; 2013a; Osanna and Vullo 2013; Riva 2010).

By contrast, up until now comparatively little attention has been paid to the question of how these key developments resonated across the broader social transect, and how social groups other than ruling élites both promoted these changes and experienced their effects. Studies on comparable developments in the Greek world (e.g. Morris 1998) have already stressed the need to move beyond traditional approaches to state formation, and examine the phenomenon as involving not only top-down institutional structures, but also particular ways of thinking and of understanding 'community' and the individual's role – a nexus of ideological and cultural values (*cf.* Cuozzo 2003; 2005).

Although agency is sometimes employed as a theoretical framework by international scholars working on Italy, research on the peninsula in the first millennium BC still displays a strong emphasis on large-scale, often 'impersonal' narratives of social development and the establishment of chronologies (e.g. Bartoloni and Delpino 2005) that are sometimes obtained through schematic seriation methods, as opposed to micro-dynamics and the individual agency of those who produced the archaeological record we come to study, especially where burial rites are concerned. Sharp has been the focus on powerful or 'aristocratic' male individuals (e.g. Ampolo 1976–1977; von Eles 2002; Gleirscher and Marzatico 2004; Ruggeri 2007) and prominent social groups that are recognized as the driving forces behind socio-political change (e.g. Bartoloni 2003; von Eles 2004; Torelli 2006). Similarly strong is the emphasis on large-scale entities – such as the Villanovan or the Golaseccan 'culture' – (e.g. Bartoloni 2000a; de Marinis 1997) or social categories such as the 'aristocracy' (e.g. Bartoloni 2003), the 'queen' (d'Ercole and Martellone 2007), the aristocratic 'wife' (e.g. Bartoloni and Pitzalis 2012), the 'prince' (e.g. Bartoloni 2000b; d'Agostino 1999; Dore *et al.* 2000; Gleirscher and Marzatico 2004; Giulierini 2012), the 'warrior' (e.g. Gleirscher and Marzatico 2004; Ruggeri 2007; 2010; Tagliamonte 2003), the 'king' (Ruggeri 2007) and the 'princely' tomb phenomenon (e.g. d'Agostino 1977; Delpino 2000; Fulminante 2003), which do not fully account for the subtle variation in socio-ritual practice that characterized life in ancient Italy at the micro-level, and outside élite and prominent social circles.

As noted above, much attention has also been given to ethnic entities that might represent constructs by scholars based on the reading of Greco-Roman historical sources (e.g. Pesando 2005; for a critique *cf.* Dench 1995); furthermore, there are numerous large-scale, thematic studies dedicated to individual Italic 'peoples', sometimes taken as 'given' entities, such as the 'Etruscans' (e.g. Cristofani 1985; Torelli 2000; for more recent approaches: Belelli 2012; Naso 2015; Turfa 2013), the 'Campanians' (Cerchiai 1995), the 'Samnites' (Tagliamonte 1996), the 'Faliscans' (e.g. Maetzke *et al.* 1990), the 'Picentes' (Naso 2000) and the 'Veneti' (e.g. Capuis 2009; Fogolari and Prosdocimi 1988; Gamba *et al.* 2013) (for a critique *cf.* Zamboni this volume;

Perego 2014a; Scopacasa forthcoming; on ethnicity in Italian archaeology *cf.* also Cerchiai 2012 and the recent contributions in the *Mélanges de l'École française de Rome* 126(2), 2014). When the micro-scale level is approached, it is often only for generating catalogues, lists of finds, meticulous descriptions of archaeological layers and highly detailed accounts of classes of objects or even individual objects (e.g. Boitani 2005; Chieco Bianchi and Calzavara Capuis 1985; 2006; Colonna 1974; 2007; Delpino 2000; Lo Schiavo 2010; Quirino 2011; Sciacca 2005).[2]

Especially in the Anglophone and Francophone contexts, scholarship on agency and power has explored the complex interplay between people's active role in creating their world and the constraints posed by coercive social structures on individual lives (e.g. Dobres and Robb 2000; Foucault 1975; Gardner 2004a; 2008; Giddens 1984; Knapp and van Dommelen 2008; Robb 2005; 2010). However, such research has only sporadically influenced studies on proto-historic Italy, which nonetheless offers a unique context for exploring these issues given its great regional diversity, and the variety of community forms and networks, whose full extent remains to be explored in light of recent theoretical developments that go beyond agency itself, such as personhood (Fowler 2004), fragmentation theory (Chapman 2000; Chapman and Gaydarska 2007), postcolonial thought (van Dommelen 1997), materiality and embodiment (Crossland 2012), queer theory (Alberti 2013; Dowson 2000) and Network Theory (Blake 2014; Malkin 2011; *cf.* also Castells 2000; Granovetter 1973).[3]

The concept of agency that we advocate in this volume provides a powerful analytical tool with which to investigate the entanglement between people's ability to act, and the social rules and forces that both enable and constrain human action (*cf.* Gardner 2004b, 2–3; Giddens 1984, 1–14, 220), sometimes creating niches of extreme powerless and marginalization. As we shall see in many chapters from this book, individual action is shaped by the social structures and norms that are in place in society: in first-millennium BC Italy, these structures and social norms – which usually included deeply ingrained ideas about gender, age, ethnicity, rank and social inclusion – often moulded the way in which people approached and reproduced funerary rites over time; in turn, ritual itself became a means to perpetuate the structures of power (and oppression) in which these people thrived or declined. Yet at the same time, social agents can be aware of these structures and deliberately seek to change them (Giddens 1984, 220; *cf.* also Bourdieu 1977, who argues that social actors are at once products and creators of history): as many of our authors will show, attempts at modifying ritual – and the social norms behind it – can be easily identified in the funerary record of proto-historic Italy; these efforts may include attempts at modifying 'structure' by social actors who did not belong to the highest echelons of society. As Gardner (2004b, 5) notes, humans act "... in the sense that they select particular ways of engaging with the world on a moment-by-moment basis, albeit constrained by both past traditions and future goals." Whether archaeologists can ever hope to recover *individual* action is debatable (e.g. Dobres and Robb 2000). However, given that agency is a social phenomenon, the archaeological evidence can reveal patterns in social practice that transcend individual action, and indicate the balance between the forces of tradition and change (Gardner 2004b, 5): indeed, the material patterns in funerary ritual that are debated in this book provide powerful insights into the rise of new socio-political forms in Italy, c. 1000–300 BC.

The chief aim of this volume, therefore, is to harness innovative approaches to the exceptionally rich mortuary evidence of first-millennium BC Italy, in order to investigate the roles and identities of social actors who either struggled for power and social recognition, or were manipulated and exploited by superior authorities in a phase of tumultuous socio-political change throughout the entire Mediterranean basin. Our purpose is to promote an exploration of socio-cultural change at both the grass-root and the top-down level in different regions of Italy before, during and after the political transformations that scholars conceptualize as state formation, urbanization and increased socio-political complexity. In order to fully develop this research approach, we believe it is necessary to shift the focus of inquiry directly onto social groups such as women, children and marginal individuals, whose changing roles within processes of growing social complexity in first-millennium BC Italy have often been poorly addressed. Such an approach offers a coherent and unifying focus on funerary data, as well as a more richly textured analysis of phenomena of social development in ancient Italy. This includes a detailed exploration of socio-ritual practices and dynamics of power negotiation in regions where statehood and urbanization may not have developed, or developed in forms that were different from those identified in mainstream scholarship focusing on the most prominent regions of central Tyrrhenian and southern Italy.

Notably, funerary remains represent a substantial evidence base for the period, and offer a unique opportunity to explore how individuals and communities represented and re-created themselves in the rites of passage generated by the supreme crisis of death, often leading to significant socio-cultural adjustments for families and wider social segments (e.g. Morris 1992; Parker Pearson 1999). Whereas previous scholarship has generally focused on wealthy or élite graves (e.g. Bartoloni 2000b; Bianchin Citton *et al.* 1998; d'Agostino 1977; Fulminante 2003; Silvestrini and Sabbatini 2008; von Eles 2002; *cf.* also above and Morris 1999a on Greece), this volume seeks to consider the broader spectrum represented in the funerary record, including demographic groups (e.g. women, children and the non-élite) that until recently have rarely been the *primary* subject of research in late prehistoric and Iron Age Italy or – even when this was the case – were often just considered against the background of the actions of powerful 'aristocratic' men, and not as *social agents* in their own right.[4] Furthermore, we try to disclose evidence relating to individuals left at the margins of – or excluded from – privileged social networks, such as people who were denied formal cemetery burial or became the victims of ritual violence and extreme ritual exploitation.[5]

In addition to agency, identity and ethnicity (Insoll 2007; Jones 1997), connectivity and networks (Horden and Purcell 2000; Knapp and van Dommelen

2014; Malkin 2003; 2011), gender and childhood (Butler 1990; Carroll 2011; Carroll and Graham 2014; Gero and Conkey 1991; Morgan 1997; 2009; Morris 1999b), *habitus* (Bourdieu 1977; 1990; Bourdieu and Wacquant 1992), materiality (Miller 2005), commensal politics (Bray 2003), social exclusion and personhood (Conklin and Morgan 2006; Fowler 2004; Morgan 2006; Strathern 1988) are some of the key conceptual lenses through which the contributors to this volume approach the changing notions of power, community and the individual's role in social transformation in first-millennium BC Italy. Within this framework, we address questions such as: how can the social role of women, children and non-élite individuals be reconstructed from the way in which these roles are expressed and negotiated through mortuary ritual in increasingly complex social contexts? How does the status of both élite and supposedly 'marginal' social groups change across time and space within the framework of evolving socio-political structures? To what extent can the analysis of funerary evidence offer reliable information on the forms of power and authority emerging in societies where inequality is a pervasive social feature? To what extent do alternative social practices and identities, as opposed to élite ones, become archaeologically visible when one explores the less 'prestigious' funerary evidence that is often neglected?

The chapters in this volume, therefore, aim to provide a diverse range of approaches to the Italian funerary evidence, which have been at the forefront of archaeological debates on a broader scale. At first sight, the individual chapters might appear to differ substantially from each other because of their regional and thematic focus. However, what they have in common is their attention to how power operated in society, how it was exercised and resisted and how this can be studied through mortuary archaeological evidence. As we noted above, the underlying theme throughout the volume is the idea of agency, intended as an exploration of the subtle interplay between people's creative behaviour in both society and the funerary sphere, and the increasingly complex articulation of coercive power throughout first-millennium BC Italy. In their study of power and social transformation, the authors in this volume explore different kinds of archaeological correlates and case studies to concepts that have undergone increasing re-assessment in theoretical archaeology in recent years, such as identity and ethnicity (*cf.* chapters by Cuozzo, Shipley, Morris, Rajala, Zamboni and Scopacasa), *habitus* (*cf.* chapters by Cuozzo, Iaia and Perego), gender, childhood, the life-cycle and masculinity (*cf.* chapters by Cuozzo, Iaia, Di Lorenzo and colleagues, O'Donoghue, Faustoferri and Zanoni), personhood (*cf.* chapters by Shipley, O'Donoghue and Perego) and social inclusion and exclusion (*cf.* especially the chapters by Scopacasa, Zanoni, Perego and the finale by Perego and Scopacasa, but also the contributions by Cuozzo and Iaia). The chapters also address issues that are increasingly at the forefront of research but remain widely under-studied in Iron Age Italian archaeology, such as the ideological construction of extreme social marginality (*cf.* especially the chapters by Perego, and Perego and Scopacasa) and the manipulation of material culture by non-élite (or sub-élite) social segments, or by faltering élite groups that had to cope with the anguish of the dissolution of their power (*cf.* especially the chapters by Iaia and Scopacasa, but also Perego).

In exploring these issues, this book is twofold. Section 1 addresses the construction of identity by focusing mainly on the manipulation of age, ethnic and gender categories in society. Most contributions in Section 1 still focus on identity negotiation among the prominent groups living in regions and sites that reached notable power and splendour in first-millennium BC Italy. These include Etruria, Latium, Campania and the rich settlement of Verucchio, close to the Adriatic coast in Emilia Romagna. In all these chapters, however, strong is the awareness by the authors (Cuozzo, Shipley, O'Donoghue, Faustoferri, Morris and Rajala) of the delicate socio-political mechanisms creating and sustaining power in the study area; furthermore, vivid is the description of power dynamics among 'unexpected' social actors such as non-élite or sub-élite individuals, including women, in the chapter on commensality and alcohol consumption by Iaia. Reaching farther, Section 2 is particularly concerned with the concepts of 'periphery', marginality, social exclusion and the frailty of élite (or sub-élite) power in phases of dramatic socio-political change. Furthermore, this Section approaches the idea of identity construction in supposedly 'fringe' geographical areas such as the Veneto region (Perego), Samnium (Scopacasa), western Emilia (Zamboni) and Trentino–South Tyrol (Zanoni).

Crucially, each chapter in Section 2 offers a counterpoint to a contribution in Section 1, and vice-versa. The exploration of age and child identities among the Verucchio élite presented by Di Lorenzo and colleagues in Section 1 can be read together with Zanoni's contribution on northern Italy in Section 2, where 'being (ideologically) young' is seen as a potential criterion for social exclusion or social diversity. The focus on thriving forms of sub-élite self-representation in central Tyrrhenian Italy, proposed by Iaia in Section 1, is set against a depiction of obsolete forms of sub-élite self-representation in a 'peripheral' region of central-southern Italy, provided by Scopacasa in Section 2. In Section 1, Shipley and O'Donoghue focus on the personhood status of socially significant individuals from the powerful settlements of Tarquinia and Chiusi: their work is offered a counterpoint by Perego's alternative interpretation of the concept of 'personhood' in Section 2, where she explores the link between social exclusion, violence and coercion, in a 'peripheral' region of ancient Italy. Perego also explores the role of ritual in constructing social meaning and the imaginary through *habitus*, a connection that surfaces also in the chapters by Cuozzo and Iaia in Section 1. While the ideas of multiculturalism, connectivity, interaction and ethnicity run – in different forms – in the chapters by Cuozzo, Morris and Rajala in Section 1, a critical reassessment of these concepts is offered in the opening chapter of Section 2, where Zamboni provides a counterpoint to identity studies more in general. By noting the absence of a 'commensal ideology' in the tombs of sixth-century BC western Emilia, Zamboni also provides a counterpoint to the chapters by Cuozzo, O'Donoghue, Faustoferri, Di Lorenzo and colleagues, and especially Iaia, which in Section 1 all emphasize the key role of wine-drinking and food consumption in the burial rites of Etruria, Campania, Abruzzo and eastern Emilia. For the Abruzzo region, the emphasis on élite burial that we find in Section 1 in the chapter by Faustoferri (albeit with a focus on women, unusual for this region), is counterpointed by Scopacasa in the second part of the volume, where he focuses not on splendour and supremacy, but on anxiety and the dissolution of power. With her focus on 'forgotten' social actors in a peripheral region of Italy, Faustoferri also anticipates the 'fringe' theme, which is more widely addressed in Section 2.

The volume's overall emphasis on scholarly multivocality, and the multiplicity of the theoretical approaches that can be used to read the archaeological evidence, are exemplified by the very different impressions one may have in reading the chapters by Shipey and Iaia: these largely focus on the same archaeological material and geographical contexts, and yet provide alternative interpretations of the funerary evidence from early first-millennium BC central Italy. Finally, the volume's journey from the élite context to marginality is a common thread that runs from start to finish, starting off with the exquisite 'princely tombs' described by Cuozzo in Chapter 1, and ending with the victims of ritual violence, stripped of their meaningfulness as human beings, that are among the protagonists of Perego's work in Chapter 12. And yet this thread can also run in individual chapters, such as that by Iaia, where the extravagant rituals of wine-drinking harnessed by the highest echelons of society find a more humble and yet highly significant counterpart in alcohol consumption by sub-élite or non-élite social strata. This journey from élite power, to resistance, to misery is described in more detail in the following section, and is critically assessed in the finale, which will conclude this volume.

From élite identities to marginality

The chapters in Section 1 all shift their research emphasis from élite identities to more nuanced understandings of how child, adult, ethnic and gender identities were constructed in burial. While still focusing on funerary contexts that in first-millennium BC Italy are generally associated with the ruling élite, or at least with prominent social groups, the authors develop engaging new ways of addressing the changes in the articulation of individual, collective and personal identities in contexts of growing social complexity and – potentially – inequality. This is achieved by harnessing different methodologies, theoretical frameworks and research themes – from the investigation of women's active role in ritual practices of great political importance such as ritual drinking, to the way in which the bodies of children and adults alike became the fulcrum of diverging and evolving forms of power negotiation from the Early Iron Age to the Orientalizing and Archaic periods (tenth–ninth to sixth centuries BC).

In the dense initial research chapter, Mariassunta Cuozzo proposes a review of recent archaeological work exploring the negotiation of identity as well as the construction of power and consensus in the burial rites of complex societies. By drawing on key notions and theoretical frameworks in the humanities and social sciences, such as semiotics, agency, *habitus*, symbolic violence, gender, *culture metisse* and Godelier's notion of the "monopoly of the imaginary" (Godelier 1985; 1999), Cuozzo revisits both her own work on the important archaeological site of Pontecagnano near Naples and Salerno (e.g. Cuozzo 2003; 2005; 2007), and previous interpretations of the archaeological record of Iron Age and Orientalizing Etruria and Campania (e.g. Cerchiai 1995; d'Agostino 1977; 1999; Torelli 2000). In her view, the funerary rite represents a privileged domain for the construction and domination of the social imaginary. The interpretation of burial sites, however, often presupposes "contradictory and misleading aspects", which may derive from the conflicting needs and desires experienced by the different groups and social agents that create the ritual. Within this framework, Cuozzo addresses some crucial issues for the study of cemeteries in first-millennium BC central and southern Italy – did the exclusion from formal burial become an instrument of domination in contexts of increasing social inequality? How were sophisticated practices of manipulation of human remains and grave goods exploited by competing élite groups to sustain their unstable prominence between the ninth–eighth and seventh–sixth centuries BC? Did some high-ranking women from ancient Campania gain a crucial role in their community as active agents of cultural hybridization or *métissage*? Rather than providing simple answers to the challenges posed by the archaeological evidence, in her chapter Cuozzo endeavours to raise questions and indicate possible lines of inquiry for future research on ancient Italy.

In the second chapter, Cristiano Iaia develops a fascinating study of the material culture associated with the consumption of alcohol and other sophisticated beverages in Early Iron Age central Italy, where drinking practices and meat consumption were greatly emphasized in the rich burial record of Etruria. By challenging the modern consensus that drinking alcohol – especially in a ritual context – was part of an aristocratic warrior *ethos*, with roots to be identified outside Italy, Iaia suggests that wine consumption may have started in the peninsula much earlier than previously thought, presumably as an indigenous practice (*cf.* also Iaia 2013b). Furthermore, he demonstrates that in Early Iron Age central Italy the distribution of drinking assemblages among the graves of males, females and sub-adults, either belonging to the same social group or to different social 'classes', was influenced by complex social rules that changed over time and in different geographical areas – often in response to increasing social complexity and inequality. In particular, he confronts how lavish élite graves (both male and female) that included luxurious metal drinking equipment differed from what he identifies as "secondary élite" graves, which contained specific classes of pottery usually not present in the richest tombs, and – only rarely – some isolated bronze drinking vessels. Through an in-depth analysis of the data, Iaia identifies different levels of wine consumption, which were expressed through the adoption of different types of material culture linked to specific rules of drinking etiquette. Far from excluding women and individuals not belonging to the highest élite from alcohol consumption, the socio-ritual practice that evolved in Early Iron Age central Italy allowed different social agents to actively negotiate diverging forms of self-representation, and strive for social recognition, in the funerary arena.

Some of the key issues about identity, power and mortuary practice touched by Cuozzo and Iaia in Chapters 1 and 2 are carried further in Lucy Shipley's discussion of the link between materiality and personhood in the context of changing mortuary practices at Tarquinia from the tenth–ninth to the eighth–seventh centuries BC. By zooming in on this key Villanovan and Etruscan site, Shipley examines how the development of individuality in the mortuary expression of identity may be related to growing socio-political complexity. By drawing on concepts such as object biography (e.g. Kopytoff 1986), the agency of objects (e.g. Gell 1998) and personhood (e.g. Fowler 2004; Strathern 1988), Shipley addresses the crucial role held by biconical cinerary urns and grave goods in substantiating the role and identity of the Tarquinian dead during the tenth–ninth century BC: while the urns, universally present in each sampled tomb and similar to each other in their shape, came to embody the communal identity of the deceased as part of their community, the variation and diversity in grave assemblages and urn decoration allowed for an expression of individuality by each single person and burying group. Shipley's ultimate question is whether the changing funerary record of Tarquinia, both over time and in the two cemeteries of Le Rose and Villa Bruschi Falgari, can be seen as a movement from a 'dividual' towards an individual conception of personhood, where 'dividuality' – the expression of the relationships between the deceased and the community – is gradually subsumed (or replaced) by élite individual identities in the rising proto-urban community. By noting the increasing emphasis on diversified and richer grave assemblages, as well the late eighth-century BC shift from cremation to inhumation in several communities of central Italy, Shipley argues that the change in the construction of personhood embodied in these new funerary practices, is indicative of the fragmentation of group identities in the face of increased socio-economic inequality – a phenomenon that might be already incipient in the slightly different ritual practices attested at Le Rose and Villa Bruschi Falgari during the ninth century BC.

Shipley's study of personhood, individuality and collective identity in Iron Age Tarquinia provides a thought-provoking counterpoint to Eóin O'Donoghue's discussion of gender identities, personhood and mortuary practices at Chiusi, another key Etruscan centre, in the later seventh and sixth centuries BC. By drawing on the more rarely addressed notion of masculinity (e.g. Connell 1995; Knapp 1998), O'Donoghue approaches gender and personhood as two central features of social differentiation in Chiusine burials, and of the changing ways in which this differentiation was articulated through ritual practice over time. As a key aspect of élite identities, the construction of highly specific gender identities and personhood forms involved manipulating not only the grave goods but every aspect of the burial process, including cinerary urns, tomb architecture and grave iconography. By focusing on the changing treatment of the human body in relation to these variables, O'Donoghue is able to identify changing notions of personhood and male self-identity from the seventh to the sixth century BC. In particular, he identifies a general shift from a sharp ritual focus on élite male individuals, who are often represented in burial as warriors and banqueters, to an emphasis on the leading person's inclusion in broader familial and groups connections. Complementing Shipley's hypothesis that growing social complexity brought about a focus on individuality in the mortuary practice of Tarquinia after the ninth–eighth century BC, O'Donoghue recognizes a subsequent stage in the ever-changing process of identity and personhood construction in first-millennium BC central Italy – or rather just a highly contextualized regional pattern of it?

The issue of gender emerges also in the chapter by Amalia Faustoferri, which presents the preliminary results of her work on some newly discovered burial contexts from Iron Age central Adriatic Italy, with a focus on Abruzzo. In her contribution, Faustoferri notes how the archaeological investigation of this area has centred almost exclusively on male tombs, with an emphasis on the study of weaponry and armour. This, in conjunction with the fact that classical sources describe the warriors from this area as Rome's most resilient enemies, has led many researchers to overlook some of the less 'conspicuous' social groups represented in the mortuary record of ancient Abruzzo, including women and children. However, new excavations at the burial sites of Fossa and Avezzano have revealed the existence of wealthy women's tombs, many of which stand out for containing elaborate bronze discs that had previously been regarded as 'male' breastplates. These new data – as well as the presence of other potential insignia of rank and role (e.g. knives and axes) in female graves – raise compelling questions about the social standing of some women, and even some female children, in a world that up until now has been conceptualized as essentially masculine. In focusing on women, Faustoferri's chapter offers a counterpoint to O'Donoghue's discussion of masculinity; also, her argument that certain women carried out key roles in central Italian society is coherent with Cuozzo and Iaia's observations about women's crucial involvement in ritual (including ritual drinking) in the better-known regions of Etruria and Campania.

Further to the previous chapter's discussion of gender, Giorgia di Lorenzo, Patrizia von Eles, Claudio Negrini, Paola Poli, Lisa Manzoli and Elena Rodriguez offer a much-needed reassessment of the issue of age, and socio-cultural attitudes to age, as seen through the funerary record of Iron Age and Orientalizing Italy. Their focus is on the exceptionally well-documented cemeteries around Verucchio near Rimini, where the availability of detailed information on the spatial arrangement of grave goods in the tomb allows for an in-depth analysis of how funerary space was used to articulate social status amongst the members of élite families in this key area of central-northern Italy – thereby taking further issues of mortuary symbolism that we find in the earlier chapters by Cuozzo and Iaia. Di Lorenzo and colleagues approach these issues by focusing on the burials of children, which they argue are pivotal to understanding the expression of familial identity and status, given the very tangible social expectations and cultural conventions regarding the future role of young people in the powerful Verucchio community. By developing a highly sophisticated approach to the mortuary material, Di Lorenzo and co-authors argue that it is possible to identify a 'personal' funerary apparatus, which was burnt with the dead person on the pyre and subsequently placed inside the cremation urn along with the bones. Notably, this grave set was perceived to be different from a secondary funerary apparatus that was deposited in the tomb outside the cinerary vessel, and was indicative of what the authors refer to as the "symbolic representation" of the deceased – which did not always coincided with the image of the dead conveyed by the 'personal' set of grave goods in the urn. In the close-knit, evolving community of Iron Age and Orientalizing Verucchio, the powerful social actors that created the opulent graves studied in this chapter were expressing very sophisticated ideas about family membership, and what their children were supposed to grow up to be. And yet, in our opinion, this tale of privilege and splendour raises compelling questions about social inclusion, free will and power: were the élite children and pre-adolescents buried in Verucchio the fortunate beneficiaries of complex ritual practices that underlined their social meaningfulness – or were they the silent cogs in structures of power expression that they couldn't control to any extent?

By further tackling some theoretical concerns raised by Cuozzo in the first research chapter, the last two contributions in Section 1 focus on issues of connectivity and interaction, and how cultural contact shaped the cultural identity of communities where social change was not necessarily driven only by the highest echelons of society. We begin with Owain Morris and his critical reading of the spread of so-called 'princely tombs' in Campania – which feature prominently in Cuozzo's chapter, but are analysed here from the vantage point of collective agency and connectivity. In traditional literature on death and burial in the Iron Age central Mediterranean, the term 'princely tomb' is used to indicate a sample of exceptionally rich graves from Italy and Greece, which have been attributed to dominant individuals and social groups (e.g. Cerchiai 2010; d'Agostino 1977; 1999; Morris 1999a). As Morris notes, the appearance and dissemination of this tomb type in Italy is normally seen as the result of external influence, such as the influx of Greek settlers and the spread of Greek culture. Furthermore, this phenomenon has been connected to the rise of a specific form of social organization – the so-called *gens* of the later Roman tradition (*cf.* discussion in Smith 2006) – which need not be present in Iron Age and Orientalizing Campania, as well. By moving away from traditional evolutionist approaches and shifting the focus onto local communities and their role as social agents, Morris offers a fresh reading of the development of élite burial rites in Iron Age and Orientalizing Campania. As he draws on wider theoretical approaches to the movement of goods and people, such as connectivity (e.g. Horden and Purcell 2000), materiality (e.g. Miller 2005), and networks (e.g. Malkin 2011), as well as on innovative research on ancient

Mediterranean dynamics (e.g. Hales and Hodos 2010; Riva 2010), Morris provides a more nuanced understanding of the subtle forms of social networking and cultural re-elaboration that brought about change in key sites of ancient Campania. There, crucial developments in ritual and social structuring might not have been determined directly (or solely) by the influence of Greek newcomers and the individual agency of powerful 'princes". Rather, social change might have been the result of complex dynamics of competition and adaptation that originated in the local communities as a whole, when élite and non-élite social segments aside became increasingly entangled in the networks of relations that came to embrace the entire Mediterranean basin.

Moving north along the Tyrrhenian coast, Ulla Rajala draws on the concepts of 'nested identities' and 'mental distance', both taken from social psychology, to bring about new ways of understanding the formative interaction of city-states in Archaic Latium. Rajala starts by noting that funerary remains in Latium are fragmentary and highly diverse, and consequently pose considerable analytical challenges. The region was home to communities that played a key role in the early development of Rome, but how culturally cohesive were they to begin with? In order to identify patterns of social and cultural connectivity, Rajala focuses on the degree of cultural proximity and distance between different communities as seen through the mortuary record. Her main theoretical basis is the work of Bjerring Olsen (2004), who argues that people belonging to different systems of socialization are culturally 'programmed' to exhibit differences in behavioural patterns, including mortuary practices, because of differences in collectively shared values. By drawing also on theory-informed archaeological research on ethnicity (e.g. Jones 1997), Rajala systematically compares different burial customs and tomb types in central Italy during the Orientalizing and Archaic periods. The outcome is a thought-provoking picture of cultural connectivity and ethnicity in Latium, with links very often crossing the political boundaries of independent city-states and stretching beyond the confines of the region. Notably, Rajala's discussion of 'outspoken' community self-definition, with an emphasis on both region-wide networks and the micro-level of the single cemetery, is complemented by the opening chapter of Section 2, where Zamboni offers a critical take on the concept of identity in view of the multifaceted and more elusive forms of cultural interaction in ancient Emilia.

Indeed, whereas the chapters in the first section deal with issues of gender, age, ethnicity and connectivity head-on, those in Section 2 address phenomena of social change and identity construction on the fringe. The term 'fringe' is deliberately given a double meaning in this volume. On the one hand, it refers to the 'out-of-the-way' geographical location of the study areas, which do not tend to feature very prominently in Anglophone scholarship on first-millennium BC Italy – such as several parts of northern Italy, and to a lesser degree regions further south such as the central Apennines. Yet 'fringe' also refers here to the focus on 'marginality', 'exclusion' and 'diversity' as they might have been defined in social and cultural terms, both in these regions and in the critical investigation of the evidence provided by the scholars writing here.

As previously noted, Section 2 starts with Lorenzo Zamboni's work on sixth-century BC western Emilia, which complements some key issues regarding ethnicity, connectivity and interaction raised in Section 1 by Cuozzo, Morris and especially Rajala. Contrary to previous Italian scholarship, which has attempted to pigeonhole the Emilian communities into ethnic categories such as 'Etruscans', 'Celts' and 'Ligurians', Zamboni adopts a new perspective on the peculiar and diverse archaeological evidence of this region, by focusing on the complex patterns of cultural acceptance vis-à-vis rejection that emerge from the local funerary record. On the one hand, for example, female ornaments often bear similarities, or derive from, models and typologies that display a vast regional distribution. However, there is a peculiar absence in western Emilia of grave goods relating to socio-ritual practices and ideologies, such as ritual food consumption and the 'symposium', which are widespread both in the same areas that were often sources of inspiration for the female costume, and in regions that were geographically very close to Emilia itself. These findings raise interesting questions about the mechanisms of identity construction and interaction amongst social agents in a sub-region of Italy which has gained comparatively scanty attention in international scholarship to date. From these premises, Zamboni demonstrates how a comprehensive review of earlier findings, taken together with the results of recent excavations, affords a basis for rethinking some deeply ingrained assumptions about the study of identity, ethnicity and self-representation through mortuary evidence. Working from recent anthropological and sociological research that questions the value of 'identity' and 'ethnicity' as research frameworks, and uncovers their potentially dangerous ideological load (*cf.* Remotti 2010), Zamboni's reflections are not limited to this particular region of ancient Italy, but have an important bearing on how we think about both the peninsula's past and identity studies more generally.

The three final chapters in Section 2 assess long-term patterns in funerary practice and their implications regarding ritual expressions of ideas of community, and the degree of inclusiveness and exclusiveness that these ideas entailed. In doing so, they critically complement the chapters by Cuozzo, Iaia, Shipley, and Di Lorenzo and colleagues in Section 1, and take further some crucial ideas about social exclusion and power negotiation already emerging there. First, Rafael Scopacasa discusses how long-term changes in access to formal burial allow us to explore the link between mortuary practice and élite self-legitimization in periods of accelerated socio-political change. Through a systematic approach to the mortuary evidence of Samnium, in central Italy, Scopacasa argues that a restriction of access to formal burial between the sixth and third centuries BC may have been an attempt by some élite or sub-élite groups to assert their faltering pre-eminence in a time of growing socio-political complexity, which arguably involved the rise of the first state-level polities in the region. With the aid of quantitative analysis, he shows that graves become less numerous and, on average, more lavish between the sixth and third centuries BC. This transformation may indicate that some of the local élites, who had traditionally asserted their authority through funerary ritual, began to develop a tighter control over the old cemeteries, so as to try and preserve some of their exclusive status in a rapidly changing world, but in a way that was not particularly up to speed with the times. In their struggle for survival, some segments of the local élites would have emphasized traditional ideas about social status and boundaries through funerary ritual, which had been prominent during the Iron Age, but were not necessarily as effective after the fifth century BC.

The issue of identity construction in fringe contexts emerges also in Vera Zanoni's study of selected practices of bodily manipulation in north-east Italy. Zanoni explores a fascinating yet poorly understood type of ritual site known as the *Brandopferplätze*, the 'places of fire sacrifice', which were characteristic of the communities living in the Alpine region from late prehistory to the early Roman period. In northern Italy, late prehistoric Trentino–South Tyrol was a relatively secluded and largely mountainous area, where the harsh terrain and regional peculiarity of burial rites have often hampered the identification of rich formal cemeteries such as those discovered in central Italy. By focusing on a sample of human bones from Iron Age *Brandopferplätze* in this region and nearby areas, Zanoni is able to identify a predominance of subjects classified as 'sub-adults' and 'young adults' amongst the individuals recovered from these ritual sites. Through careful contextual analysis of the finds, she suggests that there may have been a connection between the tendency to situate the *Brandopferplätze* in threshold places such as remote mountain areas, and the presence in these sites of individuals belonging to age classes that might have been considered 'marginal' or 'liminal', such as children, adolescents and young adults who might have failed to reach full social integration. In approaching the issue of past age identities in a way that complements Di Lorenzo and colleagues' work in Section 1, Zanoni's findings raise intriguing questions about the social agents that operated in the *Brandopferplätze* of first-millennium BC northern Italy: why only some individuals were selected for deposition in the 'places of fire sacrifice'? Was age the only selection criterion? Who did carry out the selection? Was violence a feature of the practices performed in the *Brandopferplätze*, as suggested by Perego for some selected ritual sites of first-millennium BC Veneto? Were the ideas of 'liminality' and 'difference' that might have been constructed through ritual in *Brandopferplätze* also markers of extreme social exclusion?

In the concluding research chapter, Elisa Perego harnesses the concepts of *habitus* (Bourdieu 1977), agency (Dobres and Robb 2000) and personhood (e.g. Conklin and Morgan 2006) to shed light on social change in Veneto *c*. 800–500 BC. By proposing a different formulation of the concept of 'personhood' vis-à-vis that usually adopted in mainstream Anglophone archaeology (e.g. Fowler 2004), Perego explores the relation between non-normative funerary treatment, the construction of ideological notions of what 'being human' means, and the rise of increasingly sophisticated socio-political structures in a crucial phase of development for the entire peninsula. In particular, Perego discusses how ritual practices of appropriation and abuse of the human body, presumably developed by prominent social groups practicing cremation as their burial rite of choice, can be recognized in relation to a sample of inhumation burials which display marked abnormal features, including mutilation, prone burial, careless interment, exclusion from the formal burial ground, location in marginal cemetery areas and association with probable sacrificial remains such as broken pottery, food and incomplete animal carcasses. By exploring how social recognition and full social integration were granted (or denied) through ritual, Perego debates the hypothesis that in Iron Age Veneto human sacrifice and the ritual exploitation of marginalized individuals by the élite developed as a form of reiterated instilling of social norms – *habitus* – in which the perpetrators themselves became entrapped in their spasmodic strive for power and social control. Crucially, Perego emphasizes how these phenomena of ritual violence are often attested in an important phase of accelerated development and dramatic change, which immediately preceded and accompanied the rise of new forms of socio-political organization in the Veneto region. Did this novel political power need new forms of control and appropriation of the human body to affirm itself?

Notes

1. The three phenomena of state formation, urbanization and ethnogenesis (i.e. ethnic formation) are often connected in Italian scholarship focusing on the first millennium BC (*cf.* Carandini 2012 for an example and Perego 2014a for a critical evaluation of this trend, with additional bibliography).

2. Obviously, this is not to deny the usefulness of these studies, which are necessary to provide the evidence base for further investigation of the archaeological material. What we advocate in this volume is a sophisticated approach to social change in the study area, one taking into account both recent developments in archaeological theory, and the crucial role of social actors and social dynamics that have received comparatively less attention in scholarship to date.

3. For some exceptions regarding agency *cf.* for example Perego 2011 on Iron Age Veneto; Robb 2007 on the Italian Neolithic. Fragmentation and personhood theory have been used by Perego (e.g. 2011; 2012; 2014b; forthcoming) to investigate burial rituals and social change in late prehistoric and early Roman Veneto. In recent years, Network Theory has enjoyed increasing success among scholars working on ancient Italy (e.g. Blake 2014; Fulminante 2012; 2014) while postcolonial thought has informed much work by van Dommelen (e.g. 1997; 2012). For theory-laden approaches to the Italian evidence *cf.* also Cuozzo 1996; Gleba and Horsnaes 2011; Riva 2010; Robb 2002 and selected essays in Knapp and van Dommelen 2014; on gender *cf.* for example Herring and Lomas 2009; Perego 2011; forthcoming; Robb 1994; Saltini Semerari and Sojc forthcoming; Scopacasa 2014; Whitehouse 1998; 2001; 2013.

4. This issue is also considered in the volume's finale. We anticipate here that our critique to the current status of the discipline does not imply that such groups were never considered in Italian scholarship before. For example, literature addressing the social status and role of women in first-millennium BC Italy is quite rich (e.g. Bietti Sestieri 1992; Bonfante 2013; Coen 2008; von Eles 2007). However, many studies still maintain a strong focus on high-status women or women that are somewhat 'trapped' in the traditional roles of wives, mothers, daughters, 'princesses'

and 'priestesses'. What we seek to promote through our work is a more nuanced reflection on both women's and men's identities in a context where gender archaeology has failed to have a major impact until recently (*cf.* Dommasnes and Montón-Subiás 2012; Whitehouse 2013). Questions concerning past sexualities and bodily experiences, as well as the nature of the sex/gender dichotomy and the possible existence of ambiguous and multiple genders, are now commonplace in gender archaeology (e.g. Bolger 2013); however, they remain largely unanswered in the Italian context. Rare or absent are also studies considering how gender and age identities were constructed in marginal contexts and among marginal social groups in late prehistory and proto-history (*cf.* Perego 2014a for further discussion).

5. On the issue of abnormal burial and funerary deviancy in ancient Italy *cf.* however Bartoloni and Benedettini 2007/2008; Belcastro and Ortalli 2010; Perego 2014b; Perego *et al.* 2015; Saracino 2009; Zanoni 2011, and the early study by d'Agostino 1985; on the nascent debate on marginality and social exclusion in Italian archaeology *cf.* Perego 2012; 2014a; 2014b; forthcoming; and Perego and Scopacasa this volume; Perego *et al.* 2015; Saracino and Zanoni 2014; Saracino *et al.* 2014.

Bibliography

Alberti, A. (2013) Queer prehistory: Bodies, performativity and matter. In D. Bolger (ed.) *Blackwell Companion to Gender Prehistory*, 86–107. Oxford, Blackwell.

Ampolo, C. (1976–1977) Demarato. Osservazioni sulla mobilità sociale arcaica. *Dialoghi di Archeologia* 9–10, 333–345.

Ampolo, C. (2013) Il problema delle origini di Roma rivisitato. Concordismo, ipertradizionalismo acritico, contesti. *Annali della Scuola Normale Superiore di Pisa. Classe di Lettere e Filosofia* 5(1), 217–248.

Balista, C. and Ruta Serafini, A. (2004) Primi elementi di urbanistica arcaica a Padova. In M. Luni (ed.) *I Greci in Adriatico 2* (Hesperia 18), 291–310. Roma, L'"Erma" di Bretschneider.

Balista, C. and Ruta Serafini, A. (2008) Spazi urbani e spazi sacri a Este. In *I Veneti Antichi: Novità e Aggiornamenti. Atti del Convegno di Studi (Vò di Isola della Scala, Verona, 15 Ottobre 2005)*, 79–100. Sommacampagna, Cierre Edizioni.

Bartoloni, G. (1984) Riti funerari dell'aristocrazia in Etruria e nel Lazio. L'esempio di Veio. *Opus* 3, 13–25.

Bartoloni, G. (1987) Esibizione di ricchezza a Roma nel VI e V sec. a. C.: Doni votivi e corredi funerari. *Scienze dell'Antichità* 1, 143–159.

Bartoloni, G. (2000a) The origin and diffusion of Villanovan culture. In M. Torelli (ed.) *The Etruscans*, 53–71. Milano, Bompiani.

Bartoloni, G. (2000b) (ed.) *Principi Etruschi: Tra Mediterraneo ed Europa. Catalogo della Mostra (Bologna, 2000-2001)*. Venezia, Marsilio.

Bartoloni, G. (2003) *Le Società dell'Italia Primitiva. Lo Studio delle Necropoli e la Nascita delle Aristocrazie*. Roma, Carocci.

Bartoloni, G. (2006) L'inizio del processo di formazione urbana in Etruria. Analogie e differenze venute in luce nei recenti scavi. *Quaderni di Acme* 77, 49–82.

Bartoloni, G. and Benedettini, M.G. (2007–2008) (eds) *Sepolti tra i Vivi. Evidenza e Interpretazione di Contesti Funerari in Abitato. Atti del Convegno Internazionale (Roma, 26-29 Aprile 2006)*. Roma, Quasar.

Bartoloni, G. and Delpino, F. (2005) (eds) *Oriente e Occidente: Metodi e Discipline a Confronto. Riflessioni sulla Cronologia dell'Età del Ferro in Italia. Atti dell'Incontro di Studi (Roma, 30-31 Ottobre 2003)* (Mediterranea 1, 2004). Pisa-Roma, Istituti Editoriali e Poligrafici Internazionali.

Bartoloni, G. and Pitzalis, F. (2012) Mogli e madri nella nascente aristocrazia tirrenica. In V. Nizzo and L. La Rocca (eds) *Antropologia e Archeologia a Confronto: Rappresentazioni e Pratiche del Sacro. Atti del Convegno (Roma, Museo Preistorico Etnografico "Luigi Pigorini", 20–21 Maggio 2011)*, 137–160. Roma, E.S.S. Editorial Service System.

Belcastro, M.G. and Ortalli, J. (2010) (eds) *Sepolture Anomale. Indagini Archeologiche e Antropologiche dall'Epoca Classica al Medioevo in Emilia Romagna. Giornata di Studi (Castelfranco Emilia, 19 Dicembre 2009)* (Quaderni di Archeologia dell'Emilia Romagna 28). Borgo S. Lorenzo, All'Insegna del Giglio.

Bellelli, V. (2012) (ed.) *Le Origini degli Etruschi: Storia, Archeologia, Antropologia*. Roma, "L'Erma" di Bretschneider.

Bianchin Citton, E., Gambacurta, G. and Ruta Serafini, A. (1998) (eds) *Presso l'Adige Ridente... Recenti Rinvenimenti Archeologici da Este a Montagnana. Catalogo della Mostra (Este, Museo Nazionale Atestino, 21 Febbraio 1998–21 Febbraio 1999)*. Padova, ADLE.

Bietti Sestieri, A.M. (1992) *The Iron Age Community of Osteria dell'Osa: A Study of Socio-Political Development in Central Tyrrhenian Italy*. Cambridge, Cambridge University Press.

Blake, E. (2014) *Social Networks and Regional Identity in Bronze Age Italy*. Cambridge, Cambridge University Press.

Boaro, S. (2001) Dinamiche insediative e confini nel Veneto dell'Età del Ferro: Este, Padova e Vicenza. *Padusa* 37, 153–197.

Boitani, F. (2005) Le più antiche ceramiche greche e di tipo greco a Veio. In G. Bartoloni and F. Delpino (eds) *Oriente e Occidente: Metodi e Discipline a Confronto. Riflessioni sulla Cronologia dell'Età del Ferro in Italia. Atti dell'Incontro di Studi (Roma, 30–31 Ottobre 2003)*, 319–332. Pisa–Roma, Istituti Editoriali e Poligrafici Internazionali.

Bolger, D. (2013) Introduction: Gender prehistory – The story so far. In D. Bolger (ed.) *Blackwell Companion to Gender Prehistory*, 1–20. Oxford, Blackwell.

Bonfante, L. (2013) Mothers and children. In J.M. Turfa (2013) *The Etruscan World*, 426–446. London–New York, Routledge.

Bourdieu, P. (1977) *Outline of a Theory of Practice*. Cambridge, Cambridge University Press.

Bourdieu, P. (1990) *The Logic of Practice*. Cambridge, Polity Press.

Bourdieu, P. and Wacquant, L.J.D. (1992) *An Invitation to Reflexive Sociology*. Cambridge, Polity Press.

Bourdin, S. (2012) *Les Peuples de l'Italie Préromaine: Identités, Territoires et Relations Inter-ethniques en Italie Centrale et Septentrionale (VIIIe–1er s. av. J.-C.)*. Rome, École française de Rome.

Bradley, G. (2000) *Ancient Umbria. State, Culture and Identity in Central Italy from the Iron Age to the Augustan Era*. Oxford, Oxford University Press.

Bray, T.L. (2003) (ed.) *The Archaeology and Politics of Food and Feasting in Early States and Empires*. New York–London, Kluwer Academic/Plenum.

Butler, J. (1990) *Gender Trouble: Feminism and the Subversion of Identity*. New York, Routledge.

Bjerring Olsen, K. (2004) *Economic Cooperation and Social Identity: Towards a Model of Economic Cross-Cultural Integration* (Department of Economics, Aarhus School of Business. Working Papers 04-10). Aarhus, Department of Economics, Aarhus School of Business.

Capuis, L. (1998–1999) "Città", strutture e infrastrutture "urbanistiche" nel Veneto pre-romano: Alcune note. *Archeologia Veneta* 21/22, 51–57.

Capuis, L. (2009) *I Veneti. Civiltà e Cultura di un Popolo dell'Italia Preromana*. Milano, Longanesi (third edition).

Carandini, A. (2006) *La Leggenda di Roma. Dalla Nascita dei Gemelli alla Fondazione della Città*. Milano, Einaudi.

Carandini, A. (2007) *Roma: Il Primo Giorno*. Roma–Bari, Laterza.

Carandini, A. (2012) Urban landscapes and ethnic identity of early Rome. In G. Cifani and S. Stoddart (eds) *Landscape, Ethnicity and Identity in the Archaic Mediterranean Area*, 5–20. Oxford, Oxbow Books.

Carroll, M. (2011) Infant death and burial in Roman Italy. *Journal of Roman Archaeology* 24, 99–120.

Carroll, M. and Graham, E.-J. (2014) (eds) *Infant Health and Death in Roman Italy and Beyond* (Journal of Roman Archaeology Supplementary Series 96). Portsmouth, RI, Journal of Roman Archaeology.

Castells, M. (2000) Toward a sociology of the network society. *Contemporary Sociology* 29(5), 693–699.

Cerchiai, L. (1995) *I Campani*. Milano, Longanesi.

Cerchiai, L. (2010) *Gli Antichi Popoli della Campania. Archeologia e Storia*. Roma, Carocci.

Cerchiai, L. (2012) L'identità etnica come processo di relazione: Alcune riflessioni a proposito del mondo italico. In V. Bellelli (ed.) *Le Origini degli Etruschi. Storia, Archeologia, Antropologia*, 345–357. Roma, "L'Erma" di Bretschneider.

Chapman, J. (2000) *Fragmentation in Archaeology*. London, Routledge.

Chapman, J. and Gaydarska, B. (2007) *Parts and Wholes. Fragmentation in Prehistoric Context*. Oxford, Oxbow Books.

Chieco Bianchi, A.M. and Calzavara Capuis, L. (1985) *Este I. Le Necropoli di Casa di Ricovero, Casa Muletti-Prosdocimi, Casa Alfonsi*. Roma, Giorgio Bretschneider Editore.

Chieco Bianchi, A.M. and Calzavara Capuis, L. (2006) (eds) *Este II. La Necropoli di Villa Benvenuti*. Roma, Giorgio Bretschneider Editore.

Cifani, G. (2003) *Storia di una Frontiera. Dinamiche Territoriali e Gruppi Etnici nella Media Valle Tiberina dalla Prima Età del Ferro alla Conquista Romana. Archeologia del Territorio*. Roma, Libreria dello Stato, Istituto Poligrafico e Zecca dello Stato.

Cifani, G. and Stoddart, S. (2012) (eds) *Landscape, Ethnicity and Identity in the Archaic Mediterranean Area*. Oxford, Oxbow Books.

Confini 1999 = *Confini e Frontiera nella Grecità d'Occidente. Atti del 37° Convegno di Studi sulla Magna Grecia (Taranto, 3-6 Ottobre 1997)*. Taranto, Istituto per la Storia e l'Archeologia della Magna Grecia.

Coen, A. (2008) Il banchetto aristocratico e il ruolo della donna. In M. Silvestrini and M. Sabatini (eds) *Potere e Splendore. Gli Antichi Piceni a Matelica. Catalogo della Mostra (Matelica, Palazzo Ottoni, 19 Aprile-31 Ottobre 2008)*, 159–165. Roma, "L'Erma" di Bretschneider.

Colonna, G. (1974) Su una classe di dischi-corazza centro-italici. *In Aspetti e Problemi dell'Etruria Interna. Atti dell'VIII Convegno di Studi Etruschi e Italici (Orvieto, 1972)*, 193–205. Firenze, L.S. Olschki.

Colonna, G. (2007) Dischi-corazza e dischi di ornamento femminile: Due distinte classi di bronzi centro-italici. *Archeologia Classica* 58, 3–30.

Connell, R.W. (1995) *Masculinities*. Cambridge, Polity Press.

Conklin, B.A. and Morgan, L.M. (1996) Babies, bodies and the production of personhood in north America and a native Amazonian society. *Ethos* 24(4), 657–694.

Cristofani, M. (1985) (ed.) *Civiltà degli Etruschi*. Milano, Electa.

Crossland, Z (2012) Materiality and embodiment. In M.C. Beaudry and D. Hicks (eds) *The Oxford Handbook of Material Culture Studies*. Oxford, Oxford University Press (online edition).

Cuozzo, M. (1996) Prospettive teoriche e metodologiche nell'interpretazione delle necropoli: La Post-Processual Archaeology. *Annali di Archeologia e Storia Antica* 3, 1–37.

Cuozzo, M. (2003) *Reinventando la Tradizione: Immaginario Sociale, Ideologie e Rappresentazione nelle Necropoli Orientalizzanti di Pontecagnano*. Paestum, Pandemos.

Cuozzo, M. (2005) Community norms and inter-group dialectics in the necropoleis of Campania, during the Orientalizing. In P.A.J. Attema, A. Nijboer and A. Zifferero (eds) *Papers in Italian Archaeology VI: Communities and Settlements from the Neolithic to the Early Medieval Period* (BAR S1452). Oxford, Archaeopress.

Cuozzo, M. (2007) Ancient Campania: Cultural interaction, political borders and geographical boundaries. In G.J. Bradley, E. Isayev and C. Riva (eds) *Ancient Italy. Regions without Boundaries*, 224–267. Exeter, Exeter University Press.

Dore, A., Morigi Govi, C., Delpino, F., von Hase, F-W., Bartoloni, G., Colonna, G., Minarini, L., Marchesi, M., Liverani, M., Gras, M., Flourentzos, P. and Karageorghis, V. (eds) (2000) *Principi Etruschi tra Mediterraneo ed Europa. Catalogo della Mostra (Bologna, Museo Civico Archeologico, 1 Ottobre 2000–1 Aprile 2001)*. Venezia, Marsilio.

d'Agostino, B. (1977) *Tombe Principesche dell'Orientalizzante Antico da Pontecagnano* (Monumenti Antichi 49, Serie Miscellanea 2/1). Roma, Accademia Nazionale dei Lincei.

d'Agostino, B. (1985) Società dei vivi, comunità dei morti: Un rapporto difficile. *Dialoghi di Archeologia* 1(3), 47–58.

d'Agostino, B. (1999) I principi dell'Italia centro-tirrenica in epoca orientalizzante. In P. Ruby (ed.) *Les Princes de la Protohistoire et l'Émergence de l'État. Actes de la Table Ronde Internationale Organisée par le Centre Jean Bérard et l'École française de Rome (Naples, 27–29 Octobre 1994)*, 81–88. Napoli, Centre Jean Bérard.

d'Agostino, B. and Cerchiai, L. (2004) I Greci nell'Etruria campana. In G.M. Della Fina (ed.) *I Greci in Etruria. Atti dell'XI Convegno Internazionale di Studi sulla Storia e l'Archeologia dell'Etruria*, 271–289. Roma, Quasar.

Delpino, F. (1986) Rapporti e scambi nell'Etruria meridionale villanoviana con particolare riferimento al Mezzogiorno. *Archeologia nella Tuscia II* (Quaderni del Centro di Studio per l'Archeologia Etrusco-Italica 13), 167–176. Roma, CNR.

Delpino, F. (1997) I Greci in Etruria prima della colonizzazione euboica: Ancora su crateri, vino, vite e pennati nell'Italia centrale protostorica. In G. Bartoloni (ed.) *Le Necropoli Arcaiche di Veio. Giornata di Studio in Memoria di Massimo Pallottino*, 185–194. Roma, Università degli Studi di Roma "La Sapienza", Dipartimento di Scienze Storiche, Archeologiche e Antropologiche dell'Antichità.

Delpino, F. (2000) Il principe e la cerimonia del banchetto. In A. Dore, C. Morigi Govi, F. Delpino, F-W. von Hase, G. Bartoloni, G. Colonna, L. Minarini, M. Marchesi, M. Liverani, M. Gras, P. Flourentzos and V. Karageorghis (eds) *Principi Etruschi tra Mediterraneo ed Europa. Catalogo della Mostra (Bologna, Museo Civico Archeologico, 1 Ottobre 2000–1 Aprile 2001)*, 193–195. Venezia, Marsilio.

Delpino, F. (2002) Brocchette a collo obliquo dall'area etrusca. In O. Paoletti and L. Tamagno Perna (eds) *Etruria e Sardegna Centro-Settentrionale tra l'Età del Bronzo Finale e l'Arcaismo. Atti del XXI Convegno di Studi Etruschi ed Italici (Sassari-Alghero-Oristano-Torralba, 13–17 Ottobre 1998)*, 363–385. Pisa–Roma, Istituti Editoriali e Poligrafici Internazionali.

d'Ercole, V. and Martellone, A. (2007) *Regine d'Abruzzo. La Ricchezza nelle Sepolture del I Millennio a.C.*. L'Aquila, Soprintendenza per i Beni Archeologici dell'Abruzzo.

de Marinis, R.C. (1997) La civiltà di Golasecca: I più antichi Celti d'Italia. In M.V. Antico Gallina (ed.) *Popoli Italici e Culture Regionali*, 11–42. Cinisello Balsamo, Silvana Editoriale.

De Min, M., Gambacurta, G. and Ruta Serafini, A. (2005) (eds) *La Città Invisibile. Padova Preromana: Trent'Anni di Scavi e Ricerche. Catalogo della Mostra*. Bologna, Tipoarte.

Dench, E. (1995) *From Barbarians to New Men. Greek, Roman and Modern Perceptions of the Central Apennines*. Oxford, Clarendon.

Dobres, M.-A. and Robb, J. 2000 (eds) *Agency in Archaeology*. London, Routledge.

Dommasnes, H. and Montón-Subiás, S. (2012) European gender archaeologies in historical perspective. *European Journal of Archaeology* 15(3), 367–391.

Dowson, T.A. (2000) (ed.) *Queer Archaeologies* (World Archaeology 32). New York, Taylor & Francis.

Eles, P. von (2002) (ed.) *Guerriero e Sacerdote. Autorità e Comunità nell'Età del Ferro a Verucchio. La Tomba del Trono* (Quaderni di Archeologia dell'Emilia Romagna 6). Borgo S. Lorenzo, All'Insegna del Giglio.

Eles, P. von (2004) Verucchio: Aristocrazia, rango e ruoli in una comunità dell'età del Ferro. In F. Marzatico and P. Gleirscher (eds) *Guerrieri, Principi ed Eroi fra il Danubio e il Po dalla Preistoria all'Alto Medioevo*, 259–261. Trento, Castello del Buonconsiglio.

Eles, P. von (2007) (ed.) *Le Ore e i Giorni delle Donne. Dalla Quotidianità alla Sacralità tra VIII e VII Secolo a.C.. Catalogo della Mostra (Museo Civico Archeologico di Verucchio, 14 Giugno 2007-6 Gennaio 2008)*. Verucchio, Pazzini Editore.

Fogolari, G. and Prosdocimi, A.L. (1988) *I Veneti Antichi. Lingua e Cultura*. Padova, Editoriale Programma.

Foucault, M. (1975) *Discipline and Punish: The Birth of the Prison*. New York, Random House.

Fowler, C. (2004) *The Archaeology of Personhood: An Anthropological Approach*. London, Routledge.

Fulminante, F. (2003) *Le Sepolture Principesche nel Latium Vetus. Tra la Fine della Prima Età del Ferro e l'Inizio dell'Età Orientalizzante*. Roma, "L'Erma" di Bretschneider.

Fulminante, F. (2012) Social network analysis and the emergence of central places. A Case study from Bronze and Early Iron Age central Italy. *Babesch* 87, 1–27.

Fulminante, F. (2014) *The Urbanization of Latium Vetus: From the Bronze Age to the Archaic Era*. Cambridge, Cambridge University Press.

Gamba, M., Gambacurta, G., Ruta Serafini, A., Tiné, V. and Veronese, F. (2013) (eds) *Venetkens. Viaggio nelle Terra dei Veneti Antichi. Catalogo della Mostra (Padova, Palazzo della Ragione, 6 Aprile-17 Novembre 2013)*. Venezia, Marsilio.

Gardner, A. (2004a) (ed.) *Agency Uncovered. Archaeological Perspectives on Social Agency, Power, and Being Human*. Walnut Creek, Left Coast Press.

Gardner, A. (2004b) Introduction: Social agency, power, and being human. In A. Gardner (ed.) *Agency Uncovered. Archaeological Perspectives on Social Agency, Power, and Being Human*, 1–18. Walnut Creek, Left Coast Press.

Gardner, A. (2008) Agency. In R.A. Bentley, H.D.G. Maschner and C. Chippindale (eds) *Handbook of Archaeological Theories*, 95–108. Lanham, MD, AltaMira Press.

Gell, A. (1998) *Art and Agency*. Oxford, Clarendon Press.

Gero, J.M. and Conkey, M.W. (1991) (eds) *Engendering Archaeology: Women and Prehistory*. Oxford, Blackwell.

Giddens, A. (1984) *The Constitution of Society. Outline of the Theory of Structuration*. Cambridge, Polity Press.

Giulierini, P. (2012) (ed.) *Restaurando la Storia. L'Alba dei Principi Etruschi. Catalogo della Mostra (Cortona, Palazzo Casali, 18 Novembre 2012-5 Maggio 2013)*. Cortona, Tiphys Edizioni.

Gleba, M. and Horsnaes, H. (2011) (eds) *Communicating Identities in Italic Iron Age Communities*. Oxford, Oxbow Books.

Granovetter, M. (1973) The strength of weak ties. *American Journal of Sociology* 78(6), 1360–1380.

Guidi, A. (2006) The archaeology of the early state in Italy. *Social Evolution and History* 5(2), 55–89.

Guidi, A. (2010) The archaeology of early state in Italy: New data and acquisitions. *Social Evolution and History* 9(2), 12–27.

Hales, S. and Hodos, T. (2010) (eds) *Material Culture and Social Identities in the Ancient World*. Cambridge, Cambridge University Press.

Herring, E. and Lomas, K. (2000) (eds) *The Emergence of State Identities in Italy in the First Millennium BC*. London, Accordia Research Institute.

Herring, E. and Lomas, K. 2009 (eds) *Gender Identities in Ancient Italy* (BAR S1893). Oxford, Archaeopress.

Horden, P. and Purcell, N. (2000) *The Corrupting Sea: A Study of Mediterranean History*. Oxford, Blackwell.

Iaia, C. (1999) *Simbolismo Funerario e Ideologia alle Origini di una Civiltà Urbana. Forme Rituali nelle Sepolture "Villanoviane" a Tarquinia e Vulci, e nel loro Entroterra* (Grandi Contesti e Problemi della Protostoria Italiana 3). Borgo S. Lorenzo, All'Insegna del Giglio.

Iaia, C. (2005) *Produzioni Toreutiche della Prima Età del Ferro in Italia Centro-Settentrionale. Stili Decorativi, Circolazione, Significato* (Biblioteca di Studi Etruschi 40). Pisa–Roma, Istituti Editoriali e Poligrafici Internazionali.

Iaia, C. (2006) Servizi cerimoniali e da "simposio" in bronzo del Primo Ferro in Italia centro-settentrionale. In P. von Eles (ed.) *La Ritualità Funeraria tra Età del Ferro e Orientalizzante in Italia. Atti del Convegno (Verucchio, 26–27 Giugno 2002)*, 103–110. Pisa–Roma, Istituti Editoriali e Poligrafici Internazionali.

Iaia, C. (2007) Prima del "simposio": Vasi in bronzo e contesto sociale nell' Etruria meridionale protostorica. *Revista d'Arqueologia de Ponent* 16–17, 261–270.

Iaia, C. (2013a) Warrior identity and the materialisation of power in Early Iron Age Etruria. *Accordia Research Papers* 12[2009–2012], 71–95.

Iaia, C. (2013b) Drinking in times of crisis: Alcohol and social change in late Bronze Age Italy. In S. Bergerbrant and S. Sabatini (eds) *Counterpoint: Essays in Archaeology and Heritage Studies in Honour of Professor Kristian Kristiansen* (BAR S2508), 373–382. Oxford, Archaeopress.

Insoll, T. (2007) (ed.) *The Archaeology of Identities: A Reader*. London, Routledge.

Jones, S. (1997) The *Archaeology of Ethnicity: Constructing Identities in the Past and Present*. London, Routledge.

Lo Schiavo, F. (2010) *Le Fibule dell'Italia Meridionale e della Sicilia dall'Età del Bronzo Recente al VI Sec. a.C.*. Stuttgart, Steiner Verlag.

Luni, M. (2004) (ed.) *I Greci in Adriatico 2* (Hesperia 18). Roma, L'"Erma" di Bretschneider.

Knapp, B. (1998) Boys will be boys: Masculinist approaches to a gendered archaeology. In K. Hays-Gilpin and D.S. Whitley (eds) *Reader in Gender Archaeology*, 365–373. London–New York, Routledge.

Knapp, A.B. and van Dommelen, P. (2008) Past practices: Rethinking individuals and agents in archaeology. *Cambridge Archaeological Journal* 18(1), 15–34.

Knapp, A.B. and van Dommelen, P. (2014) (eds) *The Cambridge Prehistory of the Bronze and Iron Age Mediterranean*. New York, Routledge.

Kopytoff, I. (1986) The cultural biography of things. In A. Appadurai (ed.) *The Social Life of Things: Commodities in Cultural Perspective*, 64–91. Cambridge, Cambridge University Press.

Maetzke, G., Paoletti, O. and Tamagno Perna, L. (1990) (eds) *La Civiltà dei Falisci. Atti del XV Convegno di Studi Etruschi ed Italici. (Civita Castellana-Forte Sangallo, 28–31 Maggio 1987)*, 61–102. Firenze, L.S. Olschki.

Malkin, I. (2003) Networks and the emergence of Greek identity. *Mediterranean Historical Review* 18(2), 56–74.

Malkin, I. (2011) *A Small Greek World: Networks in the Ancient Mediterranean*. Oxford, Oxford University Press.

Mandolesi, A. (1999) *La "Prima" Tarquinia. L'Insediamento Protostorico sulla Civita e nel Territorio Circostante*. Borgo S. Lorenzo, All'Insegna del Giglio.

Menichetti, M. (1994) *Archeologia del Potere. Re, Immagini e Miti a Roma e in Etruria in Età Arcaica*. Milano, Longanesi.

Miller, D. (2005) (ed.) *Materiality. Politics, History and Culture*. Durham–London, Duke University Press.

Morgan, L.M. (1997) Imagining the unborn in the Ecuadoran Andes. *Feminist Studies* 23(2), 323–350.

Morgan, L.M. (2006) "Life begins when they steal your bicycle": Cross-cultural practices of personhood at the beginnings and ends of life. *Journal of Law, Medicine & Ethics* 36(2), 193–218.

Morgan, L.M. (2009) *Icons of Life: A Cultural History of Human Embryos*. Berkeley, University of California Press.

Morris, I. (1992) *Death-Ritual and Social Structure in Classical Antiquity*. Cambridge, Cambridge University Press.

Morris, I. (1998) Archaeology and Archaic Greek History. In N.R.E. Fisher and H. van Wees (eds) *Archaic Greece: New Approaches and New Evidence*, 71–74. London, Duckworth.

Morris, I. (1999a) Iron Age Greece and the meanings of "princely tombs". In P. Ruby (ed) *Les Princes de la Protohistoire et l'Émergence de l'État. Actes de la Table Ronde Internationale Organisée par le Centre Jean Bérard et l'École française de Rome (Naples, 27-29 Octobre 1994)*, 57–80. Napoli, Centre Jean Bérard.

Morris, I. (1999b) Archaeology and gender ideologies in Early Archaic Greece. *Transactions of the American Philological Association* 129, 305–317.

Naso, A. (2000) *Piceni: Storia e Archeologia delle Marche in Epoca Preromana.* Milano, Longanesi.

Naso, A. (2015) *Etruscology.* Berlin, De Gruyter.

Osanna, M. and Vullo, S. (2013) (eds) *Segni del Potere. Oggetti di Lusso dal Mediterraneo nell'Appennino Lucano di Età Arcaica.* Venosa, Osanna Edizioni.

Pacciarelli, M. (1991) Territorio, insediamento, comunità in Etruria meridionale agli esordi del processo di urbanizzazione. *Scienze dell'Antichità* 5, 163–208.

Pacciarelli, M. (2001) *Dal Villaggio alla Città. La Svolta Protourbana del 1000 a.C. nell'Italia Tirrenica.* Borgo S. Lorenzo, All'Insegna del Giglio.

Paoletti, O. (2000) (ed.) *Dinamiche di Sviluppo delle Città nell'Etruria Meridionale. Veio, Caere, Tarquinia, Vulci. Atti XXIII Convegno di Studi Etruschi e Italici (Roma-Cerveteri-Tarquinia-Montalto di Castro-Viterbo, 1-6 Ottobre 2001).* Pisa–Roma, Istituti Editoriali e Poligrafici Internazionali.

Parker Pearson, A. (1999) *The Archaeology of Death and Burial.* Stroud, Sutton.

Perego, E. (2011) Engendered actions: Agency and ritual in pre-Roman Veneto. In A. Chaniotis (ed.) *Ritual Dynamics in the Ancient Mediterranean: Agency, Emotion, Gender, Reception*, 17–42. Stuttgart, Steinar.

Perego, E. (2012) *The Construction of Personhood in Veneto (Italy) between the Late Bronze Age and the Early Roman Period.* Unpublished thesis, University College London.

Perego, E. (2014a) Final Bronze Age and social change in Veneto: Group membership, ethnicity and marginality. *Mélanges de l'École française de Rome* 126(2) (online version).

Perego, E. (2014b) Anomalous mortuary behaviour and social exclusion in Iron Age Italy: A case study from the Veneto region. *Journal of Mediterranean Archaeology* 27(2), 161–185.

Perego, E. (forthcoming) Gendered powers, gendered persons. Gender and personhood in a case study from Iron Age Veneto, Italy. In G. Saltini Semerari and N. Sojc (eds) *Investigating Gender in Mediterranean Archaeology.*

Perego, E., Saracino, M., Zamboni, L. and Zanoni, V. (2015) Practices of ritual marginalisation in protohistoric Veneto: Evidence from the field. In Z.L. Devlin and E.J. Graham (eds) *Death Embodied: Archaeological Approaches to the Treatment of the Corpse*, 129–159. Oxford, Oxbow Books.

Pesando, F. (2005) (ed.) *L'Italia Antica.* Roma, Roma, Carocci.

Quirino, T. (2011) Le case F I e F II del Forcello di Bagnolo San Vito (MN): Analisi preliminare di due abitazioni etrusche di fine VI secolo a.C.. *Notizie Archeologiche Bergomensi* 19, 379–390.

Rawlings, L. (1999) *Condottieri and clansmen:* Early Italian raiding, warfare and the State. In K. Hopwood (ed.) *Organised Crime in Antiquity*, 97–127. London, Duckworth.

Remotti, F. (2010) *L'Ossessione Identitaria.* Bari, Laterza.

Rich, J. (2007) Warfare and the army in early Rome. In P. Erdkamp (ed.) *A Companion to the Roman Army*, 7–23. Oxford, Blackwell.

Riva, C. (2010) *The Urbanisation of Etruria: Funerary Ritual and Social Change, 700-600 BC.* Cambridge, Cambridge University Press.

Robb, J. (1994) Gender contradictions, moral coalitions, and inequality in prehistoric Italy. *Journal of European Archaeology* 2(1), 2–49.

Robb, J. (2002) Time and biography. Osteobiography of the Italian Neolithic lifespan. In Y. Hamilakis, M. Pluciennik and S. Tarlow (eds) *Thinking Through the Body: Archaeologies of Corporeality*, 153–171. New York, Kluwer/Plenum.

Robb, J. (2005) Agency. In A.C. Renfrew and P.G. Bahn (eds) *Archaeology: The Key Concepts.* London, Routledge.

Robb, J. (2007) *The Early Mediterranean Village: Agency, Material Culture and Social Change in Neolithic Italy*. Cambridge, Cambridge University Press.

Robb, J. (2010) Beyond agency. *World Archaeology* 42, 493–520.

Ruggeri, M. (2007) (ed.) *Guerrieri e Re dell'Abruzzo Antico*. Pescara, Carsa.

Ruggeri, M. (2010) L'Abruzzo dei guerrieri: Da Comino a Capestrano. In L. Franchi dell'Orto (ed.) *Pinna Vestinorum e il Popolo dei Vestini*, 274–285. Roma, "L'Erma" di Bretschneider.

Ruta Serafini, A. (2002) (ed.) *Este Preromana: Una Città e i Suoi Santuari*. Treviso, Canova.

Saltini Semerari, G. and Sojc, N. (forthcoming) (eds) *Investigating Gender in Mediterranean Archaeology*.

Saracino, M. (2009) Sepolture atipiche durante il Bronzo Finale e la seconda Età del Ferro in Veneto. *Padusa* 45, 65–72.

Saracino, M., Zamboni, L., Zanoni, V. and Perego, E. (2014) Investigating social exclusion in late prehistoric Italy: Preliminary results of the 'IN or OUT' Project (Phase 1). *Papers from the Institute of Archaeology* 12(1), 1–12.

Sassatelli, G. and Govi, E. (2005) (eds) *Culti, Forma Urbana e Artigianato a Marzabotto. Nuove Prospettive di Ricerca. Atti del Convegno di Studi (Bologna, S. Giovanni in Monte, 3-4 Giugno 2003)*. Bologna, Ante Quem.

Silvestrini, M. and Sabbatini, T. (2008) (eds) *Potere e Splendore. Gli Antichi Piceni a Matelica. Catalogo della Mostra (Matelica, Palazzo Ottoni, 19 Aprile-31 Ottobre 2008)*. Roma, L'"Erma" di Bretschneider.

Saracino, M. and Zanoni, V. (2014) The marginal people of the Iron Age in north-eastern Italy: A comparative study. i.e. The Iron age written by the losers. *Revue Archéologique de l'Est (36e Supplément)*, 535–550.

Sciacca, F. (2005) *Patere Baccellate in Bronzo. Oriente, Grecia, Italia in Età Orientalizzante* (Studia Archaeologica 139). Roma, L'"Erma" di Bretschneider.

Scopacasa, R. (2014) Gender and ritual in ancient Italy: A quantitative approach to grave goods and skeletal evidence in pre-Roman Samnium. *American Journal of Archaeology* 188(2), 241–266.

Scopacasa, R. (2015) *Ancient Samnium. Settlement, Culture and Identity between History and Archaeology*. Oxford, Oxford University Press.

Scopacasa, R. (forthcoming) Ethinc identity. In G.J. Bradley and G. Farney (eds) *A Handbook of Ancient Italic Groups*. Berlin, De Gruyter.

Smith, C.J. (1996) *Early Rome and Latium. Economy and Society c. 1000 to 500 BC*. Oxford, Clarendon.

Smith, C.J. (2005) The beginnings of urbanization at Rome. In B.W. Cunliffe and R. Osborne (eds) *Mediterranean Urbanization 800-600 BC*, 91–111. Oxford, Oxford University Press.

Smith, C.J. (2006) *The Roman Clan: The Gens from Ancient Ideology to Modern Anthropology*. Cambridge, Cambridge University Press.

Smith, C.J. (2012) Comment on Carandini. In G. Cifani and S. Stoddart (eds) *Landscape, Ethnicity and Identity in the Archaic Mediterranean Area*, 20–23. Oxford, Oxbow Books.

Strathern, M. (1988) *The Gender of the Gift*. Cambridge, Cambridge University Press.

Tagliamonte, G. (1996) *I Sanniti. Caudini, Irpini, Pentri, Carricini, Frentani*. Milano, Longanesi.

Tagliamonte, G. (2003) La terribile bellezza del guerriero. In *I Piceni e l'Italia Medio-Adriatica. Atti del XXII Convegno di Studi Etruschi e Italici (Ascoli Piceno-Teramo-Ancona, 9-13 Aprile 2000)*, 533–550. Pisa–Roma, Istituti Editoriali e Poligrafici Internazionali.

Terrenato, N. and Haggis, D. 2011 (eds) *State Formation in Italy and Greece. Questioning the Neoevolutionist Paradigm*. Oxford, Oxbow Books.

Torelli, M. (2000) *Gli Etruschi*. Milano, Bompiani.

Torelli, M. (2006) *Insignia imperii*. La genesi dei simboli del potere nel mondo etrusco e romano. *Ostraka* 15, 407–430.

Trentacoste, A. (2013) Faunal remains from the Etruscan sanctuary at Poggio Colla (Vicchio di Mugello). *Etruscan Studies* 16(1), 75–105.

Turfa, J.M. (2013) *The Etruscan World*. London–New York, Routledge.

van Dommelen, P. (1997) Colonial constructs: Colonialism and archaeology in the Mediterranean. *World Archaeology*, 305–323.

van Dommelen, P. (2012) Colonialism and migration in the ancient Mediterranean. *Annual Review of Anthropology* 41, 93–409.

Zanoni, V. (2011) *Out of Place. Human Skeletal Remains from Non-Funerary Contexts: Northern Italy during the 1st Millennium BC* (BAR S2306). Oxford, Archaeopress.

Zifferero, A. (2005) Economia, divinità e frontiera: Sul ruolo di alcuni santuari di confine in Etruria meridionale. *Ostraka* 2, 333–350.

Whitehouse, R.D. (1998) (ed.) *Gender and Italian Archaeology: Challenging the Stereotypes.* London, Accordia Research Institute and Institute of Archaeology, University College London.

Whitehouse, R.D. (2001) Exploring gender in prehistoric Italy. *Papers of the British School at Rome* 69, 49–96.

Whitehouse, R.D. (2013) Gender in central Mediterranean prehistory. In D. Bolger (ed.) *Blackwell Companion to Gender Prehistory*, 480–501. Oxford, Blackwell.

Section 1

Funerary symbolism and ritual practice:
from élite identities to gender, age,
personhood and connectivity

Chapter 1

Theoretical issues in the interpretation of cemeteries and case studies from Etruria to Campania

Mariassunta Cuozzo

Introduction

> "(...) the socially constituted classificatory schemes through which we actively construct society tend to represent the structures out of which they are issued as natural and necessary, rather than as the historically contingent fallouts of a given balance of powers between classes, "ethnic" groups, or genders. But if we grant that symbolic systems are social products that contribute to making the world, that they do not simply mirror social relations but help constitute them, then one can, within limits, transform the world by transforming its representation" (Wacquant 1992, 13–4).

As is well-known, for over 30 years the question of whether funerary practices can provide an 'accurate' image of society, its stratification and its complexity, has been the central issue in the archaeological study of funerary sites (*cf.* Cuozzo 1996; 2000 for a discussion and review of previous bibliography; below). This has been one of the most hotly debated topics in the context of the New Archaeology, and one of the chief challenges taken on by post-processual archaeologists in their radical critique of previous paradigms. Today, approaches to the study of cemeteries should reject any equivalence between social structure and funerary representation, as well as between funerary complexity and social complexity. The gauging of wealth, and the reconstruction of social hierarchies, are – in my opinion – no longer the key concerns in current research on funerary customs.

This chapter investigates the construction of élite ideologies, gender and collective identities in Italian burial sites of the so-called 'Orientalizing' period (*c.* 725–575 BC), while also addressing some theoretical issues concerning cemeteries dating from the Iron Age (*c.* ninth–eighth centuries BC). From a theoretical standpoint, my approach is to regard funerary performances and cemeteries as active ritual contexts, and as the material outcome of mentalities, identities, ideologies, political and religious cosmologies, social strategies and technologies of power. Funerary rites and cemeteries can constitute a privileged domain for the construction of the social imaginary. Nevertheless, the debate on the interpretation of funerary sites has shown that the analysis of burials involves multiple and often contradictory and misleading aspects. The focus on social agents that is advocated in this volume allows laying special stress on the tensions that develop between the rules of a community, and the strategies of negotiation and resistance upheld by minority groups, specific social segments such as gender and age groups, and even single individuals. From this perspective, this chapter will focus on case studies from Etruria and Campania (Fig. 1.1). As regards gender identity, some space will be devoted to the controversial issue of women's role in Etruscan and Italic societies.

Theoretical perspectives

In the last 30 years, an important strand of archaeological literature focusing on mortuary practice has stressed the active and productive role of ritual. From this perspective, funerary rites can never be regarded as a mere way of communicating the values of a community in a straightforward manner (e.g. Cuozzo 1996; 2000; 2003; d'Agostino 1985; d'Agostino and Schnapp 1982; Hodder 1982; Morris 1987; Parker Pearson 1999). Instead, what is crucial within this theoretical framework is to investigate funerary practices in view of their multiple layers of meaning as well as their semantic oppositions or ambiguities; furthermore, it is important to focus on how the burying group manipulates the multiple meanings of burial rites in order to construct particular images of itself. One of the most important contributions of Ian Hodder's work (1982) was to recognize the active role of material culture in structuring society and human interaction (on this issue *cf.* also an alternative approach based on object biography and the agency of objects in Shipley, this volume, with bibliography). This research generated one of the most significant debates within post-processualism, which led to a radical change in perspective in archaeological studies on death and burial (e.g. Cuozzo 1996; 2000, and Hodder 2012, all with bibliography). The focus of research carried out within this framework is no longer on the extent to which funerary rites may reflect the society of the living; rather, the main concern is to understand how funerary rites (like other types of ritual) can form an integral part of socio-political, cultural and religious constructs, as well as a component of the mind-sets/thought-worlds and ideologies of the burying community. Funerary performances can play an active role in perpetuating, legitimizing and crystallizing social structures. They also have the power to convey new mentalities, ideologies and technologies of power, as well as different social identities, and different conceptions of the body and the individual.

An adequate interpretation of burial sites should approach the funerary context as the outcome of social performance, which is often extended through time and renewed at regular intervals. Scholars must look at material culture in order

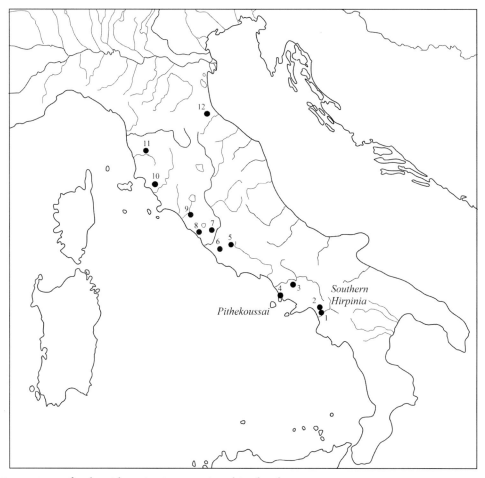

Fig. 1.1: Map of Italy with main sites mentioned in the chapter: 1. Pontecagnano; 2. Monte Vetrano; 3. Capua; 4. Cumae; 5. Praeneste; 6. Castel di Decima; 7. Veii; 8. Caere; 9. Tarquinia; 10. Vetulonia; 11. Volterra; 12. Verucchio (elaboration R. Scopacasa, base map by C. Iaia).

to reconstruct the complex sequence of "words, silences, gestures, behaviours" (d'Agostino 1985, 52; *cf.* also Cuozzo 2003) that the deceased person is granted at the funeral, and that come to represent the social, ceremonial and cultic actions through which the dead person's image is memorialized. Ceremonial performances allow for multiple layers of meaning and multiple interpretations. They also bring into play the relationship with the group's ancestors and the supernatural. At all stages of the funerary performance, the strategies of the deceased individual's group take priority. In each context, a community's system of values, mental attitudes and conceptions of the border between the living and the dead, inform funerary practice and its relationship with society.

As noted above, the interpretation of funerary contexts is framed with difficulties and involves contradictory and misleading aspects. In my previous analysis of the ancient cemeteries of Pontecagnano in Campania, I suggested the possibility that contemporaneous and potentially conflicting social dynamics existed there, in relation to four principal 'fields of action', which might have been developed by different social groups and different social agents (Cuozzo 2003; on ancient Campania and Pontecagnano *cf.* also for example Cerchiai 2010; d'Agostino 1977; 2011a; 2011b; below; Morris this volume). These 'fields of action' – which promoted the creation of different ideologies in funerary representation – are

a. the field of action of the *community*, which is manifested in the rules and prohibitions determining the basic code of funerary practice;
b. the field of action of *different or antagonist groups*, which is manifested through the accentuation of differences in funerary practice;
c. the field of action of the so-called *transversal social segments*, which involves the negotiation of gender, age and ethnic identities;
d. the field of action of the *individual(s)*, which can encompass a wide range of ritual variations determined by individual actions, as well as abnormal funerary behaviour and the adoption of uncommon funerary practices.

The ritual and socio-political dynamics created at the time of the funeral – and the ways in which they manifest themselves as one field of action (e.g. the burial strategies enacted by selected segments of the community) prevails over others (e.g. collective norms or the needs of individuals) – depend on the degree and forms of social control that develop in different historical and political contexts. We first need to ascertain whether – on the basis of the 'mentality' and values prevailing in any given social context – priority is given to ritual practices reflecting the construction of wider social hierarchies, or whether other aspects are enhanced (for example, the personal needs of an individual). We may then investigate how different ideologies develop and are negotiated in any given context (Bourdieu and Waquant 1992).

In light of these premises, this chapter draws on Godelier's notion of "monopoly of the imaginary" (Godelier 1985). Godelier has suggested that the preservation of a particular social order does not depend entirely on the degree to which élite groups control the material means of production. Instead, it is the control over the community's relations with the outside world, the divine, the ritual sphere and cosmological forces that guarantees the élite's power and legitimacy in the long term, rather than wealth *per se* (*cf.* also Godelier 1999).

Often, funerary rites are carried out by the people who had a special connection with the deceased. These 'burying groups' who are in charge of burial rituals are interested in presenting the deceased in a particular manner, and therefore may manipulate the deceased person's identity in view of their own agendas – to the point where the deceased sometimes become what they had not been in life (Hodder 1982). The collective nature of funerary practice has raised some controversial questions: to what extent can we apply the notion of the 'individual' to our analysis of funerary practice? Is it possible to identify individual agency in the mortuary record? Scholars have offered different and contentious answers to this question (*cf.* Knapp and van Dommelen 2008, and Thomas in Knapp and van Dommelen 2008 for an example of diverging views on the subject).

In view of this debate, the following issues are central to my present argument:

1. the symbolism that can be encoded in burial sites (i.e. the 'semiology' of cemeteries);
2. the demographic and social representativeness of a burial site, and the distinction that may arise between a "visible élite and a largely invisible majority" (e.g. Morris 1987, 94–5);
3. gender dynamics;
4. the active role of material culture in burial rituals, and the presence of several ideologies at work in the same funerary context.

The semiology of burial sites

Already in the late 1970s and the 1980s, scholars such as d'Agostino and Schnapp provided a definition of funerary ideology emphasizing the alterations, differences and antagonisms that exist in funerary practices. This definition laid the foundation for a 'semiotics of cemeteries' based on the acknowledgment of the multifunctionality of funerary symbols, whereby graves cannot be regarded as inert clues, but as key components of modes of expression that need to be understood in their diversity and polysemy (e.g. d'Agostino and Schnapp 1982; d'Agostino 1985). These considerations led to a second highly significant development: authors working within this research framework rejected any simplistic equivalence between funerary customs and social structure, as funerary rituals can never be regarded as univocal reflections of selected models of social organization (*cf.* also the discussion above and Cuozzo 1996; 2000, with bibliography). Following U. Eco's work on semiology, a 'semiotics of cemeteries' calls indeed for a shift away from the analysis of 'sign systems' to an investigation of the modes of 'sign production' (e.g. Eco 1975).

Demographic and social representativeness of funerary sites

The absence of a direct and neutral relationship between society and ritual has been noted in studies on the demographic and social representativeness of cemeteries. Notably, funerary strategies based on discrimination and exclusion reserve formal burial only for specific categories of people (on this issue *cf.* also Iaia, Scopacasa, Zanoni, Perego, and Perego and Scopacasa this volume, all with additional bibliography). This selection is usually grounded in criteria such as the age, gender and/or social standing of the deceased. It was Morris (1987) who introduced this important issue into the archaeological debate, although some earlier paleo-demographic studies had already broached it. Morris showed that, in many cases, it is far from granted that a cemetery is fully representative of a community, not only from the standpoint of social composition, but also from that of demography. The exclusive representation of privileged social segments – as well as of select gender and/or age groups – depends on political, social and ideological mechanisms that need to be investigated in each individual context. For example, Morris' studies revealed a rigid subdivision of the population of ancient Attica. In some periods, formal burial appears to have been reserved for only a quarter of the adult population, as the result of a rigid subdivision of the community into a "visible élite and a largely invisible majority" (e.g. Morris 1987, 94–5; review and discussion in Cuozzo 2000, 7, with additional bibliography). The small number of children that may be found in formal burial areas is one of the clearest indications of selectivity in formal burial, as children may represent up to 40–50% of the population in pre-industrial agricultural societies (*cf.* also Zanoni, this volume, on the same issue; *cf.* however the chapter by Di Lorenzo *et al.* on the widespread burial of children in formal cemeteries at Iron Age and Orientalizing Verucchio, in Emilia Romagna). For Morris, the representativeness of a cemetery needs to be ascertained beforehand in two main ways: first, by examining the demographic composition of the buried groups, namely the ratio between sexes and different age groups: this analysis should be carried out by using parameters that are adequate for pre-industrial agricultural societies (or any society form comparable to the archaeological context under consideration); secondly, by examining funerary variability to reveal the social makeup of the burying group.

As previously noted, the insufficient presence of children/sub-adults in funerary sites is regarded as one of the clearest indicators of selectiveness in formal burial. This is a highly relevant aspect that should be considered central to the archaeological inquiry, and should be the first step in any study of cemeteries. Notably, however, this issue has often been ignored or underestimated, even in recent studies on Etruscan and Italic cemeteries.

Gender identity

Archaeological research carried out in Italy, unlike academic work carried out in English-speaking countries and several European countries, has not yet developed a true theoretical debate on gender (*cf.* also Dommasnes and Montón-Subías 2012 on this issue). This situation contrasts with theoretical developments in other fields in the humanities, such as history, anthropology and sociology, where an interesting debate on gender is under way in Italian universities. In these fields, interdisciplinary studies, meetings and seminars on the subject have been recently promoted, while doctoral and master's courses are focusing on the themes of gender and equal opportunities for women. The near-absence of a debate on gender in Italian archaeology is possibly due to the anomalous character of the Italian theoretical debate on the ancient world. The 1970s and 1980s witnessed significant Marxist-inspired discussion mainly through the journal *Dialoghi di Archeologia*: however, in subsequent years the theoretical debate waned and scholars became reluctant to address themes whose implications reached beyond the confines of the discipline – with a few exceptions, especially in the field of mortuary archaeology. Here I cannot go into the complex implications of these issues, which deserve further reflection in the future.

Nevertheless, some recent research has called into question any approach to past gender dynamics that seeks to extol the role of women at all costs. These analyses have also questioned the methodology of some studies, notably those based on characterizations of women by certain Greek and Roman authors (e.g. Izzet 2007; Riva 2010).

In the international scene, gender archaeology is increasingly evolving into an 'archaeology of differences', based on the analysis of variable and multidimensional aspects of identity (e.g. Díaz-Andreu *et al.* 2007; Nelson 2006), another issue scarcely tackled in archaeological research carried out in Italy (on this issue *cf.* also Zamboni this volume). Gender research in archaeology has also addressed socio-political issues such as gender bias or equal professional opportunities for women in the field (e.g. Hamilton *et al.* 2007). By contrast, comparatively few Italian studies have focused on these issues, as well as on the construction of gender identity in the burial context, or on past conceptions of women (among these *cf.* for example Bietti Sestieri 1992; Cuozzo and Guidi 2013; Herring and Lomas 2009; Perego 2011; Riva 2010; Scopacasa 2014; Whitehouse 1998, as well as Faustoferri, O'Donoghue, the introduction, and Perego and Scopacasa this volume, all with discussion and additional bibliography).

As regards the situation outlined so far, caution is called for before we can say that fundamental research questions such as gender bias in the interpretation of archaeological contexts have been answered or superseded. I must also stress the importance of promoting studies on gender and the role of women in antiquity in Italy, where consideration for women has possibly reached its lowest ebb in the last few years – as Italy lags far behind other European countries with regard to equal opportunities for women (on the same issue, and on the impact that the socio-political situation of the country may have in affecting gender research in Italian archaeology *cf.* Perego 2011).

As regards Etruscan and Italic archaeological contexts, discussion by scholars working in Italy should be resumed on a new basis. This should be done, for example, by drawing on recent developments in gender theory. In particular, I regard two research themes in international gender studies to be especially worthy of future investigation: (*a*) the construction of feminine identity and the negotiation of women's roles through an analysis of funerary evidence – a theme that often involves taking into consideration other forms of identity, such as those based on the dead person's age or ethnicity (on the issues inherent to the notion of multiple identities *cf.* however Zamboni this volume); (*b*) the ambiguity arising from the overlap between gender and social status.

Interesting results can be achieved by examining gender dynamics in Italian cemeteries dating from the Early Iron Age onwards (*c.* ninth–eighth centuries BC). As far as the research theme that I mentioned as (*b*) above is concerned, Díaz-Andreu and Tortosa (1998) and Arnold (1996) have proposed a gender-based perspective that

I find especially interesting. These authors investigate the semantic ambiguities arising from the connection between gender and status. In the case studies they discuss, the gender that is equivalent to the 'high-status female' is ideologically constructed through an appropriation, negotiation and re-working of typically male symbols on the one hand, and through iconographic codes usually reserved for female deities, on the other. In Italy, some studies on 'princely' female figures in Etruria and Campania have already adopted this line of inquiry (e.g. Cuozzo 2003), and this is the interpretive path I choose to follow here (on the 'princely' burial phenomenon *cf.* also Morris this volume).

Active material culture and the presence of different ideologies within the same context
No less relevant in analyses of funerary contexts is the study of the mechanisms through which ideology is constructed by social actors. Also worthy to consider is the possibility that different ideologies may coexist within the same context. This complicates the analysis of archaeological evidence, as it highlights the possibility that material culture can be used by different social actors to support diverging or even conflicting ideologies at the same time. As hinted above, I am especially interested in the 'field of action' developed by different/individual social agents, who may promote the creation of several different ideologies in the same burial context.

Based on this premise, I shall focus on some aspects of the mortuary archaeological evidence between the second half of the eighth century BC (*c.* 750–725 BC) and the Orientalizing period (*c.* 725–575 BC), with particular emphasis on selected case studies. Given the scope of this chapter, I have decided to focus on two significant examples. The first case study, set in the context of the Etruscan Orientalizing culture, illuminates the central themes of (*a*) the social selectiveness of burial sites, and (*b*) the gradual stiffening of the rules of access to formal burial over time, marking a split between a "visible élite and a largely invisible majority" (on the issue of funerary visibility and practices of inclusion and exclusion from formal burial *cf.* also Scopacasa, Perego and Scopacasa, Zanoni, Di Lorenzo *et al*, Perego and Iaia, especially endnote 3, this volume). The second case study, on the other hand, will focus on the intersection between status and gender in relation to élite burials in contexts of cultural hybridization or *métissage*; in particular, the creation of new symbolic strategies is exemplified by an analysis of some 'princely' graves in Campania, on which recent finds have shed new light.

Etruria: visible élites, invisible majorities
In Etruria, the construction of new forms of social imaginary, which were connected to new forms of power at the start of the Orientalizing period, was certainly not led by new élite groups (on burial rites and social complexity in Etruria from the Iron Age to the Archaic period *cf.* also Iaia, Shipley and O'Donoghue this volume; on Latium *cf.* the chapter by Rajala). On the contrary, these new forms of social imaginary were rooted in

the long process of transformation that preceded this phase and stretched back into the Iron Age. However, the élite groups that spearheaded this process did seek to represent themselves as new, by constructing a language of power that re-worked older ideas, artefacts and technologies to express new meanings (e.g. Cuozzo 2003). The purpose of the new symbolic apparatus was to display power, but even more so to connect the community with the cosmological sphere, the gods and the external world, which in this period coincided with the Mediterranean (e.g. Godelier 1985; 1999; Horden and Purcell 2000). Ideologies conventionally labelled as 'princely' provided the basis for the development of new forms of social imaginary and processes of social reproduction, which took over at a time when the old symbolic apparatus of the Iron Age was in crisis. The symbolism of the Iron Age, even in its expanded form observable during the eighth century BC, was no longer adequate for the expression of new forms of power. This required a shift in the social imaginary, a transition towards an ideology that we may define as that of the "living ancestor" (e.g. Antonaccio 2002). The construction of both a funerary representation and a material culture exclusively reserved for the élite seems to go hand in hand with the virtual disappearance of subordinate social groups from formal burial sites, reflecting a rigid split between "a visible élite and a largely invisible majority" (Cuozzo 2003; Morris 1987).

Thus, following the approach of Bourdieu (Bourdieu 1977; Bourdieu and Wacquant 1992; Godelier 1999), we might argue that a social order founded on the long-term hegemony of aristocracies is primarily legitimized (or its instability concealed) through forms of 'symbolic violence' (e.g. Cuozzo 2003). In Etruria, this symbolic violence was implemented through practice and *habitus*, namely the everyday instilling of social norms, and through the ideological construction of the image of a balanced social system (on the use of the notion of *habitus* to address the issue of violence and explain aspects of the funerary record of Iron Age Italy *cf.* also Perego this volume).

A debated theme is that of the social organization and the role of rulers in Orientalizing Etruria. According to a widespread view (e.g. Colonna 2002; Torelli 2000; *cf.* additional discussion and bibliography in Morris, this volume), the gentilicial or 'patron-client' organization that prevailed in the Roman world also existed in Etruria as early as the Iron Age, and especially in the Orientalizing period. In his relationship with the other members of his aristocratic group, the head of the aristocratic clan – or *princeps gentis* – was a *primus inter pares* or 'first among equals'. I share the concern expressed by Smith (2006), among others, about the risks of projecting the historical tradition and vocabulary of the Roman *gens* onto the archaeological evidence, and especially the application of these categories to the Etruscan funerary evidence and social milieu. It is true that the rise in Etruria of 'gentilicial' forms of organization recalling those of the Roman world is borne out by the appearance of the *nomen gentilicium* (the name of one's *gens*) in the epigraphy of the Orientalizing period (e.g. Colonna 2002; Torelli 2000). However, subaltern social classes comparable to the Roman clients are invisible in the archaeological record of the period, and only make an appearance in the epigraphic record at the end of the Archaic period. In spite of all these challenges, the concepts of 'prince' and 'princely' are in my opinion still useful as a means to summarize the complexity of how leading social figures represented themselves in the Orientalizing period. These 'living ancestors' were the 'princes' of groups that competed for the monopoly over political and social power, rather than kings wielding a centralized power – as is the case in later periods.

One of the main issues I have investigated is that of the strategies for controlling the collective imaginary. From this perspective, it is arguable that the real strength of Etruscan aristocracies in the Orientalizing phase was their ability to fashion their identity through a number of different cultural inputs. This composite material image was built on a set of symbols conventionally defined as 'princely', which were partly based on the circulation of gifts among aristocrats (as well as on war and piracy), but were reinforced and amplified by an increase in craft production. This phenomenon reflects the interconnection and competition between the élite groups of the Tyrrhenian area of Italy, which transcended ethnic and gender distinctions. From the main centres of Etruria (Caere, Veii, Tarquinia, Vetulonia, Volterra etc.) to Latium (Praeneste, Castel di Decima, Laurentina etc.), to the Greek colonies and the Etruscanized centres of Campania (Cumae and Pontecagnano), the élites of this period were connected by a shared material culture of luxury and by shared symbolic discourses (e.g. Bartoloni 2003; d'Agostino 1977; Riva 2010). The similarities between the 'princely' tombs that emerged from these shared practices are rooted in a selected set of symbols: the evocation of a 'Homeric' material culture and funerary ritual, with the adoption of cremation; the deposition of cremated remains in a metal vase; the multiplication of the ceremonial insignia of power and the sacred (such as thrones, fans, sceptres, the *lituus* etc.); the adoption of ritual forms of drinking that evoked privileged forms of commensality (such as the seated banquet, the Greek symposium and Oriental banqueting styles) and were alluded to by the deposition of selected sympotic equipment (on ritual drinking in Iron Age Etruria and Latium *cf.* also Iaia this volume); the presence of chariots; the burial of multifunctional sets of implements connected to the spheres of the sacrifice, the hearth and the banquet (e.g. axes, knives, spits, andirons etc.); the display of similar or even identical types of luxury 'Orientalizing' objects, many imported from the Phoenician or Greek eastern Mediterranean, but more often produced locally (e.g. golden silver wine jugs or *oinochoai*, cups and dishes or *paterae* with figurative decoration in the so-called 'Phoenician-Cypriot style'; bronze cauldrons and tripods with appliqués shaped as gryphons, sirens or other fantastical creatures; wrought ivory; jewellery and the like: *cf.* for example Bartoloni 2000; d'Agostino 1977). A splendid example of the fluidity of ethnic and cultural boundaries between Tyrrhenian élite groups is the use of Etruscan shields as lids for the bronze cauldrons containing the urns in which the cremated remains of the earliest Greek colonists of Cumae were placed, as the 'Homeric' ritual prescribed. The best-known case is that of the exceptional Tomb 104 at Fondo Artiaco (Cuozzo 2007).

However, the main Etruscan centres and élite groups also display an accentuated particularism and identity (e.g. d'Agostino 1999a; 1999b), or conservative attitudes which find expression in ritual, and especially in the choice of local pottery. In particular, the use of local ceramics involved either traditional wares such as impasto, or newly created ones such as *bucchero*, which combined the adoption of traditional techniques with technological, morphological and stylistic innovations.

As I have stressed above, an integral part of the domination strategies and forms of 'symbolic violence' enacted by the Etruscan aristocracies during the Orientalizing period was the virtual disappearance of subordinate social groups from the cemeteries. An illuminating example of this phenomenon is offered by burial sites that were exclusively reserved for a very restricted élite. Such cemeteries often feature chamber tombs – as well as other tomb types – which are surmounted by monumental *tumuli*. These *tumuli* are attested in different but equally significant forms in southern and northern Etruria, from Caere (Cerveteri) to Vetulonia (e.g. Fig. 1.2; for a discussion of burial in chamber tombs in central Italy *cf.* Rajala this volume, with one chamber tomb seen in Fig. 8.2; also O'Donoghue this volume). Although they apparently consisted of multiple graves housing several family or clan members, the rare cases where human remains are preserved (especially in the earlier phases) point to the careful selection of very few individuals, possibly belonging to privileged descent lines.

However, the general lack of visibility of the tombs of non-élite or subordinate groups may partially result from the lack of systematic excavations of Orientalizing cemeteries, especially since many of these sites were excavated in the nineteenth and early twentieth centuries. A further issue that has been recognized, but is often underestimated, involves the reliability of past excavation methods. Indeed, the techniques used in earlier archaeological investigations have often caused not only the loss of important contextual information about grave goods, but also the complete loss of skeletal remains, and all the information about the buried individuals, excepting only a few cases. This is a significant problem, especially when we consider the elaborate rituality and individuality of body treatments that have been revealed in the few cases where osteological analysis is available.

The Monte Michele cemetery at Veii contains an excellent example of the ambiguity of social selectiveness through funerary ritual, and of the stiffening of the rules of access to formal burial (on Veii *cf.* also briefly Iaia and Rajala this volume). Tomb 5 at Monte Michele dates from *c.* 675–650 BC, and is surrounded by a group of more recent graves (Sgubini Moretti 2000). It is a square chamber tomb with two smaller rooms opening onto the *dromos*. The grave contained three or possibly four burials, presumably belonging to members of the same family. In the room on the left was a very young sub-adult, inhumed and lacking grave goods, except for three lead plates. These were possibly used to hold in place a mortuary shroud. The room on the right housed a cremated young man, about 18–20 years old at death, whose remains were collected in an Italo-Geometric jar along with two iron spearheads and a sober but significant set of vases; the latter included a Protocorinthian ovoid *aryballos*

Fig. 1.2: Cerveteri: a. Tumulus and entrance to the chamber tombs; b. interior of the Regolini Galassi Tomb (both after Lawrence 1932 in Project Gutenberg Australia: http://gutenberg.net.au/).

(c. 670 BC) placed inside a large impasto *dolium*. The main chamber is believed to have been reserved for a couple of individuals of 'princely' status. On the left must have been a female whose skeletal remains were not found; her presence, however, is indicated by 'female-type' fibulae made of precious materials, as well as by textile instruments found in association with a knife, and an elaborate set of vases. On the right was a cremated adult whose grave goods suggest the male gender.

The first consideration that comes to mind is that the number of individuals buried in this tomb is very small, especially in comparison with contemporaneous graves, such as the Regolini–Galassi Tomb in south Etruria (*cf.* Fig. 1.2b). In view of the choice of specific burial rites for the sub-adult deceased, the osteological evidence from Tomb 5 at Monte Michele may actually bear witness to the dying out of a direct line of descent in less than a generation. Along the path leading from biological death to 'social death', the individual and collective tragedy of the group is reinterpreted, adapted and reformulated in conformity with a funerary ideology that celebrates the myth of lineage continuity. This is achieved through the lavishness of grave goods and funerary ritual, and by portraying the aristocratic group as 'living ancestors'.

Another equally important aspect is the extremely elaborate ritual adopted, which makes this tomb an emblematic case study, shedding light on burial practices whose various phases of development elude us at most Etruscan sites. This evidence reminds us of how the human body is central to mortuary ritual – a fact often obscured by the pre-eminence accorded to grave goods or grave architecture in Italian archaeology (Cuozzo 2003; *cf.* for example Parker Pearson 1999 with bibliography on research in Anglophone countries). In the case of Monte Michele Tomb 5, although two of the dead individuals were cremated, the charred bones were reassembled in order to create a fictitious reproduction of anatomical connection. The cremated human remains from the main chamber, for example, were placed in a cloth that was fastened with three silver 'serpentine' fibulae and a golden silver ornament of the *affibbiaglio a sbarre* type – a typical ornament of the 'princely' attire. The cloth was then placed in a bronze box with a double-pitched roof harking back to the burial customs of the Iron Age. In the case of Monte Michele Tomb 5, however, the urn is made of metal rather than clay, and displays the image of a Gorgon, which suggests connections with the Greek world. The urn itself was placed on a four-wheeled chariot that functioned as a hearse. The composite nature of the funerary ceremony and treatment of the corpse is evident in the contradiction between the active appropriation of a Homeric 'heroic' rite – a choice of many Mediterranean and Tyrrhenian élite groups – and a reluctance to accept the loss of the body as an indivisible entity (for examples of similarly complex, and sometimes contradictory, dynamics in the treatment of the body and the development of funerary rituals, *cf.* the Tomba del Duce at Vetulonia and Tomb 4461 at Pontecagnano; *cf.* also Bartoloni 2000; Cerchiai 1995; on attitudes towards the dead body and its manipulation for different ritual purposes *cf.* also Perego, Shipley, Di Lorenzo *et al.* and Zanoni this volume). As regards Monte Michele Tomb 5, a tension between the appropriation of Mediterranean symbols of power and the negotiation of individual identity is evident in the grave-good associations. Here, the symbols of power and social prerogatives (including a sceptre, a fan or *flabellum*, weapons, the set connected with the sacrifice, hearth and banquet, a grater, a censer and imported Orientalizing-style objects) are associated with a large and typically local set of drinking and eating vessels made of brown impasto and *bucchero sottile* (a type of thin-walled *bucchero*: Sgubini Moretti 2000).

What is especially striking about the burials in Monte Michele Tomb 5 is that they clearly indicate the deployment of very strict forms of selection. As I have stressed above, the construction of a funerary image of the deceased, and the display of a material culture that was exclusively reserved for the élite, should be regarded as part of a mechanism that represented a form of 'symbolic violence' and strengthened the exclusion of subordinate groups from the centre of society through ideology and ritual practice (on similar issues in the Veneto region *cf.* Perego this volume).

Campania: gender and status between the Iron Age and the Orientalizing period

The complex dynamics of the peopling of ancient Campania make this region in southern Italy a frontier zone, and an area characterized by complex cultural interactions. The composite cultural background of ancient Campania has been recently reconsidered from a perspective that emphasizes the constant interaction and reciprocal influences between the area's different cultural components, instead of searching solely for hegemonic trends. Many Campanian communities seem indeed, for most of their history, to fit the definition of 'mixed cultures' or *culture métisse* proposed by some archaeologists (e.g. Cerchiai 2010; Cuozzo 2012; d'Agostino and Cerchiai 2004), in the wake of recent anthropological reflections by scholars such as Amselle (1990; 2009) and Fabietti (1998).

On this subject, other scholars have brought into play the notion of 'middle ground' (Malkin 2011) and the controversial concept of 'hybridization', both of which originate in post-colonial literature (e.g. Krishnaswamy and Hawley 2009; van Dommelen 2006). The cultural complexity of Campania, rather than being explainable in terms of ethnic juxtaposition, reflects a dynamic situation whose multiple aspects are hard to categorize in the present state of research (Cuozzo 2012, and Morris this volume, with additional bibliography).

As several authors have already stressed, these intense cultural dynamics of interchange between Greek, Etruscan and indigenous populations can never be regarded as one-way. This is borne out by the complexity of the material culture of the isle of Pithekoussai, where indigenous and Levantine cultural elements are present in a manner that was not necessarily subordinate to the Greek element. Furthermore, the repertoire of fibulae and ornaments is hybrid (Lo Schiavo 2010). Cultural diversity is present in the material culture of many Campanian communities in this phase – hence the controversy over Tomb 104 in the Fondo Artiaco cemetery at Cumae, which has been variously ascribed to a Greek, an Etruscan and an indigenous chieftain.

Yet concepts such as hybridization, however intriguing, threaten to obscure the complex and multivocal character of cultural responses to changes in the population makeup and the social systems of ancient Campania. We should be careful not to generalize this "idyllic absence of conflict" (*cf.* Fabietti 1998). The responses to change that have been recognized in Campania and the Tyrrhenian region as a whole cannot be taken for granted or regarded as univocal. Some Campanian communities responded to change by opening up to external stimuli. In other cases, however, the complex intercultural dynamics set in motion by stable contact with the Greeks, and the redefinition of the balance between indigenous and Etruscanized social groups, appear to give rise to conservatism, a reaction which possibly reflects what Scott calls "silent resistance" (Scott 1985; van Dommelen 2006). This is borne out by complex dynamics of socio-political negotiation among emergent social groups, a phenomenon which, as I observed above, has implications for the creation of gender identities (Cerchiai 1999; Cuozzo 2007).

The emergence of the so-called 'princely tombs' of the Orientalizing period in Campania has attracted renewed interest from scholars, who are trying to re-examine this issue in light of agency theory, as advocated in this volume, or through approaches connected to globalization theories such as Network Theory (*cf.* also Morris this volume). Here I do not intend to re-examine the question of 'princely' tombs and gentilicial social organization in Campania. Instead, I focus on gender dynamics and the intersection between gender and status, which even the most recent literature on the subject has generally overlooked (but *cf.* Riva 2010 on Orientalizing Etruria). Gender relations are the underlying theme in the analysis I propose here, although I also consider how the construction of gender was intertwined with the development and negotiation of other forms of collective or individual identities.

As I have stressed above, Godelier's notion of the "monopoly of the imaginary" (Godelier 1985; 1999) is of central importance to my analysis. According to Godelier, the rule of aristocracies in the middle- and long-term is legitimized not by the sheer exercise of violence or the accumulation of riches, but by controlling the social imaginary, and by managing the community's relations with the outside world, the divine and the cosmological and sacred spheres. Of fundamental importance is also the ability of aristocratic groups to represent themselves as irreplaceable guarantors of the reproduction of society and life in general.

As this web of ideologies was articulated in the funerary context of ancient Campania, very high-ranking women appear to have played an essential role in the various Campanian settlements. The site of Pontecagnano and the surrounding territory (*agro picentino*) provide an ideal evidence base for testing some theories and methods outlined here. It surely helps that Pontecagnano is the most thoroughly published site of ancient Campania, thanks to an ongoing joint research project between the archaeological *Soprintendenza* of Salerno and different Italian research institutions (e.g. Cerchiai 2010; Cuozzo 2003).

From its very beginning, the history of Pontecagnano provides an excellent outline of mixed cultures or *culture métisse*, revealing openness and interaction among the various peoples who lived in or frequented Campania. Notably, between the ninth–eighth centuries BC and the Orientalizing period, Pontecagnano gained a leading role in the broader Tyrrhenian scenario, commanding a strong network of relationships with Etruria, Greek settlements, as well as Phoenician, Near Eastern and Italic communities.

The 'Etrusco-Campanian' centre of Pontecagnano developed near the Picentino River, 10 km south of Salerno (*cf.* Fig. 1.1 and Fig. 1.4a), on a plain bounded by mountains known as the *Monti Picentini*. The site is mainly known for its vast burial sites (e.g. Bonaudo *et al.* 2009; Cinquantaquattro 2000; Cuozzo 2003; 2007; d'Agostino and Gastaldi 1988). Until today, these cemeteries have yielded tombs that are mainly datable between the ninth and fourth centuries BC. Little is presently known about the ancient town, in spite of important finds in recent years (e.g. Cerchiai 2010; Pellegrini and Rossi 2011). Nevertheless, a recent excavation of the settlement area (Pellegrini and Rossi 2011), and an ongoing research project led by the University of Molise, have yielded important evidence of the composite material culture at the ancient town, which is comparable with the artefact types found in the main burial site.

The main cemeteries at Pontecagnano are located to the west and east of the ancient town, in the locality of S. Antonio a Picenza, on a platform of 80 ha in extent, whose limits have been identified through surveys and recent excavations. The settlement occupied a strip of land that today is almost entirely bounded on the north by the Salerno-Reggio Calabria motorway (*autostrada*) and to the south by the SS 18 trunk road. To the west and south the ancient boundary followed natural ravines, which correspond to the bed of the Picentino River.

As I stressed above, at Pontecagnano (and in Campania in general) the affirmation of powerful hereditary aristocracies in the Orientalizing period is attested in the funerary sphere by the well-known phenomenon of the 'princely tombs' (*cf.* also Morris this volume). As noted above, these tombs can be seen as a sign of supra-local recognition, and of the comprehensive solidarity that bound together the Tyrrhenian élite groups, whether of Greek, Etruscan, or indigenous origin. This solidarity transcended ethnic differences in favour of the expression of privileged social status, and the capacity to monopolize the various connections with the broader Mediterranean world. This type of funerary display is found in different corners of Campania. Particularly good examples are Fondo Artiaco Tomb 104 at Cumae, as well as female Tomb 2465, and male Tombs 926, 928 and 4461 at Pontecagnano (*cf.* Cuozzo 2004–2005; 2012; Fig. 1.3). In some respects, some women's tombs in the indigenous centres of southern Hirpinia and the Campanian plain might also be classified as 'princely' in nature (Cuozzo 2007). In contrast, 'princely' tombs seem until now to be absent from Capua during the Orientalizing period. It is possible, however, that this absence simply reflects the current state of research, and the vast backlog of unpublished evidence.

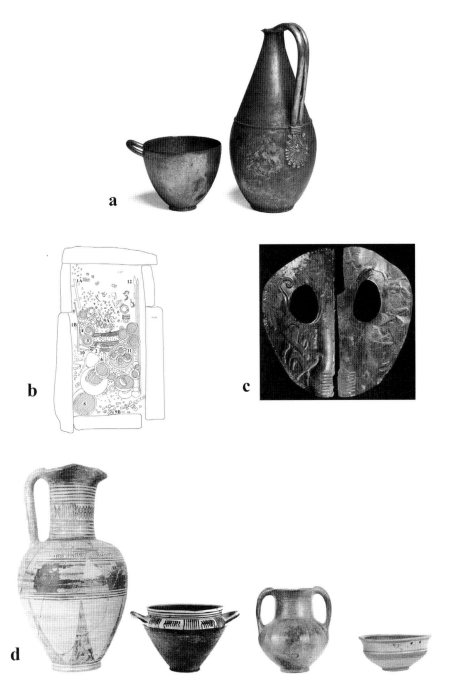

Fig. 1.3: a. Silver vessels from Pontecagnano Tomb 928; b. plan of Pontecagnano Tomb 4265; c. bronze horse frontpiece from Pontecagnano Tomb 4461; d. Pontecagnano: the 'basic' vessel set (all images modified after Cuozzo 2007).

Up until now, Orientalizing Pontecagnano has mostly been known for its 'princely' Tombs 926, 927, 928 and 4461, all of which belong to male individuals and are located in the western cemetery. The partial publication of Tomb 2465, the so-called 'Tomb of the Princess', together with the systematic survey of the cemetery, have however revealed the complex socio-political and ideological structuring of the community. This has enhanced previous readings of the local funerary record, and raised questions about the diversity of the identities that were constructed in the mortuary arena at this site (Cuozzo 2003). Furthermore, the picture outlined so far for the 'princely' burials of the Orientalizing period in Campania has been called into question by some very recent finds, datable to the transition phase between the end of the Iron Age and the Orientalizing period. These recent discoveries may challenge the currently accepted date of the onset of the 'princely' tomb phenomenon in Campania, which can now be pushed back to the ninth–eighth centuries BC, based on the evidence of tombs containing Greek pottery from *c.* 750–725 BC, buried together with impasto pottery dating to the ninth–eighth centuries.

These discoveries indicate that the first graves to display evidence of 'princely' status are exceptional female tombs. In other words, the suggested changes to the chronology of the appearance of 'princely' burials in the study area would mean that, in Campania, gender dynamics involving a crucial ritual emphasis on women's graves played an important role in the construction of the 'princely' symbolic apparatus from the outset. In the midst of the profound changes that mark the crucial passage from the ninth–eighth centuries BC to the Orientalizing period, a tension seems to emerge between conservatism and innovation. Notably, such a tension might have had its roots in the interplay between internal developments and external stimuli. It is interesting to observe how these dynamics take on gender connotations. This phenomenon can be observed not only in those corners of ancient Campania that were traditionally less open to external contact, such as southern Hirpinia or the Sarno Valley (on which *cf.* Cuozzo 2007), but also in centres such as Pontecagnano, which actively engaged with external cultural elements ever since the Iron Age, and developed dynamics of hybridization – albeit with different degrees of nuance.

At Pontecagnano and the surrounding territory (*agro picentino*), unlike other areas, the funerary treatment given to males included the use of imported artefacts as grave goods – namely pottery and luxury bronze vases, which symbolized privileged relations with the Greek world and the East. These innovations, however, were accepted within the limits of an overall traditional form of self-representation that stressed the ideological 'soberness' of the warrior and the 'hardiness' or *duritia* connected with subsistence activities; an important focus was also placed on certain types of craftsmanship, as indicated by a specific set of tools to which recent studies have called attention (d'Agostino and Gastaldi 2012; Iaia 2006).

At Pontecagnano, both male and female individuals were buried with Greek wine and table vessels, which became an integral part of the basic burial equipment in the Orientalizing period (Cuozzo 2003; 2007; 2012; Fig. 1.3d). This vessel set programmatically integrated aspects of the local tradition (i.e. the small impasto amphora) and the active appropriation of material culture from the Greek settlements in south Italy, including the drinking cup and the wine jug (*oinochoe*). This was a communal norm extended to all social groupings attested in the Pontecagnano cemeteries, whether status-, gender- or age-based.

Very different considerations apply to luxury objects made of metal or precious materials. These are found in exceptionally wealthy women's tombs found at Pontecagnano and Monte Vetrano, in the surrounding area (Fig. 1.4). These graves suggest a deep ideological renovation, a true experimentation with a new symbolic apparatus that acts as a prelude to the 'princely' burial customs of the Orientalizing phase, which appear at the same time in Tyrrhenian Etruria, particularly in male graves. A good example is offered by the female burials in Tomb 7178 at Pontecagnano and Tomb 74 at Monte Vetrano (Fig. 1.4), which are generally similar in terms of grave furnishings, including certain types of imports. These common traits could point to special ties between the two women in question, their social groups and/or their external connections (d'Agostino and Gastaldi 2012; *cf.* also below). The abundance and variety of references evoked by the exceptional selection of imported bronzes is not merely a show of luxury, but the sign of the concentration of long-distance relations within a few aristocratic groups. The recurrent presence, both in these tombs and in other eminent female tombs in Pontecagnano (*cf.* for example Tomb 7765, discussed below) of andirons and/or fire tongs, along with knives and spits (which are also documented in male graves) points to the crystallization of an iron tool set connected to sacrifice and the sacred hearth of the clan and the community. Notably, this set is often found in Orientalizing 'princely' tombs, where it has been read as a symbolic guarantee of the relation with the divine, as well as of the continuity of the group, the lineage and the community itself.

The evidence seems to suggest a scenario where high-ranking women could have been active agents of cultural hybridization or *métissage* – as Bagnasco Gianni has suggested with regard to the introduction and spread of writing in Etruria (Bagnasco Gianni 1999). Studies on colonial encounters in the modern world have shown that high-ranking indigenous women can gain remarkable social prestige by acting as linguistic interpreters and/or cultural go-betweens (e.g. Hodder 1982; Migden Socolow 2000; Moore 1994). These women are regarded as primary agents of hybridization, integration and formation of new aristocratic groups, especially by marrying and bearing progeny. This is, however, a complex and multifaceted process of social change, which needs to be investigated carefully in view of context-related social developments that may vary depending on the circumstances. In this part of my chapter, I shall use the concept of gender as a theoretical lens for the analysis and discussion of a range of graves that date from between the Iron Age and the Orientalizing period. Several scholars have drawn attention to these tombs because of their peculiar features, which challenge received wisdom (e.g. Cerchiai 2010).

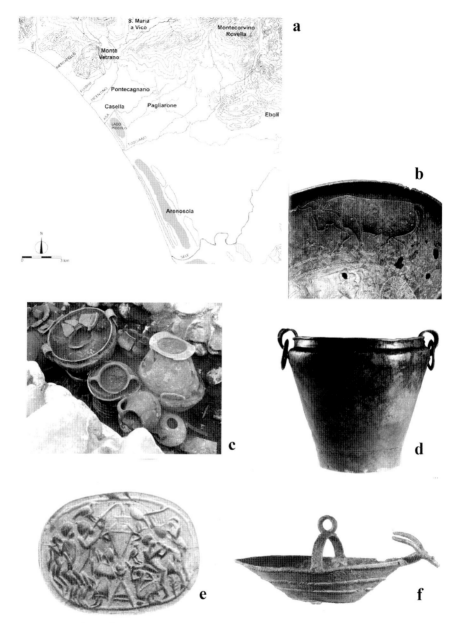

Fig. 1.4: a. Map of southern Campania; b. detail of silver bowl (Monte Vetrano Tomb 74);
c. vessel set (Monte Vetrano Tomb 74); d. Bronze Kurd-type situla (Monte Vetrano Tomb 74); e. faience
scarab (Monte Vetrano Tomb 74); f. Nuragic model ship (Monte Vetrano Tomb 74) (modified after Cuozzo
and Pellegrino 2016; d'Agostino and Gastaldi 2012; Cerchiai and Nava 2009).

Firstly, it is worth dwelling on recent archaeological discoveries near Pontecagnano, in the so-called Picentine area or *agro picentino*, which allow us to explore the link between élite self-assertion and gender dynamics. The burial sites at Monte Vetrano (already mentioned above) are situated *c.* 2 km from Pontecagnano (Fig. 1.4a), on the other side of the Picentino River. Recent excavations provide an initial overview of this settlement, which occupied a strategic position by the river, close to a mooring spot near the mouth (Cerchiai 2010; d'Agostino and Gastaldi 2012). Early in its development, Monte Vetrano already appears to be characterized by cultural diversity, with a material culture resembling that of Pontecagnano but also showing affinities with areas further inland, especially the southern Hirpinian hinterland. It is still not clear, however, whether Monte Vetrano was an important hub in the territory of Pontecagnano, or at least a semi-independent centre (*cf.* Pellegrini and Rossi 2011).

More than 300 tombs were found at Monte Vetrano (Fig. 1.4). The individual tombs seem to have been grouped according to kinship, with a larger number of graves arranged around central tombs of male and/or female individuals. The tombs date from *c.* 750–725 BC to the threshold of the Orientalizing period, when the cemetery ceased to be used. The site is of special interest because of its surprising Tyrrhenian and Mediterranean connections, which are revealed by the concentration of luxury imports of great symbolic value in the tombs of pre-eminent individuals.

Although some male graves at Monte Vetrano stand out for containing lavish furnishings (*cf.* for example Tomb 51, which yielded a pair of bronze basins, weapons, spits and iron tools: Campanelli 2011; d'Agostino and Gastaldi 2012), women's tombs are by far the most conspicuous. Some of these women were buried with symbols of exceptional status and power, which suggest their capacity to monopolize the various social relations within the groups to which they belonged, and in the community as a whole. Good examples are Monte Vetrano Tombs 74 and 111, datable to 750–725 BC, both of which must have belonged to women. Tomb 111 is a cremation in a bronze vase (*lebes*) imported from Euboea, accompanied by a Greek chevron cup. Its furnishings, which were partly lost, included iron tools, personal ornaments and imported pottery.

Monte Vetrano Tomb 74 (Fig. 1.4) is currently unmatched in terms of the abundance of prestige goods. The structure of the tomb and the arrangement of the grave goods suggest that it contained an inhumation burial. The biconical vase of sheet metal with embossed bird motifs lacks immediate parallels and therefore may not have been an urn (Campanelli 2011; d'Agostino and Gastaldi 2012). A use of the vase for sacral and ritual activities is suggested by the presence of an aromatic substance inside, instead of the cremated remains. Other bronze objects found in the tomb might have had a ritual and ceremonial function. These include a censer of southern Etruscan origin and a tray or *presentatoio* made of sheet metal decorated with small circles. This tray, possibly from Capua, is similar to a specimen found in Tomb 7765 at Pontecagnano, which I discuss below. Monte Vetrano Tomb 74 also shows similarities with Pontecagnano Tomb 7178, in view of objects that were previously thought to be exclusive to Pontecagnano (*cf.* further information on Pontecagnano Tomb 7178 below). These artefacts include a cist vase of Adriatic origin (*cista cordonata*) and the Kurd-type situla vase of southern Etruscan manufacture (Fig. 1.4d). These numerous similarities may suggest direct connections between the deceased individuals at Monte Vetrano and Pontecagnano, and their respective families and/or social affiliates. However, Monte Vetrano Tomb 74 also suggests some more exceptional long-distance Mediterranean connections. The hemispheric cup of sheet metal, embossed with a procession scene of bulls and heifers nursing calves, is an Oriental import previously unattested in the western Mediterranean area (Fig. 1.4b). A Nuragic miniature ship (Fig. 1.4f), which might have carried complex sacred overtones, is also the first of its kind to be found near Pontecagnano until now. The sphere of ritual and cult is also evoked by instruments connected with sacrifice and the hearth. This extraordinary grave assemblage seems to herald, already in the mid-eighth century BC, the elaborate forms of self-assertion that find full expression in the Orientalizing period. Among the Greek-type pottery in Tomb 74, a jar that was probably produced locally by Pithekoussan craftsmen closely recalls the vessel with 'Cesnola-type' decoration from Tomb 538 at Pontecagnano (Cerchiai 1995).

We also have prestige imports that are sporadic finds and therefore devoid of context. One of these is a remarkable faience scarab of the Lyre-Player group, decorated with a complex symposium scene. The fact that scarabs and other Eastern ornaments at Pontecagnano are mainly found in graves belonging to female individuals and sub-adults, could indicate that the scarab from Monte Vetrano (Fig. 1.4e) belonged originally to the tomb of a high-ranking female individual (Cerchiai 2010).

Given the present state of the evidence, we cannot be certain about the nature of the connection between Monte Vetrano and Pontecagnano. It also remains unclear how the ruling élites in these two settlements interacted with each other. At Pontecagnano, unlike other areas of Campania, the spread of Orientalizing culture from *c.* 725–700 BC onwards represents a marked and intentional break with the previous Iron Age period. This break is clearly indicated by the appearance of new burial grounds that remained in use until the fourth century BC. A second innovation is the appearance of a new basic set of grave goods (Fig. 1.3d).

However, despite the clear and intentional break with earlier traditions, this new social imaginary of Orientalizing Pontecagnano – which I have discussed elsewhere (Cuozzo 2003) – had already developed its key features by the end of the Iron Age. Some eighth-century BC female tombs at Pontecagnano already stand out for including status markers that were 'unusual' for their time. These graves suggest that the eighth-century BC élites at Pontecagnano were experimenting with new symbols of power and status, which would later characterize the Orientalizing 'princely' tombs. In Pontecagnano Tomb 7178, for example, a large bronze *lebes*, probably imported from Euboea, was associated with a Kurd-type situla from north Etruria, a pair of cists (*ciste cordonate)* from the Adriatic area, and two bronze cups that were probably imported from south Etruria and the Levant. Tomb 7178, therefore, is an instance where status symbols are combined with the management of supra-local networks, and the assertion of socio-economic power, in a way that recalls Tomb 74 at Monte Vetrano, which I have already discussed above (d'Agostino and Gastaldi 2012; above). Tomb 7178 also contained a set of impasto vessels that were probably more ancient than the burial context, pieces of jewellery, traditional weaving instruments and a set of multifunctional tools – a knife, fire tongs and andirons. Iron spits are the only prestige items in this grave that are also found in men's tombs.

Another 'princely' tomb at Pontecagnano – Tomb 7765 – yielded artefacts presumably alluding to the sacrificial prerogatives of the deceased woman and/or her burying group, including the feast (which involved the roasting of meat), and the safeguarding of the clan hearth (on the possible role of women from ancient central Italy in these ritual practices *cf.* also Iaia and Faustoferri this volume). One significant item found in this grave was a sheet-bronze tray (*presentatoio*: d'Agostino and Gastaldi 2012). This object, whose precise function is unclear, is also attested in Monte Vetrano Tomb 74, and in lavish graves around Capua, where it must have been originally produced. Finally, the presence of Greek pottery and Eastern imports, namely a scarab and ivory handles (d'Agostino and Gastaldi 2012), indicates that the burying group responsible for Tomb 7765 was able to harness long-distance connections, and participated in wide-ranging social and commercial networks.

In contrast to the intense cosmopolitanism that we see at Monte Vetrano and Pontecagnano, the area of inland Campania known as south Hirpinia (comprising the sites of Oliveto–Citra, Cairano, Calitri and Bisaccia) is characterized by what appears to be an acute conservatism. This conservatism may be likened to forms of "silent resistance"(*cf.* Scott 1985) and suggests that gender dynamics may have played a role in both the construction of the local social imaginary and the intentional manipulation of material culture by social agents (Cerchiai 2010; Cuozzo 2007; d'Agostino 1964). Although the material culture of the earliest phases of the Iron Age in south Hirpinia is still poorly known, many of the object types appear to continue into the later Iron Age, showing an extraordinary long-term persistence, the only (partial) exception being the grave goods found in a single rich female tomb (Cerchiai 1995; Cuozzo 2007). Likewise, a strong conservatism is present in the funerary sites in the area of S. Valentino Torio, which date to the third quarter of the eighth century BC. This conservatism is revealed by the fact that Greek and Phoenician imports, including scarabs and ornaments, occur exclusively in female and child tombs. Male funerary customs seem impermeable to these external influences (Cerchiai 1995; d'Agostino 1988). Indeed, contact with the early Greek colonists seems to have provoked a reaction among the male ranks of the local dominant groups, who decided to fashion their own image according to traditional forms of self-representation (such as 'the male as warrior'), possibly reflecting complex forms of cultural "silent resistance" (*cf.* Scott 1985).

Lastly, I shall tackle a controversial issue regarding one of the funerary sites at Capua, which has been repeatedly addressed by scholars over the last few years (e.g. d'Agostino 2011b; Melandri 2011). Tomb 722 in the Fornaci cemetery, which belonged to a woman, is outstanding for its concentration of status symbols, and for the ostentation of the burying group's network connections. Indeed, the richness of the grave furnishing and their potential symbolic value, indicate the complexity of the social dynamics involved in the formation of this grave assemblage, including the openness shown by the deceased and/or her burying group towards the earliest Greek colonists. Tomb 722 may dates around 750 BC in view of a Pithekoussan-made Aetos 666-type cup (for a different view *cf.* Melandri 2011, 715). This grave, therefore, appears to document the formative moment of the Orientalizing culture, and the rise of the 'princely' symbolic apparatus in Campania. The fact that the grave belonged to a woman also sheds light on the complexity of the gender dynamics that characterized this region in this pivotal moment in history. Furthermore, the presence of such a grave in Capua is surprising, because so far no 'princely' tombs from the Orientalizing period have been found there.

The attribution of Capua Fornaci Tomb 722 to a woman is suggested by both the burial equipment and the osteological analysis of the skeletal remains. The deceased was deposited in a large trench and granted an elaborate funerary ritual that might have taken a relatively long period of time to be performed (d'Agostino 2011b). The funerary treatment of the corpse could be evidence of a secondary burial ritual accompanied by sacrifices, as attested by the number of faunal remains found in the tomb, including pig, sheep and goat bones. While the funerary rite and treatment of the body reflect an exclusive ceremony that recalls Orientalizing examples (e.g. Pontecagnano Tomb 4461, on which *cf.* most recently Cerchiai 2010), Fornaci Tomb 722 is also well-known for its exceptional grave goods. These included imported jewellery (e.g. Egyptian-type scarabs and personal ornaments made of materials such as gold, silver and amber), rare and exotic objects (a faience statuette and wrought ivory), a rich local repertoire of impasto pottery of high quality and, above all, a hemispherical silver cup with embossed decoration. This type of silver cup is attested in Orientalizing 'princely' tombs at Cumae, as well as in Latium and Etruria. Although there are still doubts that the silver cup actually came from Tomb 722, the exceptional character of this burial suggests that this might have been the case. This would make the silver cup the earliest known example of this vessel type, which is otherwise found only in tombs from about 50 years later (d'Agostino 2011b).

The prerogatives of the woman in Tomb 722 are ideologically reinforced by the occurrence in her grave of a set of instruments presumably connected to sacrificial practices and the hearth. This symbolic apparatus – as I stressed above – appears to be closely associated with high-status female burials from around 750 BC, moving on to become one of the recurrent traits of 'princely' graves between the late eighth and early seventh centuries BC.

Conclusion

In this chapter, I have reviewed and discussed some theoretical approaches to the interpretation of burial sites that might produce fruitful insights into the social and ideological organization of Italy's communities during the Iron Age and the

Orientalizing period. In particular, I have highlighted how research produced in the humanities and social sciences on semiotics, gender, agency, *habitus* and cultural hybridization or *métissage* may help shed light on the complex dynamics of power negotiation and identity construction that took place in Etruria and Campania in the crucial historical phase under consideration here.

The case studies presented in this chapter have cast light on the complex ritual dynamics that contributed to set apart prominent social groups in ancient Italy from their invisible and marginalized social counterparts, which might often been denied formal burial, or at least burial in prominent cemetery sites.

Another issue that I have touched in this chapter is the role of women in Campania and Etruria during the Iron Age and the Orientalizing period. In the context of key Campanian cemeteries, during the transition phase from the Iron Age to the Orientalizing period, it appears that female figures of exceptionally high status stood as guarantors, in the funerary context, of the far-reaching relations (in the broader Tyrrhenian and Mediterranean scenes) of the groups to which they belonged. Such women acted either alongside their male counterparts or by themselves. They may have also played an active role in the construction and reworking of the ideologies of power that we see in action during the Orientalizing period.

Indeed, two interpretations of this phenomenon are possible. In the first case, these high-status women had a passive role. They were mere instruments of their family or group of affiliation, who chose to entrust the display of luxury, as well as the display of their economic and relational capacity, to such women, at least in the funerary context. The funerary treatment given to these women's male counterparts does not incorporate most or any of these external influences. As noted above, this might reflect complex forms of cultural resistance enacted in the funerary sphere, although this remains unproven. From a different perspective, however, these high-status women can be seen as active social agents that played an important role in the construction of the new ideologies of the nascent aristocracies in Campania, as well as agents of intercultural mediation, social renewal and social promotion. Here, rather than simple answers, I have endeavoured to pose questions and indicate possible lines of inquiry for future research.

Bibliography

Amselle, J-L. (1999) *Logiche Meticce. Antropologia dell'Identità in Africa e Altrove* (Traduzione e presentazione di Marco Aime). Torino, Bollati Boringhieri.

Amselle, J-L. (2009) *Il Distacco dall'Occidente*. Roma, Meltemi.

Antonaccio, C. (2002) Warriors, traders, ancestors: The 'heroes' of Lefkandi. In J. Munk Hotje (ed.) *Images of Ancestors* (Arhus Studies in Mediterranean Archaeology), 12–42. Arhus, Arhus University Press.

Arnold, B. (1996) 'Honorary male' or women of substance? Gender, status and power in Iron Age Europe. *Journal of European Archaeology* 3(2), 153–168.

Bagnasco Gianni, G. (1999) L'acquisizione della scrittura in Etruria: Materiali a confronto per la ricostruzione del quadro storico e culturale. In G. Bagnasco Gianni and F. Cordano (eds) *Scritture Mediterranee tra il IX e il VII Secolo a.C.. Atti del Seminario (Università degli Studi di Milano, Istituto di Storia Antica, 23-24 Febbraio 1998)*, 85–106. Milano, Edizioni ET.

Bartoloni, G. (2000) (ed.) *Principi Etruschi: Tra Mediterraneo ed Europa. Catalogo della Mostra (Bologna, 2000-2001)*. Venezia, Marsilio.

Bartoloni, G. (2003) *Le Società dell'Italia Primitiva. Lo Studio delle Necropoli e la Nascita delle Aristocrazie*. Roma, Carocci.

Bietti Sestrieri, A.M. (1992) (ed.) *La Necropoli Laziale di Osteria dell'Osa*. Roma, Quasar.

Bonaudo, R., Cuozzo, M., Mugione, E., Pellegrino, C. and Serritella, A. (2009) Le necropoli di Pontecagnano: Studi recenti. In R. Bonaudo, L. Cerchiai and C. Pellegrino (eds) *Tra Etruria, Lazio e Magna Grecia: Indagini sulle Necropoli. Atti dell'Incontro di Studio 2009*, 169–208. Paestum, Pandemos.

Bourdieu, P. (1977) *Outline of a Theory of Practice*. Cambridge, Cambridge University Press.

Bourdieu, P. and Wacquant, L.J.D. (1992) *An Invitation to Reflexive Sociology*. Cambridge, Polity Press.

Campanelli, A. (2011) (ed.) *Dopo lo Tsunami. Salerno Antica. Catalogo della Mostra (Salerno, 18 Novembre 2011-28 Febbraio 2012)*. Napoli, Prismi.

Cerchiai, L. (1995) *I Campani*. Milano, Longanesi.

Cerchiai, L. (1999) I vivi e i morti: I casi di Pitecusa e Poseidonia. In *Confini e Frontiera nella Grecità d'Occidente. Atti del 37° Convegno di Studi sulla Magna Grecia (Taranto, 3-6 Ottobre 1997)*, 658–670. Taranto, Istituto per la Storia e l'Archeologia della Magna Grecia.

Cerchiai, L. (2010) *Gli Antichi Popoli della Campania. Archeologia e Storia*. Roma, Carocci.

Cerchiai, L. and Nava, M.L. (2009) Uno scarabeo del lyre player group da Monte Vetrano (Salerno). Annali dell'Istituto Orientale di Napoli, Serie Archeologia e Storia Antica 16, 97–114.

Cinquantaquattro, T. (2000) *Pontecagnano. II.6. L'Agro Picentino e la Necropoli di Località Casella* (Annali dell'Istituto Orientale di Napoli, Serie Archeologia e Storia Antica 13). Napoli, Istituto Universitario Orientale.

Colonna, G. (2002) Gli Etruschi nel Tirreno meridionale: Tra mitistoria, storia e archeologia. *Etruscan Studies. Journal of the Etruscan Foundation* 9, 191–206.

Cuozzo, M. (1996) Prospettive teoriche e metodologiche nell'interpretazione delle necropoli: La Post-Processual Archaeology. *Annali di Archeologia e Storia Antica* 3, 1–37.

Cuozzo, M. (2000) Orizzonti teorici e interpretativi, tra percorsi di matrice francese, archeologia post-processuale e tendenze italiane: Considerazioni e indirizzi di ricerca per lo studio delle necropoli. In N. Terrenato (ed.) *Archeologia Teorica*, 323–360. Borgo S. Lorenzo, All'Insegna del Giglio.

Cuozzo, M. (2003) *Reinventando la Tradizione. Immaginario Sociale, Ideologie e Rappresentazione nelle Necropoli Orientalizzanti di Pontecagnano*. Paestum, Pandemos.

Cuozzo, M. (2004-2005) Ripetere, moltiplicare, selezionare, distinguere nelle necropoli di Pontecagnano. Il caso della tomba 4461. In L. Cerchiai and P. Gastaldi (eds) *Pontecagnano: La Città, il Paesaggio e la Dimensione Simbolica* (Annali di Archeologia e Storia Antica 11-12), 145–154. Napoli, Istituto Universitario Orientale.

Cuozzo, M. (2007) Ancient Campania: Cultural interaction, political borders and geographical boundaries. In G.J. Bradley, E. Isayev and C. Riva (eds) *Ancient Italy. Regions without Boundaries*, 224–267. Exeter, Exeter University Press.

Cuozzo, M. (2012) Gli Etruschi in Campania. In G. Bartoloni (ed.) *Introduzione all'Etruscologia*, 189–226. Milano, Hoepli.

Cuozzo, M. and Guidi, A. (2013) *Archeologia delle Identità e delle Differenze*. Roma, Carocci.

Cuozzo, M. and Pellegrino, C. (2016) Culture meticce, identità etnica, dinamiche di conservatorismo e resistenza: questioni teoriche e casi di studio dalla Campania. In L. Donnellan, V. Nizzo and G.-J. Burgers (eds) *Conceptualising Early Colonisation*, 117–136. Roma, Istituto Storico Belga di Roma.

d'Agostino, B. (1964) Oliveto Citra – Necropoli arcaica in località Turni. *Notizie degli Scavi* 18, 40–99.

d'Agostino, B. (1977) *Tombe Principesche dell'Orientalizzante Antico da Pontecagnano* (Monumenti Antichi 49, Serie Miscellanea 2/1). Roma, Accademia Nazionale dei Lincei.

d'Agostino, B. (1985) Società dei vivi, comunità dei morti: Un rapporto difficile. *Dialoghi di Archeologia* 1(3), 47–58.

d'Agostino, B. (1988) Le genti della Campania antica. In A.M. Chieco Bianchi (ed.) *Italia Omnium Terrarum Alumna. La Civiltà dei Veneti, Reti, Liguri, Celti, Piceni, Umbri, Latini, Campani e Iapigi* (Antica Madre 11), 529–589. Milano, Garzanti/Scheiwiller.

d'Agostino, B. (1999a) I principi dell'Italia centro-tirrenica in epoca orientalizzante. In P. Ruby (ed.) *Les Princes de la Protohistoire et l'Émergence de l'État. Actes de la Table Ronde Internationale Organisée par le Centre Jean Bérard et l'École française de Rome (Naples, 27-29 Octobre 1994)*, 81–88. Napoli, Centre Jean Bérard.

d'Agostino, B. (1999b) La ceramica greca e di tipo greco dalle necropoli della I Età del Ferro di Pontecagnano. In G. Bailo Modesti and P. Gastaldi (eds) *Prima di Pithecusa: I più Antichi Materiali Greci del Golfo di Salerno. Catalogo della Mostra (Pontecagnano Faiano, Museo Nazionale dell'Agro Picentino, 1999)*, 13–24. Napoli, Arte Tipografica.

d'Agostino, B. (2011a) Pithecusae e Cumae nel quadro della Campania di età arcaica. *Römische Mitteilungen* 117, 35–53.

d'Agostino, B. (2011b) La tomba 722 di Capua loc. Le Fornaci e le premesse dell'Orientalizzante in Campania. In D. Maras (ed.) *Corollari. Scritti di Antichità Etrusche e Italiche in Omaggio all'Opera di G. Colonna*, 33–45. Pisa, F. Serra.

d'Agostino, B. and Cerchiai, L. (2004) I Greci nell'Etruria campana. In G.M. Della Fina (ed.) *I Greci in Etruria. Atti dell'XI Convegno Internazionale di Studi sulla Storia e l'Archeologia dell'Etruria (Orvieto, 12-14 Dicembre 2003)*, 271–289. Roma, Quasar.

d'Agostino, B. and Gastaldi, P. (1988) (eds) *Pontecagnano II. La Necropoli del Picentino. 1. Le Tombe della Prima Età del Ferro* (Annali dell'Istituto Orientale di Napoli, Serie Archeologia e Storia Antica 5). Napoli, Istituto Universitario Orientale.

d'Agostino, B. and Gastaldi, P. (2012) Pontecagnano nel terzo quarto dell'VIII secolo a.C.. In C. Chiaramonte Treré, G. Bagnasco Gianni and F. Chiesa (eds) *Munera Amicitiae* (Quaderni di Acme 134), 343–387. Milano, Cisalpino.

d'Agostino, B and Schnapp, A. (1982) Les morts entre l'object et l' image. In G. Gnoli and J.P. Vernant (eds) *La Mort, les Morts dans les Sociétés Anciennes*, 18–25. Paris, Éditions de la Maison des Sciences de l'Homme.

Díaz-Andreu, M. and Tortosa, T. (1998) Gender, symbolism and power in Iberian societies. In P.P. Funari, M. Hall and S. Jones (eds) *Historical Archaeology. Back from the Edge*, 99–121. London, Routledge.

Díaz-Andreu, M., Lucy, S., Babić, S. and Edwards, D.N. (2005) *The Archaeology of Identity. Approaches to Gender, Age, Status, Ethnicity and Religion*. Oxford, Routledge.

Dommasnes, H. and Montón-Subiás, S. (2012) European gender archaeologies in historical perspective. *European Journal of Archaeology* 15(3), 367–391.

Eco, U. (1975) *Trattato di Semiotica Generale*. Milano, Bompiani.

Fabietti, U. (1998) *L'Identità Etnica*. Roma, Carocci.

Godelier, M. (1985) *L'Ideale e il Materiale*. Roma, Editori Riuniti.

Godelier, M. (1999) Chefferies et États, une approche anthropologique. In P. Ruby (ed.) *Les Princes de la Protohistoire et l'Émergence de l'État. Actes de la Table Ronde Internationale Organisée par le Centre Jean Bérard et l'École française de Rome (Naples, 27-29 Octobre 1994)*, 19–30. Napoli, Centre Jean-Bérard.

Hamilton, S., Wright, K.I. and Whitehouse, R. (2007) (eds) *Archaeology and Women: Ancient and Modern Issues*. London, Left Coast Press.

Herring, E. and Lomas, K. (2009) (eds) *Gender Identities in Ancient Italy* (BAR S1893). Oxford, Archaeopress.

Hodder, I. (1982) *Symbols in Action. Ethnoarchaeological Studies of Material Culture*. Cambridge, Cambridge University Press.

Hodder, I. (2012) (ed.) *Archaeological Theory Today*. Cambridge, Polity Press.

Horden, P. and Purcell, N. (2000) *The Corrupting Sea: A Study of Mediterranean History*. Oxford, Blackwell.

Iaia, C. (2006) Strumenti da lavoro nelle sepolture dell'Età del Ferro italiana. *In Studi di Protostoria in Onore di Renato Peroni*, 190–201. Borgo S. Lorenzo, All'Insegna del Giglio.

Izzet, V. (2007) *The Archaeology of Etruscan Society*. Cambridge, Cambridge University Press.

Knapp, A.B. and van Dommelen, P. (2008) Past practices: Rethinking individuals and agents in archaeology. *Cambridge Archaeological Journal* 18(1), 15–34.

Krishnaswamy, R. and Hawley, J.C. (2009) (eds) *The Postcolonial and the Global*. Minneapolis, University of Minnesota Press.

Lawrence, D.H. (1932) *Etruscan Places*. New York, Vikings.

Lo Schiavo, F. (2010) *Le Fibule dell'Italia Meridionale e della Sicilia dall'Età del Bronzo Recente al VI Sec. a.C.*. Stuttgart, Steiner Verlag.

Malkin, I. (2011) *A Small Greek World: Networks in the Ancient Mediterranean*. Oxford, Oxford University Press.

Melandri, G. (2011) *L'Età del Ferro a Capua. Aspetti Distintivi del Contesto Culturale e suo Inquadramento nelle Dinamiche di Sviluppo dell'Italia Protostorica* (BAR S2265). Oxford, Archaeopress.

Migden Socolow, S. (2000) *The Women of Colonial Latin America*. Cambridge, Cambridge University Press.

Moore, H. (1994) *A Passion for Difference: Essays in Anthropology and Gender*. Bloomington–Cambridge, Polity Press.

Morris, I. (1987) *Burial and Ancient Society: The Rise of the Greek City-State*. Cambridge, Cambridge University Press.

Nelson, S.M. (2006) (ed.) *Handbook of Gender in Archaeology*. Lanham, Alta Mira Press.

Parker Pearson, M. (1999) *The Archaeology of Death and Burial*. Stroud, Sutton.

Perego, E. (2011) Engendered actions: Agency and ritual in pre-Roman Veneto. In A. Chaniotis (ed.) *Ritual Dynamics in the Ancient Mediterranean: Agency, Emotion, Gender, Reception*, 17–42. Stuttgart, Steinar Verlag.

Pellegrino, C. and Rossi, A. (2011) *Pontecagnano I.1. Città e Campagna nell'Agro Picentino (Gli Scavi dell'Autostrada 2001-2006)*. Fisciano, Dipartimento di Scienze del Patrimonio Culturale dell'Università degli Studi di Salerno.

Riva, C. (2010) *The Urbanisation of Etruria: Funerary Ritual and Social Change, 700-600 BC*. Cambridge, Cambridge University Press.

Scopacasa, R. (2014) Gender and ritual in ancient Italy: A quantitative approach to grave goods and skeletal data in pre-Roman Samnium. *American Journal of Archaeology* 118(2), 241–266.

Scott, J.C. (1985) *Weapons of the Weak: Everyday Forms of Peasant Resistance*. New Haven, Yale University Press.

Sgubini Moretti, A.M. (2000) (ed.) *Villa Giulia. Dalle Origini al 2000*. Roma, "L'Erma" di Bretschneider.

Smith, C.J. (2006) *The Roman Clan: The Gens from Ancient Ideology to Modern Anthropology*. Cambridge, Cambridge University Press.

Torelli, M. (2000) *Gli Etruschi*. Milano, Bompiani.

van Dommelen, P. (2006) Colonial matters: Material culture and postcolonial theory in colonial situations. In C. Tilley, W. Keane, S. Küchler, M. Rowlands and P. Spyer (eds) *Handbook of Material Culture*, 104–124. London, Sage.

Wacquant, L.J.D. (1992) The structure and logic of Bourdieu's sociology. In P. Bourdieu and L.J.D. Wacquant (eds) *An Invitation to Reflexive Sociology*, 2–59. Cambridge, Polity Press.

Whitehouse, R.D. (1998) (ed.) *Gender and Italian Archaeology: Challenging the Stereotypes*. London, Accordia Research Institute and Institute of Archaeology, University College London.

Chapter 2

Styles of drinking and the burial rites of Early Iron Age Middle-Tyrrhenian Italy

Cristiano Iaia

Introduction

Ever since the influential papers by A. Sherratt, M. Dietler and B. Arnold in the 1980s and 1990s (e.g. Arnold 1999; Dietler 1990; Sherratt 1987), alcohol consumption has been recognized as a 'total social fact', even in the archaeological discourse. Indeed, drinking alcohol is a sphere that encompasses functions of solidarity and hospitality, as well as reciprocal exchange flows, but also competitive behaviour and inequality (*cf.* also Hamilakis 1999). In particular, transformations in drinking practices, and the ideological constructs linked to them, have many implications for collective action and agency, and can provide notable insights into social change and politics more in general. However, from the perspective of an archaeologist involved in standard analyses of archaeological materials and contexts, further research is desirable on the material aspects of commensality. In particular, further work would be necessary on the stylistic variability seen in vessels used for serving and drinking alcohol. In this regard, some ethnoarchaeological works (e.g. Dietler and Herbich 1998) have stressed that 'style' should be conceived not as a simple means of communication, but rather as the complex outcome of structural processes which include those relating to the context of an object's manufacture. This consideration stems from the assumption that (a) both producers and consumers are social actors and (b) our investigation of material culture has to take into account the relationships that develop between these two categories of agents, who share the same cognitive attitudes and perceptions within a definite socio-cultural context (i.e. P. Bourdieu's notion of *habitus*: e.g. Bourdieu 2009[1994]; on *habitus cf.* also Cuozzo and Perego this volume, with additional bibliography). In complex societies, craftspeople play the fundamental – and undervalued – role of those who actively give material form and shape to rituals, religious and ideological symbols, and notions of social identity, power and interaction (Costin and Wright 1998).

Within this theoretical framework, therefore, I shall explore the burial record of some areas of Early Iron Age central Italy (c. 930–730 BC, with particular regard to south Etruria: Fig. 2.1), in order to start asking, through a comparative approach, the following questions:

1. What role did ceremonial drinking have within the rising politically centralized communities of this region?
2. Were coexisting styles in vessel forms and/or design linked to different drinking practices?
3. Did non-élite groups and/or specific gender or age groups (e.g. women, children) play any role in the creation of these hypothetically diverging commensality patterns?

Although I am aware that the data and analytical work so far available are not always sufficient to answer these questions in full, I shall argue that it is now possible to provide a picture of alcohol consumption in Early Iron Age middle-Tyrrhenian Italy that is much more nuanced than previously conceived. In particular, the archaeological record suggests that the traditional linkage between top-level élite groups and alcohol consumption might not have been as straightforward and exclusive as often argued in the current scholarly debate.

Growing archaeobotanical evidence datable from the Middle and Recent Bronze Age is shedding light on the earliest stages of grape domestication in north-central Italy (c. sixteenth–twelfth centuries BC: Aranguren et al. 2007; Iaia 2013a). Furthermore, a development and intensification of wine production is attested – both directly and indirectly – in the Final Bronze Age (twelfth–tenth centuries BC: Delpino 2007). For instance, a substantial quantity of pips pertaining to wild, intermediate and domesticated forms of vitis vinifera has been recovered in the Final Bronze Age settlement of Livorno-Stagno in coastal northern Etruria (Giachi et al. 2010). Among the Early Iron Age data, two finds are especially remarkable: these are the many grapevine pips from the ninth-century BC village of Gran Carro near Bolsena, in south Etruria (Costantini and Costantini Biasini 1995), and the eighth-century BC wine-making press from the riverside settlement of Longola di Poggio Marino in Campania (Cicirelli et al. 2008). The hypothesis that wine was traded across the Tyrrhenian Sea at the beginning of the first millennium BC is also suggested by other data. Worth noting is the fact that, according to residue analyses, the so-called 'nuragic askoid-jugs', either imported from Sardinia or locally imitated in Etruria, were presumably used for wine consumption (Delpino 2002; Santoni 2010). At the same time, archaeobotanical and chemical analyses are starting to disclose evidence of vine cultivation and wine production at indigenous contexts of Final Bronze Age and Early Iron Age Sardinia (Santoni 2010, 27). Notably, mainstream research keeps emphasizing the acquisition of wine as a chiefly 'Greek gift' dating to the eighth century BC (even though with a timid acknowledgment of some precedents dating to the Final Bronze Age: Bartoloni et al. 2012; Zifferero 2012). However, the evidence mentioned above contributes to

Fig. 2.1: Main sites mentioned in the chapter: 1. Livorno-Stagno; 2. Murlo; 3. Gran Carro; 4. Poggio Montano; 5. Tarquinia; 6. Caolino del Sasso; 7. Cerveteri; 8. Narce; 9. Veii; 10. Ficana; 11. Castel di Decima; 12. Osteria dell'Osa; 13. Longola di Poggio Marino (elaboration C. Iaia).

change our perspective on the socio-cultural meaning of alcohol consumption in pre-Roman Italy: the latter had a rather long history with indigenous or central Mediterranean roots, and was not the result of a sudden introduction from abroad (as argued for other cultural contexts in Dietler 1990; on the role of local Italian communities as social agents in phases of cultural contacts with the Greeks *cf.* also Cuozzo and Morris this volume).

This is not to say that wine was a widespread and common foodstuff in Etruria since its introduction and earliest use. On the contrary, it is well known that wine production is a time-consuming process, which requires complex labour management from cultivation to processing, and which not every social group and socio-political entity can afford (Dietler 1990; Hamilakis 1999). Despite the lack of data for assessing the scale and extension of this kind of secondary subsistence production, the impact of alcohol production and consumption on the burial rites examined here appears remarkable. In particular, the material repertoire of Early Iron Age central Italy shows an increasing emphasis on drinking practices versus the consumption of solid food. This is the reason why I shall not employ here the term 'banquet', which encompasses a broader range of collective ritual situations.[1] Nonetheless, major innovations can be observed in regards to ritual drinking in the context considered in this chapter. These innovations focused on the much more widespread presence, vis-à-vis the previous Final Bronze Age period, of indigenous vessel shapes, whose ties with alcohol consumption were to become increasingly explicit by the following Orientalizing period (c. 720–570 BC). These vessel shapes, which were often found reciprocally associated in grave assemblages, include amongst others handled cups, krater-like vessels, globular jars, small amphorae and jugs with a narrow neck. Obviously, we do not have any assurance that all these vessels were closely connected to wine consumption. However, the specialized character of the shapes (cf. below) makes their use implausible for beverages other than alcohol.[2] This hypothesis is reinforced by the key role played by drinking in the social life of ancient Etruria and Latium – a role that one may presume in light of the qualitative and quantitative prominence of drink consumption in Early Iron Age burial rituals.

Early stages of ritualized alcohol consumption

Starting from the tenth–ninth centuries BC (corresponding to the so-called 'Latial Period II'), probable cases of ritualized alcohol consumption can be recognized at Osteria dell'Osa, a cemetery located in Latium Vetus not far from Rome (Bietti Sestieri 1992a; 1992b). There, among the 450 graves dating to this period, a remarkable differentiation can be noted between the vessel sets deposited in a restricted group of cremation graves, and those deposited in association with the much more numerous inhumations. These 16 cremation tombs mostly belonged to adult male individuals of remarkable standing, and contained complete sets of miniature, non-functional impasto pots. These services included vessels for food consumption and miniature reproductions of huge storage containers, the so-called *ollette a rete*, that can be linked to burial traditions dating back to the Final Bronze Age. Conversely, the inhumations largely belonged to women and infants, and were accompanied by new associations of normal-size pots, undeniably used for serving and drinking liquids (Bietti Sestieri 1992b, 103). As A.M. Bietti Sestieri pointed out, although drinking vessels are not exclusive of female graves, at Osteria dell'Osa a connection is evident between some groups of young and adult female individuals and some specific kinds of drinking sets. In particular, one set composed of a cup and jugs of two different shapes (i.e. biconical and globular) is closely associated with young women characterized in burial as weavers (Bietti Sestieri 1992b, 108). Moreover, a specific task of controlling and redistributing beverages has been attributed to 'old adult' women furnished with a drinking set that included a cup and a two-handled globular jar on high foot. Also remarkable is that pottery vessels at Osteria dell'Osa usually display use-wear traces (Bietti Sestieri 1992b, 87). This evidence possibly indicates that such vessels were actual possessions of the dead, or were at least mementoes of their family life. Hence, it is possible to conjecture that in this community, probably structured into kinship groups, women may have held some roles in managing drinking occasions in the household context. On the other hand, there is no clear evidence that these drinking sets were used as markers of social distinction. This is suggested by the fact that the impasto vessels as a whole do not exhibit any considerable differentiation in technological characteristics and style; furthermore, their production apparently took place in a domestic environment (Bietti Sestieri 1992a, 445).

In the same chronological period, the burial record of south Etruria shows a greater complexity and diversification of grave goods and rituals. First, understanding this specific context is impossible without taking into account the birth and subsequent dramatic growth, in the ninth century BC, of the substantial demographic agglomerations known in Italian scholarship as 'proto-urban centres', *centri protourbani*, later to become the major Etruscan cities (Pacciarelli 2001). In these territorial entities, which from their onset were characterized by processes of rapid centralization of people, productive forces and power, it is not surprising to find a broad range of ritual practices relating to commensality, as a consequence of increasing complexity in social relations.

Tarquinia, located near Viterbo in Latium, holds most of the earlier evidence for these phenomena (on the funerary ritual of Iron Age Tarquinia *cf.* also Shipley this volume). Since the beginning of the Early Iron Age (Tarquinia Phase 1, *c.* late tenth–late ninth century BC and chronologically coincident with the Latial Period II), Tarquinia developed into a huge proto-urban agglomeration, surrounded by several cemeteries, largely composed of cremation tombs (Iaia 1999; Mandolesi 1999). The cremation tombs excavated between the late nineteenth and the first half of the twentieth centuries yielded mainly vessels for solid food consumption, such as bowls and plates, the latter sometimes forming abundant services composed of up to about ten exemplars (Iaia 1999, 49). The presence of such vessel shapes in these cremation graves has been extensively confirmed by recent excavations (Trucco 2006; Trucco *et al.* 2005). In the diagram presented below (Fig. 2.2), the percentage of the main vessel forms from the graves of Tarquinia is plotted and compared primarily with gender distinctions (source of data: Iaia 1999). Sex determination is mainly based here on archaeological indicators, a fact that does not constitute a severe limitation, as some gender-related grave goods are recognizable in this period without great difficulty. For example, spinning implements and fibulae are associated with female burials, while razors, vase lids in the shape of helmets and/or the less common weapons are associated with male burials. The diagram clearly shows that in Early Iron Age Tarquinia (for the so-called IA–IB Phases: Fig. 2.2A) pottery assemblages were frequently composed of small plates, while definitely rarer were vessels linked

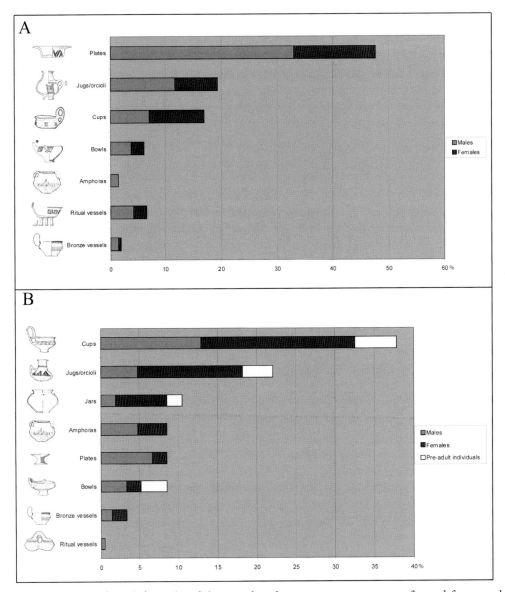

Fig. 2.2: Tarquinia (Viterbo), tombs of the initial Early Iron Age: percentages of vessel forms and relationship with the gender of the deceased. A: IA–IB Phases (total number of tombs: 56). B: IC–IIA Phases (total number of tombs: 85) (source: Iaia 1999; elaboration: C. Iaia).

with drinking, such as cups, jugs and small amphorae. Moreover, male graves dating to this period were more likely to contain complex burial assemblages than the female ones; some of these male graves also included ritual paraphernalia, such as multiple vessels (kernoi), votive ceramic boats and bronze cups (Iaia 2007).

A more unambiguous change in practices of commensality can be recognized in the graves of south Etruria dating to the transition period between the so-called Phase 1 and Phase 2 of the Early Iron Age (*c.* 825–800 BC; for more information on the chronology of this period, with a focus on the chronological framework developed by R. Peroni, *cf.* Toms 1986, 41–97; also Pacciarelli 2001, 50–69). In the wealthy cemeteries of Tarquinia, we are able to analyse this transformation in some detail. The assemblages associated with cremation burials show a new type of material culture connected to the consumption of liquids, which displays some stylistic variability. In order to clarify this point, we can compare the diagram above, which provides the percentage of the main artefact classes for the IA–IB Phases (Fig. 2.2A), with the same diagram for the subsequent period, corresponding to the IC–IIA Phases (Fig. 2.2B). In these later phases, the picture changes abruptly. The most widespread pottery form is now the cup, followed by different types of jugs/*orcioli*, jars and small amphorae; the same pattern is attested at Veii in the local IC–IIA Phases (*cf.* Toms 1986). Significantly, these same vessels are widely present in female and, secondarily, infant tombs. In particular, when we take into account the whole repertoire of vessels from the Tarquinia cemeteries dating to this period, drinking vessels in female tombs represent about 45% of the total, while those present in male tombs account for no more than 26% (Fig. 2.2B: analytical data from Iaia 1999, tab. 6). Worth considering is also the percentage of 'sub-adult' graves, mainly attributable to female children, which yielded about 11% of these vessel forms. The impression is of a sudden, radical transformation in the ritual role of drinking (Iaia 1999, 65), in which women may have gained a greater importance than in the earlier period.

Let us take a closer look at these changes in material culture. A first striking feature is the appearance of totally new pottery classes, such as the globular or round-belly jars, generally of red impasto ware. As F. Delpino pointed out (Delpino 1986; 1997), these vessels bear some morphological similarities to Greek kraters. However, although this similarity is undeniable, in my opinion it should be understood more as a functional parallel, rather than as indicative of a cultural borrowing from the Aegean world. At Tarquinia this type of jar, far from being an exotic status symbol, is recurrent in several graves furnished with local drinking vessels, such as impasto jugs and cups (Iaia 1999, 65); its relation with the act of dipping is clear, since in many cases the cup was found inside the jar. In fact, the simple drinking set including one jar – sometimes of the krater-like shape – and a cup is the one most frequently attested at Tarquinia in this period. There is also evidence suggesting that the same set was especially used during the funerary ceremony or at its conclusion. For example, the couple of vessels were sometimes placed on top of the cinerary urn, perhaps in order to offer liquids to the deceased or make a toast in their honour. Interestingly, this service can recur in graves belonging to individuals of different social standings, from high-status warriors to middle- or high-rank women. These women may include for instance those associated in burial with bronze distaffs or spindles. Such implements, even though representing individuals holding an important social role in the household context, may or may not be associated with explicit signs of élite membership (e.g. wealthy sets of ornaments, golden pendants or bronze vessels: Iaia 1999, 57). Drinking, and especially the act of serving the beverage, are also alluded to by the presence of exotic pots in female graves probably pertaining to sub-adults. These vessels include jugs painted in the 'Oenoetrian' geometric style, which might have been imported from southern Italy (*cf.* in particular the modest infant Impiccato Tomb 78 from Tarquinia: Bartoloni 1971; Iaia 1999, 61, fig. 16a; *cf.* also Sopra Selciatello Tomb 140, dating to the early eighth century BC: this grave yielded a wealthier assemblage including a complete pottery drinking service with krater-like jars, mugs and a cup: Iaia 1999, 65, fig. 15a).

In interpreting this evidence, we should consider that most cemeteries from the Early Iron Age proto-urban centres of Etruria seem to be largely representative of wide sections of the overall community, or at least of its outright members (on the issue of inclusion and exclusion from formal burial *cf.* also the chapters by Cuozzo, Di Lorenzo *et al.*, Scopacasa, Perego, Zanoni, and Perego and Scopacasa).[3] In this context, drinking sets, in light of their wide diffusion in graves with heterogeneous socio-ritual characteristics, could testify to the inclusive significance of drinking for the inhabitants of these large settlements. In other words, although the management of vine cultivation and wine production was probably in the hands of the élite, the introduction of wine into commonly shared burial rituals (for instance in the form of limited funerary libations) can be interpreted as the mark of a circulation of this precious commodity. This circulation might have taken place, for example, through gift exchange and/or some mechanisms of redistribution involving people belonging to different social levels.

A complementary facet of this pattern can be recognized in relation to a small group of graves belonging to the top-level of the political echelon, such as the well-known Impiccato Tombs I and II from Tarquinia (Delpino 2005; Iaia 1999; 2007; 2013a). These two graves yielded cremation burials, pertaining to male individuals, which sharply differed in their ritual treatment from the other burials attested at Tarquinia in the same period (*cf.* the above-mentioned tombs with ceramic drinking assemblages). This diversity is evidenced by their complex and lavish ritual: the urns, laid on their sides in a rectangular cist or pit, were dressed with clothes adorned with fibulae and gold plates; furthermore, they were complemented by prestigious weapons and bronze armour. In these graves drinking is alluded to by very rare sets of bronze vessels, including a cup of the 'Stillfried-Hostomice type' and an incense burner; the latter was possibly used as a ritual device to accompany codified acts of libation (Iaia 2006; 2007). These items were the outcome of very specialized processes of production that helped placing a greater emphasis on the symbolic and political implications of the act of drinking. This new emphasis on ritual drinking was achieved through the display of prestigious vessels, a practice meant as an exclusive privilege of powerful individuals (compare the early Celtic customs: Arnold 1999). This is a key aspect of drink consumption that was to assume a greater importance during the following period.

To summarize, the burial data from south Etruria in the central phases of the Early Iron Age disclose a complex picture in which alcohol consumption was gaining a major importance in the ceremonial sphere of the whole proto-urban community. In this framework, grave goods relating to drinking are much more widespread than before. Furthermore, these drinking sets are constructed through different configurations of material culture, possibly corresponding to different rituals. The standard drinking set included vessels (e.g. red impasto and sheet bronze vessels) that were at the same time the outcome of a new style of commensality and the products of new and sometimes highly specialized processes of manufacture. For the first time (but with precedents in Latium), female individuals of variable social standing seem to have played a key role in the framework of these rituals of commensality – rituals that seem to have facilitated the development of key social relations, which especially included mechanisms of group inclusion (on the social role of women in first-millennium BC Italy *cf.* also the chapters by Cuozzo and Faustoferri; on gender more in general *cf.* also Di Lorenzo *et al.*, Perego and Scopacasa, and O'Donoghue, this volume, the latter with a focus on masculinity). In this regard, however, we should raise doubts as to whether this apparent mechanism of inclusion through drinking rituals was only an ideological attempt at masking competition for the control over wine, which was still a rare and added-value commodity at the time. This attempt might have occurred through the fictitious construction and naturalization of ideas of solidarity, hospitality (through gifts exchange) and redistribution in the funerary arena (*cf.* Hamilakis 1999).

High variety of commensal practices in the eighth century BC

The second phase of the Early Iron Age in south Etruria and Latium (c. 800–725 BC) witnessed radical transformations in every aspect of the archaeological record (for a general overview *cf.* Bartoloni 2003). With regards to territorial dynamics, the processes of centralization that took place in Etruria at the onset of the Early Iron Age were followed by a trend of territorial expansion aimed at founding new secondary settlements on defensible positions. These new settlements were especially concentrated in the hilly hinterland, with the clear purpose of controlling crucial areas for resource exploitation and strategic needs (Iaia and Mandolesi 2010). Another major aspect of the same process was the highly competitive nature of the social context in which the interment of weaponry and war-related symbols played an essential, albeit not unique, role in driving socio-political dynamics (Iaia 2013a; Pacciarelli 2001). It is within this economically and politically much more diversified framework, directly conducive to the subsequent process of urbanization of the southern Etruscan communities (Riva 2010), that wine production and consumption came to play an even more important socio-political role.

In this period the use of sheet bronze vessels in Middle-Tyrrhenian Italy became the chief medium for expressing participation in elaborate rituals of commensality that appear to have been the preserve of privileged social groups. The characteristics of exclusiveness and separateness manifested by these products were enhanced by the adoption of heterogeneous ritual models, which indicate the involvement of the first urban aristocrats in a wide network of long-distance connections (Iaia 2005; 2006; 2010). I suggest that one of the most important innovations in this regard was the adoption of a new vessel shape, namely the amphora or bucket with a cylindrical neck and embossed decoration (Fig. 2.3A.10). These amphorae were fitting in the act of dipping liquids with ladles or cups. This ritual act, which also had deep social significance, presupposed the generous dispensing – analogous to gift-giving behaviours – of a quantity of alcoholic beverage by a wealthy patron to a collective entity, such as a family or retinue group, according to hospitality relationships. The function of this kind of vessel, similar to that of the Greek krater, was charged with additional symbolic meanings by technical and formal features influenced by the bronze-working industries of central and northern Europe (Iaia 2006, 105), intermixed with increasing Near Eastern stimuli. It is at Veii and Tarquinia, in tombs belonging to high-ranking warriors and their spouses, that one can observe the most spectacular associations between this vessel shape and a series of very sophisticated bronze vases, partly inspired by Eastern models (Iaia 2010): among them we should cite basins, the so-called 'pilgrim flasks', tripod stands and different types of ceremonial bronze cups on foot (e.g. Fig. 2.3A.6–9, 11).

Another significant phenomenon, albeit very restricted in scale, was the interment of tools for meat consumption, a practice that occurred at Veii and in Latium since the late ninth century BC. These tools included in particular spits and knives that must have been adopted in ceremonial practices reserved for privileged individuals (Bartoloni 1988; 2003, 123; Iaia 2007, 266; Riva 2010). The earliest examples have been found in female tombs with an explicit élite character. These graves included Tomb OP 4–5 from the Quattro Fontanili cemetery at Veii (*Quattro Fontanili* 1972, 295) and the well-known Tomb 132 of Castel di Decima in Latium (Nijboer 2006), both dating approximately to the late ninth–early eighth century BC. This kind of association, rather than being a mere indication of the role played by some women in food dispensing, has evident links to the sacrificial sphere, as more explicitly attested in the burial record of the Orientalizing period (on the presence of knives and axes in female tombs *cf.* also Faustoferri, this volume, with a focus on Abruzzo and additional bibliography).[4] This hypothesis is reinforced by the additional presence at Veii of bronze axes – a typical implement for the sacrificial killing of animals – and ritual paraphernalia, such as a bronze incense-burner. A relationship between these sets for meat consumption and drinking is also made clear from the bronze cups found in the same tombs. It is noteworthy that all these assemblages, far from being exclusive of female graves, cut across gender distinctions. Hence, these objects were clearly intended to express the close relation between cultic functions and an entire status group (whatever its definition could be), in M. Weber's sense of collective groups sharing lifestyles and honours (for a recent thorough discussion: Riva 2010).

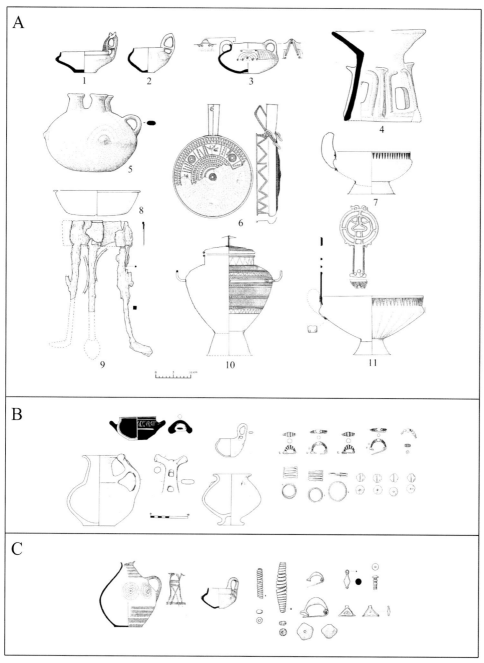

Fig. 2.3: Veii (Rome), Phase 2 of Early Iron Age, drinking sets from female tombs. A: vessel assemblage from Quattro Fontanili Tomb FF 7–8 (modified after Quattro Fontanili 1967). B: grave set, Grotta Gramiccia Tomb 779 (modified after Berardinetti and Drago 1997). C: grave set, Quattro Fontanili Tomb HH 15 (modified after Quattro Fontanili 1965).

This status group was increasing its own "symbolic capital" (according to the notion in Bourdieu 2009[1994]), namely its legitimized capacity of managing and/or controlling immaterial spheres (e.g. links to deities) and esoteric wisdom.

In order to highlight the complexity of practices of ritual drinking in this chronological phase, I shall now turn to the vivaciously debated issue of Greek or Greek-type ceramics found in Middle-Tyrrhenian Italian tombs dating to c. 830/800–720 BC. This class of vessels occurs in south Etruria, Latium, Campania and – more rarely – Sardinia (e.g. Boitani 2005; Ridgway 2000; 2002; Rizzo 2005). Most of these vessels were wheel-made and painted pots in depurated clay used for drinking or dispensing liquids. The vessel shapes are mainly represented by *skyphoi* (e.g. Fig. 2.4a), and less frequently by handled cups and jugs. The introduction of kraters, *stamnoi*/jars and stands (*holmoi*) took place only by the third quarter of the eighth century BC (c. 750–725 BC). Unfortunately, there is no space here to examine this later evidence.

Archaeometric analyses have revealed that these vessels, especially the *skyphoi*, were to some extent imported from Greece. Others, however, were manufactured in Italy – possibly in south Etruria and/or Campania – by expert Greek potters (Boitani 2005, with references). Clearly, they represented highly specialized products and an abrupt technological change in respect to the native impasto pottery. Setting aside an analysis of the vast hyper-specialized literature on this topic, we should at least take into account that scholars have expressed various opinions on the function and significance of this ceramic class. These opinions have generally focused on a truly generic concept of acculturation from the Greek 'civilized' world and have persistently favoured an interpretation of these objects as markers of élite trade (e.g. Nizzo and ten Kortenaar 2010). Most of the Italian classicists simply link them to the introduction of wine consumption in central Italy, according to ceremonial customs stimulated by the Greek *symposion* (e.g. Bartoloni 2003, 32, 196; Boitani and Berardinetti Insam 2001). Conversely, one of the greatest authorities in the field, D. Ridgway, was more sceptical about this notion of transmission through acculturation. In particular, he wondered whether the *skyphoi*, imported or imitated in a different cultural context, could still be considered drinking pots in the same fashion as in Iron Age Greece (Ridgway 2002, 220).

I think that only a different approach to the indigenous cultural context in which this phenomenon took place might provide some contribution to the debate (for a non-traditional approach to banqueting and drinking in Orientalizing Etruria cf. also Riva 2010). To reassess this evidence in a new light, therefore, I have collected a geographically large sample of graves from south Etruria that yielded at least one such pot of Greek-type ceramic. This sample mainly comprises tombs from Veii, but also evidence from Tarquinia, Cerveteri, Poggio Montano, Narce and Caolino del Sasso.[5] The number of the sampled tombs is 29 (the sample does not include robbed graves or graves whose funerary assemblage was not fully recovered or published).

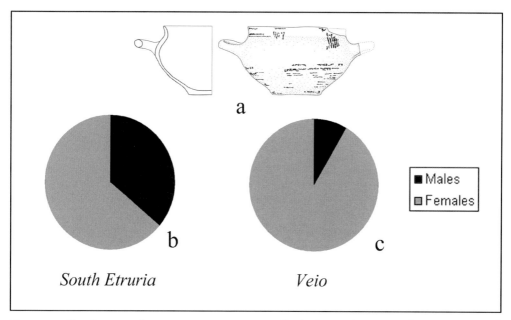

Fig. 2.4: a: Skyphos *cup from Poggio Montano-Vetralla (redrawn from Cristofani Martelli 1971); b: percentages of tombs with Greek-type pottery in South Etruria, according to gender distinctions; c: the same at Veii–Veio (elaboration: C. Iaia).*

A 'sociological' understanding of the burial record dating to the second phase of the Early Iron Age in south Etruria (*c.* 830/800–720 BC) is facilitated by some specific features of the mortuary ritual. Most important of all are (a) the dominant adoption of the inhumation rite, with its emphasis on the visibility of the corporeal and individual dimension of the dead person (notably, the few exceptions known still imitate the tombs in which inhumation is adopted in their arrangement and grave goods), and (b) the possibility of recognizing a full range of combinations in the grave assemblages (for example, on Veii *cf.* Pacciarelli 2001; on Veii in the following Orientalizing and Archaic periods *cf.* briefly Rajala this volume). The analysis of this evidence, which cannot be considered comprehensive, shows that the early Greek-type pottery consisted of a very limited range of ceramic forms, almost all clearly linked to drinking practices. They were regularly part of vessel associations comprising a great majority of impasto pots (Fig. 2.3B, C). In several cases, these assemblages included a variable number of cups and other basic vessels for drinking and containing liquids, such as jugs, mugs, small amphorae and globular jars (for example, for the Veian cemetery of Grotta Gramiccia *cf.* Berardinetti and Drago 1997, 52). Bronze vessels were rare and limited to the less sophisticated forms, such as cups, while a direct co-occurrence between sheet bronze neck-amphorae and ceramics of depurated clay is nearly non-existent. Overall, a close connection between Greek-type pottery and alcohol consumption seems the most reasonable hypothesis; conversely, a relationship with Hellenic sympotic rituals is debatable, in view of the characteristics of the burial assemblages, well grounded in the local socio-cultural milieu. Moreover, prior to the latest developments of the late eighth century BC, there is scarce evidence of the employment of these vessel forms in elaborate ceremonial practices.

The social environment that favoured this pottery class seems to have been noticeably different from that of the aristocrats buried with costly sets of bronze vessels. Unfortunately, the lack of evidence from settlement sites is a serious obstacle to an in-depth understanding of the socio-economic significance of these practices of consumption. Some limited clues might be provided by sites such as Ficana, in Latium, where a remarkable quantity of fragments of this pottery class was recovered from some eighth-century BC domestic layers (Brandt *et al.* 1997; below). However, as they still have to be subject to accurate scrutiny, we have to confine ourselves to the funerary record. As indicated by the diagrams presented here (Fig. 2.4a, b), the burials associated with services including Greek-type pottery mainly belonged to women, and only secondarily to male individuals; furthermore, numerous infants or adolescents are recognizable among those associated with these vessels on the basis of osteological analyses published in the 1960s and the 1970s (Boitani and Berardinetti Insam 2001, 110, with references). As shown by the diagrams with the percentages of the main categories of objects, personal grave goods are generally of 'humble' or 'medium' level (Fig. 2.5). The few male tombs can include standard associations of weapons, mainly spear-heads and knives, and only exceptionally swords and other markers of high social standing (Fig. 2.5A). Female tombs, whose number is definitely higher than that of male graves (*cf.* Nizzo and ten Kortenaar 2010 on the case of Veii), are mainly characterized by standard assemblages of ornaments, mostly made up of necklaces and fibulae (Figs 2.3C; 2.5B).

A particularly neat pattern is attested at Veii. Here, most graves comprising Greek-type ceramics can be classified as belonging to low- or middle-rank women and infants (two instances in Fig. 2.3B–C) whose grave assemblages contrast with the sumptuous grave-sets that have also been found in Veii in the same period, and which include bronze vessels and other status symbols. The scanty data available from other sites, such as Tarquinia, Cerveteri and Narce, show a similar pattern, though with some local variation. In particular, burial furnishing seems peculiar at the small site of Poggio Montano, in the hinterland of Tarquinia. Here, *skyphoi* and other vessels of depurated clay (Fig. 2.4a) are widely present in graves of both men and women, without any close relation with a specific social level, though with a somewhat more explicit link to burials belonging to the members of social segments that might be defined as 'peripheral élite groups' (Colini 1914; Cristofani Martelli 1971; Piergrossi 2002). This dissimilarity with the situation attested at major centres such as Veii is probably due also to the definitely minor importance of Poggio Montano in the hierarchical scale of settlements that developed in this area in the period under consideration here (Iaia and Mandolesi 2010). Although a more accurate characterization of these social strata

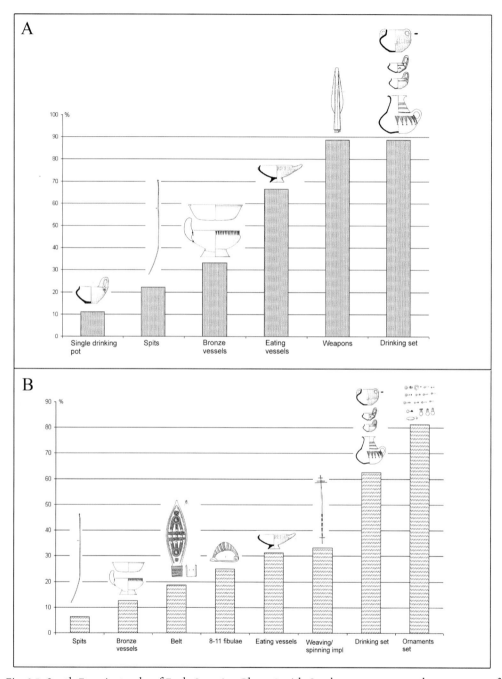

Fig. 2.5: South Etruria, tombs of Early Iron Age Phase 2 with Greek-type pottery, and percentages of the main grave-good categories; A: male tombs; B: female tombs (elaboration: C. Iaia).

is needed, I think that a possible definition for them would be that of 'sub-élites'. These 'sub-élite' groups might represent social groups of an intermediate standing that tended to emulate, but not necessarily to imitate rigorously, the lifestyles and consumption habits of top-level social strata (for a definition of 'sub-élites' in the Late Bronze Age eastern Mediterranean *cf.* Sherratt 1993).

Further research on this topic should attempt to shed light on the relationship between these 'sub-élites' and the wider context in which the production of wine and wheel-made painted ceramics, as two distinct but interrelated domains, took place.

Conclusion

In conclusion, I suggest that at least two different patterns in the use of material culture linked to drinking can be envisaged in the central and late phases of the southern Etruscan Early Iron Age, approximately corresponding to the whole eighth century BC.

The first pattern was characterized by the adoption of plenty of metal ceremonial equipment and a greater concern with ritual practices presumably connected to cult. In the same context, wine might often be consumed in association with cooked meat, possibly with an emphasis on sacrificial rites. Sophisticated bronze containers, such as the necked amphorae (which recurred in some graves in two exemplars) or the 'pilgrim flasks', might have symbolized the possession of considerable quantities and/ or different varieties of the beverage. Notably, in such cases a clear connection with the highest levels of the social hierarchy is evident.

The second pattern was mainly centred on plain pottery services and could involve the adoption of some Greek-type ceramics. Furthermore, it was characterized by the absence of fixed rules and by more mundane qualities, and seems to correspond to lower social contexts, ranging from 'poor' subordinated individuals to members of 'sub-élite' social strata (on social marginality and subordination in pre-Roman Italy *cf.* also Perego, Perego and Scopacasa, and to a less extent, Cuozzo and Zanoni, this volume). It is reasonable to assume that drinking with *skyphoi* and impasto pots was physically and symbolically a different matter than carrying out the same action with a huge bronze cup and bronze containers. Thus, highly diverse was the material dimension of production and consumption, ranging from a sophisticated bronze industry to the use of Greek-type fine ceramics and simple local impasto. Whether this could have corresponded to different rules of codification of the wine consumption etiquette seems now highly probable, although not easy to demonstrate beyond any doubt. A later parallel could be found in the early sixth-century BC terracotta relief of Murlo in central Tuscany, where the aristocratic participants to a banquet were differentiated between men holding Oriental-type bronze bowls and women and servants associated with Ionic-type *skyphoi*. This evidence might indicate a hierarchical arrangement of banqueting and drinking practices, which however took place in a different, more stratified social context (Rathje 1995, 173). In Early Iron Age Etruria the situation seems still fluid and variable, and reveals some extent of social mobility, in agreement with the whole archaeological record of this period.

In both models of ritual drinking, women seem to have played a central role in managing the consumption of alcohol, seemingly in continuity with a regional trend going back to the late ninth century BC (compare the evidence from Tarquinia). It is among the burials associated with Greek-type pottery that the female deceased was indeed given a strong preponderance, at least in the best documented case, namely that of Veii. Even though this phenomenon could effectively correspond to a special proclivity by women to manage hospitality in the framework of commensal practices in Iron Age Middle-Tyrrhenian Italy (as is commonly noted in specific literature *cf.* for example Bartoloni 2003, 123), there are other implications to be considered. In fact, the wide diffusion of drinking vessels, such as Greek-type *skyphoi* and the like, in female graves, rather than being linked to the simple task of serving or dispensing in a household context, is symptomatic of women's involvement in the actual consumption of alcohol in various social occasions.

I think that, because of the incompleteness of the archaeological record and a lack of sufficient data from settlement sites, the explanations of this phenomenon could be manifold and only cautious. First, we should take into account any possible kind of cultural inheritance of social institutions, unknown to us in their specific features, from the Italian Late Bronze Age, when comparable female roles in managing commensal occasions did emerge (on the Terramare culture: Iaia 2013b). Secondly, in eighth-century BC south Etruria (as also attested in seventh-century BC Picenum: Coen 2008) women could have participated in the political and symbolic dimension of commensal practices. Hence, serving and dispensing, but especially drinking alcohol, could have been a counterpart to the dominance of maleness and warrior symbolism in local material culture and burial rituals (Iaia 2013a; Riva 2010). A further outcome of this phenomenon can be seen by the final decades of the eighth century BC, when outstanding female burials associated with elaborate equipment for ceremonial banqueting (initially still focused on drinking) appeared in Middle-Tyrrhenian cemeteries (for one among several examples *cf.* Olmo Bello Tomb 2 from Bisenzio: Iaia 2006). This phenomenon, alongside others such as the spread of wagons in female graves (Riva 2010, 95), raises questions about the role of aristocratic women as agents of hereditary transmission of paramount statuses, as argued for the West-Hallstatt 'princely' contexts in central Europe (Chaume 2007; *cf.* also Cuozzo and Faustoferri this volume). Indeed, it seems to me that the Early Iron Age burial record of south Etruria, not being confined to the élite echelons, has yielded evidence of a deeply rooted role of women in the drinking rituals of these communities. Possibly, this might be in accordance with the special importance of wine production and consumption for the societies of central Italy, which becomes especially evident from the seventh century BC onwards. Moreover, this scenario may shed new light on the ideological and social dimension of wine consumption in classical times. This might be particularly significant as regards ancient Rome, where wine drinking by women was strictly forbidden by consuetudinary laws, which likened it to adultery and sexual transgression.[6]

Conclusively, other observations on wine production and consumption in the study area are possible, though only tentative. The wide recurrence of Greek-type pots even in infant graves, sometimes pertaining to the above-mentioned 'sub-élite' groups, could suggest the existence of a distinct socio-economic milieu, possibly the same that engaged in trade exchange with Aegean immigrants and the production of wheel-made pottery. In this light, some underestimated archaeological contexts might provide useful insights into the socio-economic framework of these phenomena. I would mention again, for instance, the settlement of Ficana, in the area of Latium closer to the territory of Veii: there, several Greek-type ceramics were found, with a particularly high concentration in a settlement area presumably devoted to iron working (Brandt *et al.* 1997, 225). This evidence might allow us to link Greek-type pottery at Ficana to corporate groups involved in production and trade activities. These supposedly distinct social strata (or, possibly, a subordinated component of the same stratum that consumed sophisticated beverages in prestigious bronze vessels) developed not only a different sphere of circulation of goods, but even autonomous modes of alcohol consumption. In other words, we are not dealing with classical mechanisms of emulation of lifestyles from bottom to top (as for example in the Celtic context mentioned above, where bronze and precious metal paraphernalia for drinking, typical of a top-level social stratum, were imitated in ceramic by low-status groups). Rather, it would be more a matter of competition and antagonism between distinct social groups, or just between different factions within the élite (on the possible competition between different élite sub-strata *cf.* also Scopacasa this volume, with a focus on Samnium). New social groups, characterized by a special inclination to external relationships, particularly with the western Greek world, and/or perhaps via south Italic intermediaries chiefly positioned in Campania, experimented convivial attitudes that were very different from the male-dominated Greek *symposion*. In particular, they might have been managing the incorporation of alien modes of social drinking into pre-existing local customs through ways of transmission closer to a form of hybridization than to typical processes of acculturation (on the idea of cultural hybridization, with a focus on ancient Campania, *cf.* also Cuozzo and Morris this volume; on connectivity and interaction *cf.* also the chapters by Zamboni and Rajala). In the context of these practices, technological traits, decorative styles (introduced via the immigration of potters) and possibly even the first spreading of a formerly luxurious and rare drink, namely wine, constituted a totality difficult to disentangle.

A better comprehension of this 'package' deserves serious reassessment, aiming to turn the attention from the traditional issue of élite consumption to a more articulated and nuanced manipulation of material symbols and rituals of commensality by various and alternative social actors.

Acknowledgements

This chapter is a modified version of the paper presented at the workshop 'Burial and Social Change in Ancient Italy, 9th–5th century BC: Approaching Social Agents' held at the British School at Rome in 2011. It was a nice and stimulating occasion, during which young and lesser young people from all over the world debated on topics without the concern of academic constraints, a very rare instance currently in Italy. I am thankful to my colleagues Rafael Scopacasa and Elisa Perego, with whom I have had interesting discussions on this same topic, for giving me this opportunity. Elisa, Rafael, the anonymous reviewer(s) and Corinna Riva of UCL stimulated me to enrich and improve the text in a decisive way, especially from the point of view of consistency and intelligibility.

Notes

1. On the importance of banqueting in the funerary rituals and socio-political transformations dating to the Orientalizing period *cf.* for example Coen 2008; Delpino 2000; Rathje 1995; Riva 2010.

2. For a number of reasons the use of these vessel associations for consuming more common and basic beverages, such as water or milk, is highly unlikely. Ritual consumption of water presumably had a greater importance in Europe throughout the Bronze Age, as documented in cult sites (for continental Europe *cf.* Vencl 1994, 300). In Italy the consumption of water in caves for cultic purposes was especially popular during *c.* the mid-second millennium BC. For instance, the acts of dipping and drinking water with ceramic cups have been convincingly postulated for the Pertosa cave in southern Italy: Trucco 1992. On the contrary, in the Early Iron Age the use of water in ritual contexts seems to have been occasional and complementary to wine. Villanovan biconical urns, secondarily used as cinerary urns, were possibly water containers (Iaia 1999), although their use for containing milk is also recorded (*cf.* the bronze biconical vessel found in an eighth-century BC *Picene* grave: Coen 2008, n.19). The consumption of milk in proto-historic and early historic times, though rarely demonstrated by textual and archaeological sources, seems to be mainly restricted to the sacrificial sphere. According to Bettini (1995, 232) in Rome there was an original opposition between milk and wine. In particular, milk was the substance connected to the earliest ritual acts in Rome's foundation legends (i.e. Romulus making sacrifices with milk) (on these issues *cf.* Coen 2008, n.19).

3. Osteological analyses of an extended sample of bones from the Villa Bruschi Falgari cemetery at Tarquinia have demonstrated that Villanovan cemeteries provide a quasi-complete demographic spectrum, with some limited exceptions relating to infant burials, which however remain largely represented in the sample (Trucco 2006, 189; on Villa Bruschi Falgari *cf.* also Shipley this volume). On the other hand, scanty evidence exists for burials outside formal interment areas, either attributable to socially marginal individuals or not (*cf.* for example the few 'deviant' inhumation burials found in the 'sacred-institutional area' on La Civita plateau at Tarquinia: Bonghi Jovino 2010). Although this may be due to the rarity of settlement investigations, the difficult interpretation and the limited extent of the latter evidence does not affect the overall coherence of the picture presented here (on settlement burial and burial outside the formal cemetery in Iron Age north-east Italy *cf.* also Perego, Zanoni this volume).

4. Between the late eighth and the seventh century BC aristocratic graves in central Italy were characterized by the dramatic emergence of an elaborate apparatus for consuming solid food and beverages. This apparatus included the equipment for roasting and consuming meat in a sacrificial context. An extended critical review of this topic for Etruria and the Middle-Tyrrhenian area is in Riva 2010, 91–3 (with references). The Italian scholarly perspective on the same phenomenon (especially relating to wealthy female graves in Picenum) is well epitomized in Coen 2008.

5. For the data *cf.* Baglione and De Lucia Brolli 1990; Boitani 2005; Brusadin Laplace *et al.* 1993; Cristofani Martelli 1971; Piergrossi 2002; Rizzo 2005.

6. Bettini 1995. In this sense, restriction of consumption might represent a reaction to women's larger freedom in proto-historic and early historical times. I owe this suggestion to prof. Christopher Smith.

Bibliography

Aranguren, B., Bellini, C., Mariotti Lippi, M., Mori Secci, M. and Perazzi, P. (2007) L'avvio della coltura della vite in Toscana: L'esempio di San Lorenzo a Greve (Firenze). In A. Ciacci, P. Rendini and A. Zifferero (eds) *Archeologia della Vite e del Vino in Etruria. Atti del Convegno (Scansano, 9–10 Settembre 2005)*, 88–97. Siena, Ci.Vin.

Arnold, B. (1999) 'Drinking the feast': Alcohol and the legitimation of power in Celtic Europe. *Cambridge Archaeological Journal* 9(1), 71–93.

Baglione, M.P. and De Lucia Brolli, M.A. (1990) Nuovi dati sulla necropoli de "I Tufi" di Narce. In G. Maetzke, O. Paoletti and L. Tamagno Perna (eds) *La Civiltà dei Falisci. Atti del XV Convegno di Studi Etruschi ed Italici (Civita Castellana-Forte Sangallo, 28–31 Maggio 1987)*, 61–102. Firenze, L.S. Olschki.

Bartoloni, G. (1971) La tomba 78 di Poggio dell'Impiccato (Tarquinia). *In Nuove Letture di Monumenti Etruschi dopo il Restauro*, 13–16. Firenze, L.S. Olschki.

Bartoloni, G. (1988) A few comments on the social position of women in the proto-historic coastal area of western Italy made on the basis of a study of funerary goods. In A. Bietti, R. Macchiarelli, G. Manzi and L. Salvadei (eds) *Physical Anthropology and Prehistoric Archaeology: Their Interaction in Different Cultural Contexts in Europe from the Late Upper Palaeolithic to the Beginning of the Historical Times. Atti del Simposio Internazionale (Roma, 5–8 Ottobre 1987)* (Supplemento di Rivista di Antropologia LVI), 317–336. Roma, Istituto Italiano di Antropologia.

Bartoloni, G. (2003) *Le Società dell'Italia Primitiva. Lo Studio delle Necropoli e la Nascita delle Aristocrazie.* Roma, Carocci.

Bartoloni, G., Acconcia, V. and ten Kortenaar, S. (2012) Viticoltura e consumo del vino in Etruria: La cultura materiale tra la fine dell'età del Ferro e l'Orientalizzante antico. In A. Ciacci, P. Rendini and A. Zifferero (eds) *Archeologia della Vite e del Vino in Toscana e nel Lazio. Dalle Tecniche dell'Indagine Archeologica alle Prospettive della Biologia Molecolare*, 201–275. Borgo S. Lorenzo, All'Insegna del Giglio.

Berardinetti, A. and Drago, L. (1997) La necropoli di Grotta Gramiccia. In G. Bartoloni (ed.) *Le Necropoli Arcaiche di Veio. Giornata di Studio in Memoria di Massimo Pallottino*, 39–61. Roma, Università degli Studi di Roma "La Sapienza", Dipartimento di Scienze Storiche, Archeologiche e Antropologiche dell'Antichità.

Bettini, M. (1995) In vino stuprum. In O. Murray and M. Tecuşan (eds) *In Vino Veritas*, 224–235. London, British School at Rome.

Bietti Sestieri, A.M. (1992a) (ed.) *La Necropoli Laziale di Osteria dell'Osa.* Roma, Quasar.

Bietti Sestieri, A.M. (1992b) *The Iron Age Community of Osteria dell'Osa. A Study of Socio-Political Development in Central Tyrrhenian Italy.* Cambridge, Cambridge University Press.

Boitani, F. (2005) Le più antiche ceramiche greche e di tipo greco a Veio. In G. Bartoloni and F. Delpino (eds) *Oriente e Occidente: Metodi e Discipline a Confronto. Riflessioni sulla Cronologia dell'Età del Ferro in Italia. Atti dell'Incontro di Studi (Roma, 30–31 Ottobre 2003)*, 319–332. Pisa–Roma, Istituti Editoriali e Poligrafici Internazionali.

Boitani, F. and Berardinetti Insam, A. (2001) La ceramica greca e di tipo greco a Veio nell'VIII secolo a.C.. In A.M. Sgubini Moretti (ed.) *Veio, Cerveteri, Vulci. Città d'Etruria a Confronto. Catalogo della Mostra (Roma, Museo Nazionale Etrusco di Villa Giulia, Villa Poniatowski, 1 Ottobre–30 Dicembre 2001)*, 106–111. Roma, "L'Erma" di Bretschneider.

Bonghi Jovino, M. (2010) The Tarquinia project: A summary of 25 years of excavation. *American Journal of Archaeology* 114(1), 161–180.

Bourdieu, F. (2009[1994]) *Ragioni Pratiche*. Bologna, Il Mulino (Italian edition).

Brandt, J., Jarva, E. and Fisher-Hansen, T. (1997) Ceramica di origine e d'imitazione greca a Ficana nell'VIII sec. a.C.. In G. Bartoloni (ed.) *Le Necropoli Arcaiche di Veio. Giornata di Studio in Memoria di Massimo Pallottino*, 219–231. Roma, Università degli Studi di Roma "La Sapienza", Dipartimento di Scienze Storiche, Archeologiche e Antropologiche dell'Antichità.

Brusadin Laplace, D., Patrizi Montoro, G. and Patrizi Montoro, S. (1992) Le necropoli protostoriche del Sasso di Furbara. III. Il Caolino ed altri sepolcreti villanoviani. *Origini* 16, 221–294.

Chaume, B. (2007) Essai sur l'évolution de la structure sociale hallstattienne. In H.-L. Fernoux and C. Stein (eds) *Aristocratie Antique: Modèles et Exemplarité Sociale. Actes du Colloque Organisé à l'Université de Bourgogne (25 Novembre 2005)*, 25–55. Dijon, Editions Universitaires de Dijon.

Cicirelli, C., Albore Livadie, C., Costantini, L. and Delle Donne, M. (2008) La vite a Poggiomarino, Longola: Un contesto di vinificazione dell'Età del Ferro. In P.G. Guzzo and M.P. Guidobaldi (eds) *Nuove Ricerche Archeologiche nell'Area Vesuviana (Scavi 2003–2006). Atti del Convegno Internazionale (Roma, 1–3 Febbraio 2007)*, 574–575. Roma, "L'Erma" di Bretschneider.

Coen, A. (2008) Il banchetto aristocratico e il ruolo della donna. In M. Silvestrini and M. Sabatini (eds) *Potere e Splendore. Gli Antichi Piceni a Matelica. Catalogo della Mostra (Matelica, Palazzo Ottoni, 19 Aprile–31 Ottobre 2008)*, 159–165. Roma, "L'Erma" di Bretschneider.

Colini, G.A. (1914) Vetralla – Necropoli di Poggio Montano. *Notizie degli Scavi 1914*, 297–362.

Costantini, L. and Costantini Biasini, L. (1995) I resti vegetali del villaggio del «Gran Carro», Bolsena (VT): Scavo 1974. In P. Tamburini (ed.) *Un Abitato Villanoviano Perilacustre: Il «Gran Carro» sul Lago di Bolsena (1959–1989)*, 325–333. Roma, Giorgio Bretschneider.

Costin, C. and Wright, R. (1998) (eds) *Craft and Social Identity* (Archaeological Papers of the American Anthropological Association 8). Washington DC, American Anthropological Association.

Cristofani Martelli, M. (1971) La tomba XXX di Poggio Montano (Vetralla). *In Nuove Letture di Monumenti Etruschi dopo il Restauro*, 17–23. Firenze, L.S. Olschki.

Delpino, F. (1986) Rapporti e scambi nell'Etruria meridionale villanoviana con particolare riferimento al Mezzogiorno. *Archeologia nella Tuscia II* (Quaderni del Centro di Studio per l'Archeologia Etrusco–Italica 13), 167–176. Roma, CNR.

Delpino, F. (1997) I Greci in Etruria prima della colonizzazione euboica: Ancora su crateri, vino, vite e pennati nell'Italia centrale protostorica. In G. Bartoloni (ed.) *Le Necropoli Arcaiche di Veio. Giornata di Studio in Memoria di Massimo Pallottino*, 185–194. Roma, Università degli Studi di Roma "La Sapienza", Dipartimento di Scienze Storiche, Archeologiche e Antropologiche dell'Antichità.

Delpino, F. (2000) Il principe e la cerimonia del banchetto. In A. Dore, C. Morigi Govi, F. Delpino, F-W. von Hase, G. Bartoloni, G. Colonna, L. Minarini, M. Marchesi, M. Liverani, M. Gras, P. Flourentzos and V. Karageorghis (eds) *Principi Etruschi tra Mediterraneo ed Europa. Catalogo della Mostra (Bologna, Museo Civico Archeologico, 1 Ottobre 2000–1 Aprile 2001)*, 193–195. Venezia, Marsilio.

Delpino, F. (2002) Brocchette a collo obliquo dall'area etrusca. In O. Paoletti and L. Tamagno Perna (eds) *Etruria e Sardegna Centro-Settentrionale tra l'Età del Bronzo Finale e l'Arcaismo. Atti del XXI Convegno di Studi Etruschi ed Italici (Sassari-Alghero-Oristano-Torralba, 13–17 Ottobre 1998)*, 363–385. Pisa–Roma, Istituti Editoriali e Poligrafici Internazionali.

Delpino, F. (2005) Dinamiche sociali e innovazioni rituali a Tarquinia villanoviana: Le tombe I e II del sepolcreto villanoviano. In O. Paoletti (ed.) *Dinamiche di Sviluppo delle Città nell'Etruria Meridionale. Veio, Caere, Tarquinia, Vulci. Atti XXIII Convegno di Studi Etruschi e Italici (Roma-Cerveteri-Tarquinia-Montalto di Castro-Viterbo, 1-6 Ottobre 2001)*, 343–358. Pisa-Roma, Istituti Editoriali e Poligrafici Internazionali.

Delpino, F. (2007) Viticoltura, produzione e consumo del vino nell'Etruria protostorica. In A. Ciacci, P. Rendini and A. Zifferero (eds) *Archeologia della Vite e del Vino in Etruria. Atti del Convegno Internazionale di Studi (Scansano, Teatro Castagnoli, 9-10 Settembre 2005)*, 133–146. Siena, Ci.Vin.

Dietler, M. (1990) Driven by drink: The role of drinking in the political economy and the case of Early Iron Age France. *Journal of Anthropological Archaeology* 9(4), 352–406.

Dietler, M. and Herbich, I. (1998) Habitus, techniques, style: An integrated approach to the social understanding of material culture and boundaries. In M. Stark (ed.) *The Archaeology of Social Boundaries*, 232–263. Washington DC, Smithsonian Press.

Giachi, G., Mori Secci, M., Pignatelli, O., Gambogi, P. and Mariotti Lippi, M. (2010) The prehistoric pile-dwelling settlement of Stagno (Leghorn, Italy): Wood and food resource exploitation. *Journal of Archaeological Science* 37(6), 1260–1268.

Hamilakis, Y. (1999) Food technologies/technologies of the body: The social context of wine and oil production and consumption in Bronze Age Crete. *World Archaeology* 31(1) (Special Issue: Food Technology in its Social Context: Production, Processing and Storage), 38–54.

Iaia, C. (1999) *Simbolismo Funerario e Ideologia alle Origini di una Civiltà Urbana. Forme Rituali nelle Sepolture "Villanoviane" a Tarquinia e Vulci, e nel loro Entroterra* (Grandi Contesti e Problemi della Protostoria Italiana 3). Borgo S. Lorenzo, All'Insegna del Giglio.

Iaia, C. (2005) *Produzioni Toreutiche della Prima Età del Ferro in Italia Centro-Settentrionale. Stili Decorativi, Circolazione, Significato* (Biblioteca di Studi Etruschi 40). Pisa–Roma, Istituti Editoriali e Poligrafici Internazionali.

Iaia, C. (2006) Servizi cerimoniali e da "simposio" in bronzo del Primo Ferro in Italia centro-settentrionale. In P. von Eles (ed.) *La Ritualità Funeraria tra Età del Ferro e Orientalizzante in Italia. Atti del Convegno (Verucchio, 26-27 Giugno 2002)*, 103–110. Pisa–Roma, Istituti Editoriali e Poligrafici Internazionali.

Iaia, C. (2007) Prima del "simposio": Vasi in bronzo e contesto sociale nell' Etruria meridionale protostorica. *Revista d'Arqueologia de Ponent* 16–17, 261–270.

Iaia, C. (2010) Fra Europa Centrale e Mediterraneo: Modelli di recipienti e arredi in bronzo nell'Italia centrale della prima età del Ferro. In H. Di Giuseppe and M. Dalla Riva (eds) *Meetings Between Cultures in the Ancient Mediterranean. Proceedings of the 17th International Congress of Classical Archaeology (Roma, 22-26 Settembre 2008)*, 31–44 (Bollettino di Archeologia Online I) [http://www.bollettinodiarcheologiaonline.beniculturali.it/bao_document/articoli/4_IAIA.pdf].

Iaia, C. (2013a) Drinking in times of crisis: Alcohol and social change in late Bronze Age Italy. In S. Bergerbrant and S. Sabatini (eds) *Counterpoint: Essays in Archaeology and Heritage Studies in Honour of Professor Kristian Kristiansen* (BAR S2508), 373–382. Oxford, Archaeopress.

Iaia, C. (2013b) Warrior identity and the materialisation of power in Early Iron Age Etruria. *Accordia Research Papers* 12[2009–2012], 71–95.

Iaia, C. and Mandolesi, A. (2010) Comunità e territori nel Villanoviano evoluto dell'Etruria meridionale. In N. Negroni Catacchio (ed.) *Preistoria e Protostoria in Etruria. L'Alba dell'Etruria. Fenomeni di Continuità e Trasformazione nei Secoli XII-VIII. Ricerche e Scavi. Atti del Nono Incontro di Studi (Valentano-Pitigliano, 12-14 Settembre 2008)*, 61–78. Milano, Centro Studi di Preistoria e Archeologia.

Mandolesi, A. (1999) *La 'Prima' Tarquinia. L'Insediamento Protostorico sulla Civita e nel Territorio Circostante*. Borgo S. Lorenzo, All'Insegna del Giglio.

Nijboer, A.J. (2006) Coppe di Tipo Peroni and the beginning of the Orientalizing phenomenon in Italy during the late 9th century BC. *In Studi di Protostoria in Onore di Renato Peroni*, 288–304. Borgo S. Lorenzo, All'Insegna del Giglio.

Nizzo, V. and ten Kortenaar, S. (2010) Veio e Pithekoussai: Il ruolo della comunità pithecusana nella trasmissione di oggetti, tecniche e 'idee'. In H. Di Giuseppe and M. Dalla Riva (eds) *Meetings between Cultures in Ancient Mediterranean. Proceedings of the 17th International Congress of Classical Archaeology (Roma, 22-26 Settembre 2008)*, 50–68 (Bollettino di Archeologia Online I) [http://www.bollettinodiarcheologiaonline.beniculturali.it/bao_document/articoli/7_NIZZO.pdf].

Pacciarelli, M. (2001) *Dal Villaggio alla Città. La Svolta Proto-Urbana del 1000 a.C. nell'Italia Tirrenica.* Borgo S. Lorenzo, All'Insegna del Giglio.

Piergrossi, A. (2002) Una comunità di frontiera: Poggio Montano. *Archeologia Classica* 53, 1–63.

Quattro Fontanili (1965) Veio (Isola Farnese). Continuazione degli scavi nella necropoli villanoviana in località «Quattro Fontanili». *Notizie degli Scavi* 1965, 49–263.

Quattro Fontanili (1967) Veio (Isola Farnese). Continuazione degli scavi nella necropoli villanoviana in località «Quattro Fontanili». *Notizie degli Scavi* 1967, 87–286.

Quattro Fontanili (1972) Veio (Isola Farnese). Continuazione degli scavi nella necropoli villanoviana in località «Quattro Fontanili». *Notizie degli Scavi* 1972, 195–384.

Rathje, A. (1995) Il banchetto in Italia Centrale: Quale stile di vita? In O. Murray and M. Tecuşan (eds) *In Vino Veritas*, 167–175. London, The British School at Rome.

Ridgway, D. (2000) The first Western Greeks revisited. In D. Ridgway, F.R. Serra Ridgway, M. Pearce, E. Herring, R. Whitehouse and J. Wilkins (eds) *Ancient Italy in its Mediterranean Setting: Studies in Honour of Ellen Macnamara*, 180–191. London, Accordia Research Institute.

Ridgway, D. (2002) Rapporti dell'Etruria con l'Egeo e il Levante. Prolegomena Sarda. In O. Paoletti and L. Tamagno Perna (eds) *Etruria e Sardegna Centro-Settentrionale tra l'Età del Bronzo Finale e l'Arcaismo. Atti del XXI Convegno di Studi Etruschi e Italici (Sassari-Alghero-Oristano-Torralba, 13-17 Ottobre 1998)*, 215–223. Pisa–Roma, Istituti Editoriali e Poligrafici Internazionali.

Riva, C. (2010) *The Urbanisation of Etruria. Funerary Ritual and Social Change, 700-600 BC.* Cambridge, Cambridge University Press.

Rizzo, M.A. (2005) Ceramica greca e di tipo greco da Cerveteri (dalla necropoli del Laghetto e dall'abitato). In G. Bartoloni and F. Delpino (eds) *Oriente e Occidente: Metodi e Discipline a Confronto. Riflessioni sulla Cronologia dell'Età del Ferro in Italia. Atti dell'Incontro di Studi (Roma, 30-31 Ottobre 2003)*, 333–378. Pisa–Roma, Istituti Editoriali e Poligrafici Internazionali.

Santoni, V. (2010) Gonnesa, Nuraghe Serucci. IX Campagna di scavo 2007/2008. Relazione e analisi preliminare. *Fasti Online. Documents and Research* 2010-198, 1–53 [http://www.fastionline.org/docs/FOLDER-it-2010-198.pdf].

Sherratt, A. (1987) Cups that cheered. In W.H. Waldren and R.C. Kennard (eds) *Bell Beakers of the Western Mediterranean: Definition, Interpretation, Theory and New Site Data. The Oxford International Conference 1986* (BAR S331), 81–106. Oxford, Archaeopress.

Sherratt, S. (1993) Commerce, iron and ideology: Metallurgical innovation in 12th–11th century Cyprus. In V. Karageorghis (ed.) *Cyprus in the 11th Century B.C. Proceedings of the International Symposium Organized by the Archaeological Research Unit of the University of Cyprus and the Anastasios G. Leventis Foundation (Nicosia, 30-31 October 1993)*, 59–10. Athens, A.G. Leventis Foundation.

Toms, J. (1986) The relative chronology of the Villanovan cemetery of Quattro Fontanili at Veii. *AION. Annali dell'Università degli Studi di Napoli L'Orientale* 8, 41–97.

Trucco, F. (1992) Revisione dei materiali di grotta Pertosa. *Rassegna di Archeologia* 10[1991–1992], 471–479.

Trucco, F. (2006) Indagini 1998–2004 nella necropoli tarquiniese di Villa Bruschi-Falgari: Un primo bilancio. In M. Pandolfini Angeletti (ed.) *Archeologia in Etruria Meridionale. Atti delle Giornate di Studio in Ricordo di Mario Moretti (Civita Castellana, 14-15 Novembre 2003)*, 183–198. Roma, "L'Erma" di Bretschneider.

Trucco, F., De Angelis, D., Iaia, C. and Vargiu, R. (2005) Nuovi dati sul rituale funerario di Tarquinia nella prima età del Ferro. In O. Paoletti (ed.) *Dinamiche di Sviluppo delle Città nell'Etruria Meridionale. Veio, Caere, Tarquinia, Vulci. Atti XXIII Convegno di Studi Etruschi e Italici (Roma-Cerveteri-Tarquinia-Montalto di Castro-Viterbo, 1-6 Ottobre 2001)*, 359–369. Pisa–Roma, Istituti Editoriali e Poligrafici Internazionali.

Vencl, S. (1994) The archaeology of thirst. *Journal of European Archaeology* 2(2), 299–326.

Zifferero, A. (2012) Il primo vino degli etruschi: Vitigni, vigneti e modi di consumo. In A. Mandolesi and M. Sannibale (eds) *Etruschi. L'Ideale Eroico e il Vino Lucente. Catalogo della Mostra (Asti, Palazzo Mazzetti, 17 Marzo-15 Luglio 2012)*, 67–85. Milano, Electa.

Chapter 3

Potting personhood: biconical urns and the development of individual funerary identity

Lucy Shipley

Introduction

Objects are the primary vehicle through which people negotiate the material world. By encountering things: touching them, seeing them and living with them, we experience the world outside our bodies, whether through the warmth of a blanket or the sharp pain of a stinging nettle. Through creating and choosing objects, bringing them into or pushing them far from ourselves, the experience of being in the world is curated (Gosden and Marshall 1999, 169–70; for different approaches to materiality *cf.* also Cuozzo, Iaia and Rajala this volume). After death, the objects that others choose to allow the dead to keep, or choose to remove for themselves, are all that is left to construct a final physical presence in the world. These objects are those that will be brought to light centuries later by curious strangers, the only remnants of a series of choices undertaken on and around an individual body by those who buried it. To try and reconstruct these choices, to unpick the structure and potential meaning of mortuary ritual in an effort to seek out the rhythms of past lives, is a difficult task (Parker Pearson 1999, 3). This book chapter suggests that through a biographical, object-focused analysis of burial practice, the relationships between the dead and living in the Italian Iron Age can be examined more clearly, through an analysis of material from two biconical urn cemeteries from Tarquinia (on the funerary record of Tarquinia *cf.* also Iaia this volume, with a map for the general positioning of Tarquinia in Italy in Fig. 2.1). The differences between burial practice at the sites of Le Rose and Villa Bruschi Falgari form the centre of a discussion of processes of mortuary ritual, examining to the construction of identity in death.

Biconical urn burial is characteristic of the later stages of a phenomenon of object placement which was commonly practised in central Italy from the late tenth century BC, and continued until the late eighth century. This type of funerary assemblage is formed of a large ceramic vessel with a single handle, made of dark impasto ware decorated with geometric incised designs, and accompanied by a bowl placed upside-down as a cover over the urn itself (Fig. 3.1). The lower vessel contains the burnt bone and ash remains of the dead person, which is sometimes accompanied by the scorched remains of objects associated with dress, such as fibulae. Other metal artefacts and additional ceramics may be added, while the cover-bowl may be replaced with a bronze helmet or a ceramic representation

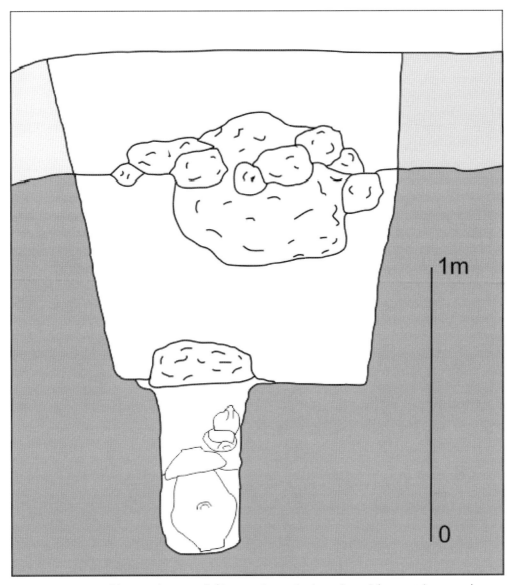

Fig. 3.1: Typical biconical urn tomb (drawing by L. Shipley, adapted from Leighton 2004).

of such a helmet. The urn itself may also be made of bronze, but is more usually ceramic (for a more detailed discussion of typical biconical urn burials *cf.* Hencken 1968, 462–4). This type of burial was dominant over the area of northern Lazio, Tuscany and Umbria which would later come to be associated with Etruscan communities, and has become a key aspect of the definition of what has been termed 'Villanovan' material culture (Pallottino 1939, 86; Di Lorenzo *et al.* this volume). Using burial evidence to examine the social activities of the living is a pattern of archaeological practice which has been dominant in analyses of the late Italian Iron Age and Etruscan period (Damgaard Andersen 1997, 345; Izzet 2007, 16) and elsewhere in the Mediterranean (*cf.* Morris 1987; 1991; 1992). The gradual replacement of biconical urn burial by inhumation in the late eighth century BC has been a particular focal point for the discussion of potential changes in societal organization (Giardino *et al.* 1991; Pacciarelli 1991; Riva 2010; Stoddart 1990).

The use of funerary material to consider the activities of the living has a long pedigree in Italian archaeology, dating back to antiquarian studies focused upon new discoveries, primarily of tombs (Cristofani 1983, 33). The continued occupation of ancient settlement locales, combined with the visibility of mortuary sites, resulted in excavation of the latter across Etruria on an exploitative scale throughout the nineteenth century (Paolucci 2005). The application of these findings to the formation of cultural and ethnic groups grew with Italian nationalism in the latter nineteenth and early twentieth century, in the wake of the Risorgimento and under Mussolini (Guidi 1996, 108), resulting in the use of Villanovan burial material as evidence for an indigenous origin for the Etruscans (Pallottino 1947; on ethnicity and material culture *cf.* also Zamboni this volume, with a critical approach and additional bibliography). While culture history is no longer explicitly used, typological and stylistic analyses remain important methods used to connect funerary objects with the lives of their original owners (e.g. Colonna 1986, 395; Mansuelli 1985, 111). As observed by Robb (1996), a more recently developed approach, influenced by work at the Campanian site of Pontecagnano (Bietti Sestieri 1992; Cuozzo 1994; 2003; d'Agostino 1977; Robb *et al.* 2001; Vida Navarro 1992) has been to use burial material as a source of information relating to the identity of the deceased while alive, examining their potential experiences as a member of a particular social group based on age, gender or status, using osteological work, analyses of grave goods, or a combination of both methods (Becker 1993; 2000; 2007; Bietti Sestieri and de Santis 2006; Toms 1992–1993). While these studies have focused on the experience of the deceased while alive, and the organization of the society in which they lived, another group has focused on death ritual itself, particularly during the later Etruscan period (Krauskopf 2006; Taylor 2011; Tuck 1994; 2012), in addition to the aforementioned socio-economic works based on burial evidence.

This chapter brings together the socio-economic and identity-based approaches in an analysis of mortuary practice through an examination of material from two small cemeteries at Tarquinia, namely the burial sites of Villa Bruschi Falgari (Trucco 1999;

2006a; 2006b) and Le Rose (Buranelli 1984). It begins with an examination of the similarities and differences between the two sites, with the primary research question being what these shared and divergent characteristics may mean. To answer this question, the objects which make up each individual burial are considered in a biographical analysis of the assemblage as a whole, to untangle the actions which created each collection of things in their original deposition. Connerton (1989, 54) observes that rituals focus the attention of their attendees on particular "objects of thought and feeling which are held to be of special significance." Which objects these were, and how they gained significance, is examined through using the idea of personhood (Brück 2001; 2006; Fowler 2001; 2004; Gillespie 2001; Jones 2002; 2005; *cf.* also O'Donoghue, Perego, the introduction and Perego and Scopacasa this volume, with additional bibliography) to consider the materials which form biconical urn burials at each site. The different combinations of objects which were brought together in each ritual is used to suggest a view of funerary identity as represented in the grave based upon a dual system combining both communal and individual types of personhood to distinguish the dead. The implications of such a system on the experience of the living, and its relationship to other intersecting aspects of identity form a conclusion.

Two cemeteries

The cemeteries of Villa Bruschi Falgari and Le Rose are located in one of the most well-known areas of Iron Age, Villanovan and later Etruscan activity, that surrounding the ancient city of Tarquinia on the southern Tyrrhenian coast of Etruria. Excavations on the hill of the Civita, opposite the medieval and modern city, have revealed an extensive settlement, and included the excavation of continually occupied ritual complexes (Bonghi Jovino 1986; 1989; 2008; 2010; Bonghi Jovino *et al.* 2001). The area was a centre for activity from the Neolithic onwards, but around the early ninth century BC there is evidence for the first buildings on the Civita plateau, including house structures and pits containing pottery and animal remains (Mandolesi 1999; Sgubini Moretti 2001, 30–2). However, there is also evidence for settlement in the form of pottery remains scattered across the opposite hilltop, where modern Tarquinia now stands (Leighton 2004, 41). It is these smaller settlements which are in the closest vicinity to the two cemeteries of Le Rose and Villa Bruschi Falgari, located nearest to the settlements of Santa Maria in Castello and Infernaccio respectively (Fig. 3.2). The distance between the two groups of burials is less than 2 km – an easy walk, with the settlements and cemeteries possibly within sight of each other on the western scarp of the hill. The other contemporaneous settlements of Villanovan Tarquinia would also have been within walking distance, as would the coastal resources of the Tyrrhenian littoral strip.

Excavations at the cemetery of Villa Bruschi Falgari are among the most recent explorations of burials in Tarquinia, and took place during the late 1990s and early 2000s. As a result, they provide some of the most accurate data available for biconical

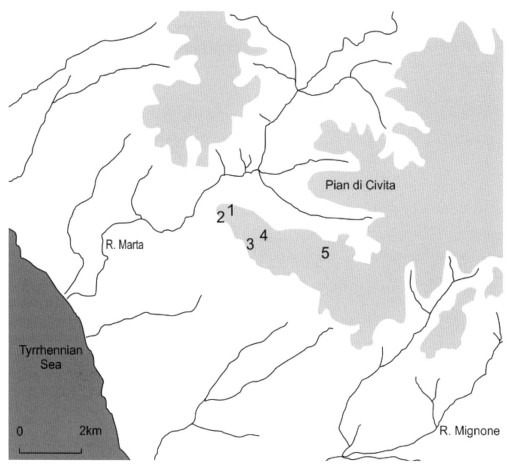

Fig. 3.2: Map of Tarquinia and surrounding area (map by L. Shipley, adapted from Mandolesi 1999, figs 63–4). 1. Santa Maria in Castello; 2. Le Rose; 3. Villa Bruschi Falgari; 4. Infernaccio; 5. Monterozzi.

urn burial as a phenomenon. While the presence of tombs in the area was first recorded by Mario Moretti in 1959 (Moretti 1959, 137–8), it was during work on the roadway which transects the site that the latter excavation began. It was soon clear that the cemetery, located just below the hill of the large and famous Etruscan burial ground of Monterozzi, close to the modern city of Tarquinia, was in a good state of preservation. While 75 graves had been disturbed, of which 30 were completely empty, there remained 228 tombs which were relatively intact (Trucco 2006a, 187). The recent discovery of the cemetery has resulted in a number of scientific examinations of the material, including radiocarbon dating, which has provided one of the first absolute dates for the Early Italian Iron Age. Based on a fragment of human bone from Tomb 103, typologically dated to Tarquinia Phase IC (Trucco 2006a, 188), a radiocarbon date of 1130–990 cal BC was produced (Nijboer and van der Plicht 2008, 105). The provision of this absolute date suggests that the burial ground was used earlier than previously thought. Osteological analysis (Trucco *et al.* 2002; Vargiu *et al.* 2010) has presented the biological sex of the remains recovered from the cemetery, which have been used to develop an interpretation of ritual behaviour and social identity at the site (Trucco 2006b; Trucco *et al.* 2005) while further analyses (Trucco 1999; 2002; Trucco *et al.* 2001; 2003) have examined the spatial placement of the tombs and their structural composition. While no complete catalogue of the remains from Villa Bruschi Falgari has been published, this is unsurprising in light of the weight of material from the site. However, the contents of a single exceptional grave, Tomb 182 (Barbaro *et al.* 2008) and a summary of ritual objects associated with tombs (Iaia 2002) complete the sizeable publications of the site, all of which are sources for the data used here.

The cemetery of Le Rose lies less than 500 m away from the medieval walls of the city of Tarquinia. It was discovered in 1953, after the landowner brought a selection of impasto fragments to the *Museo Nazionale* of Tarquinia after finding them in the course of digging a trench. Further digging in the area was supervised by archaeologists, who uncovered four biconical urn burials, described as being in "the best possible condition" (Buranelli 1983, 1). Excavations continued into 1954, exposing an area of around 3000 m2, alongside unmistakeable signs of past disturbance of the cemetery. An incomplete catalogue of these objects was published soon after the discovery, providing the first glimpse of the burial group as a whole (Moretti 1959), while a complete catalogue was made available in 1984 (Buranelli 1983), in addition to more detailed analyses of the ceramics (De Angelis 2001; 2002; Guidi 1980) and the spatial distribution of graves at the site in terms of social status (Pacciarelli 2001, 247–8; Sgubini Moretti 2001). In his catalogue, which forms the base for the data in this paper, Buranelli notes that 33 tombs from Le Rose fall into two clear groups, differentiated by typological dating as belonging to Phases IA and IB (Buranelli 1983, 115–6), with approximate dates of between 950–925 and 925–900 BC respectively, based on the radiocarbon dates from similar burials at Villa Bruschi Falgari (Nijboer and van der Plicht 2008, 105). The remaining 34 graves, while lacking objects to tie them closely into this chronology, are nonetheless similar in date to the diagnostic remains.

The two neighbouring cemeteries, which are approximately contemporaneous according to stylistic dating, form an ideal comparison of two burying communities. The two have been compared previously in terms of the spatial distribution of particular individuals differentiated by grave goods considered indicative of high social status (Trucco *et al.* 2005, 366). However, with a total of 297 assemblages of undisturbed grave goods from the Early Iron Age between the two, the variations between individual graves in each cemetery and between the two sites provide through direct comparison an opportunity to examine in detail the shared and divergent characteristics of late tenth- and early ninth-century BC burial practice at Tarquinia. Unsurprisingly, for two sites located so near to each other, there are several shared connections between them: notably, the almost universal use of biconical urns as containers for cremation burials. Seven burials from Villa Bruschi

Falgari were later inhumations (Trucco 2006a, 288), as were two cases at Le Rose, a small proportion of the overall 228 and 69 intact tombs respectively located in each cemetery. The consistency of practice at the two sites is striking: each burial comprised the cremation of the corpse, followed by its placement inside a ceramic vessel and eventual placement in the earth. Three examples from Le Rose were placed in pots aside from the standard urn, of which all three were jug forms, but the overall ritual is markedly similar between the two sites. The individual urns are decorated with geometric motifs which differ in individual graves, while retaining a shared repertoire of images and shapes. The presence of the central urn is, however, the only part of burial ritual which is so commonly practiced at Le Rose and Villa Bruschi Falgari: around and about it are distinctly different objects marking practices which occurred at divergent rates at the two sites.

The first of these is the placement of the urn. While the majority of tombs at Le Rose and Villa Bruschi Falgari are simple *tomba a pozzo* graves placed in a pit, 26 urns (11%) were entombed in *nenfro* stone cists of a circular shape, while a further three were positioned in similar cists of a semi-rectangular shape (Trucco 2002; 2006a, 188). Further differences between tombs were marked out by the placement of objects additional to the biconical urn in the grave. The first of these artefacts is the choice of covering used to seal the urn itself. While certain coverings of cloth, wickerwork or wood may not have survived, ceramic examples, whether in the form of a helmet or bowl, have done so. The proportions of different urn coverings are the first point at which the two sites seriously diverge: at Le Rose, 18 tombs, or 26% of the assemblage, had no extant cover at all, while only three urns (1.3%) from Villa Bruschi Falgari were left uncovered. Of those which had a cover, at Le Rose the majority of urns (43 examples, or 64%) were covered by a bowl, with 17 bowls differentiated further by the presence of finials. Ceramic helmets were only present in four graves, or 5.9%. At Villa Bruschi Falgari, however, ceramic helmets were present in 9.6% of graves, double the rate of their appearance at Le Rose. The discrepancy between urn coverings continues in the presence of grave goods additional to the urn and cover: at Villa Bruschi Falgari, 83% of tombs contained some form of personal adornment item such as a fibula or spiral, while at Le Rose only 22% did so while additional ceramics were found in 19% of graves at Le Rose, and 41% from Villa Bruschi Falgari. Why are the two cemeteries, so united in the practice of cremation and biconical urn burial, yet so different in the additional goods placed with burials? How can this difference contribute to a discussion of the treatment of the dead, and the experiences of the living at these two sites?

Tomb biography: constructing funerary identity

The concept of object biography, developed from the work of Kopytoff (1986), conceives of objects as having life cycles and identities in a similar way to people, moving from creation (birth) to use (life) to deposition (death). The connections between persons and objects forged over this period of use define and re-define the meaning of the object, marking it as part of both identity creation and ascription (Gosden and Marshall 1999, 174). Biographical approaches were primarily deployed in studies of exchange (Peers 1999; Rainbird 1999), but have also been applied in context to funerary artefacts and sites (Mytum 2003–2004; Roymans 1995). Recently, Jody Joy (2009, 543) has revisited object biography and critiqued the tendency of prehistorians in particular to use the concept in a solely linear fashion, perhaps relying all too heavily on the familiar idea of *chaine-operatoire* developed from the work of Mauss (1990) and Leroi-Gourhan (1977). Joy suggests moving beyond simple progression to envisioning the surrounding actions in which an object is enveloped, not only at moments which are more obvious to the modern viewer such as production and deposition, but also through using the properties of the object itself to arrive at a better understanding of the nature of use (Joy 2009, 550). A focus on physical properties is allied to a continuing movement away from textual metaphor in post-processual archaeology, and towards a more object-centred approach which has been termed post-textual archaeology (Alberti *et al.* 2013; Boivin 2005; Jones 2004; Preucel and Mrozowski 2011). This philosophy is heavily influenced by the work of Gell (1992; 1993; 1998) on object agency. In his initial work on Trobriand *kula* canoes, Gell noted that imagery used to decorate the canoes was neither solely decorative nor symbolic, but designed to create an effect upon the viewer (Gell 1992). In his later work, Gell argues that other images are equally endowed with power, not only to evoke emotions in those utilising them, but also to impact upon the world in which they are made (Gell 1998, 66).

In terms of analysing the material from Le Rose and Villa Bruschi Falgari, a biographical and post-textual approach can be applied. While a biography may appear textual by nature, it is physically expressed in a firmly material way. Each grave within the two cemeteries is composed of a group of objects, as outlined above. The physical forms of each object relate a series of decisions made by those who chose each item and placed it in the ground, and also to a series of tasks which the objects were expected to perform. From urn to fibula, each artefact has its own biography, characteristics and agency, while also contributing to the shared biography of the tomb assemblage as a whole. The physical properties of each type of object used in the two cemeteries allow for a consideration of the process of burial, and for the recognition of each object in the burial biography as meaningful and purposeful in the construction of a funerary identity for the deceased, and by extension in the mourning process of the living. The biography of the tomb assemblage begins with the production of human remains of the dead person themselves at the moment of death. Through a series of object-layers, from container for remains to further ceramic objects to minute fibulae and jewellery, these central human objects are bounded and clarified by the use of things. By analysing the deployment, the presence or absence of these layers, the most significant of them can be identified: the things that must be included in a burial, the objects that create a formal grave from a dead body. The biography of a grave is made up through each object layer, with each item forming part of the identity of the deceased. Through recognizing the different phases in tomb biographies, and the material connections of each accompanying object, the affective purpose for each object can be established, and the reasons for their presence or absence in an individual tomb approached. In turn, the difference in identity between the buried communities of Le Rose and Villa Bruschi Falgari can be understood not in terms of attributes, but in terms of actions and choices.

Communal persons, ubiquitous objects

The most obvious object required for a grave is the presence of the dead person themselves. However, as observed by Trucco *et al.* (2002, 721), the human body at the centre of a tomb is often the least documented aspect of a burial, in spite of some remnants of their physical presence in the majority of graves. While cenotaph burials are known in Etruria, particularly in the case of later *tumuli* (Camporeale 2005, 15–7), and biconical urn graves may be looted to the point of destruction of human remains, in these cases the abstract presence of the dead nonetheless dominates the tomb in the same way as physical human remains. In the case of the two cemeteries at Tarquinia, aside from the 70 looted graves at Villa Bruschi Falgari, human remains are present in almost every burial assemblage, forming the most dominant object within the corpus. The remains themselves are the centre of the tomb, the most important part of the assemblage. Without the presence of the dead, abstract or concrete, a burial does not exist. Tomb biography begins with the death of an individual, whether projected into the future and prepared for, or hurriedly commenced in the wake of sudden bereavement. Objects may be put aside and designated appropriate for later burial, or chosen after an individual has died: with or without the physical corpse, it is the knowledge of a death which sets off the process of tomb assemblage. Where the remains of the dead are present, as at Le Rose and Villa Bruschi Falgari, the life history of each burial group of materials commences as a human being becomes a thing, and the life of a tomb begins with the actual or projected death of its occupier.

The remains of the dead become lumpen objects, once the animation of life is over: *rigor mortis* sets in, the smell of rot creeps and seeps from beneath what was once alive. The primary identity of a corpse is that it is separate from the living, transformed into a shell vacated by the owner. This does not deny agency to the objectified body of the deceased – whether through metaphysical intervention or physical acts, the dead can (and do) interfere with and structure the lives of the living (Williams 2004, 264). The dead body is a site of memory (Battaglia 1990; Connerton 1989), a place of interaction with other worlds, as well as an increasingly repulsive decaying object which has to be physically removed or adapted. The process of cremation at Tarquinia is the one method for this negotiation and transformation of the dead which is essential to continuity among the living. The physical remains in biconical urn graves are the final product of this process, burned in a pyre heated to temperatures of 600°C and 900°C, costing a huge effort in terms of the collection and manipulation of wood, and creating an intense experience for living viewers. After the pyre goes out, the collected cremated remains no longer visibly decay, but are transformed into a fragile heap. The physical features of the dead person are gone, and cannot be retrieved, yet as Tuck (2012, 64) observes, the rotting corpse has been transformed into a new form which can be manipulated, moved and re-formed. A new identity can be created for these burnt bones and ashes, beginning with the most fundamental ascriptions of the living. The deceased is now a group of separate objects, broken and fragmentary.

The formation of each of the broken groups of cremated remains from the 288 burials from Le Rose and Villa Bruschi Falgari into a single body is done through their placement in the biconical urn. There are three key aspects of the urn which impact upon its role in forming funerary identity: form, fabric and decoration. Each of these features is incorporated through the design and making of the urn, part of its biographical birth, and itself a meaningful process (Barley 1994; Hamilton 2002). The design of the shape of the urn itself is distinctive: it provides a secure bowl for cremated remains at the bottom, while the elongated upper portion allows for any longer fragments. The presence of a non-functional single handle is more perplexing: a single handle could not be used to pick up and move an urn securely, it demands the placement of hands around the base to be held safely. The single handle also has connotations of fragmentation in the case of urns which are made and fired with two handles are buried only after one has been removed (Tuck 1994, 623). Three graves at Le Rose do not use the traditional shape of the biconical urn (Tombs 49, 59 and 62), yet all retain this feature of the single handle, perhaps a contributing factor in the choice of the container. These characteristics are important: they are the first aspect of the rebuilding of dead identity, and mark out the urn-under-construction as an object for burial.

Through placement within the completed object, the dead person is re-made into a form which remains, while less unwieldy than the original corpse, nonetheless difficult to interact with. The lack of paired handles demands that an individual carrying the urn holds it close to their body, embracing the pot in an enclosing grasp. During burial and movement, these pots appear designed to be held close to the body – their short use-life above ground enabling physical closeness between mourners and corpse. Prior to the movement of urn to grave, the urn itself has to be filled with physical remains, and in doing so reshapes the cremated pieces into a single entity once more, after their separation and disintegration in the flames. The biography of the pot itself resembles, in many ways, that of the human corpse it contained: both have been re-made and transformed through fire, in the kiln and on the pyre. Although there are no examples of bronze vessels used as urns at Le Rose or at Villa Bruschi Falgari, the same connections between flame and reconstruction remain relevant to the process of bronze production, perhaps a consideration in the use of both metal and pottery for the placement of human remains. These vessels, however, retain their shapes in firing, unlike their contents, providing a new body for the deceased. The urn-as-body connection is most obvious in Archaic period Chiusi in the form of clearly anthropomorphic canopic urns (on the canopic urns of Chiusi *cf.* also O'Donoghue this volume). Even without the addition of obviously human features, the urns from Villa Bruschi Falgari and Le Rose demonstrate the commitment of the burying communities to the reproduction of the bodies of the dead in clay: a form of body which can be inscribed and manipulated to express personal and communal identity through decoration.

The placement of decoration on the surface of the urn, alongside the type of decoration used, provides a way to differentiate the container for the deceased – the first point in the biography at which burned bones were provided with a specific identity. Up until this point in the production and design process, the urn is a blank canvas of a body – it is now ready for the addition of markers. Previous analyses of decorative styles have been used to create networks of shared designs, based on the presence of motifs at cemeteries. De Angelis (2001, 298) notes a preference at Le Rose for small impressed dots above the cornice – a decorative decision which is much less marked at the neighbouring tombs from Villa Bruschi Falgari. She also demonstrates connections between larger communities: for example, the collective cemeteries from Tarquinia share designs only with the neighbouring proto-city to the north, Vulci (De Angelis 2001, 301). Guidi, too, has used urn decoration to argue for urn decoration as emblematic of local decorative styles, with accompanying connotations of identity ascription (Guidi 1980). The correlation between individual communities and decorative patterns, even when divided by so short a distance as Le Rose and Villa Bruschi Falgari, is convincing evidence for the function of biconical urn decoration. The unique combinations of shapes and their layout mark out the individual connections and place in the community of the deceased, demonstrating their position in both their immediate group and relationship to wider connections. In terms of urn decoration, the deceased is represented as the sum of their connections, while the urn itself provides a unifying base, connecting all the dead through their identical bodies. Iaia (1999, 22) has described the decoration of biconical urns as representative of an "unchanging cosmic order." Rather than placing this order in the realms of gods, however, I suggest that it is more a cosmology of belonging. The place of the deceased in terms of family and community is the primary focus of buried identity: it is these pieces of information which are the most important in the making of the dead.

This conception of funerary identity based upon a communal sense of personhood is drawn from Strathern's recognition of the phenomenon of partible personhood, or dividuality (Strathern 1988). Through ethnographic fieldwork in Hagen, Papua New Guinea, primarily working on trade and gift giving, Strathern recognized that individuals were being conceived of as divisible, with different parts of themselves attached to the objects they made, received and gave away. These divided identities attached to objects were themselves split through the relationships the person at the centre themselves carried – their connections to family members, trading partners and allies. As such, while the body of the central figure is singular, it is only one of a number of objects which carry these multiple connections, which Strathern describes as a "social microcosm" (Strathern 1988, 14). While it is impossible to know whether the inhabitants of Le Rose and Villa Bruschi Falgari consciously used dividual concepts to order their living world, the attachment of personhood to objects, and the transfer of this microcosmic site of social relationships onto a singular object in death provides a social meaning for the biconical urn and its universality. The urn-as-body theme is not only symbolic: through using dividuality as a base for interpretation, the connections and position of a person's body can also be transferred to the urn for burial. Whether identity for the living was communal and divisible, the central representation of identity of the dead was presented in the shared form of the urn, universally present in each tomb, suggesting the centrality of partible personhood in the identity of the dead.

The role of the urn in the replacement of the body as site for dividual connections can be elaborated further with reference to another Melanesian ethnographic phenomenon: that of Malanggan funerary sculptures, produced on the island of New Ireland off the coast of Papua New Guinea. Made from intricately carved wood, these objects (shown in Fig 3.3) are emphatically not portraits of a dead person: they are rather "likenesses" drawn from the world of the ancestors (Küchler 2002, 13). Nor are Malanggan decorative objects, rather powerful agents which control and structure the mourning process through images (Gell 1998, 223–7). Küchler observes that Malanggan are used to "build up chains of memory" about a deceased person, with their carvings representing layers of relationships and connections to living members of the community (Küchler 2002, 6). The process of creating a sculpture allows for the broken fabric of social life to be repaired through the recording of a person's identity in a spiritually secure and appropriate fashion, providing a product of mourning. This activity is described as "finishing the dead," while the eventual deposition of Malanggan to decay in the forest represents the safe removal of the dead person from social interaction (Küchler 2002, 81). The sculpture is the container of the deceased, with its decoration demonstrating their communal identity, and its production and disposal moderating grief and loss. Although made of clay and not wood, the geometric decorations shared between communities noted on biconical urns provide a similar process of "finishing" the identity of the dead: marking out the connections which characterized a person during life. The permanence of clay, rather than perishable wood, suggests a desire for this shared identity not to be forgotten, placed out of sight beneath the earth, but contained and marked for eternal memory. The same negotiation of grief in a small community affected by death is present in the making of the urn, and in marking it with the relationships which constituted the dead individual. The urn is not a symbol of a person's body: it has become their body, and the decorated clay which contains their physical remains is as singular as their original flesh and features.

While neither the phenomenon of Malanggan nor Hagen dividuality can be used as a direct analogy to burial practice at Tarquinia, relevant shared themes can be observed which suggest a social role for biconical urns beyond containment of

Fig. 3.3: Malanggan figures collected in the early twentieth century
(British Museum photograph Oc, B58.3. Image © Trustees of the British Museum).

remains. The cosmological power of the biconical urn recognized by Iaia (1999, 22) is also to be found in Malanggan: the sculptures are closely tied to seasonal movements, and are seen as having the power to move the calendar forward when deposited (Küchler 2002, 68). Urns, too, may have performed a similar function: their burial taking place at particular moments, with the emotional ripples and social consequences of death seen as mirrored in changes in the physical or spiritual world. The actions of urn creation, possible curation and burial form a series of processes which, like Malanggan, record and commemorate the shared identity of the deceased, while simultaneously differentiating the living from the dead. Through the clay skin of their container, memories central to the identity of the dead person can be made permanent, in a way that their physical remains cannot, while the potential of the living body is expressed through the agency of their clay effigy. While a record of a 'distributed person' conceived of through relationships with people and things, urns themselves were simultaneously a consolidation of personhood, a powerful site at which cosmology and communal identity are fused with the physical remains of a singular individual. The importance and centrality of biconical urns to burial practice at Villa Bruschi Falgari and Le Rose (and elsewhere in both Tarquinia and Italy) can be used to suggest that this process of negotiation and reformation of the corpse, and the representation of communal identity was the most important aspect of burial ritual. The position of the deceased in relation to the living left behind, and their power to impact upon the living necessitated the containment and reconstitution of the urn in order to protect the living and correctly identify the dead.

Singular memories, variable things

The process of cremation and placement of human remains into a biconical urn may have taken place either before or after the creation of the pit into which the urn would eventually be placed. The decision over whether or not to elaborate the pit by the addition of a stone cist is, whenever it was taken in the burial ritual, the first point in the process at which a tomb can be differentiated from its fellows. The physical characteristics of stone cists act to perform a purpose in the burial: they separate the urn from the surrounding earth, clarifying the space in which the dead person is placed. The stone holds back the soil, forming an additional piece of protection for the fragile pieces of burnt bone and ash contained within the urn. A stone layer defines the limits of the tomb beyond the digging of a hole, which must be customized to fit around it. Stone is also permanent and strong, providing an ideal security that the ceramic body contained inside will survive. The decision to make the effort to create and bury a stone cist, while probably symptomatic of higher social status, may not have been necessarily caused by the economic trappings of such an élite role. The small number of individuals who are bestowed a stone resting place at Villa Bruschi Falgari must have made such investment in the tomb a requirement. The stone container, as already suggested, emphasizes the space for the dead below ground, and the people who were placed within it are marked with a permanent place in the burial ground, their reconstituted communal bodies protected by stone walls. The role of the stone cist as a marker of élite burial may not have been solely as an act of conspicuous consumption, but possibly more closely linked to ensuring the continuation of the communal identity of the dead, in the form of the urn. Their reformed physical body cannot be marked by the earth, ensuring that the dead person continues to have a presence. In the case of individuals whose connections with the living were important, the continuity of their body as a site of containment of social relationships is essential to sustaining those relationships after death. Through the stone container, memories bound up in the communal ties of the biconical urn could be protected and made immortal, allowing for relationships based upon them to continue without damaging the social fabric. Individuals with a significant influence over the community in which they lived needed to be preserved and protected in death to ensure the continuity of their influence upon the living: whether in terms of trading relationships, family ties or political power.

Through recognizing the individual body as the site for relationships and memories, stone cists provide a meeting point for two different forms of funerary identity: the communal person made manifest in the body of the biconical urn, and the individual person as a particular, unique point of reference for relationships and activities. The next phase of the tomb biography is dominated by objects which demonstrate the growing importance of the latter in the construction of funerary identities at Le Rose and Villa Bruschi Falgari: things placed in the grave which augment and personalize the burial. The first of these, which can be assumed to have been chosen and made alongside the urn, are the urn covers. Helmets and bowls, and perhaps other objects which have not survived, are used to protect the human remains inside the urn, and form part of its structure. While the lower urn itself references communal identity, the cover begins to contribute to an idea of individuality. While the association of helmets with male burials may indicate a concern with the representation of warrior ideals in death associated with masculinity (Treherne 1995), they appear in only one in three male graves at Villa Bruschi Falgari (Trucco 2006a, 188), and in even smaller numbers at Le Rose, where no anthropological study has yet been done (on masculinity cf. also O'Donoghue this volume, with additional bibliography). While assimilating living and dead identities to suggest that these few are the graves of proven warriors is tempting, it may be more important to recognize that these individuals were differentiated in death, and provided with personal, rather than communal, funerary identity. Whether or not helmets are a marker of success in violence or a mark of family associations or symbols is secondary to their role demonstrating the individual agency and identity of the dead person. The subtle differences in the choice of cover-bowls are less obvious statements of a similar idea – the presence or absence of finials may relate to particular familial or personal roles or choices, but helmets provide a more obvious moment in which communal funerary identity is overwhelmed by the power of the individual.

The shift in balance between individual and communal identity continues with the addition of objects aside from the urn, cover and container: smaller, portable materials placed in the tomb aside from those seemingly required by the burial ritual. These optional choices form an opportunity in the biography of the tomb for the mourners to demonstrate their agency in choosing particular things to place in the grave – or to leave absent. One of the features of these additional objects is their own previous life histories – in addition to contributing to the biography of the tomb, the ceramics, ornaments, weapons and implements may in many cases have had extensive use prior to their deposition. It is this previous use, and its nature, which makes these objects appropriate to be placed in the grave: through their association with particular activities and persons, they can be used both as receptacles for memories of the dead person, and for the association of their identity in death with particular tasks. Their presence or absence is a marker of whether the inhabitant of a grave was permitted to be represented as something more than their connections and place in the community. The number of graves without any form of grave goods at Le Rose is 22, only 32% of the total graves, while almost every tomb at Villa Bruschi Falgari was distinguished by additional grave goods. The two cemeteries present completely different funerary identities for their inhabitants: those at Le Rose primarily represented through their communal identity in the form of the urn, those at Villa Bruschi Falgari as individuals in addition to their shared connections.

Of the objects used to establish this individual funerary identity, all share a common characteristic. They are all closely associated with the physical body of the living person, from ornaments worn on the body, to personal toilet items used to maintain its appearance, to ceramics which are used to bring liquids and foods into the body. Weapons and weaving implements, too, are deeply physical objects, held in the hand and incorporated as extensions of the body of their user. The relationship between the body and the additional grave goods is further demonstrated by the dressing of urns, a phenomenon in evidence at Villa Bruschi Falgari in the placement of a necklace around the neck of an urn in Tomb 182. The communal identity of the urn is literally overlaid by the individual statement made by the additional goods, emphasizing the dual nature of funerary identity in these more personalized burials. The choice of these objects, or a selection of them in graves is a statement about which materials became imbued with memories and associations of their owner. However, ownership and memorialization should not be assimilated to use, and thence to activities undertaken in life associated with particular identity facets such as age or gender, rightly critiqued by Toms (1998) and Whitehouse (2001). The memories contained in objects used to personalize the tomb are as individual as the person they were buried with and should be recognized as such. A particular person may be buried with objects associated with a variety of identities, some of which may appear contrasting – yet the connections imbued in them were clearly relevant to the burying community and were used as an expression of an individual's complex and multi-faceted personhood, rather than as a code for their attributes. The close connection between additional objects and the body, as well as their potential for use in life, provides an explanation for potentially confusing objects and combinations: through use or association, all were relevant to the individual being buried, and to their individuality. The dominant presence of such objects in graves at Villa Bruschi Falgari demonstrates the importance of individual funerary identity to the burying community, as defined through the memories and experiences contained in each personalized group of grave goods, as unique as the dead person themselves.

Conclusion

The purpose of comparing and contrasting the objects which made up tombs at Le Rose and Villa Bruschi Falgari was to examine the reasons behind their placement in the grave. The use of a biographical approach has allowed for the identification of a dual system of funerary identity being expressed in the assemblages of objects at both sites. Communal, shared identity, possibly akin to Melanesian ideas of dividuality, is demonstrated in the universal presence of the biconical urn, the reconstitution of the deceased in a shared form which unites them with the other dead. The centrality of the biconical urn, and its longevity as a burial rite at Tarquinia and elsewhere, can be perhaps explained with reference to the strength of this shared identity in death. The force of representing the deceased in a way which recognizes their position within society and their connections with others held together biconical urn burial as a focal ritual in the negotiation of the social impact of death. This form of representation of the dead is dominant at Le Rose, although in the coverings of urns and the presence of additional objects the second form of funerary identity is also present: individual personhood, and the recognition of the deceased as a unique being, rather than as a distributed presence constituted through relationships. At Villa Bruschi Falgari, the personality of the deceased is celebrated in addition to their communal self, allowing for the investment of memories of a particular person in objects heavily associated with the body accompanying its reconstitution in the form of the urn. Through recognizing the complex nature of the relationship between these objects and this personalized funerary identity as based on memory and association rather than literal use, sweeping generalizations about object associations with single aspects of living identity can be avoided. The central celebration of communal identity present in the biconical urn burial can be recognized as the most important aspect of the ritual to these burying communities.

However, this situation of prioritizing communal identity in funerary identity at Tarquinia was not a lasting one. The seeds of change are already visible in the growing preference for objects memorializing individual identity at Villa Bruschi Falgari. The difference between the two cemeteries could be one of status, where élite individuals were represented in a more customized fashion recognizing their sole agency in life, or one of tradition, where the inhabitants of Le Rose preferred to continue expressing the identity of their dead through communal identity alone. Whichever is the case, the personal approach to funerary identity, although incorporating old ideas of immortal bodies inherent in biconical urn burial, would become dominant over the eighth century BC and onwards into the seventh, surely a key factor in the change from cremation to inhumation as a burial practice. It is tempting to suggest that the increasing interest in personal over communal identity could be connected to increasing urbanization, and the accompanying opportunities for individual aggrandisement. The objects from Le Rose and Villa Bruschi Falgari present a moment at which changes to the lives of the living and the disposal of the dead are beginning to transform the representation of the latter in the ground, with potential connotations for the livings' own conception of personhood.

Acknowledgements

I would firstly like to thank Rafael and Elisa for inviting me to participate in the original workshop, and to contribute to this volume. I would also like to thank the other contributors for their feedback and ideas during a very enjoyable conference.

The British School at Rome formed a perfect venue for the workshop, and made staying in Rome even more of a pleasure. My doctoral supervisor, Dr Yvonne Marshall, provided a great deal of help in the design of the original paper, as did Professor Simon Keay, in addition to their continued support: thank you both.

Bibliography

Alberti, B., Jones, A. and Pollard, J. (2013) (eds) *Archaeology after Interpretation: Returning Materials to Archaeological Theory*. Walnut Creek, Left Coast Press.

Barbaro, B., De Angelis, D. and Trucco, F. (2008) La tomba 182 della necropoli di Villa Bruschi Falgari a Tarquinia. In P. Petitti and F. Rossi (eds) *AES. Metalli Preistorici dalla Tuscia. Catalogo della Mostra*, 32–39. Valentano, Museo della Preistoria della Tuscia e della Rocca Farnese.

Barley, N. (1990) *Smashing Pots: Feats of Clay from Africa*. London, British Museum Press.

Battaglia, D. (1990) *On the Bones of the Serpent: Person, Memory and Mortality in Sabarl Island Society*. Chicago, University of Chicago Press.

Becker, M.J. (1993) Human skeletons from Tarquinia: A preliminary analysis of the 1989 Cimitero site excavations with implications for the evolution of Etruscan social classes. *Studi Etruschi* 58, 211–248.

Becker, M.J. (2000) Reconstructing the lives of south Etruscan women. In A.E. Rautman (ed.) *Reading the Body: Representations and Remains in the Archaeological Record*, 55–67. Philadelphia, University of Pennsylvania Press.

Becker, M.J. (2007) Childhood among the Etruscans: Mortuary programs at Tarquinia as indicators of the transition to adult status. In A. Cohen and J.B. Rutter (eds) *Constructions of Childhood in Ancient Greece and Italy* (Hesperia Supplement 41), 281–292. Princeton, American School of Classical Studies at Athens.

Bietti Sestieri, A.M. (1992) *The Iron Age Community of Osteria dell'Osa. A Study of Socio-Political Development in Central Tyrrhenian Italy*. Cambridge, Cambridge University Press.

Bietti Sestieri, A.M. and de Santis, A. (2006). Il rituale funerario nel Lazio tra il bronzo finale e prima età del ferro. In P. von Eles (ed.) *La Ritualità Funeraria tra Età del Ferro e Orientalizzante in Italia. Atti del Convegno (Verucchio, 26-27 Giugno 2002)*, 41–79. Pisa–Roma, Istituti Editoriali e Poligrafici Internazionali.

Boivin, N. (2005) Comments I: Post-textual archaeology and archaeological science. *Archaeometry* 47, 175–179.

Bonghi Jovino, M. (1986) *Gli Etruschi di Tarquinia*. Modena, Panini.

Bonghi Jovino, M. (1989) Scavi recenti nell'abitato di Tarquinia. In G. Maetzke (ed.) *Atti del Secondo Congresso Internazionale Etrusco (Firenze, 26 Maggio-2 Giugno 1985)* (Vol. 1), 315–319. Roma, "L'Erma" di Bretschneider.

Bonghi Jovino, M. (2008) *Tarquinia Etrusca: Tarconte e Il Primato della Città*. Roma, "L'Erma" di Bretschneider.

Bonghi Jovino, M. (2010) The Tarquinia Project: A summary of 25 years of excavation. *American Journal of Archaeology* 114, 161–180.

Bonghi Jovino, M., Chiaramonte Treré, C. and Bagnasco Gianni, G. (2001) (eds) *Tarquinia: Scavi Sistematici nell'Abitato, Campagne 1982-1988: I Materiali*. Roma, "L'Erma" di Bretschneider.

Brück, J. (2001) Monuments, power and personhood in the British Neolithic. *The Journal of the Royal Anthropological Institute* 7, 649–667.

Brück, J. (2006) Fragmentation, personhood and the social construction of technology in middle and late Bronze Age Britain. *Cambridge Archaeological Journal* 16, 297–315.

Buranelli, F. (1983) *La Necropoli Villanoviana "Le Rose" di Tarquinia* (Quaderni del Centro di Studio per l'Archeologia Etrusco-Italica). Roma, Consiglio Nazionale delle Ricerche.

Colonna, G. (1986) Urbanistica e architettura. In M. Pallottino and G. Pugliese Carratelli (eds) *Rasenna: Storia e Civiltà degli Etruschi*, 371–530. Milano, Scheiwiller.

Connerton, P. (1989) *How Societies Remember*. Cambridge, Cambridge University Press.

Cristofani, M. (1983) *La Scoperta degli Etruschi: Archeologia e Antiquaria nel 700*. Roma, Consiglio Nazionale delle Ricerche.

Cuozzo, M. (1994) Patterns of organisation and funerary customs in the cemetery of Pontecagnano (Salerno) during the Orientalising period. *Journal of European Archaeology* 2(2), 263–298.

Cuozzo, M. (2003) *Reinventando la Tradizione: Immaginario Sociale, Ideologie e Rappresentazione nelle Necropoli Orientalizzanti di Pontecagnano*. Paestum, Pandemos.

d'Agostino, B. (1977) *Tombe Principesche dell'Orientalizzante Antico da Pontecagnano* (Monumenti Antichi 49, Serie Miscellanea 2/1). Roma, Accademia Nazionale dei Lincei.

Damgaard Andersen, H. (1997) The archaeological evidence for the origin and development of the Etruscan city in the 7th to 6th centuries BC. In H. Damgaard Andersen, H.W. Horsnaes, S. Houby-Nielsen and A. Rathje (eds) *Urbanization in the Mediterranean in the 9th to 6th Centuries BC* (Acta Hyperborea 7), 343–382. København, Museum Tusculanum Press.

De Angelis, D. (2001) *La Ceramica Decorata di Stile "Villanoviano" in Etruria Meridionale*. Soveria Mannelli, Rubbettino.

De Angelis, D. (2002) Ricerche sulla decorazione villanoviana: I biconici di Tarquinia. In N. Negroni Catacchio (ed.) *Paesaggi d'Acque. Ricerche e Scavi. Atti del Quinto Incontro di Studi "Preistoria e Protostoria in Etruria" (Sorano-Pitigliano-Farnese, 12-14 Maggio 2000)*, 739–747. Milano, Centro Studi di Preistoria e Archeologia.

Fowler, C. (2001) Personhood and social relations in the British Neolithic with a study from the Isle of Man. *Journal of Material Culture* 6, 137–163.

Fowler, C. (2004) *The Archaeology of Personhood: An Anthropological Approach*. London, Routledge.

Gell, A. (1992) The technology of enchantment and the enchantment of technology. In J. Coote and A. Shelton (eds) *Anthropology, Art and Aesthetics*, 40–63. Oxford, Oxford University Press.

Gell, A. (1993) *Wrapping in Images: Tattooing in Polynesia*. Oxford, Clarendon Press.

Gell, A. (1998) *Art and Agency*. Oxford, Clarendon Press.

Giardino, C., Belardelli, C. and Malizia, A. (1991) Power and the individual in funerary ideology: The emergence of the aristocracy in the Villanovan period in the Bologna region. In E. Herring, R. Whitehouse and J. Wilkins (eds) *Papers of the Fourth Conference of Italian Archaeology Part 2: The Archaeology of Power*, 9–19. London, Accordia Research Centre.

Gillespie, S.D. (2001) Personhood, agency, and mortuary ritual: A case study from the ancient Maya. *Journal of Anthropological Archaeology* 20(1), 73–112.

Gosden, C. and Marshall, Y.M. (1999) The cultural biography of objects. *World Archaeology* 31(2), 169–178.

Guidi, A. (1980) *Studi sulla Decorazione Metopale nella Ceramica Villanoviana*. Firenze, L.S. Olschki.

Guidi, A. (1996) Nationalism without a nation: The Italian case. In T. Champion and M. Díaz-Andreu (eds) *Nationalism and Archaeology in Europe*, 108–118. London, University College London Press.

Hamilton, S. (2002) Between ritual and routine: Interpreting British prehistoric pottery production and distribution. In A. Woodward and J.D. Hill (eds) *Prehistoric Britain: The Ceramic Basis*, 38–53. Oxford, Oxbow Books.

Hencken, H. (1968) *Tarquinia and Etruscan Origins*. London, Thames and Hudson.

Iaia, C. (1999) *Simbolismo Funerario e Ideologia alle Origini di una Civiltà Urbana. Forme Rituali nelle Sepolture "Villanoviane" a Tarquinia e Vulci, e nel loro Entroterra* (Grandi Contesti e Problemi della Protostoria Italiana 3). Borgo S. Lorenzo, All'Insegna del Giglio.

Iaia, C. (2002) Oggetti di uso rituale nelle sepolture "villanoviane" di Tarquinia. In N. Negroni Catacchio (ed.) *Paesaggi d'Acque. Ricerche e Scavi. Atti del Quinto Incontro di Studi "Preistoria e Protostoria in Etruria" (Sorano-Pitigliano-Farnese, 12-14 Maggio 2000)*, 729–738. Milano, Centro Studi di Preistoria e Archeologia.

Izzet, V. (2007) *The Archaeology of Etruscan Society*. Cambridge, Cambridge University Press.

Jones, A. (2002) A biography of colour: Colour, material histories and personhood in the early Bronze Age of Britain and Ireland. In A. Jones and G. MacGregor (eds) *Colouring the Past: The Significance of Colour in Archaeological Research*, 159–174. Oxford, Berg.

Jones, A. (2004) Archaeometry and materiality: Materials-based analysis in theory and practice. *Archaeometry* 46, 327–338.

Jones, A. (2005) Lives in fragments? Personhood and the European Neolithic. *Journal of Social Archaeology* 5(2), 193–224.

Joy, J. (2009) Reinvigorating object biography: Reproducing the drama of object lives. *World Archaeology* 41(4), 540–556.

Kopytoff, I. (1986) The cultural biography of things. In A. Appadurai (ed.) *The Social Life of Things: Commodities in Cultural Perspective*, 64–91. Cambridge, Cambridge University Press.

Krauskopf, I. (2006) The grave and beyond in Etruscan religion. In N.T. De Grummond and E. Simon (eds) *The Religion of the Etruscans*, 66–89. Austin, University of Texas Press.

Küchler, S. (2002) *Malanggan: Art, Memory and Sacrifice*. Oxford, Berg.

Leighton, R. (2004) *Tarquinia: An Etruscan City*. London, Duckworth.

Leroi-Gourhan, A. (1977) *La Geste et la Parole*. Paris, A. Michel.

Mandolesi, A. (1999) *La "Prima" Tarquinia: L'Insediamento Protostorico sulla Civita e nel Territorio Circostante*. Borgo S. Lorenzo, All'Insegna del Giglio.

Mansuelli, G.A. (1985) L'organizzazione del teritorio e la città. In M. Cristofani (ed.) *Civiltà degli Etruschi*, 111–120. Milano, Electa.

Mauss, M. (1990) *The Gift: The Form and Reason for Exchange in Archaic Societies* (Translated by W.D. Halls). New York–London, WW Norton.

Morris, I. (1987) *Burial and Ancient Society: The Rise of the Greek City-State*. Cambridge, Cambridge University Press.

Morris, I. (1991) The archaeology of ancestors: The Saxe-Goldstein Hypothesis revisited. *Cambridge Archaeological Journal* 1(2), 147–169.

Morris, I. (1992) *Death Ritual and Social Structure in Classical Antiquity*. Cambridge, Cambridge University Press.

Mytum, H. (2003–2004) Artefact biography as an approach to material culture: Irish gravestones as a material form of genealogy. *Journal of Irish Archaeology* 12/13, 111–127.

Nijboer, A. and van der Plicht, J. (2008) The Iron Age in the Mediterranean: Recent radiocarbon research at the University of Groningen. In D. Brandherm and M. Trachsel (eds) *A New Dawn for the Dark Age? Shifting Paradigms in Mediterranean Iron Age Chronology. Proceedings of the XV UISPP World Congress (Lisbon, 4–9 September 2006)*, 103–118. Oxford, Archaeopress.

Pacciarelli, M. (1991) Territorio, insediamento, comunità in Etruria meridionale agli esordi del processo di urbanizzazione. *Scienze dell'Antichità* 5, 163–208.

Pacciarelli, M. (2001) *Dal Villaggio alla Città. La Svolta Protourbana del 1000 a.C. nell'Italia Tirrenica*. Borgo S. Lorenzo, All'Insegna del Giglio.

Pallottino, M. (1939) Sulle facies culturali arcaiche dell'Etruria. *Studi Etruschi* 13, 85–129.

Pallottino, M. (1947) *L'Origine degli Etruschi*. Roma, Tumminelli.

Paolucci, G. (2005) *Documenti e Memorie sulle Antichità e il Museo di Chiusi*. Pisa–Roma, Istituti Editoriali e Poligrafici Internazionali.

Parker Pearson, M. (1999) *The Archaeology of Death and Burial*. Stroud, Sutton.

Peers, L. (1999) 'Many tender ties': The shifting contexts and meanings of the S BLACK bag. *World Archaeology* 31(2), 288–302.

Preucel, R. and Mrozowski, S. (2011) (eds) *Contemporary Archaeology in Theory: the New Pragmatism*. London, Wiley Blackwell.

Rainbird, P. (1999) Entangled biographies: Western Pacific ceramics and the tombs of Pohnpei. *World Archaeology* 31(2), 214–224.

Riva, C. (2010) *The Urbanisation of Etruria: Funerary Ritual and Social Change, 700-600 BC*. Cambridge, Cambridge University Press.

Robb, J. (1996) Review Article: New directions in Italian burial studies: A disorganized Renaissance? *American Journal of Archaeology* 100(4), 773–776.

Robb, J., Bigazzi, R., Lazzarini, L., Scarsini, C. and Sonego, F. (2001) Social "status" and biological "status": A comparison of grave goods and skeletal indicators from Pontecagnano. *American Journal of Physical Anthropology* 115(3), 213–222.

Roymans, N. (1995) The cultural biography of urnfields and the long-term history of a mythical landscape. *Archaeological Dialogues* 2, 2–24.

Sgubini Moretti, M. (2001) *Tarquinia Etrusca: Una Nuova Storia*. Roma, "L'Erma" di Bretschneider.

Stoddart, S.K.F. (1990) The Political Landscape of Etruria. *Journal of the Accordia Research Centre* 1, 39–51.

Strathern, M. (1988) *The Gender of the Gift*. Cambridge, Cambridge University Press.

Taylor, L. (2011) Mourning becomes Etruria: Ritual, performance and iconography in the seventh and sixth centuries. *Etruscan Studies: Journal of the Etruscan Foundation* 14(1), 39–54.

Toms, J. (1992-1993) Symbolic expression in Iron Age Tarquinia: The case of the biconical urn. *Hamburger Beiträge zur Archäologie* 19–20, 139–161.

Toms, J. (1998) The construction of gender in Iron Age Etruria. In R. Whitehouse (ed.) *Gender and Italian Archaeology: Challenging the Stereotypes*, 157–179. London, Accordia Research Institute and Institute of Archaeology, University College London.

Treherne, P. (1995) The warrior's beauty: The masculine body and self-identity in Bronze Age Europe. *Journal of European Archaeology* 3(1), 105–144.

Trucco, F. (1999) Tarquinia (Viterbo). Località Villa Bruschi Falgari. La necropoli della prima Età del Ferro. *Bollettino di Archeologia* 28–30, 79–84.

Trucco, F. (2002) Strutture funerarie e uso dello spazio nella necropoli della prima Età del Ferro di Villa Bruschi Falgari a Tarquinia. In N. Negroni Catacchio (ed.) *Paesaggi d'Acque. Ricerche e Scavi. Atti del Quinto Incontro di Studi "Preistoria e Protostoria in Etruria" (Sorano-Pitigliano-Farnese, 12-14 Maggio 2000)*, 709–720. Milano, Centro Studi di Preistoria e Archeologia.

Trucco, F. (2006a) Indagini 1998–2004 nella necropoli tarquiniese di Villa Bruschi-Falgari: Un primo bilancio. In M. Pandolfini Angeletti (ed.) *Archeologia in Etruria Meridionale. Atti delle Giornate di Studio in Ricordo di Mario Moretti (Civita Castellana, 14-15 Novembre 2003)*, 183–198. Roma, "L'Erma" di Bretschneider.

Trucco, F. (2006b) Considerazioni sul rituale funerario in Etruria meridionale all'inizio dell'Età del Ferro alla luce delle nuove ricerche a Tarquinia. In P. von Eles (ed.) *La Ritualità Funeraria tra Età del Ferro e Orientalizzante in Italia. Atti del Convegno (Verucchio, 26-27 Giugno 2002)*, 95–102. Pisa–Roma, Istituti Editoriali e Poligrafici Internazionali.

Trucco, F., De Angelis, D. and Iaia, C. (2001) Villa Bruschi Falgari: Il sepolcreto villanoviano. In A.M. Moretti (ed.) *Tarquinia Etrusca. Una Nuova Storia. Catalogo della Mostra*, 81–93. Roma, "L'Erma" di Bretschneider.

Trucco, F., Vargiu, R. and Mancinelli, D. (2002) Il trattamento dei resti incinerati nella necropoli della prima Età del Ferro di Villa Bruschi Falgari a Tarquinia. In N. Negroni Catacchio (ed.) *Paesaggi d'Acque. Ricerche e Scavi. Atti del Quinto Incontro di Studi "Preistoria e Protostoria in Etruria" (Sorano-Pitigliano-Farnese, 12-14 Maggio 2000)*, 721–727. Milano, Centro Studi di Preistoria e Archeologia.

Trucco, F., De Angelis, D., Iaia, C. and Vargiu, R. (2005) Nuovi dati sui rituali funerari della prima Età del Ferro a Tarquinia. In *Dinamiche di Sviluppo delle Città nell'Etruria Meridionale: Veio, Caere, Tarquinia e Vulci. Atti del XXIII Convegno di Studi Etruschi ed Italici (Roma, 1-6 Ottobre 2001)*, 359–369. Pisa–Roma, Istituti Editoriali e Poligrafici Internazionali.

Tuck, A.S. (1994) The Etruscan seated banquet: Villanovan ritual and Etruscan iconography. *American Journal of Archaeology* 98(4), 617–628.

Tuck, A.S. (2012) The performance of death: Monumentality, burial practice, and community identity in central Italy's urbanizing period. In M.L. Thomas, G.E. Meyers and I.E.M. Edlund-Berry (eds) *Monumentality in Etruscan and Early Roman Architecture: Ideology and Innovation*, 61–81. Austin, University of Texas Press.

Vargiu, R., Mancinelli, D., Paine, R.R. and Trucco, F. (2010) Condizioni di vita e stato di salute a Tarquinia (Viterbo) nella fase iniziale della prima età del Ferro. In N. Negroni Catacchio (ed.) *L'Alba dell'Etruria. Fenomeni di Continuità e Trasformazione nei Secoli XII-VIII a.C.. Atti del IX Incontro di Studi "Preistoria e Protostoria in Etruria" (Valentano-Pitigliano 2008)*, 247–255. Milano, Centro Studi di Preistoria e Archeologia.

Whitehouse, R. (2001) Exploring gender in prehistoric Italy. *Papers of the British School at Rome* 69, 49–96.

Williams, H. (2004) Potted histories – Cremation, ceramics and social memory in Early Roman Britain. *Oxford Journal of Archaeology* 23, 417–427.

Chapter 4

Somebody to love: gender and social identity in seventh- and sixth-century BC Chiusi

Eóin O'Donoghue

Introduction

This chapter investigates changes in burial practices in north inland Etruria in the seventh–sixth centuries BC, with a focus on Chiusi (Rastrelli 2000; Fig. 4.1). Over these two centuries funerary traditions were transformed in the region of Chiusi with a move from a focus on the individual, as manifested in separate burial depositions and anthropomorphic urns, to the introduction of chamber tombs and urns mimicking house design that emphasized the place of the individual within both the familial group and wider Chiusine society (on a possible shift from collective to individual identities in the funerary record of Iron Age Tarquinia *cf.* Shipley this volume). A by-product of these changes was a shift in how gender and social identities were memorialized. This may be interlinked with whole-scale changes in the conception of the afterlife.

A considerable amount of recent scholarship has been dedicated to social and cultural changes in Etruria between the seventh and fifth centuries BC (e.g. Izzet 2007; Riva 2010). Examinations of previously known and recently discovered burial and settlement evidence, have challenged the view that the inhabitants of ancient Etruria passively absorbed models of eastern Mediterranean culture during the so-called 'Orientalizing period'. It has long been recognized that the inhabitants of central Italy during this period were conscious consumers of foreign ideas; they adopted and adapted external technological and artistic models for their own benefit (e.g. Ridgway 2002, 21–31). Indeed, Riva (2010) has recently reemphasized through an analysis of seventh-century BC élite funerary practices that developments in material culture, and consequently of socio-political identities in the region, were the result of long-term processes stretching back to the Bronze Age. It is possible to see in the archaeological evidence the crystallization of these changes in the material culture of the sixth century BC, during what is normally termed the 'Archaic period',

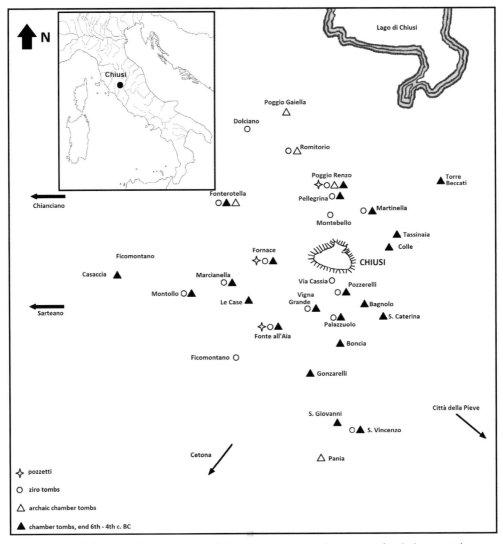

Fig. 4.1: Map of Chiusi and its cemeteries (after Banti 1973, 165; base map of Italy by C. Iaia).

and sometimes understood as the high-point of Etruscan cultural influence in the Italian peninsula (on the Archaic period in western Emilia, with a critical discussion concerning the possible influence or expansion of Etruscan people in this region, *cf.* Zamboni this volume; on the Archaic period in Latium Vetus *cf.* the chapter by Rajala). Izzet (2007, 43–5) has argued that a greater stress is apparent from the funerary evidence on personal identity, especially gender identity, in the late sixth century BC throughout Etruria, and that this is apparent through the deposition of mirrors as grave goods. While there certainly is an emphasis on personal and gender identity during the sixth century BC, it was not a sudden occurrence, and one of the aims of this chapter is to investigate the beginnings of certain features of social and gender identity from earlier periods.

In concert with the initial stages of urbanization and transformations in how personal identity was conveyed there was also considerable change in burial practices between the seventh and fifth centuries BC (e.g. Izzet 2007, 87–119). Within this context it is possible to observe how gender differences were highlighted in mortuary rituals. This paper explores how gender differences were maintained and distinguished through these two centuries with particular reference to burial practices at Chiusi. The settlement of Chiusi was situated in the southern part of north inland Etruria on a hill that dominates the Chiana Valley. It was connected to southern and coastal areas via a network of rivers. The economy of the area was similar to others in the region and was markedly different from opulent coastal cities like Tarquinia (on Tarquinia *cf.* also Iaia and Shipley this volume). It appears to have been based on agricultural practices. Indeed, a number of later writers comment on this. Livy (28.45.5) notes wheat production, Dionysius of Halicarnassus (*Ant.Rom.* 13.10.11) comments on its wine and oil, and Strabo (5.2.9) mentions Chiusi's fish and game.

Gender archaeology and Italian archaeology

In contrast to most studies relating to issues of gender identity the focus of this paper is on aspects of masculine identity (on gender in first-millennium BC Italy *cf.* also Cuozzo, Fuastoferri, Di Lorenzo *et al.* and Perego and Scopacasa this volume, with additional bibliography). Until comparatively recently gender archaeology and gender studies were focused on female identity.[1] R. Connell (1995) expounded the concept of hegemonic masculinities, which attempted to explain the present and historical domination of societies by men, and to offer a new framework for scholars to investigate gender identities. Within archaeology B. Knapp (e.g. 1998) has highlighted the need to consider both men and masculinities in gender archaeology. In contrast within the field of pre-Roman Italian archaeology, comparatively little work has been produced on this topic with regard to the first millennium BC. However, a few articles have addressed gender and masculine identity in prehistory (e.g. Treherne 1995). In Etruscan studies the most relevant scholarship is that of V. Izzet (2007, 51), who argues that it was during the Archaic period that the body increased in social importance, and consequently a new stress was placed on defining the gender identities of men and women during this time. There is much merit in Izzet's arguments; nevertheless the timeframe for this change in emphasis on the human body will be challenged in this chapter. Instead, it is argued throughout that the body, particularly that of an élite male, was the locus of social and gender differentiation from at least the end of the Bronze Age onwards. Following on from this it is apparent that considerations of personhood have been overlooked in Italian archaeology also; indeed it is only comparatively recently that this has become a new vector of investigation (on personhood *cf.* also Shipley, Perego, and Perego and Scopacasa this volume, with additional bibliography). With regard to funerary archaeology it is accepted that death involves the transformation of the person, and conceptions of this transformation are central to comprehending personhood (*cf.* Fowler 2004, 44–55). One common manner in which this is done is the dissolution and subsequent redistribution or reconstitution of the person by the community burying him or her. The concept of the recomposition of the person as an ancestor is of particular relevance to this chapter, with the 'new' social and gender status of the dead being a key component of the reconfigured identity.

Chiusi

As previously introduced, Chiusi is the focus of this investigation. In contrast with some of the other major sites from central Italy, comparatively little is known about the topography of the ancient settlement and surrounding area. A comprehensive account of Chiusi and its environs complied by R. Bianchi Bandinelli (1925) remains the essential introduction. However, excavations since then, along with recent studies, have done much to develop a more detailed picture of the landscape in the region.[2] At its most expansive the city seems to have been around 25 ha, and was small in comparison to other settlements in inland Etruria such as Volsinii (modern Orvieto) which was up to 85 ha (Bloch 1972). It has been suggested that the ancient city that lies under modern Chiusi only developed late on in the fifth century BC (Banti 1973[1968], 163). Prior to this Chiusi comprised a series of distinct smaller settlements in the surrounding hills of Montevenere (Fig. 4.1). Therefore, the powerful city-state of Clusium, as described in later Roman literary sources (Pol. 2.25.2; Livy, numerous references in Book 2), should not be confused or imposed on the limited settlement evidence that exists, especially for the earlier periods. Despite this we do know from the wealth of archaeological material from the area that Chiusi did wield considerable power and influence in inland Etruria. It stood as the only major settlement in the region, and it has been accused of the destruction of numerous minor settlements in north inland Etruria, including Poggio Civitate (Edlund-Berry 1994). Even if such conclusions are seen as overly speculative, the archaeological record of sixth-century BC central Italy preserves the demolition of a number of smaller settlements, and often large ones, as in the cases of Acquarossa and Bisenzio in south Etruria. This indicates that the world of sixth-century central Italy was a fierce and competitive landscape in which interstate rivalries were a reality. As Stoddart (1990) notes, the socio-political environment of Etruria was also becoming increasingly complex. Coupled with increased regional and external trade and interaction (Izzet 2007, 223; Malone and Stoddart 1994, 136–41; Roth-Murray 2007, 135–6), this resulted in city-states, such as Chiusi, becoming places of regional significance.

Burial practices at Chiusi

Just as the settlement evidence appears to be atypical with respect to its size and centralization, burial practices at Chiusi were distinctive also, and did not follow the more general trends in the rest of central Italy. From the eleventh to seventh centuries BC Chiusi was an innovative centre in which funerary sculpture developed (Haynes 1973, 16). Throughout Early Iron Age central Italy biconical urns were employed to conceptualize the deceased (*cf.* Shipley this volume; on the urn as the dead person's embodiment *cf.* also the chapter by Di Lorenzo *et al.*). After this was abandoned elsewhere, a new and more deliberate anthropomorphizing rendering of the deceased was made through the introduction of so-called 'canopic urns' at Chiusi (Gempeler 1974, 251–2). The burial evidence shows continuity of the Villanovan practice of cremation all the way through to the Hellenistic period (ninth–second centuries BC). Additionally, a special emphasis was always placed on the personal identity of the deceased in the region. From the ninth and eighth centuries BC there are examples of a few shaft graves – *pozzetto* tombs – and during the seventh century the so-called *tombe a ziro* generally outnumber simple trench graves (*tombe a fossa*) which were more common in Etruria at the time (Minetti 2004, 511–9; Steingräber 1995, 54).

A *ziro* itself was a jar that was placed in connection to the burial pit, but was on a level above the pit itself and served to protect the burial below. The monumental *tumuli* (usually covering chamber tombs) that are found at other settlements in Etruria during this period are not as numerous or as conspicuous today in the Chiusine area, possibly due to their deterioration over time (for an example of a monumental *tumulus* and for the chamber of the Regolini Galassi Tomb from Cerveteri *cf.* Fig. 1.2, in the chapter by Cuozzo; on burial architecture and its variability in Latium *cf.* Rajala this volume, with a chamber tomb seen in Fig. 8.2). However, a handful of well-known examples existed, or must have existed, nearby Chiusi and in the Chiusine territory as well, such as the Poggio Gaiella *tumulus* (still visible today and dating to the sixth century BC) and the Pania *tumulus* (Minetti 2004). As Tuck (2012, 53) notes, the monumentality of these tombs covered by *tumuli* does not represent a deviation from the norm, but rather a vector through which the region's aristocratic families could engage in competitive displays through the increase and amplification of the common ritual framework. The simpler *ziro* tombs themselves allowed for exhibitions of wealth and status as well as for indications of the gender roles of the deceased. A *ziro* burial assemblage from Ficomontano near Chiusi provides a relatively typical example (Barbagli and Iozzo 2007, 245–54). A canopic urn with a male head was enthroned on a cylindrical ceramic throne; included in the assemblage was a range of ceramic and bronze vessels, as well as bronze implements. A well-known, but controversial and distinctive example of a *ziro* burial was reputedly excavated late in the nineteenth century near Chiusi (Hall-Dohan 1935); however, the bronze table and chair that Hall-Dohan described are now accepted as fakes (Warden 2002–2003). Moreover, complete *ziro* grave assemblages are rare and there exists no reliable report of graves containing tables and thrones (Tuck 1994, 98, no. 26). The urn in Hall-Dohan's reconstruction is represented as enthroned on a bronze chair covered with a cloth and a bronze belt symbolically adorning the deceased's remains (Fig. 4.2). Also placed in the grave was a censer resting on a tripod, a table upon which apparently lay the

Fig. 4.2: Reconstruction of ziro tomb (after Hall-Dohan 1935, 202).

remains of the funeral banquet and an axe. Surmounting the burial was the *ziro*, in this case a large vase decorated with griffins and figurines upon which was a lid that acted as a pediment for a large figure of a human body. It may be surmised that the figure was intended to have an apotropaic function with the griffins protecting the deceased below. In each of the known surviving examples, the figure makes distinctive gestures with its arms. Most common is the placing of the arms resting on the chest with the hands joined, or the placing of the right hand over the chest with the left one raised in a gesture of salutation. It is possible to see this section of the structure, above the space that is the tomb proper, as a liminal dimension between the worlds of the living and the dead. Within this space the terracotta figures may represent generic members of the burying community and consequently are manifestations of their agency in perpetually guarding their ancestor. Moreover, architecturally this elaborate and especially complex construction of *ziro* tombs sought to insulate, preserve, and protect the cremated remains of the deceased. Therefore, in the urbanizing period at Chiusi the tomb represents the underworld and the final space the deceased inhabits.

The use of urns imitating the body is generally considered to have revitalized the deceased by re-establishing the body after cremation (Tuck 1994, 626–7). The urn containing the remains was thus the central feature in a signification system involving grave goods arranged around and upon it. Items such as jewellery, arms and even clothing articulated the social and gendered identities of the deceased individual. There is a consequent stress on the individuality of the deceased; therefore, their re-appearance in the tomb in this manner can be interpreted as another stage in the process of the preservation of personhood. Yet, it can be assumed that while idealized, the meaning of the grave goods reflected on the roles of the deceased in life. The burying community shared a concern for commemorating the deceased in a particular manner. Most obvious is the connection to the banquet (Rathje 1990; Tuck 1994) where we may surmise that the deceased was celebrated as an élite male (on ritual alcohol and food consumption in Early Iron Age central Italy *cf.* Iaia this volume). This is enhanced through the emphasis on the miniaturized chairs and tables (manufactured to suit the scale of the urn) and more commonly banqueting sets. Although not unique by any means in central Italy, the creation of objects specifically for the burial lays stress on the process and value placed on the memorialization of the individual in this period. The seated funeral banquet of this type, as has been shown by De Marinis and Tuck, was characteristic of the later seventh century BC throughout central Italy (De Marinis 1961; Tuck 1994). Another similar example from a tomb group at Poggio alla Sala in Chiusi contains bronze and ceramic vessels that formed the banqueting set (Randall-MacIver 1924, 241). Again the validity of the make-up of the tomb-group has been questioned (Tuck 1994, 622, no. 26) as it strongly appears that some of the components are combinations of two separate graves. Nevertheless, it remains likely that *ziro* tombs contained numerous examples of the seated banquet burial type. Therefore, it should be understood that the deceased is memorialized banqueting in death. While it is not necessarily an idealized representation of real-life banqueting, the similarity of the banqueting equipment to that recovered from domestic contexts indicates these were the dining practices of high status groups. Moreover, the axe and bronze belt around the urn can be seen to contribute another facet to our understanding of high status male identity at Chiusi as it can be appreciated to signify the deceased's role as a warrior.

The deposition of these objects can be seen as related to, and are perhaps the remnants of the Bronze Age phenomenon of the so-called *kriegergrab*, common throughout central Europe, including Italy (Treherne 1995). This concept could be described more simply as a 'warrior grave' or even a 'princely grave', but in doing so it loses part of its meaning (on the 'princely' tomb phenomenon *cf.* also Cuozzo and Morris this volume; on warriorhood in the Bronze Age *cf.* Harrison 2004). It encapsulates the ideals of the warrior aristocracy, and the material representation of it through objects that include weapons, drinking equipment and toilet articles. A fine example from Chiusi is the seventh-century BC Tomba del Principe from Morelli, being distinct in itself in the form of an early chamber tomb in this region (e.g. Minetti 2004). Not only did the grave goods include a large number of drinking vessels and valuable goods, but additionally this grave yielded a bronze shield and lances with iron blades. In addition, vessels were deposited that contained glass paste for scented oils as well as a fibula. In this case the deceased is clearly represented as a member of the warrior aristocracy. As P. Treherne (1995) has shown with regard to the earlier Bronze Age, these burials were not as much about an ideological expression, but more about the development and maintenance of a 'life style' specific to an élite male status group. This included the philosophy of the Homeric banquet, but also at Chiusi this focused on the re-vitalized body of the deceased. The deposition of objects for bodily ornamentation along with spears and shields suggests the commemoration of an individual subject bound up in the trappings of the *heroic warrior*. It is of course not possible to show that the deceased achieved a so-called "beautiful death" but he was certainly immortalized in this fashion.[3] Indeed from the Greek literary tradition of this period we have manifestations of similar concepts with both Homer (*Illiad* 22.71–76) and Tyrtaios (10.21–30) describing the disgraceful deaths of old men and praising the heroic, and consequently, beautiful deaths of young men on the battlefield (Shanks 1999, 212). It is likely that Chiusine élites appropriated such values into their social and cultural system. The seventh century BC saw the widespread adoption and adaption of elements of Near Eastern and Greek culture in inland Etruria; this is evident in the iconography of 'Orientalizing' *bucchero* at Chiusi through the introduction of the iconography of the *potnia theron* (Valentini 1969). In a similar way the ideology of the heroic warrior, as memorialized in death, was another element of an exotic foreign culture that was attractive to aristocratic groups seeking to maintain their status and hegemony.

These manifestations of the eternalized individual gradually became more anthropomorphized through the development of so-called 'canopic' urns at Chiusi and in the surrounding region during the seventh century BC. These urns, too, were frequently enthroned in *ziro* tombs. The some 150 urns of this kind known to date display a high level of individualism with no one being exactly like the other (Gempeler 1974). The vessels in these instances were covered with modelled images of human heads and, in some examples, arms and other anatomical attributes were added to accentuate the re-vitalized body of the deceased (Tuck 2012, 52). Most of the heads tend to emphasize idealized youthful persons and all are stylized; there are no blemishes, and the faces are represented as fresh and without fault. It has been suggested that these heads may well be an early example of a mask, and indeed in some cases bronze masks were attached onto the urn as well (Phillips 1984; 1986; Tuck 2012). It can, therefore, be suggested that these burials centred on the individual, a concern that was evident from earlier periods manifested through biconical urns. There was a particular concern to ensure the permanence of the deceased's identity as personal and singular, and this was reinforced through the inclusion of burial assemblages unique to each individual. This contrasts with the concept of generic ancestor figure, which can be observed through the representational evidence of the dead at Cerveteri and Tarquinia for instance. At the former site the production of a number of fictile ash-urns with generic figures attest to this, including most famously two near identical urns commonly referred to as the 'Sarcophagi of the Married Couple' (Nielsen 2009, 79). Meanwhile, at Tarquinia the abundance of figures in tomb-painting from the earlier phases does not become personalized until much later in the Hellenistic period, and then 'portraits' are supplemented with inscriptions identifying the individual represented (Steingräber 2006, 191).

The burying community went to great lengths to stress the status and roles of the deceased. While high status and wealth are not necessarily indicators of real power, it can be assumed, through the considerable effort manifested in these memorials, that some at least were political and military leaders of the communities that made up Chiusi in the eighth and seventh centuries BC. Therefore, central to male identity during this period, in Chiusi and throughout its hinterlands, was membership of a warrior élite. This was not just confined to Chiusi, but was a broader phenomenon throughout pre-Roman central Italy (e.g. Riva 2010). The Greek and Roman literary traditions emphasize the warring nature of the early Etruscans, although details of this are not clear and usually refer to the later centuries of the first millennium BC during the Roman conquest (Eckstein 2006, 123). They even allege the existence of a league in the form of a *dodecapolis* (Livy 7.2.1), yet there is no reason to believe that had this even existed it was some form of a military alliance. Moreover, for this period questions of state formation are far from clear (Bradley 2000), and in most cases the first urban centres were only taking form. Therefore, warfare was most likely a regional and local phenomenon and not a large-scale enterprise.

Another consideration is the efficacy of the funeral on the burying community. The group of signs that made up the funeral process were designed to fix in the minds of the onlookers an image of the deceased, but this all happened during the comparatively brief duration of the funeral ceremony. Moreover, the material evidence that survives in the form of the tomb represents the very final stage of the funeral ritual. The identity of the deceased became fixed at this moment and could not be altered through sustained revisiting. Tombs of *pozzeto*, *ziro* and *fossa* types were not designed to be re-opened for further depositions, the addition of other members of the social group, or even for continued visiting unlike later chamber tombs. Therefore, the spectacle of the burial, and of the deceased as an individual subject became inscribed in the collective memory of the group during the funeral itself. In a recent reconsideration of Etruscan funeral practices Tuck (2012, 52) notes that on many examples of canopic urns there are perforations on the lower edge of the canopus that correspond to perforations on the upper neck of the cinerary urn, with the obvious explanation being that the perforations were designed to ensure the lid remained joined to the urn. The necessity for such stability implies that the series of activities that took place prior to the final deposition of the urn were such that the lid may become detached from the urn. This allows for the possibility that the display of the canopic urn in a procession of some form was a feature of the spectacle associated with the funeral. In this case, the urn can be understood to have had the dual function of a container for the deceased individual's cremated remains, but also as an effigy of the dead. Although separated by time and place, the Roman tradition of parading ancestral death masks at funerals may be a later variation of this practice (Flower 1996, 97–106). Moreover, the continuity of the body in another space and form also enabled the community to develop what Vernant (1991b, 76) termed an "acculturation of death": that is a means by which such loss could be explained and even celebrated through ritual formulation, therefore partially overcoming the discontinuity and finite nature of death. These practices and beliefs are probably similar to preceding Villanovan traditions throughout central Italy and the symbolic status of biconical urns has received similar attention at Tarquinia (Toms 1992–1993; *cf.* also Shipley this volume).

Maintaining tradition in a time of change

It is possible to discern that these features of masculine identity were maintained in a different form in the sixth and early fifth centuries BC in Chiusi. There are again new developments in funerary practices in the region with a move away from anthropomorphic cineraria to ash chests that mimic house design (Banti 1973[1968], 264). Indeed, this is a phenomenon that occurs in various forms throughout central Italy, with tomb architecture at Tarquinia from this period clearly mimicking house design as well (Leighton 2004, 90). Alongside the ash chests *cippi* (stone tomb markers) became important features in the funerary landscape. However, despite these changes, it is possible to examine the reliefs of ash chests and *cippi* that have been recovered from the cemeteries in the region of Chiusi. It should be noted, however, that canopic urns did not disappear immediately and they continued to be employed during the sixth century BC, albeit to a lesser extent. As noted above, it is well established that the sixth century was a time of considerable change in central Italy, and Chiusi was no exception to this (e.g. Becker 2007). While the process of urbanization was more gradual here in the seventh century BC, it intensified in the sixth century and the city probably reached its greatest extent around this time (Steingräber 1995, 59). Increased urbanization must have brought with it changes, or acted as a catalyst for such, in the socio-political landscape through the increased visibility of an aristocratic élite. The increase in the population and the adoption of high-status Chiusine burial practices between Trasimeno, Orcia and Paglia attest to this (Steingräber 1995, 60). The sphere of influence of Chiusi also expanded during this time as can be seen through the distribution of the distinctive sixth-century BC Chiusine pottery, *bucchero pesante*, in north inland Etruria (Del Verme 1998, 193–216). Chiusi can be considered to have existed in splendid isolation as one of the dominant 'city-states' in the region of inland Etruria. Indeed, the literary tradition detailing the exploits of the king of Chiusi, Lars Porsenna, perhaps preserves at least fragments of truth, and the status of Chiusi as an economic and political power was preserved and later recognized in Roman memory (Livy 2.9). The social delineation evident in the seventh century BC became more pronounced but population growth and increased wealth and power forced the aristocratic class to ensure their status was memorialized through other mechanisms. The gradual introduction of chamber tombs, as can be observed in a most dramatic form at Poggio Gaiella, became more frequent (Rastrelli 1998, 57–80; on the 'chamber tomb' grave type *cf.* also Rajala this volume). This type of tomb was formed by carving rooms out of the soft calcareous *tufo*. The potential for more than one chamber to be constructed also brought about a change in the position of the individual during the sixth century BC – or at least a change concerning how the individual was memorialized within the broader social group. Chamber tombs offered the potential for familial or other groupings to be buried together. A shift from a concern for individual identity to that of group identity can be observed through funerary architecture alone. Yet the best evidence for this is through the gradual introduction of ash urns. Often imitating house forms themselves, they signify a different meaning in this changing socio-political environment. There is no longer a stress on individuality and, therefore, there is potentially a change in the notion of personhood, as the emphasis is now situated on the individual's place within the social group, presumably that of the family. These house urns can be understood to represent the familial group as the fundamental unit of Chiusine society with the deceased being memorialized in death as a member of that group. The symbolic depth of meaning may be further understood when the placement of the urns within the chamber tomb, itself mimicking house design, is considered.

While these changes are evident, as in the case of the anthropomorphic urns, a certain degree of continuity can be observed, in particular with respect to the ideals of male gender identity. The aspects of masculine identity present before continue in an altered format in the iconography of the urn and *cippus* reliefs. The funeral banquet is memorialized in a different form through the carved reliefs as can be seen on this example in Dublin (Fig. 4.3). In a sample of nearly 150 ash urn and *cippi* reliefs the funeral banquet recurs as the primary iconographic theme on just fewer than 20% of the examples.[4] Furthermore, as can be seen on the example from Dublin considered here, the deceased is no longer represented dining alone. Instead the focus is on numerous participants, reinforcing the change in the stress on the individual to the broader familial and social group. Again it can be assumed that this is not just an ideological statement, but one that reflects a life style change amongst élite groups. Such statements are visible in non-funerary evidence, too, in inland Etruria, with sites such as Poggio Civitate providing evidence for the ideology of élite banqueting through the discovery of banqueting wares and in the iconography of architectural terracottas (Berkin 2003, 118–26; Rathje 1994). Despite this, the identity of men as warriors is not as persistent, with just a few urns and *cippi* – less than ten – alluding to this through depictions of combat scenes; and even within this group the emphasis is no longer on the solitary hero, but instead on groups of men fighting or performing

Fig. 4.3: Ash urn from Chiusi, sixth century BC (National Museum of Ireland, inv. 1893.2).

the so-called 'armed-dance' (Spivey 1988) as well as through the introduction of the imagery of the hoplite (Rich 2007, 16). However, the emphasis on related traits of strength and virility does persist through the theme of athletics and games – the singularly most popular motif occurring on a quarter of the examples of urns and *cippi* considered. It is well established that there is a certain corollary between warfare and games – both activities focusing on competiveness and dexterity. Thus, perhaps athletic prowess or being honoured through funeral games replaced this aspect of masculine identity in the middle of the Archaic period in Chiusi and its territories. Additionally, the comparatively few painted tombs from Chiusi also stress this imagery, such as the athletic contests in the Tomba della Scimmia (Steingräber 1986, no. 25).[5] There is, thus, a continuation of certain ideals in masculine identity that were present during the seventh century BC through displays that focused on the male body. In addition we can observe the enthronement of figures on a number of reliefs, perhaps a continuation of the concept of the enthroned person evident in earlier graves. For example, a *cippus* in Munich contains a scene of five men, two of whom are seated on ornately carved stools and hold staffs, presumably as symbols of elevated social standing (Jannot 1984, 165–6).

This partially counters V. Izzet's belief that it was during the sixth century BC that the body and the individual became the locus of social change. Central to Izzet's argument is an apparent sudden increase in the deposition of bronze mirrors as grave goods in Etruria, coupled with the relationship between the iconography of Etruscan mirrors and that of bodily transformation though adornment. While Izzet is correct that there was an increase in the production of mirrors, it remains that only about 3,000 mirrors are definitively known from central Italy and the vast majority of these date to the Classical and Hellenistic period (mid-fifth–first century BC). From a sample of 976 mirrors published in the *Corpus Speculorum Etruscorum* series, less than 1% come from the sixth century; moreover, most of the mirrors from this period are undecorated. Therefore, it can be suggested that issues such as adornment and bodily manipulation did not become a significantly new concern around this time. However, Izzet's argument that there was a concern for adornment and an idealized form of male beauty is not entirely inaccurate; however it can instead be identified much earlier than the sixth century BC and through other forms of evidence. It stretches back further into the eighth and seventh centuries through the reforming of the cremated body in anthropomorphizing urns, together with the deposition of suitable objects with it. During the sixth century, while an emphasis on the ideals of a masculine life style and male identity continued, there was (as suggested already) an emphasis placed upon the integration of the previous concern for individual identity into group and particularly familial identity. This corresponds with issues of female gender identity where female beauty and the female role within the family are given special prominence (Izzet 2007, 55–74). The burying community, primarily consisting of the dead individual's kin group, were aware that their status, and consequently their importance, was contingent upon that of the deceased. As noted above, the maintenance of their familial group within an ever more competitive socio-political environment, both at intra- and inter-community levels, was a significant concern. It seems likely that within what were now urban settlements, there was much competition between different factions. Moreover, the accounts of sixth-century BC Rome, as provided by Livy for instance, although probably nearer to legend than fact, are likely to preserve a shadow of such a reality (*cf.* Smith 2011). Thus, the construction of chamber tombs, as was being done elsewhere in central Italy, was one way of physically manifesting an élite group's importance. In addition, the employment of previously used ideas, such as banquets, to display status was continued through other media.

In addition to this, the funeral ritual itself no longer was the last point in which the remains of the deceased were seen – the consignment to memory of the image of the tomb was no longer the final encounter with the deceased. The chamber tomb allowed for the potential visits to the deceased to make offerings or for the visibility of the ash urns during the course of other funerals. Therefore, the deceased could be viewed sharing in funerary banquets with extended members of their family. The Inghirami Tomb from Volterra as reconstructed in the *Museo Archeologico* in Florence presents an idea of how this could have been done. Here it has been shown (Maggiani 1977) that positions of urns in relation to one another were altered in antiquity, a practice which allowed for the alteration of the identities of the deceased with respect to other members of the family through association or indeed disassociation with particular ancestors. Consequently, while certain aspects of identity were fixed in memory through the iconographic programme, others could – potentially at least – be subtly manipulated. However, the Inghirami Tomb is exceptional in offering potential insights like this. Moreover, it is mere speculation that practices at Chiusi several centuries earlier may have followed a similar route.

This change is also significant as it is entirely different to the *ziro* graves discussed above. In *ziro* burials the tombs represented the underworld itself, with the space above containing the figurine being the actual liminal sphere of interaction. In contrast, the chamber tomb itself became the locus of interaction between the world of the living and that of the dead. It became the liminal space. The decoration of the ash urns with apotropaic imagery in this sphere supports this interpretation, as do false doors represented in tomb paintings from Etruria more generally marking the threshold to the underworld.[6] These deviations from practices attested in the eighth and seventh centuries BC must be linked to a changing belief system in the Etruscan afterlife. Jannot (2000, 85) observes that in the earlier phases it is undeniable that the dead could enjoy an afterlife and that this was explicitly expressed through anthropomorphic urns. However, by the Archaic period and in later periods it can be argued that the physical tomb acted as a gateway to the next world. The tomb was no longer the final place where the deceased dwelt, but rather it was an intermediary space in which the living could come to make offerings or simply 'visit' ancestors. The impetus for this change must be linked to socio-political developments and urbanization in particular. Developing urban spaces brought about greater competition between aristocratic groups, and monuments – such as chamber tombs – provided a vector through which familial lineage could be advertised in a more conspicuous manner than before. Additionally, increased contact with the Greek world, both that in south Italy and the Aegean, seems to have effected this change, too, and perhaps catalyzed a fundamental shift in the conception of the afterlife to one where the deceased lived in an Etruscan equivalent of the underworld.[7] Consequently, through the construction of chamber tombs, the aristocratic groups in Chiusi and its hinterland during the sixth century BC did not depart from common ritual practices. Rather they subtly manipulated the traditional framework and adapted belief systems to express previously established aspects of social and gender identity, along with carefully chosen new ones, in an increasingly inter-connected Mediterranean world.

Conclusion

From this brief overview of burial practices at Chiusi a number of observations can be made. The seventh-century BC groups at Chiusi were concerned with stressing the individual in death. With respect to male identity this involved an emphasis on the persona of the warrior. This may be linked to the survival of the paradigm of the Bronze Age heroic warrior from central Europe (Treherne 1995). But central to this display of a particular life style is the body. Although by no means unique to Chiusi, the partial anthropomorphization of the urn underscores this belief. The reformed body with the accoutrements representing the career and exploits of a warrior became an extension to the body. The self-identity is further cultivated through objects of banqueting and ornamentation and the often personalized and youthful heads on canopic urns, which combined with the warrior status help presuppose a position of privilege. The community, therefore, employed the body to display the life style of what is described by Riva (2010, 84) as the "civilised" warrior. In other words, the definition of warriorhood itself was broadened and became synonymous with high status.

While many of the changes in burial practices in Chiusi may have been induced by the process of urbanization and growing socio-political complexities, there may well have been other factors also. The move from a focus on the individual to that on the family and the broader social group also indicates a modification in belief systems or at least in attitudes to death. This may be linked to changes that had already occurred and were continuing to occur in other parts of central Italy. The relationship between what may be labelled 'city-states' by the sixth century BC can be observed through the later introduction of painted tombs in Chiusi, which are similar in conception and execution to those at Tarquinia and Cerveteri. The different polities can be observed endeavouring to imitate and emulate one another. But critically, within them the role of the body and the gender roles as memorialized in death remained important in an alternative format, through commemoration in the developing concept of funerary art. Through the creation of a group of individuals, the creation of an aristocratic family became important in a constantly evolving political environment. The concept of the individual warrior hero was no longer sufficient, but instead the construction of chamber tombs enabled the continued display of wealth and status that enabled manifestations of familial status – and like their late earlier eighth- and seventh-century BC predecessors, ideals of masculine prowess were central themes therein.

Acknowledgements

I would like to thank the editors for their assistance and patience during the course of preparing this paper. I also acknowledge the helpful criticisms of the anonymous reviewer(s) which have greatly improved many of the arguments. Thanks are also due to Edward Herring, Theresa Huntsman and Lucy Shipley for their individual comments. Needless to say those that have provided criticisms and assistance do necessarily agree with all the opinions I have expressed, and similarly all remaining errors and omissions are mine alone.

Notes

1. In archaeology the seminal works on gender have been focused on women; for instance, the contributions to Gero and Conkey (1991), and more recently, the edited volume by Hamilton and co-authors had as their primary focus women in archaeology (Hamilton *et al.* 2007). However, there have been a number of contributions on masculinities and masculine identity, such as Harrison's (2004) monograph on Bronze Age Europe, which places particular emphasis on warrior identity. With regard to ancient Italy there has been a near total focus on female identity in the scholarship on gender. Most notable is the valuable work of Larissa Bonfante (e.g. 1989; 1994; 1997) on Etruscan women. Furthermore, a number of edited volumes, such as Whitehouse (1998) and Herring and Lomas (2009), while worthy efforts at raising issues of male, female and other possible gender groups, remain proportionally dominated by papers concerned with female identity.

2. A considerable bibliography has emerged on the landscape and region of Chiusi in the last fifteen years with contributions that focus on specific localities, time-periods and excavations. A good introduction is the collection of papers edited by Rastrelli (2000), while Minetti (2004) considers the Orientalizing period and Gastaldi (1998) looks at the region during the Archaic period. Separate studies on Chianciano Terme (Paolucci 1988 and 2007), on recent excavations around Sarteano (Minetti 2012) and Chiusi (Gastaldi 2009) have done much to illuminate the ancient topography.

3. The concept of the "beautiful death" is usually associated with the Homeric Greek world, especially that discussed by Vernant (1991a). Although it is not a concept that can be definitely shown to have existed in early Italy, it seems likely that similar socio-political and cultural values prevailed, not only in Italy, but also across much of Europe. Indeed, Treherne (1995, 130, no. 8) notes that many of the characteristics of a heroic society feature widely in Indic, Nordic and Celtic epic, and must have their roots in the late Bronze Age.

4. This is based upon an analysis of Jannot's (1984) catalogue, in addition to a number of more recently discovered urns and *cippus* reliefs.

5. Indeed, athletic imagery is the most recurrent theme in the iconography of Archaic tomb-paintings at Chiusi. From the ten tombs of this period six of them contain images of games: Tomba della Scimmia, Tomba di Poggio al Moro, Tomba di Poggio Gaiella, Tomba Paolozzi, Tomba di Montollo and Tomba del Colle Casuccini.

6. Much has been written on 'false' doors in Etruscan art and architecture, e.g. d'Agostino 1987 and Camporeale 1993. At Chiusi two contemporary tomb-paintings, Tomba di Poggio al Moro and Tomba del Colle Casuccini, contain such imagery.

7. The Greek concept of the afterlife was by no means homogenous (Felton 2007, 86). However, in most literary sources the deceased was thought to live in an underworld, and not one associated with the tomb. Perhaps the most famous example of this is the description of the underworld in *Odyssey* Book 11. The conception of the Etruscan underworld is debatable. Serra Ridgway (2007) argued for continuity in beliefs of the afterlife between the Archaic period and Hellenistic period in Tarquinia, and one element of this is the existence of the false door in Etruscan art across this time span, as well as epigraphic references to the chthonic deities Charun and Vanth.

Bibliography

Banti, L. (1973[1968]) *Etruscan Cities and their Culture*. Berkely, University of California Press (first published as *Il Mondo degli Etruschi*, Roma).

Barbagli, D. and Iozzo, M. (2007) *Etruschi. La Collezione Bonci Casuccini tra Chiusi, Siena e Palermo, Catalogo della Mostra (Siena-Chiusi, 2007-2008)*. Siena, Protagon.

Becker, H.W. (2007) *Production, Consumption and Society in North Etruria during the Archaic and Classical Periods: The World of Lars Porsenna.* PhD thesis, University of North Carolina, Chapel Hill.

Berkin, J. (2003) *The Orientalizing Bucchero from the Lower Building at Poggio Civitate (Murlo).* Philadelphia, The University of Pennsylvania Museum of Archaeology and Anthropology.

Bianchi Bandinelli, R. (1925) Ricerche archeologiche e topografiche su Chiusi e il suo territorio in età etrusca. *Monumenti Antichi* (pubblicati per cura della R. Accademia Nazionale dei Lincei) 30, coll. 209–578.

Bloch, R. (1972) *Recherches Archeologiques en Territoire Volsinien de la Protohistoire à la Civilisation Étrusque.* Paris, E. de Boccard.

Bonfante, L. (1989) La moda femminile etrusca. In A. Rallo (ed.) *Le Donne in Etruria*, 157–172. Roma, "L'Erma" di Bretschneider.

Bonfante, L. (1994) Etruscan women. In E. Fantham, H.P. Foley, N.B. Kampen, S.B. Pomeroy and H.L. Shapiro (eds) *Women in the Classical World: Image and Text*, 243–259. Oxford, Oxford University Press.

Bonfante, L. (1997) Nursing mothers in classical art. In A.O. Koloski-Ostrow and C.L. Lyons (eds) *Naked Truths: Women, Sexuality and Gender in Classical Art and Archaeology*, 174–196. London–New York, Routledge.

Bradley, G. (2000) *Ancient Umbria. State, Culture and Identity in Central Italy from the Iron Age to the Augustan Era.* Oxford, Oxford University Press.

Camporeale, G. (1993) Aperture tarquiniese nella pittura tardoarcaica di Chiusi. *In La Civiltà di Chiusi e del suo Territorio. Atti del XVII Convegno di Studi Etruschi e Italici (Chianciano Terme, 28 Maggio–1 Giugno 1989)*, 183–192. Firenze, L.S. Olschki.

Connell, R.W. (1995) *Masculinities.* Cambridge, Polity Press.

d'Agostino, B. (1987) L'Immagine, la pittura e la tomba nell'Etruria arcaica. *Prospettiva* 32, 2–12.

De Marinis, S. (1961) *La Tipologia del Banchetto nell'Arte Etrusca Arcaica.* Roma, "L'Erma" di Bretschneider.

Del Verme, L. (1998) La ceramica di bucchero. In P. Gastaldi (ed.) *Studi su Chiusi Arcaica* (Annali di Archeologia e Storia Antica Nuova Serie 5), 193–216. Napoli, Istituto Universitario Orientale.

Eckstein, A.M. (2006) *Mediterranean Anarchy, Interstate War, and the Rise of Rome.* Berkeley–Los Angeles, University of California Press.

Edlund-Berry, I.E.M. (1994) Ritual destruction of cities and sanctuaries: The 'un-founding' of the archaic monumental building at Poggio Civitate (Murlo). In R. De Puma and J.P. Small (eds) *Murlo and the Etruscans: Art and Society in Ancient Etruria*, 16–28. Madison, University of Wisconsin Press.

Felton, D. (2007) The dead. In D. Ogden (ed.) *A Companion to Greek Religion*, 86–99. Oxford, Blackwell.

Flower, H.I. (1996) *Ancestor Masks and Aristocratic Power in Roman Culture.* Oxford, Clarendon Press.

Fowler, C. (2004) *The Archaeology of Personhood: An Anthropolgical Approach.* London, Routledge.

Gastaldi, P. (1998) (ed.) *Studi su Chiusi Arcaica* (Annali di Archeologia e Storia Antica Nuova Serie 5). Napoli, Istituto Universitario Orientale.

Gastaldi, P. (2009) (ed.) *Chiusi: Lo Scavo del Petriolo (1992-2004).* Chiusi, Edizioni Luì.

Gempeler, R.D. (1974) *Die Etruskischen Kanopen: Herstellung, Typologie, Entwicklungsgeschichte.* Einsiedeln, Benziger.

Gero, J.M. and Conkey, M.W. (1991) (eds) *Engendering Archaeology: Women and Prehistory.* Oxford, Blackwell.

Hall-Dohan, E. (1935) A *ziro* burial from Chiusi. *American Journal of Archaeology* 39(2), 198–209.

Hamilton, S., Whitehouse, R.D. and Wright, K.I. (2007) (eds) *Archaeology and Women: Ancient and Modern Issues.* Walnut Creek, Left Coast Press.

Harrison, R.J. (2004) *Symbols and Warriors: Images of the European Bronze Age.* Bristol, Western Academic and Specialist Press.

Haynes, S. (1973) *Etruscan Sculpture.* London, Trustees of the British Museum.

Herring, E. and Lomas, K. (2009) (eds) *Gender Identities in Italy in the First Millennium BC* (BAR S1983). Oxford, Archaeopress.

Izzet, V.E. (2007) *The Archaeology of Etruscan Society*. Cambridge, Cambridge University Press.

Jannot, J.R. (1984) *Les Reliefs Archaïques de Chiusi*. Rome, École française de Rome.

Jannot, J.R. (2000) The Etruscans and the Afterworld. *Etruscan Studies: Journal of the Etruscan Foundation* 7, 81–99.

Knapp, B. (1998) Boys will be boys: Masculinist approaches to a gendered archaeology. In K. Hays-Gilpin, and D.S. Whitley (eds) *Reader in Gender Archaeology*, 365–373. London–New York, Routledge.

Leighton, R. (2004) *Tarquinia: An Etruscan City*. Duckworth, London.

Maggiani, A. (1977) Analisi di un contesto tombale. La tomba Inghirami di Volterra. In M. Martelli and M. Cristofani (eds) *Caratteri dell'Ellenismo nelle Urne Etrusche. Atti dell'Incontro di Studi (Università di Siena, 28-30 Aprile 1976)*, 124–136. Firenze, Centro DI.

Malone, C. and Stoddart, S.K.F. (1994) (eds) *Territory, Time and State: The Archaeological Development of the Gubbio Basin*. Cambridge, Cambridge University Press.

Minetti, A. (2004) *L'Orientalizzante a Chiusi e nel suo Territorio*. Roma, "L'Erma" di Bretschneider.

Minetti, A. (2012) (ed.) *La Necropoli delle Pianacce nel Museo Civico Archeologico di Sarteano*. Milano, Silvana Editoriale.

Nielsen, M. (2009) One more Etruscan couple at the Museum of Fine Arts, Boston. In S. Bell and H. Nagy (eds) *New Perspectives on Etruria and Early Rome*, 171–181. Madison, University of Wisconsin Press.

Paolucci, G. (1988) *Il Territorio di Chianciano Terme dalla Preistoria al Medioevo*. Roma, Multigrafica Editrice.

Paolucci, G. (2007) *Carta Archeologica della Provincia di Siena Vol. IX: Chianciano Terme*. Siena, Nuova Immagine.

Phillips, K.M. Jr (1984) Protective masks from Poggio Civitate and Chiusi. In M.G. Marzi Costagli and L. Tamagno Perna (eds) *Studi di Antichità in Onore di Guglielmo Maetzke*, 413–417. Roma, Giorgio Bretschneider Editore.

Phillips, K.M. Jr (1986) Masks on a canopic urn and an Etrusco-Corinthian perfume pot. In J. Swaddling (ed.) *Iron Age Artefacts in the British Museum: Papers of the Sixth British Museum Classical Colloquium*, 153–155. London, British Museum Press.

Randall-MacIver, D. (1924) *Villanovans and Early Etruscans*. Oxford, Oxford University Press.

Rastrelli, A. (1998) La necropoli di Poggio Gaiella. In P. Gastaldi (ed.) *Studi su Chiusi Arcaica* (Annali di Archeologia e Storia Antica Nuova Serie 5), 57–86. Napoli, Istituto Universitario Orientale.

Rastrelli, A. (2000) (ed.) *Chiusi Etrusca*. Chiusi, Edizioni Luì.

Rathje, A. (1990) The adoption of the Homeric banquet in central Italy in the Orientalizing period. In O. Murray (ed.) *Sympotica: A Symposium on the Symposium*, 279–289. Oxford, Clarendon Press.

Rathje, A. (1994) Banquet and ideology. Some new considerations about banqueting at Poggio Civitate. In R. De Puma and J.P. Small (eds) *Murlo and the Etruscans. Art and Society in Ancient Etruria*, 95–99. Madison, Wisconsin.

Rich, J. (2007) Warfare and the army in early Rome. In P. Erdkamp (ed.) *A Companion to the Roman Army*, 7–23. Oxford, Blackwell.

Ridgway, D. (2002) *The World of the Early Etruscans*. Jonsered, Paul Åström.

Riva, C. (2010) *The Urbanisation of Etruria: Funerary Ritual and Social Change, 700-600 BC*. Cambridge, Cambridge University Press.

Roth-Murray, C. (2007) Élite interaction in Archaic Etruria: Exploring the exchange networks of terracotta figured frieze plaques. *Journal of Mediterranean Studies* 17(1), 135–160.

Serra Ridgway, F.R. (2007) Revisiting the Etruscan underworld. *Accordia Research Papers* 10, 127–142.

Smith, C.J. (2011) Citizenship and community: Inventing the Roman Republic. In N. Terrenato and D. Haggis (eds) *State Formation in Italy and Greece: Questioning the Neoevolutionist Paradigm*, 217–230. Oxford, Oxbow Books.

Spivey, N.J. (1988) The armed dance on Etruscan vases. In J. Christiansen and T. Melander (eds) *Proceedings of the 3rd Symposium on Ancient Greek and Related Pottery (Copenhagen, 31 August–4 September 1987)*, 593–603. København, Nationalmuseet, Ny Carlsberg Glyptotek.

Steingräber, S. (1995) Funerary Architecture at Chiusi. *Etruscan Studies: Journal of the Etruscan Foundation* 2, 53–84.

Steingräber, S. (1986) (ed.) *Etruscan Painting. Catalogue Raisonné of Etruscan Wall Painting* (English-language edition edited by David and Francesca R. Ridgway). New York, Harcourt Brace Jovanovich.

Steingräber, S. (2006) *Abundance of Life: Etruscan Wall Painting.* Los Angeles, J. Paul Getty Museum.

Stoddart, S.K.F. (1990) The political landscape of Etruria. *Journal of the Accordia Research Centre* 1, 39–51.

Thomas, M.L., Meyers, G.E. and Edlund-Berry, I.E.M. (2012) (eds) *Monumentality in Etruscan and Early Roman Architecture: Ideology and Innovation.* Austin, University of Texas Press.

Toms, J. (1992–1993) Symbolic expression in Iron Age Tarquinia: The case of the biconical urn. *Hamburger Beiträge zur Archäologie* 19–20, 139–161.

Treherne, P. (1995) The warrior's beauty: The masculine body and self-identity in Bronze Age Europe. *Journal of European Archaeology* 3(1), 105–144.

Tuck, A.S. (1994) The Etruscan seated banquet: Villanovan ritual and Etruscan iconography. *American Journal of Archaeology* 98(4), 617–628.

Tuck, A.S. (2012) The performance of death: Monumentality, burial practice, and community identity in central Italy's urbanizing period. In M.L. Thomas, G.E. Meyers and I.E.M. Edlund-Berry (eds) *Monumentality in Etruscan and Early Roman Architecture: Ideology and Innovation*, 61–81. Austin, University of Texas Press.

Valentini, G. (1969) Il motivo della potnia theron sui vasi di bucchero. *Studi Etruschi* 37, 413–442.

Vernant, J.P. (1991a) A 'beautiful death' and the disfigured corpse in Homeric epic. In J.P. Vernant (ed.) *Mortals and Immortals: Collected Essays* (English-language edition edited by F.I. Zeitlin), 27–29. Princeton, Princeton University Press.

Vernant, J.P. (1991b) *Mortals and Immortals: Collected Essays* (English-language edition edited by F.I. Zeitlin). Princeton, Princeton University Press.

Warden, P.G. (2002–2003) The anatomy of an Etruscan tomb forgery: Case unresolved. *Journal of the International Foundation for Art Research* 5(4), 36–42.

Whitehouse, R.D. (1998) (ed.) *Gender and Italian Archaeology: Challenging the Stereotypes.* London, Accordia Research Institute and Institute of Archaeology, University College London.

Chapter 5

Women in a warriors' society

Amalia Faustoferri

Introduction

In the ninth century BC, central Adriatic Italy (Fig. 5.1) was home to the people that defined themselves as the *Safini*, as A. La Regina recently (2010) argued. Archaeological investigation in the region has focused almost exclusively on graves of adult male individuals, which as a rule contain weapons and/or armour. This, in conjunction with the fact that classical accounts describe the local communities as Rome's most resilient enemies, has led scholars to overlook some of the less 'conspicuous' social groups represented in the funerary record of the region, such as women and children. However, new excavations at the funerary sites of Fossa and Avezzano have revealed the existence of wealthy women's graves, many of which stand out for containing elaborate bronze discs that had previously been regarded as 'male' breastplates. These new data – discussed here by presenting the preliminary results of ongoing research on female graves in this area – raise questions about the social role of high-standing women in a world that until now has been conceptualized as essentially masculine (on the issue of gender in first-millennium BC Italy *cf.* also Cuozzo, Iaia and O'Donoghue this volume; on mortuary rituals in Apennine central Italy and Samnium *cf.* also Scopacasa this volume).[1]

Weaponry in a warrior society

The image of Abruzzo as a land of strong warriors is deeply rooted in our imagination. Already in the first century AD, the Elder Pliny described the region's inhabitants as "the toughest peoples of Italy" (*gentes fortissimae Italiae*: NH 3.11.106). This image was strengthened by the discovery of the Archaic (sixth century BC) funerary statue known as the 'warrior of Capestrano' in central Abruzzo in 1934. The 'warrior' has become a symbol of Abruzzo, as well as the logo of the region's archaeological *Soprintendenza*. It is the main attraction in the *Museo Archeologico Nazionale d'Abruzzo*, where it can be seen in the new and striking display by Mimmo Paladino (Pessina and Simongini 2011).

Fig. 5.1: Map of Italy showing the main sites mentioned in the chapter: 1. Capracotta; 2. Alfedena; 3. Barrea; 4. Opi-Val Fondillo; 5. Luco dei Marsi; 6. Avezzano (Cretaro); 7. Scurcola Marsicana; 8. Celano; 9. Molina Aterno; 10. Capestrano; 11. L'Aquila; 12. Bazzano; 13. Fossa; 14. Campovalano; 15. Pieve Torina (elaboration R. Scopacasa, base map by C. Iaia).

The 'warrior' of Capestrano is one of many statues and *stelai* from Abruzzo that depict adult males in armour (Ruggeri 2007; some of these sculptures are also housed in Chieti). What is special about the Capestrano statue is its excellent state of preservation, including traces of paint that reveal interesting details of the figure's apparel. Yet it would be wrong to see this sculpture as the image of 'the Warrior' par excellence: the individual in question was most likely a person of authority, possibly a 'lord', because his weapons and armour – the sword, the axe and the breastplate – were all emblems of high social standing in the context under study.[2] Such artefacts, however, were not part of the usual set of weapons found in Abruzzo during the seventh and sixth centuries BC.

Owing to the systematic excavation of cemeteries by the *Soprintendenza* of Abruzzo, we know that males were most often buried with iron spears and daggers, while only a few graves included swords, breastplates and axes. Such graves are mostly found in the funerary sites of the upper Sangro Valley, namely Alfedena, Opi and Barrea. In particular, Tomb D^{IV} 388 at Alfedena (Mariani 1901, fig. 75) closely recalls the Capestrano statue in view of the shape, style and position of the weapons and breastplate. The same is true of Tomb 2 at Opi (Grossi 1988) and Tomb 96 at Barrea, which contained an adult male that displayed remarkable similarities to the Capestrano statue, from the bronze breastplate worn diagonally over the chest, to details such as the shape and position of the bracelets (Riccitelli 2011). We may conclude that the Capestrano 'lord' and the individual in Barrea Tomb 96 were associated to items that might be indicative of a specific social standing and/or role.

Axes, such as the one held by the Capestrano figure, occur in a small number of male graves in the Sangro area; all of these graves also include daggers (Mariani 1901: Alfedena Tombs B^{II} 52 and 71, C 3, D^{II} 192 and F 1). The only exception is Tomb 67 at Alfedena, which contained an axe, a dagger and an iron spear that was placed right outside the grave (Parise Badoni and Ruggeri Giove 1981, 43). It must be noted that the grave was sealed with a single slab. This feature is significant, since investigations carried out at Opi and Barrea have shown that the presence of a monolithic cover is normally associated with richly outfitted graves.

Overall, research on the funerary evidence from these sites suggests that the type of weaponry, and its position in relation to the grave, indicated the deceased individual's social role (Ruggeri 2010, 282; Ruggeri *et al.* 2009, 49). There appears to have been some sort of hierarchy among the weapons as insignias of power; only a few men had the privilege of 'taking' these weapons with them to the grave, as they 'embarked' on their last journey.[3] Axes, however, also occur in women's graves. These include Tomb 183 at Opi (*cf.* below) and probably Tomb B 17 at Alfedena, where no other weapons were found, but which featured a separate compartment with plenty of pottery. Such compartments, especially those containing large amounts of vessels, are likely to indicate social distinction. In cases where weapons are absent from such tombs, we might infer that the deceased was a woman – although in the Sarno Valley, in nearby Campania, both men and women were buried with axes of different types (Gastaldi 1979, 22).

The scabbard of the sword depicted on the Capestrano 'warrior' occurs in a grave at Alfedena (Mariani 1901, fig. 81a), as well as further north at Campovalano (d'Ercole 2010, 231, e.g. Tomb 69; *S.O.S.* 2010, 57 n. 8), Molina Aterno (Riccitelli 1998) and Scurcola Marsicana (Lapenna 2004, 53 n. 59, 83 n. 1, a specimen from Rome-Riofreddo). Breastplates are also rare. Regardless of how these artefacts were used in a functional sense (*cf.* Weidig 2011, 25, 30, who sees them as objects of everyday life), it is clear that at least in the funerary context they were restricted to a select group of people. The total number of breastplates from Abruzzo is quite small, compared to the number of graves in the cemeteries where they were found.

For example, Alfedena, which includes a total of over 1000 graves, yielded only nine pairs of breastplates (*cf.* Mariani 1901, 353 n. 5, who mentions two additional pairs in the De Amicis collection, and a sample from Barrea owned by the Di Loreto family). Only two pairs have been found at Opi (Tombs 2 and 48: Riccitelli 2000) and at least three at Barrea.[4] Given their very small numbers, it is difficult to generalize about these breastplates. As noted above, the rarity of these objects suggests that they were not part of the standard military panoply of the seventh and sixth centuries BC, but were the preserve of a restricted group – at least as far as their funerary use is concerned. It is unclear whether breastplates were meant to indicate the rank of the deceased and their family, or instead the social role of the deceased individual. Probably they signified both role and rank, as there are instances where breastplates were placed over the bodies of children – a strong indication of inherited or 'ascribed' rank (e.g. Mariani 1901, Tombs D[III] 210, E 98, D[IV] 389, 468 and 471; the case of Alfedena Tomb C[I] 75 is uncertain; the observations in Mariani 1901 have been confirmed by the scientific analysis of Tomb 48 at Opi: *cf.* Riccitelli 2000).

Until recently, many scholars placed in the category of 'breastplates' a particular series of metal discs with punctured or fretwork decoration (i.e. an interlaced decorative design that is either carved or cut out). These discs are found throughout the central Apennines between Capracotta (south) and Monte Tezio (north), but are especially common in the Fucine basin (modern Avezzano). Although they have been interpreted as a type of breastplate (Tomedi 2000), they were not included in Colonna's (1974) pioneering typology of breastplates in Italy. A turning point in the study of these artefacts has come in recent years, with the excavation of funerary sites in the province of L'Aquila. Of particular interest is the cemetery at Fossa, where such discs (including iron ones) could be contextualized in detail. These discoveries have brought about a new discussion on metalworking in ancient Abruzzo, and have revived debates on gender, since the punctured and fretwork-decorated discs were part of women's outfits (d'Ercole and Copersino 2004, 180; *cf.* below).

Breastplates in female graves

More recently, the Cretaro (Avezzano) cemetery has yielded some of the clearest evidence that the metal discs with fretwork or punctured decoration were not breastplates. These artefacts were found in women's graves, and were mostly intact (Ceccaroni 2009; 2010; Di Giandomenico 2006; *S.O.S.* 2010, 82–5 nn. 23–8). Indeed, some scholars had already suggested that these discs were personal ornaments (*cf.* Faustoferri 2008; also Colonna 2007a; 2007b). Some of the first discs that were brought to light came from a woman's grave in Pieve Torina (Marche). The woman in question was buried with two such discs next to her body, one larger and one smaller, which were initially interpreted as parts of a *stole* – a long rectangular garment worn over the chest and/or abdomen (Lollini 1976, 175). This interpretation was neglected at first (e.g. Colonna 1991, n. 42) but is now widely accepted. Discussion has focused on whether the larger disc on the *stole* was meant to be placed over the chest (Colonna 2007a; 2007b) or the abdomen (Papi 2007, 79; unfortunately, the data from Cretaro add little to this discussion as none of the *stolai* were worn by the deceased at the time of interment: Ceccaroni 2009, 19).

The graves at Cretaro also included large iron rings, which were initially interpreted as head ornaments: this is because in one instance this object was placed around the head of the inhumed individual (Ceccaroni 2009, 20, fig. 13). Similar rings are seen as being connected with the worship of the sun, and as prestige items of high-ranking females (Fogolari 1975, 174). Yet it is difficult to interpret the rings from Cretaro as head ornaments, since the nature and meaning of these artefacts are still unclear. Most of the women's graves at Cretaro (14 out of 18) include iron rings, so these objects may not have been wholly exclusive to 'prominent individuals' (Ceccaroni 2009, 19). On the other hand, we cannot rule out the possibility that this area of the Cretaro cemetery (which was large and organized into separate grave clusters: *cf.* Ceccaroni 2009, 15) was reserved for 'special' women. It seems more appropriate, for the time being, to regard these iron rings as "diacritical insignia" (following the definition in Dietler 1999, 145 n. 10) awarded to women who had a special role in the community – possibly as priestesses, as the presence of an adolescent amongst them might suggest. Unfortunately, the religious beliefs of Italic communities, and their attitudes towards the sacred, are still shrouded in uncertainty (the problem is masterfully framed in von Eles 2007, 149). Nevertheless, in light of comparisons with other societies from different periods and places, we can assume that certain people in ancient Italy were responsible for managing the community's relationship with the divine. Therefore, we may attempt to recognize such individuals in the archaeological record in view of certain outward signs.

Regardless of how we interpret the social role of women buried with metal discs, it seems clear that only a small number of these objects may be regarded as breastplates. The breastplate types in first-millennium BC Italy include only the rectangular and Übergangsform types (or 'Bolsena' type: *cf.* Colonna 1991, 101; Tomedi 2000, 25), the so-called 'Mozzano group', which includes the 'Cittaducale' group (according to Weidig 2011, 5) and the circular breastplates with iron reinforcements and the image of the so-called 'fantastic animal'.[5] Such images were more than just a decorative motif: they were part of the 'insignias of power' that high-ranking individuals in ancient Abruzzo displayed (Faustoferri 2011). To fully understand the 'fantastic animal' iconography, we need to take into account the prestigious artefacts on which these images occur, and the fact that the figures remain essentially unchanged for a very long time, from the Orientalizing to the late Archaic period (i.e. seventh–late sixth centuries BC: Tagliamonte 2003, 539). As a general assessment, the 'fantastic animal' iconography was most likely a type of socio-political status marker, a prestigious visual convention that may have operated on the supra-local level of ethnic belonging.

What concerns us here, however, is the fact that the metal discs with fretwork or punctured decoration, previously thought to belong to 'warriors', are now seen as women's apparel. This calls for a new focus on these women who wore elaborate disc *stolai* and belts as a means of flaunting their role, perhaps even more than their rank. On closer inspection, it would appear that some kind of differentiation existed between women buried with *stolai* and women buried with belts, since graves that contain disc *stolai* do not include belts (and vice-versa). This has been confirmed by the excavations at Cretaro (Ceccaroni 2009, 20): the only exception to this pattern seems to be Tomb 365 at Fossa. Furthermore, graves with *stolai* and graves with belts were contemporaneous. Hence, it remains unclear how to account for these differences in the funerary assemblages of certain women, although contextual analysis can provide some initial clues. At Fossa, for example, the graves with belts also contain spindle whorls (d'Ercole and Benelli 2003: Tombs 47, 61, 152 and 387). It is important to note, however, that none of the women were wearing any of the items in question at the time of their burial – even in cases where only the buckle was made of metal as in Tomb 2 at Cretaro (Ceccaroni 2009, fig. 12). Possibly, therefore, we are dealing with a type of funerary display that may not reflect how these women actually dressed in life. In the seventh and sixth centuries BC, women's belts are attested only in north Abruzzo (Weidig 2005, fig. 1; these belts were lined with metal either wholly or in part). Excavations at Fossa and Bazzano have increased considerably the pre-existing sample of women's belts from Campovalano, and it is now believed that at least some of these artefacts were produced locally (*cf.* Weidig 2005; 2010, 10). The same applies to the iron discs with punctured or fretwork decoration, especially since the latter recall the type of fretwork seen on fibulae (Acconcia and d'Ercole 2012, 34; two striking bow-arch fibulae were found in Tomb 551 at Fossa, together with fretwork-decorated discs: d'Ercole and Benelli 2003, 229–31).

In the Orientalizing period (seventh century BC), some of the punctured and fretwork-decorated discs feature images of animals drawn in thick dotted lines (the so-called 'Alba Fucens' group: Tomedi 2000, 72). Among the animals depicted are ducks and four-footed beasts, either standing still or on the move, occasionally facing each other. In some cases, they are so schematic as to resemble squiggles. The heads in particular tend to be highly stylized, to the point where they look like harps or lyres (e.g. Tomedi 2000, nos 319–20). A special case is the bronze disc from Luco dei Marsi, which shows 'fantastic' animals at the centre and in a band outlined by cantilever pearls (Tomedi 2000, no. 328). In a society where figurative decoration is rarely attested, such an imaginative visual repertoire seems significant. Furthermore, it is notable that these animal figures usually decorate the bronze breastplates worn by élite men that some scholars regard as the 'lords' of ancient Abruzzo (Weidig 2005, 476). How, then, should we understand the presence of these images on metal discs that were worn by women?

Women in ancient Abruzzo

I suggest that one possible solution to this problem involves exploring the roles that women had in this society. As was rightly pointed out by von Eles (2007, 83) about high-ranking women at the Iron Age centre of Verucchio: "It is likely that [these women's] prestige did not derive entirely from their relationship with prominent male members of the community, but also from the important roles that they performed, probably in connection with the sacred, but perhaps also in the political sphere" (on Verucchio *cf.* also Di Lorenzo *et al.* this volume; on the role of women in Iron Age and Orientalizing Campania and central Italy *cf.* also Cuozzo and Iaia this volume). This intuition may be extended to the Abruzzo case as well.

The available written sources on Abruzzo are meagre and biased, as they all date from later periods; furthermore, they are Rome-centred and generally unreliable. Archaeological sources, however, provide a better evidence base. One very important piece of evidence is the fragmentary stone statue of a woman, of which only the torso survives. Like the 'warrior', this statue was found in Capestrano and dates to the sixth century BC. There has been some scholarly debate concerning this woman's relationship with the 'warrior'. Indeed, the female statue has been approached as subordinate to the Capestrano figure, as his 'wife' or 'daughter' (*cf.* the contrasting views of Franchi dell'Orto 2010, 224 n. 87, and d'Ercole and Martellone 2007, 24), with little thought given to the nature of the family group that one is attempting to reconstruct. First, the statue as a monument might have referred to a ruling élite family or dynasty, and is therefore a key element in any reconstruction of the society of the time. In addition to the commonplace (but necessary) observation that the honour of having one's statue made presupposes an exceptional social and political standing, what is truly remarkable is that, in the present case, the person who received such an honour was a woman. Yet despite the statue's uniqueness and importance, it has attracted surprisingly little attention – which is symptomatic of the silence that surrounds women in what has often been characterized as a 'society of warriors'.

Many tombs from Abruzzo that are considered to belong to women include grave goods that might have been associated to the deceased individual's gender and/or status. Yet in interpreting this evidence the concept of 'wealth' has prevailed over nuanced reflections concerning the social role of these women. Scholars have therefore imagined a plethora of 'queens' and 'princesses' (depending on the presumptive age at death suggested by osteological analysis) who parade around in scenarios that are seldom defined (e.g. d'Ercole and Martellone 2007, 14, who describe the woman buried in Tomb 4 at Celano as the oldest queen of Abruzzo). What is missing from these reconstructions is a social context for such characters.

Unfortunately, the 'lady' of Capestrano is too fragmentary to support inferences about her social role, in view of her clothing, attributes or insignia (but *cf.* Franchi dell'Orto 2010, 212). Nevertheless, the statue itself is indicative of how the social position of women in Abruzzo had changed since the Early Iron Age (ninth–eighth centuries BC), when even the wealthiest females were denied the honour of a *stele*. This change appears to be connected with another important transformation, namely the reuse of Iron Age burial mounds in the late seventh century BC. During the Early Iron Age, the burial mounds in Abruzzo were built for selected individuals only; in the seventh century BC, however, they started to include more numerous graves of men, women and children. The conversion of the mounds into collective burial plots suggests that a funerary ideology more concerned with the concepts of family, ancestry and lineage became important for élite self-legitimization (*cf.* Faustoferri and Riccitelli 2007, 165). By placing their burials together and next to earlier ones, these later élite groups may have been attempting to claim descent from prestigious 'ancestors', either real or imagined. As part of this new funerary ideology, female 'ancestors' started to be honoured alongside male ones, possibly because of the lustre that these women were considered to bestow on their progeny. The issue remains to be explored, but the best evidence comes from the upper Sangro Valley, where it has been possible to investigate large sections of major funerary sites (Opi, Barrea and Alfedena) that were used from the late seventh to the end of the sixth century BC.[6] This is precisely the period when powerful individuals such as the 'warrior' of Capestrano rose to prominence. Although the evidence is limited geographically, it is qualitatively significant: the sample is homogeneous and allows us to approach questions of social organization – in full awareness of theoretical debates regarding the difficulties of seeking to reconstruct social organization through the material remains of ritual practice, which are part of the social structuring of reality, rather than a passive reflection of social organization (e.g. Morris 1987, 39; on the same issue *cf.* also Cuozzo this volume, with additional bibliography).

From the second half of the seventh century BC until the end of the sixth, the upper Sangro cemeteries (Alfedena: *cf.* Mariani 1901; Parise Badoni and Ruggieri Giove 1981; Ruggieri *et al.* 2009; Opi: *cf.* Morelli 1998; 2000; Barrea: Faustoferri and Riccitelli 2007) were divided into circular grave clusters, the central areas of which included the tomb of the deceased individual that was the most important person in the group (Faustoferri and Riccitelli 2007). Because these clusters were probably used by kinship groups, they provide some information on the internal structure of extended families during this period. A good example is Cluster 9 at Opi. This mound included nine male graves, eight female graves, and nine children's graves occupying the edge of the mound, closer to the surface. At the highest point of the mound, near the centre, was Tomb 179. This grave probably belonged to an accomplished hunter, as is suggested by the presence, beside the dagger, of three bear nails, originally stored in a container made of organic material. The remaining tombs contained fairly simple and homogeneous grave goods, suggesting that the mound was used by a middling family. Yet one grave, Tomb 183, is somewhat surprising, as it contained an adult woman that was buried holding a large iron axe in her left hand. As noted above, axes are rare in cemeteries from this period, which suggests that the woman buried in Tomb 183 had a relevant social role. This is further indicated by her carefully made coffin, and by the presence in the tomb of a compartment containing four-handled impasto vases (*olle*), covered by a bowl and a stone plate. Of particular significance is the fact that the woman was buried holding the axe: such a position suggests that this item was not a mere funerary offering, but was directly linked with the deceased woman.[7] Given the axe's shape and large size, it is also difficult to think of it as a mere symbol of power, as has been suggested regarding axes in women's graves elsewhere in Italy (e.g. von Eles 2004, 259). By contrast, the axe buried in Opi Tomb 183 was most likely a functional instrument connected to the woman's social role. Axes were used to sacrifice animals, but while in the Homeric world this was a man's job (*Odyssey* 3, 448–52), in Italy it would appear that certain women could also perform this important social and ritual function.

Like axes, knives may also have been associated with ritual activity. Some of the women's graves at Fossa and Bazzano include iron knives with bone and wooden handles. Such artefacts have been described as "an element of differentiation that begins to characterize a small segment of the feminine world from the mid-eighth century BC" (Cosentino *et al.* 2001, 189). The fact that some women might have been in charge of "dividing and distributing the flesh" (d'Ercole and Martellone 2007, 18; *cf.* also Acconcia and d'Ercole 2012, 9) should probably not be regarded as a general trend in the construction of gender identities in ancient Abruzzo. Moreover, the specific social status and role of women buried with knives is not completely clear. At Fossa, for example, the women's graves with knives are not especially well furnished; furthermore, they belonged to individuals from different age classes, namely an elderly woman, two adults and a child of 6–8 years (Cosentino *et al.* 2001, 181). Consequently, it is possible that these knives refer to the sphere of the sacred, as has been suggested with regard to Iron Age Latium and the Venetic world, where knives are more frequent in women's graves between the seventh and sixth centuries BC (e.g. von Eles 2007, 45).

The distance (both geographical and chronological) between the knives from L'Aquila and the axe from Opi is surely great. It is nevertheless significant that, in both cases, the use of objects with a probable ritual function was delegated by the community to certain women, whose 'training' or preparation to hold such a role might have begun at an early age, as is shown by the child grave from Fossa. In the case of the axe from Opi, we can assume a more particular use, not connected to the domestic killing of animals for food, but rather to cultic events. This interpretation is consistent with the view put forward by other scholars, that axes in female graves are an indication that the women in question belonged to a type of 'priestly class' (Torelli 2006, 418–22; also von Eles 2007, 155).

There is another exceptional grave from Opi that demands attention. Tomb 124 contained the remains of a 'girl' buried with lavish grave goods that occur nowhere else in the cemetery, namely a long *châtelaine* with pendants, various personal ornaments possibly meant to adorn a complex hairstyle or veil and an iron chain with wrought bone appendages. The grave also included a clay spindle whorl, an object that scholars normally regard as a strong gender indicator. Yet this does not seem to be the case at Opi (for a similar problem regarding Fossa, *cf.* Acconcia and d'Ercole 2012, 13; Cosentino *et al.* 2001, 188), where spindle whorls are only present in three graves (Tombs 40, 124 and 170). Tomb 40 contained an elderly woman who, like the young female in Tomb 124, was buried with a set of lavish and unusual grave goods, including the long *châtelaine* with chains and pendants. Tomb 170 yielded the remains of a 'girl' whose body was covered with iron and bronze buckles, conical pendants, two bracelets and a veil with various decorative attachments. There was also a globular pendant with an iron suspension ring; the function of this pendant is not quite clear, but we may assume that it resembled that of Tomb 124. A spindle whorl was placed on the left side of the girl's body. This item was not a gender marker, but instead was probably related to the dead girl's social role or function. We can infer that such a role may have been inherited, given that Tomb 170 is very close to the grave of an adult woman (Tomb 169) with similarly rich furnishings, including an amber necklace, a bronze *châtelaine* and an iron object shaped as a half-moon with an attached pendant. Spindle whorls are also very rare at Alfedena, where they occur in only 12 of *c.* 1500 graves, eight of which belonged to infants, and date to the cemetery's later phases (mid-late fifth century BC). In these graves, the spindle whorls were used as personal ornaments, such as necklace pendants (*cf.* Mariani 1901, 338), whereas spindle whorls actually used to spin were found only in four of the graves at Alfedena, all of which were richly outfitted (Tombs D^{IV} 364, 434 and 30, D^{II} 77).

As other scholars have noted (e.g. Murphy 2008), the occurrence of unusual grave goods suggests that 'something different' was at work with regard to certain individuals in a community. The young females in Tombs 124 and 170 at Opi probably had a significant, and possibly hereditary, role to perform (Faustoferri and Riccitelli 2007, 167). It was not uncommon in antiquity for highborn women to be trusted with religious duties, and for these duties to have been transmitted in a hereditary manner (*cf.* Langdon 2003, 17). The most likely hypothesis is that the two young females at Opi were associated with initiation rituals, in view of their age. Based on criteria that are unknown to us, but which probably involved rank, these girls may have been chosen to perform certain duties at a sanctuary. Because of their premature death, which probably happened when they were still in office, both girls might have had the right to be buried in their ceremonial attire.

The fact that the two girls at Opi were also buried with spindle whorls suggests that they were associated with weaving and spinning, which were hugely important activities in the ancient Mediterranean (e.g. Gleba 2008). As some scholars have argued (e.g. van Wees 2005, 10), clothes were not simply functional items but also status symbols meant to be displayed at important social events, such as funerary ceremonies. In addition, fine clothes were often exchanged as lavish gifts among aristocrats (*cf.* also Torelli 1997, 63 on the social and economic role of textiles in the Italic world). In the Odyssey (15, 104–8), Helen is noted for the beautifully decorated tunics that she herself weaves. This introduces an element of social hierarchy to the activity of weaving: the 'lady' of the house produced only the finest garments, and mastered the 'true art' of weaving. We can identify a very similar link between weaving and high-status women in Orientalizing and Archaic Italy, in view of the iconography displayed on the throne of Verucchio and the *tintinnabulum* of Bologna (*cf.* Torelli 1997, 57; 2006; von Eles 2002). Further evidence of this link is present in Basilicata (for the Alianello cemetery *cf.* Bottini 2000), Daunia (e.g. the image of a little girl sitting on her mother's lap, and learning to weave: D'Ercole 2000, 332, fig. 1b) and the Venetic world (Ruta Serafini 2004, 280).

Also in Abruzzo there were high-raking women who spun and wove, as is suggested by the ivory spool in Tomb 2 at Capestrano (d'Ercole and Martellone 2007, fig. 29), but especially by the glass spindles from Tombs 119 and 415 at Campovalano, which have been described as "authentic feminine symbols of royalty" (d'Ercole and Martellone 2007, 22). Similarly, Boccolini (2003, 159) argues that the presence of spindles and/or distaffs in women's graves in Abruzzo should be seen "...not so much as a reference to these objects' practical fuction, but as symbolic of the deceased woman's control over weaving activities". Despite the controversy about the actual function of the glass spindles from Campovalano (Chiaramonte Treré *et al.* 2010, 238), what matters here is that these were very unusual and valuable objects, in view of their material and the fact that they were probably imported. Yet, as mentioned above, a study of individual objects must consider the complex relationship between all of the grave goods in the cemetery as a whole. Such a task, however, is beyond the scope of this preliminary work, which has outlined the possibilities offered by an investigation of the roles of women in a 'society of warriors'.

Notes

1. The reflections proposed here are not meant to be comprehensive, as they are work in progress, the initial results of which were presented at the 'Burial and Social Change' workshop.

2. I use the word 'emblem' here in the sense of Colburn 2008, 203 n. 7: "... by 'emblem' I mean any object that plays an active role in signifying personal or social identity."

3. This implies a distinction between privately owned objects and those referring to the political status of the individual, which no doubt had to be indicated very visibly. It is important to stress that knowledge of a weapon's shape can provide important clues as to its possible function. To give one example, Tomb 100 at Campovalano included what appears to be a kind of axe, along with a chariot, and a vase that featured the only inscription found in the cemetery (d'Ercole 2010, 228).

4. These include the pair of breastplates in Tomb 96, a fragment from the same mound and the pair recovered thanks to an official seizing (*S.O.S.* 2010, 95 nn. 3 and 4). Mariani (1901) mentions several breastplates from Barrea, and Grossi (1988) notes numerous specimens that are now in private collections. The cemetery of Barrea was looted for decades, and much of its material is now in the illegal market.

5. These breastplates have been divided into the so-called 'Numana', 'Paglieta' and 'Alfedena' groups (Colonna 1974); the latter group was subdivided into two further subsets (Colonna 2007b), with the second subset including the plain discs worn by the Capestrano figure. The 'fantastic animal' imagery is attested in Abruzzo from the seventh century BC onwards (mid-seventh century according to Weidig 2011, n. 46).

6. In fact, the basin of the upper Sangro River housed a nearly continuous series of large cemeteries which remain only partly investigated: recently, some excavations have been carried out at Opi and Barrea, while none was conducted in the area between the current Civitella Alfedena and Villetta Barrea, from which also comes a bronze disc (Grossi 1988, 92, pl. xvii.1). For reasons yet unclear, there appears to be a gap in the funerary record in this area between the eighth and the mid-seventh centuries BC. None of the graves at Alfedena, Barrea and Opi can be dated securely to the early–mid seventh century BC.

7. So as to avoid the kind of risk discussed by Langdon (2003, 13).

Bibliography

Acconcia, V. and d'Ercole, V. (2012) La ripresa delle ricerche a Fossa. L'Abruzzo tra il Bronzo Finale e la fine dell'età del Ferro: Proposta di periodizzazione sulla base dei contesti funerari. *Archeologia Classica* 63, 7–53.

Boccolini, P. (2003) Note sul rituale funerario femminile. In C. Chiaramonte Treré and V. d'Ercole (eds) *La Necropoli di Campovalano. Tombe Orientalizzanti e Arcaiche I* (BAR S1177), 153–159. Oxford, Archaeopress.

Bottini, A. (2000) *Kestos himas poikilos. Ostraka* 9, 273–279.

Ceccaroni, E. (2009) Archeologia preventiva nella Marsica: Lo scavo della necropoli in località Cretaro-Chiusa dei Cerri-Brecciara di Avezzano (AQ). *Quaderni di Archeologia d'Abruzzo* 1, 15–24.

Ceccaroni, E. (2010) La necropoli in loc. Cretaro Brecciara di Avezzano (AQ): Primi dati e nuove prospettive. *Quaderni di Archeologia d'Abruzzo* 2, 341–446.

Chiaramonte Treré, C., d'Ercole, V. and Scotti, C. (2010) (eds) *La Necropoli di Campovalano. Tombe Orientalizzanti e Arcaiche II* (BAR S2174). Oxford, Archaeopress.

Colburn, C. (2008) Exotica and the early Minoan élite: Eastern imports in Prepalatial Crete. *American Journal of Archaeology* 112(2), 203–224.

Colonna, G. (1974) Su una classe di dischi-corazza centro-italici. In *Aspetti e Problemi dell'Etruria Interna. Atti dell'VIII Convegno di Studi Etruschi e Italici (Orvieto, 1972)*, 193–205. Firenze, L.S. Olschki.

Colonna, G. (1991) Gli scudi bilobati dell'Italia centrale e l'*ancile* dei Salii. In *Miscellanea Etrusca e Italica in onore di Massimo Pallottino* I, 55–122. Roma, "L'Erma" di Bretschneider.

Colonna, G. (2007a) Migranti e ornato femminile (a proposito di Perugia e dei Sarsinati *qui Perusiae consederant*). *Ocnus* 15, 89–116.

Colonna, G. (2007b) Dischi-corazza e dischi di ornamento femminile: Due distinte classi di bronzi centro-italici. *Archeologia Classica* 58, 3–30.

Cosentino, S., d'Ercole, V. and Mieli, G. (2001) (eds) *La Necropoli di Fossa I. Le Testimonianze più Antiche*. Pescara, Carsa.

d'Ercole, M.C. (2000) Immagini dall'Adriatico antico. Su alcuni temi iconografici delle stele daunie. *Ostraka* 9, 327–349.

d'Ercole, V. (2010) Le armi e gli armati. In C. Chiaramonte Treré, V. d'Ercole and C. Scotti (eds) *La Necropoli di Campovalano: Tombe Orientalizzanti e Arcaiche II* (BAR S2174), 223–234. Oxford, Archaeopress.

d'Ercole, V. and Benelli, E. (2003) (eds) *La Necropoli di Fossa II. I Corredi Orientalizzanti e Arcaici*. Pescara, Carsa.

d'Ercole, V. and Copersino, M.R. (2004) (eds) *La Necropoli di Fossa IV. L'Età Ellenistico-Romana*. Pescara, Carsa.

d'Ercole, V. and Martellone, A. (2007) *Regine d'Abruzzo. La Ricchezza nelle Sepolture del I Millennio a.C.*. L'Aquila, Soprintendenza per i Beni Archeologici dell'Abruzzo.

Dietler, M. (1999) Rituals of commensality and the politics of state formation in the 'princely' societies of early Iron Age Europe. In P. Ruby (ed.) *Les Princes de la Protohistoire et l'Émergence de l'État. Actes de la Table Ronde Internationale Organisée par le Centre Jean Bérard et l'École Française de Rome (Naples, 27-29 Octobre 1994)*, 132–152. Napoli, Centre Jean Bérard.

Di Giandomenico, L. (2006) Una necropoli dell'età del Ferro. In A. Campanelli (ed.) *Poco Grano Molti Frutti. 50 Anni di Archeologia ad Alba Fucens. Catalogo della Mostra (Avezzano, Villa Torlonia, 13 Maggio–15 Agosto 2007)*, 165–169. Sulmona, Synapsi.

Eles, P. von (2002) (ed.) *Guerriero e Sacerdote. Autorità e Comunità nell'Età del Ferro a Verucchio. La Tomba del Trono* (Quaderni di Archeologia dell'Emilia Romagna 6). Borgo S. Lorenzo, All'Insegna del Giglio.

Eles, P. von (2004) Verucchio: Aristocrazia, rango e ruoli in una comunità dell'età del Ferro. In F. Marzatico and P. Gleirscher (eds) *Guerrieri, Principi ed Eroi fra il Danubio e il Po dalla Preistoria all'Alto Medioevo*, 259–261. Trento, Castello del Buonconsiglio.

Eles, P. von (2007) (ed.) *Le Ore e i Giorni delle Donne. Dalla Quotidianità alla Sacralità tra VIII e VII Secolo a.C.. Catalogo della Mostra (Museo Civico Archeologico di Verucchio, 14 Giugno 2007-6 Gennaio 2008)*. Verucchio, Pazzini Editore.

Faustoferri, A. (2008) 15. Bronzescheibe. In Bentz, M. (ed.) *Rasna. Die Etrusker: Eine Ausstellung im Akademischen Kunstmuseum, Antikensammlung der Universität Bonn (15. Oktober 2008-15. Februar 2009)*, 26–27. Petersberg, Imhof Verlag.

Faustoferri, A. (2011) Riflessioni sulle genti della valle del Sangro. *Quaderni di Archeologia d'Abruzzo* 3, 153–168.

Faustoferri, A. and Riccitelli, P. (2007) I Safini del Sangro. In A.M. Dolciotti and C. Scardazza (eds) *L'Ombelico d'Italia. Popolazioni Preromane dell'Italia Centrale. Atti del Convegno (Roma, 17 Maggio 2005)*, 161–175. Roma, Gangemi.

Fogolari, G. (1975) La protostoria delle Venezie. In G. Fogolari and F. Rittatore Vonwiller (eds) *Popoli e Civiltà dell'Italia Antica 4*, 61–222. Roma, Biblioteca di Storia Patria.

Franchi dell'Orto, L. (2010) Il Guerriero di Capestrano e la statuaria medio adriatica. In Franchi dell'Orto (ed.) *Pinna Vestinorum e il Popolo dei Vestini*, 180–225. Roma, "L'Erma" di Bretschneider.

Gastaldi, P. (1979) Le necropoli protostoriche della valle del Sarno: Proposta per una suddivisione in fasi. *Annali dell'Istituto Orientale di Napoli, Archeologia e Storia Antica* 1, 13–57.

Gleba, M. (2008) *Textile Production in Pre-Roman Italy*. Oxford, Oxbow Books.

Grossi, G. (1988) Il territorio del Parco nel quadro della civiltà safina (X–IV secolo a.C.). *In Il Territorio del Parco Nazionale d'Abruzzo nell'Antichità. Atti del I Convegno Nazionale di Archeologia (Villetta Barrea, 1-3 Maggio 1987)*, 65–108. Civitella Alfedena, Edizioni L'Orsa.

Langdon, S. (2003) Views of wealth, a wealth of views: Grave goods in Iron Age Attica. In D. Lyons and R. Westbrook (eds) *Women and Property in Ancient Near Eastern and Mediterranean Societies*, 1–27. Cambridge MA, Harvard Center for Hellenic Studies.

Lapenna, S. (2004) (ed.) *Gli Equi tra Abruzzo e Lazio*. Sulmona, Synapsi.

La Regina, A. (2010) Il Guerriero di Capestrano e le iscrizioni paleosabelliche. In L. Franchi dell'Orto (ed.) *Pinna Vestinorum e il Popolo dei Vestini*, 230–272. Roma, "L'Erma" di Bretschneider.

Lollini, D. (1976) La civiltà picena. In V. Cianfarani, D. Lollini and M. Zuffa (eds) *Popoli e Civiltà dell'Italia Antica 5*, 109–195. Roma, Biblioteca di Storia Patria.

Mariani, L. (1901) Aufidena. *Monumenti Antichi dell'Accademia Nazionale dei Lincei* 10, 225–638.

Morelli, C. (1998) Dalle comunità tribali all'egemonia romana. In F. Pratesi and F. Tassi (eds) *Parco Nazionale d'Abruzzo. Alla Scoperta del Parco più Antico d'Italia*, 107–117. Pescara, Carsa.

Morelli, C. (2000) La necropoli arcaica di Val Fondillo a Opi. In A. Bietti-Sestieri (ed.) *Piceni. Popolo d'Europa, Guida alla Mostra di Teramo*, 31–36. Roma, De Luca.

Morris, I. (1987) *Burial and Ancient Society: The Rise of the Greek City-State.* Cambridge, Cambridge University Press.

Murphy, E.M. (2008) (ed.) *Deviant Burial in the Archaeological Record.* Oxford, Oxbow Books.

Papi, R. (2007) Produzione metallurgica e mobilità nel mondo italico. Nuovi dati dal Fucino sui dischi di bronzo laminato. *Abruzzo* 45, 3–153.

Parise Badoni, F. and Ruggeri Giove, M. (1981) *Alfedena: La Necropoli di Campo Consolino. Scavi 1974-1979.* Chieti, Soprintendenza Archeologica dell'Abruzzo.

Pessina, A. and Simongini, G. (2011) (eds) *Al di là del Tempo. Mimmo Paladino e il Guerriero di Capestrano: La Nuova Sala.* Torino, Allemandi.

Riccitelli, P. (1998) L'uso funerario di Campo Consolino. In V. d'Ercole and R. Cairoli (eds) *Archeologia in Abruzzo. Storia di un Metanodotto tra Industria e Cultura*, 81–86. Montalto di Castro, Arethusa.

Riccitelli, P. (2000) La tomba 48. In A. Bietti-Sestieri (ed.) *Piceni. Popolo d'Europa, Guida alla Mostra di Teramo*, 37–40. Roma, De Luca.

Riccitelli, P. (2011) Barrea (AQ). La campagna di scavo del 2011. *Quaderni di Archeologia d'Abruzzo* 3, 285–288.

Ruggeri, M. (2007) (ed.) *Guerrieri e Re dell'Abruzzo Antico.* Pescara, Carsa.

Ruggeri, M. (2010) L'Abruzzo dei guerrieri: Da Comino a Capestrano. In L. Franchi dell'Orto (ed.) *Pinna Vestinorum e il Popolo dei Vestini*, 274–285. Roma, "L'Erma" di Bretschneider.

Ruggeri, M., Cosentino, S., Faustoferri, A., Lapenna, S., Sestieri, A.M. and Tuteri, R. (2009) Dai circoli ai tumuli: Rilettura di necropoli abruzzesi. *Quaderni di Archeologia d'Abruzzo* 1, 39–52.

Ruta Serafini, A. (2004) Il mondo veneto nell'età del Ferro. In F. Marzatico and P. Gleirscher (eds) *Guerrieri, Principi ed Eroi fra il Danubio e il Po dalla Preistoria all'Alto Medioevo*, 277–283. Trento, Castello del Buonconsiglio.

S.O.S. 2010 = *S.O.S. Arte dall'Abruzzo. Una Mostra per non Dimenticare.* Roma, Gangemi.

Tagliamonte, G. (2003) La terribile bellezza del guerriero. *In I Piceni e l'Italia Medio-Adriatica. Atti del XXII Convegno di Studi Etruschi e Italici (Ascoli Piceno-Teramo-Ancona, 9-13 Aprile 2000)*, 533–550. Pisa–Roma, Istituti Editoriali e Poligrafici Internazionali.

Tomedi, G. (2000) *Italische Panzerplatten und Panzerscheiben.* Stuttgart, Steiner.

Torelli, M. (1997) *Il Rango, il Rito, l'Immagine. Alle Origini della Rappresentazione Storica Romana.* Milano, Electa.

Torelli, M. (2006) *Insignia imperii.* La genesi dei simboli del potere nel mondo etrusco e romano. *Ostraka* 15, 407–430.

van Wees, H. (2005) The invention of the female mind: Women, property and gender ideology in Archaic Greece. In D. Lyons and R. Westbrook (eds) *Women and Property in Ancient Near Eastern and Mediterranean Societies*, 1–26. Cambridge MA, Harvard Center for Hellenic Studies.

Weidig, J. (2005) Der Drache der Vestiner. Zu den Motiven der durchbrochenen Bronzegürtebleche vom "Typ Capena". *Archäologisches Korrespondenzblatt* 35, 473–492.

Weidig, J. (2010) Aufnahme und Modifikation etruskischer Sachgüter in den nordwestlichen Abruzzen. In A. Kieburg and A. Rieger (eds) *Neue Forschungen zu den Etruskern, Beiträge der Tagung (Bonn, 7-9 November 2008)* (BAR S2163), 9–15. Oxford, Archaeopress.

Weidig, J. (2011) Nur glänzendes Blech oder echter Schutz? Die ältesten italischen Panzerscheiben (Mozzano, Cittaducale, Capena) und die Frage der Kampfesweise in Zentralitalien. *Jahrbuch des Römisch-Germanischen Zentralmuseums* 58, 1–63.

Chapter 6

Verucchio. The social status of children: a methodological question concerning funerary symbolism and the use of space within graves

Giorgia Di Lorenzo, Patrizia von Eles, Lisa Manzoli, Claudio Negrini, Paola Poli and Elena Rodriguez

Introduction

Recent excavations in the cemeteries of Verucchio (Rimini) have not only improved our knowledge of the community that lived in this major cultural crossroads of central Italy, but also led to important methodological breakthroughs that have a bearing on funerary archaeology in Italy more generally. A wealth of newly generated data, including skeletal analysis and a detailed study of metal finds and pottery, provide a solid basis for tackling the question of how the interment of grave goods was linked to personal identity, social status and community self-assertion in Iron Age and Orientalizing Italy. In addition to the quantity and quality of grave goods, it became evident that the use of space within the grave, and the way in which grave goods were positioned in the tombs, are key elements for understanding the funerary symbolism at Verucchio. Our analysis has suggested that different forms or levels of identity were being expressed simultaneously in the same burial. In this chapter we shall focus on a sample of graves of infants and children from ninth- to seventh-century BC Verucchio, whose furnishings are compared to those of adults. The results of our research revealed the intentional expression of family status in burial, in conjunction with more intricate symbolic representations of identity in terms of age groups and the social standing of each individual within the family group.

Current research into the Villanovan cemeteries of Verucchio: evidence and methods

During the Iron Age, several different archaeological 'cultures' developed and spread throughout Italy, including the so-called 'Villanovan culture' which is attested in Etruria and Campania, as well as Bologna, Fermo and Verucchio near the Adriatic coast of Emilia Romagna (on the Iron Age in central-southern Italy *cf.* also Cuozzo, Morris, Iaia and Shipley this volume, with additional bibliography). In Etruria, Campania and Bologna, the communities associated with Villanovan material culture were already organized as proto-urban centres by the ninth century BC. Verucchio, on the other hand, was the focus of a territorial organization that remained stable until the second half of the seventh century, although the site never developed into an urban centre. Verucchio is located on a high hill just inland of Rimini, a strategic position that afforded control over the nearby Adriatic coast, and enabled the community to engage in commercial exchange with northern and central Europe (Fig. 6.1). Such exchange links are evident in the fact that amber, a north European import, became a primary factor in Verucchio's economic development during the eighth century BC (Boiardi *et al.* 2006; von Eles *et al.* 2009).

Little information is available on the settlement at Verucchio. Most of our information on Iron Age Verucchio comes instead from four partly excavated cemeteries located on the hillsides around the Pian del Monte plateau, namely the burial sites of Lavatoio (Campo del Tesoro and Fondo Ripa), Lippi, Moroni and Le Pegge (e.g. von Eles 2006; Gentili 1985; 1986; 2003; Tamburini Müeller 2006). A total of 580 graves has been excavated; these date between the Early Iron Age (ninth century BC) and the Orientalizing period (second half of the seventh century BC).

Although a detailed chronology is still being developed, a preliminary chronological sequence of the Villanovan archaeological culture or '*facies*' at Verucchio has been put forward (von Eles 2014; von Eles *et al.* 2015; von Eles and Pacciarelli in press). This sequence is based on five phases which are anchored to the Bologna sequence (for previous discussion on the chronology of Bologna's Villanovan *facies cf.* for example Morigi Govi 1976; Panichelli 1990; Peroni and Dore in Bartoloni and Delpino 2005, 255). The five phases are: Verucchio I (ninth century BC, corresponding to Bologna I); Verucchio II (first decades of the eighth century BC = Bologna IIA); Verucchio III (mid–third quarter of the eighth century BC = Bologna 2B1); Verucchio IV (last quarter of the eighth century BC = Bologna 2B2); Verucchio V (first half of the seventh century BC = Bologna 3A).

Once the artefact types that could provide chronological information had been identified (Lo Schiavo 2010, 1; Peroni 1994, 25–30, 90–4) it proved impossible to use a classical seriation method based on types association, because of the excessively high number of variables. We therefore preferred to use a limited number of artefact classes and significant artefact types, considering their associations whilst assessing

Fig. 6.1: Map of Italy with main sites mentioned in the chapter (elaboration R. Scopacasa, base map by C. Iaia).

external comparisons. The results were then validated by comparison with other categories of data such as ritual practice, grave structure, grave-good assemblages, as well as the age and gender of the buried individuals.[1]

The determination of the gender of the deceased has taken into account all the available data, both archaeological and anthropological (i.e. osteological). Osteological analysis was carried out for 253 of the 580 graves. The sampled graves include almost all those from Gentili's excavations, but unfortunately none from the Lavatoio cemetery which was excavated in 1893–4, or from the Brizio and Scarani excavations dating to 1894 and 1962–3, respectively. This means that the sampled graves amount to approximately 44% of the graves from all burial sites, or almost 55% if we consider only the better-known Lippi cemetery (which includes 397 graves, of which 217 had their human remains analysed: Fig. 6.2). Osteological analysis was carried out by the anthropologists without previous knowledge of the grave assemblages and their interpretation by the archaeologists. In spite of uncertainties concerning the application of osteological analysis to cremated remains (e.g. Quesada Sanz 2012, 317–8), at Verucchio a significant correspondence was detected between osteological and archaeological gender indicators, which strengthens the credibility of both methods. This correspondence suggests that the archaeological criteria used in identifying the gender of the deceased at Verucchio are reliable, particularly for the later phases. This allowed us to suggest a gender attribution for an additional 20% of the graves where skeletal remains were insufficient (Onisto 2015).

The total number of buried individuals does not correspond to the total number of graves, as many urns contained more than one individual,[2] mostly two but in some cases even three (for similar cases in Iron Age Veneto *cf.* Perego this volume, with additional bibliography). This is indicated by the osteological analysis and by the archaeological record in all of the cemeteries. Instances of re-opening of the urn after primary deposition have not been verified stratigraphically in the recent excavations at Verucchio, as has been the case at the site of Este in Veneto (Bianchin Citton *et al.* 1998; Gambacurta and Ruta Serafini 1998). The hypothesis that some graves in our sample may have been re-opened for subsequent burials could be put forward for some tombs containing items from different chronological phases or periods. However, at present such cases mainly concern the graves in the Lavatoio cemetery, which was excavated in the nineteenth century, and are therefore subject to doubt (Tamburini Müeller 2006).

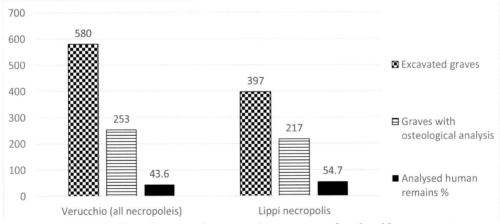

Fig. 6.2: Total number of excavated graves and percentages of analysed human remains (drawn by the authors).

Our research team is currently investigating the diverse combinations of gender-related archaeological attributes, searching for reliable criteria that might allow us to identify multiple burials using both archaeological and osteological data. Gender-specific objects can sometimes indicate multiple burials in the same grave. This might be the case when one object is at odds with the overall gender associations of the grave assemblage as a whole. Such cases have been evaluated separately.

At present, children's graves have been identified on the basis of osteological data. This is because in Verucchio it is difficult to use the archaeological record for this purpose. As will be discussed below, objects that are exclusively associated with children seem to be rare, although a preliminary study of 'small' or 'miniature' items has been carried out. Only in three cases it has been possible to attribute graves to children in the absence of skeletal remains. These are Lippi Tombs 3/1972 and 64/1972 (given the presence of very small bracelets) and Lippi Tomb 26/1972 (because of a small cinerary urn). We are aware of the difficulty in determining the gender of children, considering that gender is a social construct that differs from biological sex (e.g. Díaz-Andreu *et al.* 2005; Sofaer Deverensky 1997). Whenever we refer in this chapter to the gender of children, we mean only that which can be deduced from archaeological gender indicators.

The study of skeletal remains is particularly challenging in Verucchio (Onisto 2015). In addition to well-known problems concerning the study of cremated human remains, a further difficulty is caused by the selection of bones from the pyre for burial in the grave, a common practice in other Iron Age cemeteries in Italy (e.g. Cavazzuti 2015). As a result, the cremated human remains found in the urn often do not allow us to determine the age and biological sex of the deceased with precision. Furthermore, as noted above, it is impossible for physical anthropologists to determine the biological sex of young children. Bearing these challenges in mind, the children sampled from Verucchio have been classed in three conventional age groups, namely *infans* 1 (under 3 years at death), *infans* 2 (3–7 years) and *infans* 3 (7–14 years).[3] Often the age of the deceased could only be approximately determined, and in many cases it could not be clearly situated in the three *infans* classes. However, there were only four examined burials that could not be attributed either to adults or children. Another important issue to consider is that some children were given individual burial whilst others were included in graves that contained more than one individual. By 'individual burial' we mean individual deposition and individual funerary rites, which were generally carried out in relation to an individual grave pit, where the deceased was buried alone. The issue of 'multiple burial' has been repeatedly examined in scholarship on Italian proto-history (e.g. Bartoloni 2003, 97–101; Belardelli *et al.* 1990, 19–73; Peroni 1981, 133; Vanzetti 1992, 116–8).

As noted above, it is impossible to determine the biological sex of children on the basis of osteological analysis. For this reason, in cases where the bones of children were mixed with the bones of adults, and where the grave furnishings include objects that are typical of both sexes, we presently have no way to determine which grave assemblage was associated with the adults, and which with the children. Such cases are numerous and are already present in the first chronological phase. One example is Lippi Tomb 39/1972, where the bones belong to an adult of undetermined sex and to a small child whose remains are limited to a few cranial bones. The grave can be dated to the Early Iron Age (ninth century BC) and is the earliest child burial at Verucchio known to date. The presence of two fibulae suggests that one of the deceased may have been a female, as in this period the male 'costume' at Verucchio usually involved the use of only one fibula. The other individual is almost certainly a male given the presence of a razor in the grave. It would be extremely interesting if a child burial contained such a distinctive object at this early stage, but unfortunately we cannot safely attribute one set of grave goods to the adult and the other to the child. Differences in how age groups are defined in scholarship, though sometimes determined by differences in the available data (e.g. skeletal remains from inhumations vis-à-vis skeletal remains from cremations), make it difficult to compare the data from Verucchio to the information from other Italian sites. One example is the age grouping proposed for the cemetery of Osteria dell'Osa in Latium, where children between 1 and 6 years are considered as a single group (Nizzo 2011a, 56, note 16).

In this chapter we shall analyse both individual child burials and the presence of children in multiple burials, by relating any quantifiable information to the chronology and, whenever possible, to the topographical placement of the tombs in the cemetery. In particular, the spatial distribution of children's graves will be examined in relation to the burial ground's topographical organization. The Lippi cemetery is the only site where such an approach is feasible. This is because the exploration of the Moroni and Le Pegge cemeteries has been very limited, whereas at the Lavatoio cemetery only two graves have had their human remains preserved from the 1893–4 excavations (Fig. 6.3).

The study of children in antiquity is often done within the framework of gender studies, especially in French and Anglophone scholarship (e.g. Becker 2007; Lucy 1997; 2000; Parker Pearson 1999, 95–7; on the issue of 'age' in funerary archaeology *cf.* also Zanoni this volume; on gender and/or the role of women in Iron Age and Orientalizing Italy *cf.* the chapters by Cuozzo, Iaia, Faustoferri and the finale, with additional bibliography and discussion). Recent French symposia on archaeological approaches to childhood, especially in ancient Greece and Rome, have focused on issues of mortality, age classes, rites of passage, family, motherhood, and ritual practices. Anglophone literature has often discussed the issue of gender as both a biological phenomenon and a social construct. Research focusing on ancient Greece and Rome has centred on aspects of infant marginality and the representation of children in art.[4] Other studies have concentrated on

Fig. 6.3: Plan of Lippi cemetery from Verucchio: spatial distribution of children's graves (drawn by the authors).

the social context of families and on socio-political attitudes towards children. Biological age groups as they are currently understood (e.g. infants/children/ adolescents/adults) do not necessarily correspond to one's 'social' age, which refers to attitudes towards the lifecycle that are culturally and historically specific. Children of the same age can receive different treatments at death even in the same cultural context, due to differences in family lineage and rank (Dedet 2008b, 143). Children are often represented in ancient art as 'miniature adults' (Cohen and Rutter 2007, 6–7), and one might wonder if, how and when such images correspond to reality. Is it possible, for example, to identify objects, clothes and costumes that are exclusive to children and make them socially visible (Sofaer Derevenski 1997, 195–9; on the same issue *cf.* Zanoni this volume)?

Italian proto-historians have dealt with many aspects of social strategies concerning death; particular attention has been paid to the treatment of children in different contexts, the concept of 'danger' and ritual strategies of inclusion vis-à-vis discrimination (e.g. Nizzo 2011b, with a discussion of previous bibliography; for the issue of exclusion from formal burial *cf.* also Perego, Scopacasa, Iaia, Cuozzo, Zanoni, and Perego and Scopacasa this volume). According to Nizzo, in the earliest phases of the Italian Iron Age exclusion from formal burial seems to concern children who died before developing the ability to communicate, i.e. before 3 or 4 years of age. He supports his claim with a careful assessment of some important child burials (Nizzo 2011a, 51–93). As Nizzo argues, the ritual adopted for a 7-year-old child at Castel di Decima (near Rome) may have expressed the idea that the child was not able to achieve in life the role that he was socially expected to fulfil (Nizzo 2011a, 60). This is suggested by the deposition in the tomb of objects indicating a clear and remarkable social role, which were intentionally broken or placed in non-functional positions (*defunzionalizzazione*). Nizzo also points out that in the cemetery of Quattro Fontanili at Veii, during the early eighth century BC children were often buried together with other children or adults – which he sees as an early indication that familial groups were being articulated. He notes the case of inhumation Tomb HH 6–7 (Veii Phase IIC), where a 5-year-old child was buried with an older one aged 9–11, in association with a rich set of grave goods apparently meant to denote the family's lineage, including weapons and tools (axe, skewers) as well as a chariot. A change in burial practices at Veii can be detected at the end of the eighth century in the Orientalizing period, when child as well as adult graves are distinguished in view of exceptional and 'princely' characteristics that were meant to underline the social standing of the family (Nizzo 2011a, 62–3, 68; on the 'princely' burial phenomenon *cf.* also Cuozzo, Morris this volume; Veii is also briefly discussed in the chapters by Iaia and Rajala).

In light of the new data that has been made available at Verucchio, it is now possible to re-evaluate previous work through an integrated multidisciplinary approach. One of the objectives of this research concerns the representation of identity in the funerary context, and related changes associated with social dynamics. Traditional quali-quantitative analysis of funerary material culture considers only the number of grave goods and their quality in terms of rarity and prestige. However, this traditional approach does not take into account where and how the objects were placed in the grave, and the ritual significance of these specific funerary practices.

In contrast, in this chapter we shall examine possible differences in grave structure, furnishing and ritual practices in children's versus adults' graves. These aspects will be considered also from the perspective of the symbolic use of space within the grave. One of the primary aims of the recent excavations at Verucchio has been to gather information on the exact location of grave goods in the tombs. By paying close attention to depositional and post-depositional processes, we have been able to put forward a new viewpoint concerning what we have defined as the 'symbolic representation' of the dead. In particular, this specific methodological approach, which takes into consideration the ritual use of space within the grave in relation to various categories of grave goods, has allowed us to draw a distinction between: a) burial assemblages that might correspond to the deceased's personal belongings in life, or those which may have been attributed to them shortly before (or on) death; these are usually placed inside the urn, generally after being burnt with the deceased on the pyre; and b) a second set of grave goods, external to the urn or deposited in connection to the cinerary vessel, expressing the 'symbolic representation' of the deceased, which can differ from their identity as constructed through the burial assemblage placed in the urn.

It is worth stressing that our idea of 'symbolic representation' does not refer to the mere attribution of a symbolic value to artefacts. It has long been recognized that the urn could virtually recreate the body of the deceased through its shape, as in the case of anthropomorphic urns such as the canopies of Chiusi (on Chiusi *cf.* O' Donoghue this volume), or through the so-called practice of 'urn dressing' (Bentini *et al.* 2015; von Eles *et al.* 2015; *cf.* also Shipley this volume). We suggest that the 'symbolic representation' of the deceased had an additional meaning: as part of the funeral rite, it was a message addressed to the community of onlookers; as such, it was part of a communication system that served to preserve the social equilibrium among the different family groups that buried their dead in Verucchio's cemeteries, but also to promote social change.

A few specific and complex burials, recently excavated, are presented as 'case studies' below, with a focus on the markers of rank and role exhibited by children. All the data resulting from the various approaches detailed above will be considered together, in light of the social significance of the funerary treatment of children in Verucchio between the eighth and the first half of the seventh centuries BC.

Quantitative data and children's graves in Verucchio

Skeletal remains from 253 graves at Verucchio (almost all cremations) have been analysed by anthropologists, and the results revealed the presence of 71 children out of 296 individuals. These children were distributed in dozens of graves, most of which contained more than one person. Three more graves without human remains were attributed to children based on archaeological data (i.e. Lippi Tombs 3/1972 and 64/1972, which contains small bracelets, and Lippi Tomb 26/1972, with a small urn). Given the sample size, it is clear that children represent approximately one quarter of the buried population, and that more than half of these children were buried alone or with other children (as opposed to other adults).

As mentioned above, in the case of children the determination of sex can only be done archaeologically. At Verucchio the application of this method has suggested the presence of a large majority of females in the sample. It is difficult to interpret this information at present, which could depend on the fact that 'female' grave assemblages are more visible in the archaeological record. However, it is worth remembering that the greater presence of adult females in the cemeteries pertaining to many Iron Age Italian communities has been repeatedly discussed (e.g. von Eles in von Eles 2006, 148–50).

In order to shed light on the chronological distribution of child burials, some issues must be taken into account. Firstly, although the number of examined graves is considerable, many of them yielded no human remains. Secondly, none of the Verucchio cemeteries has been explored completely. For a large number of graves, very limited or no information is available (Lippi Podere Dolci 1984, 28 tombs; Lippi Podere Gardini 1962, 18 tombs), and the archaeological materials are often not preserved (Gentili 1985, with a review of previous bibliography). Thirdly, most graves dating from the earliest phase (ninth century BC) are concentrated in the Lavatoio cemetery, which was excavated in the nineteenth century. Here no human remains are available, with only two exceptions, one of them concerning a child (Lavatoio Fondo Ripa Tomb 64/1894). Only few graves in the Lippi cemetery have been dated to the first phase. These are insufficient for a general evaluation, as only two children are included (i.e. Lippi Tomb 39/1972, a double burial with an adult and a child, and Lippi Tomb 3/1972). Hence the detailed chronological analysis in this chapter does not take into account the ninth-century BC phase.

Most of the data examined in this chapter comes from the Lippi cemetery, where large numbers of graves from the eighth century BC have been explored, some of them recently and with particular attention paid to their ritual and depositional features. Before recent excavation campaigns, it was generally believed that the Lippi cemetery had been completely explored. It is now clear that the geomorphologic movements of the hill have caused the disappearance of many graves. The extent of the burial ground has also turned out to be larger than expected. Table 6.1 offers a summary of the available data.[5] These are almost exclusively from the Lippi, Moroni and Le Pegge cemeteries. Although we are conscious of the reduced statistical value of the data, we have nonetheless tried to evaluate some developments in the later phases (III to V; cf. Tables 6.2 and 6.3). Percentages have not been evaluated for the Le Pegge cemetery because of the low number of graves with analysed human remains.

Tables 6.1 and 6.2 show that the highest percentage (41.6%) of children appears in Phase II, whereas in Phase III the percentage of children is lower (23%). A significant change appears to occur in Phase IV: there is a consistent increase in the number of individuals that can be identified as either adults or children, although the great majority are adults, with children accounting for only 18.1% of the total. Yet the final phase (V) sees a new increase in the percentage of children in the sample (30.5–31%).

Before discussing how we might interpret these patterns, it is helpful to make some preliminary observations on multiple burials, individual child burials and the rituals and grave assemblages that characterize children's graves, whilst comparing

Table 6.1: Graves attributed to children, with indication of age and gender.

Necropolis	Grave No.	Child age	Depositions with children only (no. children in grave)	Depositions of children with adults
Ripa Lavatoio 1894	64	infans 2 ♀	1	
Lippi 1970	VII	infans 3 ♂		1
Lippi 1970	VIII	infans 1♀	2	
Lippi 1970	XI	infans 1 ND		1
Lippi 1970	XVI	ND ?		1
Lippi 1970	XVII	infans 1 ♀		1
Lippi 1970	XVIII	infans 2♀	1*	
Lippi 1972	1	ND ?	1	
Lippi 1972	2	infans 1 ?		1
Lippi 1972	3	ND ♀	1**	
Lippi 1972	6	infans 1♂		1
Lippi 1972	7	ND ?		1
Lippi 1972	10	ND ♀	1	
Lippi 1972	16	ND ?		1
Lippi 1972	18	infans 2 ?		1
Lippi 1972	26	ND ♀	1**	
Lippi 1972	34	ND ?		1
Lippi 1972	39	ND ?		1
Lippi 1972	55	ND ?	1*	
Lippi 1972	57	ND ♂	1*	
Lippi 1972	61	infans 3 ♀	1	
Lippi 1972	63	infans 1 ♀	1	
Lippi 1972	64	ND ♀	1**	
Lippi 1972	65	infans 2 ?		1
Lippi 1972	73	infans 2 ?		1
Lippi 1972	74	infans 2 ?	1	
Lippi 1972	75	infans 2 ♀	1	
Lippi 1972	76	infans 2 ♀	1	
Lippi 1972	77	infans 2 ♀	1	
Lippi 1972	81	infans 1 ?	1	
Lippi 1972	86	ND ♂	1	
Lippi 1972	88	infans 1 ?		1

(*Continued*)

Necropolis	Grave No.	Child age	Depositions with children only (no. children in grave)	Depositions of children with adults
Lippi 1972	92	ND ?		1
Lippi 1972	96	ND ?		1
Lippi 1972	100	infans 1 ♂		1
Lippi 1972	102	infans 1 ♀		1
Lippi 1972	111	infans 2 ♀	1	
Lippi 1972	116	ND ♀	1	
Lippi 1972	122Bis	infans 1 ?	1	
Lippi 1972	123	infans 1 ♂	1	
Lippi 1972	125	infans 1 ♂	1	
Lippi 1972	128	infans 2 ?	1	
Lippi 1972	129	infans 1 ?	1	
Lippi 1972	133	infans 3 ?	1	
Lippi 1972	134	ND ♂	1	
Lippi 1972	138	infans 3 ♂	1	
Lippi 1972	142	ND. ♀	1	
Lippi 1972	143	infans 1 ♀		1
Lippi 1972	147	infans 3 ♀	1	
Lippi 1972	158	infans 2 ?		1
Lippi 1972	162	ND ?		1
Lippi 2005	8a	infans 1 ♀	1*	
Lippi 2005	9	ND ?		1
Lippi 2005	18	infans 2 ♀	1	
Lippi 2005	20	infans 1 ♂	1	
Lippi 2005	20 bis	infans 2 ♂	1	
Lippi 2006	41	infans 2 ♀	1	
Lippi 2008	73	infans 2 ♂	1	
Lippi 2008	78	infans 1		
Lippi 2008	81	infans 2		1
Le Pegge 1970	3	1 infans 1 ♀2 infans 3	3	1
Le Pegge 1970	5	infans 2 ♀	1	
Moroni Semprini 1969	14	ND ♀		1
Moroni Semprini 1969	22	ND ♂		1

(Continued)

Necropolis	Grave No.	Child age	Depositions with children only (no. children in grave)	Depositions of children with adults
Moroni Semprini 1969	25	ND ?		1
Moroni Semprini 1969	26	infans 1 ♀	1	
Moroni Semprini 1969	27	ND ?		1
Moroni Semprini 1969	28	ND ♀	1	
Moroni Semprini 1969	32	infans 1 ?		1
Moroni Semprini 1969	36	infans 2 ♀	1	

Key: ND = not determined; gender: ♂ male ♀ female ? undetermined; * doubtful presence of a second individual; **archeological identification

Table 6.2: Numbers of identified individuals (adults and children) per phase and necropolis.

Phase	No. anthropologically identified individuals (adults and children)								
	Lippi			Moroni			Le Pegge		
	No. Ident.	Adults	Children	No. ident.	Adults	Children	No. ident.	Adults	Children
I	9	8	1	0	0	0	0	0	0
II	36	20	15	0	0	0	0	0	0
III	34	27	7	4	3	1	1	0	1
IV	101	82	17	20	16	4	5	5	0
V	58	37	17	11	8	3	4	1	3
?	12	3	1	0	0	0	0	0	0
Total	250	177	58	35	27	8	10	6	4

Table 6.3: Number of children in the cemetery and of burials including only children per phase.

Phase	No.anthropologically ident. (adults & children)	Total % children	% children in individual burials or with other children	% children with adults
II	36	41.6	80	4
III	39	23	77	2
IV	127	18.1	47,6	9
V	73	30.5–31	36.3	13
Total				28

them with adult burials. In Phase II, most of the child burials are either individual or include children only (80%). This situation is similar to that of Phase III, when despite the presence of fewer child burials, the percentage of graves including only children is only slightly lower than in Phase II (77%). As we have seen, Phase IV (Early Orientalizing period) shows a significant change in the cemetery population, with adults far outnumbering children. There is also a significant decrease in the number of individual child burials (41.1%). In the final phase (Phase V) there is an increase in the number of children but a lower number of individual child burials (36.3%), which continues the trend seen in previous phases.

Among the children's graves, different types of burials are attested: a) children buried alone; b) children buried with other children; c) children buried with adults. We shall only consider those graves where the presence of more than one individual is securely attested. This leaves out four graves (i.e. Lippi Tombs XVIII/1970, 55/1972, 57/1972 and 8/2005) where the presence of a second individual is possible but far from certain, as it is suggested only by the presence of one artefact that is at odds with the gender indicated by the overall grave assemblage (*cf.* above; a different case is that of the graves which contain several artefacts relating to different genders, even if the human remains do not confirm the presence of multiple burials).

The few cases of children buried with other children can be taken together with the 34 children who are buried individually. We therefore consider separately the 28 cases of children buried with adults or young adults (Table 6.3). In assessing the gender of adults when the results of the osteological analysis were uncertain, the archaeological indicators have been accepted, considering the high level of coincidence of the two methods at Verucchio (*cf.* above). In cases where the two methods provide different information, we base our analysis on the archaeological indicators whenever the anthropologists failed to offer a secure result. For reasons previously explained, the graves with no physical determination of biological sex, but which contain only 'feminine' funerary equipment, have been attributed to females. By considering all the data, we can presently say that in 15 cases the sampled children appear to have been buried with women, in five cases with men, whilst in other eight cases the gender of the adult cannot be determined. There are few cases of burials which contain three individuals including children. In Le Pegge Tomb 3/1970, one cinerary urn contained the remains of a newborn and two older children. Whilst all the deceased are of undetermined sex, the grave goods are exclusively 'feminine' (Fig. 6.4). We will discuss this case in more detail later, but for now we can put forward the hypothesis that, whilst two of the children were buried together, the third child might represent a previous deposition, given that the tomb contained fragments of a typologically older cinerary urn. All the three children possibly belonged to the same family group.

A different situation is offered by Lippi Tomb 18/1972, which contains the remains of three individuals all placed inside the same urn. These are one child and two adults, the latter possibly being a man and a woman who are not clearly identified from an archaeological point of view. No indication is given by the excavator (Gentili) as to whether the grave might have been 're-opened' at some point. Indeed, despite the attention paid to this issue during recent excavations, clear stratigraphic evidence of such a practice was never recognized. At present, therefore, we can only suggest that the individuals died at around the same time. These people might have belonged to the same family, although this cannot be proved. As is well known (e.g. Harbeck *et al.* 2011, 191–200), it is impossible to carry out DNA analysis on

Fig. 6.4: Selection of grave goods from Le Pegge Tomb 3/1970.

cremated bones that have undergone burning at high temperatures (above 800°C), which is the case of the Verucchio burials (Onisto 2015).

Another aspect to be examined is the distribution of age groups in child graves in relation to the chronological development of the burial areas (Table 6.4). At Verucchio, there does not seem to be marked variation in the presence of very young children through time (*infans* 1 and *infans* 2: cf. Table 6.5). From Phase II to Phase V, very young children are present in similar numbers. The difference seems to be more in the features of the graves, with some children being associated with very clear rank indicators, mainly in Phase IV, but at least once also in Phase V (Lippi Tomb 41/2006).

A topographical analysis of the distribution of child burials is feasible only for the Lippi cemetery. It is possible to offer some preliminary considerations on the general development of this cemetery in the ninth and eighth centuries BC (Boiardi and von Eles 1996; von Eles *et al.* 2015). We have considered the spatial distribution of child burials in view of all the different variables discussed above: chronology, age groups, presence of individual child graves, and presence of children in adult graves. Throughout the period in question, child burials are equally well distributed in all areas of the cemetery. No significant differences can be seen in the placement

Table 6.4: Graves where children are buried with adults.

Phase	Children buried with females (N = 15)	Children buried with males (N = 5)	Children buried with undetermined adult (N = 8)	Children buried with two adults (male and female) (N = 1)
I			Lippi 39/1972	
II	Lippi 2/1972 Lippi 92/1972	Lippi XI/1970		
III	Lippi XVI/1970	Lippi 102/1972		
IV	Lippi 34/1972 Lippi 65/1972 Lippi 73/1972 Lippi 88/1972 Lippi 96/1972 Lippi 143/1972 Moroni 27/1969		Lippi VII/1970 Lippi XVII/1970 Moroni 22/1969	Lippi 18/1972
V	Lippi 7/1972 Lippi 16/1972 Lippi 78/2008 Lippi 81/2008 Moroni 25/1969	Lippi 158/1972 Lippi 162/1972 Lippi 9/2005	Lippi 6/1972 Lippi 100/192 (possibly adult female) Moroni 14/1969 (possibly adult female) Moroni 32/1969	

Table 6.5: Distribution of children's age groups (individual burials).

Phase	Infans 1	Infans 2	Infans 3	Infans undetermined age	Total
I					0
II	Lippi 81/1972 Lippi 122 BIS/1972 Lippi 123/1972 Lippi 129/1972	Lippi 74/1972 Lippi 128/1972 Lippi 136/1972	Lippi 133/1972 Lippi 147/1972	Lippi 1/1972 Lippi 134/1972 Lippi 142/1972	12
III		Le Pegge 5/1970 Lippi VIII/1970 Lippi 111/1972	Lippi 138/1972	Lippi 86/1972 Moroni 28/1969	6
IV	Lippi 63/1972 Lippi 20/2005 Moroni 26/1969	Ripa 64/1894 Lippi 75/1972 Lippi 77/1972 Lippi 20Bis/2005 Lippi 73/2008 Moroni 36/1969		Lippi 10/1972 Lippi 64/1972	11
V		Lippi 76/1972 Lippi 18/2005 Lippi 41/2006	Lippi 61/1972	Lippi 116/1972	5
ND	Lippi 125/1972				1
Total					34

of children who are buried alone or with other children, and in the placement of children buried with adults. There is only a small group of tombs (10 graves) located at some distance from the others, where three small children are present (Lippi Tombs 122/1972, 123/1972 and 125/1972). All the three children in this group were granted individual burial, although this can hardly be considered significant from a statistical point of view.

Adult and child burials: small items and ritual differences

As a preliminary approach to the identification of archaeological indicators of child burials in Verucchio, we have taken into account individual child graves on the one hand, and the use of certain objects which are functional, but are of reduced size, on the other.

The presence of certain types of small (but not miniature) objects is not necessarily indicative of the deceased being a child. For example, a couple of small horse bits are present in Moroni Tomb 37/1969, a multiple grave containing two adults. A very small horse bit is also found in Le Pegge Tomb 9/1970, which includes an adult individual. Some helpful results can be gained from the analysis of individual child graves where small items are frequent, although such graves appear to be rare. Out of all the 34 individual child burials, eight include a small cinerary urn (Fig. 6.5; height <40 cm). Another possible case is that of Lippi Tomb 26/1972, where no bones are preserved. The personal ornaments placed in this grave are 'small' rather than 'miniature' items: bracelets with a diameter under six cm are generally considered one of the best archaeological indicators of child burials, and are certainly present in five child graves. There is, however, one case where a couple of small spiralled bracelets are associated with an adult male (Lippi Tomb 71/2008): the bracelet typology, however, might have determined the reduced diameter. More complicated is the case of earrings: Le Pegge Tomb 3/1970 yielded a couple of very small amber earrings that seem to integrate a set of very small objects. This set includes items such as spindle whorls and bobbins that can be considered miniature copies of functional items. Small amber earrings are present in other three graves. The difficulty arises from the fact that children are also sometimes buried with 'adult-size' ornaments. For example, Moroni Tomb 26 /1969 yielded not only 'normal-size' fibulae but also bronze belts, whilst two Moroni Semprini graves (Tombs A and B, with no preserved human bones) contained more than a couple of amber earrings of different size.

Fig. 6.5: Different-sized funerary urns: Lippi Tombs 122/1972 (adult) and 122B/1972 (child).

When comparing adult and child graves, no great differences are evident at first sight, particularly with regard to markers of prestige or rank. The 'symbolic representation' of children follows the same pattern adopted for adults, and does not seem to be connected with the real age and the role that the deceased had in life. No clear differences are apparent in the choice of grave structure: the most complex ones, with a *dolium* vase and separate spaces for the grave goods (*nicchia laterale*), are apparently the same for adults and children. This seems only partly related to the chronological development of the burial site, as simple pit graves continue to exist in the later phases.

The 'symbolic representation' of the dead person, obtained through the so-called practice of 'urn dressing' (*vestizione del cinerario*) and the placing of objects (weapons, tools and the like) outside the urn but in connection with the latter, involves similar percentages of children and adults (between 50% and 60% if one considers the undamaged graves) from Phase II to Phase V.[6] The children granted this ritual appear to have been both male and female.

It is in the selection of grave goods that some differences can be found, although these differences are not the most obvious or expected ones. For example, horse bits are present in 16 graves containing children but only three of these are individual burials of children (Lippi Tombs 111/1972 and 73/2008, and Le Pegge Tomb 5/1970). In some female graves there is indirect evidence for the use of chariots, as is shown by a special type of ringing pendant that is present only in women's graves. It is interesting to note that even some very rich and 'princely' graves such as Moroni Tomb 26/1969 did not yield artefacts associated with the possession or use of horses. This cannot be due to the owner of the grave being a female, as in Verucchio the number of horse bits in female graves is practically equal to that in men's graves. In contrast, weaving tools are very frequent in tombs pertaining to little girls.

Some interesting differences between children and adults appear in connection with the ritual funerary banquet. Bronze vessels apt to contain liquids are present in both children's and adults' graves, but no child granted an individual burial was associated with bronze vessels for solid food consumption (von Eles 2007). Some age-related differences concerning apparel have already been noted and discussed (Bentini and Boiardi in von Eles 2007), but we can now identify additional items that also appear to be age-specific. For example, amber fibulae are rare in adult male graves but never appear in association with male child burials. Little girls were never associated with a very particular type of belt buckle which is found in adult female graves (Bentini *et al.* in press; von Eles and Trocchi 2015). Extremely rare is a type of amber fibula apparently produced only in Verucchio upon specific request for certain 'princely' women's graves (i.e. *fibule ad arco rivestito cavo*: Boiardi and von Eles 2003).

Rituals in children's graves: the use of space and the 'symbolic representation' of males and females

During recent excavations and research, attention has been given to the structure and spatial organization of the graves. Hence, evidence is now available suggesting that the objects were deposited during the funeral according to precise rules distinguishing between burned objects collected from the pyre, and other artefacts used to 'symbolically represent' the dead social person.

Out of 13 children identified as males on the basis of archaeological gender markers, seven were buried with weapons. These children were generally represented as warriors with real-size weapons, which could not have been used by the children in question. These grave assemblages occasionally include ornaments such as serpentine fibulae, the so-called *fibule serpeggianti*, that in Verucchio do not appear to be part of the 'feminine' costume.

In the earlier phases, male child grave assemblages included javelins or spearheads and knives. Lippi Tomb 123/1972 (*infans* 1), which can be dated to the early eighth century BC (Phase II), contained a knife placed outside the urn. Inside the urn was a javelin or spearhead. An analogous set of weapons appears in an adult grave dating to the same period (Lippi Tomb 32/1972). In both cases the placement of the weapons inside the urn suggests (in our view) the intention of attributing these artefacts to the dead as their personal belongings (von Eles *et al.* 2015). Probably to the same period and to the same family group belongs another male child grave (Lippi Tomb 125/1972) also containing a javelin or spearhead, as reported by Gentili (Gentili 2003, 352). In Verucchio Phase III, Lippi Tomb 86/1972 includes a knife and a bronze axe. Unfortunately, the lack of precise information on the funerary ritual does not allow us to understand whether the objects were treated in death as personal belongings of the deceased.

In Phase IV there are four burials belonging to young males. Lippi Tomb 19/1972 belonged to a 15-year-old (±36 months) individual, strictly speaking not an *infans* and possibly already considered an adult; his set of weapons includes one javelin point and two knives. Lippi Tomb 73/2008, belonging to a 6–8-year-old boy (*infans* 2), is a very peculiar 'princely' grave. Inside the pit was a *dolium* containing a biconical urn; beside the *dolium*, in a lateral separate space, was a wooden throne (Mazzoli and Pozzi 2015), above which a bronze vase was deposited (Fig. 6.6). The weapons were disposed of in the grave according to a clearly planned sequence of actions: a high crested bronze helmet and a spear were placed in the most visible external space outside the *dolium*; a knife was placed near the urn, and inside the urn was the 'personal panoply' including a javelin point, two more knives and a spear. The 'symbolic representation' of the dead is emphatically that of a warrior, obviously beyond what the dead person's young age would have allowed, whilst the throne and bronze vessel show him as a member of an important family who probably played a significant role in ritual ceremonies.

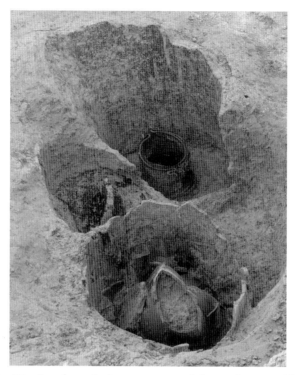

Fig. 6.6: Lippi Tomb 73/2008 during excavation; dolium, *throne and bronze vase.*

Lippi Tomb 20/2005 (*infans* 1, approximately 5 months at death) and Lippi Tomb 20BIS/2005 (*infans* 2: 3–5-year-old child) represent another peculiar situation. Two *dolia* were placed in the same pit at the same time, or one shortly after the other, each containing a cinerary urn. In both cases the 'symbolic representation' of the dead was constructed through the deposition of a small-sized shield, associated to a bronze crested helmet in Tomb 20/2005 and to a knife in Tomb 20BIS/2005, which also yielded a spear deposited outside the *dolium*. In Tomb 20/2005 a sword and a spear were among the burnt remains from the pyre, which suggests that they may have been considered personal belongings of the neonate. By contrast, Tomb 20BIS yielded a group of bronze broken objects including the fragments of an axe and small bronze ingots, which would have possessed some economic value like a 'hoard'. Tomb 20/2005, belonging to the younger child, also contained a complete banqueting pottery set which is not present in Tomb 20BIS. Similarities in the complex structure and in the grave-good sets are apparently due to both children sharing the same ascribed aristocratic rank, while their different 'symbolic representation' probably suggests differences in their future roles as 'warriors', which were already defined at an early age.

Judging from the archaeological data alone, females are much better represented among the children buried at Verucchio. Among all the sampled children's graves, there might be 31 females, 20 of whom were given individual burials. Seven graves date to Phases II and III, eight to Phase IV and five to Phase V. Among the age groups, the better represented is the *infans* 2 age class (3–7-year-old children). However, there are also children under the age of 3 and 'adolescents'. Furthermore, in all phases there are some children whose age cannot be determined.

Children are among some of the most lavishly buried individuals at Verucchio. In the early eighth century BC, when grave furnishings were still generally simple in terms of personal ornaments, Lippi Tomb 134/1972 (*infans* of undetermined age) featured precious fibulae and amber beads. Weaving tools are very rare (one spindle whorl in Lippi Tomb 147/1972). In Phase III (central decades of the eighth century BC) the 'costume' seems to change: for example, Lippi Tomb 111/1972 (*infans* 2), contained a high number of bronze and amber fibulae. It also yielded a scarab and a rich set of weaving tools. A similar case is that of Le Pegge Tomb 5/1970 (*infans* 2), whereas Lippi Tomb 138/1972 (*infans* 3) contained a less distinguished set of grave goods.

As already noted with regard to male child burials from Phase IV, the high social standing of the family is strongly stressed in child tombs. Moroni Tomb 26/1969, belonging to a little girl under 3 years of age, can be regarded as a truly 'princely' grave: in addition to an extremely rich set of personal ornaments and tools, and a pottery banquet set, there were an engraved wooden throne and additional wooden furniture (footstool, table, box and musical instrument: von Eles 2012). Moroni Tomb 36/1969 is not quite as rich, but clearly belonged to an élite family as well.

In the final phase (Phase V), the graves for which the gender of the dead was determined are all female burials. There are no truly 'princely' graves. However, Lippi Tomb 41/2006 belongs to a 4-year-old child, buried in an individual urn, but in the same pit with an adult female; both were buried with high status markers. We have already mentioned Le Pegge Tomb 3/1970, which presumably belonged to three girls buried inside one cinerary urn with precious objects of reduced size. Many other objects are of normal size and it cannot be excluded that one of the older individuals was a pre-adolescent girl. This is also suggested by a small clay statuette clearly showing a lying female, who does not seem to be a child as the breasts are clearly indicated.

Also from Phase V is Lippi Tomb 9/2005, where the remains of an adult and a child have been identified in the same urn. This grave poses an additional problem concerning the use of space within the grave. Two separate groups of burnt and broken metal objects (*defunzionalizzati*) were placed outside the *dolium*: one contains personal ornaments and weapons (an iron sword and a large knife), whilst the second group only contains items connected with the use of horses. It is likely that the separate deposition had a ritual meaning which is difficult to understand at present.

Discussion and conclusion: the social status of children in Villanovan Verucchio

Summarizing the data discussed above, we can note a number of key points. In Verucchio Phase I, children are present but the data available are insufficient to determine their percentage. During Phase II (early eighth century BC) the percentage of children is close to what is usually expected in pre-Jennerian societies (50%: Morris 1987). Surprisingly, in the later Phases III and IV the percentage is definitely lower than expected, with a limited increase in Phase V (*cf.* Table 6.2). As apparently there are no observable differences in the treatment of children during the different phases (e.g. presence of children in single or double graves, topographical distribution of child burials in the cemetery space), we believe that the lower percentage of child burials may be due to a lower mortality rate. Indeed, the parallel increase in adults who reach older ages in Phases IV and V may suggest improved living conditions for the élite groups of that time.

The number of very young children (*infans* 1) does not vary significantly from the early eighth century BC to Phase V (Table 6.3). Also, the 'honour' of being buried individually (or with other children, but not in adult graves) is awarded to children from the early eighth century BC onwards. The incidence of this custom follows a different pattern, with a continuing decrease as time goes on, from 80% in the early eighth century to much lower percentages at the end of the eighth and in the seventh centuries BC. Particularly important seems to be the high percentage of individual burials given to children under 3 years of age.

The number of multiple burials, which is small in the first phase, sees an increase that peaks in the final phase (Phase V), suggesting that this was a deliberate ritual choice and not merely a reflection of chance events. The issue of multiple burials involving not only children buried with adults, but also different combinations of age categories (i.e. children buried with other children, children buried with adults, adults buried with other adults) is difficult to explain, but could be related to a wish to emphasize family relations.

Judging from the funerary ideology, between the ninth and seventh centuries BC children were considered full members of the community, or at least of their families. These families were probably a select minority that used the burial grounds that have thus far been discovered in Verucchio. There is a real possibility that the groups who first settled on the Verucchio hill in the Early Iron Age might have already been structured in socially stratified families: in the earliest Lavatoio cemetery, the graves with a complex structure and rich furnishings form separate clusters which include distinguished female tombs.

The situation in Verucchio seems quite different from what has been suggested for the Iron Age in Latium and Pontecagnano (Bartoloni 2003; Nizzo 2011a). In the Tyrrhenian and southern Villanovan cemeteries, it is only at the end of the eighth century BC that children start to be regularly included in the burial ground, thereby highlighting the importance of family ties and family rank. In Verucchio, however, children are definitely not excluded from formal burial already in the Early Iron Age.

When considering the ritual practice and grave assemblages, there is no clear difference between the tombs of adults and children. Childhood does not seem to have been considered as a distinct category in the context of burial. Children seem to have been recognized from an early age as members of the social group and treated as such. The funerary treatment given to children at Verucchio can be read as a projection of social expectations about the children's future role and status in the community. High-standing families at Verucchio had very clear ideas about what their children should grow up to be, and the funerary context afforded an ideal venue for these ideas and expectations to be expressed to an audience of onlookers. This is why the grave structure, the 'symbolic representation' of the dead and the selection of grave goods all become in time more and more important and functional to the expression of family status. This is particularly clear in the case of young boys who are buried with all the attributes of warriors, or in the case of little girls who are associated with personal ornaments usually linked to adults. Even extremely significant items such as wooden thrones are sometimes included in tombs belonging to children of both genders.

In the case of multiple burials, the most prestigious grave goods cannot always be attributed to the adult. The existence of family relations between the deceased can be suggested for multiple burials, or when children are buried in individual cinerary urns placed inside or very close to burial structures reserved for adults. Within the family groups, there certainly were individual differences in role, which were probably already defined at an early age. This is shown, for example, by Lippi Tombs 20 and 20BIS/2005, both of which share the same aristocratic status but are characterized by different 'symbolic representations' of the dead. Overall, in the Early Orientalizing period the aristocratic families of Verucchio used funerary rituals as a key means of emphasizing their social standing and power, probably within a 'dynamic equilibrium' involving different groups. Attempts at expressing the potential of children as full members of the aristocratic community through funerary rites and the 'symbolic representation' of the deceased, formed an essential part of the communication system that developed in Verucchio, and was crucial to the negotiation of power in this community of first-millennium BC Italy.

Notes

1. Work by our team on the funerary rituals and structures in Verucchio started with the publication of Lippi Tomb 89/1972 (von Eles 2002; 2006; also Boiardi and von Eles 2006) and continued with a conference held in Verucchio in 2011 (von Eles *et al.* 2015). All the work has been supported by the *Soprintendenza per i Beni Archeologici dell'Emilia Romagna* and by the Verucchio Municipal Archaeological Museum. Photos courtesy of the *Soprintendenza*. Preliminary reports of the 2005–2009 excavation campaigns, soon to be published, will offer many new data.

2. The situation from this point of view is highly variable: for examples in Etruria *cf.* Trucco 2006, 97. In Bologna, at the recently excavated Iron Age cemetery of Borgo Panigale, the number of examined urns was the same as that of the individuals identified (i.e. 167: Cavazzuti 2015).

3. It was possible to use dental eruption as an age indicator, after Ubelaker (1989). The dental germs were well preserved in children compared with the teeth of adults, since children's teeth are more resistant to combustion because they are still inside the jaws. As Holck (1997) argues, the accuracy of age estimates based on human skeletons decreases proportionally with age: hence children's ages can be determined with relatively high precision.

4. Dasen 2004, 9; Dedet 2008a, 6; 2008b; Guimier-Sorbets and Morizot 2010, 11–17; Papaikonomou 2006, 239. For a general discussion on issues concerning pregnancy, breastfeeding and child mortality *cf.* Rollet and Morel 2000; Margaret Mead's influence (*Coming of Age in Samoa*) can be clearly seen in recent studies: Cohen and Rutter 2007; Neils and Oakley 2006.

5. We are aware that the numbers are extremely limited for statistical analyses, even as regards the Moroni cemetery, but we believe it can be useful to examine these numbers in comparison with the fuller dataset from Lippi.

6. Phase II: Lippi Tombs 123/1972, 129/1972 and 143/1972; Phase III: Lippi Tombs 11/1972, 138/1972, Le Pegge Tomb 3/1970, and Moroni Tomb 28/1969; Phase IV: Lippi Tombs 63/1972, 20/2005, 20BIS/2005 and 73/2005, and Moroni Tombs 26/1969 and 36/1969; Phase V: Lippi Tombs 116/1972, 18/2005 and 41/2006.

Bibliography

Bartoloni, G. (2003) *Le Società dell'Italia Primitiva. Lo Studio delle Necropoli e la Nascita delle Aristocrazie*. Roma, Carocci.

Bartoloni, G. and Delpino, F. (2005) *Oriente e Occidente: Metodi e Discipline a Confronto. Riflessioni sulla Cronologia dell'Età del Ferro in Italia. Atti dell'Incontro di Studi (Roma, 30–31 Ottobre 2003)* (Mediterranea 1, 2004). Pisa–Roma, Istituti Editoriali e Poligrafici Internazionali.

Becker, M.J. (2007) Childhood among the Etruscans: Mortuary programs at Tarquinia as indicators of the transition to adult status. In A. Cohen and J.B. Rutter (eds) *Constructions of Childhood in Ancient Greece and Italy* (Hesperia Supplement 41), 281–292. Princeton, American School of Classical Studies at Athens.

Belardelli, C., Giardino, C. and Malizia, A. (1990) *L'Europa a Sud e a Nord delle Alpi alle Soglie della Svolta Protourbana. Necropoli della Tarda Età dei Campi di Urne dell'Area Circumalpina Centro-orientale*. Treviso, Edizioni Unigrafica.

Bentini, L. and Boiardi, A. (2007) Le ore della bellezza. Mundus muliebris: Abito, costume funerario, rituale della personificazione, oggetti da toletta. In P. von Eles (ed.) *Le Ore e i Giorni delle Donne. Dalla Quotidianità alla Sacralità tra VIII e VII Secolo a.C.. Catalogo della Mostra (Museo Civico Archeologico di Verucchio, 14 Giugno 2007–6 Gennaio 2008)*, 128–138. Verucchio, Pazzini Editore.

Bentini, L., Boiardi, A., Di Lorenzo, G., von Eles, P., Di Penta, S., Mazzoli, M. and Trocchi, T. (in press) Verucchio tra X e VII sec. a.C.: Identità culturale, èlites e produzioni artigianali. *In Atti della XLV Riunione Scientifica Istituto Italiano di Preistoria e Protostoria (Modena, 26–31 Ottobre 2010)*. Firenze, Istituto Italiano di Preistoria e Protostoria.

Bentini, L., Boiardi, A., Di Lorenzo, G., von Eles, P., Rodriguez, E., Cerruti, G., Di Penta, S., Ossani, M. and Ghini, L. (2015) Tra simbolo e realtà. Identità, ruoli, funzioni a Verucchio. In P. von Eles, L. Bentini, P. Poli and E. Rodriguez (eds) *Immagini di Uomini e di Donne dalle Necropoli Villanoviane di Verucchio. Giornate di Studio Dedicate a Renato Peroni (Verucchio, 20–22 Aprile 2011)*. Borgo S. Lorenzo, All'Insegna del Giglio.

Bianchin Citton, E., Gambacurta, G. and Ruta Serafini, A. (1998) (eds) *...Presso l'Adige Ridente...Recenti Rinvenimenti Archeologici da Este a Montagnana. Catalogo della Mostra (Este, Museo Nazionale Atestino, 21 Febbraio 1998-21 Febbraio 1999)*. Padova, ADLE.

Boiardi, A. and von Eles, P. (1996) Verucchio, la comunità villanoviana: Proposte per un'analisi. In A.M. Bietti Sestrieri and V. Kruta (eds) *The Iron Age in the Mediterranean Area: Archaeological Materials as Indicator of Social Structure and Organization. Congresso Internazionale di Scienze Preistoriche e Protostoriche (Forlì, 1996)*, 45–66. Forlì, A.B.A.C.O.

Boiardi, A. and von Eles, P. (2003) Fibule in ambra di Verucchio: Appunti per uno studio sulla produzione e la tecnologia. In E. Formigli (ed.) *Fibulae. Dall'Età del Bronzo all'Alto Medioevo. Tecnica e Tipologia*, 107–124. Firenze, Polistampa.

Boiardi, A. and von Eles, P. (2006) Codici funerari: Dalle 'regole' alla situazione 'eccezionale' o viceversa? *In Studi di Protostoria in Onore di Renato Peroni*, 602–608. Borgo S. Lorenzo, All'Insegna del Giglio.

Boiardi, A., von Eles, P. and Poli, P. (2006) Ornamenti e non solo. L'uso ed il significato dell'ambra nelle produzioni di Verucchio. In D. Cocchi Genick (ed.) *Atti della XXXIX Riunione Scientifica dell'Istituto Italiano di Preistoria e Protostoria (Firenze, 25-27 Novembre 2004)*, 1590–1597. Firenze, Istituto Italiano di Preistoria e Protostoria.

Cavazzuti, C. (2015) Aspetti del rituale crematorio nella necropoli dell'età del ferro di Borgo Panigale. Ossilegi differenziati. In P. von Eles, L. Bentini, P. Poli and E. Rodriguez (eds) *Immagini di Uomini e di Donne dalle Necropoli Villanoviane di Verucchio. Giornate di Studio Dedicate a Renato Peroni (Verucchio, 20-22 Aprile 2011)*. Borgo S. Lorenzo, All'Insegna del Giglio.

Cohen, A. and Rutter, J. (eds) *Constructions of Childhood in Ancient Greece and Italy* (Hesperia Supplement 41). Princeton, American School of Classical Studies at Athens.

Dasen, V. (2004) *Naissance et Petite Enfance dans l'Antiquité. Actes du Colloque de Fribourg (28 Novembre-1er December 2001)*. Fribourg, Academie Press.

Dedet, B. (2008a) *Les Enfants dans la Société Protohistorique: L'Exemple du Sud de la France* (Collectiòn dell' École francaise de Rome 396). Roma, École française de Rome.

Dedet, B. (2008b) La mort du nouveau-nè et du nourrisson dans le sud de la France protohistorique (Ixe-I siècles avant J.C.). In F. Gusi Jener, S. Muriel and C. Olària (eds) *Nasciturus, Infans, Puerulus Vobis Mater Terra: La Muerte en la Infancia*, 143–182. Castellò, Diputacio de Castello.

Díaz-Andreu, M., Lucy, S., Bacić, S. and Edwards, D.N. (2005) (eds) *The Archaeology of Identity: Approaches to Gender, Age, Status, Ethnicity and Religion*. London–New York, Routledge.

Dore, A. (2005) Il villanoviano I-III di Bologna, problemi di cronologia relativa e assoluta. In G. Bartoloni and F. Delpino (2005) *Oriente e Occidente: Metodi e Discipline a Confronto. Riflessioni sulla Cronologia dell'Età del Ferro in Italia. Atti dell'Incontro di Studi (Roma, 30-31 Ottobre 2003)* (Mediterranea 1, 2004), 252–292. Pisa-Roma, Istituti Editoriali e Poligrafici Internazionali.

Eles, P. von (2002) (ed.) *Guerriero e Sacerdote. Autorità e Comunità nell'Età del Ferro a Verucchio. La Tomba del Trono* (Quaderni di Archeologia dell'Emilia Romagna 6). Borgo S. Lorenzo, All'Insegna del Giglio.

Eles, P. von (2006) (ed.) *La Ritualità Funeraria tra Età del Ferro e Orientalizzante in Italia. Atti del Convegno (Verucchio 26-27 Giugno 2002)*. Pisa-Roma, Istituti Editoriali e Poligrafici Internazionali.

Eles, P. von (2007) (ed.) *Le Ore e i Giorni delle Donne. Dalla Quotidianità alla Sacralità tra VIII e VII Secolo a.C.. Catalogo della Mostra (Museo Civico Archeologico di Verucchio, 14 Giugno 2007-6 Gennaio 2008)*. Verucchio, Pazzini Editore.

Eles, P. von (2012) Necropoli Moroni, Tomba 26/1969. La tomba della 'principessina'. In N.C. Stampolidis and M. Yannopulou (eds) *Principesse del Mediterraneo all'Alba della Storia. Catalogo della Mostra (Atene, 2012)*, 241–242. Athens, Museum of Cycladic Art.

Eles, P. von (2014) Research in Villanovan necropoleis of Verucchio, 9th to 7th century BC. In A.J. Nijboer, S.L. Willemsen, P.A.J. Attema and J.F. Seubers (eds) *Research into Pre-Roman Burial Grounds in Italy* (Caeculus: Papers in Medierranean Archaeology and Greek & Roman Studies), 83–102. Leuven, Peeters.

Eles, P. von, Bentini, L., Poli,, P. and Rodriguez, E.(2015) (eds) *Immagini di Uomini e di Donne dalle Necropoli Villanoviane di Verucchio. Giornate di Studio Dedicate a Renato Peroni (Verucchio, 20-22 Aprile 2011)*. Borgo S. Lorenzo, All'Insegna del Giglio.

Eles, P. von and Pacciarelli, M. (in press) La Romagna dal Bronzo Finale all'età orientalizzante. *In Atti della XLV Riunione Scientifica Istituto Italiano di Preistoria e Protostoria (Modena, 26-31 Ottobre 2010)*. Firenze, Istituto Italiano di Preistoria e Protostoria.

Eles, P. von and Trocchi, T. (2015) Artigiani e committenti: Officine locali e produzioni specializzate a Verucchio tra VIII e VII sec. a.C.. In P. von Eles, L. Bentini, P. Poli and E. Rodriguez (eds) *Immagini di Uomini e di Donne dalle Necropoli Villanoviane di Verucchio. Giornate di Studio Dedicate a Renato Peroni (Verucchio, 20-22 Aprile 2011)*. Borgo S. Lorenzo, All'Insegna del Giglio.

Eles, P. von, Siboni, M. and Zanardi, M. (2009) Verucchio, a center of amber craftmanship and distribution in Iron Age Italy. In A. Palavestra, C.W. Beck and J.M. Todd (eds) *Amber in Archaeology. Proceedings of the Fifth International Conference on Amber in Archaeology (Belgrade, 2006)*, 210–219. Belgrade, Belgrade National Museum.

Formigli, E. 2003 (ed.) *Fibulae. Dall'Età del Bronzo all'Alto Medioevo. Tecnica e tipologia*. Firenze, Polistampa.

Gambacurta, G. and Ruta Serafini, A. (1998) Être reliés dans la mort: Deux exemples du rituel funéraire de l'Âge du Fer de Padua et d'Este. *European Journal of Archaeology* 1(1), 91–115.

Gentili, G.V. (1985) *Il Villanoviano Veruchiese nella Romagna Orientale ed il Sepolcreto Moroni* (Studi e Documenti di Archeologia I). Bologna, Nuova Alfa Editoriale.

Gentili, G.V. (1986) L'età del ferro a Verucchio: Cronologia degli scavi e scoperte, ed evoluzione della letteratura archeologica. *In Studi e Documenti di Archeologia II*, 1–44. Bologna, Nuova Alfa Editoriale.

Gentili, G.V. (2003) *Verucchio Villanoviana. Il Sepolcreto in Località Le Pegge e la Necropoli al piede della Rocca Malatestiana*. Roma, Giorgio Bretschneider.

Guimier-Sorbets, A.M. and Morizot, Y. (2010) *L'Enfant et la Mort dans l'Antiquitè I. Nouvelles Recherches dans les Nècropoles Grecques. Le Signalement des Tombes d'Enfants. Actes de la Table Ronde Internationale Organisèe à Athènes-Ecole Francaise d'Athènes (29-30 Mai 2008)* (Travaux de la Maison René Ginouvès 12). Paris, De Boccard.

Harberck, M., Schleuder, R., Schneider, J., Wiechmann, I., Schmahl, W.W. and Grupe, G. (2011) Research potential and limitations of trace analyses of cremated remains. *Forensic Science International* 204, 191–200.

Holck, P. (1997) *Cremated Bones. Antropologiske Skrifter nr. 1c*. Oslo, Anatomical Institute, University of Oslo.

Lucy, S.J. (1997) Housewives, warriors and slaves? Sex and gender in Anglo-Saxon burials. In J. Moore and E. Scott (eds) *Invisible People and Processes: Writing Gender and Childhood into European Archaeology*, 150–168. London–New York, Leicester University Press.

Lucy, S.J. (2000) Sviluppi dell'archeologia funeraria negli ultimi 50 anni. In N. Terrenato (ed.) *Archeologia Teorica: 10.mo Ciclo di Lezioni sulla Ricerca Applicata in Archeologia (Certosa di Pontignano, Siena, 9-14 Agosto 1999)*, 311–322. Borgo S. Lorenzo, All'Insegna del Giglio.

Mazzoli, M. and Pozzi, A. (2015) I troni di Verucchio tra archeologia e iconografia. In P. von Eles, L. Bentini, P. Poli and E. Rodriguez (eds) *Immagini di Uomini e di Donne dalle Necropoli Villanoviane di Verucchio. Giornate di Studio Dedicate a Renato Peroni (Verucchio, 20-22 Aprile 2011)*. Borgo S. Lorenzo, All'Insegna del Giglio.

Morigi Govi, C. (1976) La prima età del ferro in Emilia Romagna. *In Atti della XIX Riunione Scientifica dell'Istituto Italiano di Preistoria e Protostoria in Emilia Romagna (Forlì, 11-14 Ottobre 1975)*, 163–180. Firenze, Istituto Italiano di Preistoria e Protostoria.

Morris, I. (1987) *Burial and Ancient Society. The Rise of the Greek City-state*. Cambridge, Cambridge University Press.

Neils, J. and Oakley, J.H. (2003) *Coming of Age in Ancient Greece: Images of Childhood from the Classical Past*. New Haven, Yale University Press.

Nizzo, V. (2011a) «Antenati bambini». Visibilità e invisibilità dell'infanzia nei sepolcreti dell'Italia tirrenica dalla prima età del Ferro all'Orientalizzante: Dalla discriminazione funeraria alla costruzione dell'identità. In V. Nizzo (ed.) *Dalla Nascita alla Morte: Antropologia e Archeologia a Confronto. Atti dell'Incontro Internazionale di Studi in Onore di Claude Lévi-Strauss (Roma, Museo Nazionale Preistorico Etnografico "Luigi Pigorini", 21 Maggio 2010)*, 51–94. Roma, E.S.S. Editorial Service System.

Nizzo, V. (2011b) (ed.) *Dalla Nascita alla Morte: Antropologia e Archeologia a Confronto. Atti dell'Incontro Internazionale di Studi in Onore di Claude Lévi-Strauss (Roma, Museo Nazionale Preistorico Etnografico "Luigi Pigorini", 21 Maggio 2010)*. Roma, E.S.S. Editorial Service System.

Onisto, N. (2015) Lo studio antropologico dei resti cremati di Verucchio. In P. von Eles, L. Bentini, P. Poli and E. Rodriguez (eds) *Immagini di Uomini e di Donne dalle Necropoli Villanoviane di Verucchio. Giornate di Studio Dedicate a Renato Peroni (Verucchio, 20-22 Aprile 2011)*. Borgo S. Lorenzo, All'Insegna del Giglio.

Panichelli, S. (1990) Sepolture bolognesi dell'VIII secolo a.C.. In G.L. Carancini (ed.) *Miscellanea Protostorica* (Archeologia Perusina 6), 187–408. Roma, Giorgio Bretschneider.

Parker Pearson, M. (1999) *The Archaeology of Death and Burial*. Stroud, Sutton.

Papaikonomou, I.D. (2006) L'interprétation des "jouets" trouvés dans les tombes d'enfants d'Abdère. In A.M. Guimier-Sorbets, M.B. Chatzopoulos and Y. Morizot (eds) *Rois, Cités, Nécropoles: Institutions, Rites et Monuments en Macédoine. Actes des Colloques de Nanterre (Décembre 2002) et d'Athènes (Janvier 2004)* (MELEMATA 45), 239–248. Paris–Athènes, De Boccard.

Peroni, R. (1981) (ed.) *Necropoli e Usi Funerari nell'Età del Ferro*. Bari, De Donato.

Peroni, R. (1994) *Introduzione alla Protostoria Italiana*. Bari, Laterza.

Peroni, R. and Ferrante, F. (2005) Discussione e interventi. In G. Bartoloni and F. Delpino (2005) *Oriente e Occidente: Metodi e Discipline a Confronto. Riflessioni sulla Cronologia dell'Età del Ferro in Italia. Atti dell'Incontro di Studi (Roma, 30-31 Ottobre 2003)* (Mediterranea 1, 2004), 387–388. Pisa–Roma, Istituti Editoriali e Poligrafici Internazionali.

Quesada Sanz, F. (2012) Mujeres, amazonaz, tumbas y armas: Una aproximación transcultural. In L. Prados, C. Lopez and J. Parra (eds) *La Arquelogia Funeraria Desde una Perspectiva de Género* (Colección Estudios 145), 317–364. Madrid, Universidad Autónoma de Madrid.

Rollet, C. and Morel, M.F. (2000) *Des Bébés et des Hommes: Tradition et Modernité des soins aux Tout-pètits*. Paris, Editeur Albin Michel.

Sofaer Derevenski, J. (1997) Engendering children, engendering archaeology. In J. Moore and E. Scott (eds) *Invisible People and Processes: Writing Gender and Childhood into European Archaeology*, 192–202. London–New York, Leicester University Press.

Sofaer Derevenski, J. (2000) (ed.) *Children and Material Culture*. London–New York, Routledge.

Tamburini Müeller, M.E. (2006) *La Necropoli Campo del Tesoro-Lavatoio di Verucchio (RN)*. San Lazzaro di Savena (BO), Campomarzo Editore.

Trucco, F. (2006) Considerazioni sul rituale funerario in Etruria meridionale all'inizio dell'Età del Ferro alla luce delle nuove ricerche a Tarquinia. In P. von Eles (ed.) *La Ritualità Funeraria tra Età del Ferro e Orientalizzante in Italia. Atti del Convegno (Verucchio, 26-27 Giugno 2002)*, 95–102. Pisa–Roma, Istituti Editoriali e Poligrafici Internazionali.

Ubelaker, D.H. (1989) *Human Skeletal Remains*. Taraxacum, Washington.

Vanzetti, A. (1992) Le sepolture a incinerazione a più deposizioni nella protostoria dell'Italia nordorientale. *Rivista di Scienze Preistoriche* 44, 155–209.

Chapter 7

Quid in nomine est? What's in a name: re-contextualizing the princely tombs and social change in ancient Campania

Owain Morris

Introduction

The term 'princely tomb' is used to refer to a series of élite graves found around the Mediterranean that are of an especially rich and ostentatious character (on the 'princely tomb' phenomenon in Campania and Etruria *cf.* also Cuozzo this volume). Such tombs are in striking contrast to their more humble contemporaries due to the standardized set of luxurious objects they include. The presence of Orientalizing imports, for example, attest to pan-Mediterranean connections and signal a period of heightened connectivity. The prominence of these so-called 'princes' in the cemeteries of Etruria, Latium and Campania from the mid-eighth century BC, has led to their association with the visible social transformations in Early Iron Age Italy (Fig. 7.1). Furthermore, an absence of any concrete evidence for the élite during the earliest phases of these communities has favoured the notion of egalitarianism (e.g. Cerchiai 1994; d'Agostino 1988). This was apparently followed by a phase of social stratification and the emergence of these 'princely' individuals. The traditional interpretation of these figures posits them as a key stage along a one-way evolutionary scheme from primitivism to the state (Morris 1999, 57). An evolution towards the state is viewed as a "natural conclusion to this long process" of social change (d'Agostino 1999a, 82). This long process begins in the ninth century BC and although it is believed to result from internal social changes, these dynamics apparently accelerate with the assistance of external catalysts (e.g. Cerchiai 2005; d'Agostino 1988).

Princely burials in Greece and Cyprus are widely held up as the prototypes behind a pan-Mediterranean phenomenon. Many scholars argue that the 'princely' burial type was exported to Italy by the Euboeans who established themselves at Pithekoussai and Cumae. Fondo Artiaco Tomb 104 at Cumae (*c.* 725 BC) is generally assumed to be the inspiration behind other similar graves in Campania, Latium and Etruria (Cuozzo 2007, 250; d'Agostino 2011, 45–8; Frederiksen 1984, 71–2). The transmission of these new funerary practices supposedly provoked a cultural revolution in Italy (Cerchiai 1995, 69–8; d'Agostino 1999a). Though the indigenous settlements

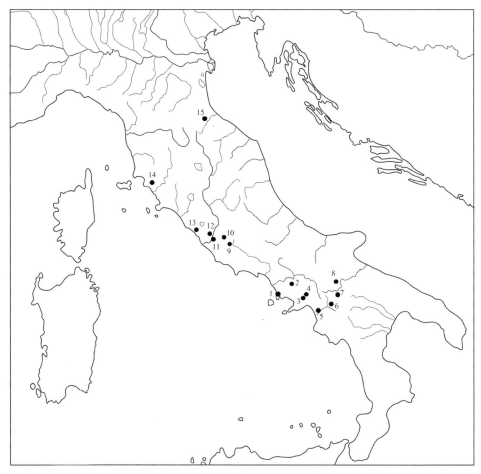

Fig. 7.1: Map of Italy with main sites mentioned in the chapter: 1. Cumae (facing the Isle of Ischia); 2. Calatia; 3. San Marzano; 4. San Valentino Torio; 5. Pontecagnano; 6. Oliveto-Citra; 7. Cairano; 8. Bisaccia; 9. Praeneste; 10. Osteria dell'Osa; 11. Rome; 12. Veii; 13. Caere; 14. Vetulonia; 15. Verucchio (elaboration R. Scopacasa, base map by C. Iaia).

of Campania were apparently in a stage of early development, some believe that contact with the nearby Euboeans brought about the "birth of the élite" within these communities (*cf.* Cerchiai 2010, 22–8; d'Agostino 1988, 537–44). The emergence of élite burials in Italy is thereby associated with the formation of the *gens*, a later Roman political term that signified a patron-client relationship (Colonna 2002a, 198–9).

Such a normative explanation presents a series of issues, especially with regard to the use of nomenclature. By adhering to a strict definition of what constitutes a 'princely' tomb, scholars have imposed a "single abstract model on the data" (Morris 1999, 57–8) and permitted a diffusionist interpretation of the geographic distribution of these burials. This view smacks of unilateral Hellenization: the supposedly more advanced Greeks brought this burial type to Italy and became the catalysts behind social change. The adoption of Greek customs by élites in Italy apparently requires no further explanation, the process seems to occur mechanically leaving many issues on local agency unconsidered. The notion of these 'princes' constituting a key stage in a larger evolutionary process towards the state is especially problematic when we recall that the sources on these figures largely refer to Republican Rome and Latium. While many identify an egalitarian society preceding the emergence of the élite, others believe that social stratification was present in central Italy from at least the tenth century BC (Smith 1996, 106–25; 1998, 33). An analysis of settlements based on their levels of progress owes much to a neo-evolutionary view on state formation which has since been exposed as a self-referential teleology (Terrenato and Haggis 2011; Yoffee 2005). The picture is therefore not as clear as current interpretations assert.

As the title of this study indicates, I intend to question the current focus on the *gens* through a reassessment of these 'princes' in the light of new ideas on the ancient Mediterranean, including research drawing on Network Theory, connectivity and materiality (e.g. Horden and Purcell 2000; Malkin *et al.* 2009; Riva 2010). In order to re-contextualize these 'princely' figures within this burgeoning framework, further analysis is needed of the roles played by other social actors in the community and how their own struggle for recognition may have shaped new forms of élite representation. Aside from work by Cuozzo (2003) little attention has been given to the kinds of non-élite social actors in Iron Age Campania that this volume seeks to consider. Many scholars appear unaware of recent debates concerning identity, gender and agency. My intention, therefore, is to eschew a top-down approach to social change by examining how the actions of individuals across the community led to these ostentatious graves in Campania.

The role of Cumae

As Iron Age Campania is largely known through its funerary contexts there has been a focus on reconstructing the social fabric of the diverse communities in the region. Three cultural groups have been identified in Campania based on their burial rituals: the *fossakultur*; the Villanovan/proto-Etruscan; and the Oliveto–Cairano culture (for an overview *cf.* Cerchiai 2010, 13–20; Cuozzo 2007, 227). Though the foundation of Greek Cumae in the eighth century BC had consequences for these three cultural groups, there is a tendency to explain this event as taking the form of a violent conquest against the indigenous occupants of the site. Indigenous communities are placed onto a hierarchy based on their apparent level of political and technological development. Local settlements are thus viewed as 'open' or 'closed', which act as synonyms for advanced or primitive status (Cerchiai 2005, 188). At the top of this evolutionary scheme was pre-Hellenic Cumae, which apparently controlled all maritime traffic along the Tyrrhenian coast in partnership with Castiglione on the island of Ischia/Pithekoussai (Cerchiai 1995, 13–4; d'Agostino 1988, 534). From Pithekoussai, the Euboeans traded with Italic communities on the mainland in order to obtain food. This interpretation can acquire Hellenocentric connotations, however, especially in the formulation of d'Agostino: "these rather backward ... farming communities were stimulated into rapid social change through the more advanced Greek culture" (d'Agostino 2006, 231–2, translation by the author). Despite these initially friendly relations, the Euboean Greeks apparently destroyed the indigenous site at Cumae through a process that has been described as a "show of strength" (Cerchiai 2005, 190; Cuozzo 2007, 248; d'Agostino 2011, 44). Quickly establishing a colony, they then supposedly transplanted their burial practices from their Greek homeland to Cumae. The 'princely' burial phenomenon consequently spread into Campania. Four tombs at Pontecagnano (namely Tombs 4461, 2465, 926 and 928; *cf.* also Cuozzo and Fig. 1.3 this volume) are believed to be the inspiration behind the emergence of similar élite graves at other sites in Campania and adjoining regions, such as Bisaccia (Tomb 66), Calatia (Tomb 201) and the Sarno Valley (San Marzano Tomb 232, San Valentino Torio Tomb 168) (Cerchiai 1995, 71–5, 90–4).

However, this traditional interpretation can be challenged in view of recent evidence. The destruction of pre-Hellenic Cumae is now questioned by the discovery of a domestic structure at Cumae in use from *c.* 725–550 BC, which included both Greek and local Italic pottery (Greco 2010). Such ceramics strongly suggest that Greeks and locals lived side-by-side, which is not unusual, as evidence exists for similar cohabitation at Pithekoussai prior to the move to Cumae (Kelley 2012). Moreover, material evidence is rarely provided for the proposed defensive system between indigenous Cumae and Castiglione, the need for the Greeks to obtain food or for the destruction of pre-Hellenic Cumae. With Cumae's earliest phases possibly being a mixed character of Greek and local, the idea of an exclusively Greek 'princely' burial form exported into Italy from Cumae needs reassessment. While Cumae played a role in the formation of the 'princely' burial phenomenon in Italy, the possibility of a local Italic component calls for further investigation.

Princely tombs: similarity and difference

Despite the expression 'princely tomb' being widely used, many scholars decline to offer a definition of exactly what makes such tombs 'princely' in character (e.g. d'Agostino 1999a, 81; Fulminante 2003, 21; Winther 1997, 423, 434). While these tombs often exhibit common traits, particularly amongst their grave goods, many variations can be observed in both the assemblages and the structure of the tombs themselves. This section, therefore, aims to review the main tombs that are associated with the idea that this burial form was exported from Greece to Italy. Due to spatial constraints only a sample of these will be examined here but the focus will be on illustrating their affinities and variations.

Although there is a tendency to identify a standard set of 'princely' grave goods, close inspection indicates that the 'princely' grave assemblages rarely include exactly the same number or type of objects. A cursory glance at the assemblages suggests that precious Orientalizing metal vessels, the presence of a chariot and sacrificial objects are the most frequently found objects. Imported and local ceramics, jewellery and weapons appear less important. The metal vessels deposited are often imports from the east Mediterranean (such as silver and gold drinking vessels) which along with spits and firedogs constitute the 'princely' objects par excellence. The treatment of the corpse is also an indication of a 'princely' grave, especially in the case of the cremations that used bronze cauldrons as containers for the deceased's cremated remains. Similarly, the position of the tomb in the cemetery and the landscape could be a further indicator of pre-eminent status. Unfortunately, the exact position of such tombs is rarely apparent from published data (Winther 1997, 424) and in some cases, such as the Praeneste tombs, other graves in the cemetery were ignored (Smith 1996, 93). This is often a consequence of the rudimentary excavation methods used in the nineteenth century where the recovery of ceramics was a low priority when compared with luxury metal vessels (Winther 1997, 423).

The so-called 'royal' tombs uncovered in Greece and Cyprus were well excavated and metal vessels figured prominently. Despite such ostentation, the Greek 'princely' tombs have been described as poor in comparison with those found in Latium, Etruria and Campania (Morris 1999, 63). A rich group of tombs near the West Gate at Eretria in Greece included cremations where the remains were placed in bronze urns. Weapons, bronze cauldrons and precious metal objects featured amongst the grave goods. These graves were later enclosed by a triangular stone monument suggesting that some form of cult was performed at the tombs (Berard 1970, 13–7; Walker 2004, 107). In Cyprus, another prominent group of élite tombs at Salamis featured similar assemblages of bronze cauldrons, tripods and chariots (Karageorghis 1967). These built chamber tombs were cut into the ground and covered by *tumuli*. Some of these graves included the deposition of horses and chariots (such as Tombs 1, 2 and 79) and – in terms of body treatment – were a mix of both inhumation and cremation. Although the *heroon* from Eretria and the royal tombs at Salamis date to *c.* 700 BC, they are seen as the inspiration behind similar tombs at Cumae and Pontecagnano (d'Agostino 1977).

Tomb 104 from the Fondo Artiaco site at Cumae dates to *c.* 730–720 BC and was located close to the city's acropolis. Cut into the rock, this trench grave held a stone cist with a central depression for the cinerary urn (Strøm 1971, 146). The silver vessel held the deceased's cremated remains and was itself placed inside a bronze *lebes* (a deep bowl with rounded bottom). This *lebes* was then wrapped in a purple cloth, placed within a larger *lebes* and then covered by a Villanovan shield (Strøm 1971, 146–8; Buchner 1979, 130–1). The objects uncovered from the grave are largely linked to Etruria, which led Strøm to view the deceased as an Etruscan prince buried at Greek Cumae (1971, 147; *contra* Buchner 1979, 131–3). Six other cremation burials placed in cauldrons were found at Cumae during Stevens' excavations of 1896 (Buchner 1979, 130). Whether they came from similar 'princely' tombs cannot be confirmed, however, due to their unpublished state.

This burial type apparently spread from Cumae to Pontecagnano, where four similar tombs were found. Pontecagnano Tomb 2465 dates to the end of the eighth century BC, but is unfortunately unpublished. Lined with travertine slabs, this female *cassa* inhumation was probably covered by a *tumulus* (Fig. 7.2; Cuozzo 2003, 108–12).

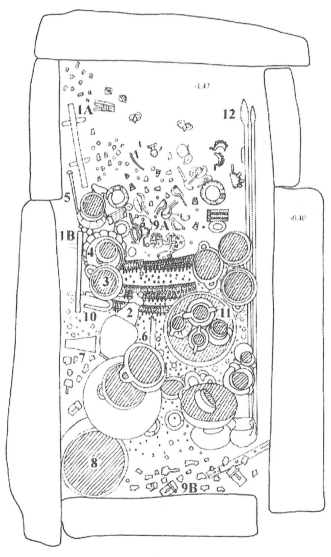

Fig. 7.2: Plan of Pontecagnano Tomb 2465 (after Cuozzo 2003).

Cuozzo notes that this tomb lay in an area of the eastern cemetery that was reserved for female burials, and no male burial in this area received the same level of ostentation (Cuozzo 2007, 235). Covered by a large *tumulus*, the earliest of the male 'princely' burials, interred in Pontecagnano Tomb 4461, also dates to the late eighth century BC. Although incorporating a similar enclosure to Cumae Fondo Artiaco Tomb 104, the corpse received an entirely different treatment. The flesh was removed from the bones before interment (Cerchiai 1987, 29). The bones of the deceased were then collected, wrapped in a cloth alongside selected goat bones and placed inside a bronze *lebes*. This unusual form of secondary burial has no clear precedent in the Iron Age, and is therefore connected with the burials of people killed in wars and/or in foreign lands mentioned in the Twelve Tables, a law code issued in Rome in the mid-fifth century BC (*bellicam peregrinamque mortem*: Cic. *Leg.* 2.24.60).[1] Because the skull was missing this burial is interpreted as a death in war or in foreign lands, with only a few bones available for a funeral by the individual's *gens* (Cerchiai 1995, 86; Cuozzo 2004–2005). Bronze vessels and horse masks from Vetulonia (Fig. 7.3), imported pottery (Proto-Corinthian and Phoenician) and weaponry were among the grave goods.

Pontecagnano Tombs 926 and 928 date to *c.* 670 BC and exhibit similarities to Pontecagnano Tomb 4461 and Cumae Fondo Artiaco Tomb 104. After cremation the bones of the deceased were collected, wrapped in a cloth and then enclosed by two arch serpentine fibulae. The remains were finally placed inside a bronze *lebes*. These two tombs were placed side-by-side and both feature an additional travertine

Fig. 7.3: Horse masks from Pontecagnano Tomb 4461 (after Cerchiai 1987).

recinto or *ricettacolo* inside the monumentalized *recinto* where the bronze cauldron and other objects were placed, segregating them from the rest of the assemblage (d'Agostino 1977, 9–13). The method of deposition in Potencagnano Tombs 4461, 926 and 928 is linked to the heroic burial ritual bestowed upon Patroclus (Hom. *Il.* 23.702). These tombs are therefore seen as "ideological models [elaborated] from the Greek élites at Cumae" (Cerchiai 1995, 89; 2010, 39–42; d'Agostino 1977, 59–60).

The 'princely' tombs from Etruria and Latium Vetus extend the use of inhumation and cremation to both males and females. Moreover, the chosen tomb structure shows degrees of regional variation (on Latium Vetus *cf.* also Rajala this volume, with a chamber tomb seen in Fig. 8.2). The Barberini and Bernardini Tombs from Praeneste (Palestrina) in Latium both yielded male inhumations dating to 675–650 BC. They were unfortunately the subject of unscientific excavation in the nineteenth century and although little information is available on the Barberini Tomb, it may have been a chamber tomb (Winther 1997, 439). The Bernardini Tomb was conversely a tufa-lined trench (Holloway 1994, 156–7). Also the Regolini Galassi Tomb at Caere (Cerverteri) dates from 650 to 625 BC and has a completely different structure, consisting of a large chamber tomb covered by a *tumulus* containing three burials (*cf.* Fig. 1.2 in Cuozzo this volume): a female inhumation (650 BC) in the so-called *cella*, and two later male burials, one cremation (650–625 BC, in the antechamber) and the other an inhumation (625 BC, in a side chamber: Winther 1997, 440). The so-called 'Tomba del Duce' at Vetulonia in Etruria dates from 700 to 650 BC and was actually a large trench containing five burial groups (I–V), which included both inhumations and cremations, and were situated at different depths and in different areas of the trench. The burials were then surrounded by a stone circle (Strøm 1971, 178–80; Winther 1997, 436). Interestingly, the bones of the male cremation in burial group V were wrapped in a cloth and then placed in a silver urn, similar to the aforementioned examples at Cumae and Pontecagnano (Sciacca 2005, 305).

Although these élite graves exhibit different tomb structures, they do include similar sets of grave goods. Within all of these tombs were silver vessels and bronze bowls or basins (produced in the eastern Mediterranean), chariots, bronze shields, bronze cauldrons with lion or griffin attachments and some form of chair or throne decorated in bronze. Some of these assemblages include objects that are absent in other tombs, such as ivory objects (from the eastern Mediterranean) in the Barberini and Bernardini Tombs, spits and firedogs in the Regolini Galassi Tomb and the 'Tomba del Duce' (burial group II) and imported pottery (Proto-Corinthian *kotylai* and *bucchero*) in the Tomba del Duce (burial group VI; for all these assemblages *cf.* Holloway 1994, 156–60; Riva 2010, 151–3; Smith 1996, 93–7; Strøm 1971, 150–68, 178–80; Winther 1997, 436–40).

While the tombs discussed above share similar objects, not one of these assemblages is exactly the same. Furthermore, the tomb structures of 'princely' graves in Etruria, Latium Vetus and Campania show much variation. For example, the construction of chamber tombs, where space was created for further burials after the initial 'prince', appears to be common to southern Etruria and Latium but absent from Campania. Such visible differences in rite and tomb structure illustrate the difficulties in defining these 'princely' graves (although Winther 1997, 424–32 proposes a common tomb type). Furthermore, the four 'princely' tombs at Pontecagnano are not only different from the 'princely' graves in Latium and Etruria, but also exhibit differences between each other. This suggests adaptation of a common burial type rather than the diffusion of a specifically Greek funerary model. The need for a more balanced view, that eschews the notion of an Euboean way of life that was exported to the west, has been increased by the aforementioned discoveries at Cumae. Before examining the emergence of this burial type at Pontecagnano in more depth, I intend to review some recent theoretical approaches to the study of the ancient Mediterranean and their implications for current interpretations of Iron Age Campania.

Reassessing the ancient Mediterranean

As noted above, the communities of Iron Age Campania are often explained as given an impetus by the Greeks, who established themselves in the region. This view derives from a primitivist approach to the ancient Mediterranean, where mobility was limited and Greece was emerging from a 'Dark Age'. However, not only has the Bronze to Iron Age transition been recently reassessed but also a consideration of space has returned to the fore. This shift in focus has been termed "the spatial turn" and is part of a wider trend across the humanities (Warf and Arias 2009). Such new perspectives have literally shrunk space and promoted the idea of an interconnected Mediterranean. Horden and Purcell's *The Corrupting Sea* (2000) played a key role in prompting new approaches to emerge. Furthermore, there is now an increased awareness of the mobility of objects that traversed this interconnected arena. Behind such mobility was a series of connections that literally entangled objects, peoples and ideas. A recent approach to the ancient world has been the use of Network Theory, which offers a fluid, dynamic view of space and depends on many variables (Malkin *et al.* 2009). From the end of the Bronze Age, these networks shifted from the eastern to the western Mediterranean as Cypriots, Phoenicians, Syrians, Sardinians, Euboeans and Corinthians tied the region together during a period of heightened connectivity (Riva 2010, 47–59). For Malkin, the Iron Age Mediterranean underwent a transition from a "many-to-many type network" to a more homogeneous structure by 500 BC (Malkin 2011, 40).

The realisation that objects played a central role in forging these network connections has emerged from a heightened focus on material culture. Because objects are frequently the medium through which social relations are constituted, both objects and humans can therefore be entangled and "entwined, involved with each other, dependent on each other [and] tied together" (Hodder 2012, 95). Such understandings come under the rubric of 'material culture studies' or 'materiality', areas of research that have yet to be considered for Campania. The 'princes' of Pontecagnano need further reassessment against this backdrop and a more balanced synthesis. Riva (2010) has examined the emergence of these 'princely' figures and their role in the urbanization of Etruria. She highlights a shift in funerary ideology from the individual male warrior in the Iron Age, to an ideology that encompassed the élite as a group, with warrior attributes extended to both men and women in the Orientalizing period (Riva 2010, especially 72–105). According to Riva, the élite created a "new material aesthetics" based upon a common culture comprising objects from the eastern Mediterranean. While Etruscan élites were actively appropriating Orientalizing culture, they were not aware of the origins of the objects they used: this was a consequence of a proximate rather than ultimate knowledge of the East (Riva 2010, 47). These eastern objects enabled the Etruscan élites to create new rituals and these in turn institutionalized the power of the élite through their exclusive ability to obtain them. Although these élites transformed Orientalizing objects and ideas through their use, these same individuals were themselves transformed by the new power structures they created (Riva 2010, 47). This common culture can be recognized beyond Etruria and was therefore constructed by Greeks, Phoenicians, Etruscans and others in the Mediterranean. Alongside Orientalizing objects, this shared *koine* included ideas and practices, such as writing and the alphabet, symposiastic dining and the spread of the Homeric myths, new technologies (filigree and granulation, fast potter's wheel), and burial practices (Riva 2010, 55–9).

Central to the formation of this common culture, therefore, was the increased mobility of the relevant specialists required for the transfer and adaptation of new skills into each locale. The specialized artisan was key to the spread of this culture and to the élite who held the exclusive access to it. While it is often difficult to distinguish between the movement of objects and artisans in archaeological terms (Smith 1998, 32), scholars of Campania frequently acknowledge the presence of resident itinerant artisans (especially of Near Eastern origin) within the various communities in the region (*cf.* Cerchiai 1995, 67–8 on the *ollae* from Pontecagnano Tombs 3892 and 538; d'Agostino 1999b, 20). Although caution is needed when attaching material culture to specific ethnicities (e.g. Jones 1997; *cf.* also Rajala and Zamboni this volume, with additional bibliography), there is a strong case for artisan mobility at this time. In terms of approaching the social agents involved at Pontecagnano from 900–675 BC, it is perhaps best to understand the common culture, and the ideas and individuals that led to its formation, as a network of relationships and dependencies. This requires further analysis.

Burial practices at Pontecagnano, 900–675 BC

The main cemeteries at Pontecagnano are located to the east (S. Antonio) and west (Picentino) of the ancient settlement, which is unfortunately unexplored. During Phase IA (900–850 BC) the graves are simple pit cremations (*a pozzo*), which has led to the conclusion that Pontecagnano was initially marked by egalitarianism (Cerchiai 1994; d'Agostino 1988). Changes occur at the end of this phase when tombs come to include the *a ricettacolo* type cremation and male warrior inhumations (d'Agostino and Gastaldi 1988). This is the start of a gradual shift from cremation to inhumation that continues into the Orientalizing period. Such changes have prompted the use of an evolutionary narrative to explain the settlement's development on a phase-by-phase basis. The male figures in Phase IA are thus understood as the first stage in this evolutionary scheme.

During Phase IB (850–780 BC) these male warriors apparently controlled all forms of trade and exchange in the community through political intermarriages with neighbouring regions which correspond to modern-day Basilicata and Sicily; this is attested by the imported vessels from these areas in female Pontecagnano Tombs 166 and 174 (Cerchiai 1995, 59). The first signs of monumentalization are visible in this phase, such as the cabin-type structure above Tomb 2145, which is compared to the Roman *bustum* rite (d'Agostino and Gastaldi 1988, 197–8). Furthermore, this tomb has been linked to the "birth of the élite" at Pontecagnano as four other later tombs were placed around it, and this family plot has been interpreted as evidence for the Roman-type *gens* (Cerchiai 1995, 60; 2010, 22; d'Agostino and Gastaldi 1988, 236–8). As will be discussed below, it is too early to speak of the *gens* at this stage. Similarly, the idea of egalitarianism is simplistic and the presence of the élite in some form at the start of phase IA is likely. Nevertheless, the various graves show a series of connections with Basilicata, Sicily, Calabria, Sardinia, Latium and Etruria (d'Agostino and Gastaldi 1988).

This picture changes in Phase II (780–720 BC) with the establishment of Pithekoussai and Cumae. A period of trade and contact had preceded these permanent settlements; this trade included the exchange of Middle and Late Geometric drinking cups as gifts to members of the local élite. These were luxury items due to their connection with wine consumption, which probably occurred for the first time during furtive ceremonial encounters between the local élite and the visiting Greeks (Cerchiai 2010, 23; on the key socio-political role of wine drinking in proto-historic central Italy *cf.* also Iaia this volume). Such vessels and the access to wine were powerful symbols for the local aristocracy and must have served to assert their position. When deposited in tombs they would have further accentuated this hegemony, as funerals were probably communal events. A considerable number of Late Geometric and Middle Geometric cups have been found at Capua, Pre-Hellenic Cumae and Veii (d'Agostino 2006). Both the published and unpublished tombs at Pontecagnano have also produced a large number of examples (d'Agostino 1999b; d'Agostino and Gastaldi 1988; De Natale 1992). Greek drinking cups also include motifs that were not present in the local ceramic repertoire, such as chevrons, meanders and a single bird between vertical lines. It is therefore interesting that these vessels are imitated almost immediately and this indicates their appeal. It is not clear if these were produced by local artisans or resident Greeks and attempts to attach ethnic labels to material culture have been highly criticized in recent years (e.g. Jones 1997). I will not attempt to answer this here. While some have argued that these imitations reflect a demand for Greek vessels that was not being met by the available supply (Cerchiai 1995, 82), this hypothesis misses an important detail. Indeed, it is notable that these imitations ignore the Greek shape and instead adapt the geometric motifs to local shapes, as is the case of an olla in Pontecagnano Tomb 3892, an amphora in Pontecagnano Tomb 3288, and a couple of bowls (*scodella* and *scodellone*) in Pontecagnano Tombs 211 and 266 (Cerchiai 1995, 67–8; d'Agostino and Gastaldi 1988, 48). Despite these hybrid practices, this contact is still viewed as Greek-dominated with the local community dependent on the Pithekoussai–Cumae milieu (Cerchiai 1995, 82; Cuozzo 2007, 232–4). It is true that the connections with the wider Mediterranean in Phase I are replaced with contact and trade with the Greeks in Phase II, but this does not necessarily equate to dependency. Instead, the rise in both imported Greek ceramics and local imitations may result from internal group dynamics. The increase in the number of these vessels throughout Phase II and into the Early Orientalizing period (roughly 730–675 BC) may have been a consequence of competition, resulting from the élite's main funerary symbol becoming available to the whole community. If this hypothesis is acceptable, then it may explain the emergence of the 'princely' tombs at Pontecagnano from the late eighth century BC.

The 'princes' of Pontecagnano

If there were increased competition in the community then some evidence of tension would need to be found. Tension in the Orientalizing period is exactly what Cuozzo's (2003) commendable study of a series of unpublished tombs at Pontecagnano has revealed. She indicates how the Iron Age cemeteries were abandoned at the end of the eighth century BC and new burial grounds were inaugurated by élite groups (Cuozzo 2007, 234). This represented a break with tradition where new prominent tombs were surrounded by enclosures to allow funerary cults. Cuozzo compares these individuals to the powerful *gentes* of Etruria and Latium (Cuozzo 2007, 234). This new funerary ideology also saw the extension of full burial to infants and children for the first time, while the lower strata of society were excluded (on the issue of formal cemetery burial *cf.* also Cuozzo, Iaia, Scopacasa, Perego, Zanoni, and Perego and Scopacasa this volume; on formal burial granted to children in Iron Age and Orientalizing Verucchio, in Emilia Romagna, *cf.* Di Lorenzo *et al.* this volume). Furthermore, many graves contained a basic vessel service comprising a Greek *oinochoe*, *skyphos* or *kylix* alongside a local amphora and bowl, indicating the popularity of Greek vessels in the Early Orientalizing period (Fig. 7.4; Cuozzo 2007; on the issue of internal community tension at Pontecagnano *cf.* also Cuozzo this volume).

Two groups in the Orientalizing cemetery further indicate this internal tension. Firstly, the western cemetery was dominated by a small group of adult male graves that include the three 'princes' (Pontecagnano Tombs 926, 928 and 4461). Secondly,

Fig. 7.4: Standard vessel service (after Cuozzo 2007).

in clear contrast, the eastern cemetery has a closer relationship with female figures. The female 'princely' inhumation (Pontecagnano Tomb 2465) held a central place in the eastern cemetery and no male was allowed similar ostentation. Furthermore, the INA CASA area in the eastern cemetery is open to imports, such as the aforementioned basic ceramic set, while the Chiancone IV area is conservative, possibly due to the presence of an enclave from the Oliveto–Cairano area further inland (Cuozzo 2007, 234–8). There is therefore evidence that competition led to restructuring processes where diverse groups sought to differentiate themselves from each other. Amongst these groups, the so-called 'princes' distinguished themselves from the rest of the community by creating a common culture similar to that found in coeval Etruria.

The first aspect that made these tombs stand out from their contemporaries was the burial itself. As outlined above, the unique burial form in Pontecagnano Tomb 4461 saw the bones of the deceased mixed with a goat and placed in a cauldron. Pontecagnano Tombs 926 and 928 also saw the bones placed in a cauldron and objects placed in two distinct enclosures within the tomb. In addition, the use of cremation, at a time when inhumation was the main rite at Pontecagnano, further indicates the significance of these figures. Importantly the élite at Pontecagnano appears to have shifted from Greek to Orientalizing material culture as their objects of choice. Though the two earliest tombs contain imported Greek pottery (Pontecagnano Tomb 4461 has a Proto-Corinthian *oinochoe* and *aryballos*: Cerchiai 1987; Pontecagnano Tomb 2465 has two Proto-Corinthian *kylikes* and four Thapsos cups: Cuozzo 2003, 108–12), they are absent in the later Pontecagnano Tombs 926 and 928 (aside from a solitary Corinthian amphora in Tomb 926). D'Agostino speculates as to whether this absence of Greek vessels (when the rest of the community included them) indicates a reaction against the Greek world, articulated through a conservative warrior ideology (d'Agostino 1977, 56). I believe instead that this was most likely a reaction against what the rest of the community were doing. For these 'princes', Greek pots were no longer in fashion.

These élites utilized heroic rites that were focused on "ceremonial wine drinking, sacrifices and meat banquets" that had their origins in both the Greek and Oriental worlds (Cuozzo 2007, 233). In the place of Greek drinking vessels, the 'princes' were buried with a silver banqueting service. Both Pontecagnano Tombs 926 and 928 included silver *skyphoi*; the latter tomb also contained a silver *phiale* and *oinochoe* with palmette handle, whose closest parallels lie in Cyprus or Nimrud, but was apparently produced by an Oriental artisan resident in Etruria (Fig. 7.5; d'Agostino 1977, 37–9; Sciacca 2005, 409). This *oinochoe* finds affinities with similar vessels in Fondo Artiaco Tomb 104 from Cumae, the Bernardini, Barberini and Regolini Galassi Tombs from Praeneste and Cerveteri and the Tomba del Duce from Vetulonia (d'Agostino 1977, 38). Pontecagnano Tomb 928 also held a silver *kotyle* with a 'false' hieroglyph inscribed around the rim that recalls the shape of the *kotylai* in the Bernardini and Barberini Tombs (d'Agostino 1977, 31–6). As a series of random symbols, this hieroglyph is not translatable. While it could be argued that the artisan copying the Egyptian hieroglyph failed to produce an actual text, I believe that the act of copying offered the effect of writing, which was more than enough to associate the owner with the wider cultural transformation taking root in the western Mediterranean: the emergence of literacy and the alphabet.

Bronze vessels were also used in 'princely' tombs as funerary containers, a practice that has no parallel in the Villanovan sphere. Three of the four tombs at Pontecagnano contained bronze *patere* or *phialai* that were either made in Italy by Oriental craftsmen, or imported directly from the eastern Mediterranean (Sciacca 2005, 198–200). Also included were bronze serving vessels such as the *oinochoai* in

Fig. 7.5: Silver oinochoe *and inscribed silver* kotyle *in Pontecagnano Tomb 928 (after Cuozzo 2007).*

Pontecagnano Tomb 2465, including examples with three-lobed rims in Pontecagnano Tombs 926 and 928. Pontecagnano Tomb 4461 includes a bronze biconical amphora and a bronze Kurd-type situla probably imported from Vetulonia (Cerchiai 1987, 41; 1995, 87). These vessels are associated with the banquet, as are the bronze cauldron and basins found in Tombs 2465, 926 and 928 (Cuozzo 2003, 108–12). Bronze or iron spits and firedogs are also connected to the banquet (Riva 2010, 92) and these were also deposited in Tombs 2465, 926 and 928. A rise in funeral banqueting is observed in coeval Etruria, where the use of bronze vessels indicated the scale of these new funerary consumption practices (Riva 2010, 149; *cf.* also Iaia this volume). There is a case for similar rites in the 'princely' tombs of Campania.

Such new rites literally transformed the way in which the élites constructed and represented themselves, as in the case of the bronze grater deposited in Pontecagnano Tomb 928. The adoption of this object by the élites at Pontecagnano connected them with the wider Euboean ritual of adding spices and cheeses to wine (Hom. *Il.* 11.628–643; Ridgway 1997, 331–4). Such rituals and their paraphernalia constituted new food technologies that transformed the local élite by encouraging new conceptions of the self and the body (Riva 2010, 55, 144 and 147). The body was further transformed through the use of cremation and interment of the remains in the metal vessels of Pontecagnano Tombs 926 and 928. In Homer, the roasting of meat on spits was reserved for the aristocratic warrior group, while the boiling of meat in cauldrons was for the wider community (Detienne 1979, 77). The combined deposition in the tomb of cauldrons and spits/firedogs connected the deceased with a Homeric burial, such as that bestowed upon Patroclus (Hom. *Il.* 23.702), where an *oinochoe* was used to quell the flames of the funeral pyre with wine and the cremated remains were wrapped up in a cloth (Riva 2010, 158). All of these elements are present in the 'princely' tombs at Pontecagnano. It is also possible that the use of metal cauldrons and basins (*bacini*) as cremation urns symbolically conflated the prince with the sacrifice and transformed him from a male warrior into a sacrificial victim for the gods (Riva 2010, 158–9). While the exact nature of this ritual cannot be confirmed, it is interesting to recall that the bones of the deceased male in Pontecagnano Tomb 4461 were mixed with those of a goat or sheep, the Homeric animal of sacrifice.

Such ostentatious funerals would have sent a profound message to the rest of the community that was further accentuated by the use of equestrian themes. Although all four 'princely' graves at Pontecagnano feature the remains of chariots (Cerchiai *et al.* 1997, 25), these were not war chariots but rather the funeral carriages to transport the corpse to its final resting place. While this indicates a very public procession there is unfortunately a lack of adequate information on the use of the contemporary landscape to understand how this procession may have taken place. Nevertheless, visible chariot funeral processions may have further asserted the hegemony of these figures within the community. Similarly, the deposition of the horse masks in Pontecagnano Tomb 4461 (Cerchiai 1987, 31–42) may have served as a "part taken for the whole" in the absence of the horse and chariot (Riva 2010, 98–9; Winther 1997, 428), or even attest to remnants of the funeral procession or *ekphora* (Cerchiai 1995, 87). Furthermore, three of the Pontecagnano 'princely' tombs (2465, 926, 928) include a *scodellone con ansa a cavallini*, an impasto bowl with a zoomorphic horse figure on the handle (Cuozzo 2003, 112; d'Agostino 1977). This figure is reminiscent of the 'Lord of the Animals' motif that was prevalent in antiquity. Such symbols reflect the position of the élite, who received extravagant funerals and also possessed horses, an important aristocratic symbol in many ancient societies.

In terms of social agents, these aristocrats would have required access to the skills necessary to produce a new funerary ideology. Artisans and experts were therefore sought from around the Mediterranean in order to create the common culture that is recognized along the Tyrrhenian coast. These specialists were pivotal to the transformation of these élites, as was the community at Pontecagnano as a whole, for without their competition such new élite ideologies may not have come into being. The need to demonstrate power and status was further extended to the 'prince''s family. Not only were females permitted similar heroic burials to the males (e.g. Pontecagnano Tomb 2465) but children also received some of the 'princely' objects described above, such as spits and metal vessels. This has led Cuozzo to refer to them as *piccoli principi* or 'little princes' (Cuozzo 2003, 199–202, 194–6 on Pontecagnano Tombs 5867 and 5926 for example). The question that needs to be asked, however, is how far can such developments be equated with the *gens*?

Che cos'è una gens?

The apparent emergence of the élite during the transition from the Iron Age to the Orientalizing period coincides with the appearance of clusters of later burials around many prominent tombs in Etruria, Latium and Campania. These have been interpreted as evidence for familial or clan groups who traced their patrilineal descent to a shared ancestor. Such clans were called the *gens* in antiquity and because all agricultural land was under their control this was essentially a client-based economy. The 'princes' emerged from this larger clan or *gens* and as important patrons they held power over their clients. These clients were dependent on the 'prince' and were obliged to provide military support to this figure when required (Cerchiai 2010, 35–6). The root of the 'princes'' ancestral power was manifest in the two-name system or *nomen gentilicium*, which demonstrated their link to a real or mythical ancestor.

The concept of 'gentilicial society' is widespread in Italian scholarship and although it is regularly used to explain social change in Etruria, problems exist with the phrase *società gentilizio-clientelare* (Riva 2010, 7). For example, the proposed presence of a *gens* in the Iron Age at the Osteria dell'Osa cemetery in Latium has been questioned (Smith 2006, 147–50), while some argue that the two-name system tells us little aside from who the deceased's parents were (Riva 2010, 7). Despite such criticism, Cerchiai (2010, 35–6) and others maintain that the *gens* existed in coeval Campania, with Pontecagnano Tombs 926 and 928 upheld as its physical manifestation.

Key to this argument is the nearby Tomb 3509 where a vessel inscribed in Etruscan provides evidence for a *gens* at Pontecagnano. This impasto chalice provides what are interpreted as the parent's names of the infant interred. The inscription reads **mi mulu venelasi velχaesi rasuniesi**, or "I am given by **Venela** and **Velchae Rasunies**" (*REE* 2002 no.84). Alongside their *praenomina* is the *nomen gentilicium* "**Rasunies**" which Colonna argues can be traced to an Etruscan root signifying "those able to carry arms within the community" and potentially an Etruscan military office (Colonna 2002b, 387). Scholars utilize this to argue for a *nomen gentilicium*, the emergence of the élite and the prince-client system at Pontecagnano (Cerchiai 2010, 36; Colonna 2002a, 199). Furthermore, this tomb is seen to be associated with 'princely' Tombs 926 and 928 and so they too are assumed to be part of this *gens* (Cerchiai 2010, 36).

On closer inspection, Pontecagnano Tomb 3509 dates to *c.* 650 BC, which at 20 years later than Tombs 926 and 928 is in keeping with the idea that the infant was a member of the 'princely' family buried next to the 'prince'. However, the plan of this area of the cemetery shows that Tomb 3509 does not clearly form part of a cluster around the two 'princely' graves (*cf.* Pellegrino 2010, 4 which includes a cemetery plan). The lack of similar inscriptions in all four 'princely' tombs from Pontecagnano eliminates their potential link to a *nomen gentilicium* (gentilicial name) or with the name **Rasunies** in Tomb 3509. Other tombs in this area of the cemetery have Etruscan inscriptions but only Tomb 3509 gives a *nomen*, making it the sole possible claim to a *gens* in the cemetery. Therefore even if **Rasunies** is a *gens* it still cannot be directly connected to Tomb 926 or 928, nor the earlier 'princely' tombs at Pontecagnano, as Cerchiai has done.

Even if the gentilicial name **Rasunies** might indicate an Etruscan military office, it is still not certain that the vessel was deposited by the deceased's parents, that it belonged to the deceased, that it named the parents, or that any of them were able to read Etruscan. Inscribed vessels were deposited in other infant graves in Campania for other reasons, most notably the so-called Nestor's Cup, which has been linked to the symposium. It is no longer acceptable to attribute ethnicity on the basis of one object (*cf.* Jones 1997) as the rest of the assemblage in Pontecagnano Tomb 3509 indicates. Alongside the inscribed chalice were other impasto, Italo-Geometric and Proto-Corinthian vessels (Pellegrino 2002, 384–5), none of which support an Etruscan ethnicity for the deceased. The chalice may therefore have been acquired through gift exchange, trade or deposited after commensal rites rather than *a priori* inscribed and interred by the infant's parents.

In addition, the *gens* is not as clearly definable as scholars suggest. The ancient sources are actually quite vague on its nature and nowhere do they describe membership of the *gens* as key to political power, nor do they describe the *princeps* of the *gens* as a formal office (Smith 2006, 34, 64). Many of the associations with mythical *principes* were made in the late Republic and earlier links could be subject to reinvention or realigned with an alternate *princeps* (Smith 2006, 40–1). Modern interpretations of the *gens* frequently place it as a stage in the history of human progress, a tendency characterizing Italian archaeology and its Marxist orientation towards material culture (Smith 2006, 65–111). These modern ideas are based on erroneous anthropological and historical constructs of the *gens* that make it a "shadowy institution", extremely problematic for early Rome and Latium, let alone Campania (Smith 1996, 189–90).

Similarly for Etruria, Riva has accused scholars of retrojecting later political institutions back onto the Orientalizing period (Riva 2010, 7). With the considerable problems in identifying the *gens* in Latium and Etruria, it is unreasonable to extend this interpretation to Campania, a different context where different socio-political structures may have existed. Cerchiai's interpretation owes much to a later Roman Republican understanding of political institutions and therefore cannot account for the complex socio-political changes of the Iron Age to the Orientalizing period.

Conclusions

The question *what's in a name*, as posed in the title of this paper, has brought forward a series of issues with current scholarship of the 'princely' tombs. First of all, the use of the term 'prince' to refer to these figures is problematic. It cannot be proven that all societies possessed monarchical structures in antiquity. The associations that the name 'prince' has with the later Roman *rex* in Latium and Etruria do not permit its extension to the settlements of Campania, merely on the assumption that they too were Etruscan. Despite the similarities between many assemblages, the 'princely' burial type has no fixed form in the Mediterranean, so surely it is more productive to view its physical manifestation as connected to a common élite culture, as Riva (2010) has proposed for Etruria.

The role played by Cumae in the transmission of these tombs also needs further reconsideration. There is ample evidence emerging at both Pithekoussai and Cumae that these were not pure Greek settlements but involved some form of cohabitation with locals and others. This seems perfectly acceptable when we also consider recent debates on the multiplicity of Greek ethnicity itself (Dougherty and Kurke 2003).

Furthermore, as the Cumae Fondo Artiaco Tomb is actually earlier than its apparent predecessors in Greece and Cyprus, these graves may therefore have been a new ideology that began in the west. Such new ideas were attractive to local élites for the potential they allowed for reinvention (Cuozzo 2003). When asking "what's in a name", perhaps the best names for these developments are competition, adaptation and dynamism over the use of the rather static 'prince', *gens* and 'state' that currently prevail. This dynamism was permitted by, and expressed through, the network changes occurring in the Iron Age Mediterranean, where a thickening of contact saw many ideas, practices and values transgress cultural boundaries. At Pontecagnano, this was not a result of individual agency as it was not led by the 'princes'. The whole community was a social actor; group consumption patterns led to increased competition in the funerary sphere. In turn the élite reacted by creating a new funerary ideology in order to maintain their position which they extended to their family. Consequently, there was an increased presence for once silent actors such as the 'little princes' and ostentatious female burials to promote this common culture. Alongside them were newly arrived resident or itinerant foreign specialists, who further enabled the élite transformations that convention calls 'princes'. Regardless of their name, these individuals were transformed through the material culture they used, and in the process transformed their own communities.

Acknowledgements

This paper is dedicated to the memory of my Grandparents, J.R. and A.H. Brice.

Note

1. In this passage, Cicero explains that one of the funerary laws determined that the bones of the deceased were not to be collected and given a second burial, excepting the bones of those who had died in war and/or foreign lands.

Bibliography

Bérard, J. (1970) *L'Hérôon à la Porte de l'Ouest. Eretria III*. Berne, Éditions Francke.

Buchner, G. (1979) Early Orientalising: Aspects of the Euboean connection. In D. Ridgway and F. Ridgway (eds) *Italy Before the Romans. The Iron Age, Orientalizing and Etruscan Periods*, 129–144. London, Academic Press.

Cerchiai, L. (1987) Una tomba principesca del periodo orientalizzante antico a Pontecagnano. *Studi Etruschi* 53, 28–42.

Cerchiai, L. (1995) *I Campani*. Milano, Longanesi.

Cerchiai, L. (2005) Le regioni dell'Italia meridionale e le isole. In F. Pensando (ed.) *L'Italia Antica. Culture e Forme del Popolamento nel I Millennio a.C.*, 181–202. Roma, Carocci Editore.

Cerchiai, L. (2010) *Gli Antichi Popoli della Campania*. Roma, Carocci Editore.

Cerchiai, L., Colucci Pescatori, G. and D'Henry, G. (1997) L'Italia antica: Italia meridionale. In A. Emiliozzi (ed.) *Carri da Guerra e Principi Etruschi. Catalogo della Mostra (Viterbo, 24 Maggio–31 Gennaio 1998; Roma, 27 Maggio–4 Luglio 1999)*, 25–32. Roma, "L'Erma" di Bretschneider.

Colonna, G. (2002a) Gli Etruschi nel Tirreno meridionale: Tra mitistoria, storia e archeologia. *Etruscan Studies: Journal of the Etruscan Foundation* 9, 191–206.

Colonna, G. (2002b) Tomba 3509. *Studi Etruschi* 65–68, 385–388.

Cuozzo, M. (2003) *Reinventando la Tradizione: Immaginario Sociale, Ideologie e Rappresentazione nelle Necropoli Orientalizzanti di Pontecagnano*. Paestum, Pandemos.

Cuozzo, M. (2004–2005) Ripetere, moltiplicare, selezionare, distinguere nelle necropoli di Pontecagnano. Il caso della tomba 4461. In L. Cerchiai and P. Gastaldi (eds) *Pontecagnano: La Città, il Paesaggio e la Dimensione Simbolica* (Annali di Archeologia e Storia Antica 11–12), 145–154. Napoli, Istituto Universitario Orientale.

Cuozzo, M. (2007) Ancient Campania: Cultural interaction, political borders and geographical boundaries. In G.J. Bradley, E. Isayev and C. Riva (eds) *Ancient Italy. Regions without Boundaries*, 224–267. Exeter, Exeter University Press.

d'Agostino, B. (1977) *Tombe Principesche dell'Orientalizzante Antico da Pontecagnano* (Monumenti Antichi 49, Serie Miscellanea 2/1). Roma, Accademia Nazionale dei Lincei.

d'Agostino, B. (1988) Le genti della Campania antica. In A.M. Chieco Bianchi (ed.) *Italia Omnium Terrarum Alumna. La Civiltà dei Veneti, Reti, Liguri, Celti, Piceni, Umbri, Latini, Campani e Iapigi* (Antica Madre 11), 529–589. Milano, Garzanti/Scheiwiller.

d'Agostino, B. (1999a) I principi dell'Italia centro-tirrenica in epoca orientalizzante. In P. Ruby (ed.) *Les Princes de la Protohistoire et l'Émergence de l'État. Actes de la Table Ronde Internationale Organisée par le Centre Jean Bérard et l'École française de Rome (Naples, 27–29 Octobre 1994)*, 81–88. Napoli, Centre Jean Bérard.

d'Agostino, B. (1999b) La ceramica greca e di tipo greco dalle necropoli della I Eta del Ferro di Pontecagnano. In G. Bailo Modesti and P. Gastaldi (eds) *Prima di Pithecusa: I Più Antichi Materiali Greci del Golfo di Salerno. Catalogo della Mostra (Pontecagnano Faiano, Museo Nazionale dell'Agro Picentino)*, 13–24. Napoli, Arte Tipografica.

d'Agostino, B. (2006) The first Greeks in Italy. In G.R. Tsetskhladze (ed.) *Greek Colonisation: An Account of Greek Colonies and Other Settlements Overseas* (Vol. I), 201–237. Leiden, Brill.

d'Agostino, B. (2011) Pithecusae e Cumae nel quadro della Campania di età arcaica. *Römische Mitteilungen* 117, 35–53.

d'Agostino, B. and Gastaldi, P. (1988) *Pontecagnano II. La Necropoli del Picentino. 1. Le Tombe della Prima Età del Ferro* (Annali dell'Istituto Orientale di Napoli, Archeologia e Storia Antica, Quaderno 5). Napoli, Istituto Universitario Orientale.

De Natale, S. (1992) *Pontecagnano II. La Necropoli di S. Antonio: Propr. ECI. 2. Tombe della Prima Età del Ferro* (Annali dell'Istituto Orientale di Napoli, Archeologia e Storia Antica, Quaderno 8). Napoli, Istituto Universitario Orientale.

Detienne, M. (1979) *Dionysius Slain*. Baltimore, Johns Hopkins University Press.

Dougherty, C. and Kurke, L. (2003) (eds) *The Cultures within Greek Culture: Contact, Conflict, Collaboration*. Cambridge, Cambridge University Press.

Frederiksen, M. (1984) *Campania*. London, British School at Rome.

Fulminante, F. (2003) *Le Sepolture Principesche nel Latium Vetus. Tra la Fine della Prima Età del Ferro e l'Inizio dell'Età Orientalizzante*. Roma, "L'Erma" di Bretschneider.

Greco, G. (2010) Dalla città greca alla città sannitica: Le evidenze della Piazza del Foro. *In Atti del XLVIII Convegno di Studi sulla Magna Grecia (Taranto, 2008)*, 385–431. Napoli, Arte Tipografica.

Hodder, I. (2012) *Entangled. An Archaeology of the Relationships between Humans and Things*. Oxford, Wiley-Blackwell.

Horden, P. and Purcell, N. (2000) *The Corrupting Sea: A Study of Mediterranean History*. Oxford, Blackwell.

Jones, S. (1997) *The Archaeology of Ethnicity. Constructing Identities in the Past and Present*. London, Routledge.

Karageorghis, V. (1967) *Excavations in the Necropolis of Salamis* (Vol. I). Nicosia, Department of Antiquities, Cyprus.

Kelley, O. (2012) Beyond intermarriage: The role of the indigenous Italic population at Pithekoussai. *Oxford Journal of Archaeology* 31(3), 245–260.

Malkin, I. (2011) *A Small Greek World. Networks in the Ancient Mediterranean*. Oxford, Oxford University Press.

Malkin, I., Constantakopoulou, C. and Panagopoulou, K. (2009) (eds) *Greek and Roman Networks in the Mediterranean*. London, Routledge.

Morris, I. (1999) Iron Age Greece and the meanings of "princely tombs". In P. Ruby (ed) *Les Princes de la Protohistoire et l'Émergence de l'État. Actes de la Table Ronde Internationale Organisée par le Centre Jean Bérard et l'École française de Rome (Naples, 27–29 Octobre 1994)*, 57–80. Napoli, Centre Jean Bérard.

Pellegrino, C. (2002) Tomba 3509. *Studi Etruschi* 65–68, 384–385.

Pellegrino, C. (2010) Pontecagnano: L'uso della scrittura tra Etruschi, Greci e Italici. *Bollettino di Archeologia Online I (2010), Volume Speciale F/ F3/ 2*. [http://www.bollettinodiarcheologiaonline. beniculturali.it/bao_document/articoli/2_PELLEGRINO.pdf].

REE (2002) *Rivista di Epigrafia Etrusca* 2002.

Ridgway, D. (1997) Nestor's cup and the Etruscans. *Oxford Journal of Archaeology* 16(3), 325–344.

Riva, C. (2010) *The Urbanisation of Etruria: Funerary Ritual and Social Change, 700-600 BC*. Cambridge, Cambridge University Press.

Ross Holloway, R. (1994) *The Archaeology of Early Rome and Latium*. London, Routledge.

Sciacca, F. (2005) *Patere Bacellate in Bronzo. Oriente, Grecia, Italia in Età Orientalizzante*. Roma, "L'Erma" di Bretschneider.

Smith, C.J. (1996) *Early Rome and Latium. Economy and Society c. 1000-500 BC*. Oxford, Clarendon Press.

Smith, C.J. (1998) Traders and artisans in archaic central Italy. In H. Parkins and C.J. Smith (eds) *Trade, Traders and the Ancient City*, 31–50. London, Routledge.

Smith, C.J. (2006) *The Roman Clan: The Gens from Ancient Ideology to Modern Anthropology*. Cambridge, Cambridge University Press.

Strøm, I. (1971) *Problems Concerning the Origin and Early Development of the Etruscan Orientalizing Style*. Odense, Odense Universitetsforlag.

Terrenato, N. and Haggis, D. (2011) (eds) *State Formation in Italy and Greece: Questioning the Neoevolutionist Paradigm*. Oxford, Oxbow Books.

Walker, K. (2004) *Archaic Eretria. A Political and Social History from the Earliest Times to 490 BC*. London, Routledge.

Warf, B. and Arias, S. (2009) (eds) *The Spatial Turn. Interdisciplinary Perspectives*. London, Routledge.

Winther, H.C. (1997) Princely tombs of the Orientalising period in Etruria and *Latium Vetus*. In H. Damgaard Andersen, H.W. Horsnaes, S. Houby-Nielsen and A. Rathje (eds) *Urbanization in the Mediterranean in the 9th to 6th Centuries BC* (Acta Hyperborea 7), 423–446. København, Museum Tusculanum Press.

Yoffee, N. (2005) *Myths of the Archaic State: Evolution of the Earliest Cities, States, and Civilizations*. Cambridge, Cambridge University Press.

Chapter 8

Nested identities and mental distances: Archaic burials in Latium Vetus

Ulla Rajala

Introduction

This paper expands on my previous theoretical discussions on funerary identities (Rajala 2011; 2012). It is a twin piece to a paper presented in the Groningen workshop *Current Research into Pre-Roman Burial Grounds in Italy* (Rajala 2014), which discusses the use of biographical metaphor in interpreting funerary remains. Here I explore the concepts of nested identity and mental distance, with a focus on Latium Vetus (Fig. 8.1). For analytical purposes, I define 'identity' as an acceptance of a group membership that is demonstrated through mutually recognized codes and symbols. An individual or a group can have a number of social identities that are based on gender, age, status, ethnicity, shared culture and religion. While these can be observed and defined with relative certainty across living populations, the boundaries between different identities are more difficult to detect in archaeological assemblages (Díaz-Andreu *et al.* 2005). The identities presented in burials are further blurred by the difficulty of separating the self-representation of the deceased from the representations by the living who stage the funeral (*cf.* Morris 1987, 40; Parker Pearson 1999, 7–11). Nevertheless, 'funerary identities', namely the representations of individual and/or group identities through funerary practice, can be assessed by comparing the similarities and differences between individual tombs and cemeteries, within and between communities. These identities are multifaceted and nested, depending on individual and group values.

Livy and other ancient authors gave different ethnic labels to central Italian regions. As a consequence, the Latin, Etruscan and Sabine areas are generally seen to possess linguistic, historic and material cohesion. However, I argue that 'nested identities', which describe unevenly nested self-definitions relating to geographical entities (Kaplan 1999, 31; Kaplan and Herb 1999, 4), allow us to identify a hierarchy in the different social identities that are detectable in the material assemblages of these

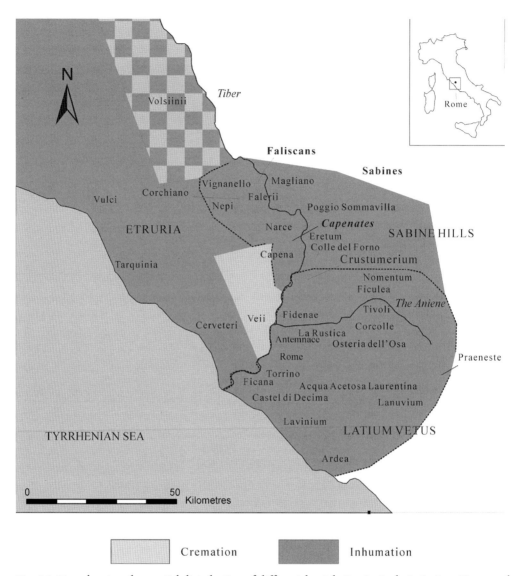

Fig. 8.1: Map showing the spatial distribution of different burial rites in Archaic Latium Vetus and southern Etruria (map: U. Rajala).

regions. Even at the cemetery level, an individual tomb is a geographic entity and a cemetery as a whole reflects different identities in the local community. In addition, the concept of 'mental distance', namely the relative closeness or distance between communities in terms of socio-cultural practices (Bjerring Olsen 2004), can be used to evaluate similarities or differences in material culture between communities and regions. These concepts used in combination help assess the relative conformity or independence of different city-states that, according to the historical record, were included in the 'Latin League' and other 'ethnic' alliances (on the Latin League of cities *cf.* Dion. Hal. *Ant.Rom.* 3.57, 8.18, 9.1; Livy 4.23.4–24.2, 4.25.7–8, 4.31.6, 5.1.3–7, 5.17.6–16; *cf.* also Eckstein 2006, 120).

This discussion is a result of the *Remembering the Dead* Project that excavated in the cemetery area of Cisterna Grande at Crustumerium between 2004 and 2008, in collaboration with the *Soprintendenza* of Rome and Dr Francesco di Gennaro. The main aim of the project was to study the metaphorical funerary representations of a Latin Orientalizing and Archaic community. Tombs were seen as part of a wider ritual landscape (*cf.* Naso 1996a; Riva and Stoddart 1996) and studied at a local micro-level using digital and traditional methods (*cf.* Fulminante 2008; Rajala 2008a). The first tombs exposed at Cisterna Grande were chamber tombs, which had been rarely stratigraphically excavated (Rajala 2007): thus the project prioritized their study. Due to their collapsed state, the number of excavated tombs is limited; however, they form an interesting chronological series (Rajala 2011). The architecture of different tomb types has been ignored in many discussions on funerary identities (*cf.* Izzet 2007a, 88–90), but the variability at Cisterna Grande suggests that local and regional identities may have been reflected in and marked by the physicality of the tombs. Even if Stoddart (1990), Izzet (2007a) and Riva (2010) put tomb architecture at the forefront of funerary studies, they only discussed the Etruscan area. Stoddart (1990, 47) considered funerary architecture as an indicator of political boundaries, similarly to his Italian colleagues (e.g. Colonna 1990), whereas Izzet (2007a, 87–121) discussed the ontological difference and social relationship between the living and the dead. Riva (2010, 109–25) addressed the connection between the late Orientalizing mortuary and domestic architectures and how the resulting funerary ideology affirmed the identity and authority of the élite. In contrast, my intention is to compare the differences and similarities across the traditional ethnic areas along the downriver of the Tiber, in order to deconstruct nested identities and mental distances. The well-documented drop in the number of grave goods in Latium Vetus by the Archaic period (580–475/450 BC; *cf.* Bartoloni 1987; Carafa 1995, 11–2; Colonna 1977; 1981; Naso 1990) suggests that these similarities and differences can only be properly understood by comparing Archaic architecture and burial practices with those of the preceding Orientalizing period (730/720–580 BC), when the data are more plentiful.

The general development of tomb architecture in central Italy reveals a sequence where Iron Age pit cremations were followed by trench tombs with inhumations, which represent the dominant burial type during the Orientalizing period (on the funerary rite in Iron Age to Orientalizing central Italy *cf.* also Iaia and Shipley this volume, while the chapter by O'Donoghue also covers the Archaic period). Later, trench tombs were followed by chamber tombs, which are the norm during the Archaic period (e.g. Potter 1976, 14–6). However, mounds (*tumuli*) with chambers were the dominant tomb type across much of southern Etruria during the Orientalizing period (Izzet 2007a, 87; *cf.* also Cuozzo this volume, with the Regolini Galassi Tomb from Cerveteri seen in Fig. 1.2). At Cisterna Grande the oldest tomb was a trench tomb, a mid/late Orientalizing example of the so-called *tomba a loculo tipo Narce* type (Fulminante 2008; Fig. 8.2A). Another grave, namely a late Orientalizing chamber tomb, was similar to the early chambers excavated at Monte Del Bufalo at Crustumerium (*cf.* for example Belelli Marchesini 2008; Fig. 8.2B), while five of the six chambers excavated in their entirety were Archaic. In what follows, I will first discuss the concepts of nested identity and mental distance and how they can help us understand the identities that are reflected in tombs and burial rituals. I will then discuss the distribution of different Orientalizing and Archaic tomb types across central Italy. In this way, I will place the case study of Cisterna Grande in its regional context. Finally, I will summarize the main arguments of this paper.

Nested identities and burial customs

Lucy (2005, 100) suggested that the study of past collective identities, in view of their social and territorial aspects, may facilitate our understanding of how material culture is actively used for different purposes and in different ways depending on the context (on materiality and the active use of material culture in burial *cf.* also Cuozzo and Shipley this volume, both with additional bibliography). In the contemporary world, cultural identity is relational, and its definition is based on an individual's or a group's

Fig. 8.2: On the left the partially looted Orientalizing tomba a loculo tipo Narce *at Cisterna Grande, and on the right the Orientalizing simple chamber tomb from the same cemetery area (photos: U. Rajala).*

understanding of themselves and, reciprocally, on other people's understanding of themselves (Jenkins 1996, 5; Ziller 1973). Juxtaposing 'us' with 'them' requires the existence of boundaries, either real or imaginary (on this issue *cf.* also Zamboni this volume). Boundaries function as the most visible apparatus for making sense of the world. Indeed, they feed into the social identity of people by establishing shared values, which can be compared to similar values on the other side of the boundary (*cf.* Bjerring Olsen 2004; Paasi 2000). In archaeology, we aim to reconstruct past ideologies through material culture – if and when they were consciously or unconsciously represented with objects or symbols. We also look for differences that stand for distance and boundaries as well as for similarities that stand for closeness. The analysis of geographic distributions of funerary architecture can help us in this pursuit.

The existence of different contemporaneous tomb types in a single community suggests different preferences. In a ritual context, the choice of a design can suggest that groups and individuals identified a shared symbol that signalled an identity. Funerary architecture in central Italy has often been connected to a specific city-state or an ethnic area (e.g. Cifani 2003; Colonna 1990). State and ethnic identities are geographic identities that Kaplan (1994) called "spatial identities", namely identities that are defined through a group's collective consciousness of their locational context against other groups. Geographically defined identities have a hierarchy that may relate to the scale of their respective geographical extent. Different entities (e.g. empire, state, region and locality) are nested within one another and each may gain salience as aspects of identity. Notably, spatial identities tend to be unevenly nested and viewed differently by various people (Kaplan 1999, 31; Kaplan and Herb 1999, 4). Hence, the assessment of the levels of hierarchy in both the spatial and political organization of territories as well as their bearing on the construction of identity (Knight 1999), can be done in archaeology by interpreting the geographic distributions of material evidence. Tombs, their architecture and their contents are likely to contain representations of cultural identities on both a personal/familial level and a communal level (*cf.* Lomas 2011, 9).

The presence of common denominators between different neighbouring sites means that we can call some areas 'regions' (Paasi 2001). These need to be recognized as real entities in the supra-regional system and in the social consciousness of interacting societies. As suggested earlier, in central Italy ethnicity has traditionally been seen as the shared identity defining different regions (on ethnicity, connectivity and interaction *cf.* also Cuozzo, Morris and Zamboni this volume, with additional bibliography). However, Jones (1997) and Hall (1997, 2–33) have shown that an ethnic identity is an inter-subjective reality defined by the group itself, and not a static but a dynamic category that is negotiable, situational and enhanced by conflict. The misuse of the notion of 'ethnic social identity' by nationalistic movements and ideologies has rendered it a controversial concept (Hakenbeck 2004; Zamboni this volume). However, this article cannot ignore discussing Latin, Etruscan or Sabine identities together with sub-ethnic identities within city-states, since these macro-categories are part of local history and archaeology, and make sense when comparing funerary architecture in different neighbouring areas.

Shared burial customs and funerary architecture are signs of interaction and common identities within and between communities. During the excavations at Cisterna Grande, the variability among the chamber tombs was an unexpected discovery, given the relative standardization of the chambers at Colle del Forno in the Sabine area (Santoro 1977; 1983), which at that time was the best-known Archaic chamber tomb cemetery east of the Tiber. Comparisons within Latium Vetus (Rajala 2007; 2008b; 2011; 2012) have suggested that this variability in funerary architecture and burials practices existed at the micro-regional scale between different city-states. The comparison of funerary architecture across the Tiber, within and between the supposed ethnic areas, allows us to evaluate the prevalence of different nested identities, and the creation of family and group affinities in the funerary sphere both locally and across the region. However, I will first assess in theoretical terms the variability caused by interaction across perceived boundaries.

Mental distances and burial customs

Boundaries do not necessarily coincide with physical border lines, but are everywhere in society and can therefore be based on various institutions such as diverging social practices, languages and discourses (*cf.* Bjerring Olsen 2004; Paasi 2000). The relativity of cultural borders implies that they may be represented as cultural or mental distances (Bjerring Olsen 2004, 3). Van Houtum (1999; 2001) observed that people's mental distance towards the other side, as well as their perception of the border's symbolic value, may affect significantly the kinds of relationships that develop across the boundary. Thus, if individuals or communities feel closeness with the other side, they are more likely to adopt influences, but if they feel distinctively separate, their response tends to be negative.

Bjerring Olsen (2004, 4) suggests that human beliefs, knowledge and behaviour are guided by universal, collective and individual values. Universal values are related to feelings of pain and pleasure. Collective values can be a shared set of norms, rules and beliefs within a group, whereas individual values are unique to a person due to their history. These values can underpin different types of identity, partly because of their nested nature. Therefore, even within a group there may be different representations of identities due to different experiences and interpretations of the group's norms. This notion can be used in interpreting the variability in funerary architecture in the area under examination.

Bjerring Olsen (2004, 5) concludes that people who belong to different systems of socialization are culturally programmed to exhibit differences in mental and behavioural patterns, owing to differences in collectively shared values. Because of the socially constructed nature of culture, the mental distance between two parties is not necessarily uniform. Thus, the influences or cultural loans can be unilateral: in a context such as Latium Vetus, with a federation of independent city-states, neighbouring centres or even individuals within those communities may have chosen not to adopt a given custom or architectural design. However, if the group allowed deviations from the norm, it would be easier for different alternatives to be chosen and therefore to be present in the archaeological record. Thus, mental distance reveals the habitual dispositions and the ways in which different cultural practices are experienced at the 'ethnic' and community level (*cf.* Bentley 1987; Bourdieu 1977).

The concept of mental distance suggests that cultural interaction may have both positive and negative outcomes, and different parties may perceive the possibility of interaction in different terms. The outcomes of cultural interactions depend on the agents' social attachment to different groups, and the cultural distances between these groups. Single individuals and communities may decide either to emphasize or to downplay their contacts and relationship to other entities or communal identities, and accordingly adopt or reject different customs or innovations. In addition, a 'distance' can be real or mental, and neighbouring communities may feel – and therefore display – closeness or distance depending on their perception of each other and what the boundary represents for them. The Tiber may have represented a natural boundary between the Latins, Etruscans, Sabines and Faliscans (*cf.* Livy 1.3.6), but different crossings (*cf.* for example Quilici Gigli 1986) probably offered an opportunity for contact, bringing people together. The same can be said of the Aniene River, which both joined and separated Latin communities at a different nested level.

Mental distances between regions can explain the strength or weakness of interaction. Archaeological finds can be used to evaluate the cultural closeness or remoteness of different centres in a regional setting. Thus, I suggest that mental distance between neighbours can be defined on the basis of different distributions of material culture and potential symbols of identity. In the following section, I will consider how burial customs and funerary architecture may have reflected cultural distances inside Latium Vetus and across the ethnic boundaries of Orientalizing and Archaic central Italy.

Mental distances in Orientalizing and Archaic central Italy

The overall archaeological evidence for Orientalizing and Archaic funerary practices in central Italy is fragmentary. The publication of historical and modern excavations at centres such as Veii, Eretum and Castel di Decima is far from complete. In addition, it is quite clear that sites such as Torrino or Tor de' Cenci in Latium were not on the same hierarchical level as the large cities of Rome or Crustumerium. Major/minor or primary/secondary centres are generally discussed separately; for example, Colonna (1991, 212–14) regarded Acqua Acetosa Laurentina and La Rustica as aristocratic centres that related to the boundaries of Archaic Rome (*ager antiquus romanus*). Considering the poor publication record of the vast Orientalizing cemeteries from the area, the amount of material still under study, as well as the patchiness of Archaic funerary evidence, especially in Latium, the significant evidence from minor centres, which are perceived as dependent on larger centres, is considered here independently in order to understand the distribution and range of different tomb types in the region.

Riva (2010) has emphasized the hybrid, Mediterranean-wide nature of Etruscan élite culture. The existence of the rich Tomba Barberini (Curtis 1925), Tomba Bernardini (Curtis 1919; Canciani and von Hase 1979) and other so-called 'princely tombs' in Latium Vetus (*cf.* Fulminante 2003) indicates that the same phenomenon was at work there (on the notion of 'princely tomb' *cf.* also Cuozzo and Morris this volume). The drop in the size of funerary assemblages in Latium Vetus by the Archaic period took place against this background. Given that different burial customs persisted or disappeared at different paces in different regions, this variability (*cf.* Figs 8.1 and 8.3–8.5) allows us to assess the fluidity and nested tendencies in cultural and funerary identities.

Burial rites in central Italy

During the Orientalizing and Archaic periods the dominant rite in central Italy was inhumation (Fig. 8.1); furthermore, the settlement areas were physically separate from the burial sites (e.g. Bartoloni 2003, 20–7). However, in Latium small infants could be buried inside settlements, a custom that is unattested in the adjacent areas. Thus, Brandt (1996, 115) has suggested that this burial practice can be used to define the boundaries of the Latin area.

All burials excavated at Cisterna Grande were inhumations; similarly, inhumations prevailed at Monte Del Bufalo (*cf.* Belelli Marchesini and Pantano 2014; Willemsen 2014). In neighbouring areas (Fig. 8.1) cremation was the dominant burial rite only in Veii (Drago Troccoli 1997, 269) and coexisted with inhumation to a relatively equal extent at Volsinii (modern Orvieto; Bonamici *et al.* 1994, 28–9). In the Faliscan area cremations appeared occasionally in the fifth century BC, with the cremated remains placed in prestige bronze or pottery vessels (De Lucia Brolli 1991, 29).

Veii shared with the Latin area the decline in the number of Archaic grave goods (Fig. 8.3; Drago Troccoli 1997). Yet the abolition of funerary opulence did not happen everywhere (Fig. 8.3; *cf.* for example Alvino 2009, 68; Rizzo 2006). For instance, there was a drop in the southern Sabine area, but the Archaic tombs in the north continued to include rich ceramic grave goods (Alvino 1985; 1987; 2009, 68; Alvino and Santoro 1984). The lack of records from the early excavations at Veii, the distribution of their material all over the world (*cf.* for example Bartoloni and Delpino 1979, 17–32) and the continuous reburial and reuse of tomb contexts that took place especially in the Faliscan area (*cf.* for example De Lucia Brolli 1991, 29–30) complicate the assessment of the relative richness of sixth- and fifth-century BC tombs in south-eastern Etruria. However, the wealth of painted Greek vases found at Vulci and Cerveteri (e.g. Colonna 1974, 254; Leighton 2004, 93–4) and the imports at Falerii Veteres in the Faliscan area (*cf.* Carlucci and De Lucia 1998, 16–8; De Lucia Brolli 1991, 28–37) suggest that grave

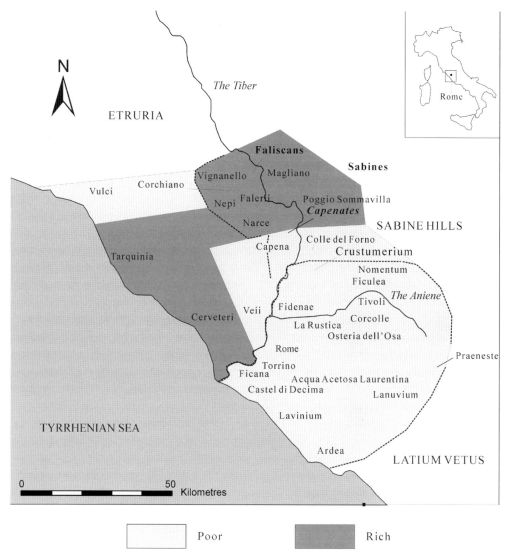

Fig. 8.3: Map showing the spatial distribution of tombs with different quality of grave goods in Archaic Latium Vetus and southern Etruria (map: U. Rajala).

goods were deposited in tombs in most of southern Etruria during this period. Yet no grave goods were found at Vulci in the later tombs from the second half of the fifth century BC (Gsell 1891, 528–32).

Veii is an interesting case. Its cremation rite stood apart from the customs of its Etruscan, Faliscan, Sabine and Latin neighbours. This suggests a strong local identity. However, the Archaic period witnessed a drop in the number of grave goods deposited in Veii, a pattern consistent with the burial data from the Latin and southern Sabine communities. These patterns reveal the nested nature of the different identities that can be recognized in these burials. Local funerary identity in Veii was clear, but some values were shared with the Latins, probably reflecting both the contradictions of the geographical proximity and political confrontation between Veii and Rome, as well as the alliances with the northern Latins and Sabines (*cf.* Livy 1.10.1–3; 1.15.1–6; 1.30.6–7; 2.53.1).

Funerary architecture in Latium Vetus

The Orientalizing tombs at Crustumerium continue the tradition of simple Iron Age trenches (*fosse*), some with stone lining (*cassa*) and more complex trenches with an apsidal niche for the many ceramic grave goods. The tombs that have been classified as *tombe a loculo tipo Narce*, with a longitudinal niche (*loculus*) for the corpse and grave goods, appeared during the seventh century BC (Belelli Marchesini 2008; Belelli Marchesini and Pantano 2014; di Gennaro 1999). Double tombs (*tombe a loculo tipo Monterosi*) with two *loculi* along the long sides of the shaft (*caditoia*) are of similar date. The first chamber tomb, from the mid-seventh century BC at Sasso Bianco, had a *caditoia* instead of a proper entrance corridor or *dromos* (Paolini 1990). At Monte Del Bufalo the chamber tombs date to the last quarter of the seventh century BC (Belelli Marchesini and Pantano 2014). The later Orientalizing chambers were simply rectangular or square with burials placed on the floor, whereas the dominant Archaic chamber type had *loculi* on the walls (di Gennaro 1999; *cf.* also Belelli Marchesini 2008; Belelli Marchesini and Pantano 2014; Rajala 2008b; 2011; 2012; Willems 2014).

Despite their different layouts, the Archaic chamber tombs at Cisterna Grande seem to fall into two main categories. The first has large, rectangular chambers with one or more *loculi*, while the second has small, low, rounded chambers with two irregular *loculi* on the opposite sides of the chamber. Both types have burials also on the chamber floor and secondary burials in the *loculi*, which are most often closed with tiles. All chamber tombs yielded the remains of blocking elements that closed the entrance, and most were reinforced with a heap of stones. The location of some ceramic grave goods, such as jars placed just behind the doors of late Orientalizing chambers, suggests that closing rituals took place, even when there was no evidence of offerings in the *dromoi*.

At Fidenae the Orientalizing tombs were very similar to each other, as at Crustumerium. The famous rich Archaic female inhumation inside the ancient town was exceptional (di Gennaro 1990). Recent excavations have revealed two cemetery areas outside the town. In the north-eastern cemetery area, numerous tombs included simple *fosse* and *tombe a grande fossa con loculo absidale* from the eighth century BC, *tombe a loculo tipo Narce* from the late eighth and seventh centuries BC, and chamber tombs, some with *loculi* (di Gennaro *et al.* 2007, footnote 20, 141) showing closeness to Crustumerium.

Little is known about the cemeteries of Nomentum. An Orientalizing tomb with a stone lining (*cassa*) contained black *bucchero*, Italo-Corinthian and local wares and dated to the last quarter of the seventh century BC (Pala 1976, *sito* 1.78, 61–3). However, no tombs securely datable to the Archaic period are known. A constructed chamber, later used as a chapel, has been dated to the fourth century BC on the basis of its architecture (Pala 1976, *sito* 1.39, 37). Some *fossa* tombs, covered with stones and containing pottery as grave goods, date to the fourth and third centuries BC (Pala 1976, *sito* 1.51, 98–9).

The evidence from Ficulea is meagre apart from an Orientalizing *tumulus* near Torre S. Giovanni (Quilici and Quilici Gigli 1993, 463), which is similar to the *tumulus* on the road towards Ficulea near Crustumerium (Quilici and Quilici Gigli 1980, *sito* 88, 278–9; *cf.* also Zifferero 1991, 123, fig. 14). At Antemnae, south of the Aniene, there are no excavated cemeteries. The only known burial appears to be an Orientalizing child *enchytrismos* (a burial in a pottery jar) from the urban area (Quilici and Quilici Gigli 1978, 42–3).

At the famous Iron Age cemetery of Osteria dell'Osa at ancient Gabii, Tomb 62 is the only excavated chamber tomb,[1] and is dated to 630/620–580 BC (De Santis 1992, 864–74; tav. 50–2). This tomb had two separate chambers, one aligned with the *dromos* and the other oriented perpendicularly towards north-north-west. Both chambers had U-shaped benches. The tomb contained 13 relatively rich burials. One of the male skeletons was apparently cremated *in situ* according to a burial rite that appears to have been Etruscan (Bietti Sestieri and De Santis 2000, 28–9, 69–70; De Santis 1992, 867–8). This probably reflects closeness among different élite groups that were adopting a new tomb type.

The evidence from Rome itself is very fragmentary and the nineteenth-century excavations were not properly recorded. The Orientalizing tombs on the Esquiline included constructed and dug chambers (Cifani 2008, 323–4; Pinza 1905, 149–53, 194–5), but there is no evidence for Archaic chamber tombs. Simple *fosse*, stone-lined *casse* and *sarcophagi*, the finest of which are in marble, were customary (*cf.* Cifani 2008, 326; Naso 1990). The simpler *sarcophagi* of *pietra gabina* stone date from the end of the sixth century BC, but the ones of *peperino* stone are from the late fifth century BC (Colonna 1977, 136–49).

Tivoli partook in the use of *sarcophagi*, including a marble one. The burials were placed in trenches (*fosse*) similar to those at Praeneste (*cf.* Faccenna 1957, 123; Pensabene 1983, 260–8). The Tivoli *sarcophagi* date from the fifth or fourth centuries BC. Thus, Colonna (1977, 155) has suggested that *peperino sarcophagi*, together with the *tombe a loculo* without finds from the Orientalizing cemetery of La Rustica, nearer Rome, could be Archaic.

At Praeneste the rich Orientalizing graves known as Tomba Barberini (Curtis 1925) and Tomba Bernardini (Canciani and Von Hase 1979; Curtis 1919) were 'pseudo-chambers'. The details of Tomba Barberini are sketchy,[2] but the tomb is considered to have been built after an Etruscan model with local material (Curtis 1925, 9–11). More is known of

Tomba Barberini (Canciani and Von Hase 1979; Curtis 1919); it had a large rectangular trench with a smaller 2 m-long *fossa* dug into its base. The walls of the smaller *fossa* were lined with tuff blocks. Canciani and Von Hase (1979, 4) compared the tomb with the princely tombs at Pontecagnano, but these are all 'simpler' *cassa fossa* tombs (Cuozzo 2003; on Pontecagnano *cf.* also Cuozzo and Morris this volume). 'Pseudo-chambers' are also known from Acqua Acetosa Laurentina (Bedini 2000) and Vivaro in the Alban Hills (Arietti and Martellotta 1998) as well as from Satricum in *Latium adiectum* (Waarsenburg 1995, 293–8; *cf.* also Cifani 2008, 323). More modest trenches with *fosse* dug into their bases are present at Osteria dell'Osa (e.g. Bietti Sestieri 1992, fig. 3.c.45) and Crustumerium (di Gennaro 1999). At Pontecagnano the dead were still buried in *fosse* during the Archaic period (Cerchiai 1995). The dominance of Archaic *fosse* in Campania, Abruzzo (D'Ercole and Benelli 2004) and along the Adriatic coast (Scopacasa 2015) may have had an impact on eastern Latium.

The famous 'warrior' at Lanuvium in the Alban Hills was buried in a *sarcophagus*. This burial dates from around 480 BC (Zevi 1990, 251). Zevi (1993) suggested that the tomb was a *tomba ipogea* (namely a subterranean grave), but the published records show no ceiling. The tomb had a *dromos* (*l'accesso a scivolo*), but it lacked the blocking elements that are customary in proper chambers. At Corcolle, north-east of Rome, tuff *sarcophagi* were found in chamber tombs from the mid-sixth century BC (Reggiani *et al.* 1998). A series of *fosse* with no surviving grave goods were found in a separate area at the same site, but their chronology remains unclear. Finds from these two ancient towns show that the *sarcophagi*, which are common in north-eastern Latium, were combined with chamber architecture and may have been followed by *fosse*, which were also a local preference.

At Ardea a group of miniature objects and a Latial *fossa* belonging to a child point to early infant burials on the acropolis (Andrén 1961, 33–4). A few fragments of Orientalizing pottery (Andrén 1961, 47) have been interpreted as the remains of a cemetery area (Colonna 1977, 132; Naso 1990, 250–1). Additional unstratified objects from the northern edge of the acropolis were seen as the continuation of this possible cemetery (Morselli and Tortorici 1982, *sito* 57). Poor *fosse* were interpreted as later child burials (Tortorici 1983, 54).

Outside Ardea a double grave from the transition between the Orientalizing and Archaic periods at Campo del Fico, south of the town, is a late example of the continuing tradition of trench burial, with some imported wares from Vulci or Cerveteri (*cf.* Bartoloni *et al.* 2009, 76; Tortorici 1983, 81–3). The north-eastern cemetery revealed a series of *fosse* with no surviving grave goods, as well as chamber tombs (Morselli and Tortorici 1982, *sito* 155, 130–1; Pasqui 1900). The *fosse* were filled only with soil. The chambers were either rectangular or square in shape with a short *dromos*. Some had *loculi* or benches inside (Morselli and Tortorici 1982, footnote 539), with finds dating from the Iron Age to the third century BC. At Ardea two chamber tombs with two columns supporting the ceiling reveal clear Etruscan influences (Morselli and Tortorici 1982, 110–1; Quilici and Quilici Gigli 1977).

The excavated tombs at Lavinium, from the so-called 'Heroon' and 'Tumulo Trovalusci', are exceptional. The 'Heroon' is a commemorative monument that incorporated an Orientalizing *cassa* tomb from *c.* 670/660 BC. The site of Lavinium was monumentalized around 570–560 BC, but the 'Heroon' chamber and the *tumulus* atop were added only in the fourth century BC (Fulminante 2003, 207; Sommella 1971–1972). The Tumulo Trovalusci incorporated a two-room chamber, dated between the mid-sixth and mid-fourth century BC (Cifani 2008, 326; Guaitoli 1995, 557–62). It also contained a cremation burial in a *cappellaccio cassa* as well as a black *bucchero* amphora with a dedication from an Etruscan individual called **Mamarce Apunie**, who is also known from a votive offering at the sanctuary of Portonaccio in Veii (Bartoloni *et al.* 2009, 76, 78; Guaitoli 1995). This 30 m-wide and 3 m-high mound clearly belongs to the Orientalizing mound tradition (*cf.* Naso 1990; Zifferero 1991) and suggests a range of Etruscan contacts.

Ficana has the clearest evidence for the continuation of different *fossa* and *tomba a loculo* tomb types into the Archaic period.[3] These tombs include simple *fosse* with soil fills, *tombe a loculo tipo Narce* (called *fosse munite di grande loculo laterale*) filled with stones, *tombe a cassone*, tombs covered with slabs *alla cappuccina* and *fosse* covered with roof tiles. Bartoloni and Cataldi Dini (1978, 41) have suggested that the last three tomb types were the most recent. The total lack of grave goods separates the later tombs from the earlier ones (Bartoloni and Cataldi Dini 1978; Cataldi Dini 1980). In addition, children's *fosse* and *enchytrismos* burials (Brandt 1996, 115–64; Jarva 1980) were found in the settlement area.

At Torrino, just north of Ficana, two chambers contained Orientalizing material. The larger tomb looked like a conglomerate of later, smaller 'pod-like' chambers that are also found at Acqua Acetosa Laurentina and Tor de' Cenci (*cf.* below). The smaller chamber was used around 630–600 BC in the late Orientalizing period (Bedini 1981, 60). The assemblage of vases from the larger tomb can be compared in terms of its chronology and composition to the one from Tomb 62 at Osteria dell'Osa. Bedini (1981, 61) has interpreted this group as a repository for earlier burials, since other 'pods' were sealed and without surviving grave goods, a ritual feature suggesting that they date from the Archaic period.

At Acqua Acetosa Laurentina further inland, several Archaic tomb types were in use in the same period. These included a 'pod-like' chamber and a rectangular chamber tomb (Bedini 1983, Fig. 8.3), both with one *loculus* on the right-hand side. Moreover, Acqua Acetosa Laurentina yielded *tombe a loculo* closed with roof tiles, simple *fosse*, tile cists or *cassoni* and infant burials (Bedini 1980). At Casale Massima nearby, approximately 20 Archaic chamber tombs with no surviving grave goods disturbed earlier Orientalizing *fosse* and have been dated loosely to the sixth and fifth centuries BC (Bedini 1980, 58–60). The area north of the fortification or *agger* at Acqua Acetosa Laurentina revealed an additional tomb type, namely a *dromos a loculo* (Bedini 1983, fig. 11, 36).[4] Both Archaic *tombe a loculo* and *dromoi a loculo* were found at La Rustica, too (*cf.* Cifani 2008, 326; Colonna 1977, 155; di Gennaro 2007, footnote 2), and apparently also at Gabii (di Gennaro 2007, footnote 2).

At Tor de' Cenci (Bedini 1990a), approximately 2 km from Castel di Decima south of Rome, eight chamber tombs with a similar 'pod-like' design were situated at a crossroads as at Acqua Acetosa Laurentina and seem to avoid disturbing earlier Orientalizing *fosse*. These 'pods' had a narrow chamber, hardly wider than the *dromos*, and one *loculus* on the right-hand side, except in one case where two *loculi* opposite each other were created (Bedini 1990a, fig. 9). Two tombs had no surviving grave goods. Two deep trenches had large stones lining the walls near the base and are similar to the *cassoni* or pseudo-*cassoni* of Ficana and north-eastern Latium; furthermore, a *tomba a loculo* with no surviving grave goods recalls those at Ficana and Acqua Acetosa Laurentina.

There are no confirmed Archaic tombs at Castel di Decima itself, although one *fossa* tomb had no surviving grave goods and displayed an anomalous orientation (Bartoloni *et al.* 1975, 367). Tombs with no surviving grave goods were interpreted as lower-class or slave burials (Bartoloni *et al.* 2009, 85; on the issue of inequality and marginality in the funerary record *cf.* also Cuozzo, Iaia, and especially Perego, Zanoni, and Perego and Scopacasa this volume). The Orientalizing *tumulus* of Castel di Decima contained an unusual burial, either a special kind of cremation or a cenotaph (*cf.* Bartoloni 1984, 16; Bedini 1977; Colonna 1989, 465); this *tumulus* may be comparable to the *tumuli* at Lavinium and Vulci (*cf.* below).

The data from Latium Vetus shows that during the Orientalizing period the élite groups at Osteria dell'Osa and Torrino chose chamber structures for their new communal graves. The Archaic evidence reveals the presence of areas in which different dominant tomb types spread during the same period. The chamber tomb grave type with *loculi* was dominant north of the Aniene, with additional occurrences at Corcolle, Ardea and Acqua Acetosa Laurentina. *Fossa* and *tomba a loculo* types were common especially in the south-west and north-east, while *fosse* with *sarcophagus* and *cassa* tomb types were dominant in Rome, farther northeast and possibly in the Alban Hills. The southern coast showed Etruscan contacts suggesting cultural closeness to Etruria. The nested identities are shown in (a) the acceptance of infant burials inside the settlements, a practice which can relate to the development of identities that can be verified on an ethnic or regional level; (b) different preferences regarding tomb types attested at the city-state level; (c) intra-site variability at many settlements, disclosing the negotiation of identities at the family and individual level.

Chronological differences remain slightly unclear, partly due to the fact that many tombs have no surviving grave goods. The chamber tombs with *loculi* seem to date from the sixth century BC, whereas the *sarcophagi* at Rome, Lanuvium and the northeast date from the fifth century BC. The *tombe a loculo* at Ficana and Acqua Acetosa Laurentina, as well as similar structures at La Rustica and Gabii, show that the trench tradition continued into the Archaic period, with simple *fosse* and *sarcophagi* following a simpler 'trench tradition'. The local funerary traditions (*cf.* also Bedini 1983, 37; di Gennaro 2007, footnote 2; on the Laurentina *cf.* also Bedini 1990b) reflect the local identities of different Latin centres (*cf.* Rajala 2007; 2008b; 2011; 2012), even if a wider regional identity, revealed by the distribution of infant burials, is apparent. The later *sarcophagi* are often referred to as 'Archaic tombs' in the literature, even if their dating is late Archaic or Classical. These, together with the possibly of mid-Republican simple *fosse* at Ardea and Corcolle, may highlight an expanding 'Roman' identity that was shared under Roman supremacy.

Tomb architecture in the Sabine area

Eretum was the nearest Sabine centre from Crustumerium and other northern Latin settlements. The Archaic material culture in the cemetery of Eretum at Colle del Forno was very similar to that at Cisterna Grande, as indicated by identical grave good assemblages from the Archaic tombs (Rajala *et al.* 2012). However, the tomb architecture at these two centres differs. At Colle del Forno only individuals of exceptional social standing were granted monumental tombs that were different from the commonest types (Benelli and Santoro 2006; 2009). Tomb 36 dated to the late sixth century BC and yielded fewer high-status symbols than Tomb 11 from the Orientalizing period. Notably, however, Tomb 36 combined the Latin lack of opulence with an Etruscan cruciform chamber tomb layout (*cf.* below). This suggests the existence of a supra-ethnic, regional élite identity. On the other hand, the standard rectangular chambers with multiple *loculi* and simple grave goods were similar to those in northern Latium, but the lack of variability contrasts with Cisterna Grande.

Little is known about the cemeteries of the settlement of Cures Sabini (*cf.* Guidi 1997). Muzzioli (1980) listed only sporadic pre-Roman chamber tombs (nos 142 and 143), with the exception of the cemetery at Campo del Pozzo by the Tiber (no. 123).[5]

The cemetery of Poggio Sommavilla in the north revealed 48 tombs (Alvino 1985; 1987; Alvino and Santoro 1984; Santoro 1981), most of which were chamber tombs. The cemetery started to be used in the second half of the seventh century BC with *tombe a fossa* that are seemingly contemporaneous with chamber tombs. Tomb 2 (Santoro 1981, fig. 3) is very similar to the 'pod-like' single chamber at Torrino and similarly contained late Orientalizing pottery, whereas the dating and layout of Tomb 4 (Alvino and Santoro 1984, fig. 4) recall those of Tomb 62 at Osteria dell'Osa.[6] One prominent chamber type had a relatively long *dromos* and squarish chamber, whereas another type had a rectangular chamber with *loculi* on three sides. However, some layouts diverted from the norm, partly due to their protracted use over time. Tomb 16, for example, displayed a central column and *loculi* at five different points. It was first used during the early sixth century BC and was reused towards the end of the fourth century (Alvino 1985, 93; Alvino and Santoro 1984, 79). Only Tomb 27 was a single-period tomb with an individual late Orientalizing burial (Alvino 1985, 96). This tomb was characterized by a *fossa* dug into the base of a larger *fossa*, a design familiar from the Tomba Bernardini at Palestrina.

Tomb finds are rarer further north, but cemeteries are known at Magliano Sabina (Alvino 1997, 19; Santoro 1997a, 22–7). At Colle del Giglio pilasters were constructed with tuff blocks (Santoro 1997b, 76), whereas chambers with funerary benches and rich male burials from the second half of the seventh century BC were found in the survey of Magliano (Santoro 1997a, 27). However, the use of *tombe con loculo* continued throughout the sixth century (Santoro 1997c, 82), with imported Etrusco-Corinthian pottery from Vulci found at Colle del Giglio and San Biagio.

The southern Sabine area had close contacts with Veii, Cerveteri and the *ager capenas*, whereas the northern areas turned towards the Faliscan area, Volsinii and Vulci (Alvino 2009, 68). The clearest difference between these two areas is the quantity of grave goods deposited in Archaic tombs. The so-called *anfore sabine* ('Sabine' amphorae) have been seen as related to Sabine identity (Cristofani Martelli 1977), but their distribution is concentrated in the northern Sabine area (*cf.* Alvino 1997, 21; Santoro 1997d). Thus, the tombs showed nested identities reflecting belonging to an ethnic group which was signalled with chamber tombs, whilst also presenting different mental distances and affinities at the city-state level in terms of architectural detail and grave goods.

Funerary architecture of the Faliscans and the Capenates

The main Orientalizing tomb type in the Faliscan area and at Capena was the *tomba a loculo*. The chamber tombs with *loculi* date to the late seventh and sixth centuries BC (Naso 1996b, 311–2). While the full understanding of funerary customs from this area is hindered by the partial publication of old excavations,[7] funerary architecture can be easily evaluated from plans and descriptions.

Cifani (2003, 99) and Ceccarelli and Stoddart (2007, 143–4) argued that the equal dimensions of chamber tombs at Falerii Veteres reflected the equal statuses of the deceased. Most chambers were either simple square or rectangular-shaped rooms with *loculi* on three walls, and appear to have been standardized like at Colle del Forno. However, some tombs diverted from the norm with additional rows of *loculi* or other features (*cf.* Cozza and Pasqui 1981, 100, 146, 188, 206). The finds from Celle (Cozza and Pasqui 1981, 102–4) suggest a momentary drop in the number of grave goods, perhaps coinciding with the late Orientalizing period, when the poorer *fosse con loculi* and richer chamber tombs with Corinthian vases coexisted.[8] The sixth-century BC chamber tombs once again contained lavish grave goods such as Greek metalwork and red-figure pottery.

The tomb typology at Narce ranged from Iron Age pits to Orientalizing *tombe a loculo tipo Narce* and Archaic chamber tombs. Chamber tombs were present in 15 different cemetery areas (*cf.* Barnabei *et al.* 1894; Pasqui 1902; Potter 1976, table 1). These chamber tomb typologies were more varied than at Falerii,[9] and included different Etruscan types, but also tomb types familiar from Osteria dell'Osa and southern Latium.[10] The *fosse* and chamber tombs at Narce are also known to have contained tuff *sarcophagi* (e.g. Barnabei *et al.* 1894, colls 437–8, 464, 515, 531–2, 541–2). Their dating is unclear due to the long period of reuse of the tombs; a few seem to be from the Orientalizing period.

At Corchiano different cemetery areas reflected different identities at the community level, as well as different histories of use of the cemeteries. Orientalizing tombs were mainly *tombe a loculo* and simple squarish chambers, whereas most chamber tombs had *loculi*, sometimes with Etruscan features. The site of *Il primo di Caprigliano* revealed mainly *tombe a loculo* and simple Orientalizing squarish chambers. The site of *Il secondo di Caprigliano* had a variety of different types, whereas the cemeteries at Vallone contained mainly chamber tombs with *loculi*, similar to those found elsewhere in the Faliscan area. Both areas yielded Orientalizing and Archaic grave goods. At the site of *Il primo di S. Antonio* the chamber tombs with *loculi* had Etruscan-style pre-chambers, whereas *Il secondo di S. Antonio* included also Classical and Hellenistic tombs (Cozza and Pasqui 1981, 219–311).

At Vignanello little is known about the Orientalizing tombs (Giglioli 1924). The chamber tombs were rectangular, squarish or trapezoid. The chambers were of different sizes, some without *loculi*. There were unique tombs, such as a chamber with a *colonna tuscanica* (Tuscan column) supporting the ceiling, showing an Etruscan design similar to that of the chambers at Ardea. Other exceptional architecture types included a tomb with funerary beds and one with two large *loculi*. There is also evidence of *ad hoc* reparations and the cutting of *loculi* on demand. Most chamber tombs had both Archaic and Hellenistic phases, with merely three tombs displaying evidence of use in a single period only. The tombs at Vignanello also included Orientalizing and Archaic *sarcophagi* (Giglioli 1924, 236–44). The three small *sarcophagi* found at this site were positioned onto two cut shelves on two sides of the steps leading to a well in Cavo N. These tuff *sarcophagi* were clearly for children and probably contained inhumations. A Corinthian *pyxis* suggests a transitional or early Archaic date (*cf.* Giglioli 1924, 242; Szilágyi 1998, 675). However, the two other *sarcophagi* contained only Orientalizing pottery.

Recently, Cifani (pers. comm.) has suggested that the frontier town of Nepi was an Etruscan centre, not a Faliscan one, with close ties with Cerveteri. However, the burial sites at Nepi resemble the Faliscan cemeteries (*cf.* Carlucci and De Lucia 1998, 28–9; De Lucia 1991, 94–7; Rizzo 1996; 2006), with unusual layouts suggesting a diverse population.[11] Rizzo (1996, 479) also compared the local tomb typology found at Nepi to the Sabine typology. Different pottery types show contacts with Veii and Cerveteri, but these are commonly shared with the Sabine area and the *ager capenas* (Rizzo 2006). The supposed influences from Cerveteri are most evident outside Nepi, in view of the funerary beds found at Tenuta Franca in the north and the presumed *tumulus* found to the west at Monte del Tufo (Cifani 2003, 95). This may suggest that the 'funerary identity' (i.e. the set of funerary practices and material culture) in Nepi was Faliscan, but that the population, contacts and power relations were in flux.

At Capena and the *ager capenas* the tomb typology spans the long interval from the Iron Age to the Roman period (*cf.* Paribeni 1906; Stefani 1958).[12] The early chambers were simple, shallow and irregularly trapezoid, with funerary benches and occasionally with trenches for earlier burials that were re-deposited. Most chamber tombs had a *dromos* and three or more *loculi* that were closed with tiles. However, there were also many tombs that displayed unusual features. A limited number of tombs were cruciform, or with a pair of *loculi* in the *dromos* opposite each other like at Vulci (Gsell 1891, 14, 16).

Chamber tombs were introduced across the *ager capenas* and the Faliscan area at the end of the Orientalizing period, when the *tomba a loculo tipo Narce* was the dominant type. The most common type of Archaic chamber tomb was the chamber with *loculi*, suggesting mental closeness with the Sabine area. Nevertheless, the tombs presented many *ad hoc* features, irregular plans and even transitional forms and signs of reuse. Cruciform tombs and antechambers show Etruscan influences, even if their number is limited. The partly constructed chambers emphasize links across the Tiber (Santoro 1997a, 26), whereas the differences in variability between Falerii Veteres and Narce show local funerary identities, in contrast with what is suggested by the more regional and later *tombe a portico falische* (Colonna 1990, 129–35). This evidence reveals the changing nested identities in the Faliscan funerary contexts: initially the tombs reflected local independence at the city-state level and then regional Faliscan identity.

Funerary architecture in southern Etruria

In general, the Etruscan tomb types reflected the identity of every city-state; in particular, the architecture and rites follow local norms that Stoddart (1990, 47) saw as distinctions between competing city-states. The Orientalizing *tombe a loculo*, which are common in the Latin, Sabine and Faliscan areas, concentrate in two areas in Etruria with sporadic examples in Cerveteri, near Civitavecchia, and at Bisenzio. The northern concentration is around Pitigliano, Poggio Buco and Cellano and the southern is around Veii, Trevigliano and Poggio Montarano (Naso 1996b, 311–2, n. 478).

Some of the most interesting evidence from Etruria comes from Veii. The Orientalizing tombs at this site included *tombe a loculo* and later simple chambers with a long *dromos* and burials on the chamber floor (Colini 1919). The Orientalizing *tumuli*, the most famous of which is located at Vacchareccia, were a funerary feature that Veii shared with northern Latium Vetus (*cf.* Zifferero 1991). Similarly, the practice of cremating the corpse *in situ* is known from Monte Michele (Bietti Sestieri and De Santis 1992, 207; Boitani 1985). Furthermore, one small chamber tomb near the Veian north-eastern Gate (Ward Perkins 1961, 78, fig. 25, pl. 18a) is very similar to the later Archaic 'pod-like' chambers attested in southern Latium. It did not have a *dromos*, but its door was cut directly into the rock face. The chamber inside was narrower than the architectural framing outside (*cf.* Naso 1996b, fig. 3; Ward Perkins 1961, 78, fig. 25, pl. 18a). It is dated to the seventh century BC (Boitani 1985, 556; Naso 1996b, 21), which suggests it was contemporaneous with the tombs at Terrino; however, its similarity to the 'pods' at Tor de' Cenci and Acqua Acetosa Laurentina is more striking.

As far as later chronological phases are concerned, Drago Troccoli (1997, 269) has suggested that the dominant tomb type at Veii during the Archaic and Classical periods was a *tomba a fossa con loculi a cremazione con o senza gradini* (*fossa* tomb with *loculi* and cremation burials, with or without steps). It is not clear if the *tombe a loculo* without grave goods also found at this site date from this period. Nevertheless, the Archaic *tomba a fossa* and *tomba a tipo Monte Michele* types had parallels in Latium Vetus, although the prevalence of cremation meant that the tomb design could be very different (Drago Troccoli 1997, fig. 2).

Overall, the number of known sixth- or fifth-century BC graves from Veii is just over 40 (Drago Troccoli 1997, 269). Approximately 30 are *tombe a fossa con loculi* and ten simple pit tombs (Bartoloni *et al.* 1994, 38–9). These graves were located in different cemetery areas. The tomb structures were very conservative and uniform (Drago Troccoli 1997, 269–70). The oldest Archaic tombs lacked surviving grave goods altogether. The number of grave goods increased later, generally with the presence of ceramic objects in small quantities and a few pieces of jewellery; however, very few fibulae or Greek imports are attested. The urns tended to be *stamnoi* of *bucchero grigio*. The occurrence of pit tombs characterized by the adoption of a different burial rite (i.e. cremation) makes Archaic Veian tomb architecture truly original in the region and distances it from the surrounding areas. Naturally, the small number of burials that can safely be dated to the Archaic period (as many are found in chamber tombs excavated in the nineteenth century) does not allow us to fully evaluate to what extent Veii was different from nearby settlements in this phase. This leaves room for the possibility that a greater closeness with neighbouring centres persisted – as was the situation during the Orientalizing period. Nevertheless, the adoption of a distinct burial practice and architecture suggests that at a certain point Veii may have indeed developed an independent funerary identity.

As in the Faliscan area, *sarcophagi* were present at Veii (Bartoloni and Delpino 1979). Two tuff *sarcophagi con coperchio* (i.e. with a lid) at Valle la Fata contained inhumations.[13] The meagre grave goods match those in Archaic Latium. If they date to the fifth century BC, this suggests that the diffusion of *sarcophagi* was not necessarily related to the dominance of Rome, since they occurred simultaneously or earlier among its rivals.

Another notable site is Cerveteri. The typological series of chamber tombs at this settlement suggests that the Orientalizing chambers were generally cruciform and developed slowly into a tomb type characterized by a rectangular *atrio* and two *cubicula* (Izzet 2007a, fig. 3.2; Prayon 1975, pl. 85; for the chamber types *cf.* Naso 1996b). The earliest rounded chambers, which appear to have developed from *fosse* (Prayon 1975, 16), were very similar to the 'pods' at Torrino. The Orientalizing tombs at Banditaccia were predominantly covered by a mound. These chambers and those found in Latium Vetus were very different. However, the monumental mounds from the sites of Lavinium and Decima in Latium may have been influenced by these Early Orientalizing monumental mounds (Zifferero 1991, 111, figs 3 and 4). The Denti di Lupo Tomb at Cerveteri, dated to 630–620 BC, had a very similar layout to Tomb 62 at Osteria dell'Osa, despite having separate funerary beds (Naso 1996b, 38–41, fig. 11). Parallels between Cerveteri and Latium Vetus become more common at the end of the sixth century BC, with the late square chambers with or without a supporting central column, and funerary beds that recall those at Ardea. These cube tombs (*tombe a dado*) lined the roads at Bandidaccia outside Cerveteri (Izzet 2007a, 117).

At Tarquinia chambers were more versatile. They were often squarish or rectangular and sometimes featured *loculi* or a U-shaped bench. There were also cruciform types and tombs characterized by a rectangular *atrio* and two *cubicula* (Steingräber 1985, 386–7; for the chamber types *cf.* Naso 1996b). Most chambers at Monterrozzi were covered by a small mound. These show affinity to the types present at Cerveteri, whereas the simpler chambers with and without *loculi* have parallels in the Faliscan, Sabine and Latin areas.

At Vulci the Orientalizing tombs were mainly *fosse*, although small elongated apsidal chambers were cut from the sixth century BC onwards (Gsell 1891). During the Archaic period the dominant tomb type was the *tomba a cassone* (Falconi Amorelli 1987). The *tumulus* of Cuccumella, with at least part of the decorative sculptures dated from the Archaic period (van Kempen 2009, 145–8), belong to the élite mound tradition of central Italy. The fifth-century BC 'pod-like' chambers with or without a *loculus* and with very poor inhumation depositions (Gsell 1891, 528–9, figs 19 and 73) were very similar to those around Acqua Acetosa Laurentina.

The urban cemetery located along the Via Cassia at Sutri, west of Nepi, is Roman (Morselli 1980, 54–77, site no. 2). The lack of tombs in a historically known Etruscan centre (*cf.* for example Duncan and Reynolds 1958) is puzzling, but many of these may have been remodelled in Roman and Medieval times. The only certain pre-Roman tomb was located in the northern side of the town and has been partly destroyed (Morselli 1980, 85–6). It featured two consecutive chambers with two funerary beds, which are dated on the basis of their architectural features between the sixth and fourth centuries BC. There are further small groups of chambers with *loculi* and funerary benches located farther east of the town itself (*cf.* Cifani 2003, 90, footnote 426; Morselli 1980, site nos 30, 37, 67, 84, 173). The tombs near Sutri differ from the Faliscan chambers and are similar to those at Cerveteri. The funerary identity was clearly Etruscan.

Morselli (1980, 88–92, site nos 37, 41 and 48) has suggested that the *loculi* at Sutri were late for the Etruscan context, perhaps dating to the fifth or fourth century BC. This evidence suggests that the chambers with *loculi* were adopted from the east at the time when trenches with *sarcophagi* became dominant in Rome and the central Latin area. This shows mental closeness between Sutri and the Faliscan and Sabine areas, in a period when most Latin city-states had lost their independence, and just before or around the time when Sutri became a Latin colony in 383 BC (Vell. Pat. 1.14.2).

In inner Etruria the diffusion of *tombe a facciata* during the sixth century BC has been interpreted as reflecting the increased influence of Cerveteri (Colonna 1967, 17–30; 1974), with the design modelled after the *tombe a dado*. The funerary beds cut into tuff were widely distributed near Blera (Quilici Gigli 1976, 13) and along the Tiber near Torrimpietra (Tartara 1999, 102–5, fig. 126, site no. 113). They did not really penetrate into Latium, which suggests that this burial feature may indicate Etruscan identity or influence.

At the Cannicella cemetery near Volsinii the chamber tombs were either constructed or cut into large tuff blocks (Bonamici *et al.* 1994, 21–3). These had Orientalizing features and some originated from the late seventh century BC onwards. Later constructed chambers from the sixth century were built from tuff blocks. From a chronological view point, they were followed by *tombe a cassone* in the sixth and fifth centuries BC. These graves contained both cremations and inhumations, often in the same tomb (Bonamici *et al.* 1994, 28–9). The presence of *both* the burial rites that are generally attested separately in southern Etruscan centres reveals an independent identity from any southern neighbours.

An overall comparison of southern Etruscan tomb architecture shows that different centres adopted different dominant types reflecting their own funerary identity. However, the Orientalizing tombs were more uniform across the wider region with simple *fosse, tombe a loculo* and early chambers. In addition, mound building connected the higher echelons of society. By contrast, the sixth century BC seems to have been the time when local identities were the strongest in the Etruscan area and the mental distance from the neighbours was at its clearest. As suggested above, the Faliscan area showed greater permeability to the Archaic Etruscan chamber designs than the Latin area. This may suggest more nested identities in that area. The only clearly Etruscan chamber tombs in Latium are the ones at Ardea. However, it is important to note that the use of tuff *sarcophagi* seems to have originated on the western side of the Tiber, and shows continued closeness between Veii and the central Latin area before the Roman expansion and in spite of it.

The mental distances of the Latins

The Orientalizing *tombe a loculo* were common in Latium Vetus (*cf.* Naso 1996b, 311–2, footnote 478) and show closeness with Veii in Etruria and the Faliscan and Sabine areas (Fig. 8.4). This tomb type and its derivates were still in use during the Archaic period in Veii, Ficana, Tor de' Cenci and La Rustica in Latium, at the time when the northern areas had adopted the chamber tomb, similarly to the Faliscan and Sabine areas.

The Latin tomb types from the Archaic period show clear local traditions and different mental distances with neighbouring areas (Fig. 8.5). The northern city-states shared the chamber type with *loculi* with the Faliscan and Sabine areas. The southern and central Latin areas characterized by Archaic *tombe a loculi, dromoi con loculi* and perhaps also the 'pod-like' chambers show closeness with Veii. The coastal areas at Lavinium and Ardea reveal closeness with coastal southern Etruria. However, chambers with *loculi* are present also at Ardea: this suggests that this tomb type was not restricted to the north. The chambers at Corcolle seem to combine different funerary elements, namely the northern tomb typology of chambers, the use of *sarcophagi*, which are widely attested in central Latium, and the presence of more numerous ceramic grave goods. The overall predominance of *sarcophagi* and

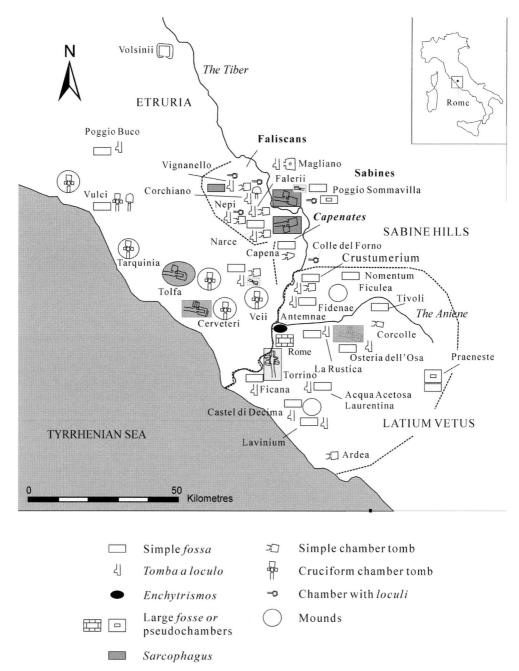

Fig. 8.4: Map showing the spatial distribution of tomb types in Orientalizing Latium Vetus and southern Etruria (map: U. Rajala).

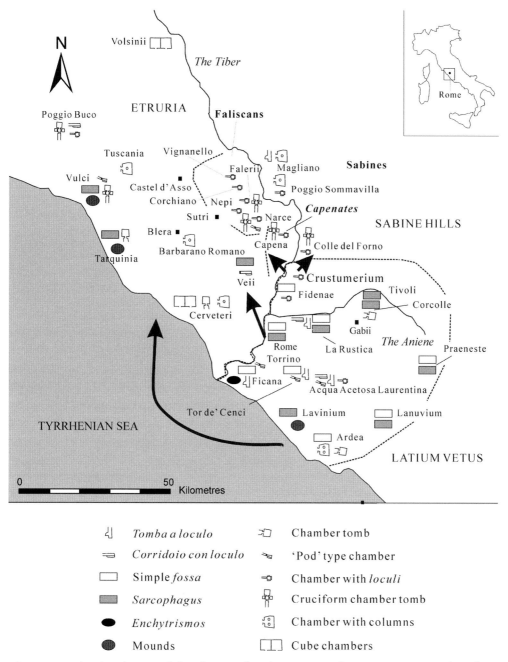

Fig. 8.5: Map showing the spatial distribution of tomb types in Archaic Latium Vetus and southern Etruria (map: U. Rajala).

casse from Rome to Praeneste and Lanuvium in a slightly later period may indicate close cultural ties and new power structures.

The nested nature of different identities in Latium is shown by the fact that even if the custom of infant burial was shared, there was no clear Latin tomb type. Instead, more localized designs are attested, reflecting local identities in funerary contexts. Adult burials were more likely to reflect individual and family identities at the city-state level rather than ethnic identity. The same is true with regard to all 'ethnic' areas in question. The only tomb type that appears to have been shared in the Faliscan area can be recognized at the time when the Romans were securing their dominance over central Italy, with this conflict fuelling the development of opposing identities on a regional level. However, the earlier distribution of chambers with *loculi* suggests close contacts in the central Tiber Valley.

Chamber tomb types of Etruscan inspiration seem to have had more influence in Latium during the late Orientalizing period. The similarity between Tomb 62 at Osteria dell'Osa and chamber tombs with two chambers at Cerveteri, Narce and Poggio Sommavilla is notable, and suggests that interregional élite groups were sharing status markers. This can also be seen in the distribution of large mounds in Etruria and Latium Vetus down to the Archaic period. Archaic plurality in mortuary practices in some centres reveals the nested nature of funerary identities, which made it possible to advertize belonging to different groups, but generally demonstrating clear separation from the Etruscans.

Several lines of evidence show how tomb types and funerary architecture crossed the Tiber and ethnic areas. Good examples are the clear differences between northern, central and southern Latin centres; the differences found among Faliscan centres; the more tangible differences between the dominant tomb types attested in different Etruscan city-states; and finally the distribution of Orientalizing *tombe a loculi* and later chambers with *loculi* and *sarcophagi*. These tomb types were not just shared cultural traits. Rather, they show closeness between communities that were geographically connected but independent. Mental closeness seems to follow the known pre-Roman road network and river crossings (*cf.* Figs 8.4 and 8.5; Quilici Gigli 1986). The coastal road brought the Etruscan and Latin coastal cities into closer contact. The roads and crossings at Ficana and Rome towards Veii resulted in similar funerary architecture on both sides of the Tiber. Similarly, the crossings at Fidenae, Campo del Pozzo and Poggio Sommavilla seem to have strengthened the interaction between the *Capenates*, Latins, Sabines and Faliscans, and to a lesser degree between these centres and Veii. Internally, the Aniene River and its crossings seem to have brought together different centres in central and northern Latium. The similarities with the Sabine area may be explained by the Latins' need to buffer ideologically against the Roman expansion. This may be compared to the seventh- and sixth-century BC buffer zones of central Etruria, where cities of medium importance wedged their own identities between the great city-states (*cf.* Izzet 2007b, 119; Stoddart 1990, 48). However, in the case of Latium the closeness with other ethnic areas and city-states can be seen as a stand against the expanding Roman state.

Acknowledgements

This article is a result of the *Remembering the Dead* Project, carried out in collaboration with the *Soprintendenza* of Rome. I wish to thank all who contributed to the project. Attending the workshop and the preparation of the first draft of this paper were made possible by a grant from the Kordelin Foundation and assistance from the University of Oulu. The final touches to the paper were made while I held a research position at Stockholm University in Sweden.

Notes

1. A second one was observed but not excavated (Bietti Sestieri and De Santis 1992, 217).

2. The notes published are contradictory, since they were prepared long after the excavation. It is clear that the deceased was *"sepolto con sassi"* (i.e. "buried with stones"), but if these stones were the remains of a collapsed vaulting pertaining to a constructed chamber or the cover or lining of a *fossa* is unclear (Curtis 1925, 9–10).

3. These tombs include simple *fosse* with soil fills, *tombe a loculo tipo Narce* (called *fosse munite di grande loculo laterale*) filled with stones, *tombe a cassone*, tombs covered with slabs *alla cappuccina*, and *fosse* covered with roof tiles. Bartoloni and Cataldi Dini (1978, 41) have suggested that the last three types were the most recent.

4. The *tomba a loculo* type closed with tiles continues the tradition of the *tombe a loculo tipo Narce* with the tiles as an Archaic feature, whereas the *dromos a loculo* type is similar to the so-called *tomba a loculo tipo Monte Michele* (di Gennaro 2007, fig. 1.C, footnote 2), which is known at Crustumerium from Sasso Bianco. The 'pod-like' chamber tomb at Acqua Acetosa Laurentina has been said to belong to the same type as this *dromos a loculo* (Bedini 1983, 36; *cf.* also Cifani 2008, 326; di Gennaro 2007, footnote 2). However, the published records showing its proper door blocks and a second door on the back wall (Bedini 1983, figs 2, 5 and 6) suggest that it was a chamber tomb.

5. The abbreviations "no." and "nos" refer to the numbers assigned to individual sites in Barnabei *et al.* 1894, Morselli 1980 and Tartara 1999.

6. This is described as having a *dromos*, a *fossa* and a small chamber (Alvino and Santoro 1984, 78). The published drawings suggest that the floors of all the three spaces were at the same level, which may indicate a chamber tomb with no benches.

7. Even if the records of the nineteenth-century excavations at Falerii Veteres (Cozza and Pasqui 1981, 13–211) and Narce (Barnabei *et al.* 1894; Pasqui 1902) have been published, the grave goods have never been properly edited, although some information exists in catalogues (Carlucci and De Lucia 1998; De Lucia Brolli 1991).

8. These tombs are called *tombe a fossa con loculo* in Etruscan literature. Nevertheless, in Latin contexts the term *tomba a loculo tipo Narce* is currently used (*cf.* di Gennaro 2007).

9. There were numerous squarish chambers but also wide rectangular chambers without *loculi* (Barnabei *et al.* 1894, fig. 186, site no. 1 and fig. 197, site no. 25), narrow and long chambers with two *loculi* on either side or with a U-shaped funerary bench, both long and narrow, and wide rectangular chambers with a single *loculus* and U-shaped chambers with *loculi* and anterchamber (Barnabei *et al.* 1894, fig. 192), trapezoidal chambers (Barnabei *et al.* 1894, fig. 193), cruciform chambers (Barnabei *et al.* 1894, fig. 201, site nos 39 and 208, site no. 77), chambers with two niches outside the chamber with or without *loculi* (Barnabei *et al.* 1894, fig. 197, site no. 28, fig. 201, site nos 103 and 116) and with both U-shaped bench and *loculi* (Barnabei *et al.* 1894, fig. 197, site no. 31).

10. A mirror image of Tomb 62 from Osteria dell'Osa (Barnabei *et al.* 1894, fig. 205, site no. 8) dates to the mid/late seventh century BC and contained a chariot as a status symbol (Carlucci and De Lucia 1998, 34–5). Tomb 3 (n. LXXIV) south-east of Contrada Morgi is very similar to the 'pod-like' narrow chambers, although without a *loculus*; it probably dates to the Archaic period considering the fragmentary Greek black-figured and red-figured painted pottery (Barnabei *et al.* 1894, coll. 523–4).

11. The chamber tomb at Sante Grotte was with *loculi*, although pottery fragments suggest a Late Orientalizing date for some burials (Stefani 1910, 201–2, fig. 2b). One chamber at S. Paolo revealed a *dromos* with an unusually narrow chamber with *loculi* on three sides (Stefani 1918). A recently excavated chamber tomb there contained cremation niches with a similar *bucchero* urn as at Valle La Fata at Veii; the assemblage dates to the late seventh or early sixth century BC. This tomb contained a *loculus* closed with tuff slabs, considered a combination of a funerary bed and a *loculus*. As a whole, the chambers at S. Paolo revealed material dating from the seventh century to the Hellenistic period (Rizzo 1996, 486–93). One tomb also presented two separate burials in one *loculus* (Rizzo 2006). One tomb from il Gilastro, similar to the Orientalizing chambers from Piani del Pavone, contained two tuff *sarcophagi* with at least one dating from the Archaic period (Rizzo 1996, 483–4).

12. At S. Martino a *fossa* cut a *pozzo* (well) with a chamber placed below them, whereas at Monte Cornazzo the series included a few Orientalizing *fossa* tombs and a transitional type between a *tomba a loculo* and a chamber (Paribeni 1906). At least 10 chamber tombs had constructed benches. At Contrada "La Saliere" (Stefani 1958) most tombs were simple *fosse*. The chambers were square, rectangular or trapezoidal and the series included Roman chamber tombs. Three tombs were unique; one had five separate chambers, one was an incomplete cruciform tomb and one had a curved *loculus* stretching around a corner of the chamber.

13. These were dated relatively later than Valle La Fata Tomb 15 with a *bucchero* urn (*cf.* Bartoloni and Delpino 1979, 56, 62, 93, 96). One tomb contained the remains of a small child with two glass beads (Bartoloni and Delpino 1979, 55; Stefani 1929, 340) and one the skeleton of a child, with four small white stones (Bartoloni and Delpino 1979, 56; Stefani 1929, 342).

Bibliography

Alvino, G. (1985) La necropoli di Poggio Sommavilla: Seconda campagna di scavo. In S. Quilici Gigli (ed.) *Archeologia Laziale 7. Settimo Incontro di Studio del Comitato per l'Archeologia Laziale*, 93–98. Roma, Consiglio Nazionale delle Ricerche.

Alvino, G. (1987) La necropoli di Poggio Sommavilla: Terza campagna di scavo. *Archeologia Laziale 8. Ottavo Incontro di Studio del Comitato per l'Archeologia Laziale*, 340–446. Roma, Consiglio Nazionale delle Ricerche.

Alvino, G. (1997) Un'introduzione. In G. Alvino (ed.) *I Sabini. La Vita, la Morte, gli Dei. Catalogo della Mostra (Rieti, 30 Ottobre–15 Dicembre 1997)*, 13–32. Roma, Armando.

Alvino, G. (2009) I Sabini e le evidenze archeologiche. In A. Nicosia and M.C. Bettini (eds) *I Sabini Popolo dell'Italia. Dalla Storia al Mito. Catalogo della Mostra (Roma, Palazzo del Vittoriano, 19 Marzo–24 Aprile 2009)*, 41–79. Roma, Gangemi.

Alvino, G. and Santoro, P. (1984) La necropoli di Poggio Sommavilla. In S. Quilici Gigli (ed.) *Archeologia Laziale 6. Sesto Incontro di Studio del Comitato per l'Archeologia Laziale*, 76–81. Roma, Consiglio Nazionale delle Ricerche.

Andrén, A. (1961) Scavi e scoperte sull'acropoli di Ardea. *Opuscula Romana* 3, 1–68.

Arietti, F. and Martellotta, B. (1998) *La Tomba Principesca del Vivaro di Rocca di Papa*. Roma, Istituto Nazionale di Studi Romani.

Barnabei, F., Gamurrini, G.F., Cozza, A. and Pasqui, A. (1894) *Antichità del Territorio Falisco: Esposte nel Museo Nazionale Romano a Villa Giulia*. Roma, Accademia Nazionale dei Lincei.

Bartoloni, G. (1984) Riti funerari dell'aristocrazia in Etruria e nel Lazio. L'esempio di Veio. *Opus* 3, 13–25.

Bartoloni, G. (1987) Esibizione di ricchezza a Roma nel VI e V sec. a. C.: Doni votivi e corredi funerari. *Scienze dell'Antichità* 1, 143–159.

Bartoloni, G. (2003) *La Società dell'Italia Primitiva. Lo Studio delle Necropoli e la Nascita delle Aristocrazie*. Roma, Carocci.

Bartoloni, G. and Cataldi Dini, M. (1978) La necropoli di Ficana. In S. Quilici Gigli (ed.) *Archeologia Laziale. Incontro di Studio del Comitato per l'Archeologia Laziale*, 40–41. Roma, Consiglio Nazionale delle Ricerche.

Bartoloni, G. and Delpino, F. (1979) *Veio I. Introduzione allo Studio delle Necropoli Arcaiche di Veio. Il Sepolcreto di Valle La Fata*. Roma, Accademia Nazionale dei Lincei.

Bartoloni, G., Cataldi Dini, M. and Zevi, F. (1975) Castel di Decima. La necropoli arcaica. *Notizie degli Scavi* 1975, 233–368.

Bartoloni, G., Nizzo, V. and Taloni, M. (2009) Dall'esibizione al rigore: Analisi dei sepolcreti laziali tra VII e VI sec. a.C.. In R. Bonaudo, L. Cerchiai and C. Pellegrino (eds) *Tra Etruria, Lazio e Magna Grecia: Indagini sulle Necropoli. Atti dell'Incontro di Studio (Fisciano, 5-6 Marzo 2009)*, 65–86. Paestum, Fondazione Paestum.

Bartoloni, G., Berardinetti, A., De Santis, A. and Drago, L. (1994) Veio tra IX e VI sec a.C.: Primi risultati sull'analisi comparata delle necropoli veienti. *Archeologia Classica* 46, 1–46.

Bartoloni, G., Berardinetti, A., De Santis, A. and Drago, L. (1997) Le necropoli villanoviane di Veio. Parallelismi e differenze. In G. Bartoloni (ed.) *Le Necropoli Arcaiche di Veio. Giornata di Studio in Memoria di Massimo Pallottino*, 89–100. Roma, Università degli Studi di Roma "La Sapienza", Dipartimento di Scienze Storiche, Archeologiche ed Antropologiche dell'Antichità.

Bedini, A. (1977) L'ottavo secolo nel Lazio e l'inizio dell'orientalizzante antico alla luce di recenti scoperte nella necropoli di Castel di Decima. *Parola del Passato* 32, 279–309.

Bedini, A. (1980) Abitato protostorico in località Acqua Acetosa Laurentina. In S. Quilici Gigli (ed.) *Archeologia Laziale 3. Terzo Incontro di Studio del Comitato per l'Archeologia Laziale*, 58–64. Roma, Consiglio Nazionale delle Ricerche.

Bedini, A. (1981) Contributo alla conoscenza del territorio a sud di Roma in epoca protostorica. In S. Quilici Gigli (ed.) *Archeologia Laziale 4. Quarto Incontro di Studio del Comitato per l'Archeologia Laziale*, 57–65. Roma, Consiglio Nazionale delle Ricerche.

Bedini, A. (1983) Due nuove tombe a camera presso l'abitato della Laurentina: Nota su alcuni tipi di sepolture nel VI e V secolo a.C.. In S. Quilici Gigli (ed.) *Archeologia Laziale 5. Quinto Incontro di Studio del Comitato per l'Archeologia Laziale*, 28–37. Roma, Consiglio Nazionale delle Ricerche.

Bedini, A. (1984) Scavi al Torrino. In S. Quilici Gigli (ed.) *Archeologia Laziale 6. Sesto Incontro di Studio del Comitato per l'Archeologia Laziale*, 84–90. Roma, Consiglio Nazionale delle Ricerche.

Bedini, A. (1985) Tre corredi protostorici dal Torrino: Osservazioni sull'affermarsi e la funzione delle aristocrazie terriere nell'VIII secolo a.C. nel Lazio. In S. Quilici Gigli (ed.) *Archeologia Laziale 7. Settimo Incontro di Studio del Comitato per l'Archeologia Laziale*, 44–64. Roma, Consiglio Nazionale delle Ricerche.

Bedini, A. (1990a) Un compitum protostorico a Tor de' Cenci. In S. Quilici Gigli (ed.) *Archeologia Laziale 10. Decimo Incontro di Studio del Comitato per l'Archeologia Laziale*, 121–133. Roma, Consiglio Nazionale delle Ricerche.

Bedini, A. (1990b) Le tombe della Laurentina. In M. Cristofani (ed.) *La Grande Roma dei Tarquini. Catalogo della Mostra (Roma, Palazzo delle Esposizioni, 12 Giugno–30 Settembre 1990)*, 255–260. Roma, "L'Erma" di Bretschneider.

Bedini, A. (2000) La tomba 70 dell'Acqua Acetosa Laurentina. In A. Carandini and R. Cappelli (eds) *Roma. Romolo, Remo e la Fondazione della Città. Catalogo della Mostra (Roma, Museo Nazionale Romano, Terme di Diocleziano, 28 Giugno–29 Ottobre 2000)*, 355–357. Milano, Electa.

Belelli Marchesini, B. (2008) Necropoli di *Crustumerium*: Bilancio delle acquisizioni e prospettive. In *Alla Ricerca dell'Identità di Crustumerium: Primi Risultati e Prospettive di un Progetto Internazionale. Atti della Giornata di Studio Organizzata dall'Institutum Romanum Finlandiae e dalla Soprintendenza Speciale ai Beni Archeologici di Roma (Roma, 5 Marzo 2008)*. Roma, Istitutum Romanum Finlandiae. [http://www.irfrome.org/ei/images/stories/crustumerium/Belelli.pdf].

Belelli Marchesini, B. and Pantano, W. (2014) The necropolis of Crustumerium. Preliminary results from the interdisciplinary analysis of two groups of tombs. In A.J. Nijboer, S.L. Willemsen, P.A.J. Attema and J.F. Seubers (eds) *Research into Pre-Roman Burial Grounds in Italy* (Caeculus: Papers in Mediterranean Archaeology and Greek & Roman Studies), 1–33. Leuven, Peeters.

Benelli, E. and Santoro, P. (2006) Nuove scoperte nella necropoli sabina di Colle del Forno (Montelibretti, Roma). In G. Ghini (ed.) *Lazio e Sabina 3. Atti del Convegno (Terzo Incontro di Studi sul Lazio e la Sabina, Roma, 18–20 Novembre 2004)*, 97–106. Roma, Quasar.

Benelli, E. and Santoro, P. (2009) Colle del Forno (Montelibretti, Roma). Nuovi dati dalle ultime campagne di scavo. In G. Ghini (ed.) *Lazio e Sabina 5. Atti del Convegno (Quinto Incontro di Studi sul Lazio e la Sabina, Roma, 3–5 Dicembre 2007)*, 59–63. Roma, "L'Erma" di Bretschneider.

Bentley, G.C. (1987) Ethnicity and practice. *Comparative Studies in Society and History* 29(1), 24–55.

Bietti Sestieri, A.M. 1992 (ed.) *La Necropoli Laziale di Osteria dell'Osa*. Roma, Quasar.

Bietti Sestieri, A.M. and De Santis, A. (1992) Tipi di rituali e di strutture tombali. In A.M. Bietti Sestieri (ed.) *La Necropoli Laziale di Osteria dell'Osa*, 203–218. Roma, Quasar.

Bjerring Olsen, K. (2004) *Economic Cooperation and Social Identity: Towards a Model of Economic Cross-Cultural Integration* (Department of Economics, Aarhus School of Business. Working Papers 04-10). Aarhus, Department of Economics, Aarhus School of Business.

Boitani, F. (1985) Veio: La tomba "principesca" della necropoli di Monte Michele. *Studi Etruschi* 51[1983], 535–556.

Bonamici, M., Stopponi, S. and Tamburini, P. (1994) *Orvieto: La Necropoli di Cannicella. Scavi della Fondazione per il Museo "C. Faina" e dell'Università di Perugia (1977)*. Roma, "L'Erma" di Bretschneider.

Bourdieu, P. (1977) *Outline of a Theory of Practice*. Cambridge, Cambridge University Press.

Brandt, J.R. (1996) (ed.) *Scavi di Ficana II, 1. Il Periodo Protostorico e Arcaico. Le Zone di Scavo 3b-c*. Roma, Libreria dello Stato, Istituto Poligrafico e Zecca dello Stato.

Canciani, F. and von Hase, F.-W. (1979) *La Tomba Bernardini di Palestrina*. Roma, Consiglio Nazionale delle Ricerche.

Carafa, P. (1995) *Officine Ceramiche di Età Regia: Produzione di Ceramica in Impasto a Roma dalla Fine dell'VIII alla Fine del VI secolo a.C.* Roma, "L'Erma" di Bretschneider.

Carlucci, C. and De Lucia, M.A. (1998) *Le Antichità dei Falisci al Museo di Villa Giulia*. Roma, "L'Erma" di Bretschneider.

Cataldi Dini, M. (1980) Necropolen: Ficana. In J.R. Brandt and A. Rathje (eds) *Ficana - en milesten på veien til Roma*, 129–139. København, I kommisjon hos Museum Tusculanum.

Ceccarelli, L. and Stoddart, S.K.F. (2007) The Faliscans. In G. Bradley, E. Isayev and C. Riva (eds) *Ancient Italy: Regions without Boundaries*, 131–160. Exeter, Exeter University Press.

Cerchiai, L. (1995) Modelli di organizzazione in età arcaica attraverso la lettura delle necropoli: Il caso di Pontecagnano. In P. Gastaldi and G. Maetzke (eds) *La Presenza Etrusca nella Campania Meridionale. Atti delle Giornate di Studio (Salerno-Pontecagnano, 16-18 Novembre 1990)*, 405–452. Firenze, Istituto Nazionale di Studi Etruschi ed Italici.

Cifani, G. (2003) *Storia di una Frontiera. Dinamiche Territoriali e Gruppi Etnici nella Media Valle Tiberina dalla Prima Età del Ferro alla Conquista Romana. Archeologia del Territorio*. Roma, Libreria dello Stato, Istituto Poligrafico e Zecca dello Stato.

Cifani, G. (2008) *Architettura Romana Arcaica: Edilizia e Società tra Monarchia e Repubblica*. Roma, "L'Erma" di Bretschneider.

Cifani, G. (2009) Indicazioni sulla proprietà agraria nella Roma arcaica in base all'evidenza archeologica. In V. Jolivet, C. Pavolini, M.A. Tomei and R. Volpe (eds) *Suburbium II. Il Suburbio di Roma dalla Fine dell'Età Monarchica alla Nascita del Sistema delle Ville (V-II Secolo a.C.)*, 311–324. Roma, École française de Rome.

Colini, G.A. (1919) Veio: Scavi nell'area della città e della necropoli. *Notizie degli Scavi* 1919, 3–12.

Colonna, G. (1967) L'Etruria meridionale interna dal villanoviano alle tombe rupestri. *Studi Etruschi* 35, 3–30.

Colonna, G. (1974) La cultura dell'Etruria meridionale interna con particolare riguardo alle necropoli rupestri. *In Aspetti e Problemi dell'Etruria Interna. Atti dell'VIII Convegno Nazionale di Studi Etruschi e Italici (Orvieto, 27-30 Giugno 1972)*, 253–260. Firenze, L.S. Olschki.

Colonna, G. (1977) Un aspetto oscuro del Lazio antico. Le tombe del VI–V secolo a.C.: *Parola del Passato* 32, 131–165.

Colonna, G. (1981) Ideologia funeraria e il conflitto delle culture. In S. Quilici Gigli (ed.) *Archeologia Laziale 4. Quarto Incontro di Studio del Comitato per l'Archeologia Laziale*, 229–232. Roma, Consiglio Nazionale delle Ricerche.

Colonna, G. (1989) I Latini e gli altri popoli del Lazio. In A.M. Chieco (ed.) *Italia Omnium Terrarum Alumna. La Civiltà dei Veneti, Reti, Liguri, Celti, Piceni, Umbri, Latini, Campani e Iapigi*, 409–718. Milano, Garzanti/Scheiwiller.

Colonna, G. (1991) Acqua Acetosa Laurentina. L'*Ager Romanus Antiquus* e i santuari del I miglio. *Scienze dell'Antichità* 5, 209–232.

Colonna di Paolo, E. and Colonna, G. (1970) *Castel d'Asso*. Roma, Consiglio Nazionale delle Ricerche.

Cordano, F. (1975) Castel di Decima (Roma) – La necropoli arcaica. *Notizie degli Scavi* 1975, 369–408.

Cozza, A. and Pasqui, A. (1981) *Carta Archeologica d'Italia (1881-1897). Materiali per l'Agro Falisco*. Firenze, L.S. Olschki.

Cristofani Martelli, M. (1977) Per una definizione archeologica della Sabina: La situazione storico-culturale di Poggio Sommavilla in età arcaica. In P. Santoro (ed.) *Rilettura Critica della Necropoli di Poggio Sommavilla*, 9–48. Roma, Consiglio Nazionale delle Ricerche/Istituto per l'Archeologia Etrusco-Italica.

Cuozzo, M. (2003) *Reinventando la Tradizione: Immaginario Sociale, Ideologie e Rappresentazione nelle Necropoli Orientalizzante di Pontecagnano*. Paestum, Pandemos.

Curtis, C.D. (1919) The Bernardini tomb. *Memoirs of the American Academy in Rome* 3, 9–90.

Curtis, C.D. (1925) The Barberini tomb. *Memoirs of the American Academy in Rome* 5, 9–52.

De Lucia Brolli, M.A. (1991) *Civita Castellana, il Museo Archeologico dell'Agro Falisco*. Roma, Quasar.

D'Ercole, V. and Benelli, E. 2004 (eds) *La Necropoli di Fossa. I Corredi Orientalizzanti e Arcaici* (Vol. 2). Celano, Carsa.

De Santis, A. (1992) Il II e IV periodo. In A.M. Bietti Sestieri (ed.) *La Necropoli Laziale di Osteria dell'Osa*, 815–874. Roma, Quasar.

Díaz-Andreu, M., Lucy, S., Bacić, S. and Edwards, D.N. (2005) (eds) *The Archaeology of Identity: Approaches to Gender, Age, Status, Ethnicity and Religion*. London–New York, Routledge.

di Gennaro, F. (1990) Tomba femminile da Fidenae. In M. Cristofani (ed.) *La Grande Roma dei Tarquini. Catalogo della Mostra (Roma, Palazzo delle Esposizioni, 12 Giugno-30 Settembre 1990)*, 260–262. Roma, "L'Erma" di Bretschneider.

di Gennaro, F. (1999) (ed.) *Itinerario di Visita a Crustumerium*. Roma, Comune di Roma.

di Gennaro, F. (2007) Le tombe a loculo di età orientalizzante di *Crustumerium*. In F. Arietti and A. Pasqualini (eds) *Tusculum. Storia, Archeologia, Cultura e Arte di Tuscolo e del Tuscolano. Atti del Primo Incontro di Studi (27-28 Maggio e 3 Giugno 2000)*, 163–176. Roma, Comitato Nazionale per le Celebrazioni del Millenario della Fondazione dell'Abbazia di S. Nilo a Grottaferrata.

di Gennaro, F., Amoroso, A. and Togninelli, P. (2007) *Crustumerium* e Fidenae tra Etruria e Colli Albani. In F. Airetti and A. Pasqualini (eds) *Tusculum. Storia, Archeologia, Cultura e Arte di Tuscolo e del Tuscolano. Atti del Primo Incontro di Studi (27-28 Maggio e 3 Giugno 2000)*, 136–162. Roma, Comitato Nazionale per le Celebrazioni del Millenario della Fondazione dell'Abbazia di S. Nilo a Grottaferrata.

di Gennaro, F., Rajala, U., Rizzo, D., Stoddart, S.K.F. and Whitehead, N. (2008) Nepi and territory: 1200 BC–400 AD. In H. Patterson and F. Coarelli (eds) *Mercator Placidissimus - The Tiber Valley in Antiquity. New Research in the Upper and Middle River Valley (Rome, 27-28 February 2004)*, 879–887. Roma, Quasar.

Drago Troccoli, L. (1997) Le tombe 419 e 426 del sepolcreto di Grotta Gramiccia a Veio. *In Etrusca et Italica. Scritti in Ricordo di Massimo Pallottino*, 239–280. Pisa–Roma, Istituti Editoriali e Poligrafici Internazionali.

Duncan, G. and Reynolds, J.M. (1958) Sutri (Sutrium). Notes on southern Etruria, 3. *Papers of the British School at Rome* 26, 63–134.

Eckstein, A.M. 2006. *Mediterranean Anarchy, Interstate War, and the Rise of Rome*. Berkeley, University of California Press.

Faccenna, D. (1957) Tivoli (Piazza D. Tani). Necropoli del V–IV secolo av.Cr., rinvenuta durante i lavori di ampliamento della Cartiera Aminucci. Vicolo di Santa Croce. Sarcofago di tufo in terreno di proprietà R. Porcari. *Notizie degli Scavi* 1957, 123–133.

Falconi Amorelli, M.T. (1987) *Vulci: Scavi Mengarelli (1925-1929)*. Roma, Borgia.

Fulminante, F. (2000) Tumulo/*heroon* di Indiges/Enea a Lavinio (Pratica di Mare). In A. Carandini and R. Cappelli (eds) *Roma. Romolo, Remo e la Fondazione della Città. Catalogo della Mostra (Roma, Museo Nazionale Romano, Terme di Diocleziano, 28 Giugno-29 Ottobre 2000)*, 213–214. Milano, Electa.

Fulminante, F. (2003) *Le Sepolture Principesche nel Latium Vetus: Tra la Fine della Prima Età del Ferro e l'Inizio dell'Età Orientalizzante*. Roma, "L'Erma" di Bretschneider.

Fulminante, F. (2008) Una tomba a loculo fra tombe a camera a Cisterna Grande. *In Alla Ricerca dell'Identità di Crustumerium: Primi Risultati e Prospettive di un Progetto Internazionale. Atti della Giornata di Studio Organizzata dall'Institutum Romanum Finlandiae e dalla Soprintendenza Speciale ai Beni Archeologici di Roma (Roma, 5 Marzo 2008)*. Roma, Istitutum Romanum Finlandiae. [http://www.irfrome.org/ei/images/stories/crustumerium/Fulminante.pdf].

Giglioli, G.Q. (1924) Vignanello. *Notizie degli Scavi* 1924, 179–264.

Gsell, S. (1891) *Fouilles dans la Nécropole de Vulci Exécutées et Publiées aux frais de S.E. le Prince Torlonia*. Paris, E. Thorin.

Guaitoli, M. (1995) Lavinium: Nuovi dati dalle necropoli. In S. Quilici Gigli (ed.) *Archeologia Laziale* 12(2). *Dodicesimo Incontro di Studio del Comitato per l'Archeologia Laziale*, 551–562. Roma, Consiglio Nazionale delle Ricerche.

Guidi, A. (1997) L'abitato di *Cures Sabini*. In G. Alvino (ed.) *I Sabini. La Vita, la Morte, gli Dei. Catalogo della Mostra (Rieti, 30 Ottobre-15 Dicembre 1997)*, 53–56. Roma, Armando.

Hakenbeck, S. (2004) Ethnicity: An introduction. *Archaeological Review from Cambridge* 19(2), 1–6.

Hall, J.M. (1997) *Ethnic Identity in Greek Antiquity*. Cambridge, Cambridge University Press.

Izzet, V. (2007a) *The Archaeology of Etruscan Society*. Cambridge, Cambridge University Press.

Izzet, V. (2007b) Etruria and the Etruscans: Recent approaches. In G.J. Bradley, E. Isayev and C. Riva (eds) *Ancient Italy: Regions without Boundaries*, 114–130. Exeter, Exeter University Press.

Jarva, E. (1980) Barngravar i Latium under järnålder. In J.R. Brandt and A. Rathje (eds) *Ficana - en milesten på veien til Roma*, 139–145. København, I kommisjon hos Museum Tusculanum.

Jenkins, R. (1996) *Social Identity*. London, Routledge.

Jones, S. (1997) *The Archaeology of Ethnicity: Constructing Identities in the Past and Present*. London, Routledge.

Kaplan, D.H. (1994) Two nations in search of a state: Canada's ambivalent spatial identities. *Annals of the Association of American Geographers* 84(4), 585–606.

Kaplan, D.H. (1999) Territorial identities and geographic scale. In G.H. Herb and D.H. Kaplan (eds) *Nested Identities: Nationalism, Territory, and Scale*, 31–49. Oxford, Rowman & Littlefield.

Kaplan, D.H. and Herb, G.H. (1999) Introduction: A question of identity. In G.H. Herb and D.H. Kaplan (eds) *Nested Identities: Nationalism, Territory, and Scale*, 1–6. Oxford, Rowman & Littlefield.

Knight, D.B. (1999) Afterword: Nested identities – Nationalism, territory, and scale. In G.H. Herb and D.H. Kaplan (eds) *Nested Identities: Nationalism, Territory, and Scale*, 317–329. Oxford, Rowman & Littlefield.

Leighton, R. (2004) *Tarquinia: An Etruscan City*. London, Duckworth.

Lomas, K. (2011) Communicating identities in funerary iconography: The inscribed stelae of northern Italy. In M. Gleba and H.W. Horsnaes (eds) *Communicating Identity in Italic Iron Age Communities*, 7–25. Oxford, Oxbow Books.

Lucy, S. (2005) Ethnic and cultural identities. In M. Díaz-Andreu, S. Lucy, S. Bacić and D.N. Edwards (eds) *The Archaeology of Identity: Approaches to Gender, Age, Status, Ethnicity and Religion*, 86–109. London–New York, Routledge.

Morris, I. (1987) *Burial and Ancient Society: The Rise of the Greek City-State*. Cambridge, Cambridge University Press.

Morselli, C. (1980) *Sutrium*. Firenze, L.S. Olschki.

Morselli, C. and Tortorici, E. (1982) *Ardea*. Firenze, L.S. Olschki.

Muzzioli, M.P. (1980) *Cures Sabini*. Firenze, L.S. Olschki.

Naso, A. (1990) L'ideologia funeraria. In M. Cristofani (ed.) *La Grande Roma dei Tarquini. Catalogo della Mostra (Roma, Palazzo delle Esposizioni, 12 Giugno-30 Settembre 1990)*, 249–251. Roma, "L'Erma" di Bretschneider.

Naso, A. (1996a) Osservazioni sull'origine dei tumuli monumentali nell'Italia centrale. *Opuscula Romana* 20, 69–85.

Naso, A. (1996b) *Architetture Dipinte: Decorazioni Parietali non Figurate nelle Tombe a Camera dell'Etruria Meridionale (VII-V sec. a.C.)*. Roma, "L'Erma" di Bretschneider.

Paasi, A. (2000) Re-constructing regions and regional identity. Nethur Lecture, 7.11.2000, Nijmegen.

Paasi, A. (2001) Europe as a social process and discourse: Considerations of place, boundaries and identity. *European Urban and Regional Studies* 8(1), 7–28.

Pala, C. (1976) *Nomentum*. Roma, De Luca.

Paolini, L. (1990) Crustumerium (circ. IV) – II. Scavi nella necropoli. *Bullettino della Commissione Archeologica Comunale di Roma* 92, 468–471.

Paribeni, E. (1906) Necropoli del territorio capenate. *Monumenti Antichi* 16, 277–490.

Parker Pearson, M. (1999) *The Archaeology of Death and Burial*. Stroud, Sutton.

Pasqui, A. (1900) Ardea (Comune di Genzano) – Scavi della necropoli ardeatina. *Notizie degli Scavi* 1900, 53–669.

Pasqui, A. (1902) Mazzano Romano – Scavi del principe del Drago nel territorio di questo comune. *Notizie degli Scavi* 1902, 321–355, 593–627.

Pensabene, P. (1983) Necropoli di Praeneste. Storia degli scavi e circostanze di rinvenimento dei cippi a pigna e dei busti funerari. *Archeologia Classica* 35, 228–682.

Pinza, G. (1905) Le vicende della zona Esquilina fino ai tempi di Augusto. *Bullettino della Commissione Archeologica Comunale di Roma* 42, 117–675.

Prayon, F. (1975) *Fruhetruskische Grab- und Hausarchitektur* (Mitteilungen des Deutschen Archaeologischen Instituts, Roemische Abteilung 24). Heidelberg, F.H. Kerle.

Quilici, L. and Quilici Gigli, S. (1978) *Antemnae*. Roma, Consiglio Nazionale delle Ricerche.

Quilici, L. and Quilici Gigli, S. (1980) *Crustumerium*. Roma, Consiglio Nazionale delle Ricerche.

Quilici, L. and Quilici Gigli, S. (1986) *Fidenae*. Roma, Consiglio Nazionale delle Ricerche.

Quilici, L. and Quilici Gigli, S. (1993) *Ficulea*. Roma, Consiglio Nazionale delle Ricerche.

Quilici Gigli, S. (1976) *Blera. Topografia Antica della Città e del Territorio* (Deutches Archäologische Instituts Rom, Sonderschriften 3). Mainz am Rhein, Philipp von Zabern.

Quilici Gigli, S. (1986) Scali e traghetti sul Tevere in epoca arcaica. In S. Quilici Gigli (ed.) *Il Tevere e le Altre Vie d'Acqua del Lazio Antico. Settimo Incontro di Studio del Comitato per l'Archeologia Laziale*, 71–89. Roma, Consiglio Nazionale delle Ricerche.

Rajala, U. (2007) Archaic chamber tombs as material objects: The materiality of burial places and its effect on modern research agendas and interpretations. *Archaeological Review from Cambridge* 22(1), 43–57.

Rajala, U. (2008a) Visualising Latin Archaic tombs and their postdepositional histories: The 3D modelling of the tombs from Cisterna Grande, Crustumerium (Rome, Italy). In A. Posluschny, K. Lambers and I. Herzog (eds) *Proceedings of the 35th International Conference on Computer Applications and Quantitative Methods in Archaeology (CAA) (Berlin, 2-6 April 2007)*, 127–133. Bonn, Dr. Rudolf Habelt.

Rajala, U. (2008b) Ritual and remembrance at Archaic Crustumerium: The transformations of past and modern materialities in the cemetery of Cisterna Grande (Rome, Italy). In F. Fahlander and T. Oestigaard (eds) *The Materiality of Death* (BAR S1758), 79–87. Oxford, Archaeopress.

Rajala, U. (2011) The excavations in the cemetery area of Cisterna Grande (Crustumerium, Rome, Italy): Archaic burials and funerary identities. *In Roma 2008 - International Congress of Classical Archaeology. Meetings between Cultures in the Ancient Mediterranean* (Bollettino di Archeologia Online, Volume Speciale) [http://151.12.58.75/archeologia/bao_document/articoli/4_RAJALA.pdf].

Rajala, U. (2012) Political landscapes and local identities in Archaic central Italy – Interpreting the material from Nepi (VT, Lazio) and Cisterna Grande (Crustumerium, RM, Lazio). In G. Cifani and S. Stoddart (eds) *Landscape, Ethnicity and Identity in the Archaic Mediterranean Area*, 120–143. Oxford, Oxbow Books.

Rajala, U. (2014) Biographies of tombs and the metaphorical representations of the *Crustumini*: Remembering the Dead project and the funerary excavations at Cisterna Grande at Crustumerium 2004-2008. In A.J. Nijboer, S.L. Willemsen, P.A.J. Attema and J.F. Seubers (eds) *Research into Pre-Roman Burial Grounds in Italy* (Caeculus: Papers in Medierranean Archaeology and Greek & Roman Studies), 63–81. Leuven, Peeters.

Reggiani, A., Adembri, B., Zevi, F., Benedettini, M.G. and Mari, Z. (1998) Corcolle. In L. Drago Troccoli (ed.) *Scavi e Ricerche Archeologiche dell'Università di Roma "La Sapienza"*, 120–124. Roma, "L'Erma" di Bretschneider.

Riva, C. (2010) *The Urbanisation of Etruria: Funerary Ritual and Social Change, 700-600 BC*. Cambridge, Cambridge University Press.

Riva, C. and Stoddart, S. (1996) Ritual landscapes in Archaic Etruria. In J.B. Wilkins (ed.) *Approaches to the Study of Ritual. Italy and the Mediterranean*, 91–109. London, Accordia Research Centre.

Rizzo, D. (1996) Recenti scoperte nell'area di Nepi. *In Identità e Civiltà dei Sabini. Atti del XVIII Convegno di Studi Etruschi ed Italici (Rieti-Magliano Sabina, 30 Maggio–3 Giugno 1993)*, 477–494. Firenze, L.S. Olschki.

Rizzo, D. (2006) Recenti rinvenimenti nel territorio di Nepi: Un sepolcro aristocratico. In M. Pandolfini Angeletti (ed.) *Archeologia in Etruria Meridionale. Atti delle Giornate di Studio in Ricordo di Mario Moretti (Civita Castellana, 14-15 Novembre 2003)*, 107–119. Roma, "L'Erma" di Bretschneider.

Santoro, P. (1981) La necropoli di Poggio Sommavilla. Intervento di recupero. In S. Quilici Gigli (ed.) *Archeologia Laziale 4. Quarto Incontro di Studio del Comitato per l'Archeologia Laziale*, 69–74. Roma, Consiglio Nazionale delle Ricerche.

Santoro, P. (1997a) L'insediamento di Magliano. In P. Santoro (ed.) *Magliano: Origini e Sviluppo dell'Insediamento*, 5–40. Pisa–Roma, Istituti Editoriali e Poligrafici Internazionali.

Santoro, P. (1997b) La necropoli di Colle del Ciglio. In G. Alvino (ed.) *I Sabini. La Vita, la Morte, gli Dei. Catalogo della Mostra (Rieti, 30 Ottobre-15 Dicembre 1997)*, 75–77. Roma, Armando.

Santoro, P. (1997c) Magliano: Origini e sviluppo. In P. Santoro (ed.) *Magliano: Origini e Sviluppo dell'Insediamento*, 79–85. Pisa–Roma, Istituti Editoriali e Poligrafici Internazionali.

Santoro, P. (1997d) La produzione ceramica locale. In P. Santoro (ed.) *Magliano: Origini e Sviluppo dell'Insediamento*, 41–48. Pisa–Roma, Istituti Editoriali e Poligrafici Internazionali.

Scopacasa, R. (2015). *Ancient Samnium. Settlement, Culture and Identity between History and Archaeology*. Oxford, Oxford University Press.

Sommella, P. (1971–1972). Heroon di Enea a Lavinium: Recenti scavi a Pratica di Mare. *Atti della Pontificia Accademia Romana di Archeologia* 44, 47–74.

Stefani, E. (1910) Scoperte di antichità nel territorio nepesino. *Notizie degli Scavi* 1910, 199–222.

Stefani, E. (1918) Antico sepolcro della necropoli nepesina. *Notizie degli Scavi* 1918, 16–19.

Stefani, E. (1929) Veio. Saggi e scoperte fortuite nella necropoli. *Notizie degli Scavi* 1929, 326–349.

Stefani, E. (1958) Capena: Scoperte archeologiche nell'agro capenate. Ricerche archeologiche nella contrada "Le Saliere". *Monumenti Antichi* 44, 1–204.

Steingräber, S. (1985) (ed.) *Etruskische Wandmalerei*. Stuttgart–Zurich, Belser.

Stoddart, S.K.F. (1990) The political landscape of Etruria. *Journal of the Accordia Research Centre* 1, 39–51.

Szilágyi, G. (1998) *Ceramica Etrusco-Corinzia Figurata. Parte II. 590/580-550 a.C.*: Firenze, L.S. Olschki.

Tartara, P. (1999) *Torrimpietra (IGM 149 I NO)*. Firenze, L.S. Olschki.

Tortorici, E. (1983) *Ardea. Immagini di una Ricerca. Catalogo della Mostra (Roma, Biblioteca Nazionale Centrale "Vittorio Emanuele I", Giugno 1983)*. Roma, De Luca.

Van Houtum, H. (1999) What is the influence of borders on economic internationalisation? In P. de Gijsel, M. Janssen, H.-J. Wenzel and M. Woltering (eds) *Understanding European Cross-Border Labour Markets*, 107–141. Marburg, Metropolis.

Van Houtum, H. (2001) The determinants of cross-border economic relations: The case of the Netherlands and Belgium. In M. van Geenhuizen and R. Ratti (eds) *Gaining Advantage from Open Borders: An Active Space Approach to Regional Development*, 123–146. Aldershot, Ashgate.

Van Kempen, I. (2009) Stone sculpture in the context of Etruscan tombs: A note on its position. In M. Gleba and H. Becker (eds) *Votives, Places, and Rituals in Etruscan Religion: Studies in Honor of Jean MacIntosh Turfa*, 135–155. Leiden, Brill.

Waarsenburg, D.J. (1995) *The Northwest Necropolis of Satricum: An Iron Age Cemetery in Latium Vetus*. Amsterdam, Thesis Publishers.

Ward-Perkins, J.B. (1961) Veii. The historical topography of the ancient city. *Papers of the British School at Rome* 29, 1–123.

Willemsen, S.L. (2014) A changing funerary ritual at Crustumerium (ca. 625 BC). In A.J. Nijboer, S.L. Willemsen , P.A.J. Attema and J.F. Seubers (eds) *Research into Pre-Roman Burial Grounds in Italy* (Caeculus: Papers in Medierranean Archaeology and Greek & Roman Studies), 35–50. Leuven, Peeters.

Zevi, F. (1990) Tomba del guerriero di Lanuvio. In M. Cristofani (ed.) *La Grande Roma dei Tarquini. Catalogo della Mostra (Roma, Palazzo delle Esposizioni, 12 Giugno–30 Settembre 1990)*, 264–269. Roma, "L'Erma" di Bretschneider.

Zevi, F. (1993) La tomba del guerriero di Lanuvio. In J.-P. Thuillier (ed.) *Spectacles Sportifs et Scéniques dans le Monde Étrusco-Italique. Actes de la Table Ronde Organisée par l'Équipe de Recherches Étrusco-Italiques de l'UMR (CNRS, Paris) et l École Française de Rome (Rome, 3-4 Mai 1991)*, 409–442. Roma, École française de Rome.

Zifferero, A. (1991) Forme di possesso della terra e tumuli orientalizzanti nell'Italia centrale tirrenica. In E. Herring, R. Whitehouse and J. Wilkins (eds) *Papers of the Fourth Conference of Italian Archaeology: The Archaeology of Power* (Vol. 1), 107–133. London, Accordia Research Centre.

Ziller, R.C. (1973) *The Social Self.* Oxford, Pergamon Press.

Section 2

Identities on the fringe

Chapter 9

Frontiers of the plain. Funerary practice and multiculturalism in sixth-century BC western Emilia

Lorenzo Zamboni

Introduction: fluid boundaries

In this chapter I shall propose a critical review of funerary archaeological evidence from western Emilia dating to the sixth century BC. In view of the development of scholarship on this region, my purpose is to question how funerary data can be used to study agency (e.g. Gardner 1994; Giddens 1984) and cultural connectivity in an ancient 'frontier' region such as Emilia, where cultural interchange and overlap were remarkably high (on ethnicity, connectivity and interaction *cf.* also Cuozzo, Morris and Rajala this volume, with additional bibliography). Secondly, I shall highlight some critical and unresolved issues pertaining to traditional approaches to this region, namely the problematic search for distinctive ethnic units such as the 'Etruscans' and the 'Gauls', and the inadequacy of modern historical approaches to migration and colonization. I shall conclude by suggesting some new theoretical tools that can aid our understanding of the peculiar situation in ancient Emilia, in particular the concept of 'recognition' as an alternative to identity theory.

The geographical setting under study is the Po Valley in northern Italy, more precisely the territory between the modern provinces of Piacenza and Modena, north of the Apennines and south of the Po River. The chronological period under consideration is the phase between the end of the seventh and the beginning of the fifth century BC, a time-span also known as the 'Archaic period' (on the Archaic period in central Italy *cf.* also O'Donoghue and Rajala this volume). After an apparently long period of depopulation following the collapse of the so-called 'Terramare civilization' at the end of the Bronze Age (*c.* twelfth century BC: *cf.* Bernabò Brea *et al.* 1997), from *c.* 600 BC the archaeological record of western Emilia provides evidence that communities were once again beginning to expand, with the establishment of new rural settlements which featured paved roads

(Malnati and Macellari 1989). As we shall see below, a truly multicultural society seems to have developed in this area – a society that had wide-raging connections with neighbouring communities north of the Po, along the Apennines in Liguria and in northern Etruria. In particular, among the northern Italian cultural milieus that had connections with western Emilia were the so-called 'Venetic' and 'Golasecca' cultures, the former found in an area roughly corresponding to present-day Veneto, the latter approximately corresponding to north Lombardy (for funerary rites in Iron Age Veneto and social change in this region around 625–575 BC *cf.* Perego this volume).

In my thesis for the *Diploma di Specializzazione* I collated previously published funerary evidence from western Emilia with new and unpublished data (Zamboni 2009a). The funerary data that form the evidence base of this study have been thoroughly examined, although some finds are better contextualized than others. For example, we have almost no information on the archaeological context of many of the nineteenth-century finds, whilst the data from very recent excavations are highly contextualized (Zamboni 2012). My catalogue of sites and findings is still unpublished, although some newly excavated sites in the province of Parma have been included in a recent exhibition catalogue (Locatelli *et al.* 2013).

A glance at some archaeological maps of northern Italy in the sixth and fifth centuries BC (Fig. 9.1) reveals some inconsistencies. We can observe great differences in how the presence of the Etruscans between the Po River and the Apennines is portrayed. To be sure, archaeological maps are primarily learning tools as well as constructs which reflect the most popular school of thought. In our case, the differences observed are due to several theoretical and methodological uncertainties inherent in the history of archaeological studies of western Emilia. Historical and archaeological maps are also examples of how the tracing of boundaries is not only an arbitrary exercise and often an 'invention' (both ancient and contemporary), but also reflects an intellectual predisposition to compartmentalize material and visual culture into supposedly clear-cut and regionally defined 'identities' (Barth 1969; Fabietti 2002; Rajala this volume).

Western Emilia is a good case study that allows us to move beyond this deeply ingrained tradition of studies, which remains particularly strong in non-Anglophone archaeology. This tradition consists of linking material culture assemblages to ethnic labels. According to this theoretical and ideological convention, which was strongly influenced by Classical studies and remains faithful to the culture-historical paradigm, all artefacts must be attributed to the ethnic groups that are mentioned in Classical texts, such as the 'Etruscans', the 'Celts', the 'Veneti', the 'Ligurians' and so forth.

Yet in frontier territories such as western Emilia we have instead to imagine the development of societies that were much more complex and multicultural. These are regions where different cultural traditions, fashions, goods and ideas converged from very different places, going on to form original and fluid material assemblages and cultural contexts. Furthermore, in light of recent developments in

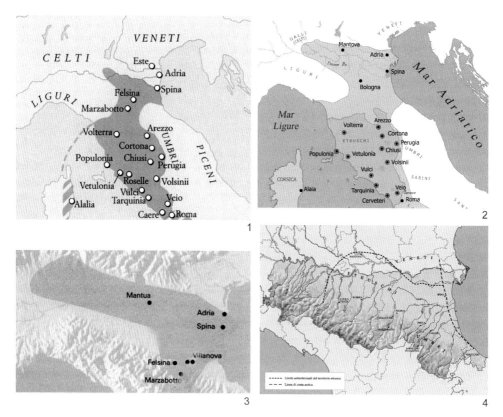

Fig. 9.1: Archaeological maps showing the supposed Etruscan expansion in northern Italy during the sixth and fifth centuries BC (1: after Camporeale 1992; 2: after Wikipedia <http://en.wikipedia.org/wiki/Padanian_Etruria>; 3: after Paolucci 2011; 4: after Sassatelli and Macellari 2011).

anthropology and the social sciences, we must question the validity and utility of concepts such as 'ethnicity' and 'identity' as used in many archaeological studies. In particular, we should be aware of their inherently contextual, performative and contrastive nature (*cf.* Fabietti 2002; Remotti 2010), as I shall attempt to explain towards the end of this chapter.

History of a problem: Etruscans, Celts or Ligurians?

Since the very beginning of archaeological research in western Emilia, archaeological finds from the pre-Roman period have raised challenging questions about cultural identity. Most difficulties were due to the fragmentary nature of the finds, but even the most complete discoveries could not be immediately attributed to any particular cultural group. There was also little information in the literary sources (Colonna 2008; Malnati and Manfredi 2003, 15–8; Sordi 1988; Uboldi 1988).

Greek and Roman authors from the second century BC onwards speak of an Etruscan expansion and domination in northern Italy, following the exploits of mythical founders such as Tarchon and Ocnus. It is interesting to note that these ancient narratives define the Etruscan communities in northern Italy in terms of their conflict with incoming 'Gauls' from across the Alps, who supposedly began to invade the Po Valley from the fourth century BC. According to Polybius (2.17.1–3):

> "... the Etruscans were the oldest inhabitants of this plain at the same period that they possessed also the Phlegraean plain in the neighbourhood of Capua and Nola, which, accessible and well known as it is to many, has such a reputation for fertility. Those therefore who would know something of the dominion of the Etruscans should not look at the country they now inhabit, but at these plains and the resources they drew thence. The Celts, being close neighbours of the Etruscans and associating much with them, cast covetous eyes on their beautiful country and on a small pretext, suddenly attacked them with a large army and, expelling them from the plain of the Po, occupied it themselves."[1]

Likewise, Livy (39.55.6–7) states that:

> "... in the same year [i.e. 183 BC] Mutina and Parma, colonies of Roman citizens, were established. Two thousand men in each case were settled on the land that had recently belonged to the Boii, and previously to the Etruscans."

He also notes that:

> "... Before the Roman supremacy, the power of the Tuscans was widely extended both by sea and land. They first settled on this side the Apennines by the western sea in twelve cities, afterwards they founded twelve colonies beyond the Apennines, corresponding to the number of the mother cities. These colonies held the whole of the country beyond the Po as far as the Alps, with the exception of the corner inhabited by the Veneti, who dwelt round an arm of the sea." (Livy, 5.33.7–10)

We have very few literary references to the Etruscan cities in northern Italy, perhaps twelve or eighteen in number (Plutarch, *Life of Camillus*, 16). One exception is Mantua, thanks to Virgil, the city's most illustrious citizen (*Aeneid* 10.198–203):

> "Ocnus, also, called up troops from his native shores, he, the son of Manto the prophetess and the Tuscan river, who gave you your walls, Mantua, and his mother's name, Mantua rich in ancestors, but not all of one race: there were three races there, under each race four tribes, herself the head of the tribes, her strength from Tuscan blood."

From an archaeological point of view, we owe the first and most important discoveries in western Emilia to Gaetano Chierici, one of the 'founding fathers' of Italian Palaeoethnology. After 1868, when he reported the first Iron Age tomb near S. Ilario d'Enza (Reggio Emilia), Chierici excavated several groups of tombs around the modern centre of S. Ilario, documenting both inhumations and cremations that were situated along a cobbled main road, probably north–south oriented. Some of the women's tombs included prestigious grave goods such as bronze belts, armrings, rings, fibulae and jewellery. Unfortunately, although these publications included one of the first stratigraphic sections ever, Chierici published almost exclusively excavation reports, with no drawings of grave goods. In 1874 he began to compare the archaeological material from S. Ilario with the material from neighbouring cemeteries. He emphasized the differences between the large domestic pottery vases (*dolia*) of S. Ilario and the urns from Villanova, which had been discovered just a few years earlier near Bologna by Giovanni Gozzadini, and had been attributed to the Etruscans (Desittere 1988, 69). For certain bronze belt plates, Chierici looked rather to graves in the Ticino area which is now southern Switzerland (Chierici 1874).

After the discovery of a second important cemetery at the Fornaci of S. Ilario d'Enza in 1878, Chierici was able to date the material to the 'second Iron Age period' (sixth to third century BC), arguing for typological parallels with the material from the Arnoaldi cemetery near Bologna, which had been published by Gozzadini in 1877. According to Chierici, except for the rectangular belt plates, "the rest is similar, except for a greater abundance of wares decorated with impressions that had never been seen in Sant'Ilario" (Cherici 1878).[2]

In attempting to attribute this material to specific cultural units, Chierici merely observed that in the absence of stratigraphic continuity, the users of the S. Ilario cemetery could not have been the Bronze Age 'Terramare' people (Chierici and Mantovani 1873, 29). In a letter from 1874 he wrote to his friend Strobel: "I begin to believe that those are Gallic tombs ..." (Macellari *et al.* 1996, 7).[3]

In the late nineteenth and early twentieth centuries, the work of Luigi Pigorini rose to prominence. By considering the findings from S. Ilario, Correggio and Casaltone, and focusing on the belt plates, Pigorini concluded that at the time when the Etruscan 'Certosa civilization' flourished in Bologna, the inhabitants of the western Emilian plain were not themselves Etruscans but were instead related to some communities in Lombardy, and were therefore 'Celts' from beyond the Alps (Pigorini 1892). Pigorini envisaged a descent of these people towards the area of Reggio Emilia, into lands that might have been uninhabited since the end of the Bronze Age. This reconstruction was important to support Pigorini's theory about the northern origin of the Etruscans. He wrote:

> "The reason why the Italics were so scarce north of the Apennines in the Early Iron Age is this, that between the end of the Bronze Age and the beginning of the Iron Age they left the Po Valley in great numbers, and settled in the Felsinean country (i.e. around Bologna) as far as Tarquinia and the Colli Albani. But the lands located left of the Po and western Emilia, whence the Italics departed, did not remain deserted and were gradually occupied by people from neighbouring countries." (Pigorini 1891)

In the first half of the twentieth century, Italian Protohistory was largely stagnant, having been marginalized by the Fascist regime (*IIPP* 2014). Archaeological activity in the Po Valley was limited to the recovery of grave goods from a few tombs in Baragalla

(Reggio Emilia) and S. Ilario d'Enza. In terms of interpretation, Pigorini's ideas remained unchallenged (Bernardi 1951–1952; Degani 1951–1952). It was only in the 1950s and 1960s that some scholars specializing in Etruscan archaeology started again to address the issue of cultural identity in western Emilia. However, they made little progress other than developing a more cautious approach. For example, G.A. Mansuelli, who was then professor in Bologna, wrote: "... the organization of this region remains protohistoric and, until it is possible to conduct new excavations, the vagueness of the cultural aspects limits our understanding of the population" (Mansuelli 1963, 149). Mansuelli was quite sceptical about a possible Etruscan presence in western Emilia, and described the region as displaying "an Etruscan veneer that covered a cultural background which was basically non-Etruscan" (Mansuelli 1960, 224–6).

The late 1970s and 1980s marked a turning point in the scholarship on ancient Emilia. New excavations and studies gave new impetus to the search for an *ethnos* to which it was possible to attribute the material culture. In particular, Giovanni Colonna (1974) and Luigi Malnati identified what they thought was "a substantially homogenous Etruscan and Etruscanized area stretching as far as the Taro River and perhaps beyond" (Bonghi Jovino 1993, 149). The epigraphic and linguistic data were taken as evidence of an 'Etruscan colonization' that was supposedly carried out by the major cities of northern and inner Etruria (initially Chiusi, then Perugia, Orvieto, Cortona, Volterra and perhaps Vulci) under the general guidance of Bologna/Felsina. With regard to the funerary record, Malnati and Macellari (1989, 32) wrote: "... the grave goods reflect wide-ranging cultural connections [...] in a frame of reference that is not distinctive [of a single cultural group] but very complex and varied". This, in their words, made it "difficult to define the ethnicity of the communities that settled between the Secchia and Enza Rivers in the sixth century BC, despite the obvious Etruscan associations of the culturally and socially dominant group".

In contrast, in the early 1980s, two professors of Protohistory in Milan and Bologna, Raffaele Carlo de Marinis and Daniele Vitali, argued for an autonomous *facies* or 'archaeological culture' in western Emilia, which they named 'S. Ilario-Correggio' or 'S. Ilario-Remedello' and saw as distinct from the Etruscan culture, named 'Marzabotto-Servirola'.

In particular, Vitali (1983, 133) argued that "in western Emilia there coexisted for some time two distinct cultural groups linked to two different cultural traditions, which perhaps began to merge in the fifth century BC". De Marinis focused on the absence of the so-called 'etrusco-padana' ware (a characteristic fine-ware pottery attested from the late sixth century BC in the Po Valley) and on the presence of elements of personal attire such as bronze belt plates, spoked-wheel pendants, open armrings and lowered arch fibulae, which are widely distributed north of the Po and across the Alps. In terms of ethnicity de Marinis was inconclusive, but suggested that the communities in western Emilia belonged neither to the 'Golasecca' culture, nor to the cultural group then known as the 'Paleoveneti', and were probably not Etruscan either (de Marinis 1988, 67).

For the last two decades the 'Etruscan colonization model' has prevailed. Debates have focused on whether colonization was carried out under the general coordination of Bologna (the Etruscan *Felsina*: Sassatelli 2008) or whether it was done independently by individual cities (Locatelli 2008). Scholars have agreed that the Etruscan 'colonizers' maintained a dominant position while interacting with neighbouring populations, and even that they integrated with 'native' substrates which remain poorly defined (Catarsi 2008; Macellari 2004). Recently, there have been many attempts to identify these 'indigenous' peoples. In the past decade there has been particular interest in the 'Ligurians', as is evident from an exhibition held in Genoa (*cf.* de Marinis and Spadea 2004), as well as from several workshops and conferences resulting in publications (e.g. Charamonte Trerè 2003; de Marinis and Spadea 2007; Venturino Gambari and Gandolfi 2004). 'Umbrians' and 'Celts' have also been mentioned as possible candidates for the role of the 'native' inhabitants of western Emilia (*cf.* Macellari 2014).

Landscape and funerary ritual

Leaving aside the attempts at cultural and ethnic interpretation, it is helpful to summarize the main archaeological features of western Emilia. From the end of the seventh century BC, the lowland territories south of the Po, between the Trebbia and Panaro Rivers, started to be intensively exploited for their rich alluvial soil, water resources and agricultural potential. The settlement organization appears to consist of groups of huts and small, scattered farmsteads, as well as small or medium-sized villages. A network of paved roads, which remains poorly documented, suggests connections between the Apennine passes and the landings along the Po River. Perhaps due to incomplete excavation, there is still very little evidence for previous occupation of the sites that went on to become Roman colonies in the third and second centuries BC (i.e. Mutina, Regium Lepidi and Placentia: Malnati and Violante 1995). Pottery from the sixth-century BC settlements is mainly local; this pottery includes domestic wares (either wheel made or handmade) and a local version of black and gray *bucchero*. By the end of the sixth century, a type of fine tableware with a thin gloss makes an appearance.[4]

Surrounding these villages and farmsteads are small clusters of graves. The main funerary sites are located east of Piacenza (Le Mose, Pontenure, Fiorenzuola and Cortemaggiore), near Parma (Baganzola, Casalora and Sorbolo), close to Reggio Emilia (S. Ilario d'Enza, Campegine, Baragalla, Villa Mancasale, Rubiera and Correggio) and west of Modena (Gaggio di Castelfranco Emilia, Nonantola and Carpi; *cf.* also a partial list in Macellari 2011, 291–8).

Although both inhumations and cremations are attested, it is more common to find cemeteries where cremation is the exclusive rite, with no apparent gender or age differentiation between the deceased (Tables 9.1 and 9.2). In some sites near Reggio Emilia (S. Ilario, Correggio and Baragalla) pebbles are used as grave markers.

Table 9.1: *Main sites (in geographical order from west to east) with numbers of identified sixth-century-BC graves categorized by ritual (inhumation or cremation). "*" indicates dubious context; "/" = uncertain or unknown.*

SITE	Cremations	Inhumations	Uncertain chronology
Piacenza, Le Mose	1		
Pontenure, Tangenziale	9	5	2 inhumations
Cortemaggiore, Chiavenna	1	2	
Fiorenzuola, Azienda Paullo	1	1	
Parma, Baganzola	6		13 inhumations
Parma, Casalora di Ravadese	2	1	
Sorbolo, Casaltone	2		
S. Ilario, Fornaci	4	21	
S. Ilario, Bettolino	7	5	
S. Ilario, Romei/Baldi	4	6	1 inhumations
Campegine (1980)	1		
Campegine, Torretta	/	/	
Campegine, La Razza	4 (*)		
Reggio Emilia, Baragalla	5		
Reggio Emilia, Villa Mancasale	1		
Rubiera, Corticella	1		
Correggio	8 (*)		
Nonantola, Redù	/	/	
Carpi, S. Croce	3		
Castelfranco, Gaggio	1		
Total	61	41	16

Overall, cremations are statistically predominant. In general the human remains were burnt with 'low energy expenditure' (Cavazzuti and Zamboni 2012)[5] and were placed together with the remains of the funeral pyre and the grave goods inside large *dolia* or, less frequently, in simple earthen pits. The main feature of these cremation tombs is the *dolium* itself (Fig. 9.2), which is typologically similar to examples from Bologna, where *dolia* are firstly used as cinerary urns in the late seventh century BC (*cf.* Locatelli and Malnati 2012). Inhumation burials, on the other hand, were usually placed in simple pits, with the exception of a single case of a burial deposited in a hollowed-out tree trunk. Many of the inhumation tombs are devoid of surviving grave goods. The preferred orientation of the body was east–west with the head pointing east.

Table 9.2: Sites and graves analysed (in geographical order from west to east).

SITE	GRAVE	RITE	GENDER	Dolium	Fibulae Bronze	Fibulae Iron	Armrings Bronze	Armrings Iron	Rings Bronze	Rings Iron	"Fermatrecce"	Belt plates	Wheel Pendant	Pendants Bronze	Pendants Glass	Pendants Amber	Pendants Bone	Pendants Stone	Toiletry items	Spinning & weaving tools	Iron knives	Pottery	Other	Total (grave goods)
Piacenza, Le Mose	1	CR	♀	1	2					1					1					1				5
Pontenure, Tangenziale	4	CR	♀?	1																2				2
	6	CR	♀	1	9	2			2			1								2				16
	9	CR		1				1																1
	10	CR		1	3		2																	5
	11	CR	♂	1	1		1																	2
	12	IN	♀		3				3	2		1		1	3	3				1				17
	14	CR	♀?					1				1												2
	17	CR	♀				1	1						1				1		3			1	8
Cortemaggiore, Chiavenna	1	CR	♂?	1																				0
	2	IN	inf		4																			4
Fiorenzuola, Azienda Paullo	1	IN			2																			2
	2	CR		1																				0
Parma, Baganzola	1	CR	♀	1	13		2		1			1	1											18
	9	CR	♀	1	5		1	1				1												8
	10	CR		1	1																			1
Parma, Baganzola	11	CR	♀	1	13	2	1		1			2	2	1	1					1				24
	12	CR	♀	1	13		4				2	2			1								1	23
	15	CR	♂	1	2			1													1	1		5

(Continued)

SITE	GRAVE	RITE	GENDER	Dolium	Fibulae Bronze	Fibulae Iron	Armrings Bronze	Armrings Iron	Rings Bronze	Rings Iron	"Fermatrecce"	Belt plates	Wheel Pendant	Pendants Bronze	Pendants Glass	Pendants Amber	Pendants Bone	Pendants Stone	Toiletry items	Spinning & weaving tools	Iron knives	Pottery	Other	Total (grave goods)
Parma, Casalora di Ravadese	1	CR		1																				0
	2	CR	♂	1				1													1			2
	3	IN			3																		1	3
Sorbolo, Casaltone	/				3				5			1											1	10
S. Ilario, Fornaci	2	IN	♀?		4		1					1												6
	3	CR	♀	1	9		2							1	2	1			1	5			5	26
	11	IN								1														1
	12	IN	♀		7	2	4								4		1			1			2	21
	13	IN	♀		13	3	4		11			1			18					4				54
	20	IN	♂					1				1									1			3
	24	IN	♀?		2		2		2			1												7
S. Ilario, Romei/Baldi	2	IN			8		1					1		1			1							12
	3	IN			8		2		5					2									1	18
	5	CR		1	7		3				2	2				4						3?	3?	19?
	9	IN	♀		2						2									1		1?		6
	11	IN	♀		6			2?			1?	1 1?								1		?	?	11?
S. Ilario, Bettolino	1	CR	♂					1													1		3	5
	2	CR	♀	1											2					1				3
	4	CR		1	1	1																		1

(Continued)

SITE	GRAVE	RITE	GENDER	Dolium	Fibulae Bronze	Fibulae Iron	Armrings Bronze	Armrings Iron	Rings Bronze	Rings Iron	"Fermatrecce"	Belt plates	Pendants Wheel Pendant	Pendants Bronze	Pendants Glass	Pendants Amber	Pendants Bone	Pendants Stone	Toiletry items	Spinning & weaving tools	Iron knives	Pottery	Other	Total (grave goods)
S. Ilario, Bettolino	5	CR	♀	1	7		4		2						4				1	12			4	34
	7	CR	♀	1	11		1		5			1			2					1			1	22
	12	CR		1																		1	1	2
Campegine, 1980	/	CR		1	2																			2
Campegine, Torretta	/	?			2		1												3					6
Reggio Emilia, Baragalla	1–5	CR		1+	2		1	1				1									1			6
Reggio Emilia, Villa Mancasale	/	CR	♂?	1	1																	3		4
Rubiera, Corticella	/	CR		1?	12								1										1	14
Carpi, S. Croce	1	CR		1	2																			2
	2	CR	♀	1	6		1					1								1				9
	3	CR	♂	1	2			1																3
Nonantola, Redù	/	?			13		2					1												16
Castelfranco Emilia, Gaggio	1	CR		1	2																			2

Key: CR = cremation; IN = inhumation; inf = sub-adult; / = number of tombs uncertain or unknown.

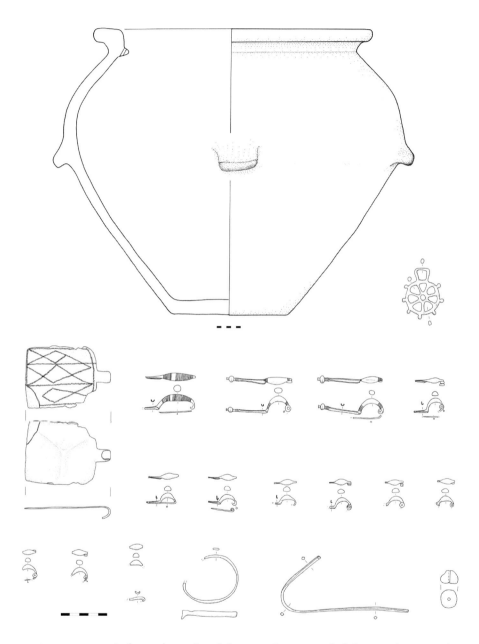

Fig. 9.2: Baganzola (Parma), Tomb 1, dolium *and grave goods (after Zamboni 2009a).*

There are differences in funerary ritual as regards gender. Grave goods that are associated with women tend to be more lavish and varied.[6] The standard grave-good assemblage associated with women (Fig. 9.3) includes a distinctive type of belt made of leather or other perishable materials, decorated with small studs of thin bronze sheet. These belts were usually fastened with a ring or a hook, and sometimes thin folded bronze rods were placed in a row along the belt, allowing for length adjustment. The main elements of the belt are the squarish bronze plate with rounded margins, and the wide, short belt hook, which is attached to the belt by the folded-over edge of the foil or with rivets. The external surface of the plate is usually decorated with embossed dots and studs or zigzag burin patterns (in the so-called *Tremolierstick* style). Typologically, this object is comparable to the triangular and rectangular Golasecca types, which derive from Bronze Age rhomboid types (Casini 1998; Damiani *et al.* 1992; Rubat Borel 2009). Outside of Emilia, this bronze belt type is widespread in the Golasecca culture area, especially in the Alpine valleys of Lombardy and Ticino (Casini 1998). Albeit less frequently, this belt type is also found in Veneto (Chieco Bianchi and Calzavara Capuis 2006, 150–2, 294–301) and in the Hallstatt region (Hodson 1990, fig. 12) (Fig. 9.4).

Another item that is distinctive to female graves is a type of bronze spoked-wheel pendant with an upper appendage for suspension; these pendants are occasionally shaped as a trapezoid human figure with open arms, or as a zoomorphic double protome. Small rings and chains are suspended from eyelets along the pendant's circumference. This type of ornament derives from prototypes belonging to the Urnfield culture (*c.* 1300–750 BC: Tramputz Orel and Heath 2001) and then to the Hallstatt 'culture' (*c.* 750–450 BC: Hodson 1990, 55). Remarkably, it is also found in some settlements in northern Italy such as Bagnolo S. Vito (Mantua), Marzabotto (Bologna) and Verucchio (near Rimini; on mortuary rites at Verucchio *cf.* also Di Lorenzo *et al.* this volume), and in a metalwork hoard near Parre (Bergamo) (Fig. 9.4; Zamboni 2012, 19–20).

Women wore other types of jewellery such as open armrings (including the 'Chiavari' type from the Golasecca area, *cf.* Fig. 9.4), necklace pendants such as the basket-shaped type (Fig. 9.4) and some other pendants made of bronze, amber or glass. Many types of fibulae are also attested (*navicella*, *sanguisuga* or 'leech-type', lowered arch, proto-Certosa and ancient Certosa), all of which are widely distributed in the Golasecca area, in Veneto and in Slovenia (Zamboni 2012, 21–2). Another ornament found in these grave assemblages is the so-called *fermatrecce*, namely a bronze ring presumably used to fasten the hair or the braid.

From the western cemeteries (Piacenza and Parma) there are items of personal adornment that pertain exclusively to the Golasecca culture. These include a bi-troncoconical bronze pendant from Pontenure (type II according to de Marinis 1981, 233), which dates from Golasecca Phase II A–B (*c.* 550–525 BC), and some disc-shaped fasteners (the so-called *fermapieghe*). Spinning and weaving instruments are often included in 'feminine' grave-good assemblages, as are toiletry items. In contrast, 'masculine' grave goods are fewer and poorer. The adult male is commonly buried with only a simple iron arm-ring, two or three iron serpentine fibulae and an iron knife that is best seen as a tool rather than a weapon. Otherwise, no weapon is attested.

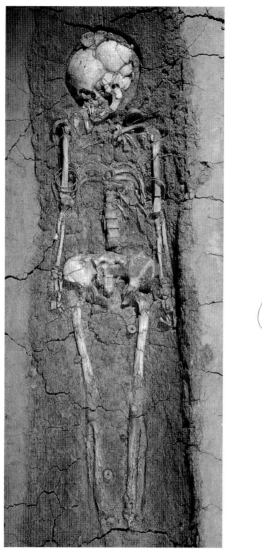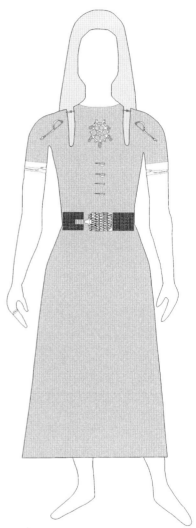

Fig. 9.3: On the left S. Ilario d'Enza, Tomb 13 (after Sassatelli et al. 1994); on the right the typical female funerary costume (after Zamboni 2012).

At a glance, we can see how the sixth-century BC funerary record in western Emilia reveals a plurality and variety of cultural connections. In particular, the bronze ornaments belonging to the 'female costume' have a wide geographical distribution that is clearly north-oriented. Yet in Emilia these objects are placed in 'Etruscan' cinerary urns (*dolia*). The cultural uniqueness of the sixth-century communities of Emilia also becomes evident in relation to some 'missing elements', as I shall explain in the following section.

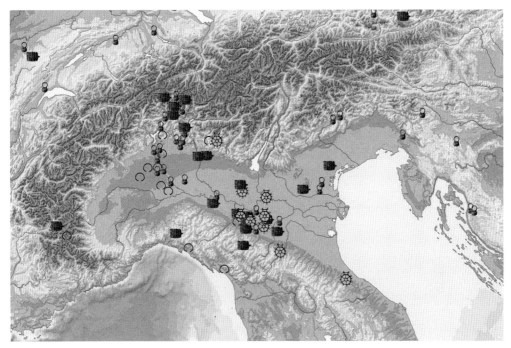

Fig. 9.4: Distribution map of distinctive female bronze ornaments in the sixth century BC: S. Ilario-type belt plates; spoked wheel-shaped pendants; Chiavari-type open armrings; basket-shaped pendant (Tessmann 2007-type 1) (elaboration: L. Zamboni).

Absences

As Siân Jones pointed out, an important aspect of ethnicity is the understanding of *differences*, namely "the possibility of exploring difference in the past, rather than merely reproducing it in the image of the present" (Jones 1997, 129, also 49).

One of the major differences we can notice between western Emilia and neighbouring regions is the almost complete absence of pottery vessels among the grave goods, both in inhumation and cremation graves.[7] This negative evidence suggests that the people buried in the western plain of Emilia during the sixth century BC did not know, or had not accepted, the funerary banquet and sympotic ideology that is a key element in many pre-Roman cultures in Italy.[8] This is a very significant aspect of mortuary practice and ideology in Emilia, which might be read as a strong and deliberate statement of differentiation in relation to neighbouring communities through funerary ritual.

It should be stressed that in the entire sixth-century BC western Emilian area, black-gloss and figured Attic pottery vessels are extremely rare, as are transport amphorae, which appear only in the fifth century at major settlements such as S. Polo Servirola (Reggio Emilia) and Siccomonte (Parma: Maggiani 1992; Sassatelli 2008). Such an absence seems odd if we consider that rich emporia flourished on the Venetian Adriatic coast and north of the Po at Adria, Spina and Bagnolo S. Vito (Mantua), particularly during the second half of the sixth century. All of these sites were busy ports of trade that imported and redistributed large amounts of fine Greek pottery (on this argument *cf.* recent work in Bentz and Reusser 2004; Paleothodoros 2012; Reusser 2002; Zamboni 2016).

The lack of tableware among the grave goods in Emilia, and the scarceness of imported pottery associated with the symposium, raise questions about what people in this region were drinking, both in their everyday life and during ceremonies. Is it possible that instead of wine they consumed other kinds of fermented beverages such as ales and mead, which might have been drunk from wood and horn containers instead of pottery vessels? Chemical and molecular analysis would be required to clarify this point (in general *cf.* McGovern 2003).

In addition to the pottery vessels, another 'absence' that characterizes sixth-century BC western Emilia is the almost complete lack of inscriptions in the Etruscan language or alphabet. The only exceptions are two funerary markers or *cippi* from Rubiera, which I briefly discuss below. It is only in the fifth and fourth centuries that we begin to see inscriptions in the Etruscan alphabet (a few names and letters) as well as some non-alphabetic signs, such as crosses, which are found only in settlements (Locatelli *et al.* 2013, 6; Macellari 2004). The epigraphic evidence therefore seems too scarce to indicate that political power in Emilia was monopolized by Etruscan speakers, especially if we compare the few inscriptions from Emilia with the more substantial Etruscan epigraphy from the contemporaneous centres of Spina, Adria, Bologna/Felsina and Marzabotto.

If we add to this picture the conspicuous absence of weapons in all the cemeteries and settlements between Bologna and the Golasecca area, plus the faint traces of cults and religious practice (Zamboni 2009b), the result seems to be a very strong 'negative' image of Emilian society (for comparisons *cf.* Fernández Götz and Ruiz Zapatero 2011, 227–8; Gassowski 2003). It is worth mentioning that the evidence from Bologna/Felsina reveals a more complex picture for the sixth and fifth centuries. For example, representations on bronze bucket-shaped vessels (situlae) and funerary *stele* suggest the image of a society in arms; however, there is little evidence supporting this representation of the local community in the rest of the archaeological record (Chierici 2008; Malnati 2008). Outside few major settlements (namely Bologna and Marzabotto), the presence of temples, sanctuaries or other cult places is yet to be recognized. Only some small bronzes and miniature domestic vessels, mostly from settlement sites, have emerged to date (*cf.* Zamboni 2009b for further discussion and references).

From an archaeological point of view, it is difficult to find comparisons for a society characterized by so many absences. Regarding the scarcity of pottery in grave-good assemblages, one possible comparison may be drawn with the La Téne graves of Casalecchio di Reno near Bologna, dating to the early stages of the so-called 'Celtic invasion' of the fourth century BC (*cf.* Ortalli 2008), and perhaps with instances from Spina (references in Zamboni 2012, 25).

"Matters of power and rhetoric"[9]

In the previous sections I demonstrated that sixth-century BC western Emilia comes across as a well-connected region with paved roads and numerous waterways, and one which was exposed to multicultural influences and different forms of mobility, but with seemingly little evidence of social differentiation in the funerary record. In these rural communities, women were buried or cremated while dressed in a typical costume that refers more or less directly to ornaments and fashion styles that are also attested in Veneto, Lombardy and 'Celtic' regions. These communities did not know or were not interested in sophisticated banquets and Greek-style symposia, as far as the funerary record is concerned.

As mentioned above, only one Etruscan inscription can be securely dated to the sixth century BC. This is a monumental funerary marker or *cippus* (unfortunately without a reliable context) which bears the name of a high-ranking woman, **Kuvei Puleisnai**. According to some scholars, this woman was 'Celtic' by name and birth, and was married to a local Etruscan king or magistrate, a **zilath**, who perhaps ruled in *Misala* (an uncertain locality), and from whom she acquired her gentilicial name or *nomen* (Amann 2008, 261; Casini 2000, 78; De Simone 1992, 10–1). From an ethnoarchaeological perspective, one might envisage strategies of exogamous marriage between the Etruscan newcomers and their northern neighbours, according to the principle of patrilocality. The 'exogamy hypothesis', which had already been proposed for other contexts in the proto-history of Europe (Kristiansen 1998, 394–402), has recently been invoked to explain the wide distribution of Golasecca personal ornaments, which is seen as evidence of the movements of women who married outside their native territory (Casini 2000; 2012).

However, besides relying on obsolete presuppositions about ethnicity, such an explanation requires us to make arbitrary assumptions about gender and class distinctions in the region under study. It is indeed possible that the presence of a **zilath** in Rubiera can be explained as a form of "mobility of the élite" (James 2000, 143–5), which does not necessarily imply an involvement of lower social strata (for an example of such an analysis *cf.* González and Ruibal 2012). However, in my opinion the archaeological data from western Emilia are still insufficient to support this sort of analysis. Moreover, in approaching a multicultural region such as western Emilia, where communities resorted to such distinctive forms of self-representation through ritual, it is no longer possible to ignore current debates in the humanities and social sciences concerning the use (and abuse) of concepts such as 'culture' and, more recently, 'ethnicity' and 'identity'. The limitations of the culture-historical paradigm become more salient when studying a boundary territory such as sixth-century BC western Emilia.

The remainder of this chapter will offer a brief overview of widespread criticisms concerning three main conceptual categories currently used in archaeology (namely culture, ethnicity and identity), which tend to be ignored by Italian scholars. I shall conclude by reflecting on whether it still makes sense to search for ethnic labels in

Iron Age societies, and whether it might be preferable to abandon the concept of identity altogether.

Interest in the problem of ethnic labels developed during the 1980s and 1990s amongst processualist and post-processualist archaeologists (e.g. Díaz-Andreu *et al.* 2005; Jones 1997, 5–6, 110; Insoll 2007). These scholars became aware of, and were affected by, the growing post-modern interest in global political changes related to post-colonialism, globalization, regionalism and super-nationalism (e.g. Dietler 2006; Hodos 2010).

In contrast, Italian archaeologists did not suffer as much from the so-called 'Kossinna syndrome' in the post-WWII period.[10] Rather, during the twentieth century Italian proto-history was mostly influenced on the one hand by the work of Gordon Childe, and on the other by the historical tradition. Thus, most Italian archaeologists still uncritically employ the culture-historical paradigm as a means of describing the various communities of late prehistoric and Iron Age Italy, which are supposed to have occupied the same geographical areas for centuries (Giannichedda 2005, 55). Among the few dissenting voices was that of Renato Peroni (1994, 22–4), who was very sceptical about traditional constructions of the concept of 'culture' in Italian archaeology, which he defined as a 'blunder'. As an alternative, he used the concept of *facies*, whose use became widespread in proto-historical studies, although in a way that complemented the traditional terminology.[11]

In Etruscan studies, Massimo Pallottino proposed a truly innovative theory regarding the complex cultural formation of the Etruscan *ethnos* as a long and multi-source formation process (Belelli 2012; Forte 2011). Yet Pallotino's theory was put forward in the 1940s, before major breakthroughs in anthropology and sociology changed our understanding of ethnic identity, and was not fully tackled by later Italian scholars. Furthermore, we should be aware today that the formation of an ethnic group is above all a discursive and contingent process (Fabietti 2002).

Put briefly, in Italian proto-history and Etruscology there was no real criticism of the traditional epistemology, as has been the case in Anglophone archaeology for the past four decades (Jones 1997, 106–10). Nor have scholars questioned seriously the culture-historical paradigm, which gives credence to the notion of a 'superior' Etruscan culture, or the existence of an Etruscan ethnic group and even an Etruscan 'nation', as instead has been the case regarding the 'Celts' (*cf.* for example Collis 2003; Dietler 2006; James 2000). In Etruscology and pre-Roman Italian archaeology, there still prevails a positivistic idea of 'Etruscization' as an inevitable and uniform process of acculturation, in the sense of a one-way influence of a people with a more advanced civilization (the Etruscans) over backward and barbarous natives (i.e. the Ligurians, the Celts, the Umbrians etc.).

As noted above, many scholars still employ the notion of colonization in discussing boundary regions such as Emilia (Della Fina 2008). Colonization is traditionally described as a mass displacement of people and/or a form of undisputed political, economic and cultural domination. It is assumed, more or less implicitly, that there was an ethnic and cultural difference between the Etruscan settlers and the nondescript 'natives'. It should also be stressed that in Italy concepts such as identity, cultural identity or ethnicity have begun to be adopted as research tools in archaeology only in the last few years (for an overview *cf.* Cuozzo and Guidi 2013). Instead, these concepts are often employed by politicians and cultural heritage managers in a positive sense, in referring to common heritage that must be preserved, or to purposes that ought to be achieved (Remotti 2010, xv). Clearly, however, the growing archaeological dataset from western Emilia offers a much more complex and heterogeneous depiction of cultural interaction in ancient Italy.

One might also mention the issue of the 'authenticity' of archaeological cultures, which might be just another modern western myth that has already been undermined by anthropological critique (Clifford 1993; Fabietti 2002). Essentially, these critics stress that 'uncontaminated' ancient peoples never existed outside of scholars' desire to legitimize certain political ideologies, as all human groups are subject to change and do not exist outside of History.

Elsewhere in western archaeology the current theoretical debate indeed focuses on ethnicity and identity. Bourdieu's concept of *habitus* (*cf.* Cuozzo, Iaia, Perego this volume with bibliography) has had a strong impact on archaeological discussions of ethnicity. According to Siân Jones (1997) the concept of *habitus* makes it possible to overcome the dichotomy between previous theoretical positions such as objectivist, subjectivist, primordialist and instrumentalist standpoints (Fernández Götz and Ruiz Zapatero 2011, 222). Jones offers a helpful definition of ethnic identity as "that aspect of a person's self-conceptualization which results from identification with a broader group in opposition to others on the basis of perceived cultural differentiation and/or common descent" (Jones 1997, xiii). Jonathan Hall, who is more interested in the creation of myths of shared origins, sees the ethnic group as "… a social collective whose members are united by their subscription to a putative belief in shared descent and to an association with a primordial homeland" (Hall 1997, 36; 2002, 9).

These approaches reject the notion of 'culture' and 'society' as monolithic, homogeneous, holistic and immutable entities. They remind us that any attempt to reconstruct the past is unavoidably influenced by contemporary historical and social contexts. The concept of 'ethnicity', redefined as a fictive and performative self-identification, an "imagined community", has been employed in many studies, especially as regards the Greek world (e.g. Hall 1997; 2002; Malkin 2001), west-central Europe (Collins 2003; Dietler 2006; James 2000[1999]), Iberia (Díaz-Andreu 1998), the Balkans (Dzino 2009) as well as the Middle Ages (Curta 2007). Nevertheless, more recently the use of the concept of ethnicity in archaeology has been criticized with the charge of oversimplification, with some scholars proposing instead a wider investigation into the various forms that 'identity' may take (e.g. Hakenbeck 2011; Mac Sweeney 2009).

Socio-cultural anthropology against identities

However, even the search for multiple identities continues to generate problems. In line with recent debates in social and anthropological studies (Bayart 1996; Bauman 2003; Boumard *et al.* 2006; Brubaker and Cooper 2000; Fabietti 2002; Maalouf 1998; Remotti 1996; 2010; Sen 2006), I would like to suggest here a critique of the concept of 'identity' and its use in archaeology.

The key problem is that identity is a modern term that refers mainly to contrastive and fictive performances, regardless if employed in relation to antiquity or the present. Human groups may often have felt the need to represent themselves in opposition to something, or to imagine 'others' to create some understanding of 'we'. Yet identity as a concept is a modern invention, leading to misunderstandings and even, in some cases, to political exploitation. Some scholars have recently argued that the concept of identity is limited because it refers to something that is non-negotiable, inalterable and makes no compromises (Remotti 2010). According to this view, identity is a 'closed' concept, which is not grounded in relationships and discussion, but in the emphasis on otherness, be it personal, social, ideological etc.

The term 'identity' – which, at its most basic, means the uniqueness and recognisability of a thing – is itself vague and indeterminate, so as to require an increasing number of adjectives. In archaeology scholars speak of many different types of identity, such as multiple, plural, mixed, hybrid, nested, situational, discrepant identities and so forth (on the concept of 'nested identities' *cf.* also Rajala this volume). The contradictions that are associated with the notion of identity were already clear to philosophers such as Hegel, who viewed identity as a "common simplification" (Remotti 2010, 47).

More recently, Lévi-Strauss claimed that identity is a "limit that does not refer to real experience" (Lévi-Strauss 1980[1977], 311). Even the concept of a unitary and immutable self was already criticized by such philosophers as Pascal, Locke, Hume and Reid (Remotti 2010, 52–79). Francesco Remotti, arguing along similar lines, pointed out that identity is a "modern myth" (Remotti 2010, 132), and that we as social scientists and citizens are invaded and possessed by the "identity obsession".[12] From an epistemological point of view, it seems that the concept of identity entered the social sciences during the 1960s in the US, and began to be questioned by historians and anthropologists since the 1980s and above all during the 1990s (Brubaker and Cooper 2000; Gleason 1983; Remotti 2010).

As regards the humanities and social sciences, another risk is to confuse 'culture' with 'identity' (Remotti 2010, 94), given that 'identity' is a 'fiction' or even an 'illusion' according to some (Remotti 2010, 119–22, 129). Furthermore, even if we want to accept the use of this term, 'identity' would be a form of (self-)definition, and as such it would require differentiating oneself from others *by contrast*. Remotti has argued that history and culture become static and closed entities, independent and self-sufficient, when seen from the perspective of identity (Remotti 2010, 137–8).

In the self-definition of a group, processes of 'identity formation' frequently involve ideas of superiority over others and of purity, becoming a form of 'cultural racism' which in extreme cases can even support racist ideologies (Remotti 1996). Indeed, recent anthropological and historical studies show that there is a close connection between ethnic identity and violence (Appadurai 2005; Remotti 2010, 48–9, 137; Sen 2006): this is because there are instances where ethnic identity is closed inward, in such a way that the ethnic group sees what stands outside as a threat to its integrity (Remotti 2010, xiii). In these instances, the idea of identity becomes an ideological weapon that closes off negotiation and compromise (Remotti 2010, 125).

The main issue for archaeologists is that identity and ethnic affiliations are not, and have never been, absolute monolithic realities, but are always fictions constructed by social actors in specific historical contexts, for various purposes of legitimacy, and with remarkable attitudes of closure against otherness. Identity is frequently constructed retrospectively in order to legitimize political claims in the present, be they racial, nationalistic or autonomist. Some of these claims are even manifest in the academic sphere. Instead, from a methodological perspective, identity should no longer be treated as a research tool (i.e. *strumento di ricerca*). Rather, it should be approached as something to be explained (i.e. as an *oggetto di ricerca*; Remotti 2010, 117–8). In other words, it is necessary to adopt an analytical or etic point of view, investigating if and why a given human group, in a specific social and historical context, has come to require some form of recognition or self-recognition, reaching the point of needing to invent (or re-invent) itself.

As alternative to the concept of identity, sociologists and anthropologists have recently proposed another concept, namely that of *recognition* (Ricoeur 2004). This concept allows for negotiable forms of social phenomena (Remotti 2010, 93). Among its many advantages is the fact that recognition is never definitive, and instead always open-ended and ongoing, based on relationships and reciprocity (Remotti 2010, 126). From this point of view, processes of identification form a case of recognition, one among many, which certainly occurred in the past as well as in the present. However, identity might be a contrastive manifestation of recognition, which some scholars see as being pursued by means of offensive tactics of closure and rejection (Remotti 2010, 95–6). Therefore, anthropological and archaeological research should no longer focus on identities alone, but rather on the various 'we's and their forms of social recognition.

To be sure, among the different types of 'identity recognition' there are also manifestations of ethnicity, which can sometimes be detected in antiquity through literary and historical sources (Hall 2002, 23–5), and through the contextual analysis of material remains (Antonaccio 2010; D'Ercole 2011). However, the effort must be directed towards inquiring when, how and why a group has come to demand an ethnic recognition, as well as the developments and relations with other social agents.

Archaeology has certainly contributed to the fiction of ethnicities and identities as well as to the "invention of traditions" (Hobsbawm and Ranger 1983), by providing legitimizing 'scientific' evidence of the supposed essence of these identities, and vouching for their presumed antiquity (Dietler 2006; Jones 1997, 135–42). Instead, by adopting the concept of recognition, we are able to inquire about relationships that are sought and obtained through exchanges, movements, integration and creations of new ideas about who 'we' are as individual members of fluid and multi-dimensional societies.

Conclusions

Sixth-century BC western Emilia was a complex and culturally mixed *milieu*, one where traditional ethnic labels and historical models are not sufficient to explain the complexities identified in the archaeological record. I argue that attempts at using this material record to identify *ethne*, as the scholars of the late nineteenth and twentieth century did, is chimeric: it is a false problem created by the historical, social and political theories that were in vogue back then.

Not even more recent models of autochthony, colonization and exogamous marriage strategies are wholly applicable, because of their inherent link to both the culture-historical paradigm and old-fashioned concepts such as the *ethnos* in the context of Italian archaeology. We should of course imagine that some episodes of mobility took place, alongside various forms of political management of the territory. However, the most important question is not which ethnic groups were involved, but rather what social agents were in place, how they interacted and renegotiated their affiliations, what connections were established and whether frontiers were created in a plain that is devoid of natural boundaries. What is interesting is to explore how and why those people decided to represent and define themselves and neighbouring 'others' through various requests for *recognition*. Finally, we must investigate how this scenario has been appropriated and elaborated by the powerful groups in society, in the past as well as in the present, and for what purposes.

Acknowledgements

This study was carried out for the preparation of a postgraduate thesis (2009) at the School of Specialization in Archaeology, Università degli Studi di Milano, under the supervision of Prof. C. Chiaramonte Treré. The opportunity to study unpublished data was offered by Dr. L. Malnati and Dr. D. Locatelli (at the former *Soprintendenza per i Beni Archeologici dell'Emilia Romagna*), to whom I extend my gratitude. A first preview of the work is in Zamboni 2012 (available at <unipv. academia.edu/LorenzoZamboni/Papers>). I would also like to thank the editors of this book, Elisa and Rafael, for their enthusiasm and their patience in organizing the workshop and reviewing my chapter.

Notes

1. English translations of ancient sources are from the following editions: *Polybius, The Histories books 1-2, translated by W.R. Paton, revised by Frank W. Walbank and Christian Habicht.* Cambridge, Mass: Harvard University Press, 2010; *Livy, History of Rome books v-vii, with an English translation by B.O. Forster.* Cambridge, Mass: Harvard University Press, 1924; *Livy, History of Rome books xxxviii-xxxix, with an English translation by Evan T. Sage.* Cambridge, Mass: Harvard University Press, 1936; *The Aeneid - Virgil. A translation into English prose by A.S. Kline.* CreateSpace Independent Publishing Platform, 2002.

2. The Italian texts are translated by L. Zamboni, R. Scopacasa and E. Perego.

3. For modern literature on the Bronze Age Terramare culture *cf.* Bernabò Brea *et al.* 1997.

4. For more information on these wares *cf.* most recently Buoite 2013, which focuses on Parma.

5. It is possible to measure the degree of 'energy expenditure' in cremations in view of the quantity of wood consumed, the duration of heat exposure and the amount of care placed in the collection of cremated bones.

6. Gender distinctions are largely based on osteological analysis, which is only partially published (Bedini 1999; Cavazzuti and Zamboni 2012; Martuzzi Veronesi 1971).

7. We currently know of only two exceptions, both in male graves: a bucchero *kantharos* and two bowls found at Villa Mancasale (Reggio Emilia, late seventh century BC) and a gray *impasto* cup covering the grave goods placed at the bottom of the *dolium* in Tomb 15 of Baganzola (Parma). Few other cases (namely S. Ilario, Romei/Baldi) were excavated in the nineteenth century and are therefore uncertain. These data are not sufficient to support any conclusions, but it seems interesting that the presence of these vessels in male graves may indicate gender differentiation through ritual.

8. For the Etruscan world *cf.* for example Mandolesi and Sannibale 2012; Riva 2010. For the Veneto region *cf.* Perego 2010.

9. Clifford 1988, 14: "Self-other relations are matters of power and rhetoric rather than essence."

10. The expression 'Kossina syndrome' refers to the attempt, within German archaeology after WWII, to reject the culture-historical paradigm as it had been appropriated by Gustaf Kossinna, whose nationalistic, racist and ethnocentric approaches were instrumental to the Nazi regime (*cf.* Fernández Götz 2009; Jones 1997, 2–5; both include references).

11. According to Peroni (1994, 24) the term *facies* means: "*L'insieme delle testimonianze archeologiche relative ad un determinato orizzonte cronologico in un dato territorio, aggregate dalle connessioni tipologiche che consentono di collegare tra loro anche fonti archeologiche pertinenti a classi eterogenee*" (i.e. "the whole assemblage of archaeological material that relates to a particular period in a given territory, which is grouped by typological connections that allow us to link together different and heterogeneous archaeological materials").

12. Although my background is not in cultural anthropology, my bibliography includes the work of two key Italian anthropologists, namely F. Remotti (1996; 2010) and U. Fabietti (2002).

Bibliography

Amann, P. (2008) Intorno al cippo II di Rubiera. In G.M. Della Fina (ed.) *La Colonizzazione Etrusca in Italia. Atti del XV Convegno Internazionale di Studi sulla Storia e l'Archeologia dell'Etruria (Orvieto, 23–25 Novembre 2007)*, 247–272. Roma, Quasar.

Antonaccio, C.M. (2010) (Re)defining ethnicity: Culture, material culture, and identity. In S. Hales and T. Hodos (eds) *Material Culture and Social Identities in the Ancient World*, 32–53. Cambridge, Cambridge University Press.

Appadurai, A. (2005) *Sicuri da Morire*. Roma, Meltemi.

Barth, F. (1969) *Ethnic Groups and Boundaries*. New York, Little Brown.

Bauman, Z. (2003) *Intervista sull'Identità* (ed. B. Vecchi). Roma–Bari, Laterza.

Bayart, J.-F. (1996) *L'Illusion Identitaire*. Paris, Fayard.

Bedini, E. (1999) Resti scheletrici umani da Cortemaggiore (Piacenza). *Archeologia dell'Emilia Romagna* 3, 29–33.

Bellelli, V. (2012) (ed.) *Le Origini degli Etruschi: Storia, Archeologia, Antropologia*. Roma, "L'Erma" di Bretschneider.

Bentz, M. and Reusser, C. (2004) (eds) *Attische Vasen in etruskischem Kontext. Funde aus Häusern und Heiligtümern*. München, Beihefte zum CVA Deutschland 2.

Bernabò Brea, M., Cardarelli, A. and Cremaschi, M. (1997) (eds) *Le Terramare. La Più Antica Civiltà Padana*. Milano, Electa.

Bernardi, W. (1951–1952) Nuova tomba dell'età del ferro a S. Ilario d'Enza. *Quaderni del Comitato di Studi Preistorici nell'Emilia Occidentale* 2, 53–61.

Bonghi Jovino, M. (1992) La testimonianza archeologica: Elementi per un approfondimento della fenomenologia storica della presenza etrusca nell'Italia settentrionale. In L. Aigner-Foresti (ed.) *Etrusker nördlich von Etrurien. Etruskische Präsenz in NordItalien und nördlich der Alpen sowie ihre Einflüsse auf die einheimischen Kulturen. Aktes des Symposions von Wien (2-5 Oktober 1989)*, 127–159. Wien, Österreichischen Akademie der Wissenschaften.

Boumard, P., Lapassade, G. and Lobrot, M. (2006) *Le Mythe de l'Identité. Apologie de la Dissociation*. Paris, Economica.

Brubaker, R. and Cooper, F. (2000) Beyond identity. *Theory and Society* 29(1), 1–47.

Buoite, C. (2013) «…Necessario è avere poi dei vasai per ogni bisogno…» (Geoponica II, 49). In D. Locatelli, L. Malnati and D. Maras (eds) *Storie della Prima Parma. Etruschi, Galli, Romani: Le Origini della Città alla Luce delle Nuove Scoperte Archeologiche. Catalogo della Mostra (Parma, Museo Archeologico Nazionale, 12 Gennaio-2 Giugno 2013)*, 23–26. Roma, "L'Erma" di Bretschneider.

Camporeale, G. (1992) Le città: Produzione e creazione artistica. In M. Pallottino (ed.) *Gli Etruschi e l'Europa. Catalogo della Mostra (Galeries Nationales del Grand Palais di Parigi, 15 Settembre-14 Dicembre 1992; Altes Museum di Berlino, 25 Febbraio-31 Maggio 1993)*, 62–71. Milano, Fabbri.

Casini, S. (1998) Ritrovamenti ottocenteschi di sepolture della cultura di Golasecca nel territorio bergamasco. *Notizie Archeologiche Bergomensi* 6, 109–161.

Casini, S. (2000) Il ruolo delle donne golasecchiane nei commerci del VI-V secolo a.C.. In R.C. de Marinis and S. Biaggio Simona (eds) *I Leponti fra Mito e Realtà: Raccolta di Saggi in Occasione della Mostra. Catalogo della Mostra (Locarno, Castello Visconteo-Casorella, 20 Maggio-3 Dicembre 2000)*, 75–100. Locarno, Dadò-GAT 2.

Casini, S. (2012) La pratica dell'esogamia nella cultura di Golasecca. In S. Marchesini (ed.) *Mixed Marriages. A Way to Integration among People. Atti del Convegno Multidisciplinare Internazionale (Verona-Trento, 1-2 Dicembre 2011)*. Trento, Provincia Autonoma di Trento.

Catarsi, M. (2008) Testimonianze dell'età del Ferro dal Parmense. In M. Bernabò Brea and R. Valloni (eds) *Archeologia ad Alta Velocità in Emilia. Indagini Geologiche e Archeologiche lungo il Tracciato Ferroviario. Atti del Convegno (Parma, 9 Giugno 2003)*, 139–146. Borgo S. Lorenzo, All'Insegna del Giglio.

Cavazzuti, C. and Zamboni, L. (2012) Tombe ad incinerazione dell'età del Ferro da necropoli dell'Emilia Occidentale: Inquadramento culturale ed analisi antropologiche. In M. Carme Rovira Hortalà, F. Javier López Cachero and F. Mazière (eds) *Les Necròpolis d'Incineració entre l'Ebre i el Tíber (segles 9.-6. aC): Metodologia, Pràctiques Funeràries i Societat*, 375–380. Barcelona, Museu d'Arqueologia de Catalunya.

Cherici, A. (2008) Armati e tombe con armi nella società dell'Etruria padana: Analisi di alcuni monumenti. In G.M. Della Fina (ed.) *La Colonizzazione Etrusca in Italia. Atti del XV Convegno Internazionale di Studi sulla Storia e l'Archeologia dell'Etruria (Orvieto, 23-25 Novembre 2007)*, 187–246. Roma, Quasar.

Chiaramonte Trerè, C. (2003) *Antichi Liguri sulle Vie Appenniniche tra Tirreno e Po. Nuovi Contributi. Atti del Convegno (Milano, 17 Gennaio 2002)* (Quaderni di Acme). Milano, Cisalpino.

Chieco Bianchi, A.M. and Calzavara Capuis, L. (2006) (eds) *Este II. La Necropoli di Villa Benvenuti*. Roma, Giorgio Bretschneider Editore.

Chierici, G. (1874) Notizie archeologiche. Un altro sepolcro della prima età del ferro a Santilario. *L'Italia Centrale* 150 (24 Dicembre 1874).

Cherici, G. (1878) Il Museo di Storia patria di Reggio nell'Emilia. *Bullettino di Paletnologia Italiana* 5, 177–197.

Chierici, G. and Mantovani, P. (1873) *Notizie Archeologiche dell'Anno 1872 Raccolte e Riferite da D. Gaetano Chierici e Pio Mantovani*. Reggio Emilia.

Clifford, J. (1988) *The Predicament of Culture: Twentieth-Century Ethnography, Literature and Art*. Cambridge, Harvard University Press.

Collis, J.R. (2003) *The Celts: Origins, Myths and Inventions*. Stroud, Tempus.

Colonna, G. (1974) Ricerche sugli Etruschi e sugli Umbri a nord degli Appennini. *Studi Etruschi* 42, 3–24.

Colonna, G. (2008) Etruschi e Umbri in Val Padana. In G.M. Della Fina (ed.) *La Colonizzazione Etrusca in Italia. Atti del XV Convegno Internazionale di Studi sulla Storia e l'Archeologia dell'Etruria (Orvieto, 23-25 Novembre 2007)*, 39–70. Roma, Quasar.

Cuozzo, M. and Guidi, A. (2013) *Archeologia delle Identità e delle Differenze*. Roma, Carocci.

Curta, F. (2007) Some remarks on ethnicity in medieval archaeology. *Early Medieval Europe* 15(2), 177–185.

D'Ercole, M.C. (2011) Sharing new worlds. Mixed identities around the Adriatic (sixth to fourth centuries B.C.E.). In E.S. Gruen (ed.) *Cultural Identity in the Ancient Mediterranean*, 428–451. Los Angeles, Getty.

Damiani, I., Maggiani, A., Pellegrini, E., Saltini, A.C. and Serges, A. (1992) *L'Età del Ferro nel Reggiano. I Materiali delle Collezioni dei Civici Musei di Reggio Emilia*. Reggio Emilia, Civici Musei.

de Marinis, R.C. (1981) *Il Periodo Golasecca III A in Lombardia* (Studi Archeologici 1). Bergamo, Musei Civici.

de Marinis, R.C. (1988a) (ed.) *Gli Etruschi a Nord del Po. Catalogo della Mostra (Mantova, Palazzo Ducale, Galleria dell'Estivale, 21 Settembre 1986-12 Gennaio 1987)* (Vols 1–2). Udine, Campanotto.

de Marinis, R.C. (1988b) I commerci dell'Etruria con i paesi a nord del Po tra IX e VI secolo a.C.. In R.C. de Marinis (ed.) *Gli Etruschi a Nord del Po. Catalogo della Mostra (Mantova, Palazzo Ducale, Galleria dell'Estivale, 21 Settembre 1986-12 Gennaio 1987)* (Vol. 1), 52–80. Udine, Campanotto.

de Marinis, R.C. and Spadea, G. (2004) (eds) *I Liguri. Un Antico Popolo Europeo tra Alpi e Mediterraneo. Catalogo della Mostra (Genova, Palazzo Ducale, 23 Ottobre 2004-23 Gennaio 2005)*. Milano–Ginevra, Skira.

de Marinis, R.C. and Spadea, G. (2007) (eds) *Ancora sui Liguri. Un Antico Popolo Europeo tra Alpi e Mediterraneo*. Genova, De Ferrari.

De Simone, C. (1992) *Le Iscrizioni Etrusche di Rubiera*. Reggio Emilia, Civici Musei.

Degani, M. (1951–1952) Ragguagli sull'età del ferro nel Reggiano alla luce di recenti ritrovamenti. *Emilia Preromana* 3, 57–62.

Della Fina, G.M. (2008) (ed.) *La Colonizzazione Etrusca in Italia. Atti del XV Convegno Internazionale di Studi sulla Storia e l'Archeologia dell'Etruria (Orvieto, 23-25 Novembre 2007)*. Roma, Quasar.

Desittere, M. (1988) *Paletnologi e Studi Preistorici nell'Emilia Romagna dell'Ottocento*. Reggio Emilia, Musei Civici.

Díaz-Andreu, M. (1998) Ethnicity and Iberians: The archaeological crossroads between perception and material culture. *European Journal of Archaeology* 1, 199–216.

Díaz-Andreu, M., Lucy, S., Babic, S. and Edwards, D.N. (2005) (eds) *The Archaeology of Identity: Approaches to Gender, Age, Status, Ethnicity and Religion*. London–New York, Routledge.

Dietler, M. (2006) Celticism, Celtitude and Celticity. The consumption of the past in the age of globalization. In S. Rieckhoff (ed.) *Celtes et Gaulois, l'Archéologie face à l'Histoire, 1, Celtes et Gaulois dans l'Histoire, l'Historiographie et l'Idéologie Moderne. Actes de la Table Ronde de Leipzig (Leipzig, 16-17 Juin 2005)*, 237–248. Glux-en-Glenne, Centre Archéologique Européen.

Dzino, D. (2008) "The people who are Illyrians and Celts": Strabo and the identities of the 'barbarians' from Illyricum. *Arheološki Vestnik* 59, 415–424.

Fabietti, U. (2002) *L'Identità Etnica*. Roma, Carocci.

Fernández Götz, M.A. (2009) Gustaf Kossinna: Análisis crítico de una figura paradigmática de la arqueología europea. *Arqueoweb. Revista Sobre Arqueología en Internet*, 11. [http://pendientedemigracion.ucm.es/info/arqueoweb/pdf/11/gotz.pdf].

Fernández Götz, M.A. and Ruiz Zapatero, G. (2011) Hacia una arqueología de la etnicidad. *Trabajos de Prehistoria* 68(2), 219–236.

Forte, V. (2011) Etruscan origins and Italian nationalism. *Studia Europaea* 1, 5–17.

Gardner, A. (2004) (eds) *Agency Uncovered. Archaeological Perspectives on Social Agency, Power and Being Human*. Walnut Creek, Left Coast Press.

Gassowski, J. (2003) Is Ethnicity Tangible? In M. Hardt, Ch. Lübke and D. Schorkowitz (eds) *Inventing the Pasts in North Central Europe. The National Perception of Early Medieval History and Archaeology*, 9–17. Frankfurt am Main, Peter Lang.

Giannichedda, E. (2005) *Archeologia Teorica*. Roma, Carocci.

Giddens, A. (1984) *The Constitution of Society. Outline of the Theory of Structuration*. Cambridge, Polity Press.

Gleason, P. (1983) Identifying identity: A semantic history. *Journal of American History* 69, 910–931.

González-Ruibal, A. (2012) The politics of identity: Ethnicity and the economy of power in Iron Age Northwest Iberia. In G. Cifani and S. Stoddart (2012) (eds) *Landscape, Ethnicity and Identity in the Archaic Mediterranean Area*, 245–266. Oxford, Oxbow Books.

Hakenbeck, S. (2011) Roman or barbarian? Shifting identities in early Medieval cemeteries in Bavaria. *Post-Classical Archaeologies* 1, 37–66.

Hales, S. and Hodos, T. (2010) (eds) *Material Culture and Social Identities in the Ancient World*. Cambridge, Cambridge University Press.

Hall, J.M. (1997) *Ethnic Identity in Greek Antiquity*. Cambridge, Cambridge University Press.

Hall, J.M. (2002) *Hellenicity: Between Ethnicity and Culture*. Chicago, Chicago University Press.

Hobsbawm, E. and Ranger, T. (1983) (eds) *The Invention of Tradition*. Cambridge, Cambridge University Press.

Hodos, T. (2010) Local and global perspectives in the study of social and cultural identities. In S. Hales and T. Hodos (eds) *Material Culture and Social Identities in the Ancient World*, 3–31. Cambridge, Cambridge University Press.

Hodson, F.R. (1990) *Hallstatt. The Ramsauer Graves. Quantification and Analysis*. Bonn, Habelt.

Insoll, T. (2007) (ed.) *The Archaeology of Identities: A Reader*. London–New York, Routledge.

IIPP (Istituto Italiano di Preistoria e Protostoria) (2014) *150 Anni di Preistoria e Protostoria in Italia. Il Contributo della Preistoria e della Protostoria alla Formazione dello Stato Unitario. Atti della XLVI Riunione Scientifica (Roma, 23-26 Novembre 2011)*. Firenze, Istituto Italiano di Preistoria e Protostoria.

James, S. (2000[1999]) *I Celti Popolo Atlantico. Antica Civiltà o Moderna Invenzione?* Roma, Newton & Compton.

Jones, S. (1997) *The Archaeology of Ethnicity. Constructing Identities in the Past and Present*. London–New York, Routledge.

Kristiansen, K. (1998) *Europe before History*. Cambridge, Cambridge University Press.

Lévi-Strauss, C. (1980[1977]) *L'Identità*. Palermo, Sellerio.

Locatelli, D. (2008) La pianura carpigiana dal controllo degli Etruschi al predominio dei Boi. In P. Bonacini and A.M. Ori (eds) *Storia di Carpi. Volume Primo. La Città e il Territorio dalle Origini all'Affermazione dei Pio*, 115–140. Modena, Mucchi.

Locatelli, D. and Malnati, L. (2012) Le necropoli ad incinerazione di età orientalizzante ed arcaica a Bologna ed in Emilia (fine VIII - VI secolo). In M. Carme Rovira Hortalà, F. Javier López Cachero and F. Mazière (eds) *Les Necròpolis d'Incineració entre l'Ebre i el Tíber (segles 9.-6. aC): Metodologia, Pràctiques Funeràries i Societat* X, 305–320. Barcelona, Museu d'Arqueologia de Catalunya.

Locatelli, D., Malnati, L. and Maras, D. (2013) (eds) *Storie della Prima Parma. Etruschi, Galli, Romani: Le Origini della Città alla Luce delle Nuove Scoperte Archeologiche. Catalogo della Mostra (Parma, Museo Archeologico Nazionale, 12 Gennaio-2 Giugno 2013)*. Roma, "L'Erma" di Bretschneider.

Maalouf, A. (1998) *Les Identités Meurtrières*. Paris, Grasset.

Mac Sweeney, N. (2009) Beyond ethnicity: The overlooked diversity of group identities. *Journal of Mediterranean Archaeology* 22(1), 101–126.

Macellari, R. (2004) Gli Etruschi del Po. *Ocnus* 12, 145–160.

Macellari, R. (2011) Memorie ricucite. Il sepolcreto preromano di San Martino di Correggio (RE) alla luce di alcune nuove acquisizioni. In S. Casini (ed.) *Filo del Tempo. Studi di Preistoria e Protostoria in onore di R.C. de Marinis* (Notizie Archeologiche Begomensi 19), 277–301. Bergamo, Civico Museo Archeologico di Bergamo.

Macellari, R. (2014) Gli Umbri a nord degli Appennini. *In Gli Umbri in Età Preromana. Atti del XXVII Convegno di Studi Etruschi ed Italici (Perugia-Gubbio-Urbino, 27-31 Ottobre 2009)*. Roma, Fabrizio Serra Editore.

Macellari, R., Stagno, E., Pinasco, M.R. and Ienco, M.G. (1996) *I Sepolcreti di Sant'Ilario d'Enza. Revisione dei Dati e Nuove Indagini (Prima Parte)* (Pagine d'Archeologia). Reggio Emilia, Civici Musei.

Maggiani, A. (1992) Ceramiche d'importazione. In I. Damiani, A. Maggiani, E. Pellegrini, A.C. Saltini and A. Serges (1992) *L'Età del Ferro nel Reggiano. I Materiali delle Collezioni dei Civici Musei di Reggio Emilia*, 83–106. Reggio Emilia, Civici Musei.

Malkin, I. (2001) (ed.) *Ancient Perceptions of Greek Ethnicity*. Cambridge, Harvard University Press.

Malnati, L. (2008) Armi e organizzazione militare in Etruria padana. In G.M. Della Fina (ed.) *La Colonizzazione Etrusca in Italia. Atti del XV Convegno Internazionale di Studi sulla Storia e l'Archeologia dell'Etruria (Orvieto, 23-25 Novembre 2007)*, 147–196. Roma, Quasar.

Malnati, L. and Macellari, R. (1989) Sant'Ilario d'Enza. Le strade, i villaggi, i sepolcreti nell'età della colonizzazione etrusca. In G. Ambrosetti, R. Macellari and L. Malnati (eds) *Sant'Ilario d'Enza. L'Età della Colonizzazione Etrusca. Strade, Villaggi, Sepolcreti. Catalogo della Mostra (Reggio Emilia, 1989)*, 27–35. Reggio Emilia, Civici Musei.

Malnati, L. and Manfredi, V.M. (2003[1991]) *Gli Etruschi in Val Padana*. Milano, Mondadori.

Malnati, L. and Violante, A. (1995) Il sistema urbano di IV e III secolo in Emilia Romagna tra Etruschi e Celti (Plut. Vita Cam. 16,3). In J.J. Charpy (ed.) *L'Europe Celtique du Ve au IIIe Siècle Avant J.-C. Actes du Deuxième Symposium International d'Hautvillers (Hautvillers, 8-10 Octobre 1992)*, 97–123. Sceaux, Kronos B.Y.

Mandolesi, A. and Sannibale, M. (2012) *Etruschi: l'Ideale Eroico e il Vino Lucente. Catalogo della Mostra (Asti, Palazzo Mazzetti, 17 Marzo-15 Luglio 2012)*. Milano, Electa.

Mansuelli, G.A. (1960) I fenomeni periferici dell'etruschismo padano. *In Mostra dell'Etruria Padana e della Città di Spina. Catalogo della Mostra (Bologna, Palazzo dell'Archiginnasio, 12 Settembre-31 Ottobre 1960)*, 224–226. Bologna, Alfa.

Mansuelli, G.A. (1963) *Lineamenti Antropogeografici dell'Emilia e Romagna dalla Preistoria alla Romanizzazione* (Preistoria dell'Emilia e Romagna 11). Bologna, A. Forni.

Martuzzi Veronesi, F. (1971) Nota sui resti scheletrici antichi di S. Ilario d'Enza (Reggio Emilia). *Atti della Società dei Naturalisti e dei Matematici di Modena* 102, 51–56.

McGovern, P.E. (2003) *Ancient Wine. The Search for the Origins of Viniculture*. Princeton, Princeton University Press.

Ortalli, J. (2008) L'insediamento celtico di Casalecchio di Reno (Bologna). In D. Vitali and S. Verger (eds) *Tra Mondo Celtico e Mondo Italico. La Necropoli di Monte Bibele. Atti della Tavola Rotonda (Roma, École française de Rome, 3-4 Ottobre 1997)*, 299–322. Bologna, Dipartimento di Archeologia.

Paleothodoros, D. (2012) (ed.) *The Contexts of Painted Pottery in the Ancient Mediterranean World (Seventh-Fourth Centuries BCE)* (BAR S2364). Oxford, Archaeopress.

Paolucci, G. (2011) L'Etruria padana. In G. Paolucci and A. Minetti (eds) *Gli Etruschi nelle Terre di Siena. Reperti e Testimonianze dai Musei della Val di Chiana e della Val d'Orcia. Catalogo della Mostra (Iseo, Palazzo dell'Arsenale, 8 Maggio-10 Luglio 2011)*, 14. Iseo, L'Arsenale.

Perego, E. (2010) Osservazioni preliminari sul banchetto rituale funerario nel Veneto preromano: Acquisizione, innovazione e resistenza culturale. In C. Mata Parreño, G. Pérez Jordà and J. Vives-Ferrándiz Sánchez (eds) *De la Cuina a la Taula. IV Reunió d'Economia en el I milleni aC (Caudete de las Fuentes, Octubre 2009)* (Saguntum. Papeles del Laboratorio de Arqueología, Extra 9), 287–294. València, Universitat de València [http://www.uv.es/fatwireed/userfiles/file/Saguntum_Extra9(1).pdf].

Peroni, R. (1994) *Introduzione alla Protostoria Italiana*. Bari, Laterza.

Pigorini, L. (1892) Tombe preromane di Correggio nella provincia di Reggio Emilia. *Bullettino di Paletnologia Italiana* 18, 40–54.

Pigorini, L. (1891) *Atti dell'Accademia Nazionale dei Lincei. Rendiconti* IV serie, VIII (1° sem. 1891), 67–68.

Remotti, F. (1996) *Contro l'Identità*. Bari, Laterza.

Remotti, F. (2010) *L'Ossessione Identitaria*. Bari, Laterza.

Reusser, Ch. (2002) *Vasen für Etrurien. Verbreitung und Funktionen attischer Keramik im Etrurien des 6. und 5. Jahrunderts vor Christus.* Zürich, Akanthus.

Ricoeur, P. (2004) *Parcours de la Reconnaissance*. Paris, Éditions du Seuil.

Riva, C. (2010) Tecnologie del sé: Il banchetto rituale collettivo in Etruria. In C. Mata Parreño, G. Pérez Jordà and J. Vives-Ferrándiz Sánchez (eds) *De la Cuina a la Taula. IV Reunió d'Economia en el I milleni aC (Caudete de las Fuentes, Octubre 2009)* (Saguntum. Papeles del Laboratorio de Arqueología, Extra 9), 69–80. València, Universitat de València [http://www.uv.es/fatwireed/userfiles/file/Saguntum_Extra9(1).pdf].

Rubat Borel, F. (2009) Note di tipologia su alcuni elementi di parure del ripostiglio di bronzi di Chiusa Pesio. *Quaderni della Soprintendenza Archeologia del Piemonte* 24, 9–28.

Sassatelli, G. (2008) Gli Etruschi nella Valle del Po. Riflessioni, problemi e prospettive di ricerca. In G.M. Della Fina (ed.) *La Colonizzazione Etrusca in Italia. Atti del XV Convegno Internazionale di Studi sulla Storia e l'Archeologia dell'Etruria (Orvieto, 23-25 Novembre 2007)*, 71–114. Roma, Quasar.

Sassatelli, G. and Macellari, R. (2009) Tuscorum Ager. Comunità etrusche fra Enza e Ongina. In D. Vera (ed.) *Storia di Parma II. Parma Romana*, 111–145. Parma, Monte Università Parma Editore.

Sassatelli, G. (1994) Gli Etruschi. In D. Vitali, G. Sassatelli, D. Scargliaini Corlaita and P. Angiolini Martinelli (eds) *Atlante dei Beni Culturali dell'Emilia Romagna. I Beni della Preistoria e della Protostoria. I Beni dell'Età. I Beni della Civiltà Bizantina e Altomedievale*, 45–98. Cinisello Balsamo, Amilcare Pizzi.

Sen, A. (2006) *Identity and Violence: The Illusion of Destiny*. New York, Norton & Co.

Sordi, M. (1988) Etruschi e Celti nella pianura padana: Analisi delle fonti antiche. In R.C. de Marinis (ed.) *Gli Etruschi a Nord del Po. Catalogo della Mostra (Mantova, Palazzo Ducale, Galleria dell'Estivale, 21 Settembre 1986-12 Gennaio 1987)* (Vol. 1), 111–115. Udine, Campanotto.

Tessmann, B. (2007) Körbchenanhänger im Süden-Goritzer Bommeln im Norden. Eine vergleichende Studie zu einem späthallstattzeitlichen Anhängertyp. In M. Blečić, M. Črešnar, B. Hansel, A. Hellmuth, E. Kaiser and C. Metzner-Nebelsick (eds) *Scripta Praehistorica "in honorem" Biba Teržan*, 667–694. Ljubljana, Narodni Muzej Slovenije.

Trampuz Orel, N. and Heath, D.J. (2001) Depo Kanalski Vrh, študija o metalurškem znanju in kovinah na začetku 1. tisočletja pr. n. š. *Arheološki Vestnik* 52, 143–171.

Uboldi, M. (1988) Le fonti antiche. In R.C. de Marinis (ed.) *Gli Etruschi a Nord del Po. Catalogo della Mostra (Mantova, Palazzo Ducale, Galleria dell'Estivale, 21 Settembre 1986-12 Gennaio 1987)* (Vol. 1), 105–110. Udine, Campanotto.

Venturino Gambari, M. and Gandolfi, D. (2004) (eds) *Ligures Celeberrimi: La Liguria Interna nella*

Seconda Età del Ferro. Atti del Convegno Internazionale (Mondovì, 26–28 Aprile 2002). Bordighera, Istituto Internazionale Studi Liguri.

Vitali, D. (1983) L'età del Ferro nell'Emilia occidentale: Dati, considerazioni e proposte. *In Studi sulla Città Antica. L'Emilia Romagna*, 129–172. Roma, "L'Erma" di Bretschneider.

Zamboni, L. (2009a) *Contesti Funerari Arcaici in Emilia Occidentale. Una Cultura di Frontiera alla Luce di Nuove Indagini.* Unpublished thesis, Università degli Studi di Milano.

Zamboni, L. (2009b) Ritualità o utilizzo? Riflessioni sul vasellame "miniaturistico" in Etruria padana. *Pagani e Cristiani* 8, 9–46.

Zamboni, L. (2012) Testimonianze arcaiche in Emilia occidentale. Una cultura di frontiera alla luce di nuove indagini. In M.P. Bologna and M. Ornaghi (eds) *Atti dei Seminari di Dipartimento di Scienze dell'Antichità* (Quaderni di Acme 129), 1–29. Milano, Cisalpino.

Zamboni, L. (2016) *Spina Città Liquida. Gli Scavi 1977-1981 nell'Abitato e i Materiali Tardo-arcaici e Classici* (Zürcher Archäologische Forschungen 3). Rahden, Marie Leidorf.

Chapter 10

Falling behind: access to formal burial and faltering élites in Samnium (central Italy)

Rafael Scopacasa

Introduction

This chapter explores the link between mortuary practice and élite self-legitimization in periods of accelerated socio-political change. In particular, I discuss how the restriction of access to formal burial in sixth–third century BC Samnium (central Italy: Fig. 10.1) may have been an attempt by élite groups to assert their pre-eminence in a time of growing socio-political complexity, which arguably involved the rise of the first state-level polities in the region.[1] During the Iron Age (*c.* 1000–400 BC) formal burial in cemeteries was an important means of indicating one's membership and role in the community, in terms of wealth, kinship and descent. However, from the fifth century BC onwards, Samnite communities embarked on a process of accelerated socio-political change, which rendered earlier forms of élite legitimacy obsolete. These changes involved the formation of larger and more complex political communities, which were headed by a select group of exceptionally powerful families (Bispham 2007; Scopacasa 2015). I will argue that some of the élites who had traditionally asserted their authority through funerary ritual, began to develop a tighter control over the old cemeteries, so as to try and preserve some of their exclusive status in a rapidly changing world, but in a way that was not particularly up to speed with the times. Essentially, these élites emphasized traditional ideas about social status and boundaries through funerary ritual, which had been prominent during the Iron Age, but were not necessarily as effective after the fifth century BC.

I will begin by presenting a brief overview of socio-political developments in Samnium *c.* 1000–400 BC, with a focus on transformations in the material evidence. This will be followed by an in-depth discussion of the long-term patterns in the funerary record during and after this period. Of importance to my argument is the theory that funerary practice is a means by which groups in society – usually the élites – express ideas about social structure (Morris 1987; 1991). In basic terms,

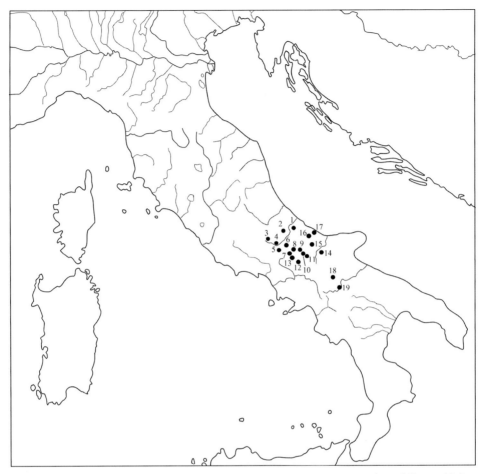

Fig. 10.1: Map of Italy with main sampled sites: 1. Gissi; 2. Atessa; 3. Opi–Val Fondillo; 4. Alfedena;
5. San Vincenzo al Volturno; 6. Capracotta; 7. Forli del Sannio; 8. Pietrabbondante; 9. Bagnoli del
Trigno; 10. Oratino; 11. Gildone; 12. Campochiaro; 13. Boiano; 14. Carlantino; 15. Larino;
16. Guglionesi; 17. Termoli; 18. Carife; 19. Castelbaronia (elaboration R. Scopacasa, base map
by C. Iaia).

by determining who is allowed to be buried how, where and with whom, people can
express notions about what the social relationships and boundaries between them
ought to be. This approach ultimately draws on the work of Edmund Leach (1954,
15–6), according to whom "the structure which is symbolised in ritual is the system of
socially approved 'proper' relations between individuals and groups." Although Leach
has been criticized for underestimating the importance of social change (e.g. Bloch
1977, 280), his approach to social structure is still useful for conceptualizing the
mainstream worldviews and ideologies in a society, which are usually constructed
by the politically and economically dominant groups.[2]

Setting the scene: socio-political developments in Samnium, *c.* 1000–400 BC

In keeping with the focus on alternative contexts that is advocated in this book (*cf.* especially the chapters by Perego, Zanoni, and the finale by Perego and Scopacasa), this chapter explores issues of burial and social change in a region of Italy for which there is very little written evidence, and which offers an alternative social and political model to that of the Greco-Roman classical polis. We hear about the communities of Samnium in classical accounts that describe their fierce resistance to the Roman expansion in the fourth and early third centuries BC, and their later role as key allies in Rome's rise as a world power (e.g. Livy 8.29.1–7; Dion. Hal. *Ant.Rom.* 15.3.7–9; Strabo 5.4.2; Plin. *HN* 3.105–7). These texts represent the outside view of Greek and Roman authors. For an inside view of ancient Samnium we depend on the archaeological record.

Graves still account for most of the available archaeological evidence. In general terms, the funerary record indicates that during the Iron Age (*c.* 1000–400 BC) local élites were closely connected with their counterparts in neighbouring regions (mainly Campania, Picenum and Umbria) in terms of cultural practices (Scopacasa 2015; for burial rites in approximately the same area *cf.* also Faustoferri this volume). Practically all of the burials are individual inhumations with the body laid in supine position. The occurrence of exceptionally wealthy graves from the seventh century BC onwards indicates that aristocratic families were increasingly differentiating themselves from the rest of the population (Barker and Suano 1995). Against a majority of simple trench graves, there is a smaller number of more elaborate cist graves (*tombe a cassone*) lined and covered with finely-cut limestone slabs, and in more select cases with travertine (Morelli 2000; Tagliamonte 1996, 88–9 includes figures). Whilst most of the graves include only a few pottery, iron and bronze objects, the more richly furnished ones contain prestige items such as bronze drinking vessels, fine-ware pottery, and a variety of bronze, amber, gold and silver jewellery (Tagliamonte 1996; Sarno 2000). Graves with weapons and armour emphasized the power of élite adult males by depicting them as warriors (*cf.* Faustoferri this volume). A good example is Alfedena Tomb D^{IV} 310, which includes a bronze breastplate and a short iron sword (Mariani 1901). Many of the cemeteries were divided into what appear to be family enclosures, which suggest a deliberate emphasis on familial ties. This type of layout is particularly clear in the upper Sangro Valley at Alfedena and Val Fondillo. The graves were grouped into large circular clusters, some of which may have been originally enclosed by stone circles or ditches (Alfedena: Mariani 1901; Parise Badoni and Ruggieri Giove 1981; Val Fondillo: Morelli 2000; Tagliamonte 1996, 88–9 includes figures). Each enclosure seems to include balanced proportions of men, women and children, and some may have been family plots (*cf.* Bondioli *et al.* 1986 on human remains at Alfedena).

From the end of the fifth century BC, these Iron Age communities began to change. Firstly, an increase in the number of rural settlements points to demographic growth, infilling of the countryside and rising levels of prosperity (Lloyd 1995; Lloyd *et al.* 1997). Some major towns, such as Larino, Monte Vairano and Benevento, underwent a process of nucleation and became exceptionally large by regional standards (*c.* 50 ha). For the people living in these towns, social interactions will have been mediated by more complex institutions. Epigraphic evidence, which begins to appear from the early third century BC, reveals that the communities that emerged from these developments were referred to by the Oscan word **touto.** Although there is still much about the **touto** that remains to be discovered, we know that it was administered by yearly-elected magistrates (Oscan **meddiss**), the head of which was the **meddiss tuvtiks** or 'magistrate of the **touto**' (La Regina 1981). It used to be thought that the Samnite **touto** was a territorial state that was coextensive with the entire Samnite ethnic group as it is described in classical sources (La Regina 1981; 1984; Musti 1984; Salmon 1967). However, Cesare Letta (1994) has convincingly argued that the term **touto** refers to smaller-scale polities which were probably coextensive with the larger nucleated settlements. These polities will have been capable of acting together as an ethnic league in key historical junctures, such as when dealing with Rome in the wars of the late fourth and early third centuries BC.[3] The recurrence of certain family names in the epigraphic record suggests that access to the **touto**'s magistracies was controlled by a select pool of élite families (La Regina 1981; 1984; *cf.* below for further discussion).

These leading families were apparently responsible for the monumentalization of sanctuary sites throughout Samnium between the fourth and second centuries BC (La Regina 1976; Scopacasa 2015; Stek 2009). Unlike the cemeteries, which would have been frequented mainly by the families of the buried individuals, these new sanctuaries were places where people from various different villages, towns and districts could meet. It is not surprising that some of the new sanctuaries became associated with new and broader ideas of community, which were grounded in ethnic membership. The large sanctuary of Pietrabbondante is the best example, since the site was probably named "the sanctuary of the Samnites (**safinim**)" at some point in the second century BC (*Imagines* Pentri/TERVENTVM 8 = *Ve* 149; *cf.* also La Regina 1981; Stek 2009, 65; Tagliamonte 1996, 156–202).[4] It is very likely that the ruling élites who embellished these sanctuaries were also responsible for the monumental building programmes that were carried out in major towns (Bispham 2007; Lloyd 1995). Monte Vairano (De Benedittis 1991), Larino (Di Niro 1980a; 1991b) and Benevento (Torelli 2002) all received paved streets, cisterns, fortifications, stone housing, intramural sanctuaries and manufacturing quarters (*cf.* Bradley 2000 for parallel developments in Umbria; on Lucania *cf.* Isayev 2007). These ambitious building programmes reflect the formation of a centralized authority, which will have been necessary for managing the large amount of manpower and resources involved in these undertakings.

It would almost seem as if the burgeoning towns and sanctuaries replaced the old cemeteries as the new focal points of community life and élite display (Bispham 2007; La Regina 1984). However, although activity at the cemeteries does decrease in the fourth and third centuries BC, they continued to function. In the remainder of this chapter I will attempt to explain this phenomenon by arguing that certain segments of the élites, who had expressed their power through funerary ritual in the Iron Age (but who did not necessarily make it to the top of the new political system), sought to assert their prominence by restricting access to formal burial.

Data and methods

The main evidence base in this study consists of 24 funerary sites, which together include nearly 2000 graves spanning the sixth–third centuries BC (Table 10.1). Practically all of these sites have been systematically excavated in the last four decades, although some were first explored in the late nineteenth century, such as Alfedena. As a result, most of the material has a secure archaeological context. The only sites in the sample that have been unsystematically excavated are Campone, Capracotta and Santo Venditti. Grave goods from these sites have recently been published and tentatively given an archaeological context (De Benedittis 2005; 2006).

Since chronology is central to my argument, a brief discussion of dating methods is needed. The currently accepted dating of graves in Samnium is grounded in diagnostic grave goods, mainly pottery vessels and bronze artefacts (e.g. Di Niro 1989; Macchiarola 1989; Parise Badoni *et al.* 1982; Suano 1986).[5] Grave goods are helpful for estimating a tomb's earliest possible date, but less so for determining the latest possible date. This is because artefacts can circulate for long periods of time before being deposited as grave goods. Heirlooms, for example, can make a grave seem a lot earlier than it actually is. In addition, some graves can be dated much more precisely than others, whereas certain tombs cannot be dated because they are devoid of surviving grave goods (*cf.* Table 10.2 below). For example, Gildone Tomb 19 can only be loosely situated in the fourth century BC, while Tombs 22 and 23 are likely to date from the last quarter of that century (Macchiarola 1989). In cases where grave goods are of little help, more information may be obtained in view of grave type. Graves that are lined and covered with stone slabs are likely to date from before the late fifth century BC, whereas graves lined with terracotta tiles are likely to date from the fourth and third centuries (Tagliamonte 1996). Stratigraphy, when known, is of course helpful. At Termoli–Porticone, a late third-century BC layer consisting of a road and manufacture debris suggests that the site was no longer used as a burial ground by that point (Di Niro 1981, 11).

A practical (if preliminary) solution is to work with the broadest time periods possible, so as to move away from precise but potentially misleading dates, and focus instead on long-term developments. Based on diagnostic grave goods as well as grave types, the tombs can be grouped into three phases: 1) *c.* 600–475 BC; 2) *c.* 500–425 BC; 3) *c.* 425–200 BC. As we shall see below, in some sites (Alfedena, Carife, Casalbore and S. Vincenzo al Volturno) there is currently no way to distinguish the first two phases securely, but this does not prevent the identification of patterns which are of interest here.

Table 10.1: Funerary record of Samnium: main published sites.

Sites	Total no. burials	individual supine inhumation	individual flexed inhumation	multiple inhumation	cremation (primary)	cremation (secondary)	trench graves	cist graves (stone)	cist graves (tile)	cremation pits
1 Alfedena	1259	100%					4%	93%	3%	
2 Atessa	4	100%					100%			
3 Bagnoli del Trigno	1	100%								
4 Campochiaro-Cerro Copponi	2	100%					50%		50%	
5 Boiano-Campone	37	n/a					n/a			
6 Capracotta	4	100%						100%		
7 Carife	97	95%				5%	n/a			5%
8 Carlantino-Santo Venditti	29	100%					80%	20%		
9 Castelbaronia	133	100%								
10 Forlì del Sannio	1	100%								
11 Gildone-Morgia della Chiusa	23	92%	4%	4%			90%		10%	
12 Gissi	6	100%					100%			
13 Guglionesi-Santa Margherita	7	100%					100%			
14 Larino-Carpineto	32	50%			20%	30%	40%		10%	50%
15 Larino-Monte Arcano	23	100%					100%			
16 Larino-Montorio nei Frentani	2					100%	100%			100%
17 Larino-Stazione	5	100%					100%			
18 Boiano- Noce di Massaro	4	100%					100%			
19 Opi-Val Fondillo	154	99%		1%			39%	61%		
20 Oratino-Pozzo Nuovo	1	100%					100%			
21 Pietrabbondante-Troccola	3	100%						100%		
22 San Vincenzo al Volturno	13	100%					100%			
23 Termoli- Difesa Grande	43	100%					100%			
24 Termoli-Porticone	49 (141 overall)	n/a					n/a			

Table 10.2: Rate of burial in sampled cemeteries, 6th–3rd centuries BC.

Funerary sites	No. burials				Rate of decrease after fifth century
	c. 600–475 BC	c. 500–425 BC	c. 425–200 BC	undated	
Alfedena	1168		55	26	97%
Atessa	0	0	4	0	–
Bagnoli del Trigno	0	0	1	0	–
Campochiaro-Cerro Copponi	0	0	2	0	–
Campone	18	3	6	10	71%
Capracotta	4	0	0	0	100%
Carife	75		22	0	70%
Carlantino-Santo Venditti	27	2	0	5	84%
Casalbore	130		3	0	97.50%
Forli del Sannio	0	0	1	0	–
Gildone-Morgia della Chiusa	0	2	21	0	–
Gissi	0	2	4	0	–
Guglionesi-Santa Margherita	5	0	4	0	20%
Larino-Carpineto	0	4	10	18	–
Larino-Monte Arcano	17	0	0	11	100%
Larino-Montorio nei Frentani	0	0	2	0	–
Larino-Stazione	4	0	1	0	80%
Noce di Massaro	6	0	0	1	100%
Opi-Val Fondillo	154	0	0	0	100%
Oratino-Pozzo Nuovo	0	0	1	0	–
Pietrabbondante-Troccola	0	1	2	0	–
San Vincenzo al Volturno	13		0	0	100%
Termoli-Porticone	40	1	8	0	80.5%
Termoli-Difesa Grande	0	9	17	17	–
Total	1685		166	88	91%

Patterns in cemetery use

Table 10.2 (below) confirms that there is a significant decrease in the number of burials per cemetery after the fifth century BC. With the sole exception of Guglionesi, the decrease rate is always over 70%. Admittedly, many of the burial sites in question are rather small to begin with (e.g. Carlantino, Campone and Larino–Monte Arcano), which suggests that they were already used by restricted groups of people before the fifth century BC.

What is particularly significant, however, is the case of cemeteries that are considerably large during the sixth and most of the fifth centuries, and where the decrease in the number of graves after the fifth century BC is more noticeable. The clearest cases are Alfedena, which is one of the largest funerary sites in the whole of Iron Age Italy (Mariani 1901; Parise Badoni and Ruggieri Giove 1981), and Casalbore (Johannowsky 1991). A third cemetery, Termoli–Porticone (Di Niro 1981; 1991c), may be included here. Even though the number of published graves is only 49, of which 41 date from the sixth–fifth centuries (Di Niro 1981), the cemetery includes a total of over a hundred graves, most of which probably date from the sixth century BC (A. Di Niro pers. comm.). A similar decline in activity has been detected at Barrea, close to Alfedena (Faustoferri 2003), although this site remains to be fully published and cannot be included in the present analysis. The fact that all of these Iron Age cemeteries continued to be used after the fifth century BC, but on a much smaller scale, sets them apart from cases such as Opi–Val Fondillo, which apparently ceased to function as a burial site altogether by the mid-fifth century BC (Morelli 2000).

Large cemeteries south of Samnium suggest a fairly similar picture of decreasing activity after the fifth century BC. Montesarchio, Sant'Agata dei Goti and Telesia are all major funerary sites where activity peaks in the seventh and sixth centuries BC, with Montesarchio housing a remarkable 3000 graves. All three sites gradually cease to receive new burials starting in the fifth century BC, and by the mid-third century BC they seem to have been all but abandoned (Sarno 2000). A similar pattern is also discernible in the central Apennines, especially in the area around the Fucine Lake (D'Ercole and Martellone 2004). After the fifth century BC, graves seem to become less frequent at Piani Pallentini, Casal Civitella, and the various cemeteries on the Borgorose plain – with the sole exception of Corvaro di Borgorose, an extremely large funerary mound where tombs from the fourth and third centuries are more numerous than earlier ones (Alvino 1996).

Another important trend (Table 10.2) is that none of the funerary sites which originate after the fifth century BC seem to develop into anything resembling the large cemeteries of the Iron Age. Gildone and Termoli–Difesa Grande, which are the largest post-fifth century BC cemeteries known, include around two dozen graves each, and are therefore on a par with the smaller Iron Age cemeteries.

It is difficult to determine if the decreasing number of graves correlates with a narrowing of the gender and age groups that were given formal burial. This is because only a small number of the graves have had their human remains subject to osteological analysis, to determine biological sex and age. In the few cemeteries where such data is available, there seems to be an overall balance among gender and age groups, both before and after the fifth century BC (Table 10.3). This would suggest that the decrease in the number of people who were given formal burial was not primarily grounded in gender and age criteria, although this must remain a tentative observation.

More significant patterns can be identified in regard to changes in grave furnishing. To be sure, determining whether a grave is 'rich' or 'poor' is a culturally specific judgment, and the identification of richly furnished graves should always be relative to the cultural context. Compared to the so-called 'princely tombs' of Etruria and Campania (*cf.* Cuozzo and Morris this volume, with bibliography) the graves in Samnium seem rather unimpressive as a whole. However, a more contextual approach reveals significant differences in furnishing and structure. Some graves stand out for containing large quantities of goods, which are not always prestige items. Others include prestige items, though not necessarily in large numbers. In view of these variations, 'richly furnished' graves can be singled out in the present sample on the basis of the following criteria: presence of ten or more grave goods (in view of an average of six per tomb: Tagliamonte 1996), and/or the presence of grave goods made of rare and probably valuable materials such as alabaster, ivory, amber, precious metals such as gold and silver, imported fine-ware pottery such as Campanian *bucchero* and/or artefacts which display sophisticated craftsmanship, such as elaborately-decorated bronze belts and pieces of armour.[6]

When we apply these criteria to the evidence base, we see that until the late fifth century BC 'richly furnished' graves tend to account for up to 15–20% of the graves in each site, and rarely exceed 40% (Table 10.4). At Alfedena, although the incidence of 'richly furnished' graves is low, most graves from before *c.* 425 BC are lined and covered with limestone slabs (*cf.* Table 10.1), which can be seen as a special investment of resources and energy. Overall, it seems fair to say that down to about 425–400 BC,

Table 10.3: *Gender and age groups (S. Vincenzo al Volturno: Bowden et al. 2006; Alfedena-Campo Consolino: Parise Badoni and Ruggieri Giove 1981; Bondioli et al. 1986; Troccola: Suano 1980; Gildone: Di Niro and Petrone 1993).*

Sites	Period BC	Sub-adults	Young/prime adults (15–40 yrs)			Mature adults (40+ yrs)			Adults (unspec.)		
			M	F	?	M	F	?	M	F	?
S.V. al Volturno	6th–late 5th cent.	4	2	5	0	0	1	0	1	0	0
Alfedena (C. Consolino only)	5th–3rd cent.	12	25	12	2	30	19	0	10	13	0
Troccola	5th–3rd cent.	1	2	0	0	0	0	0	0	0	0
Morgia della Chiusa	late 5th–3rd cent.	3	4	3	0	2	1	3	4	0	1
Total		17	33	20	2	32	21	3	15	13	1

Table 10.4: Incidence of richly-furnished burials, 6th–3rd centuries BC.

Funerary sites	c. 600–425 BC		c. 425–200 BC	
	Total burials	Richly furnished	Total burials	Richly furnished
Alfedena	1168	123 (14%)	55	5 (9%)
Atessa	0	0	4	1 (25%)
Bagnoli del Trigno	0	0	1	0
Campochiaro-Cerro Copponi	0	0	2	1 (50%)
Campone	21	0	6	1 (17%)
Capracotta	4	0	0	0
Carife	75	n/a	22	n/a
Carlantino-Santo Venditti	29	4 (15%)	2	2 (100%)
Casalbore	130	n/a	3	n/a
Forli del Sannio	0	0	1	0
Gildone-Morgia della Chiusa	2	0	21	0
Gissi	2	0	4	0
Guglionesi-Santa Margherita	5	2 (40%)	4	1 (25%)
Larino-Carpineto	4	2 (50%)	10	8 (80%)
Larino-Monte Arcano	17	7 (41%)	0	0
Larino-Montorio nei Frentani	0	0	2	0
Larino-Stazione	4	0	1	0
Noce di Massaro	6	0	0	0
Oratino-Pozzo Nuovo	0	0	1	0
Opi-Val Fondillo	154	33 (21%)	0	0
Pietrabbondante-Troccola	1	1 (100%)	2	2 (100%)
San Vincenzo al Volturno	13	2 (15%)	0	0
Termoli-Difesa Grande	9	1 (11%)	17	3 (18%)
Termoli-Porticone	41	5 (10%)	8	3 (38%)
Total	1685	180 (11%)	166	27 (16%)

people who could not afford to be buried with costly grave furnishings, or who chose not to do so, are well represented in the funerary record. After the fifth century BC, however, the proportion of 'richly furnished' graves increases, often exceeding the Iron Age average of 15–20% per site. In most cases, the very small number of graves involved (up to four) makes statistical analysis difficult. But in the cemetery at Larino–Carpineto, not only are eight of the ten tombs richly furnished, but also the grave goods in question suggest that the burying community was experimenting with a new kind of funerary ostentation. The cemetery at Carpineto originated in the fifth century BC, just 2 km east of the burgeoning town of Larino (Fardella 2003). Most of the datable graves at Carpineto (ten out of 14) post-date the fifth century BC, and many of these are secondary cremations, with cremated remains deposited in large bronze urns. The adoption of cremation as the main rite suggests an increased level of energy expenditure in burial, since it could be very expensive to cremate a corpse in antiquity (Morris 1987, 153–4). Both the cremation and the inhumation tombs at Carpineto contain grave goods that stand out either for their economic value and workmanship, or for their rarity in Samnium, such as gilt wreaths (Tombs 16, 19), bronze and iron strigils (Tomb 21), alabaster perfume bottles (Tomb 23), Gnathian pottery in the form of small ointment containers (Tomb 23) and Apulian red-figure craters (Tomb 12). These items call to mind some of the more lavish cremation tombs of south Italy, more specifically the fourth- and third-century BC cremation graves in Lucania.[7] In particular, the gilt terracotta wreath in Carpineto Tomb 19 can be seen as a smaller version of the one from Armento (De La Geniere 1989).

Other cemeteries that develop after the fifth century BC also include graves that stand out for their lavishness, especially as regards the deposition of precious metal jewellery. At the burial site of Difesa Grande near Termoli, one of the inhumation graves (Tomb 5) includes a silver fibula, a silver earring, an amber necklace and one large amber bead. The presence of two coins suggests a possible engagement with Hellenistic notions of the afterlife (Charon's obols). Hellenistic connections are also suggested by the fact that one of the coins may come from Magna Graecia. This silver coin shows a helmeted female head on the obverse, and on the reverse a dolphin, branch and scallop shell. The iconography recalls an issue of Syracusan *hemilitrae* from 405 BC, and a Tarentine issue of silver hemiobols, possibly from the fifth century BC, which shows the scallop shell and dolphin images (Head 1911, 67).

In the older cemeteries that continued to be used, the later graves and their assemblages were not much different from earlier ones, with a few exceptions. This is the case of Alfedena Tomb E65, which probably belonged to a sub-adult judging from its length (0.85 m; *cf.* Mariani 1901). This grave contained a large silver ring and a silver bracelet. Tomb E30, which is located in the same sector of the cemetery, included a large necklace of amber beads. At the Campo Consolino sector of Alfedena, there are at least three graves from after the fifth century BC (Tombs 1, 3 and 117; *cf.* Parise Badoni and Ruggieri Giove 1981). They all belong to adult males, one of whom was aged 17–25 years according to the osteological data that have been published. All three individuals were buried with elaborate bronze belts featuring cicada-shaped clasps, and one (Tomb 117) also wore a bronze chain mail. At Termoli–Porticone, the graves from the late fifth–third centuries BC tend to include the traditional set of pottery drinking vessels (usually a large container accompanied by a smaller vessel for serving or drinking) and bronze and iron jewellery such as fibulae and rings (Di Niro 1981). However, one grave (Tomb 23) stands out for including a set of large amber beads that are finely carved into women's heads (Di Niro 1980).

Lastly, there is the issue of the placement of the later graves in the funerary landscape. By the late fifth century BC, many of the cemeteries that had been used in previous centuries were still conspicuous in the landscape, owing to the practice of constructing limestone *tumuli* over individual graves, many of which were recovered intact upon excavation (Di Niro 1981; Parise Badoni and Ruggieri Giove 1981; Parise Badoni *et al.* 1982). In the older cemeteries that carried on being used, such *tumuli* will have been clearly visible, and in some cases the placement of the later graves suggests that a deliberate topographic connection with earlier funerary monuments was being attempted. In the present evidence sample, this phenomenon can be observed at Alfedena–Campo Consolino and Termoli–Porticone (*cf.*, respectively, Parise Badoni and Ruggieri Giove 1981 and Di Niro 1981, both of which include cemetery plans that show the position of later graves in relation to earlier ones).

Restricted access to formal burial?

The foregoing survey suggests that after the fifth century BC, many of the existing cemeteries in Samnium were used by smaller groups of people; none of the cemeteries that developed after the fifth century BC ever came close to their Iron Age predecessors in terms of size. In some noteworthy cases, cemetery users in the fourth and third centuries BC seem to have invested more in funerary ostentation than before, and this is particularly clear as regards Larino–Carpineto.

We should be careful in searching for a general explanation for these developments. Conditions will have varied to some extent from site to site, and each case is bound to have been influenced by local factors, such as the reorganization of communication routes, changes in settlement location and even lack of space for additional graves. Nevertheless, the data do seem to suggest a consistent trend, which makes it plausible that there were broader-ranging issues at work. Despite the decrease in grave numbers, the fact that people continued to invest energy and resources in burial suggests that these funerary sites were not simply abandoned. We are probably dealing with the deliberate actions of social agents who were experimenting with different solutions to social and political change. It is now time to consider some of the possible explanations for the decline in the number of burials, and clarify why changing rules of access to formal burial are likely to account for the pattern in question, at least to an extent.

One possibility is that the Roman expansion in the fourth and third centuries BC had a bearing on the decline in activity in certain cemeteries. Roman land confiscations and colonization may have disrupted traditional ways of life, and the changes in the funerary sphere might reflect this. In considering this hypothesis, it is important to remember that Roman intervention was more intensely felt in some parts of Samnium than in others. For example, in the upper Sangro Valley where Alfedena is located, a large but unquantifiable amount of land was confiscated after the Samnites were defeated in 290 BC (Roselaar 2010, 48–9). Yet, upon closer inspection, it is unclear whether this occurrence had a significant bearing on developments at Alfedena. To begin with, the decline in burial activity begins in the late fifth century BC, long before the start of Roman encroachment on Samnium. In addition, there is no evidence that the territory of Alfedena was confiscated. Historical accounts mention towns in the general vicinity that were conquered in the late fourth century BC, such as Venafrum, Atina and Allifae (Festus p. 262 L; Livy 9.38.1), but the closest of these to Alfedena was over 20 km away. If some form of Roman intervention did take place in the area, we might expect some degree of disruption to local daily life, such as the influx of uprooted peasants from confiscated lands who needed to be reintegrated into local society. However, Rome usually avoided interfering in the political organization of Italian communities, since it was through the cooperation of local élites that Rome tapped into local resources and manpower (Terrenato 2007). It seems more helpful to see the developments at Alfedena as part of broader social changes that affected other parts of Samnium as well.

Another possibility is that the overall decrease in burials reflects changes in settlement pattern. As noted above, survey evidence from different corners of Samnium reveals an increase in the number of small rural sites starting in the late fifth century BC. With a growing number of people living scattered throughout the countryside, one would expect that most individuals were buried next to their home villages, which would explain the decline in activity at the larger Iron Age cemeteries (*cf.* Di Niro 1991c on Termoli–Porticone). A good example of a small village cemetery is Gildone, which developed in the midst of small hamlets and farmhouses (Di Niro 1991a). But although small rural settlements did multiply in the fourth–third centuries, this happened alongside the growth of major nucleated centres, many of which were located next to the cemeteries where burial activity declines. At Alfedena, for example, a large fortified settlement developed on one of the mountains overlooking the cemetery (La Regina 1976). In other words, although there were still many people living next to Alfedena, they were no longer being buried there. Another difficulty with the 'settlement pattern' hypothesis is that small rural sites were already the majority in the Iron Age, even though their absolute numbers grew later on. Village burial grounds, of the kind we see at Gildone, already existed then – Larino–Monte Arcano and Campone are likely candidates – and cannot be seen as a later phenomenon. Therefore, the hypothesis of changing settlement patterns does not quite explain the overall decrease in the number of burials in Samnite funerary sites.

Even if allowances are made for our biased and incomplete evidence base, we must reckon with the possibility that after the fifth century BC most people in Samnium were given funerary rites that did not leave durable material traces – such as scattering cremated remains in rivers or lakes. It is certainly plausible that the socio-political developments of the fourth and third centuries BC had an impact on traditional attitudes to death and burial. And yet, in the midst of these changes, a small number of people kept on being buried in ways that were materially durable, in keeping with long-standing practices of the Iron Age. It seems plausible that some kind of distinction was being asserted between the few who continued to receive such funerary treatment, and the majority of people whose burials are invisible to us.

One hypothesis that accounts for this scenario is that there was a growing restriction of access to formal and materially durable types of burial. It seems possible that social status was among the criteria behind such a restriction. As noted in the previous section, before the late fifth century BC practically all of the known cemeteries include a majority of graves that are poorly or averagely furnished, in comparison with a smaller number of tombs that are more richly outfitted and/or elaborately built. Such a pattern could suggest that before the fifth century BC, a range of status groups were represented in the cemeteries, and not just those members of society who could afford lavish graves. As graves start to become fewer in number, it would seem that formal and materially durable burial in cemeteries became restricted to higher-status groups, especially since many of the later graves tend to display a level of ostentation that is more pronounced than before.

Admittedly, the greater or lesser wealth of a grave does not necessarily mean that the individual buried in it was rich or poor. A person's status in life may not be the same in death, especially when death is seen as a levelling of the differences among the living. In addition, graves that seem poor to us may have had different cultural meanings. For example, high-status people may have deliberately chosen to be buried without lavish furnishings for cultural, religious, or personal reasons, as is attested in numerous societies and time periods (Morris 1992, 103–27; Parker Pearson 1999, 72; Ucko 1969). That said, it is plausible that differences in wealth and structural sophistication of graves do correspond, to some extent at least, to differences in socio-economic status among the dead and their families (Wason 1994, 68).

It is therefore possible that there was a general narrowing of the groups of people in Samnite society who received formal burial in cemeteries. In basic terms, until about 425 BC there were large and thriving cemeteries where considerable numbers of people had been buried together for several centuries, in such a way as to generate the overall image of cohesive groups where the wealthy and the not-so-wealthy lay side by side. After the fifth century BC, this scenario changed in two important ways. On the one hand, only a very select few carried on using the older cemeteries. At Termoli and Alfedena, and to a lesser degree at Casalbore, these fewer cemetery users may well have claimed links between themselves and the ancient graves that were still visible in these cemeteries. Simultaneously, there appeared new and smaller burial sites where funerary ostentation reached unprecedented levels, as is best illustrated by the lavish cremation tombs at Larino–Carpineto.

Taken together, these developments seem to suggest that cemetery users were seeking to redefine social boundaries, by controlling more rigorously the people who were allowed to be buried in the cemeteries.

Formal burial and notions of exclusivity

The social and political significance of access to formal burial has been widely discussed with regard to the ancient world (for similar issues *cf.* Perego 2012, and

Cuozzo, Iaia, and Zanoni this volume; on formal infant and child burial *cf.* Di Lorenzo *et al.* this volume, all with additional bibliography). Ian Morris (1987; 1991) saw a connection between (what he identified as) a widening of access to formal burial, and the rise of the *polis* in Archaic Attica. Between the eighth and sixth centuries BC, a broader sector of the Athenian population appears to have gained access to formal burial, which had previously been a privilege reserved for the aristocracy.[8]

The link between formal burial and political participation may work in regard to Classical Athens, but in the absence of historical evidence we cannot assume that a similar connection existed in Samnium or elsewhere in central Italy. Rather than seeing formal burial as a badge of political enfranchisement, we should instead consider the different ways in which access to formal burial could have been used to negotiate community membership on a number of levels, other than that of full political participation. As noted earlier in this chapter, mortuary practice offers a means for people to construct very different ideas of community, ranging from cases where stratification is emphasized (*cf.* for example Perego 2014 and Perego this volume, on Venetic cemeteries as venues for the expression and enactment of social hierarchy), to instances where the burying group embraces 'ideologies of equality', by using funerary ritual to downplay socio-economic differences between the dead (*cf.* Morris 1992, 141–2 and Whitley 2001, 366 on Classical Athens; Dietler 1995, 70–1 on fifth-century BC southern France; Bennet 1994 discusses 'ideologies of equality' in contemporary Greece).

To understand the probable restriction of access to formal burial in Samnium, it is helpful to view this process in light of the other major changes that happen after the fifth century BC. Although we still do not know exactly what caused these changes, they probably affected the relationship between élites and the community at large, and would have transformed old ideas about community membership. References to the 'Samnites' as an ethnic group in the historical record, together with epigraphic evidence for supra-local groupings such as the state (**touto**) and the *ethnos* (**safinim**), all seem to suggest that the 'community' was now being defined in broader terms that went beyond the level of kinship, or one's relationship with local well-to-do families. The sanctuary of Pietrabbondante, for example, probably fostered belonging on a regional, ethnic level (La Regina 1976; Scopacasa 2014; 2015; Stek 2009).[9]

Some of the Samnite élites were very successful in adapting to this new socio-political environment. As we saw earlier, one noticeable change in élite behaviour after the fifth century BC is the fact that more wealth began to be invested in public rather than private contexts. Some of the élites began to underscore their power and prestige by embellishing sanctuaries and possibly also major towns. These 'benefactors' are commemorated in inscriptions at Pietrabbondante and other major cult sites. This is the case of the leading magistrates of the **touto** and their families, such as the *Staii* (*Imagines* Pentri/TERVENTVM 4-5 = *Ve* 151–2), the *Statii* (*Imagines* Pentri/TERVENTVM 12 = *Ve* 154) and the *Decitii* (*Imagines* Pentri/BOVIANVM 7 = *ST* tSa 22, Carricini/AVFIDENA 2 = *Ve* 142, Pentri/SAEPINVM 4 = *ST* Sa 59; Pentri/ TERVENTVM 20 (= *ST* Sa 24), 36 (= *ST* Sa 2)). These élites were no longer legitimizing themselves in the old Iron Age manner (i.e. by setting up ostentatious graves), but much more competitively by coming across as benefactors who directed their largesse to the wider community, in ways that were in tune with the euergetic trends of the Hellenistic world (Bispham 2007).

It is difficult to account for this change in élite behaviour without seeing it as a response to growing pressure from the non-élite sectors of society, at least to an extent. For the non-élites to be able to exercise such pressure, they will have needed to be more confident and self-reliant than before. Demographic growth, infilling of the countryside and the development of large nucleated settlements probably contributed to the formation of new types of social interactions, which will have called into question earlier forms of élite legitimacy. It is not unreasonable to infer that the world of local Iron Age clans and their retainers gradually gave way to a more complex and dynamic scenario of prospering small landowners and urban workers. These emerging social segments would have engaged in new dynamics of negotiation and compromise with the ruling élites, consequently pushing these élites to legitimize themselves in new ways.

The élites that managed to adapt to this new socio-political environment were the families who held positions of power in the **touto**, and who commemorated themselves as public benefactors in major sanctuaries. They were probably helped by their accurate perception of the times, and their quickness to respond to new challenges resulting from the new social dynamics. These people, however, seem to have been very few in number. As noted above, the same family names tend to recur in inscriptions that commemorate **touto** magistrates. This suggests a certain monopoly of political power, perhaps with each of the main families ruling over a given state or **touto**. Not all of the old Iron Age clans would have made it to the top of this new political system, and many probably faltered. It is therefore plausible that many of the people responsible for restricting access to formal burial in the cemeteries, particularly the older ones, were members of local and possibly 'minor' élites, attempting to assert some form of exclusivity in an arena which they still managed to control, but which, in the grand scheme of things, was no longer very relevant (on the issue of 'sub-élite' self-legitimization in ancient Italy *cf.* Iaia this volume; on the response of élite groups to accelerated social change *cf.* also Perego this volume).

The élites who carried on using the old cemeteries did so in a manner that suggests an effort to claim an exclusive connection with earlier generations of cemetery users. As noted above, in the seventh and sixth centuries BC limestone *tumuli* had been built to mark the graves, as can be seen at Alfedena and Termoli. The fewer people who carried on using these sites after the fifth century BC were probably aware of the antiquity of the earlier *tumuli*. The placement of later graves in proximity to the earlier *tumuli* suggests an attempt – almost an anxiety – to assert links with the 'ancient dead' through the manipulation of funerary space (for cemetery plans *cf.* Di Niro 1981; Parise Badoni and Ruggieri Giove 1981). This scenario recalls the reuse of Bronze Age Mycenaean tombs in Archaic Greece, which has been explained as an attempt by the Archaic élites to boost their authority by forging kinship links with the ancient dead, some of whom may have been perceived as belonging to the heroic past (Antonaccio 1994; Morris 1988; Whitley 1988). The Archaic Greek analogy is helpful here, as it suggests that the people who continued to use old cemeteries such as Alfedena and Termoli were attempting to create new symbols of exclusivity in a time of rapid social change. The people who carried on using Alfedena and Termoli may have tried to forge special links with the dead from previous generations, possibly by appealing to some form of perceived ancestral authority or tradition for which the earlier *tumuli* may have stood.

Conclusion

The patterns in the funerary record of Samnium suggest important changes in the way that mortuary ritual was used to construct ideas about exclusive status and élite legitimacy in a time of accelerated socio-political transformation in central Italy. Taken together, the changes in the archaeological record indicate that people were experimenting with different ways to claim exclusive status in a new socio-political order. To some, age-old cemeteries would have seemed an attractive venue for constructing and expressing ideas of exclusivity, especially since cemeteries had been key places of élite self-promotion during the Iron Age. However, this type of strategy probably became increasingly obsolete in view of the new and more competitive ways in which the more successful élites were legitimizing their status through public benefaction, which reached a broader audience and underscored a greater amount of power and wealth. We may therefore view the growing restriction of access to formal burial as a strategy through which some members of the Samnite élites – many of whom were possibly less resourceful than the 'top' people we see commemorated in the public sanctuaries – attempted to retain something of their prominence in a world that was changing rapidly. In so doing, they not only reasserted earlier forms of funerary ostentation from the Iron Age, but also transformed these long-standing practices by making them more exclusive than before. It is likely that some of these people tried to claim connections with earlier generations of cemetery users, thereby minimizing – or maybe even denying – the sense of social change. Yet if this was the case, the ideology of restricted access to formal burial was probably not entirely relevant for the new political communities that were developing. This might explain why most of the funerary sites in our sample do not appear to survive long after 200 BC. By that point, the new political order of the **touto** will have been firmly in place, and there will have been few people (if anyone) among the Samnite aristocracies who felt the need to appeal to the way things used to be.

Acknowledgements

This chapter has its origins in my PhD thesis (Exeter 2010). I was able to develop the key ideas during a research fellowship at the British School at Rome (2010–2011). The 'Burial and Social Change' workshop at the BSR was an ideal venue for exchanging ideas with colleagues. I thank my PhD supervisors at Exeter (Dr Elena Isayev and Dr Martin Pitts), the BSR staff, the two anonymous reviewers for their very helpful suggestions, and Dr Elisa Perego, who made key contributions to the argument in this chapter.

Notes

1. I am indebted to Dr Elisa Perego, who read and commented on numerous versions of this paper; any remaining errors or omissions are entirely my own. As regards the concept of state formation, I maintain the anthropological view of this process as a move towards greater complexity in the social organization of communities, in terms of size, the degree of social differentiation and stratification, and the extent to which political authority is centralized (Gledhill 1988, 2–3). There is also a territorial dimension, such as the development of a more defined sense of territorial boundaries (Claessen and Skalnik 1978, 639). Evolutionary models, which see a progression from tribe to chiefdom to state, have now been challenged. Non-state societies are not necessarily the precursors of state societies, but represent alternative forms of political organization (Gledhill 1988, 10–5). The literature on ancient states is vast, and there is no single definition of the state that suits all schools of thought; for overviews *cf.* Bradley 2000, and more recently Terrenato and Haggis 2011.

2. Whilst structures constrain the behaviour and agency of individuals, they are also transformed in the process by which individuals actively engage with them (Giddens 1984) (on this issue *cf.* also Perego, and Perego and Scopacasa this volume, with additional bibliography).

3. Letta based his argument on a set of third- and second-century BC inscriptions that record eponymous chief magistrates of the **touto (meddiss tuvtiks)** at the Samnite settlement of Boiano. Letta (1994, 387) argues that the eponymous function of these magistrates would only have made sense in a local context, since the tiles and pottery that display the inscriptions were locally produced and consumed.

4. From a linguistic point of view, the Oscan word **safinim** is akin to the Latin ethnic *Samnites* (La Regina 1970/1971; 1980; 1981; 1984; 1989; Salmon 1967, 77–95; Tagliamonte 1996). By the time the ethnic **safinim** emerged at Pietrabbondante, it had already been in use for at least three centuries. Its original geographical scope was probably very wide, encompassing not only Samnium but much of central Italy including the territory of the Sabines (Dench 1995, 206). Yet by the second century BC the term **safinim** is believed to have been largely restricted to Samnium (Dench 1995, 210).

5. Among the main sequences are De Juliis' (1977) sequence of Daunian ware (used in Di Niro 1981); Albore Livadie's (1979) sequence of Campanian *bucchero* (used in De Benedittis 2006; Di Niro 1981); and Sparkes and Talcott (1970) and Morel (1981) for Campanian and Attic black gloss (used in Macchiarola 1989). Gnathian ware, which is diagnostic of a late fourth–third century BC date, is not hugely common in Samnium (Fardella 2003; Lloyd 1995). As regards metal artefacts, certain types of fibulae can be chronologically diagnostic (Di Niro 1981, 53–5), as well as the so-called 'Samnite' bronze belts (Suano 1986, 25–8).

6. This is only a summary categorization of the data that does not do justice to the nuances and complexities of the material. For example, it would be important to distinguish between graves containing large quantities of goods that are not prestige items (such as common and coarse pottery), from graves that include smaller quantities of goods which are all prestige items. It is likely that such differences in grave-good assemblage point to different strategies of funerary display and different funerary ideologies, which were perhaps employed by competing sectors of the élite. However, such an investigation would go beyond the scope of this chapter. For the present purposes, my approach to the data – if somewhat generalizing – is geared towards identifying those graves which stand out from the rest because of a greater level of investment in funerary display, which clearly took many forms.

7. Cuozzo (2007, 235; this volume) discusses some of the distinctive features of lavish cremation tombs in Campania, which include the use of bronze cinerary vessels and the presence of 'exotic' and unique grave goods.

8. Morris (1987, 9) uses the concept of 'formal burial' to refer to the disposal of the dead in especially reserved areas. In ancient Samnium, formal burial consisted mainly of individual supine inhumation in rectangular trench graves (Tagliamonte 1996). Alternative rites – such as collective and/or secondary inhumation burial in reused graves – are very rare before the fourth century BC. Until now very few cases of non-normative burial have been securely identified, such as the double inhumations at Termoli–Porticone Tombs 14 and 14b (Di Niro 1981) (on funerary deviancy in ancient Italy *cf.* also the introduction, Zanoni, and Perego this volume, with additional bibliography). After the fifth century BC cremations become more common but they closely follow a high-status fashion which is common in south Italy (Cuozzo 2007).

9. From a different perspective, however, there is a sense in which the emergence of state and ethnic identities may have favoured adult male individuals over other gender and age groups. The monumental epigraphy at Pietrabbondante and other Samnite sanctuaries mentions only adult males, a situation that is paralleled in other regions or sub-regions of Italy such as Cadore in northern Veneto. Here, at the cult site of Lagole, where all or almost all the several dozen inscriptions found carry male names, a socio-political organization that might have been akin to the **touto** emerged in the second half of the first millennium BC (namely the **teuta**: Fogolari and Gambacurta 2001; *cf.* however the epigraphic record from the sanctuary of Baratella at Este for the presence of female inscriptions in other Venetic cult sites: Marinetti 1992). This suggests that – at least in some Italian contexts – the rise of state-level polities may have led to new ideas of community membership which favoured adult men rather than women (E. Perego, pers. comm.).

Bibliography

Albore Livadie, C. (1979) Le bucchero nero en Campanie. Notes de tipologie et chronologie. *Latomus* 160, 91–110.

Alvino, G. (1996) Alcune riflessioni sulla cultura equicola nella piana di Corvaro. In *Identità e Civiltà dei Sabini. Atti del XVIII Convegno di Studi Etruschi ed Italici (Rieti-Magliano Sabina, 30 Maggio-3 Giugno 1993)*, 415–430. Firenze, L.S. Olschki.

Barker, G. and Suano, M. (1995) Iron Age chiefdoms 1000–500 BC. In G. Barker (ed.) *A Mediterranean Valley: Landscape Archaeology and Annales History in the Biferno Valley*, 159–180. Leicester, University of Leicester Press.

Bennett, D.O. (1994) Bury me in second class: Contested symbols in a Greek cemetery. *Anthropological Quarterly* 67(3), 122–134.

Bispham, E. (2007) The Samnites. In G.J. Bradley, E. Isayev and C. Riva (eds) *Ancient Italy. Regions without Boundaries*, 179–223. Exeter, Exeter University Press.

Bloch, M. (1977) The past and the present in the present. *Man* 12, 278–292.

Bondioli, L., Corruccini, R.S. and Macchiarelli, R. (1986) Familial segregation in the Iron Age community of Alfedena, Abruzzo, Italy, based on osteodental trait analysis. *American Journal of Physical Anthropology* 71(4), 393–400.

Bowden, W., Burgess, A., Castellani, A. and Moran, M. (2006) The Samnite cemetery and the origins of the Samnite vicus. In K. Bowes, K. Francis and W. Hodges (eds) *Between Text and Territory: Survey and Excavations in the Terra of San Vincenzo al Volturno*, 49–92. London, British School at Rome.

Bradley, G.J. (2000) *Ancient Umbria. State, Culture and Identity in Central Italy from the Iron Age to the Augustan Era*. Oxford, Oxford University Press.

Chiaromonte Treré, C. and d'Ercole, V. (2003) (eds) *La Necropoli di Campovalano. Tombe Orientalizzanti e Arcaiche. Volume 1* (BAR S1177, 2174). Oxford, Archaeopress.

Claessen, H.J.M. and Skalnik, P. (1978) (eds) *The Early State*. The Hague, Mouton.

Cuozzo, M. (2007) Ancient Campania: Cultural interaction, political borders and geographical boundaries. In G.J. Bradley, E. Isayev and C. Riva (eds) *Ancient Italy. Regions without Boundaries*, 224–267. Exeter, Exeter University Press.

D'Ercole, V. and Copersino, M.R. (2004) (eds) *La Necropoli di Fossa. L'Età Ellenistico-Romana*. Celano, Carsa.

D'Ercole, V. and Martellone, A. (2004) Gli Equi prima della conquista romana. In S. Lapenna (ed.) *Gli Equi. Tra Abruzzo e Lazio. Catalogo della Mostra (Oricola, Sala dei Convegni del Comune, 2004)*, 31–59. Sulmona, Synapsi Edizioni.

De Benedittis, G. (1991) L'abitato di Monte Vairano. In S. Capini and A. Di Niro (eds) *Samnium. Archeologia del Molise. Catalogo della Mostra*, 127–130. Roma, Quasar.

De Benedittis, G. (2005) (ed.) *Prima dei Sanniti. La Piana di Bojano dall'Età del Ferro alle Guerre Sannitiche attraverso i Materiali Archeologici*. Campobasso, Iresmo.

De Benedittis, G. (2006) *Carlantino. La Necropoli di Santo Venditti*. Campobasso, Iresmo.

De Juliis, E.M. (1977) *La Ceramica Geometrica della Daunia*. Firenze, Sansoni Editore Nuova.

De La Geniere, J. (1989) Épire et Basilicate. À propos de la couronne d'Armento. *Mélanges de l'École française de Rome* 101, 691–698.

Dench, E. (1995) *From Barbarians to New Men. Greek, Roman and Modern Perceptions of the Central Appenines*. Oxford, Clarendon.

Dietler, M. (1995) Early "Celtic" socio-political relations: Ideological representation and social competition in dynamic comparative perspective. In B. Arnold and D. Blair Gibson (eds) *Celtic Chiefdom, Celtic State: Evolution of Complex Social Systems in Prehistoric Europe*, 64–71. Cambridge, Cambridge University Press.

Di Niro, A. (1980a) Larino: La città ellenistica e romana. *In Sannio. Pentri e Frentani dal VI al I sec. a.C.. Catalogo della Mostra (Isernia, Museo Nazionale, Ottobre-Dicembre 1980)*, 286–306. Roma, De Luca.

Di Niro, A. (1980b) Larino: La necropoli di Monte Arcano. *In Sannio. Pentri e Frentani dal VI al I sec. a.C.. Catalogo della Mostra (Isernia, Museo Nazionale, Ottobre-Dicembre 1980)*, 71–80. Roma, De Luca.

Di Niro, A. (1980c) La necropoli di Termoli. *In Sannio. Pentri e Frentani dal VI al I sec. a.C.. Catalogo della Mostra (Isernia, Museo Nazionale, Ottobre-Dicembre 1980)*, 53–71. Roma, De Luca.

Di Niro, A. (1981) *Necropoli Arcaiche di Termoli e Larino. Campagne di Scavo 1977-78. Catalogo della Mostra (Isernia, 1980)*. Campobasso, Soprintendenza Archeologica e per i Beni Architettonici Artistici e Storici del Molise/La Rapida Grafedit.

Di Niro, A. (1989) Il sepolcreto sannitico di Gildone. *Conoscenze* 5, 27–36.

Di Niro, A. (1991a) Cercemaggiore-Gildone: La casa, le tombe e il sacello. In S. Capini and A. Di Niro (eds) *Samnium. Archeologia del Molise. Catalogo della Mostra*, 121–126. Roma, Quasar.

Di Niro, A. (1991b) La zona frentana tra IV e I sec. a.C.. In S. Capini and A. Di Niro (eds) *Samnium. Archeologia del Molise. Catalogo della Mostra*, 131–134. Roma, Quasar.

Di Niro, A. (1991c) Le necropoli dell'area interna, le necropoli della zona costiera. In S. Capini and A. Di Niro (eds) *Samnium. Archeologia del Molise. Catalogo della Mostra*, 61–71. Roma, Quasar.

Di Niro, A. and Petrone, P.P. (1993) Gildone: Mortalità, stress nutrizionali e da attività lavorativa in un campione di Sanniti del V–IV sec. a.C.. *Papers of the British School at Rome* 59, 33–49.

Fardella, D. (2003) *La Necropoli di Carpineto*. Unpublished thesis, University of Rome "La Sapienza".

Faustoferri, A. (2003) La necropoli di Barrea. *In I Piceni e l'Italia Medio-Adriatica. Atti del XXII Convegno di Studi Etruschi ed Italici (Ascoli Piceno-Teramo-Ancona, 9-13 Aprile 2000)*, 591–598. Pisa–Roma, Istituti Editoriali e Poligrafici Internazionali.

Fogolari, G. and Gambacurta, G. (2001) (eds) *Materiali Veneti e Romani del Santuario di Lagole di Calalzo al Museo di Pieve di Cadore*. Roma, Giorgio Bretschneider Editore.

Giddens, A. (1984) *The Constitution of Society. Outline of the Theory of Structuration*. Cambridge, Polity Press.

Gledhill, J. (1988) Introduction: The comparative study of social and political transitions. In J. Gledhill, B. Bender and M.T. Larsen (eds) *State and Society: The Emergence and Development of Social Hierarchy and Political Centralisation*, 1–29. London, Allen and Unwin.

Head, B.V. (1911) *Historia Numorum. A Manual of Greek Numismatics*. Oxford, Clarendon.

Imagines = Crawford, M.H. (2011) (ed.) *Imagines Italicae*. London, Institute of Classical Studies.

Isayev, E. (2007) *Inside Ancient Lucania. Dialogues in History and Archaeology* (Bulletin of the Institute of Classical Studies Supplement 90). London, Institute of Classical Studies.

Johannowsky, W. (1991) Circello, Casalbore e Flumeri nel quadro della romanizzazione dell'Irpinia. *In La Romanisation du Samnium aux IIe et Ier Siècles av. J.-C. Actes du Colloque (Naples, Centre Jean Bérard, 4-5 Novembre 1988)*, 57–84. Napoli, Centre Jean Bérard.

La Regina, A. (1976) Il Sannio. In P. Zanker (ed.) *Hellenismus in Mittelitalien. Kolloquium in Göttingen vom 5. bis 9. Juni 1974*, 219–244. Göttingen, Vandenhoeck & Ruprecht.

La Regina, A. (1980) Dalle guerre sannitiche alla romanizzazione. *In Sannio. Pentri e Frentani dal VI al I sec. a.C.. Catalogo della Mostra (Isernia, Museo Nazionale, Ottobre-Dicembre 1980)*, 29–42. Roma, De Luca.

La Regina, A. (1981) Appunti su entità etniche e strutture istituzionali nel Sannio antico. *AION. Annali dell'Istituto Orientale di Napoli Archeologia e Storia Antica* 3, 120–137.

Leach, E. (1954) *Political Systems of Highland Burma: A Study of Kachin Social Structure*. Cambridge MA, Harvard University Press.

Letta, C. (1994) Dall'oppidum al nomen: I diversi livelli dell'aggregazione politica nel mondo osco-umbro. In L. Agnier Foresti (ed.) *Federazioni e Federalismo nell'Europa Antica*, 387–406. Milano, Vita e Pensiero.

Lloyd, J.A. (1995) Pentri, Frentani and the beginnings of urbanisation (500–80 BC). In G. Barker (ed.) *A Mediterranean Valley: Landscape Archaeology and Annales History in the Biferno Valley*, 181–212. Leicester, Leicester University Press.

Lloyd, J.A., Lock, G. and Christie, N. (1997) From the mountain to the plain: Landscape evolution in the Abruzzo. An interim report on the Sangro Valley Project (1994-95). *Papers of the British School at Rome* 65, 1–57.

Macchiarola, I. (1989) I corredi del sepolcreto di Gildone. *Conoscenze* 5, 37–79.

Mariani, L. (1901) Aufidena. *Monumenti Antichi dell'Accademia Nazionale dei Lincei* 10, 225–638.

Marinetti, A. (1992) Epigrafia e lingua di Este preromana. In G. Tosi (ed.) *Este Antica dalla Preistoria all'Età Romana*, 125–172. Este, Zielo.

Morel, J.P. (1981) *Céramique Campanienne. Les Formes*. Roma, École française de Rome.

Morelli, C. (2000) La necropoli arcaica di Val Fondillo a Opi. In A. Bietti-Sestieri (ed.) *Piceni. Popolo d'Europa. Guida alla Mostra di Teramo*, 31–40. Roma, De Luca

Morgan, C. (2003) *Early Greek States beyond the Polis*. London, Routledge.

Morris, I. (1987) *Burial and Ancient Society: The Rise of the Greek City-State*. Cambridge, Cambridge University Press.

Morris, I. (1988) Tomb cult and the Greek renaissance: The past in the present in the 8th century BC. *Antiquity* 63, 750–761.

Morris, I. (1991) The archaeology of ancestors. The Saxe-Goldstein Hypothesis revisited. *Cambridge Archaeological Journal* 1(2), 147–169.

Morris, I. (1992) *Death Ritual and Social Structure in Classical Antiquity*. Cambridge, Cambridge University Press.

Parise Badoni, F. and Ruggieri Giove, M. (1980) Alfedena: La necropoli di Campo Consolino. *In Sannio. Pentri e Frentani dal VI al I sec. a.C.. Catalogo della Mostra (Isernia, Museo Nazionale, Ottobre-Dicembre 1980)*, 84–106. Roma, De Luca.

Parise Badoni, F. and Ruggieri Giove, M. (1981) *Alfedena, La Necropoli di Campo Consolino: Scavi, 1974-1979*. Chieti, Soprintendenza Archeologica dell'Abruzzo.

Parise Badoni, F., Ruggieri Giove, M., Brambilla, C. and Gherardini, P. (1982) Necropoli di Alfedena (scavi 1974-1979): Proposta di una cronologia relativa. *AION. Annali dell'Istituto Orientale di Napoli Archeologia e Storia Antica* 4, 1–41.

Parker Pearson, M. (1999) *The Archaeology of Death and Burial*. Stroud, Sutton.

Perego, E. (2012) *The Construction of Personhood in Veneto (Italy) between the Late Bronze Age and the Early Roman Period*. Unpublished thesis, University College London.

Perego, E. (2014) Anomalous mortuary behaviour and social exclusion in Iron Age Italy: A case study from the Veneto region. *Journal of Mediterranean Archaeology* 27(2), 161–185.

Rix, H. (2002) *Sabellische Texte*. Heidelberg, Universitätsverlag C. Winter.

Roselaar, S.T. (2010) *Public Land in the Roman Republic*. Oxford, Oxford University Press.

Salmon, E.T. (1967) *Samnium and the Samnites*. Cambridge, Cambridge University Press.

Sannio 1980 = *Sannio. Pentri e Frentani dal VI al I sec. a.C.. Catalogo della Mostra (Isernia, Museo Nazionale, Ottobre-Dicembre 1980)*. Roma, De Luca.

Sarno, M.F. (2000) Il territorio caudino. In *Studi sull'Italia dei Sanniti. In Occasione della Mostra 'Italia dei Sanniti' (Roma, Museo Nazionale Romano, Terme di Diocleziano, 14 Gennaio-19 Marzo 2000)*, 56–68. Roma, Electa.

Scopacasa, R. (2014) Building communities in ancient Samnium: Cult, ethnicity and nested identities. *Oxford Journal of Archaeology* 33(1), 69–87.

Scopacasa, R. (2015) *Ancient Samnium: Settlement, Culture and Identity between History and Archaeology*. Oxford, Oxford University Press.

Sparkes, B.A. and Talcott, L. (1970) *Black and Plain Pottery of the 6th, 5th and 4th Centuries BC*. Princeton NJ, American School of Classical Studies at Athens.

ST = Rix, H. (2002) *Sabellische Texte*. Heidelberg, Universitätsverlag C. Winter.

Stek, T. (2009) *Cult Places and Cultural Change in Republican Italy. A Contextual Approach to Religious Aspects of Rural Society after the Roman Conquest*. Amsterdam, Amsterdam University Press.

Suano, M. (1986) *Sabellian-Samnite Bronze Belts in the British Museum* (British Museum Occasional Paper 57). London, British Museum Press.

Tagliamonte, G. (1996) *I Sanniti. Caudini, Irpini, Pentri, Carricini, Frentani*. Milano, Longanesi.

Terrenato, N. (2007) The clans and the peasants. Reflections on social structure and change in Hellenistic central Italy. In P. van Dommelen and N. Terrenato (eds) *Articulating Local Cultures. Power and Identity under the Expanding Roman Republic*, 13–22 (JRA Supplementary Series 63). Portsmouth RI, Journal of Roman Archaeology.

Terrenato, N. (2011) The versatile clans. Archaic Rome and the nature of early city states in central Italy. In N. Terrenato and D.C. Haggis (eds) *State Formation in Italy and Greece. Questioning the Neoevolutionist Paradigm*, 231–244. Oxford, Oxbow Books.

Terrenato, N. and Haggis, D.C. (2011) (eds) *State Formation in Italy and Greece. Questioning the Neoevolutionist Paradigm*. Oxford, Oxbow Books.

Torelli, M.R. (2002) *Benevento Romana*. Roma, "L'Erma" di Bretschneider.

Ucko, P. (1969) Ethnography and archaeological interpretation of funerary remains. *World Archaeology* 1(2), 262–280.

Ve = Vetter, H. (1953) *Handbuch der italischen Dialekte*. Heidelberg, Winter.

Wason, P. (1994) *The Archaeology of Rank*. Cambridge, Cambridge University Press.

Whitley, J. (2001) *The Archaeology of Ancient Greece*. Cambridge, Cambridge University Press.

Chapter 11

Youth on fire? The role of sub-adults and young adults in pre-Roman Italian *Brandopferplätze*

Vera Zanoni

Introduction

In a recent paper, Anna Maria Bietti Sestieri approaches the study of first-millennium BC Italy from a new perspective, by focusing on the several crisis periods which marked this chronological phase as well as on their cultural, historical and archaeological repercussions (Bietti Sestieri 2011). Bietti Sestieri uses the word 'crisis' as a synonym for social change and notes how the rise of new social forms involved a break with deeply ingrained ideological structures (such as the social organization of space, time and personal identity) and their re-negotiation among Italian communities in the first millennium BC (Bietti Sestieri 2011, 397–400; on social change and its consequences on funerary practices in first-millennium BC Italy *cf.* also Cuozzo, Iaia, Shipley and especially Scopacasa, Perego, and Perego and Scopacasa this volume). These three variables of space, time and identity overlap in archaeological sites that possess an especially powerful ritual significance, such as cemeteries and ceremonial sites. Bietti Sestieri focuses on the topographical development of pre-Roman cemeteries in Veneto, Marche and Latium to discuss the extent to which spatial data are useful to support and enrich historical and archaeological readings of the evidence, especially by making more visible the elements of rupture and continuity in the same context.

Within this theoretical and interpretative framework, ceremonial areas offer case studies of special significance. This chapter, therefore, will focus on a peculiar category of ceremonial place which developed in northern Italy and nearby regions in late prehistory, namely the *Brandopferplätze* (e.g. Gleirscher 2002a). *Brandopferplätze* ('places of fire sacrifice') are the most significant ritual manifestation of the communities that lived in and around the Alpine area during the Bronze and Iron Ages (approximately around the late third, second and first millennia BC). In *Brandopferplatz*-type sites the ceremonial activities were centred on natural features of the landscape such as peaks, rocks, fords and springs, but also involved the construction of cairns, walls, platforms and *bothroi* (ritual pits). The artefact assemblages that characterized these ritual sites consist of ceramic and bronze artefacts that were intentionally broken upon deposition, together with burnt human and animal bones. A sample of human bones recovered from some Iron Age *Brandopferplätze* in northern Italy, with a focus on the Trentino–South Tyrol region, has been subject to osteological analysis, and the resulting data add much to our understanding of this key type of ritual practice (Figs 11.1 and 11.2). In particular, osteological analysis from the sampled sites revealed the predominance of bones of individuals that may be classified as 'sub-adults' under the age of *c.* 20 years and 'young adults' in the 21–30-year-old age range. This analysis also revealed a recurrence of bones of individuals approximately aged 15–20 years at death, who represent almost half of the sample. By contrast, rare or absent is the presence – among the individuals whose age at death was estimated by osteological analysis – of subjects aged around 30 or more.

In this chapter, therefore, I shall place this osteological evidence in its archaeological context, so as to develop a more holistic approach to the *Brandopferplatz* phenomenon. In particular, I shall consider the existence of a possible connection between the tendency to situate the *Brandopferplätze* in threshold places such as natural boundaries and mountain tops, and the involvement in these rituals of individuals belonging to age classes that might have been considered liminal or even marginal, potentially because these people did not achieve full 'adulthood' and/or full social integration according to the social norms of their group of belonging. Was death in *Brandopferplätze* a 'death on the fringe'?

Background

The word '*Brandopferplatz*' was introduced into European archaeological literature in 1966 by Werner Krämer. Krämer first applied this definition to a range of ritual contexts found in the Alpine regions of Switzerland, Germany, Austria and Slovenia (Krämer 1966). According to Krämer, these contexts were characterized by the following recurring features:

a. chronological range: *Brandopferplatz*-type sites dated to the first half of the first millennium (*c.* 950/925–550/525 BC);
b. topographical location: *Brandopferplatz*-type sites were located on or near the top of mountains and hills;
c. presence of burnt bones: *Brandopferplatz*-type sites yielded bones of pigs, sheep, deer and horses;
d. presence of burnt artefacts, with particular regard to ceramic vessels and metal items such as weapons and jewellery;
e. presence of built structures such as pits, walls and cairns.

Since the appearance of Krämer's work, *Brandopferplatz*-type sites have been considered one of the most important forms of ritual practice in the northern and southern Alpine regions in the late prehistoric and proto-historic periods (e.g. Endrizzi *et al.* 2009;

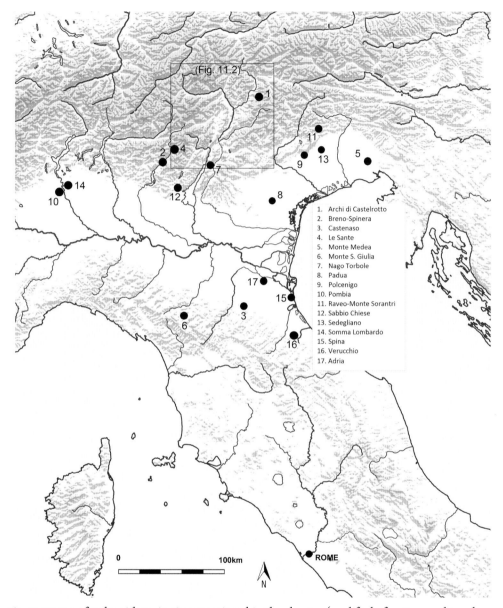

Fig. 11.1: Map of Italy with main sites mentioned in the chapter (modified after Perego this volume; base map courtesy of the Ancient World Mapping Center).

Gleirscher 2002b). At these sites, ceremonies appear to have involved the dedication of votive objects, the burning of fires and probably also blood sacrifices. Some scholars argue that these rituals may have been dedicated to a deity such as the pre-Roman god *Sethlans*, who was associated with lightening, fire and mountaintops, and was later

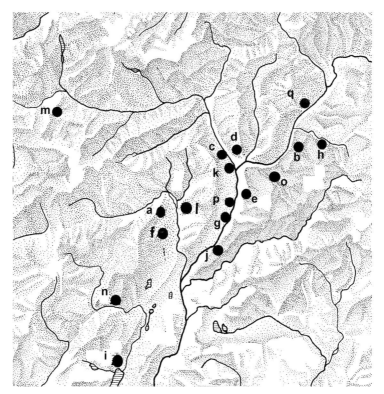

Fig. 11.2: Map of Trentino–South Tyrol with main sites mentioned in the chapter: a. Campi di Neri di Cles; b. Castelrotto; c. Greifenstein–S. Genesio; d. Noafer Bühl; e. Laives; f. Mechel; g. Montagna; h. Ortisei–Col de Flam; i. Riva del Garda; j. Salorno; k. Sanzeno; l. Sluderno; m. Stenico; n. Thalerbühel; o. Vadena; p. Velturno (modified after Bellintani 2000).

identified with the Roman god Vulcan (e.g. Valvo 1996). Others have pointed to a female deity as a possible recipient of cult at the *Brandopferplätze*: this goddess might have been one potentially sharing some similarities with the Venetic *Reitia* or the Greek Artemis, who was thought to control natural elements such as fire and water, and might have been linked to the Otherworld (De Min 2005, 117; Gleirscher 2002a, 627). On the other hand, Filippo M. Gambari has suggested that *Brandopferplätze* might have been devoted to the heroized dead (Gambari 2001, 98).

Furthermore, it has been noted that *Brandopferplatz* areas were usually wide and their elevated topographical placement made them conspicuous in the landscape. All of this suggests that the *Brandopferplätze* may have played a key socio-political role. This is further indicated by the occasional deposition of human bones in these sites, which some scholars have interpreted as belonging to outcast people (Bettencourt 2010; below). Furthermore, a relationship between *Brandopferplätze* and ritual practices possibly involving the 'cult of the dead' was found at the *Brandopferplatz*-type site of Stenico in Trentino: the area at Stenico that yielded burnt offerings occupies the southern zone of a Middle Bronze Age *tumulus* where rituals that might be classified as a form of 'skull cult' appear to have been practiced.

Italian archaeologists began to focus more consistently on *Brandopferplatz*-type sites after the excavations carried out by Paul Gleirscher in the 1980s at the Iron Age sites of Rungger Egg, near Siusi allo Sciliar/Seis am Schlern (Castelrotto/Kastelruth) in South Tyrol. Taking the archaeological and osteological data from Rungger Egg as a starting point, Gleirscher carried out a complete review of the Italian sites that displayed similar features. The result was a list of 126 sites in eastern Alpine Italy that Gleirscher identified as *Brandopferplätze* (Gleirscher 2002b). Recent discoveries in northern Italy, however, have revealed the presence of similar ceremonial places in areas previously excluded from the sample, and have opened up new perspectives for the study and interpretation of *Brandopferplatz*-type sites. New findings in Lombardy (Sabbio Chiese: Poggiani Keller and Baioni 2005; Breno–Spinera: Solano 2010), Piedmont (Pombia: Gambari 2001) and Emilia Romagna (Monte S. Giulia: Cardarelli and Pellacani 2010) show that *Brandopferplatz*-type sites are also attested in central-western Alpine, peri-Alpine and northern Apennine Italy. Moreover, we can observe a widening of the chronological range. Sites that yielded built and sometimes monumental structures, areas where fires had been burnt and burnt offerings, including burnt bones, already existed in the Late Copper Age and the Bronze Age of northern Italy (from the third millennium BC to the twelfth–eleventh centuries BC). This is indicated by the ceremonial areas of Velturno/Feldthurns-Tanzgasse, Vàdena/Pfatten-Piglonerkopf, Cles–Campi Neri, Sluderno/Schluderns–Ganglegg and Riva del Garda–Brione in Trentino–South Tyrol (Endrizzi *et al.* 2009; Mazzucchi 2010; Steiner 2007; Tecchiati 2000) and Ossimo–Pat in Lombardy (Poggiani Keller 2002). Furthermore, we now know that some *Brandopferplatz*-type sites continued to develop in later periods, from the second half of the Iron Age down to the Roman era (*c.* 550/525–50/25 BC: *cf.* Ciurletti 2007). The new data appear to confirm the persistence of *Brandopferplätze* in a wide geographical and chronological range (Endrizzi *et al.* 2009; Tecchiati 2007, 22–3). It therefore seems that *Brandopferplätze* were a cultural and ritual phenomenon that is particularly well-attested in first-millennium BC northern Italy. Probably developing in European Alpine regions from Germany to Slovenia, it may have spread to other mountain sites in peninsular Italy, involving also the presence of cultural elements that scholars have variously classed as 'Celtic' and 'Roman'. Although *Brandopferplatz*-type sites were often frequented for long periods of time, they nevertheless tended to preserve a number of shared features over time, such as the preference for prominent topographic placement, the proximity to springs, the use of fire and a predilection for certain types of animals to be placed among the offerings.

Finally, a wider application of osteological analysis both in newly discovered sites (i.e. Ortisei/Urtijëi–Col de Flam, Trentino–South Tyrol) and previously excavated sites (i.e. Stenico-Calferi, Trentino–South Tyrol: Fig. 11.3) has revealed the presence of human bones that were selected, manipulated and burnt similarly to the animal bones and the other offerings. This unexpected element has led to a general re-thinking of the *Brandopferplatz* archaeological category (Endrizzi *et al.* 2009; Tecchiati 2007). For this

Fig. 11.3: Burnt soil and broken pottery from Stenico-Calferi (after Bellintani 2000).

reason, the preliminary evaluation of these osteological samples is the main topic of this paper. It must be stressed that osteological analysis is still in progress. While with particular regard to regions such as Trentino–South Tyrol and Veneto, the recent cooperation of Italian archaeologists and bio-archaeologists has led to the adoption of a more holistic methodological approach which involves the survey, study and discussion of all the data available from any archaeological context,[1] it is still impossible to apply osteological analysis to the material found in all *Brandopferplatz*-type sites. In particular, unpublished data are often difficult to access or collect. For example, there is a significant lack of information on the western Alpine territories of Italy. Moreover, even when some preliminary data on certain sites are available, they do not include the osteological evidence. This determines disparities in collecting, analysing and interpreting archaeological and osteological data from different contexts (Zanoni 2011, 2–3). Despite these shortcomings concerning the evidence, I am able to suggest here some preliminary goals for an analysis of the *Brandopferplatz* phenomenon. My research aims are as follows:

1. to provide a list of the Italian Iron Age *Brandopferplatz*-type sites where human bones have been found;
2. to discuss and compare the published data concerning the human skeletal remains which emerged from these sites;
3. to consider archaeological, osteological and geographical data together, in order to explain the presence of human skeletal remains in these ceremonial contexts.

My preliminary analysis of the evidence will show that a wider application of bio-archaeological approaches on human burnt bones from *Brandopferplatz*-type sites in Alpine and peri-Alpine Iron Age northern Italy reveals the presence of both sub-adult individuals, including some rare children, and older individuals whose age at death, however, usually did not exceed the range of 21–30 years. This potentially suggests that a ritual selection based on the age of the deceased might have determined the choice of the categories of individuals deposited in the *Brandopferplatz*-type sites under consideration. Furthermore, the discovery of human bones in only a few of the ceremonial sites, which are also characterized by natural markers of liminality, seems to suggest a possible liminal status also for the human beings that were placed in these contexts.

Italian Iron Age *Brandopferplätze* with human bones: archaeological evidence

As mentioned above, *Brandopferplatz*-type sites can be divided into two main groups, namely those that yielded human bones and those that did not. In this chapter I shall focus on the sites where the presence of human bones has been confirmed by osteological analysis. The available data are presented here in geographical and chronological order, starting from Trentino–South Tyrol (Table 11.1).

Up until now Leimburg, Stenico–Calferi (Fig. 11.3) and Rungger Egg are the most ancient *Brandopferplatz*-type sites of interest known in Trentino–South Tyrol. They appear to have been occupied for very long periods and already hosted some forms of ceremonial activity in the Late Copper Age and in the Bronze Age. Leimburg is close to the large Vàdena/Pfatten cemetery, which was already in use between the twelfth and tenth centuries BC (*cf.* Alberti 1997). This evidence has been discussed by Umberto Tecchiati, who connected the rise of *Brandopefrplätze* with the adoption of cremation in northern Italy (Tecchiati 2007, 24). Calferi was instead occupied by a large *tumulus* dating to the fourteenth and thirteenth centuries BC, where skeletons belonging to adult and sub-adult individuals appear to have been deprived of the skull. Starting in the ninth century BC, the southern sector of this *tumulus* began to include layers of burnt soil containing coal, ash, metal and ceramic objects, as well as animal and human bones. In the first and second centuries AD, a ceremonial structure was built over the *tumulus*, which caused the partial obliteration of the area where the fires had been burnt. The site was frequented until the Middle Ages, as has been suggested in view of two inhumations without surviving grave goods (Marzatico 1992). Excavations at Rungger Egg yielded about 6 kg of copper waste and burnt flint points, which were more ancient than the *Brandopferplatz* context (Zampieri 2006). Furthermore, another ritual site that revealed evidence of long-term use was Thalerbühel, which was occupied since the twelfth century BC by a large settlement; this settlement was finally destroyed by fire in the seventh century BC (Marconi and Tecchiati 2006).

With regard to the spatial organization of these ceremonial places, they can be defined as open-air sanctuaries centred on peculiar features of the landscape that might have been of some significance for their notable spatial location (*cf.* below), even if built structures are also well attested in the same contexts. For example, at

Table 11.1: Brandopferplatz-type sites from Trentino/South Tyrol.

Site	Chronology BC	Archaeological context	Animal bones	Human bones
Vàdena/Pfatten-Leimburg (Bolzano/Bozen)	10th–9th century	Burnt soil including coal and ash	Deer	12.5 kg Cranial bones Long bones of lower and upper limbs
Stenico-Calferi (Trento)	9th–1st century	Burnt soil including coal and ash	Pig, sheep, deer	5.6 kg Cranial bones Long bones of lower and upper limbs
Castelrotto/Kastelruth-Rungger Egg (Bolzano/Bozen)	8th–6th century	Burnt soil including coal and ash	Pig, sheep, deer horse	18 kg Cranial bones Long bones of lower and upper limbs
Greis-Noafer Bühl (Bolzano/Bozen)	8th–6th century	Burnt soil including coal and ash	Pig, sheep, deer	8 kg Cranial fragments Long bones of lower and upper limbs
Leives/Leifers-via Galizia (Bolzano/Bozen)	8th–6th century	Burnt soil including coal and ash	Horse	5000 bone fragments Cranial bones Long bones of lower and upper limbs
Ortisei/Urtijëi-Col de Flam (Bolzano/Bozen)	5th–3rd century	Pits containing burnt soil including coal and ash	Pig	2 kg Cranial bones Teeth Long bones of lower and upper limbs
Tires/Tiers-Thalerbühel (Bolzano/Bozen)	1st century	Platform covered by coal and ash	Cat	Cranial fragments

Rungger Egg there were cairns and walls that delimited narrow paths leading to a water spring. The archaeological deposit was concentrated near a circular-shaped pit, the so-called *bothros*, which had a diameter of 9 m and was surrounded by two walls (Gleirscher 2002b). The case of the ritual site of Laives/Leifers–Via Galizia in Trentino–South Tyrol is also significant: the ceremonial area was constituted by four sectors with rectilinear structures parallel to each other. These structures were made of large porphyry stones and were separated by black soil including coal, ash, ceramic and metal objects, animal bones, the disarticulated bones of a horse as well as human remains (Zanforlin 2008). The large ceremonial area of Col de Flam in Trentino–South Tyrol included a few pits measuring 1–2 m in diameter, which contained coal, ash, cereals, pig bones and other organic material, perhaps a kind of brocade (Mazzucchi 2010). The site of Thalerbühel, which I have already mentioned above, featured a large platform covered by coal and ash, the disarticulated skeletons of four cats and four broken fibulae (Marconi and Tecchiati 2006).

Other *Brandopferplatz*-type sites in the Trentino–South Tyrol region have yielded human skeletal remains, but the absence of in-depth osteological analysis does not allow us to form a complete bio-archaeological profile of the deceased. At Salorno/Salurn–Dos de la Forca, layers containing coal and ash together with gold, amber and glass beads, spindle whorls, ceramic and metal objects, deer horns and human bones were discovered around a quadrangular rock with a longitudinal fissure; the deposit is datable to the ninth century BC (Alberti *et al.* 2005). Burnt human bones were also discovered at Cles–Mechel–Valemporga. The human remains, together with unburnt animal bones, were found in association with a quadrangular stone structure that was covered by coal and ash, underneath layers from the Roman period. The pre-Roman context there has been dated to the eighth century BC (Adam 1991). Disarticulated and burnt human bones were also found at S. Lorenzo di Sebato/St Lorenzen–Burgkofel, which also featured a complete and unburnt human skull. The archaeological layers, consisting of gravel and black soil, yielded carbonized wood as well as ceramic and metal objects, which include an inscribed belt. The site dates between the fifth and third centuries BC, and was located near a sulphur geyser (Constantini 2002). Other *Brandopferplatz*-type sites of this kind are also found outside Trentino–South Tyrol. For example, from the same period of S. Lorenzo date the ceremonial areas of Monte Medea–Tortul, in Friuli Venezia Giulia, and Archi di Castelrotto–Cimitero in Veneto. At both these sites, layers composed of black soil with coal and ash contained ceramic and metal artefacts, including vessels (*ollae*) broken upon deposition and burnt human skeletal remains. The latter mainly consisted of cranial bones and teeth (Furlani 1974–1975; Salzani 1978).

The site of S. Genesio/Jenesien–Greifenstein, located again in Trentino–South Tyrol and dating between the fifth and third centuries BC, also shares some similarities with *Brandopferplatz*-type sites. S. Genesio/Jenesien was characterized by a natural fissure which was filled with coal, ash, ceramic and metal objects, and glass beads, together with animal and human bones (Torggler 2002). In addition, Gleirscher tentatively identified as *Brandopferplätze* the sites of Montagna/Montan–Castelfelder and Sanzeno–Casilini, both in Trentino–South Tyrol and dating respectively from the tenth–ninth and eighth–fourth centuries BC (Gleirscher 2002b). The absence of more precise contextual data does not allow us to confirm Gleirscher's identification. Moreover, the presence of human burnt bones in these sites is only probable, even if at Montagna/Montan we have a single cremation tomb with grave goods. The burial, which was found inside a niche in the boundary walls, appears to belong to a 'sub-adult' individual (Marzoli 2004). Other sites located outside the Trentino–South Tyrol region that display *Brandopferplatz* features include the area of Capo di Ponte in Lombardy. Capo di Ponte includes significant archaeological deposits, above all at the site of Le Sante. Here the archaeological context yielded a complex of walls and two inhumation tombs with no surviving grave goods. Furthermore, a pit lined with stone slabs and dug into a layer of black soil was found. Unburnt animal bones and burnt human bones were found both in and around the pit, which dates from the second–first century BC (Solano 2010). The case of Somma Lombardo–Calzaturificio Ferrerio is also notable. The site dates from the first century BC. A black layer of soil contained ceramic and metal artefacts that were exposed to fire, as well as human bones (Bertolone 1960). Finally, some of the most interesting late Iron Age–early Roman occurrences of *Brandopferplatz*-type sites outside Trentino–South Tyrol have been discovered at Polcenigo–S. Giovanni Sottocolle and at Raveo–Monte Sorantri, in the region of Friuli Venezia Giulia, near Veneto. Both sites date from the first century BC. The ceremonial area of Polcenigo lay atop an earlier Bronze Age settlement and consisted of layers of coal and ash. These layers contained ceramic and metal objects that were broken in antiquity, in association with burnt human bones (Vitri *et al.* 2006). Also at Raveo the ceremonial site lay atop a Bronze Age settlement. In the middle of the site a pit lined with large stone slabs contained broken vases, an Arquà–Mokrong-type bronze shield, weapons and an incised gem. The pit was surrounded by black layers of soil that included human bones and ash (Petrucci *et al.* 2005).

Italian Iron Age *Brandopferplätze* with human bones: osteological evidence

Osteological analysis of the human remains from the sites under consideration was carried out by Italian bio-archaeologists. The Minimum Number of Individuals, or MNI, has been determined by taking into consideration both osteological data and the spatial distribution of the skeletal remains in their context of discovery (*cf.* Zanoni 2011, 74–5), whilst anomalies and/or stress markers on the surface of the bones have been examined at a macroscopic level. Age estimation has been done by applying the Kerley-Ubelaker microscopic method, which involves calculating osteon fragments in femurs and tibiae (Conzato *et al.* 2012, 134; Ubelaker 1978).

Thanks to this analysis, it is possible to note that human (and animal) skeletal remains at *Brandopferplatz*-type sites constituted secondary depositions. When secondary burial is carried out, the human (or animal) remains involved are placed in locations other than those where decomposition occurred, and the skeletons might be further manipulated and picked apart (Fabbri 2001, 113). In fact, in *Brandopferplatz*-

type sites we find only certain portions of the skeleton, usually the cranium and the long bones of the lower and upper limbs. The general and recurrent absence of other parts of the skeleton such as the rib-cage, the spine and the pelvis might suggest that at least in some cases disarticulation was carried out after the initial disappearance of soft tissue, resulting in exposure of underlying bones, but before cremation took place. According to some scholars, therefore, the bones might have been first selected and then burnt (Conzato *et al.* 2012, 135). Notably, this evidence also raises questions about the placing/re-location of the bones which were not deposited in *Brandopferplatz*-type sites alongside the other remains from the same individual(s), which were instead placed in the ritual area. Moreover, the prevalent white colour and the fractures caused by fire, which are visible on the skeletal remains, indicate that these were presumably burnt at temperatures of 800–1000°C (Mayne Correira 1997).

These analyses are useful to shed light on the composition of the osteological assemblages under consideration (Table 11.2). At Calferi the osteological deposit was constituted by cranial remains and long bones of the lower and upper limbs belonging to four individuals. Age was determined for two of the individuals. One cranial fragment presented a 'pitting' area, possibly indicative of a degenerative process of the cranial surface, due to increasing intra-cranial pressure. Furthermore, one femur fragment had a potential stress marker on the neck of the bone. This potential stress marker, the so-called Allen's fossa, may result from the habit of walking on rough ground or

Table 11.2: Osteological evidence from Iron Age Italian Brandopferplätze.

Site	Human bones	MNI	Age	Sex
Leimburg	12.5 kg	11	-	Both sexes
Salorno	13 kg	-	-	Both sexes
Montagna	1.7 kg	1	16–20 years old	Male
Calferi	5.6 kg	4	11±4 years old 17±8 years old	-
Rungger Egg	18 kg	20 (?)	21–30 years old	Both sexes
Noafer Bühl	8 kg	6	19–20 years old 'young adults'	Both sexes
Via Galizia	5000 fragments	3	16–20 years old 'young adults'	Female
Greifenstein	2 kg	1	20–25 years old	Male
Col de Flam	2 kg	1	17±8 years old	-
Thalerbühel	Fragments	1	7–8 years old	-
Le Sante	*c.* 5 kg	4	'young adults' 3–4 years old	-
Calzaturificio Ferrerio	*c.* 5 kg	4	3 'young adults' one 'sub-adult'	-

from a frequent hyper-flexed position such as a squatting position (on Allen's fossa *cf.* Radi *et al.* 2013). Another two fragments revealed traces of fractures. Presently, the causes of these fractures are not explicable (Mazzucchi 2010). At Noafer Bühl, the burnt cranial bones and long bones of the upper and lower limbs belonged to six subjects, apparently both males and females, who seem to have died in their young adulthood (Renhart 2002). From Rungger Egg also came cranial fragments and long bones of the upper and lower limbs. They were found in the so-called *bothros* and belonged to male and female individuals; most of these individuals appear to have been between the age of 21 and 30 at the time of death (von den Driesch and Schröter 2002). In the site of Laives/Leifers–Via Galizia the cranial fragments and the long bones of the lower and upper limbs belonged to presumptive female subjects, who died at around the age of 16–20 years (Zanforlin 2008). Osteological analysis of the human bones from Ortisei/Urtijëi has shown that the skeletal remains belonged to an individual who might have been a 'sub-adult' (Mazzucchi 2010; unfortunately, it was impossible to determine his or her age more precisely). At Salorno/Salurn 13 kg of human skeletal remains seem to belong to individuals of both sexes (Alberti *et al.* 2005). No precise age determination is presently available. The bones from Le Sante belonged to three individuals classified as 'young adults' and to a 3–4-year-old child. According to Solano (2006–2007) the bones revealed 'cut-marks' at the joints and were possibly cremated when tissue was still attached. The exact age of the 'young-adult' subjects has not been established. At Somma Lombardo–Calzaturificio Ferrerio the osteological deposit consisted of cranial bones and long bones of the upper and lower limbs that belonged to three 'young adults' and to one sub-adult (Bartolone 1960). Finally, in the natural fissure of Greifenstein were found some cranial fragments, a clavicle, a rib, cervical and thoracic vertebrae and a femur belonging to a 20 to 25-year-old male who suffered from *cribra orbitalia*, a lesion of the orbital roof, and had porosities on the frontal bone, possibly but not necessarily indicative of porotic hyperostosis (Torggler 2002). *Cribra orbitalia* and porotic hyperostosis have often been classified as markers of disturbance caused by iron-deficiency anaemia (e.g. Fornaciari and Mallegni 1980; *cf.* also discussion in Waldron 2009). Recent research, however, suggests that *cribra orbitalia* and porotic hyperostosis may have a variety of different causes, which include vitamin B12 deficiency and/or infective disease (e.g. DiGangi and Moore 2012; Walker *et al.* 2009).

The reasons for a choice: natural places of significance

The *Brandopferplatz*-type sites where human bones have been found are relatively rare if compared to the ones without human bones, and represent about 10% of the 140 locations classified as *Brandopferplätze* considered in this chapter. Therefore, it is worth investigating the reasons behind the placing of human bones in some sites but not in others.

According to Gleirscher (1991–1993), the *Brandopferplatz*-type sites with human skeletal remains are larger than those that do not include human remains, and are also located at an altitude higher than 600 m. The highest locations in our present sample are Ortisei/Urtijëi (1230 m), Rungger Egg (1004 m), S. Genesio/Jenesien (1087 m), Noafer Bühl (1000 m) and S. Lorenzo di Sebato/St Lorenzen (810 m), all of which were visible from long distances. Because of their topographical prominence, these sites could have had some kind of regional or even supra-regional relevance, while the sites with no human bones may have had only local importance (Gleirscher 1991–1993, 118–9). Noting the topographical prominence of *Brandopferplatz*-type sites with human remains, Tecchiati suggested that they might have functioned as regional sanctuaries (Tecchiati 2007). Hence, as cultural and ceremonial gathering points, these *Brandopferplatz*-type sites may have had a similar role to that of proto-urban settlements in other regions of Italy such as Etruria, which in the first millennium BC was characterized by increasing social complexity and urbanization (Tecchiati 2007, 27). For scholars such as Alessandro Guidi, the rise of proto-urban agglomerations, and the growing importance and complexity of ceremonial activities, afforded the necessary basis for the development of an early or 'Archaic' state organization in Italy (Guidi 2008, 187). However, we cannot exactly define any potential relationship between *Brandopferplätze* and urban settlements, because *Brandopferplatz*-type sites appear to be extremely isolated topographically. Those identified until now seem rather to be linked with peculiar features of the landscape such as mountaintops or water sources.

The topographical location of *Brandopferplatz*-type sites is indeed significant. If we analyse their location at the macro-level, we see that the sites with human remains are located near routes leading to key mountain passes, or occupy strategic positions commanding the road network that linked together the areas north and south of the Alps (Tecchiati 2000). Significant examples include Ortisei/Urtijëi, which is situated on the road towards the Pordoi Pass; S. Lorenzo di Sebato/St Lorenzen, located at the intersection between the Pusteria/Pustertal and Badia Valleys; and Capo di Ponte, which was near a ford on the Serio River between the Valcamonica and Trompia Valleys. Moreover, the examined *Brandopferplatz*-type sites seem to have a strong connection with water. Stenico controlled the exit of the Sarca River from the Giudicarie Alps towards Lake Garda. Laives/Leifers is right at the confluence of the Isarco and Adige Rivers, while Ortisei/Urtijëi controlled the course of the Rio Gardena River. Stenico, Noafer Bühl and Rungger Egg are all located near springs and waterfalls, while thermal springs and a sulphur geyser are present at S. Lorenzo/St Lorenzen.[2] According to Tecchiati (2000), the extreme features of the landscape around *Brandopferplatz*-type sites, their proximity to the sky and to water, as well as their geographical isolation, may have led the inhabitants of these regions to see them as portals to the Otherworld. *Brandopferplatz*-type sites may therefore have been natural places of significance, that is, locations that became important because of the presence of peculiar topographical features that functioned as territorial markers (*cf.* Knapp and Ashmore 1999). Moreover, *Brandopferplatz*-type sites may have been considered liminal places, namely locations that marked the geographical passage between different regions. Such a passage may refer to the transition between different natural habitats (e.g. mountains and hills or mountains and plains) but also between different cultural areas, with particular regard to the Hallstatt region (north of the Alps), the Fritzens-Sanzeno culture area (Trentino–South Tyrol), the Venetic culture area (roughly corresponding to present-day Veneto) and the Breno–Dos de l'Arca culture area (eastern Lombardy). It might be possible, therefore, to discuss *Brandopferplatz*-type sites within the framework of the 'frontier sanctuary' notion (*cf.* de Polignac 1987 for the use of this framework regarding ancient Greece). In Italy, the concept of 'frontier sanctuary' has been used, among others, by Andrea Zifferero (2005) to discuss several significant sanctuaries in Iron Age south Etruria. In particular, Zifferero has noted the strong connection of these religious sites with prominent topographic features such as hills, mountains and rivers, which separated not only different regions but also the areas of political influence of different settlements. These sanctuaries, therefore, constituted a kind of sacred boundary which anticipated and influenced the creation of real political frontiers (Zifferero 2005).

Finally, it is interesting to observe the coincidence of *Brandopferplatz*-type sites with previous monumental sites or long-frequented areas. These include the *tumulus* at Stenico; the areas used in prehistoric phases at Rungger Egg and Laives/Leifers, as indicated by the flint points found there; the ceremonial complex at Ortisei/Urtijëi, which was used from the late Bronze Age; the Bronze Age settlements discovered at Polcenigo and Raveo, and the large Mesolithic site at Salorno/Salurn near the Adige River. Possible interpretations for this phenomenon are, on the one hand, the casual overlapping of different archaeological deposits, or (as suggested by Endrizzi *et al.* 2009) an intentional re-occupation of places that continued to have a relevant role in the socio-cultural structuration of the geographical landscape, as well as a long persistence in the social memory of the local communities (Adams 2007; Loney-Hoaen 2005).

The reasons for a choice: human bones and age classes

The liminal aspect of *Brandopferplatz*-type sites seems to reflect also on the osteological evidence. If we consider a possible categorization of human skeletal remains on the basis of the skeletal ages that are securely attested, we may note the predominance of four age ranges (*cf.* Table 11.3).

Because of the presence of human bones, *Brandopferplatz*-type sites were long regarded as strictly funerary contexts (Nothdurfter and Schubert 1985, 250). However, it is notable that overall the human remains found at these sites do not represent the standard funerary population for a pre-jennerian and pre-industrial society.[3] In fact, if we consider that, roughly, in such societies (a) the average age at death for those who survived infancy seems to have been higher than 20–30 years (e.g. Chamberlain 2006, 53–4; Mallegni *et al.* 1999, 162–3), (b) neonatal, infant and child mortality was high, with some estimates suggesting that *c.* 30–50% of children might die before the age of 5 (e.g. Chamberlain 2006; Parkin 2013, 47–50) and (c) the minimum risk

Table 11.3: Age classes from Iron Age Italian Brandopferplätze.

0–9 years old	10–15 years old	16–20 years old	21–30 years old
1 individual from le Sante	1 individual from Calferi	1 individual from Montagna	20 (?) individuals from Rungger Egg
1 individual from Somma Lombardo		1 individual from Calferi	1 individual from Greifenstein
1 individual from Thalerbühel-Tires		1 individual from Ortisei	3 individuals from via Galizia
		1 individual from via Galizia	
		8 individuals from Noafer	

of death is on average attested in the second decade of life (e.g. Chamberlain 2006, 62, 67),[4] we can observe a significant trend at work in the *Brandopferplatz*-type sites of northern Italy. Indeed, there seems to be a predominance of specific age classes, and a general scarcity or absence of infants, children and individuals whose approximate age at death was 30+ (Table 11.3). It might also be significant that both children and individuals whose presumptive age at death exceeded 30 years have been found at several burial sites of late prehistoric and proto-historic northern Italy that do not display the features associated with *Brandopferplatz*-type sites (for Veneto *cf.* for example Onisto 2004; Voltolini 2013). This strengthens the hypothesis that (a) child mortality might have been indeed very high in late prehistoric northern Italy; and (b) once an individual survived childhood, his or her life expectancy in Iron Age northern Italy might have been higher, and even much higher, than suggested by the skeletal remains from *Brandopferplatz*-type sites.

The sites considered in this chapter include together a total of *c.* 60 individuals (for an overview of the sampled data *cf.* Mazzucchi 2010, 145). Age estimation has been carried out for 40 of them, and has determined the presence of 19 'sub-adult' individuals (49%) and 21 individuals that may be classed as 'young adults' (51%). Among the sub-adults only three are infant or children while 16 have been classed as being around 10/12 to 20 years at death (i.e. belonging to age groups that might classified as 'pubescent' [10–15 years old] and 'adolescent' [16–20 years old] in present-day western societies). As a consequence, we can suggest that there might have been active selection of the bones which constituted the osteological deposits placed in the sites examined. This selection appears to relate not only to the liminal geographical locations of these sites, but also to the kinds of people whose remains were allowed (or selected) to be placed among the votive offerings (*cf.* also Perego 2012 and Perego this volume on the ritual use of human remains in Iron Age northern Italy, with a focus on Veneto). The age profile of the adult sample is also noteworthy. The general absence of individuals older than *c.* 30 years, and comparison with other osteological samples from European ceremonial areas, such as the Iron Age sanctuary of Zàvist (Czech Republic), seem to suggest that specific cultural choices determined what categories of people could be placed in ceremonial sites such as

Brandopferplatz-type areas. One possibility is that at least some of the bones may have belonged to outcast people, such as war prisoners that might have been younger than the average adult population (on this issue *cf.* for example Chamberlain 2006, 77–80); this hypothesis, however, would need further investigation (Vanzetti 2007–2008, 758).

Discussion and conclusion: people on the fringe?

In Iron Age northern Italy – as well as in other regions of ancient Italy – sub-adult individuals and especially infants might be excluded from formal burial in cemeteries (e.g. Bonghi Jovino 2007; Zanoni 2011; 2012 but *cf.* Di Lorenzo *et al.* this volume on the formal burial of children in the Iron Age cemeteries of Verucchio, near Rimini, in Emilia Romagna). Furthermore, sub-adults, who are classed by Meyer Orlac as "negative individuals" (Meyer Orlac 1997, 2), might be shown in ethnographic and folkloric literature as being somewhat isolated from the social group because of their premature death. They seem to occupy liminal spaces between life and death or between the worldly and otherworldly spheres (e.g. Aspök 2008, 20; Nizzo 2011). With regard to these subjects, therefore, human groups might apply mortuary strategies which are different from those applied to 'adults' and which may involve burial in spaces other than formal funerary areas (e.g. settlements, ceremonial areas and natural places of significance). For example, infants and children may be buried in connection with domestic spaces. Indeed, the discovery of children's bones inside settlement areas is a widespread phenomenon in pre-Roman northern Italy as well as in other regions of the peninsula (e.g. Tecchiati 2011; Zanoni 2011). However, the simultaneous presence of children within and outside formal funerary contexts gives rise to new questions, concerning the social criteria used for determining who was granted formal burial in the cemetery space, and who was denied it (Ginzburg 1966, 23–5; on the issue of formal cemetery burial *cf.* also Cuozzo, Scopacasa, Perego, Perego and Scopacasa, and Iaia this volume).

Apart from children, individuals classed as 'pubescent' and 'adolescent' could also be buried inside settlements, sometimes in direct connection with structural features and areas of the settlement that may be considered liminal (e.g. abandoned structures or thresholds such as doorways). For example, this may have been the case of some burials from the so-called *castellieri*, namely Middle Bronze Age, Recent Bronze Age and Final Bronze Age fortified sites from northern Italy (*c.* second half of the second millennium BC). At Sedegliano, in Friuli Venezia Giulia, the bones belonging to a 15–18-year-old individual were found near the entrance ways of one of these settlements, while the skull of a 15–20-year-old subject was discovered along the fortification walls of the settlement at Siusi allo Sciliar/Seis am Schlern in Trentino–South Tyrol (Corazza and Cassola Guida 2005; Tecchiati 2011). The burial of 'adolescents' in settlement areas is also attested during the Iron Age. At Villamarzana–Campo Michela, in Veneto, the skeleton of a 16–20-year-old individual from the ninth century BC was found in the peripheral area of the settlement together with animal bones and various archaeological debris; this subject suffered from a congenital absence of some teeth, while evidence of enamel hypoplasia noticed on the remaining teeth is indicative of systemic stress (e.g. starvation, poor nutrition or disease) that occurred in childhood (Salzani and Consonni 2005; on enamel hypoplasia: Waldron 2009). This individual was buried in a layer with evidence of extensive fire, which appears to have marked the end of the use of the settlement. Notably, close to the 'adolescent' was the skeleton of an older woman who was also afflicted by trauma and disease. Her cervical, thoracic and lumbar vertebrae show evidence of Schmorl's nodules (*cf.* Waldron 2009), whilst both tibiae revealed a periostitis of possible traumatic origin (*cf.* Aufderheide and Rodriguez-Martin 1998, 179 on the possible causes of periostisis and its diagnosis in ancient skeletal material; on the possible connection between trauma, disease and abnormal burial in Iron Age Veneto *cf.* also Perego this volume, and Perego *et al.* 2015; Saracino *et al.* 2014, with additional bibliography). Another 16–18-year-old individual was recovered from a pit dug and filled with charcoal and ash at the periphery of the Castenaso settlement in Emilia Romagna (eighth century BC: Silvestri 1994). With regard to the burial of 'adolescent' individuals in natural places of significance, it is worth recalling the human skeleton found in 1972 in a deep niche at the bottom of a rock fissure at Nago Torbole, Busa Brodeghera, in Trentino. Notably, the 19–20-year-old deceased suffered from a deformation of the heads of both femurs causing a 40° opening of the hips (fifth–third centuries BC: Corrain 1983).

Although discoveries of 'pubescent' and 'adolescent' subjects in the Iron Age cemeteries of northern Italy are rare, even in funerary contexts these individuals were sometimes given different mortuary treatments in respect to the rest of the buried community. For example, they might have occupied a liminal position in the cemetery space or might be buried with peculiar kinds of grave goods. An example might be Tomb 27 in the Via Tiepolo cemetery of Padua in Veneto (sixth century BC). Here the cremated remains of a 14–17-year-old individual were found in association with grave goods that have been linked to both the sub-adult and the adult ideological spheres. These grave goods were eight shells, a biconic pendant and a bone die, on the one hand, and a *pyxis*, a distaff and a complete toiletry set on the other (Ruta Serafini and Michelini 1990, 121–8). The tomb was probably placed in relation to a small burial mound, near other child inhumation and cremation burials, and close to the skeleton of a 41–60-year-old woman unusually buried in a prone position (on the latter *cf.* also Perego this volume). Another notable case is Tomb 4 from the Vàdena/Pfatten cemetery in Trentino–South Tyrol, dating from the fourth–third century BC. In this case, the skull, hands and feet of an 18–20-year-old female individual were unusually cremated, while the rest of the body was not. Her forearms were missing and two pieces of carbonized wood had the probable function of prostheses (Dal Rì 1992, 475–7). At the cemetery of Spina Valle Trebbia, in Emilia Romagna, Tombs 83 and 528 (fourth–third century BC) may have been the only graves in this cemetery to belong to 'pubescent/adolescent' subjects. Both died around the age of 12–16 years. The grave assemblages yielded four animal-shaped vases (*askoi*) and a bone die, which have been seen as related to the childhood sphere, and two bronze arrow points, which in the Valle Trebbia context are usually found in the graves of adults (Muggia 2004, 214–15). These instances – which represent only a limited list of examples – seem to confirm the ambiguous and liminal condition that 'pubescent' and 'adolescent' subjects might have been granted in late prehistoric and proto-historic northern Italy. In pre-industrial societies, this phenomenon is also well attested outside Italy (e.g. Turner 1969) as well as in other ancient Mediterranean societies. For instance, in Greek figurative art and archaeology, 'pubescent' and 'adolescent' subjects were often associated with images of liminal creatures which could symbolize the passage to death as well as the passage between infancy and adolescence. This interpretation can be applied to the figurines of terracotta centaurs from the eleventh-century BC west shrine at Phylakopi on Melos, a probable initiation site, and from the ninth-century BC cemetery of Lefkandi (Lawton 2007, 177–8). We can notice a kind of relationship between liminal creatures in the form of *Mischwesen* and sub-adult individuals also in pre-Roman Italy. Terracotta masks of satyrs found inside graves belonging to sub-adult individuals in northern, central and southern Italy seem to suggest, on the one hand, the liminal condition of the dead, on the other, the intention to protect the passage from life to death (Zanoni 2010; for *Mischwesen* in the Greek world *cf.* Aston 2011). Notably, the liminal status often associated with puberty may sometimes extend to age groups (such as potentially the 'young adults' found in *Brandopferplatz*-type sites) that in modern western societies would be classified under the label of 'adulthood'. This may own to the elaboration of social criteria for the attainment of adulthood and full social integration other than age development (e.g. childbearing or marriage: Montgomery 2012, 229).[5]

Indeed, puberty and adolescence are problematic categories to define, as they are marked by physical and psychological changes that may create a strong discrepancy between the skeletal and socio-cultural age of an individual (Sofaer Derevenski 2000; on the same issue *cf.* Di Lorenzo *et al.* this volume). They are periods of transition that intensify the differences between boys and girls, as shown by the growth of secondary sex characteristics. From an osteological and archaeological point of view, 'pubescent' and 'adolescent' subjects are very difficult to recognize in the funerary sphere, and this has led to a perceived absence of individuals belonging to this age-range from the archaeological record (Kleijvegt 1991, 112–13). We must take into account, however, that this presumptive absence might not be real, but related to a lack of social and ritual means (e.g. specific grave goods and burial rites) to represent in the funerary arena a category of subjects that were seen as suspended between two different 'dimensions'.[6] In ancient societies, the periods of transition between different phases of the lifecycle were often considered a sort of no man's land, that is, as life stages suspended between two diverse spheres of existence, usually childhood and adulthood (Eyben 1981, 329). 'Adolescents' and even 'young adults' not fully integrated in society, therefore, may have been considered liminal people who lived between two different systems of values and were not able to break their connections with childhood and achieve full integration into the world of the adults. This abnormality might relate to their inability to complete the rites of passage which probably structured the social attitudes towards time in ancient societies (on rites of passage *cf.* Toscano 2006, 310–2; Turner 1969; van Gennep 1909). This liminal or anomalous status, which might also invest subjects with perceived magical powers or those affected by disease and disabilities, may have been associated with the liminal geographical locations and elevated territorial features that tend to characterize the *Brandopferplatz*-type sites that yielded human remains.

Notes

1. Thanks to the increasing focus of Italian archaeologists on science-based approaches to the evidence, the interpretation of the archaeological record is increasingly enhanced through the fundamental contribution of osteological data (e.g. Manacorda 2008, 230–2).

2. Springs were also associated with ritual sites that may not fit the general description of *Brandopferplätze*. In our study area these include Bolzano S. Maurizio, where about 3000 bronze rings have been found near a spring (Baggio and Dal Rì 2006, 83–8) and Telfes im Stubai, near the Brenner Pass. Telfes is located near sulphurous water sources, around which were deposited ceramic vessels and animal bones (Baggio and Dal Rì 2006, 88). Other relevant ritual sites were also located near water sources: for example, Capo di Ponte is near the Oglio and Serio Rivers, while Somma Lombardo and Polcenigo are situated along the Ticino and Degano Rivers, respectively. Furthermore, Raveo is located at the confluence of the Degano and Tagliamento Rivers. The site of Mechel was considered a spring sanctuary (*Quellenheiligtum*) by Lunz (1974, 159).

3. Obviously, the MNI from each single site considered here is not comparable to that from the largest formal cemeteries discovered at many Iron Age settlements of northern Italy. It seems still significant, however, that children and individuals older than 30 at death were generally not chosen to be placed in *Brandopferplätze*. Clearly, we must take into account that no estimate of age for adults and juveniles can be expressed without a margin of error.

4. These average estimates may be altered by socio-cultural factors and peculiar situations of high mortality (e.g. famine, natural disaster and conflict mortality: Chamberlain 2006, 69–79).

5. For example, in commenting upon the *dipo* initiation rituals of the Krobo (Ghana), Adjaye (1999, 25–6) notes "contradictions of youthhood had clearly not been resolved, as the graduates are not fully recognized as adults. Dipo does not really establish equality between an initiate and her adult counterparts in the social world. For most of the ritual subjects, physical and emotional maturity is yet to be attained, let alone adult independence. In reality, it is marriage rather than initiation that confers womanhood onto females ... Far from terminating feelings of youthhood and locating graduates into the secure state of adulthood and womanhood, *dipo* initiates find themselves indeed at a dangerous crossroad, an intersection laden with anxiety, ambiguity, and ambivalence ...".

6. However, ethnographic and historical accounts suggest that, in pre-industrial societies, individuals in their second decade of life display on average the minimum risk of death (e.g. Chamberlain 2006, 62, 67).

Bibliography

Adam, A.M. (1991) Traces de lieux de culte de l'âge du Fer en Frioul. In M. Mirabella Roberti (ed.) *Preistoria e Protostoria dell'Alto Adriatico. Atti della XXI Settimana di Studi Aquileiesi (21–26 Aprile 1990)*, 45–70. Udine, Arti Grafiche Friulane.

Adams, E. (2007) Time and chance: Unravelling temporality in North-Central Neopalatial Crete. *American Journal of Archaeology* 111(3), 391–421.

Adjaye, J.K. (1999) Dangerous crossroads: Liminality and contested meaning in Krobo (Ghana) dipo girls' initiation. *Journal of African Cultural Studies* 12(1), 5–26.

Alberti, A. (1997) New data on the Vadena (BZ) necropolis: The 1989–1997 excavations. *Preistoria Alpina* 33, 167–169.

Alberti, A., Dal Rì, L., Marzoli, C. and Tecchiati, U. (2005) Evidenze relative al X, IX, VIII sec. a.C.. nell'ambito dell'alto bacino del fiume Adige (Cultura di Luco-Meluno). In G. Bartoloni and F. Delpino (eds) *Oriente e Occidente: Metodi e Discipline a Confronto. Riflessioni sulla Cronologia dell'Età del Ferro Italiana. Atti dell'Incontro di Studi (Roma, 30-31 Ottobre 2003)*, 227–238. Pisa–Roma, Istituti Editoriali e Poligrafici Internazionali.

Aspök, E. (2008) What actually is a 'deviant burial'? Comparing German language and Anglophone research on 'deviant burials'. In E.M. Murphy (ed.) *Deviant Burial in the Archaeological Record*, 17–34. Oxford, Oxbow Books.

Aston, E. (2011) *Mixanthropoi. Animal-human Hybrid Deities in Greek Religion* (Kernos Supplement 25). Liege, Centre International d'Etude de la Religion Grecque Antique.

Aufderheide, A.C. and Rodriguez-Martin, C. (1998) (eds) *The Cambridge Encyclopedia of Human Palaeopathology*. Cambridge, Cambridge University Press.

Baggio, E. and Dal Rì, R. (2006) Ritrovamenti archeologici nella conca di Bolzano: Notizie d'archivio e dati inediti. In E. Bianchin Citton and M. Tirelli (eds) *ut...rosae... ponerentur. Scritti di Archeologia in Ricordo di Giovanna Luisa Ravagnan* (Quaderni di Archeologia del Veneto, Serie Speciale 2), 83–94. Roma, Quasar.

Bellintani, P. (2000) *Quando le Cattedrali erano Verdi. Antichi Culti del Trentino. Catalogo della Mostra Itinerante (Riva del Garda, 29 Aprile 2000-28 Febbraio 2001)*. Rovereto, Provincia Autonoma di Trento.

Bertolone, M. (1960) Vagabondaggi paletnologici e archeologici in Lombardia. *SIBRIUM* 5, 89–122.

Bettencourt, A.M.S. (2010) Burials, corpses and offerings in the Bronze Age of NW Iberia as agents of social identity and memory. In A.M.S. Bettencourt, M.J. Sanches, L.B. Alves and R. Fábregas Valcarce (eds) *Conceptualising Space and Place. On the Role of Agency, Memory and Identity in the Construction of Space from the Upper Palaeolithic to the Iron Age in Europe* (BAR S2058), 33–45. Oxford, Archaeopress.

Bietti Sestieri, A.M. (2011) Archeologia della morte fra età del Bronzo ed età del Ferro in Italia. Implicazioni delle scelte relative alla sepoltura in momenti di crisi o di trasformazione politico-organizzativa. In V. Nizzo (ed.) *Dalla Nascita alla Morte: Antropologia e Archeologia a Confronto. Atti dell'Incontro Internazionale di Studi in Onore di Claude Lévi-Strauss (Roma, Museo Nazionale Preistorico Etnografico "Luigi Pigorini", 21 Maggio 2010)*, 397–418. Roma, E.S.S Editorial Service.

Bonghi Jovino, M. (2007) A proposito di sacrifici umani e rituali sacri in area mediterranea (Tarquinia) e sepolture in abitato (Italia centro-settentrionale). In G.M. Della Fina (ed.) *Etruschi, Greci, Fenici e Cartaginesi nel Mediterraneo Centrale. Atti del XIV Convegno Internazionale di Studi sulla Storia e l'Archeologia dell'Etruria (Orvieto, Palazzo dei Congressi, 24-26 Novembre 2006)* (Annali della Fondazione per il Museo Claudio Faina 14), 455–475. Roma, Quasar.

Cardarelli, A. and Pellacani, G. (2010) Il luogo di culto del Bronzo Recente di Monte S. Giulia nell'Appennino modenese. Poster presented at the XLV IIPP Conference, Modena, 26–31 Ottobre 2010.

Cassola Guida, P. and Corazza, S. (2004–2005) Dai tumuli ai castellieri: 1500 anni di storia in Friuli (2000-500 a.C.) *Aquileia Nostra* 75, 525–552.

Chamberlain, A. (2006) *Demography in Archaeology*. Cambridge, Cambridge University Press.

Ciurletti, G. (2007) Il Monte S. Martino. Un sito archeologico tra preistoria ed età moderna. In G. Ciurletti (ed.) *Fra il Garda e le Alpi di Ledro. Monte S. Martino. Il Luogo di Culto (Ricerche e Scavi 1969-1979)*, 17–95. Trento, Soprintendenza per i Beni Archeologici.

Constantini, R. (2002) *Sebatum*. Roma, "L'Erma" di Bretschneider.

Conzato, A., Rizzi, J. and Tecchiati, U. (2012) Analisi archeozoologica, antropologica e istologica di resti cremati provenienti dai livelli dell'età del Rame di Velturno-Tanzgasse (BZ). In J. De Grossi Mazzorin, D. Saccà and C. Tozzi (eds) *Atti del 6° Convegno Nazionale di Archeozoologia (Centro Visitatori del Parco dell'Orecchiella, 21-24 Maggio 2009. San Romano in Garfagnana-Lucca)*, 131–136. Lucca, Università di Pisa.

Corrain, C. (1983) Ricerche antropologiche su resti umani antichi del Trentino del decennio 1972–1982. *Beni Culturali del Trentino* 2, 23–28.

Dal Rì, L. (1992) Note sull'insediamento e la necropoli di Vàdena (Alto Adige). In G. Metzger and P. Gleirscher (eds) *Die Räter/I Reti*, 475–522. Bolzano, Athesia.

De Min, M. (2005) Il mondo religioso dei Veneti antichi. In M. De Min, G. Gambacurta and A. Ruta Serafini (eds) *La Città Invisibile. Padova Preromana: Trent'Anni di Scavi e Ricerche. Catalogo della Mostra*, 113–121. Bologna, Tipoarte.

De Polignac, F. (1989) *Cults, Territory, and the Origin of the Greek City-State*. Chicago, University of Chicago Press.

DiGangi, E.A. and Moore, M.K. (2012) *Research Methods in Human Skeletal Biology*. San Diego, Academic Press.

Endrizzi, L., Degasperi, N. and Marzatico, F. (2009) Luoghi di culto nell'area retica. In G. Cresci Marrone and M. Tirelli (eds) Altnoi. *Il Santuario Altinate: Strutture del Sacro a Confronto e i Luoghi di Culto lungo la Via Annia. Atti del Convegno (Venezia 4-6 Dicembre 2006)*, 263–292. Roma, Quasar.

Eyben, E. (1972) Antiquity's view of puberty. *Latomus* 31, 678–697.

Eyben, E. (1981) Was the Roman youth an adult socially? *L'Antiquitè Classique* 50, 328–350.

Fabbri, F.P. (2001) Sepolture primarie, secondarie e ossari: Esempi dal cimitero medievale di Roca Vecchia (Lecce). *Rivista di Antropologia* 79, 113–136.

Fornaciari, G. and Mallegni, F. (1980) Iperostosi porotica verosimilmente talassemica in due scheletri rinvenuti in un gruppo di tombe del III secolo a.C. di S. Giovenale (Viterbo). *Quaderni di Scienze Antropologiche* 4, 21–50.

Furlani, U. (1974–1975) Una necropoli dell'età del Ferro sul Monte di Medea. *Aquileia Nostra* 45–46, 31–56.

Gambari, F.M. (2001) L'area per le offerte combuste (Brandopferplatz). In F.M. Gambari (ed.) *La Birra e il Fiume. Pombia e le Vie dell'Ovest Ticino tra VI e V secolo a.C.. Catalogo della Mostra (Oleggio, Museo Civico Etnografico "C.G. Franchini", 21 Aprile-31 Ottobre 2001)*, 85–92. Torino, CELID.

Ginzburg, C. (1966) *I Benandanti. Stregoneria e Culti Agrari tra Cinquecento e Seicento*. Torino, Einaudi.

Gleirscher, P. (1991–1993) Campo Paraiso: Un «Brandopferplatz» tipo Rungger Egg? In P. Brugnoli and L. Salzani (eds) *L'Archeologia Preistorica e Protostorica dell'Area Prealpina e Centroalpina con Particolare Riferimento alla Valpolicella e alla Valdadige*, 111–134. Annuario Storico della Valpolicella.

Gleirscher, P. (2002a) Alpine brandopferplätze. In L. Zemmer Planck (ed.) *Kult der Vorzeit in den Alpen. Opfergaben, Opferplätze, Opferbrauchtum*, 591–634. Bozen, Athesia.

Gleirscher, P. (2002b) Brandopferplätze in den Ostalpen. In P. Gleirscher, H. Nothdurfter and E. Schubert (eds) *Das Rungger Egg. Untersuchungen an einem eisenzeitlichen Brandopferplatz bei Seis am Schlern in Südtirol*, 173–258. Maeinz am Rhein, P. Von Zabern.

Guidi, A. (2008) Archeologia dell'early state: Il caso di studio italiano. *OCNUS* 16, 175–192.

Kleijvegt, M. (1991) *Ancient Youth. The Ambiguity of Youth and the Absence of Adolescence in Greek-Roman Society*. Amsterdam, Gieben.

Knapp, A.B. and Ashmore, W. (1999) Archaeological landscapes: Constructed, conceptualized, ideational. In A.B. Knapp and W. Ashmore (eds) *Archaeologies of Landscape: Contemporary Perspectives*, 1–32. Oxford, Blackwell.

Krämer, W. (1966) Prähistorische brandopferplätze. In R. Degen, W. Drak, and R. Wyss (eds) *Helvetia Antiqua. Festschrift Emil Vogt. Beiträge zur Prähistorie und Archäologie der Schweiz*, 111–123. Zürich, Conzett & Huber.

Lawton, C.L. (2007) Children in classical Attic votive reliefs. In A. Cohen and J. Rutter (eds) *Constructions of Childhood in Ancient Greece and Italy* (Hesperia Supplement 41), 41–60. Princeton, American School of Classical Studies at Athens.

Loney, H.L. and Hoaen, A.W. (2005) Landscape, memory and material culture: Interpreting diversity in the Iron Age. *Proceedings of the Prehistoric Society* 61, 361–378.

Lunz, R. (1974) *Studien zur Endbronzezeit und älteren Eisenzeit im Südalpenraum*. Firenze, Sansoni.

Mahlknecht, M. (2002) (Toten-) Kultplatz am Noafer Bühl. In U. Tecchiati (ed.) *Der Heilige Winkel. Der Bozner Talkessel zwischen der Späten Bronzezeit und der Romanisierung (13.-1. Jh. V. Ch.)*, 125–138. Bozen–Wien, FOLIO.

Mallegni, F., Bertoldi, F. and Onisto, N. (1999). I Paleoveneti: Aspetti paleobiologici e relative problematiche interpretative. In O. Paoletti (ed.) *Protostoria e Storia del "Venetorum Angulus". Atti del XX Convegno di Studi Etruschi ed Italici (Portogruaro-Quarto d'Altino-Este-Adria, 16-19 Ottobre 1996)*, 159–168. Borgo S. Lorenzo, All'Insegna del Giglio.

Manacorda, D. (2008) *Lezioni di Archeologia*. Bari, Laterza.

Marconi, S. and Tecchiati, U. (2006) La fauna del villaggio della prima età del Ferro del Thalerbühel di Tires (Bz). Economia, uso del territorio e strategie insediative tra II e I millennio a.C.. In A. Curci and D. Vitali (eds) *Animali tra Uomini e Dei. Archeozoologia del Mondo Preromano. Atti del Convegno Internazionale (8-9 Novembre 2002)*, 11–26. Bologna, Ante Quem.

Marzatico, F. (1992) Il complesso tardo La Téne di Stenico nelle Valli Giudicarie: Nuovi dati sulla romanizzazione in Trentino. *Festschrift zum 50jährigen Bestehen des Institutes für Ur- und Frühgeschichte der Leopold-Franzens Universität Innsbruck* 8, 317–338.

Marzoli, C. (2004) Castelfelder, località Falzion. *Denkmlapflege in Südtirol/Tutela dei Beni Culturali in Sudtirolo* 3, 218–219.

Mayne Correira, P.M. (1997) Fire modifications of bones: A review of the literature. In W.D. Haglund and M.H. Sorg (eds) *Forensic Taphonomy: The Post-mortem Fate of Human Remains*. Austin, CRC Press.

Mazzucchi, A. (2010) Giaciture non convenzionali nella preistoria del Trentino. In M.G. Belcastro and J. Ortalli (eds) *Sepolture Anomale. Indagini Archeologiche e Antropologiche dall'Epoca Classica al Medioevo in Emilia Romagna. Giornata di Studi (Castelfranco Emilia, 19 Dicembre 2009)* (Quaderni di Archeologia dell'Emilia Romagna 28), 141–146. Borgo S. Lorenzo, All'Insegna del Giglio.

Meyer Orlac, R. (1997) Zur Problematik von "Sonderbestattungen" in der Archäologie. In K.-F. Rittershofer (ed.) *Sonderbestattungen in der Bronzezeit im östlichen Mitteleuropa. Kolloquium der Arbeitsgemeinschaft Bronzezeit in Pottenstein 1990* (Internationale Archäologie 37), 1–10. Espelkamp, Verlag Marie Leidorf.

Montgomery, H. (2012) *An Introduction to Childhood: Anthropological Perspectives on Children's Lives*. Malden MA, Wiley Blackwell.

Muggia, A. (2004) *Impronte nella Sabbia. Tombe Infantili e di Adolescenti dalla Necropoli di Valle Trebba a Spina* (Quaderni di Archeologia dell'Emilia Romagna 9). Borgo S. Lorenzo, All'Insegna del Giglio.

Nizzo, V. (2011) «Antenati bambini». Visibilità e invisibilità dell'infanzia nei sepolcreti dell'Italia tirrenica dalla prima età del Ferro all'Orientalizzante: Dalla discriminazione funeraria alla costruzione dell'identità. In V. Nizzo (ed.) *Dalla Nascita alla Morte: Antropologia e Archeologia a Confronto. Atti dell'Incontro Internazionale di Studi in Onore di Claude Lévi-Strauss (Roma, Museo Nazionale Preistorico Etnografico "Luigi Pigorini", 21 Maggio 2010)*, 51–94. Roma, E.S.S. Editorial Service System.

Nothdurfter, H. and Schubert, E. (1985) Ein Brandopferplatz am Runggeregg in Seis. *Tutela dei Beni Culturali in Alto Adige* 1985, 243–252.

Onisto, N. (2004) Note antropologiche sugli inumati. *Quaderni di Archeologia del Veneto* 20, 95–97.

Parkin, T. (2013) The demography of infancy and early childhood in the ancient world. In J. Evans Grubbs, T. Parkin and R. Bell (eds) *The Oxford Handbook of Childhood and Education in the Classical World*. New York, Oxford University Press.

Perego, E. (2012) Resti umani come oggetti del sacro nel Veneto preromano: Osservazioni preliminari. In V. Nizzo and L. La Rocca (eds) *Antropologia e Archeologia a Confronto: Rappresentazioni e Pratiche del Sacro. Atti del Convegno (Roma, Museo Preistorico Etnografico "Luigi Pigorini", 20-21 Maggio 2011)*, 873–882. Roma, E.S.S. Editorial Service System.

Perego, E., Saracino, M., Zamboni, L. and Zanoni, V. (2015) Practices of ritual marginalisation in protohistoric Veneto: Evidence from the field. In Z.L. Devlin and E.J. Graham (eds) *Death Embodied: Archaeological Approaches to the Treatment of the Corpse*, 129–159. Oxford, Oxbow Books.

Petrucci, G., Donat, P., and Vitri, S. (2005) La fauna di età primo-medio imperiale del sito d'altura di Raveo Monte Sorantri (Carnia-UD). In G. Malerba and P. Visentini (eds) *Atti del 4° Convegno Nazionale di Archeozoologia (Pordenone, 13-15 Novembre 2003)*, 413–420. Pordenone, Comune di Pordenone, Museo Archeologico.

Poggiani Keller, R. (2002) Il sito con stele e massi-menhir di Ossimo Pat in Valcamonica (Italia): Una persistenza di culto tra età del Rame ed età del Ferro? In L. Zemmer Planck (ed.) *Kult der Vorzeit in den Alpen. Opfergaben-Opferplätze-Opferbrauchtum/Culti nella Preistoria delle Alpi. Le Offerte-i Santuari-i Riti. Catalogo della Mostra (Innsbruck, 1997)*, 377–389. Innsbruck, Tiroler Landesmuseum Ferdinandeum.

Poggiani Keller, R. and Baioni, M. (2005) Sabbio Chiese (Bs). Dos de la Rocchetta, Rasine. Sito dell'antica età del Bronzo e area di culto dell'età del Ferro. *Notiziario della Soprintendenza Archeologica della Lombardia* 2005, 83–84.

Radi, N., Mariotti, V., Riga, A., Zampetti, S., Villa, C. and Belcastro, M.G. (2013) Variation of the anterior aspect of the femoral head-neck junction in a modern human identified skeletal collection. *American Journal of Physical Anthropology* 152(2), 261–272.

Renhart, S. (2002) Menschen im Heiligen Winkel. In U. Tecchiati (ed.) *Der Heilige Winkel. Der Bozner Talkessel zwischen der Späten Bronzezeit und der Romanisierung (13.-1. Jh.V. Ch.)*, 389–398. Bozen–Wien, FOLIO.

Ruta Serafini, A. and Michelini, P. (1990) Tomba 27. In A. Ruta Serafini (ed.) *La Necropoli Paleoveneta di Via Tiepolo a Padova. Un Intervento Archeologico nella Città. Catalogo della Mostra (Padova, Via Aquileia 7, 28 Aprile-28 Giugno 1990)*, 121–128. Padova, Zielo.

Salzani, L. (1978) Un ritrovamento dell'età del Ferro presso Castelrotto. *Bollettino del Museo Civico di Storia Naturale di Verona* 5, 515–522.

Salzani, L. and Consonni, A. (2005) L'abitato protostorico di Villa Marzana-Campo Michela (RO). Scavi 1993. *Padusa* 41, 7–55.

Saracino, M., Zamboni, L., Zanoni, V. and Perego, E. (2014) Investigating social exclusion in late prehistoric Italy: Preliminary results of the "IN or OUT" Project (Phase 1). *Papers from the Institute of Archaeology* 12(1), 1–12.

Seppilli, A. (1977) *Sacralità dell'Acqua e Sacrilegio dei Ponti*. Palermo, Sellerio.

Silvestri, E. (1994) La necropoli e l'insediamento: Campagne di scavo 1972-75 e ricerche di superficie. In M. Forte and P. von Eles (eds) *La Pianura Bolognese nel Villanoviano. Insediamenti della Prima Età del Ferro. Catalogo della Mostra (Villanova di Castenaso, 24 Settembre 1994-8 Gennaio 1995)*, 139–151. Borgo S. Lorenzo, All'Insegna del Giglio.

Sofaer Derevenski, J. (2000) Material culture shock: Confronting expectations in the material culture of children. In J. Sofaer Derevenski (ed.) *Children and Material Culture*, 3–16. London–New York, Routledge.

Solano, S. (2006–2007) *Forme Minori del Popolamento della Valcamonica fra Tarda Età del Ferro e Romanizzazione. Insediamenti e Luoghi di Culto*. Unpublished thesis, Università degli Studi di Pavia.

Solano, S. (2010) Santuari di età romana su luoghi di culto protostorici: Borno e Capo di Ponte. In F. Rossi (ed.) *Il Santuario di Minerva. Un Luogo di Culto a Breno tra Protostoria ed Età Romana*, 465–480. Milano, ET.

Steiner, H. (2007) Die Bronze- und urnenfelderzeitliche Siedlung. In H. Steiner (ed.) *Die befestigte Siedlung am Ganglegg im Vinschgau, Südtirol. Ergebnisse der Ausgrabungen 1997-2001 (Bronze-Urnenfelderzeit) und natur-wissenschaftliche Beiträge*, 17–394. Bozen, Temi Editrice.

Tecchiati, U. (2000) Origine e significato dei luoghi di roghi votivi nella preistoria e nella protostoria dell'Alto Adige. Osservazioni di metodo. In J. Niederwanger and U. Tecchiati (eds) *Acqua, Fuoco, Cielo. Un Luogo di Roghi Votivi di Minatori della Tarda Età del Bronzo*, 5–8. Bolzano, Museo Archeologico dell'Alto Adige.

Tecchiati, U. (2007) Luoghi di culto e assetti territoriali nell'età del Rame della regione atesina. In S. Casini and A. Fossati (eds) *Le Pietre degli Dei. Statue-Stele dell'Età del Rame in Europa. Lo Stato della Ricerca. Atti del Congresso Internazionale (Brescia, 16-18 Settembre 2004)*, 15–30. Bergamo, Museo Civico Archeologico.

Tecchiati, U. (2011) Sepolture umane e resti sparsi in abitati della preistoria e protostoria dell'Italia settentrionale, con particolare riferimento al Trentino Alto Adige. In S. Casini (ed.) *Il Filo del Tempo. Studi di Preistoria e Protostoria in Onore di Raffaele Carlo de Marinis*, 49–63. Bergamo, Museo Civico Archeologico.

Torggler, A. (2002) Die Vorgeschichtlichenfunde von Greifenstein (Gemeinde Jenesien). In U. Tecchiati (ed.) *Der Heilige Winkel. Der Bozner Talkessel zwischen der Späten Bronzezeit und der Romanisierung (13. - 1. Jh.V. Ch.)*, 139–154. Bozen–Wien, FOLIO.

Toscano, M.A. (2006) *Introduzione alla Sociologia*. Milano, Zanichelli.

Turner, V. (1969) *The Ritual Process. Structure and Anti-Structure*. New York, Aldine de Gruyter.

Ubelaker, D.H. (1978) Human skeletal remains. Excavations, analysis, interpretations. *Manuals on Archaeology* 2, 92–94.

Valvo, A. (1996) Il bassorilievo di Bormio e il culto di Volcanus nelle Alpi retiche. *Archeologia Classica* 48, 111–141.

van Gennep, A. (1909) *Les Rites de Passage*. Paris, Nouri.

Vitri, S., Gambacurta, G., Angelini, A., Giacomello, R., Michelini, P., Spanghero, T., De Cecco, C. and Passera, L. (2006) Polcenigo (Pn). San Giovanni, località Sottocolle. "Necropoli di S. Floriano". Scavi 2006. *Notiziario della Soprintendenza per i Beni Archeologici del Friuli Venezia Giulia* 1, 24–32.

Voltolini, D. (2013) Tomba Emo 468. In M. Gamba, G. Gambacurta, A. Ruta Serafini, V. Tiné and F. Veronese (eds) *Venetkens. Viaggio nella Terra dei Veneti Antichi. Catalogo della Mostra (Padova, Palazzo della Ragione, 6 Aprile-17 Novembre 2013)*, 351. Venezia, Marsilio.

von den Driesch, A. and Schröter, P. (2002) Zu den Brandknochen von Rungger Egg. In P. Gleirscher, H. Nothdurfter and E. Schubert (eds) *Das Rungger Egg. Untersuchungen an einem eisenzeitlichen Brandopferplatz bei Seis am Schlern in Südtirol*, 33–35. Meinz am Rhein, P. Von Zabern.

Walker, P.L., Bathurst, R.R., Richman, R., Gjerdrum, T. and Andrushko, V.A. (2009) The causes of porotic hyperostosis and cribra orbitalia: A reappraisal of the iron-deficiency-anemia hypothesis. *American Journal of Physical Anthropology* 139(2), 109–125.

Zampieri, A. (2006) Manufatti litici nei corredi funebri dell'età del Ferro nell'Italia nord-orientale. *Padusa* 42, 129–148.

Zanforlin, L. (2008) Der eisenzeitlichen Fundplatz in der Galizienstraße in Leifers. *Der Schlern* 82, 22–37.

Zanoni, V. (2010) Dietro la maschera. Contesti e funzioni di modellini fittili di maschere dalla necropoli in località Calvario (Tarquinia, Viterbo). *ACME* 63(3), 309–324.

Zanoni, V. (2011) *Out of Place. Human Skeletal Remains from Non-Funerary Contexts: Northern Italy during the 1st Millennium BC* (BAR S2306). Oxford, Archaeopress.

Zanoni V. (2012) Tra la persona e l'oggetto: Giaciture infantili in abitato durante l'età del Ferro dell'Italia settentrionale. In C. Chiaramonte Trerè, G. Bagnasco Gianni and F. Chiesa (eds) *Interpretando l'Antico. Scritti di Archeologia Offerti a Maria Bonghi Jovino* (Volume 2), 699–716. Milano, Monduzzi.

Zifferero, A. (2005) Economia, divinità e frontiera: Sul ruolo di alcuni santuari di confine in Etruria meridionale. *Ostraka* 2, 333–350.

Chapter 12

Inequality, abuse and increased socio-political complexity in Iron Age Veneto, *c.* 800–500 BC

Elisa Perego

Introduction

This paper explores the relationship between agency, violence and social change in light of archaeological and osteological evidence from the region of Veneto in north-east Italy. It also explores notions of power and powerlessness by focusing on the complex ritual practices adopted by Venetic people to ensure (a) the correct location of each individual in an increasingly hierarchical social framework and (b) the persistence of the local social order in phases of dramatic socio-political transformation.

Given the emphasis of this volume on the identification of alternative social subjects vis-a-vis élite members, this chapter will explore the rise of increasingly sophisticated forms of political authority in proto-historic Veneto, *c.* 800–500 BC, by focusing on non-normative funerary treatment. In particular, I shall discuss how ritual practices of appropriation and abuse of the human body, presumably carried out by privileged social groups, are evident in relation to marginal inhumation burials which display marked anomalous features, including mutilation, careless interment, incomplete cremation, burial in a prone position, exclusion from the formal burial ground, location in marginal cemetery areas and association with probable sacrificial remains such as charcoal, broken pottery, fragmented animal bones and incomplete animal carcasses. The hypothesis that human sacrifice and forms of ritual exploitation of non-cremated human remains by the élite were not unknown practices in proto-historic Veneto will be discussed. I shall emphasize how during the Iron Age these phenomena appear to have been particularly well attested between the eighth and the sixth centuries BC, an important phase of social development that immediately preceded and accompanied the rise of new forms of socio-political organization in the region under study.

This paper is threefold. In a first section, I shall present my dataset and methodological framework. In particular, I shall discuss how personhood and agency theory, and Bourdieu's notion of *habitus* (Bourdieu 1990, 66–7), can be used to frame an investigation of violence and social change in the context under study. In a second section, I shall detail the role of Venetic funerary rituals in sustaining inequality. Furthermore, I shall discuss how the variability of Venetic funerary practices sheds light on the role of social agents in negotiating complex and diverging forms of hierarchy and social inclusion at the time of the funeral. In particular, I shall show that the rare inhumation ritual often associated with marginality was indeed linked to a variety of behaviours and individual situations ranging from the partial integration of the deceased in society, to the complete dehumanization of individuals subjected to practices of physical abuse and abnormal mortuary treatment. The exploitation of human remains in the ritual context is the subject of the following section, which focuses on evidence from the ritual site of Padua Via S. Eufemia, where human sacrifice may have been carried out alongside the slaughtering of animals and feasting. This section is completed by a discussion of social and cultural change in Veneto, *c.* 800–500 BC, which offers a reflection on the social role of violence in historical phases of instability and tumultuous socio-political transformation.

Data, theory and methodology

The analysis proposed in this chapter is based on a sample of *c.* 2000 graves from approximately 40 Venetic sites, corresponding to about 100 different cemeteries, settlement contexts and ritual areas where human remains have been found (Perego 2012a, 340–404, 417–802). The sampled sites include both some of the major Venetic settlements such as Este, Altino and Padua, and minor locales fully detailed in Perego 2012a (for the location of the main sampled sites *cf.* Fig. 12.1). The sample has been assembled for the preparation of my doctoral thesis (Perego 2012a) and covers a time-span of approximately 1200 years between the Final Bronze Age and the early Roman period (*c.* 1200/1100 BC–AD 25). This article, however, will mainly focus on funerary evidence dating to *c.* 800–500 BC. Given that the deposition of more than one individual in the same tomb or even in the same cremation urn was a relatively common feature of Venetic funerary rites, the number of sampled burials (i.e. individuals) is at least 25% higher than the number of sampled graves. This percentage, however, may vary in different locations and chronological phases (e.g. Perego 2012a, 160–89). Furthermore, an accurate estimate of the number of individuals buried in all the sampled graves is impossible because of a partial lack of osteological analysis and the poor preservation of some contexts.

The vast majority of the sampled graves are cremations, as incineration was by far the most common funerary rite in late prehistoric Veneto (e.g. Bianchin Citton *et al.* 1998; Bondini 2008; Chieco Bianchi and Calzavara Capuis 1985; 2006; Fogolari and Prosdocimi 1988; Michelini and Ruta Serafini 2005; Perego 2012a, 214–5;

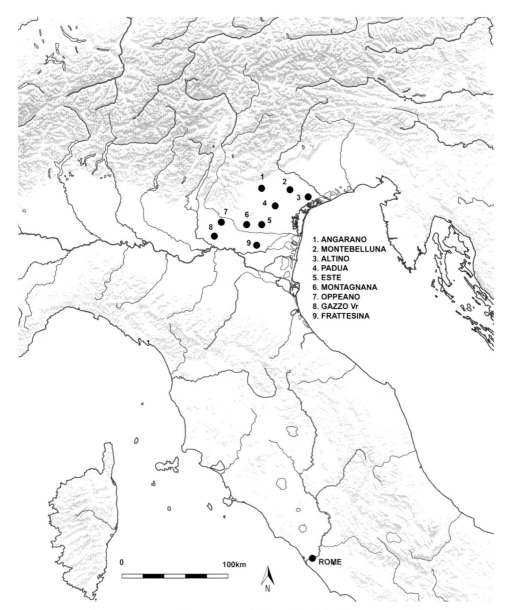

Fig. 12.1: Map of Veneto region with main sampled sites (modified by E. Perego after Perego 2014a; base map courtesy of the Ancient World Mapping Center).

Salzani 2001a; 2005; 2008a). All the cremation graves considered have been found in formal funerary areas created around the major settlements or in small clusters located near villages and farmsteads in the countryside. Inhumation tombs represent *c.* 10% of my PhD sample. However, the ratio of inhumation to cremation graves varied widely across the region (Perego 2014a). The minimum number of buried individuals is 280 (Perego 2012a, 213). These come from *c.* 270 different micro-contexts including formal graves, the floor of huts in settlement areas and discard or ritual pits where non-cremated human remains were deposited outside formal cemeteries (for burials recently published and not analyzed in Perego 2012a: e.g. Gamba *et al.* 2013; Salzani and Colonna 2010; for recent research on Veneto *cf.* IIPP 2015). The precise number of inhumation burials cannot be established because of the sporadic but sometimes intentional deposition of scattered human remains not clearly ascribable to one individual or more (Perego 2012a, 244–5; Zanoni 2011).

The scope of my doctoral research was to explore how personhood was constructed in late prehistoric, proto-historic and early Roman Veneto, especially in relation to wider socio-historical changes in Venetic society. The results of my analysis that are relevant to this article are presented below. While a discussion of Venetic personhood is beyond the scope of this chapter, personhood theory is useful to contextualize major issues of community membership, marginality and social inclusion that are widely addressed in this volume (*cf.* chapters by Cuozzo, Di Lorenzo *et al.*, Iaia, Perego and Scopacasa, Scopacasa and Zanoni). By drawing on anthropological research emphasizing the nexus between power and the construction of ideologically driven and culturally variable notions of 'humanity' and social inclusion (e.g. Bordo 1993; Morgan 1997; 2002[1989]; 2006; 2009), I define personhood as a moral categorization discriminating between those individuals that are fully or partially integrated in society and those denied such membership (Perego 2012a, 1; for alternative definitions of personhood and the current debate in archaeology *cf.* for example Brück 2004; Fowler 2004; Knapp and van Dommelen 2008; *cf.* also Shipley, O'Donoghue, the introduction and Perego and Scopacasa this volume, with additional bibliography; *cf.* also Perego 2015, forthcoming and 2014a, with bibliography). The ascription of personhood is a complex socio-political process which entails the creation of both privilege and marginality (e.g. Busby 1999; Fortes 1987; Morris 1994, 112–7). Every human group develops notions about the relative value of both its members and other human beings. Culturally variable understandings of gender, age, ethnicity, social affiliation, kinship, health and the self are among the factors that may determine the recognition of a human being as a valued member of society, or his or her exclusion from full group membership (e.g. Conklin and Morgan 1996; Lamb 1997; Morgan 1997; 2002[1989]; 2006; 2009).

In this chapter, I build upon my previous research on personhood to explore how inequality and discrimination were constructed in the context examined. Basic to my argument is the idea that power is ubiquitous in society (e.g. Bourdieu 1977; 1990; Foucault in Gaventa 2003; Navarro 2006, 18) and that ritual represents a powerful arena for the negotiation of ideologies of inequality at different levels of scale. In the Veneto region, personhood – the degree of social integration granted to people – was the outcome of struggles for power that took material form and became visible in the hierarchical arrangement of local cemeteries and cult sites.[1] An issue looming larger in the social sciences is the respective role of agents and structure in determining the hierarchical makeup of social institutions (review in Gaventa 2003). While this chapter does not aim to provide an answer to this question, I note that:

1. As suggested by a number of social scientists, the relation between agency and structure is dialectic (e.g. Giddens 1984).[2] While the identification of aspects of personal volition and individual action is often a difficult task for archaeologists (e.g. Dobres and Robb 2000; Gardner 2004), our discipline can offer powerful insights into the nature of agency as a deep entanglement between structure and praxis[3] – a reality in which 'agency' never overlaps with free will, but always emerges through the everyday struggle/engagement against/with/within the material world we live in. Material culture, which is the primary subject of archaeology, can be understood both as a reification – a materialization – of the structures (of power) that determine its production, and the making of people who act in theworld. Ritual, which I shall analyze as a means enabling authority, was reified – took a tangible form – in the material debris that archaeologists recover in the field.

2. Furthermore, archaeology favours multi-scalar analyses of social change based on an investigation of (a) both long- and short-term processes and (b) micro-, meso- and macro-contexts. This allows us to uncover both (a) large-scale social trends in the negotiation of personhood and (b) micro-scale practices meaningful to small social groups only in limited time-spans; it also allows us to develop an investigation of structure in the *longue durée*, and of individual actions in the short-term (e.g. Perego 2011). This multi-scalar analysis is pertinent to the nature of personhood itself, which is the complex interplay between largely shared social rules concerning what a meaningful human being is and personal beliefs played out by each individual on a daily basis (Perego 2012a, 101).

3. In Veneto, the nature of personhood and authority changed over time while society developed towards urbanization and presumably statehood. Coercion and violence were important aspects of this process. However, more subtle mechanisms of governance and resistance were enacted by Venetic agents in different social fields; complex strategies were probably adopted to mask – at least in certain contexts – the extent of the existing social discrimination.[4] Nonetheless, violence might have erupted in outbursts possibly representing the response of élite groups to social pressure and turmoil.[5]

4. Social actors were able to strive consciously for or against social dominance: this is indicated, for instance, by variations in the ritual practice attested at the micro-level, which suggest attempts at altering structure, or coping with social diversity, change and socio-cultural stimuli from outside Venetic society (e.g. Perego 2011).

5. However, ideologies of inequality also spread through *habitus*. *Habitus* can be defined as "the way society becomes deposited in persons in the form of lasting dispositions, or trained capacities and structured propensities to think, feel and act in determinant ways, which then guide them" (Wacquant in Navarro 2006, 16). In this chapter, I explore how *habitus* developed through exposure to ritual violence and the hierarchical structuring of funerary rituals and cemetery spaces (*cf.* also Perego 2011); in turn, this sustained the creation of ideologies of personhood based on discrimination, inequality and social exclusion.

Tensions at funerals

Research on late prehistoric and proto-historic Veneto has shown that Venetic funerary rituals were a source of legitimacy for the local dominant groups as well as an arena for the negotiation of identity and social inclusion by different social actors in phases of dramatic socio-political change (for a full overview *cf.* Perego 2012a; *cf.* also Balista and Ruta Serafini 1992; 1998; Capuis 2009; Perego 2014b). The manipulation of the funerary space was an integral feature of these processes of power and identity negotiation. From at least the Final Bronze Age to the fifth–fourth centuries BC, most of the best known Venetic cemeteries were organized around a series of low earth or stone mounds in which – or around which – the tombs were erected according to complex criteria of selection that determined the appropriate location of the dead, both in the funerary space and in the ideal social body reconstructed after death (Figs 12.2, 12.3, 12.4).[6]

Especially at main Iron Age Venetic centres such as Este and Padua, the monumentalization and rigorous arrangement of the cemetery ground, the hierarchical disposition of the graves in often accurately delimited collective mounds or burial spaces, the disproportion in wealth, structure and ritual complexity between the tombs and the appropriation of restricted segments of the graveyard by selected groups of mourners demonstrate that cemeteries were loci of construction of social disparity (e.g. Balista and Ruta Serafini 1986; 1991; 1992; 1998; Perego 2011; 2012a; 2012b; 2012c; *cf.* also Leonardi and Cupitò 2004; 2011 for a slightly different interpretation of the spatial organization of some Este and Padua cemeteries in respect to Balista and Ruta Serafini). Furthermore, the sophisticated ritual activity developed for the definition and delimitation of the funerary space suggests that Venetic mortuary practices had powerful sacral overtones and might have been performed under the aegis of the deity. These rituals often had wider resonances in Venetic religious practices carried out in sanctuary and settlement areas and included the sacrifice of horses and presumably human beings, the erection of stone and wooden boundaries to delimit *tumuli* and entire cemetery areas, the burning of fires and the interment of offerings to sacralize the erection of borders, and the creation of sacrificial sites where humans and animals were slaughtered in liminal areas between the cemetery and the settlement (Balista and Ruta Serafini 2008; Gambacurta *et al.* 2005; Michelini 2005; Michelini and Ruta

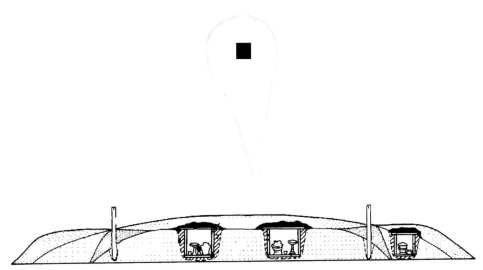

Fig. 12.2: Burial structures from pre-Roman Veneto: upper: plan with hypothetical reconstruction of a pear-shaped burial mound from the Randi cemetery of Este, with élite Randi Tomb 34/1905 (c. 635–625 BC) in the middle; lower: reconstruction of a burial mound from Iron Age Este. Tomb 34/1905 yielded the famous Randi Situla, slightly pre-dating the Benvenuti one mentioned in this chapter (modified by E. Perego after Callegari 1924 and Leonardi and Cupitò 2004).

Serafini 2005, 133; Perego 2011; 2012a; 2012b; below). Vicenza Inscription 2 – a votive inscription probably incised on a stone border marker – indicates that at least during the second Iron Age (c. 500–200 BC) the boundary itself was a deity and a sacred institution protected by supernatural powers (Pellegrini and Prosdocimi 1967, 382–7).[7] Socio-political forms of marginalization and construction of power, therefore, might have been enforced on a religious level, and cemeteries were landscapes ritually engaged to construct and normalize social inequality. Hence, the exclusion from formally delimited funerary spaces became a first means of discrimination between individuals and their ascribed social value (Perego 2014a; forthcoming).

As the *tumuli* represented the core of this system of management and appropriation of the funerary space, they can be understood as the reification of dynamics of power negotiation, which potentially reflected socio-political struggles taking place in society as a whole. Furthermore, the osteological and archaeological analysis of the funerary evidence has revealed that many graves and restricted funerary segments were presumably occupied by the components of nuclear families and extended kinship groups (e.g. Chieco Bianchi and Calzavara Capuis 2006; Perego 2011; 2012a; 2012c); hence, the *tumuli* can also be conceived as the embodiment of relations of kinship and social affiliation – or, more precisely, the embodiment of human relations as they were represented in the ideologically

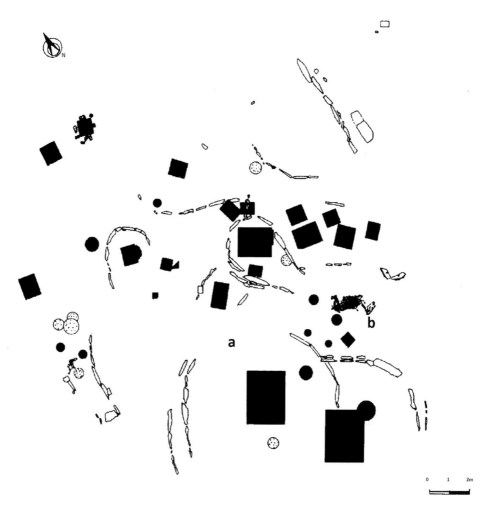

Fig. 12.3: Plan of Este Ricovero cemetery (c. 625–525 BC) with hypothetical reconstruction of Tumulus AA1 (a) and horse burial (b). The same cemetery segment is shown in a different chronological phase in Figure 12.4 (modified by E. Perego after Balista and Ruta Serafini 1998 and Leonardi and Cupitò 2004).

charged arena of the funeral. Changes in the shape, dimensions, structure and layout of the *tumuli* (or of any other form of delimitation and management of the cemetery space) have been linked to changes in both the wider social structure of proto-historic Veneto (e.g. Balista and Ruta Serafini 1992; 1998; Perego 2012a) and local conceptions of personhood, social inclusion and group membership (Perego 2012a; 2014a; 2014b).

Inside and near the *tumuli*, the tombs were often disposed of hierarchically in order to delineate the level of social inclusion granted to the deceased and the standing of their burying group. Significant evidence indicates that since at least the Final

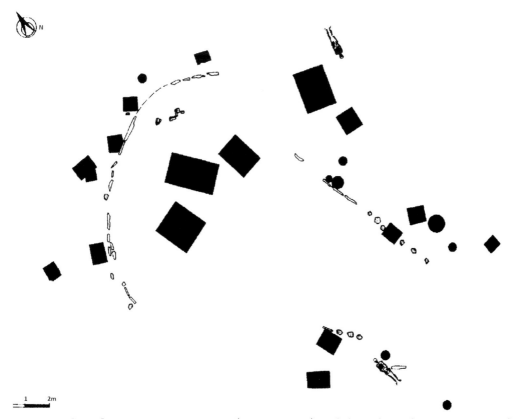

Fig. 12.4: Plan of Este Ricovero cemetery (c. 525–450 BC) with hypothetical reconstruction of Tumulus XYZ; the same cemetery segment is shown in a different chronological phase in Figure 12.3 (modified by E. Perego after Balista and Ruta Serafini 1998 and Leonardi and Cupitò 2004).

Bronze Age a dichotomy developed between inhumation and cremation rites, with the latter most likely adopted to underline the higher social standing and personhood status of the dead in respect to buried individuals (e.g. Perego 2014a; Perego *et al.* 2015; Saracino *et al.* 2014; for possible exceptions: Gamba and Tuzzato 2008; below). As further discussed below, this was often underlined by the different location of cremation vis-à-vis inhumation tombs in the funerary space, and by the exclusion of some buried individual from the formal burial ground. Significant differences between cremation and inhumation burials can also be detected in the quantity and quality of grave goods, with cremation graves being far more likely to be endowed with a grave assemblage (e.g. Bondini 2005; 2008; Perego 2014a; Perego *et al.* 2015; Salzani 2008a; Fig. 12.5). Importantly, grave goods were not only a means to emphasize the rank and wealth of the deceased, but also powerful tools to reinforce kinship affiliation in the funerary sphere; this is indicated for example by the placing in the tomb of objects probably not belonging to the dead (e.g. 'female' ornaments in a man's urn) or by

Fig. 12.5: Grave assemblage from cremation Este Ricovero Tomb 112/1989, dating to the seventh century BC (after Gamba et al. 2013, fig. 9.10).

the fragmentation of objects and the redistribution of such fragments in two or more urns in the grave as the material embodiment of kinship ties (Bianchin Citton *et al.* 1998; Perego 2011; 2012a, 190–211).[8] The importance of enhancing special relations of familial and social affiliation is also shown by the use of burying cremated individuals together, either in the same urn or in the same tomb container (e.g. Bianchin Citton *et al.* 1998; Perego 2011; 2012a, 127–88; 2012c). Osteological, archaeological and epigraphic sources indicate that people buried together were often relatives (Bianchin Citton *et al.* 1998; Chieco Bianchi and Calzavara Capuis 2006; Perego 2012a; 2012c). In particular, the placing of the bones belonging to different individuals in the same urn most likely involved the members of nuclear families, especially children and their parents (for similar occurrences at Verucchio in Emilia Romagna: Di Lorenzo *et al.* this volume). Notably, wealthy multiple tombs characterized by bone-mingling rituals and practices of grave-good manipulation were often located in prominent funerary areas, such as the centre of collective *tumuli*. By contrast, inhumations and simple cremation tombs may be placed on the *tumulus* edge or outside, in order to underline the symbolic detachment of non-élite individuals – or individuals not fully integrated in society as 'persons' – from the prominent family groups governing Venetic society.

Many inhumation burials, including those not displaying clearly deviant attributes and evidence of abuse, were characterized by potential markers of low-status and incomplete social integration (Perego 2012a; *cf.* also Bondini 2005; Michelini and Ruta Serafini 2005, 134; Perego 2014a; 2014b; Perego *et al.* 2015; Saracino 2009; Zanoni 2011). These included an association with very simple grave assemblages or a lack of any funerary provision, and a location in marginal cemetery areas and/or outside the funerary mounds were the richest cremation tombs were erected. Inhumation graves as wealthy and ritually sophisticated as the most complex cremations are yet to be discovered or published. Furthermore, there is no clear evidence of inhumation burials located in prominent locations of the funerary space, such as the centre of the most prestigious collective *tumuli*. Especially at Este, there is no proof that inhumation graves were routinely placed within the formally delimited boundaries of the mounds; however, the poor preservation of some contexts does not allow us a full evaluation of the evidence available. The intentional placing of inhumation and simple cremation graves in association with but *outside* collective mounds – in clearly subordinate positions – has been suggested for some chronological phases and micro-contexts such as *Tumulus* XYZ at the Este Ricovero cemetery (*c*. 525–450 BC; Balista and Ruta Serafini 1992; 1998; Perego forthcoming; Fig. 12.4). Further consideration, however, should be paid to funerary rites in Padua, where the percentage of inhumation in respect to cremation tombs seems higher than elsewhere, and where relatively rich inhumation burials are attested – although the precise location of many inhumation graves in respect to the mounds remains unclear because of a lack of published evidence or excavation data (e.g. Gamba and Tuzzato 2008; Michelini 2005, 158–62; Ruta Serafini 1990; Voltolini 2013a). Evidence that at least some buried individuals might have been plagued by harsh conditions of life, including food deprivation, illness, *pre-mortem* and *peri-mortem* violence and involvement in heavy and repetitive physical tasks has also been noted (e.g. Catalano *et al.* 2010; Onisto 2004). This evidence has been provisionally connected to the possibility that inhumation rites were often reserved for marginal and low-ranking social groups (e.g. Perego 2014a; Perego *et al.* 2015; Saracino 2009; Zanoni 2011; Table 12.1; on the use of osteological data for reconstructing the dead person's lifestyle *cf.* for example Blakey 2001; Danforth 1999; Robb 2002; Waldron 2009; Wilczak *et al.* 2004).

Inhumation burials found outside formal cemeteries were almost never associated with grave goods and are likely to display abnormal body positions, such as the prone posture, and evidence of disease, disability and *pre-mortem*, *peri-mortem* and *post-mortem* abuse (Perego 2014a; Perego *et al.* 2015; Saracino 2009; Zanoni 2011; Table 12.1). In some cases, such as the Oppeano and Padua burials discussed below, it is dubious whether these depositions can be classified as 'tombs', namely formal – albeit anomalous – depositions of individuals granted a funerary rite. It is more likely that these contexts represent sacrificial or discard 'deposits' connected to practices of human sacrifice (e.g. Michelini and Ruta Serafini 2005, 133), ritual exploitation of human remains (e.g. Perego 2012b) or even execution (e.g. Guidi 2010; Saracino 2009) (*cf.* also Perego 2014a; Zanoni 2011). Occurrences of abnormal – potentially sacrificial – burials inside the formal burial ground are also attested and will be discussed later in this chapter.

While an overall analysis of inhumation suggests that this ritual might have often been used to mark conditions of incomplete social integration, the variability of ritual practices surrounding each single burial sheds light on the complexity of Venetic funerary rites and society (e.g. Perego 2012a, 223–33; 2014a). In terms of agency theory, each tomb can be considered as a micro-cosmos created by different agents pursuing diverse and potentially conflicting goals in relation to the funerary practice

Table 12.1: Occurrences of abnormal burial discussed in the chapter *Minimum number of individuals. For a possible connection between handicap, disease, marginality and abnormal funerary behaviour in Iron Age northern Italy cf. Perego 2012a; 2014b; Perego et al. 2015; Zanoni 2011. **In respect to the most common arrangement of normative inhumation burials (intact supine burial in rectangular burial pit large enough to accommodate a human body). *** Osteological data unpublished or not available.

Settlement	Context	Mni*	Abnormal features of burial and health status*
Oppeano	La Montara 700–500 BC	1	Possible case of prone burial; possible case of disarticulation (according to initial assessment of the evidence: *cf.* Salzani 2008b); possible case of abnormal** re-arranging of human bones in burial pit; burial outside formal cemetery; settlement burial in anomalous** burial pit; no reported grave goods; possible association with sacrificial remains and incomplete/disarticulated animal skeletons (found in nearby pit)? ***
Oppeano	Ex Fornace 525–500/475 BC	1	Prone; burial outside formal cemetery; settlement burial in 'dump' pit; no reported grave goods; evidence of *pre-mortem* violence; partial calcification of nasal cartilages, agenesis (i.e. congenital lack) of third maxillary molars, deep carious lesion on mandibular right third molar, bone resorption and necrosis of tissue in lower incisor region, enamel hypoplasia (four episodes of systemic stress between 2 and 5 years from birth), Harris' lines (at least three episodes of systemic stress at 2, 13 and *c.* 15–20 years of age), spina bifida occulta, severe lumbar kyphosis, Schmorl's nodes (prolapse of intervertebral disc), evidence of marked development of muscles on lower limbs and marked arthritis on lumbar vertebrae probably due to excessive workloads
Gazzo Vr	Colombara *c.* 600–500 BC ?	1	Prone; hasty interment; interment in anomalous burial pit; no grave goods; association with incomplete/disarticulated animal skeleton; human skeleton found incomplete although this was attributed to post-depositional processes; evidence of musculoskeletal stress, advanced tooth wear
Padua	Via S. Eufemia *c.* 800–600 BC	10	Anomalous body postures including at least one prone burial; reported occurrences of disarticulation and/or mutilation; possible evidence of hasty interment; possible occurrence of abnormal (re-)arranging or placing of human bones in burial pit; burial outside formal cemetery; interment in anomalous burial pits; burial in sacrificial site; no reported grave goods; association with remains of sacrifice and ritual food consumption, including incomplete and disarticulated animal skeletons; possible evidence of defleshing (currently under investigation)?

Settlement	Context	Mni*	Abnormal features of burial and health status*
Padua	Via S. Eufemia *Tumulus* *c.* 600–450 BC?	2	Disarticulation and/or mutilation; possible case of abnormal re-arranging of human bones in burial pit; possible association with sacrificial remains including a disarticulated animal skeleton; no reported grave goods?
Padua	Via Tiepolo *Tumulus* A *c.* 600 BC	1/2	Anomalous body posture; no grave goods; interment in anomalous burial pit outside formally delimited burial mound; association with horse burial; possible association with sacrificial horse burial
Padua	Via Tiepolo *c.* 600–500 BC	1	Prone burial; burial partially covered with charred wood; association with simple child inhumation burials, potentially in marginal funerary segment; no reported grave goods; deposition in unusually deep and narrow burial pit
Padua	Via Umberto 1 *c.* 800–500 BC	1+	Disarticulation and/or mutilation?
Padua	Via Umberto I Tomb 306/ 2002–3 *c.* 800–500 BC	1	Disarticulation and/or mutilation; 'incomplete' cremation (vis-à-vis normative cremation burials in tomb); interment in anomalous round-shaped burial pit filled with charcoal; no reported grave goods?
Este	Nazari Capodaglio Ramini *c.* 800–600 BC	2+	At least one case of prone burial; location in marginal cemetery areas and/or near the boundary of a cemetery; possible cases of disarticulation and/or mutilation?
Este		2+	Disarticulation and/or mutilation; decapitation?
Este	Via Pra 10 *c.* 525–300 BC?		Burial outside formal cemetery; interment in sacrificial site; association with animal skeletons; no reported grave goods?
Oderzo	Via Garibaldi *c.* 625–500 BC	6	One possible case of prone burial; burial in marginal cemetery area or on the boundary of cemetery; association with pyre debris pits; grave goods scanty or absent; possible evidence of skeletal manipulation? It cannot be excluded that the adult and the infant buried together were a mother and her child who died in childbirth

(e.g. relief of bereavement, display of affection, intensification of kinship support, exhibition of wealth, enhancement of social visibility through the appropriation of space in the formal graveyard). Each social actor, however, must have operated within the framework of wider societal constraints, including the intricate web of socio-political relationships which determined the creation of Venetic cemeteries in the form they evolved. These relations must have included forms of family and kinship solidarity; they may also have included, however, potentially tenser interactions with competing peers, associates of higher social standing and the élite members who were probably able to appropriate vast areas of the mortuary space and establish the rules according to which only selected segments of the community were entitled to cremation burial in prominent funerary locations. Bone-mingling rituals fully embody the intricacies of Venetic mortuary practice: clearly intended to emphasize intimate relations of familial proximity, they also became tools of power negotiation when used to underline the rank of a family or kinship group. Similarly, the practice of inhumation – either chosen by or enforced upon selected groups and individuals – reflected a wide spectrum of social and ritual behaviours, including instances of social integration (almost) comparable to cases involving cremated individuals.

Indeed, inhumation burials apparently not conforming to the pattern delineated above are attested. For example, Emo Tomb 468/2003 from the Via Umberto I–Emo Capodilista Palace cemetery of Padua was an inhumation characterized by a grave assemblage unusually rich for this burial type (*c.* 650 BC, Voltolini 2013a, 351; Fig. 12.6). The deceased – a woman whose age at death has been suggested to range between 69 and 78 by osteological analysis – was probably interred in a wooden container, another unusual feature for the Venetic inhumations known or published to date. The corpse appears to have been wrapped in a shroud and adorned with a fibula and a necklace made of bone, amber and bronze elements. A spindle whorl, a couple of bronze rings and dog and pig bones also accompanied the burial. Particularly notable is the ceramic set, which is roughly comparable to assemblages that are found in cremation graves of good standing dating to the same phase. For example, the large round-shaped olla (*olla globosa*) placed near the hips of the deceased is not dissimilar from the vessel used as an urn for the prestigious and almost contemporaneous Emo Tomb 318/2002, a male cremation accompanied by a sophisticated drinking service and a bronze carpenter set (*c.* 650–625 BC, Voltolini 2013b, 350–1). Notably, Tomb 468/2003 is roughly contemporaneous to a phase of renovation of the Via Umberto I burial area which took place around 650 BC (Gamba and Tuzzato 2008; below). As the cemetery remains largely unpublished, it remains unclear whether the anomalous funerary ritual granted to the deceased may have been related to phenomena of unrest or accelerated social change occurring in this phase. It is however notable that the Via Umberto I cemetery had already yielded in its first phases of use inhumation tombs which do not display any clear evidence of ritual 'marginalization' vis-à-vis the cremations dating to the same phase (for a preliminary discussion: Gamba and Tuzzato 2008; *cf.* also IIPP 2015). This included

Fig. 12.6: Grave assemblage from inhumation Padua Emo Tomb 468/2003, dating to the mid-seventh century BC (after Gamba et al. 2013, fig. 9.12).

the burial of a female individual displaying peculiar features comparable to those of Emo Tomb 468/2003, but dating to the end of the eighth century BC (Voltolini 2013a, 351).

Performances of violence

The sacrificial site of Padua Via S. Eufemia

The possibility that human sacrifice and ritual violence were carried out in proto-historic Veneto is particularly consistent with evidence from the ritual site of Via S. Eufemia at Padua. This site was excavated in the 1990s between the Via Tiepolo–Via S. Massimo cemetery and the Iron Age settlement. The context is only partially preserved, as the site was used as a sand quarry in Roman times and subsequently as a dump (Michelini 2005, 157). Furthermore, the excavation remains mainly unpublished although some preliminary reports have been published (e.g. Facciolo and Tagliacozzo 2006; Michelini 2005; for a preliminary discussion of the published evidence: Michelini and Ruta Serafini 2005, 133; Perego 2012b; 2014a; Zanoni 2011). The evidence available is however sufficient to draw a preliminary description of the ritual practice carried out at the site and frame it within the themes explored in this chapter.

The earliest phase of activity, probably dating to the eighth century or the end of ninth, involved the excavation of small pits found to contain fragmented pottery, cereals, charcoal and animal bones (Facciolo and Tagliacozzo 2006; Michelini 2005, 157; Zanoni 2011, 22).[9] This evidence suggests that food might have been prepared and consumed on site, presumably on a relatively small scale, at least in respect to later phases. However, the relatively high number of pits discovered to date – 17 – may indicate that repeated ritual actions potentially involving numerous individuals were carried out. It remains unclear whether in this early phase the ritual activity was related to the commemoration of the dead buried nearby (as suggested by Facciolo and Tagliacozzo 2006, 143) and whether meat portions were brought to Via S. Eufemia from elsewhere or the slaughtering of animals for sacrificial and/or alimentary purposes was already carried out *in situ*.

During the eighth or the seventh century, the ritual practice became increasingly more conspicuous (Facciolo and Tagliacozzo 2006; Michelini 2005, 157–8; Zanoni 2011). Larger rectangular pits ('structures') were excavated, filled with several cubic meters of wood and set on fire. Burning was intense and prolonged enough to redden and harden the walls and bottoms of the pits. Subsequently, the filling of each 'installation' pit was excavated one or more times for the deposition of pottery and animal and human remains. Approximately two thirds of the 13 surviving pits have been found to contain at least one main deposition – sometimes more – represented by either a human or a horse skeleton. In the remaining structures the main depositions consisted of dog remains, which are also present in different forms (e.g. scattered, in partial anatomical connection) in the pits containing horse and human bones.

A minimum of ten/twelve human burials of both sexes have been found (Michelini 2005, 157). Although complete osteological data remain unpublished, the approximate age classes of the dead appear to range from young adulthood to old age; no child deposition is attested (Facciolo and Tagliacozzo 2006; Michelini 2005, 157). At least two individuals may have been intentionally mutilated, namely an old man interred deprived of the lower limbs, and a younger male whose incomplete skeleton was found in disarray in structure lambda, which is discussed below; furthermore, the possibility that the bodies had been defleshed is currently under investigation (Zanoni 2011, 22). The individuals sufficiently preserved for examination were found in unusual body postures (e.g. prone or with the head against the pit's walls, the torso slightly twisted and the lower limbs flexed: Michelini and Ruta Serafini 2005, 134) and were never accompanied by surviving grave goods. Overall, their ritual treatment mimics that of the horses and dogs deposited as sacrificial offerings to the point that they appear to be "the object rather than the beneficiaries of the cult practice" (Michelini 2005, 158; translated by E. Perego).

The complexity of the ritual activity at Via S. Eufemia is testified by evidence from the ritual pits better published to date, namely structures theta-xi, eta and lambda (Facciolo and Tagliacozzo 2006). The life-cycle of structure theta-xi started with the excavation and burning of the theta ritual pit, which has been almost completely destroyed by later disturbance. The xi ritual structure was excavated to overlie almost exactly the previous theta structure, then filled with wood and set on fire. This pit contained scattered dog, pig, ovicaprine and cattle remains. Subsequently, the pit was re-excavated for the deposition of a 7-year-old male horse, laid on its left side with the neck extended. The skeleton was partially damaged by the Roman excavation. A dog mandible was on the horse's right metacarpus while scattered dog bones have been found around the animal. Other dog bones pertaining to several individuals as well as pig, cattle and ovicaprine remains have been recovered from the pit filling.

Nearby structure eta was most likely part of the same theta-xi structure, but was cut by a Roman trench. The life-cycle of structure eta started with the excavation and burning of the usual 'installation' pit. The latter was subsequently re-opened to deposit an 8–10-year-old horse, found intact but with the legs flexed and the neck twisted. Some dog bones and a single deer bone accompanied this main deposition. A second pit almost exactly overlying the first was excavated after a period of time not exactly quantifiable, but presumably not long enough for the earlier pit to disappear. This second pit contained the rib cage of a second horse, buried intentionally incomplete without disturbing the previous burial. Some dog bones and a single pig bone were deposited near the horse. Apart from the usual assemblage of scattered dog, pig, cattle and ovicaprine remains, the pit filling contained the skull and neck of an 'old' dog displaying evidence of a bone degenerative process. According to Facciolo and Tagliacozzo (2006, 148), the resulting malformation must have been clearly visible when the animal was alive. Furthermore, the position of the jaws suggests that the dog's muzzle was tightly tied when placed in the pit.

Structure lambda distinguishes itself from the former for yielding two human burials; it was initially created and burnt as an 'installation' pit, which has been found to contain dog, cattle, ovicaprine and pig remains. Subsequently, the pit was re-excavated to deposit an adult woman, whose skeleton was damaged by the Roman excavation. The pit filling contained dog, ovicaprine and – diversely from the previous structures – horse scattered remains. Structure lambda was then re-excavated for the deposition of both human and dog individuals. Notably, the pit filling consisted of numerous layers of archaeological material only a few inches thick, indicating "different and close subsequent depositions" (Facciolo and Tagliacozzo 2006, 147). The lowest layer contained a dog skeleton, not in anatomical connection, and two single cattle and horse bones. Above was the skeleton of a 'young' dog, found in anatomical connection but deprived of the skull. A third layer yielded another dog skeleton, almost complete but only partially connected, and the incomplete skeleton of the man already mentioned above. Scattered remains of cattle, horse, ovicaprine and avifauna were also found. The closing layer yielded deer, dog, cattle, ovicaprine and pig scattered remains.

Presumably after 600 BC, the site was flattened out and occupied by a funerary mound which lasted up to around 450 BC. The *tumulus* might have reached a diameter of 10 m but is only partially preserved. The surviving segment yielded 35 graves, of which 29 were cremations in *dolia*, wooden containers or simple pits. The remaining six graves were the inhumation burials of two adults, one child and three infants (Michelini 2005, 158–62). Notably, while between 600–450 BC the area was used for formal burial, some rituals potentially reminiscent of the previous sacrificial practice were still carried out. In particular, one pit was used to burn a fire, a second pit yielded the 'dismembered' remains of a dog, while a third contained the lower limbs of a child, in anatomical connection but deprived of the rest of the body. Furthermore, one of the buried neonates associated with the *tumulus* had his or her legs amputated above the knees and the skull removed and disposed of in place of the feet (Michelini 2005, 158).

Sacrifice and violence: other occurrences c. 800–500 BC

Although the extent of this phenomenon cannot be precisely quantified for a lack of published data and the uneven preservation of some contexts, the evidence discussed below strongly suggests that, in the period examined, occurrences of ritual violence and human sacrifice were not unique to Via S. Eufemia.

At Padua, the intentional deposition of incomplete human bodies or isolated body parts is also documented at the Via Umberto I–Emo Capodilista Palace cemetery. This evidence most likely dates between the eighth and the sixth centuries as the cemetery was established around the end of the ninth century and is poorly documented from the fifth century onwards (Gamba and Tuzzato 2008; Zamboni and Zanoni 2011, 204–5). At least some occurrences may date to 650–600 BC as suggested by a reproduction of the funerary area published by Gamba and Tuzzato (2008, 62–3).[10] Here, some of the tombs appear to contain incomplete bodies: this, however, remains unproven (Perego 2012a, 228–9). The only occurrence that has been provisionally published is 'Tomb' 306/2002–3, an oval pit filled with charcoal, which yielded a human torso that appears to have been burnt at a lower temperature or for a shorter period of time in respect to the human remains placed in cremation graves (Gamba and Tuzzato 2008). The corpse was presumably mutilated before burial, as the pit is too small to contain an entire human body.

Around 600 BC, the sacrifice of horses and possibly human beings is attested in relation to *Tumulus* A, a 20 m-large burial mound found in the Via Tiepolo–Via S. Massimo cemetery (Gambacurta *et al.* 2005; Gambacurta and Ruta Serafini 2013a; Perego 2012a, 281–2). Here, the deposition of cremation tombs inside and near the *tumulus* border was preceded by complex practices of delimitation and sacralization of the mound, including the erection of a kerb and a wooden fence on the *tumulus* edge. Contemporary to the erection of the fence were the burial of a horse killed through skull fracturing and a second pit containing both a horse laid on its side, and a 20-year-old man; the latter was found with no grave goods in a semi-flexed, contorted posture between the legs of the horse. Although no comprehensive osteological analysis is available, the overall context of deposition and the position of the human corpse strongly emphasize the abnormal character of this burial. A fourth external 'grave' was another human skeleton, apparently incomplete and with no grave goods: unfortunately no further information is available.

Dating again to the sixth century, another anomalous inhumation from Via Tiepolo is Tomb 24/1988, the prone burial of a 41–60-year-old woman, in poor health condition, buried in an unusually deep and narrow pit and partially covered with charred wood

(Ruta Serafini 1990; Zamboni and Zanoni 2010; Zanoni this volume). Part of her right upper limb was missing. The tomb was presumably located on the edge or outside a small burial mound, close to several child tombs, including two very simple infant inhumations; one of the latter showed evidence of *cribra orbitalia*, a pitting of the orbits potentially due to malnutrition developed, in this case, *in utero* (Walker *et al.* 2009). While the overall context of deposition appears to be indicative of the woman's incomplete social integration (Perego 2012a, 283–4), it remains unclear whether she was mutilated or affected by a congenital malformation (Zanoni pers. comm.).

Outside Padua, the most notable occurrences of ritual violence attested in Veneto in this phase come from the Veronese. The prone burial of a 20-to 25-year-old woman possibly dating to the sixth century emerged at the Colombara cemetery of Gazzo Veronese (Drusini 2001; Riedel and Tecchiati 2001; Salzani 2001b; for a preliminary chronology: Guidi 2010; Fig. 12.7). The skeleton was found with the lower limbs sprawled open and the face against the bottom of a pit much larger and deeper than the average inhumation grave (4 × 4 m; 1.35 m). The right lower limb was incomplete, although this has been attributed to modern disturbance (Salzani 2001b). Notable is the association between the human burial and a largely incomplete horse skeleton, which has prompted a comparison with the Via S. Eufemia evidence (Leonardi 2004).

Two anomalous burials have recently emerged at the periphery of Oppeano (Guidi

Fig. 12.7: Prone burial from the Colombara cemetery of Gazzo Veronese (after Salzani 2008a).

and Saracino 2010). The first, possibly dating to the seventh or the sixth century, was excavated at 'La Montara', a site exploited for pottery production (Riedel and Rizzi 1999; Saracino 2009; Zamboni and Zanoni 2010; Zanoni 2011, 22; Fig. 12.8). According to a preliminary interpretation of the evidence, the skeleton was found incomplete, prone and with several skeletal districts in disarray (Salzani 2008b). Dog bones and other animal remains were interred in a second pit nearby. As both the human and animal remains were under a paved 'road', the hypothesis of a foundation sacrifice has been cautiously advanced (Guidi and Saracino 2010, 53).[11] The second burial was unearthed at the 'ex Fornace' site and may date to *c.* 525–500/475 BC (Saracino 2009, 66; Zamboni and Zanoni 2010; Zanoni 2011, 22). The dead, a man presumably in his thirties, was laid prone in a 6 × 6 m-large pit initially used for sand extraction, and then turned into a rubbish dump filled with food, metal and ceramic debris. Significant evidence of palaeopathology has been noted, including evidence of musculoskeletal and systemic or nutritional stress (Catalano *et al.* 2010). Furthermore, approximately six-eight months before death, the man was hit with a pointed tool which left a hole in his mandible and determined a flexion of the front teeth inward, with a necrosis of the surrounding tissue (Catalano *et al.* 2010, 92).

The evidence from Este and Oderzo remains ambiguous owing to a lack of published data. The presence of inhumations in marginal cemetery areas is well documented for the time-span under consideration (e.g. Gambacurta 1996) but

Fig. 12.8: Settlement burial from Oppeano 'La Montara' (after Salzani 2008b).

complete osteological and stratigraphic data are needed to clarify whether cases of ritual abuse may have occurred. Significantly, however, the first archaeologists to excavate Este between *c.* 1876–1930 have already discussed the possibility that human sacrifice and ritual violence were practiced at this site. For example, Prosdocimi (1882) and Soranzo (1885) noted the intentional association between rich cremation graves and prone – sometimes incomplete – inhumation burials. In one case, a large *dolium* vase containing a cremation urn and rich grave goods was placed on the back of a skeleton buried prone (Prosdocimi 1882, 16). Callegari (1930, 38) reported the presence of isolated human 'crania' and skeletons deprived of both the pelvis and the lower limbs at different Este sites. In the Ramini property, at least two 'crania' and other simple inhumation burials – including a prone skeleton – were found near a 'road' and the possible limit of the Capodaglio–Nazari cemetery (Callegari 1930, 33–4). Notably, Callegari's discoveries find a comparison in the Paduan occurrences detailed above; furthermore, the Ramini finds may not date after *c.* 600 BC (Callegari 1930, 37). More recent is the discovery of an incomplete human skeleton at Via Prà 10, where 34 horse burials and the remains of a pig have emerged (Balista and Ruta Serafini 2008). No cremation tomb has been found in the same area, which is interpreted as a sacrificial site potentially marking the boundary between the Nazari-Capodaglio-Morlungo burial area and the settlement (Balista and Ruta Serafini 2008). The graves have been provisionally dated between the late sixth and the fourth centuries on the basis of a pot found on site; the chronology of the human burial, however, remains unknown.

At Oderzo (an important Venetic settlement located approximately 85 km north-east of Padua), a cluster of five inhumation burials dating to *c.* 625–500 BC has been found at Via Garibaldi; this site was probably located on the margin of the Opera Pio Moro cemetery, which has recently yielded 70 cremation tombs, two inhumations and approximately 15 *tumuli* (Gambacurta 1996; Groppo 2013a). The inhumations from Via Garibaldi were close to six pyre debris pits: pits containing the remains of cremation pyres and scanty offerings were sometimes placed on the margins of *tumuli*, or outside, probably for ritual purposes (e.g. Ruta Serafini 1990). No cremation tomb was found nearby. Two skeletons appear to have been largely incomplete, although it remains unclear whether this was the result of intentional manipulation or post-depositional processes; one burial was associated with animal bones. Animal remains were also found in a third pit, which yielded the skeletons of an adult and an infant. From the cemetery map provided in Gambacurta 1996 a fourth skeleton appears to have been prone, although this remains unclear for a lack of published evidence. According to the published evidence, only the fifth burial was associated with scanty grave goods: the deceased, an adult found in a flexed position, was accompanied by a pot, and a pin and a dragon fibula probably used to fasten the burial shroud.

Social transformation c. 800–500 BC

The analysis of the archaeological and epigraphic record from the context examined discloses the picture of a society in rapid and tumultuous transformation. Firstly, social change can be traced in the funerary sphere. Significant changes in the cemetery layout and structure of the *tumuli* are clearly attested at different Venetic locales. At Padua and Este, the small burial mounds attested *c.* 825–775 BC, after 775–750 BC were progressively enlarged or substituted by more sophisticated structures clearly marked out by kerbs and fences in respect to the surrounding space; the number of graves implanted in each mound increased and a hierarchical arrangement of the space emerged (Balista *et al.* 1992; Balista and Ruta Serafini 1992; 1998; Perego 2012a, 259, 280). In the same phase, a dramatic increase in the wealth and complexity of some grave assemblages testifies to the development of a funerary ideology emphasizing inequality and social differentiation (Perego 2012a, 259). At Padua Via Umberto I, the deposition of a horse burial around 750 BC reveals the precocious adoption of sacrificial practices that would become more common in later phases, usually in association with prominent graves or *tumuli* (Millo 2013, 364); it also marked or slightly followed a phase of change in the organization of the cemetery space (Gamba and Tuzzato 2008). At Padua Via Tiepolo–Via S. Massimo, a mass grave containing six inhumation burials and pottery is also attested (Balista *et al.* 1992). This occurrence, which remains largely unpublished, may represent a communal burial, or the outcome of sacrificial practices similar to those documented at Via S. Eufemia. After a further phase of development, around 650 BC the Via Umberto I cemetery was flattened out and re-occupied according to a different spatial organization which lasted until the end of the century; a significant enhancement of the richness and variability of the grave assemblages is also attested (Gamba and Tuzzato 2008, 62–3; Michelini and Ruta Serafini 2005, 148). At Este, an interruption in the use of the Ricovero cemetery has been suggested to take place around 625 BC (Balista and Ruta Serafini 1992; 1998). This event was followed by an intense phase of activity in which the erection of new pear-shaped *tumuli* characterized by a more hierarchical disposition of the tombs in the space testifies to the further development of a funerary ideology openly discriminating between individuals (Perego 2012a, 300–2). Furthermore, the possible deposition of a horse burial in relation to one of the largest mounds of this phase – *Tumulus AA1* – indicates the adoption of grand sacrificial practices sanctioning the formal appropriation of funerary spaces where the élite deceased received formal burial (*cf.* Fig. 12.3). Another horse burial is attested at Via Umberto I in the same phase (Gamba and Tuzzato 2008).

Around 600 BC, or slightly later, the rearrangement of the funerary space resulting in the erection of *Tumulus* A at Padua Via Tiepolo–Via S. Massimo was directly marked by the deposition of sacrificial burials around the mound. Almost at the same time, a reorganization of the burial space characterized by a more evident hierarchical placing of the graves is recognizable at the Posmon–Le Rive cemetery of Montebelluna in the Piave River Valley (Manessi and Nascimbene 2003; it must be noted, however, that this burial site has yet to yield a single inhumation grave out of several hundred cremation tombs: e.g. Ceselin and Gilli 2008). The early sixth century was also characterized by further changes in the layout of the Via Umberto I cemetery and by the establishment of the Piovego cemetery near Padua (Gamba and Tuzzato 2008; Leonardi 1990). While information on the funerary record of Oppeano remains scanty, some recent discoveries from Gazzo indicate that around 600–575 BC a large burial mound associated with a minimum of four stone *stele* in the shape of female and male personages might have been erected between the Colombara and Doss del Poll cemeteries (Gamba and Gambacurta 2011). Between 575–525 BC, the creation of larger pear-shaped *tumuli* at Este Ricovero signalled the development of new forms of hierarchy; these resulted in the grouping of numerous simple cremation and inhumation tombs outside the margin of the burial mound, while rich cremation graves were placed inside or at the entrance (*cf.* Fig. 12.4). This funerary arrangement appears to have lasted until *c.* 450 BC, when the *tumuli* seem to disappear also at Padua (Balista *et al.* 1992; Balista and Ruta Serafini 1992; 1998; Perego 2012a, 268–74). Between the end of the sixth century and the mid-fifth century BC, however, a complex layout of *tumuli* emerged at the Opera Pio Moro cemetery of Oderzo, which is attested until the fourth century (Groppo 2013a, 357). To the sixth or fifth century also dates the establishment of the Via S. Eufemia *tumulus*, whose use has been provisionally dated by Michelini (2005) to 600–450 BC.

Broader phenomena of social development can also be traced outside the funerary arena. For the main Venetic centres, an increment in settlement size and complexity of layout and infrastructure is progressively attested since the eighth century BC (Balista and Gamba 2013; Bietti Sestieri and De Min 2013; Capuis 1998–1999; 2009; De Min *et al.* 2005; Malnati and Gamba 2003). The earliest evidence of formal cult activity may be found at Montegrotto Terme in the eighth or even late ninth century BC (Boaro 2001, 160). Montegrotto was probably a frontier sanctuary located halfway between Este and Padua, but linked to the latter on the basis of the material evidence attested. Although this remains unproven, the activation of the sanctuary might significantly coincide with the earliest rituals at Via S. Eufemia, the establishment of the Via Umberto I and Via Tiepolo cemeteries, and the first evidence of large-scale community work in the Paduan settlement (Malnati and Gamba 2003). At Oderzo, where evidence of sophisticated infrastructure is similarly precocious, the creation of a large pit lined with wood and used for burying huge amounts of pottery from the mid-eighth to the sixth centuries BC has been interpreted as a ritual deposit linked to communal feasting (Sainati 2013). This evidence, and the funerary material discussed above, disclose the increasing importance of cult and ritual in the socio-political life of the local communities, and testify to phenomena of centralization of power, increased social inequality and proto-urban development.[12]

From the seventh century BC, the increasing sophistication of the settlement layout and infrastructure was accompanied by the gradual infilling of the countryside with satellite sites probably depending upon central places such as Este and Padua, which produced a hierarchical organization of the territory (Balista and Gamba 2013; Boaro 2001). The 625–575 BC phase has been recognized as a focal moment of this territorial reorganization (Balista and Gamba 2013, 72). The second half and last quarter of the seventh century witnessed the development of stronger commercial ties with the Bolognese and Etruria (Vallicelli 2013a) and the introduction in the Veneto region of situla art and selected Greek pottery (Gambacurta and Ruta Serafini 2013b; Vallicelli 2013b). The most prestigious example of this earliest wave of situla art, the Benvenuti Situla, was deposited in one of the richest Este tombs around 600 BC; notably, the situla was used to contain the urn of a 1–3-year-old child, possibly a girl on the basis of the grave assemblage (Chieco Bianchi and Calzavara Capuis 2006). To this period also dates the appearance of black-and-red ware (*ceramica zonata*), a typical Venetic production that would remain popular until the third century. The same time-span is characterized by developments in textile production, the introduction of Etrusco-Padanian ware and an extraordinary opulence in the grave assemblages of Este and Padua (Chieco Bianchi and Calzavara Capuis 1985; 2006; Gamba and Tuzzato 2008; Gambacurta and Ruta Serafini 2012, 354–5; Groppo 2013b).

However, the short life-cycle of the small pear-shaped *tumuli* erected at Este and the interruption in the occupation of the Via Umberto I and Ricovero cemeteries *c.* 650–625 BC may testify to phenomena of social unrest or rapid replacement of élite groups (e.g. Balista and Ruta Serafini 1992; 1998). It is possible that these phenomena were linked to the intense technological, commercial and socio-ritual transformation attested in this phase. Similarly, it cannot be excluded that the extraordinary exhibition of funerary richness was an attempt to mask the uncertainty of faltering or resurging powers in a phase of change (on the idea of 'faltering' élite power *cf.* also Scopacasa, and Perego and Scopacasa this volume). Indeed, the transition between the seventh and the sixth century has already been recognized as a moment of rupture and socio-political reorganization in the entire peninsula (e.g. Forte and von Eles 1994; Ortalli 2002; Rossi 2009, 220).

The sixth century witnessed further steps towards urbanization for Venetic centres such as Este, Padua, Vicenza and Altino (e.g. Balista and Ruta Serafini 2004; Gamba *et al.* 2013; Malnati and Gamba 2003). The establishment of the main Venetic sanctuaries of Este Baratella, Este Meggiaro and Altino Fornace seems to date to 625–500 BC (Ruta Serafini 2002; Tirelli and Cresci Marrone 2009). The sanctuaries of Vicenza Piazzetta San Giacomo and Este Caldevigo were probably established in the following century, while evidence from the Villa di Villa and Lagole cult sites may go back to the sixth (Boaro and Leonardi 2005; Fogolari and Gambacurta 2001).[13] Significantly, the earliest evidence known to date from the Este Baratella sanctuary dates to the late seventh century – corresponding to the phase of disuse of the Ricovero cemetery mentioned above. This may testify to socio-political restructuring that impacted on both the religious and funerary arena. The introduction of writing in Veneto probably dates to *c.* 600–550 BC. Perhaps not surprisingly, the earliest written text known in the region might be a brief inscription incised on one of the *stele* from Gazzo mentioned above. The inscription may have been Venetic or Etruscan. According to Gamba and Gambacurta (2011; 2013) the *stele* themselves appear strongly influenced by Etruscan models and Gazzo was a frontier settlement open to different cultural influences and possibly characterized by a mixed ethnic background. One of the first genuine Venetic inscriptions known to date is the votive text from the Lozzo canal near Este Casale, which suggests the existence of a cult place at this site *c.* 550 BC (Marinetti and Locatelli 2002).

Roughly to the same period may date the first known example of the so-called Paduan *stele* (*stele patavine*), inscribed gravestones that were probably used to mark prestigious tombs or funerary areas and whose production would last until the first century BC; the earliest funerary *cippi* from Este are also attested in the sixth century (Gambacurta 2013; Maggiani 2013). The introduction of writing and inscribed gravestones, the development of formal cult in sanctuaries and the appearance of Attic pottery, possibly linked to the spread of drinking practices influenced by the Greek symposium (Vallicelli 2013a), indicate the development of new forms of power management and self-representation of the élite. These élite groups may or may not be the same kinship groups that dominated Venetic society in the seventh century: as noted above, reorganization in social hierarchies is testified by changes in the layout of the *tumuli* at Este Ricovero and the appearance of new cemetery sites such as Padua Piovego. Notably, the sixth century is known as a phase of turmoil and tumultuous development in the entire central (and not only central) Mediterranean (*cf.* for example the Carthaginian expansion; the Battle of Alalia in Corsica, *c.* 540–535 BC; socio-political instability and change in Athens and Rome; the development of the *emporia* of Adria and Spina on the Veneto's Adriatic shore; e.g. Aubet 2001; Gamba *et al.* 2013; Smith 1996; Statton 1991; on the sixth century BC in Emilia: Zamboni this volume). In Veneto, a possible power shift between Este and Padua may be attested from around the mid-sixth century BC (Maggiani 2013, 134), while a phase of crisis and depopulation has been recognized in the Veronese and the Lessini mountain chain (Rossi 2009, 220–1). The disappearance of many sites such as Castion di Erbé (*c.* 550 BC) was mirrored by structural changes in the settlements that survived: Oppeano developed a massive defensive system that replaced the less imposing structures dating to the seventh century, while between *c.* 600/550–475/450 BC important transformations are attested in the organization, development, material culture and potentially the ethnic makeup (e.g. Etruscan/non-Etruscan) of other frontier settlements, such as Gazzo, Castiglione Mantovano and the Castellazzo della Garolda (Bianchi 2004, 510; Guidi and Salzani 2008; Rossi 2009; Salzani 2001a; *cf.* also IIPP 2015).

Discussion and conclusion

A preliminary analysis of the Venetic evidence disclosed a complex tapestry of actions relating to power dynamics in ritual contexts, which were developed by different agents at the micro-level of individual praxis within larger phenomena of change involving society as a whole. In particular, this chapter focused on rituals resulting in abnormal mortuary treatments and probable occurrences of human sacrifice and mutilation. Particularly significant is the handling of the victims. If these people were still alive when abused, the ritual procedures adopted reveal a complete disregard for their life and pain, and resulted in a violent erasure of their personhood. The disregard for the humanity of the abused was apparently extended to their *post-mortem* treatment. Their exclusion from the formal burial ground and any prominent funerary area, complete lack of visible grave goods, deposition in abnormal body postures, evidence of skeletal manipulation and hasty interment, and the possibility they were buried naked or at least without the protection of a shroud, indicate a will to draw a strict line between victim and perpetrator, and possibly the intention to degrade the dead. No less significant are the deposition of the deceased from Oppeano 'ex Fornace' in a rubbish dump, or the potentially/presumably intentional arrangement of some abnormal inhumations such as the 'La Montara' burial and the burnt human torso from Via Umberto I – the corpses buried prone and/or incomplete, the limbs in disarray as to suggest/emphasize that the body was abnormally broken or bent. Notable is also the association of many of these burials with animal and sacrificial remains, possibly indicating their status as ritual offerings, deprived of agency and subjected to the will of the ritual practitioners, not dissimilarly from the horses mutilated at Padua Via S. Eufemia and Gazzo Colombara.

The most striking occurrences seem to suggest that violence and abuse were *performed* in the ritual context, potentially in front of several viewers and ritual practitioners, and sometimes along with food preparation and consumption, the burning of wood, and/or the slaughtering of animals. For instance, the complexity of the practices documented at Via S. Eufemia and the abundance of the remains excavated there testify to the involvement of numerous social actors, including presumably élite members, although their exact number and role remain unclear due to the preliminary publication of the evidence. The large quantities of wood, pottery and animal bones found indicate the development of complex practices of procurement, transport, management and use of these materials, which might not have been easily available to low-status social segments. For example, wood may have already been a relatively restricted resource at the beginning of the Iron Age (e.g. Motella De Carlo 2005), while the ideological connection between horses and Venetic élite groups has already been noted (e.g. Leonardi 2004; Marinetti 2003; Millo 2013).

The evidence discussed above suggests that ideologies of inequality were learnt and propagated through performances of violence carried out in the ritual setting; here, the mistreatment of both animal and human bodies might have developed as a lengthy and gruesome routine marked by the shedding of blood, the hard breaking of a living body, the screams of the victims, or the manipulation of a corpse (for the socio-political meaning of public torture and execution: Foucault 1975). Discrimination, therefore, developed as *habitus*: the immersion in a social framework praising aggression and antagonism created and reinforced a mind frame in which violence and abuse might have been perceived as valuable and necessary to maintain the local social order – and were therefore ratified on a ritual level. Even when open violence was not carried out, the hierarchical arrangement of the funerary space and the adoption of rituals, such as cremation and bone mingling, intended to enforce social discrimination, became a means to instill in people clear understandings of their different values as human beings: ritual abuse, therefore, might have represented the peak of a plateau of subjugation that also developed in people's daily lives in more 'innocent' occurrences, such as visiting a cemetery or attending a funeral.

Evidence of change in the funerary arena and the wider social setting reveals the existence – in the Venetic context – of critical episodes of development taking place in relatively shorts periods of time. These micro-phases of accelerated transformation or turmoil may have resulted in an escalation of violence and the ritual exploitation of human beings for ritual purposes. While further research is needed to substantiate this hypothesis, even a preliminary analysis of the evidence allows us to link specific cases of abuse to social change. For example, the period of technological, religious, and social innovation dating to *c.* 625–575 BC was marked by the sacrificial burials of *Tumulus* A at Padua and – potentially – other occurrences of ritual abuse still in need of full publication. The variability in practices of abuse and marginalization across the region discloses differences in the agents' response to social stress, or even attempts to innovate the ritual; this can be noted even at the micro-level when looking at differences in the 'structures' from Via S. Eufemia. It also suggests that diverse reasons deserving further investigation might have motivated the adoption of abnormal mortuary treatments or practices of abuse (e.g. exploitation of human remains to sacralize the boundary, attempts to sanction social exclusion), and that some of these reasons might be related to the status, role or even *agency* of the abused (e.g. fear of the deceased or their conditions of handicap and disease, or attempts to demean the corpse of outcasts, rivals in the political arena, or those who broke a social rule).

However, the persistence of these phenomena in the *longue durée* also reveals the existence, in the region, of general understandings of humanity and personhood entailing the creation of a gap between those given full integration in society and those denied it. At the extreme end of the social spectrum, a clear dichotomy developed between the powerful who were granted formal élite burial within the perimeter of a *tumulus* and those denied even the basic right to live – and therefore becoming the potential and real victims of sacrifice and abuse.[14] Notably, the dramatic social differences delineated through ritual appear to have been justified on an ideological level by linking violence to formal ceremonial procedures and – possibly – local religious beliefs. It is perhaps not surprising that the Benvenuti Situla – alongside with representations of drinking and aristocratic splendor – depicted a row of war prisoners taken away in captivity, their hands roped, their bodies naked.

To conclude, it is worth mentioning that in Veneto practices of abnormal mortuary behaviour and ritual abuse seems already attested in the Final Bronze Age (*cf.* the evidence from Frattesina: Salzani and Colonna 2010), with even earlier symptoms of funerary deviancy dating back to previous phases of the Bronze Age (Perego *et al.* 2015; Saracino *et al.* 2014). This evidence opens a window into the centuries-old processes of development towards social complexity that characterized Veneto in late prehistory, and might involve processes of proto-urbanization and centralization of power predating the beginning of the first millennium, or taking place at the very onset of the Iron Age (*cf.* Smith 2005 on central Italy). It also raises questions about the development of social inequality, hierarchy and coercive power in this region, as well as about the relation between power, politics and changing notions of personhood, social inclusion and group membership before the full flourishing of the so-called *Venetic* civilization in the first millennium BC (Perego 2014b; Perego and Scopacasa this volume). It is highly unlikely that instability and social change may have led to ritual and ideological violence only in the Veneto region. Evidence of anomalous funerary treatment, ritual abuse and/or human sacrifice from other regions of Italy such as Etruria, Trentino–South Tyrol, Emilia Romagna and Latium (e.g. Bartoloni and Benedettini 2007–2008; Belcastro and Ortalli 2010; Zamboni and Zanoni 2010; 2011; Zanoni 2011) would deserve further attention, in order to cast light on the complex trajectories of socio-political transformation that characterized the peninsula in crucial phases of transformation for the entire Mediterranean basin.[15] As C. Smith wrote about the urbanization of Rome (Smith 2005, 102) "the key phase is the proto-urban phase, the time of making the city rather than being a city ... Rome's coercive power over her own and other populations is a key element of the early narrative ... [monumental] display may be as much a symptom of anxiety as of confidence ...". It is then in this entanglement of fear, self-belief, potential for growth, attempts at grandeur, and crisis and dissolution of control that the exercise of power may have taken abusive forms to perpetuate or even *create* itself. An in-depth analysis of these phenomena will illuminate the micro-histories of social agents that were the victims or the creators of any new socio-political order.

Acknowledgements

This chapter partially draws on research carried out for my PhD at the Institute of Archaeology, UCL (2007–2012). I therefore want to thank my PhD supervisors and examiners – Corinna Riva, Sue Hamilton, Ruth Whitehouse and the late David Ridgway – for commenting upon my thesis. Final work leading to publication was carried out while holding a Ralegh Radford Rome Fellowship at the British School at Rome (2013–2014). My research on Veneto has also been supported by the Rotary Foundation, the Celtic Research Trust and small grants by the University of London and UCL. The latter financed my attendance to the 'Burial and Social Change' workshop. Finally, I would like to express my gratitude to those who helped me to improve this chapter or offered new information on Veneto: Massimo Saracino, Veronica Tamorri, Lorenzo Zamboni, Vera Zanoni, the audience of the Rome workshop, the anonymous reviewers and especially Rafael Scopacasa, who read this work several times and always offered me punctual and thought-provoking comments.

Notes

1. Hence, cemeteries and ritual sites represented the material correlates of ritual practice, while material culture (including human remains exploited as ritual offerings: Perego 2012b) became the means by which ritual and power were enacted in these cemeteries and ritual sites.

2. Definitions of 'structure' in sociological, anthropological, philosophical and archaeological discourse vary hugely (e.g. Dobres and Robb 2000; Giddens 1984). In agency theory, 'structure' is often used to indicate the factors that may determine or limit the agent (e.g. social norms, systems of socioeconomic stratification, gender and the like).

3. The definition of praxis in philosophical thought may vary but generally involves ideas of rational human behaviour and action (*cf.* for example Aristotle, NE: Anagnostopoulos 2009; on the idea of a 'philosophy of praxis' aimed at changing the world through political action *cf.* for example Gramsci, *Quaderni dal Carcere* (*Prison Notebooks, A Reader* available online at http://ouleft.org/wp-content/uploads/gramsci-reader.pdf).

4. Although I do not explore this issue here, examples are the banishing of weapons from grave assemblages, or the leveling of funerary richness exhibited in some chronological phases characterized by intense social antagonism (for a further discussion: Perego 2012a).

5. I mainly consider here ritualized violence whose traces can be recognized in the archaeological record, for example in the form of human remains exploited as ritual offerings. Clearly, this does not exclude that other forms of violence (e.g. gender-related or war-related violence) may have occurred in the region under study.

6. For a full discussion concerning the nature and development of the earthen funerary structures that were typical of late prehistoric and proto-historic Venetic cemeteries *cf.* on the one hand work by Balista and Ruta Serafini (e.g. 1986; 1991; 1992; 1998), on the other, two more recent essays by Leonardi and Cupitò (2004; 2011). It must be noted that the term '*tumulus*' in its more common usage – while commonly adopted by many archaeologists working on Veneto – might not be appropriate to define these structures, which, especially at Este, may have been more similar to low earthen platforms (according to Leonardi and Cupitò: *accumuli stratificati*) (*cf.* for the example the reconstruction in Fig. 12.2). Further research is needed to clarify these issues as well as to investigate the nature of the presumptive *tumuli* attested at other Venetic locales.

7. The inscription reads **osts katusiaios donasto atraes termonios deivos**: Osts Katusiaios is currently interpreted as a male onomastic formula composed of two elements, including the first name of the individual (**Osts**). **Donasto** is a common verbal form on Venetic votive inscriptions; it presumably means 'to offer' or 'to give'. **Termonios deivos** is translated as 'the deities of the boundary', with notable similarities to the Roman god *Terminus* and the Latin word *divos* (gods); unfortunately, the meaning of the word **atraes** remains unclear.

8. These practices of grave-good manipulation – as well as the bone-mingling rituals described below – generally involved the re-opening of urns and tomb containers to place the grave goods and bones of the 'new' dead with the remains and funerary equipment of the individual(s) already buried in the tomb. In other cases, the new dead individual might be buried in a single urn, but (some of) his/her grave goods were redistributed in the cinerary urn(s) already deposited in the grave (or, vice-versa, he or she might receive objects already buried in a different cinerary vase). Sometimes, grave goods were intentionally broken and only the fragments were redistributed. The presence of objects intentionally buried incomplete in some tombs (*pars pro toto*) indicates that these practices of grave-good redistribution may have also been intended to reinforce kinship ties between the dead and the living, with the dead individual's living kin retaining the missing fragments (for a full overview: Perego 2012a). A recently published example is Este Ricovero Tomb 112/1989, dating to the seventh century BC (Pirazzini 2013; Fig. 12.5). The tomb container yielded two urns with the remains of a woman and a man, respectively. While the male deposition appears to have been more ancient, and the tomb container shows

evidence of intentional re-opening, all the ornaments belonging to both the deceased have been found in the female urn, with the male assemblage placed on top the female remains and grave goods. Only a tiny element pertaining to a pin found in the woman's urn was recovered from the man's vase; according to Pirazzini (2013, 350), it may have been left there when the other items were moved to the new urn placed in the tomb.

9. According to Facciolo and Tagliacozzo (2006, 143) the earliest activity at Via S. Eufemia may date between the end of the ninth and the early eighth century BC. They also suggest that the excavation of the larger pits may have taken place around 725–675 BC. Michelini (2005) dates the excavation of the small pits to the eighth century and the 'sacrificial phase' to the seventh (*cf.* also Millo 2013, 365). Zanoni (2011, 22) suggests that the site might have been active between the eighth and the sixth centuries BC, with the human burials possibly dating to the eighth. A new publication by Ruta Serafini and Michelini may be forthcoming (Zanoni 2011, 22). Unfortunately, while Facciolo and Tagliacozzo (2006) provide a relatively detailed – albeit incomplete – description of the animal remains, information on the pottery found on site remains extremely scanty.

10. This hypothesis is reinforced by the fact that, according to preliminary research, no clear evidence of discrimination against buried individuals has been noted for the earliest phases of use of Via Umberto I (e.g. IIPP 2015; please note that this volume and other recent publications on Veneto were still in press when this chapter was written and last revised). This cemetery, however, remains partly unpublished.

11. The initial interpretation of the burial has been recently questioned (*cf.* Perego 2014a, 176). I thank V. Tamorri for her advice on this matter.

12. I use the term 'proto-urban' as a catch-term to indicate a stage in settlement development preceding the establishment of fully developed urban centres (e.g. Smith 2005, 100–1 on central Italy). However, concepts such as proto-urbanism, urbanisation and "its awkward shadow" (Smith 2005, 92), namely state formation, may be subject to question, both from an epistemological point of view and in presence of patchy archaeological and epigraphic evidence (e.g. Cunliffe and Osborne 2005; Smith 2005, 99; *cf.* also Perego and Scopacasa, this volume).

13. Vicenza – as well as other Venetic settlements such as Gazzo – is the focus of new research that may change our current understanding of this site (*cf.* IIPP 2015).

14. Most of this chapter has discussed the development – through selected ritual practices – of a potential dichotomy between prominent social segments and low-ranking or marginalized groups and individuals. However, in commenting upon my paper, Rafael Scopacasa rightly mentioned the possibility that dominant social groups occasionally directed these violent shows of power towards people from their own ranks. An in-depth analysis of skeletal specimens subjected to practices of abuse might indeed help shed light on the lifestyle and social conditions of these people before death (e.g. Table 12.1); unfortunately, such evidence is not always available. Overall, it is worth mentioning that while the degree of personhood granted to people may relate to their (high) rank or social status, this need not to be always the case: for example, little children or disabled individuals belonging to prominent social groups may be still considered nonpersons or incomplete persons because of their incomplete physical development and disability (on the potentially anomalous funerary treatment of young individuals in late prehistoric northern Italy *cf.* also Zanoni this volume). It is also important to mention that the personhood status of an individual as displayed in the funerary arena is an ideological construction not necessarily relating to his or her social standing before death (Perego 2012a). It is therefore well possible that even high-ranking individuals – when becoming the victims of ritual violence for different reasons – were stripped of their personhood in death or in the final moments of their lives.

15. This topic was the focus of my 2013–2014 research project, carried out as part of my Ralegh Radford Rome Fellowship at the British School at Rome (i.e. *Micropolitical approaches to social inequality: Case studies from first-millennium BC Italy*).

Bibliography

Anagnostopoulos, G. (2009) (ed.) *A Companion to Aristotle*. Oxford, Blackwell.

Aubet, M.E. (2001) *The Phoenicians and the West. Politics, Colonies and Trade*. Cambridge, Cambridge University Press.

Balista, C., De Vanna, L., Gambacurta, G. and Ruta Serafini, A. (1992) Lo scavo della necropoli preromana e romana tra Via Tiepolo e Via S. Massimo: Nota preliminare. *Quaderni di Archeologia del Veneto* 8, 15–24.

Balista, C. and Ruta Serafini, A. (1986) La necropoli Ricovero di Este. Primi elementi connotativi e linee di approccio metodologico allo scavo. *Aquileia Nostra* 57, 25–44.

Balista, C. and Ruta Serafini, A. (1991) Analisi planimetrico-stratigrafica del nuovo settore di scavo della Casa di Ricovero di Este (PD). *Dialoghi di Archeologia* 9(1/2), 99–110.

Balista, C. and Ruta Serafini, A. (1992) Este preromana. Nuovi dati sulle necropoli. In G. Tosi (ed.) *Este Antica dalla Preistoria all'Età Romana*, 109–123. Este, Zielo.

Balista, C. and Ruta Serafini, A. (1998) La necropoli della Casa di Ricovero. Storia della ricerca. In E. Bianchin Citton, G. Gambacurta and A. Ruta Serafini (eds) *... Presso l'Adige Ridente... Recenti Rinvenimenti Archeologici da Este a Montagnana. Catalogo della Mostra (Este, Museo Nazionale Atestino, 21 Febbraio 1998-21 Febbraio 1999)*, 17–28. Padova, ADLE.

Balista, C. and Ruta Serafini, A. (2004) Primi elementi di urbanistica arcaica a Padova. In M. Luni (ed.) *I Greci in Adriatico 2* (Hesperia 18), 291–310. Roma, L'"Erma" di Bretschneider.

Balista, C. and Ruta Serafini, A. (2008) Spazi urbani e spazi sacri a Este. *In I Veneti Antichi: Novità e Aggiornamenti. Atti del Convegno di Studi (Vò di Isola della Scala, Verona, 15 Ottobre 2005)*, 79–100. Sommacampagna, Cierre Edizioni.

Bartoloni, G. and Benedettini, M.G. (2007–2008) (eds) *Sepolti tra i Vivi. Evidenza e Interpretazione di Contesti Funerari in Abitato. Atti del Convegno Internazionale (Roma, 26-29 Aprile 2006)*. Roma, Quasar.

Belcastro, M.G. and Ortalli, J. (2010) (eds) *Sepolture Anomale. Indagini Archeologiche e Antropologiche dall'Epoca Classica al Medioevo in Emilia Romagna. Giornata di Studi (Castelfranco Emilia, 19 Dicembre 2009)* (Quaderni di Archeologia dell'Emilia Romagna 28). Borgo S. Lorenzo, All'Insegna del Giglio.

Blakey, M.L. (2001) Bioarchaeology of the African diaspora in the Americas: Its origins and scope. *Annual Review of Anthropology* 30, 387–422.

Bianchi, P.A.E. (2004) L'insediamento della fase avanzata del Bronzo Recente in località Castellazzo della Garolda (Roncoferraro, MN). In D. Cocchi Genick (ed.) *L'Età del Bronzo Recente in Italia. Atti del Congresso Nazionale di Lido di Camaiore (Viareggio, 26-29 Ottobre 2000)*, 510–520. Viareggio, Mauro Baroni Editore.

Bianchin Citton, E., Gambacurta, G. and Ruta Serafini, A. (1998) (eds) *...Presso l'Adige Ridente...Recenti Rinvenimenti Archeologici da Este a Montagnana. Catalogo della Mostra (Este, Museo Nazionale Atestino, 21 Febbraio 1998-21 Febbraio 1999)*. Padova, ADLE.

Bietti Sestrieri, A.M. and De Min, M. (2013) Il Veneto tra l'età del Bronzo Finale e il VII secolo a.C.. In M. Gamba, G. Gambacurta, A. Ruta Serafini, V. Tiné and F. Veronese (eds) *Venetkens. Viaggio nella Terra dei Veneti Antichi. Catalogo della Mostra (Padova, Palazzo della Ragione, 6 Aprile-17 Novembre 2013)*, 44–50. Venezia, Marsilio.

Boaro, S. (2001) Dinamiche insediative e confini nel Veneto dell'Età del Ferro: Este, Padova e Vicenza. *Padusa* 37, 153–197.

Boaro, S. and Leonardi, G. (2005) Il santuario di Villa di Villa a Cordignano, scavi 1997 e 2004. *Quaderni di Archeologia del Veneto* 21, 51–61.

Bondini, A. (2005) Le necropoli di Este tra IV e II secolo a. C.: I corredi dello scavo 2001/2002 in via Versori (ex Fondo Capodaglio). *Ocnus* 13, 45–88.

Bondini, A. (2008) *Il "IV Periodo Atestino": I Corredi Funerari tra il IV e II Secolo a.C. in Veneto.* Unpublished thesis, Università degli Studi di Bologna.

Bourdieu, P. (1977) *Outline of a Theory of Practice.* Cambridge, Cambridge University Press.

Bourdieu, P. (1990) *The Logic of Practice.* Cambridge, Polity Press.

Bordo, S. (1993) Are mothers persons? Reproductive rights and the politics of subjectivity. In S. Bordo and L. Heywood (eds) *Unbearable Weight: Feminism, Western Culture and the Body,* 71–97. Berkeley, University of California Press.

Brück, J. (2004) Material metaphors. The relational construction of identity in early Bronze Age burials in Ireland and Britain. *Journal of Social Archaeology* 4(3), 307–333.

Busby, C. (1997) Permeable and partible persons: A comparative analysis of gender and body in South India and Melanesia. *The Journal of the Royal Anthropological Institute* 3(2), 261–278.

Callegari, A. (1924) Este. La situla figurata Randi nel Museo di Este. *Notizie degli Scavi* 1924, 269–278.

Callegari, A. (1930) Este – Nuovi scavi nella necropoli del sud (podere Capodaglio già Nazari). *Notizie degli Scavi* 1930, 3–40.

Capuis, L. (1998–1999) "Città", strutture e infrastrutture "urbanistiche" nel Veneto pre-romano: Alcune note. *Archeologia Veneta* 21/22, 51–57.

Capuis, L. (2009) *I Veneti. Civiltà e Cultura di un Popolo dell'Italia Preromana.* Milano, Longanesi (3rd edn).

Catalano, P., Caldarini, C., De Angelis, F. and Pantano, W. (2010) La sepoltura di Oppeano (Verona): Dati antropologici e paleopatologici. In F. Candelato and C. Moratello (eds) *Archeologia, Storia, Tecnologia. Ricerche Storiche e Archeologiche dell'Università di Verona. Atti del Convegno (Verona, 23–24 Maggio 2008),* 91–99. Verona, QuiEdit.

Ceselin, F. and Gilli, E. (2008) (eds) I restauri dei reperti della necropoli di Montebelluna–Posmon (scavi 2000–2002): Un esempio di buona prassi. *Quaderni di Archeologia del Veneto* 24, 200–206.

Chieco Bianchi, A.M. (1987) Dati preliminari su alcune tombe di III secolo da Este. In D. Vitali (ed.) *Celti ed Etruschi nell'Italia Centro-Settentrionale dal V Secolo a.C alla Romanizzazione. Atti del Colloquio Internazionale (Bologna, 12-14 Aprile 1985),* 191–236. Bologna, University of Bologna Press.

Chieco Bianchi, A.M. and Calzavara Capuis, L. (1985) *Este I. Le Necropoli di Casa di Ricovero, Casa Muletti-Prosdocimi, Casa Alfonsi.* Roma, Giorgio Bretschneider Editore.

Chieco Bianchi, A.M. and Calzavara Capuis, L. (2006) (eds) *Este II. La Necropoli di Villa Benvenuti.* Roma, Giorgio Bretschneider Editore.

Cresci Marrone, G. and Tirelli, T. (2009) (eds) *Altnoi. Il Santuario Altinate: Strutture del Sacro a Confronto e i Luoghi di Culto lungo la Via Annia. Atti del Convegno (Venezia, 4-6 Dicembre 2006).* Roma, Quasar.

Conklin, B.A. and Morgan, L.M. (1996) Babies, bodies and the production of personhood in north America and a native Amazonian society. *Ethos* 24(4), 657–694.

Cunliffe, B.W. and Osborne, R. (2005) (eds) *Mediterranean Urbanization 800-600 BC.* Oxford, Oxford University Press.

Danforth, M.E. (1999) Nutrition and politics in prehistory. *Annual Review of Anthropology* 28, 1–25.

Dobres, M.-A. and Robb, J. (2000) *Agency in Archaeology.* London, Routledge.

Drusini, A. (2001) Scheda antropologica dell'inumato della tomba 61. *Quaderni di Archeologia del Veneto* 17, 83–84.

Facciolo, A. and Tagliacozzo, A. (2006) Animal burials from via S. Eufemia in the Paleovenetian context – Padova (Italia). *Journal of Intercultural and Interdisciplinary Archaeology, online repository,* 143–152 [http://eprints.jiia.it/47/1/143_152_Facciolo_Tagliacozzo_OAI.pdf].

Fogolari, G. and Prosdocimi, A.L. (1988) *I Veneti Antichi. Lingua e Cultura.* Padova, Editoriale Programma.

Fogolari, G. and Gambacurta, G. (2001) (eds) *Materiali Veneti e Romani del Santuario di Lagole di Calalzo al Museo di Pieve di Cadore.* Roma, Giorgio Bretschneider Editore.

Forte, M. and von Eles, P. (1994) (eds) *La Pianura Bolognese nel Villanoviano. Insediamenti della Prima Età del Ferro. Catalogo della Mostra (Villanova di Castenaso, 24 Settembre 1994-8 Gennaio 1995)*. Borgo S. Lorenzo, All'Insegna del Giglio.

Fortes, M. (1987) *Religion, Morality and the Person: Essays on Tallensi Religion* (ed. J. Goody). Cambridge, Cambridge University Press.

Foucault, M. (1975) *Discipline and Punish: The Birth of the Prison*. New York, Random House.

Fowler, C. (2004) *The Archaeology of Personhood. An Anthropological Approach*. London, Routledge.

Gamba, M. and Tuzzato, S. (2008) La necropoli di via Umberto I e l'area funeraria meridionale di Padova. In *I Veneti Antichi: Novità e Aggiornamenti. Atti del Convegno di Studi (Vò di Isola della Scala, Verona, 15 Ottobre 2005)*, 59–77. Sommacampagna, Cierre Edizioni.

Gamba, M. and Gambacurta, G. (2011) Le statue di Gazzo Veronese al confine tra Veneti ed Etruschi. In *Tra Protostoria e Storia. Studi in Onore di Loredana Capuis* (Antenor Quaderni 20). Roma, Quasar.

Gamba, M. and Gambacurta, G. (2013) Coppia di stele funerarie. In M. Gamba, G. Gambacurta, A. Ruta Serafini, V. Tiné and F. Veronese (eds) Venetkens. *Viaggio nella Terra dei Veneti Antichi. Catalogo della Mostra (Padova, Palazzo della Ragione, 6 Aprile-17 Novembre 2013)*, 353. Venezia, Marsilio.

Gamba, M., Gambacurta, G., Ruta Serafini, A. and Balista, C. (2005) Topografia e urbanistica. In M. De Min, G. Gambacurta and A. Ruta Serafini (eds) *La Città Invisibile. Padova Preromana: Trent'Anni di Scavi e Ricerche. Catalogo della Mostra*, 23–31. Bologna, Tipoarte.

Gamba, M., Gambacurta, G., Ruta Serafini, A., Tiné, V. and Veronese, F. (2013) (eds) Venetkens. *Viaggio nelle Terra dei Veneti Antichi. Catalogo della Mostra (Padova, Palazzo della Ragione, 6 Aprile-17 Novembre 2013)*. Venezia, Marsilio.

Gambacurta, G. (1996) Oderzo. Le necropoli. In L. Malnati, P. Croce Da Villa and E. Di Filippo Balestrazzi (eds) *La Protostoria tra Sile e Tagliamento. Antiche Genti tra Veneto e Friuli. Catalogo della Mostra (Concordia Sagittaria, Basilica Paleocristiana, 14 Settembre-10 Novembre 1996; Pordenone, ex Convento di S. Francesco, 23 Novembre 1996-8 Gennaio 1997)*, 167–173. Padova, Esedra.

Gambacurta, G. (2005) Padova, necropoli orientale tra via Tiepolo e via S. Massimo: La tomba 159/1991. In D. Vitali (ed.) *Studi sulla Media e Tarda Età del Ferro nell'Italia Settentrionale*, 325–358. Bologna, Ante Quem.

Gambacurta, G. (2013) I monumenti funerari in pietra. In M. Gamba, G. Gambacurta, A. Ruta Serafini, V. Tiné and F. Veronese (eds) *Viaggio nella Terra dei Veneti Antichi. Catalogo della Mostra (Padova, Palazzo della Ragione, 6 Aprile-17 Novembre 2013)*, 344–345. Venezia, Marsilio.

Gambacurta, G. and Ruta Serafini, A. (2012) Indicatori della lavorazione tessile nel Veneto preromano. In M.S. Busana (ed.) *La Lana nella Cisalpina Romana. Economia e Società. Studi in Onore di Stefania Pesavento Mattioli. Atti del Convegno (Padova-Verona, 18-20 maggio 2011)* (Antenor Quaderni 27), 353–365. Padova, Padova University Press.

Gambacurta, G. and Ruta Serafini, A. (2013) Il tumulo A e le tombe 57 e 117. In M. Gamba, G. Gambacurta, A. Ruta Serafini, V. Tiné and F. Veronese (eds) Venetkens. *Viaggio nella Terra dei Veneti Antichi. Catalogo della Mostra (Padova, Palazzo della Ragione, 6 Aprile-17 Novembre 2013)*, 372–373. Venezia, Marsilio.

Gambacurta, G., Locatelli, D., Martinetti, A. and Ruta Serafini, A. (2005) Delimitazione dello spazio funerario nel Veneto preromano. In G. Cresci Marrone and M. Tirelli (eds) *"Terminavit Sepulcrum". I Recinti Funerari nelle Necropoli di Altino. Atti del Convegno (Venezia, 3-4 Dicembre 2003)*, 9–40. Roma, Quasar.

Gambacurta, G. and Ruta Serafini, A. (2013) L'arte delle situle. In M. Gamba, G. Gambacurta, A. Ruta Serafini, V. Tiné and F. Veronese (eds) Venetkens. *Viaggio nella Terra dei Veneti Antichi. Catalogo della Mostra (Padova, Palazzo della Ragione, 6 Aprile-17 Novembre 2013)*, 280–281. Venezia, Marsilio.

Gardner, A. (2004) (ed.) *Agency Uncovered: Archaeological Perspectives on Social Agency, Power, and Being Human*. Walnut Creek, Left Coast Press.

Gaventa, J. (2003) Power after Lukes: An overview of theories of power since Lukes and their application to development. First note: August 2003 [http://www.powercube.net/wp-content/uploads/2009/11/power_after_lukes.pdf].

Giddens, A. (1984) *The Constitution of Society. Outline of the Theory of Structuration.* Cambridge, Polity Press.

Groppo, V. (2013a) Tomba Opera Pio Moro 32. In M. Gamba, G. Gambacurta, A. Ruta Serafini, V. Tiné and F. Veronese (eds) Venetkens. *Viaggio nella Terra dei Veneti Antichi. Catalogo della Mostra (Padova, Palazzo della Ragione, 6 Aprile-17 Novembre 2013)*, 357–358. Venezia, Marsilio.

Groppo, V. (2013b) Abitare in città. In M. Gamba, G. Gambacurta, A. Ruta Serafini, V. Tiné and F. Veronese (eds) Venetkens. *Viaggio nella Terra dei Veneti Antichi. Catalogo della Mostra (Padova, Palazzo della Ragione, 6 Aprile-17 Novembre 2013)*, 227–229. Venezia, Marsilio.

Guidi, A. (2010) The archaeology of early state in Italy: New data and acquisitions. *Social Evolution and History* 9(2), 12–27.

Guidi, A. and Salzani, L. (2008) (eds) *Oppeano. Vecchi e Nuovi Dati sul Centro Protourbano* (Quaderni di Archeologia del Veneto, Serie Speciale 3). Padova, Canova.

Guidi, A. and Saracino, M. (2010) Indagini archeologiche presso l'area "ex Fornace" di Oppeano (Verona): Questioni aperte. In Γ. Candelato and C. Moratello (eds) *Archeologia, Storia, Tecnologia. Ricerche Storiche e Archeologiche dell'Università di Verona. Atti del Convegno (Verona, 23-24 Maggio 2008)*, 41–58. Verona, QuiEdit.

IIPP (2015) *Preistoria e Protostoria del Veneto.* Firenze, Istituto Italiano di Preistoria and Protostoria.

Knapp, B.A. and van Dommelen, P. (2008) Past practices: Rethinking individuals and agents in archaeology. *Cambridge Archaeological Journal* 18(1), 15–34.

Lamb, S. (1997) The making and unmaking of persons: Notes on aging and gender in north India. *Ethos* 25(3), 279–302.

Leonardi, G. 1990 (ed.) L'area archeologica del C.U.S.-Piovego: Relazione preliminare della campagna di scavo 1989, con note metodologiche. *Quaderni di Archeologia del Veneto* 6, 11–53.

Leonardi, G. (2004) (ed.) *La Tomba Bisoma di Uomo e di Cavallo nella Necropoli del Piovego-Padova.* Venezia, Marsilio.

Leonardi, G. and Cupitò, M. (2004) Necropoli "a tumuli" e "ad accumuli stratificati" nel Veneto dell'Età del Ferro. *Padusa* 40, 191–218.

Leonardi, G. and Cupitò, M. (2011) Necropoli "a tumuli" e "ad accumuli stratificati" nella preistoria e protostoria del Veneto. In A. Naso (ed.) *Tumuli e Sepolture Monumentali nella Protostoria Europea. Atti del Convegno Internazionale (Celano, 21-24 Settembre 2000)*, 13–49. Mainz, Verlag des Römish-Germanischen Zentralmuseums.

Maggiani, A. (2013) I Veneti e l'Etruria tirrenica. In M. Gamba, G. Gambacurta, A. Ruta Serafini, V. Tiné and F. Veronese (eds) Venetkens. *Viaggio nella Terra dei Veneti Antichi. Catalogo della Mostra (Padova, Palazzo della Ragione, 6 Aprile-17 Novembre 2013)*, 133–137. Venezia, Marsilio.

Malnati, L. and Gamba, M. (2003) (eds) *I Veneti dai Bei Cavalli.* Treviso, Canova.

Manessi, P. and Nascimbene, A. (2003) (eds) *Montebelluna: Sepolture Preromane dalle Necropoli di Santa Maria in Colle e Posmon.* Montebelluna, Museo di Storia Naturale e Archeologia.

Marinetti, A. (2003) Il 'signore del cavallo' e i riflessi istituzionali dei dati di lingua. Venetico *ekupetaris.* In M. Tirelli and G. Cresci Marrone (eds) *Produzioni, Merci e Commerci in Altino Preromana e Romana. Atti del Convegno (Venezia, 12-14 Dicembre 2001)*, 143–160. Roma, Quasar.

Michelini, P. (2005) Via S. Massimo 17-19 – Angolo via S. Eufemia. In M. De Min, M. Gamba, G. Gambacurta and A. Ruta Serafini (eds) *La Città Invisibile. Padova Preromana: Trent'Anni di Scavi e Ricerche. Catalogo della Mostra*, 157–159. Bologna, Tipoarte.

Marinetti, A. and Locatelli, D. (2002) La 'coppa' dello Scolo di Lozzo. In A. Ruta Serafini (ed.) *Este Preromana: Una Città e i suoi Santuari*, 281–282. Treviso, Canova.

Michelini, P. and Ruta Serafini, A. (2005) Le necropoli. In M. De Min, M. Gamba, G. Gambacurta and A. Ruta Serafini (eds) *La Città Invisibile. Padova Preromana: Trent'Anni di Scavi e Ricerche. Catalogo della Mostra*, 131–143. Bologna, Tipoarte.

Millo, L. (2013) "Quattro cavalli dalle teste superbe gettò sulla pira". In M. Gamba, G. Gambacurta, A. Ruta Serafini, V. Tiné and F. Veronese (eds) Venetkens. *Viaggio nella Terra dei Veneti Antichi. Catalogo della Mostra (Padova, Palazzo della Ragione, 6 Aprile–17 Novembre 2013)*, 364–366. Venezia, Marsilio.

Morgan, L.M. (1997) Imagining the unborn in the Ecuadoran Andes. *Feminist Studies* 23(2), 323–350.

Morgan, L.M. (2002[1989]) When does life begin? A cross-cultural perspective on the personhood of fetuses and young children. In W.A. Haviland, R.J. Gordon and L.A. Vivanco (eds) *Talking About People: Readings in Contemporary Cultural Anthropology*, 35–46. Boston, McGraw-Hill.

Morgan, L.M. (2006) "Life begins when they steal your bicycle": Cross-cultural practices of personhood at the beginnings and ends of life. *Journal of Law, Medicine & Ethics* 36(2), 193–218.

Morgan, L.M. (2009) *Icons of Life: A Cultural History of Human Embryos.* Berkeley, University of California Press.

Morris, B. (1994) *Anthropology of the Self. The Individual in Cultural Perspective.* London, Pluto Press.

Motella De Carlo, S. (2005) La ricostruzione del paesaggio attraverso lo studio dei reperti vegetali. In M. De Min, M. Gamba, G. Gambacurta and A. Ruta Serafini (eds) *La Città Invisibile. Padova Preromana: Trent'Anni di Scavi e Ricerche. Catalogo della Mostra*, 49–55. Bologna, Tipoarte.

Navarro, Z. (2006) In search of a cultural interpretation of power: The contribution of Pierre Bourdieu. *IDS Bulletin* 37(6), 11–22.

Onisto, N. (2004) Note antropologiche sugli inumati. *Quaderni di Archeologia del Veneto* 20, 95–97.

Ortalli, J. (2002) La "rivoluzione" felsinea: Nuove prospettive dagli scavi di Casalecchio di Reno. *Padusa* 37, 57–90.

Pellegrini, G.B. and Prosdocimi, A (1967) *La Lingua Venetica.* Padova, Zielo.

Perego, E. (2011) Engendered actions: Agency and ritual in pre-Roman Veneto. In A. Chaniotis (ed.) *Ritual Dynamics in the Ancient Mediterranean: Agency, Emotion, Gender, Reception*, 17–42. Stuttgart, Steinar Verlag.

Perego, E. (2012a) *The Construction of Personhood in Veneto (Italy) between the Late Bronze Age and the Early Roman Period.* Unpublished thesis, University College London.

Perego, E. (2012b). Resti umani come oggetti del sacro nel Veneto preromano: Osservazioni preliminari. In V. Nizzo and L. La Rocca (eds) *Antropologia e Archeologia a Confronto: Rappresentazioni e Pratiche del Sacro. Atti del Convegno (Roma, Museo Preistorico Etnografico "Luigi Pigorini", 20–21 Maggio 2011)*, 873–882. Roma, E.S.S. Editorial Service System.

Perego, E. (2012c). Family relationships in late Bronze Age, Iron Age and early Roman Veneto (Italy). Preliminary considerations on the basis of osteological analysis and epigraphy. In R. Lawrence and A. Stromberg (eds) *Families in the Greco-Roman World*, 121–142. London, Continuum.

Perego, E. (2014a) Anomalous mortuary behaviour and social exclusion in Iron Age Italy: A case study from the Veneto region. *Journal of Mediterranean Archaeology* 27(2), 161–185.

Perego, E. (2014b) Final Bronze Age and social change in Veneto: Group membership, ethnicity and marginality. *Mélanges de l'École française de Rome* 126(2) (online version).

Perego, E. (2015) Bodies and persons. In A. Gardner, M. Lake, and U. Sommer (eds) *Oxford Handbook of Archaeological Theory*. Oxford, Oxford University Press (online version).

Perego, E. (forthcoming) Gendered powers, gendered persons. Gender and personhood in a case study from Iron Age Veneto, Italy. In G. Saltini Semerari and N. Sojc (eds) *Investigating Gender in Mediterranean Archaeology*.

Perego, E., Saracino, M., Zamboni, L. and Zanoni, V. (2015) Practices of ritual marginalisation in protohistoric Veneto: Evidence from the field. In Z.L. Devlin and E.J. Graham (eds) *Death Embodied: Archaeological Approaches to the Treatment of the Corpse*, 129–159. Oxford, Oxbow Books.

Pirazzini, C. (2013) Tomba Casa di Ricovero 112. In M. Gamba, G. Gambacurta, A. Ruta Serafini, V. Tiné and F. Veronese (eds) Venetkens. *Viaggio nella Terra dei Veneti Antichi. Catalogo della Mostra (Padova, Palazzo della Ragione, 6 Aprile–17 Novembre 2013)*, 349–350. Venezia, Marsilio.

Prosdocimi, A. (1882) Notizie delle necropoli euganee di Este. *Notizie degli Scavi* 1882, 3–35.

Riedel, A. and Rizzi, J. (1999) Gli scheletri di cane della prima età del Ferro di Oppeano, località Montara. *Quaderni di Archeologia del Veneto* 15, 67–72.

Riedel, A. and Tecchiati, U. (2001) Il cavallo della tomba 61. *Quaderni di Archeologia del Veneto* 17, 84–85.

Robb, J. (2002) Time and biography. Osteobiography of the Italian Neolithic lifespan. In Y. Hamilakis, M. Pluciennik and S. Tarlow (eds) *Thinking Through the Body: Archaeologies of Corporeality*, 153–171. New York, Kluwer/Plenum.

Rossi, S. (2009) *L'Abitato Arginato di Castion di Erbè (Vr) alla Luce dei Risultati dello Studio Cronotipologico della Ceramica Vascolare e Considerazioni sulla Prima Età del Ferro nel Territorio Veronese*. Unpublished thesis, Università degli Studi di Padova.

Ruta Serafini, A. (1990) (ed.) *La Necropoli Paleoveneta di Via Tiepolo a Padova. Un Intervento Archeologico nella Città. Catalogo della Mostra (Padova, Via Aquileia 7, 28 Aprile-28 Giugno 1990)*. Padova, Zielo.

Ruta Serafini, A. (2002) (ed.) *Este Preromana: Una Città e i Suoi Santuari*. Treviso, Canova.

Sainati, C. (2013) Deposito di ceramica. In M. Gamba, G. Gambacurta, A. Ruta Serafini, V. Tiné and F. Veronese (eds) *Venetkens. Viaggio nella Terra dei Veneti Antichi. Catalogo della Mostra (Padova, Palazzo della Ragione, 6 Aprile-17 Novembre 2013)*, 231–232. Venezia, Marsilio.

Salzani, L. (2001a) Tombe protostoriche della necropoli della Colombara (Gazzo Veronese). *Padusa* 37, 83–132.

Salzani, L. (2001b) Gazzo. Scavi nella necropoli della Colombara. *Quaderni di Archeologia del Veneto* 17, 83.

Salzani, L. (2005) La necropoli protostorica di Ponte Nuovo a Gazzo Veronese. *Notizie Archeologiche Bergomensi* 13, 7–112.

Salzani, L. (2008a) Necropoli dei Veneti antichi nel territorio veronese. *In I Veneti Antichi: Novità e Aggiornamenti. Atti del Convegno di Studi (Vò di Isola della Scala, Verona, 15 Ottobre 2005)*, 47–58. Sommacampagna, Cierre Edizioni.

Salzani, L. (2008b) Scavi della Soprintendenza nell'abitato. In A. Guidi and L. Salzani (eds) *Oppeano: Vecchi e Nuovi Dati sul Centro Protourbano* (Quaderni di Archeologia del Veneto, Serie Speciale 3), 21–33. Padova, Canova.

Salzani, L. and Consonni, A. (2005) L'abitato protostorico di Villamarzana-Campagna Michela (Ro). Scavi 1993. *Padusa* 41, 7–55.

Salzani, L. and Colonna, C. (2010) (eds) *La Fragilità dell'Urna. I Recenti Scavi a Narde, Necropoli di Frattesina (XII-IX sec. a.C.). Catalogo della Mostra (Museo dei Grandi Fiumi, Rovigo, 5 Ottobre 2007-30 Marzo 2008)*. Rovigo, Museo dei Grandi Fiumi.

Saracino, M. (2009) Sepolture atipiche durante il Bronzo Finale e la seconda Età del Ferro in Veneto. *Padusa* 45, 65–72.

Saracino, M., Zamboni, L., Zanoni, V. and Perego, E. (2014) Investigating social exclusion in late prehistoric Italy: Preliminary results of the "IN or OUT" Project (Phase 1). *Papers from the Institute of Archaeology* 12(1), 1–12.

Soranzo, F. (1885) *Scavi e Scoperte nei Poderi Nazari di Este*. Roma, Accademia Nazionale dei Lincei.

Smith, C.J. (1996) *Early Rome and Latium. Economy and Society c. 1000 to 500 BC*. Oxford, Clarendon.

Smith, C.J. (2005) The beginnings of urbanization at Rome. In B.W. Cunliffe and R. Osborne (eds) *Mediterranean Urbanization 800-600 BC*, 91–111. Oxford, Oxford University Press.

Stanton, G.R. (1991). *Athenian Politics c. 800-500 BC*. London, Routledge.

Vallicelli, M.C. (2013a) Venuti da molto lontano: Le importazioni. In M. Gamba, G. Gambacurta, A. Ruta Serafini, V. Tiné and F. Veronese (eds) *Venetkens. Viaggio nella Terra dei Veneti Antichi. Catalogo della Mostra (Padova, Palazzo della Ragione, 6 Aprile-17 Novembre 2013)*, 260–263. Venezia, Marsilio.

Vallicelli, M.C. (2013b) Aryballos protocorinzio. In M. Gamba, G. Gambacurta, A. Ruta Serafini, V. Tiné and F. Veronese (eds) *Venetkens. Viaggio nella Terra dei Veneti Antichi. Catalogo della Mostra (Padova, Palazzo della Ragione, 6 Aprile-17 Novembre 2013)*, 265. Venezia, Marsilio.

Voltolini, D. (2013a) Tomba Emo 468. In M. Gamba, G. Gambacurta, A. Ruta Serafini, V. Tiné and F. Veronese (eds) Venetkens. *Viaggio nella Terra dei Veneti Antichi. Catalogo della Mostra (Padova, Palazzo della Ragione, 6 Aprile–17 Novembre 2013)*, 351. Venezia, Marsilio.

Voltolini, D. (2013b) Tomba Emo 318. In M. Gamba, G. Gambacurta, A. Ruta Serafini, V. Tiné and F. Veronese (eds) Venetkens. *Viaggio nella Terra dei Veneti Antichi. Catalogo della Mostra (Padova, Palazzo della Ragione, 6 Aprile–17 Novembre 2013)*, 350–351. Venezia, Marsilio.

Waldron, T. (2009) *Paleopathology*. Cambridge, Cambridge University Press.

Walker, P.L., Bathurst, R.R., Richman, R., Gjerdrum, T. and Andrushko, V.A. (2009) The causes of porotic hyperostosis and cribra orbitalia: A reappraisal of the iron-deficiency-anemia hypothesis. *American Journal Physical Anthropology* 139(2), 109–125.

Wilczak, C., Watkins, R.C. and Blakey, M.L. (2004) *Skeletal Indicators of Work: Musculoskeletal, Arthritic, and Traumatic Events*. US Department of the Interior, National Park Service.

Zamboni, L. and Zanoni, V. (2010) Giaciture non convenzionali in Italia nord-occidentale durante l'Età del Ferro. In M.G. Belcastro and J. Ortalli (eds) *Sepolture Anomale. Indagini Archeologiche e Antropologiche dall'Epoca Classica al Medioevo in Emilia Romagna. Giornata di Studi (Castelfranco Emilia, 19 Dicembre 2009)* (Quaderni di Archeologia dell'Emilia Romagna 28), 147–162. Borgo S. Lorenzo, All'Insegna del Giglio.

Zamboni, L. and Zanoni, V. (2011) Ossa e cenere. Le pratiche di "semicombustione" o "semicremazione" nel I millennio a.C.. *Pagani e Cristiani* 10, 197–216.

Zanoni, V. (2011) *Out of Place. Human Skeletal Remains from Non-Funerary Contexts: Northern Italy during the 1st Millennium BC* (BAR S2306). Oxford, Archaeopress.

Finale

Chapter 13

Shifting perspectives: new agendas for the study of power, social change and the person in late prehistoric and proto-historic Italy

Elisa Perego and Rafael Scopacasa

Working thoughts on agency and power in ancient Italy

In his chapter about drinking practices and commensality, C. Iaia raises a question that we believe lies at the heart of this book, and underlines the significance of the issues addressed here. Iaia's question is whether non-élite groups and/or specific gender or age groups, such as women or children, played any role in the drinking and feasting events where power and status were negotiated in the proto-historic societies of central Italy.

Iaia's question encapsulates one of our chief aims: to challenge some deeply ingrained generalizations about state formation in first-millennium BC Italy, by looking beyond the élite (male) individuals who supposedly coordinated this process. We emphasize his question here because it exposes a questionable assumption that has characterized mainstream scholarship on the rise of socio-political complexity in first-millennium BC Italy: namely, that the only kind of 'serious' politics that was practiced, and is worth studying, took place amongst élite and 'aristocratic' groups, and especially among adult men, often in their capacity as 'warriors' and leaders (*cf.* the introduction by Perego and Scopacasa, with additional bibliography).

To be sure, such a notion is hard to maintain in light of all the breakthroughs in the humanities and social sciences over the past decades. Such developments have demonstrated that power and its exercise are far from constituting a neat and clear-cut mechanism that functions exclusively in a top-down manner (e.g. Bourdieu 1977; 1990; Foucault 1991; 1998; Gardner 2004; Gaventa 2003; 2006; Giddens 1984; Hayward 1998; Lukes (2005[1974]); Navarro 2006; Rabinow 1991; Scott 1985; 1992; 2009; VeneKlasen and Miller 2002). Rather, power is spread throughout the social spectrum, and the functioning of social and political systems depends on constant negotiations of empowerment and subordination between various social agents (e.g. *Pacific Affairs* 2011; Scott 1985; Tamura 2008; *cf.* also the *Powercube* 2011). In these negotiations, the non-élite, and even marginalized, dispossessed or socially excluded individuals can be driving forces of social change and resistance, in their constant struggle for survival, independence or social recognition (*cf.* different cases in Myers 2007; Pellegrino Sutcliffe 2015; Scott 1985; 1992; 2009; Winter 2004). As Foucault put it:

> "we must cease once and for all to describe the effects of power in negative terms: it 'excludes', it 'represses', it 'censors', it 'abstracts', it 'masks', it 'conceals'. In fact power produces; it produces reality; it produces domains of objects and rituals of truth. The individual and the knowledge that may be gained of him belong to this production." (Foucault 1991, 194)

C. Hayward's research (e.g. 1998; *cf.* also the *Powercube* 2011) offers another theoretical basis for developing the issues of power and society addressed in this volume. Hayward notes that social scientists tend to approach power as if it were a tool that powerful individuals use to control the independent actions of the powerless: power, therefore, would be 'exercised' in a direct exchange between two actors or groups (Hayward 1998, 16). This mainstream view of power implies that powerful people deliberately choose when, why and how to control the powerless: this narrative, therefore, makes it easier to identify "culprits" of social miseries and gives us someone "to point a finger at" (Hayward 1998, 14). In terms of archaeological analysis, such a view of power is problematic to address as it forces us to focus on individual actions and intentional choices, which are often difficult to recognize in the archaeological record (e.g. Dobres and Robb 2000; Gardner 2004). Furthermore, this notion of power downplays the fact that the actions of the powerful are just as socially conditioned as those of the powerless (Hayward 1998). As we discuss below, all individuals are socialized into identities, choices and actions: this process, according to Hayward, sets the boundaries of our freedom. Even the highest echelons of society – including the powerful 'princes' invoked in so many archaeological studies – would have been bound by practices and ideas that limited the degree to which they could exercise their authority.

Hayward, therefore, suggests that a critical analysis should redefine 'power' as a network of social boundaries that determine what is possible for all social actors, from the socially excluded to the most powerful members of a group:

> "... Power defines fields of possibility. It facilitates and constrains social action. Its mechanisms consist in laws, rules, norms, customs, social identities, and standards that constrain and enable inter- and intra-subjective action... Freedom enables actors to participate effectively in shaping the boundaries that define for them the field of what is possible." (Hayward 1998, 12)

A central aspect of analysis, therefore, should be the "unquestioned social norms which underpin possibilities for action" (Hayward 1998, 20).

Both Foucault (1991; 1998) and Hayward (1998) are cautious in drawing sharp distinctions between agency and structure: indeed, all actions and structures are conditioned by socialized norms, identities and knowledge. After recognizing the existence of social constraints that determine the limits of our freedom, Hayward (1998, 22) draws our attention to the importance of focusing on efforts to alter these constraints:

> "Freedom ... is the capacity to participate effectively in shaping the social limits that define what is possible ... Critical questions about how power shapes freedom are not, then reducible to questions about distribution and individual choice. Rather, they are questions about the differential impact of social limits to human action on people's capacities to participate in directing their lives and in shaping the conditions of their collective existence."

Furthermore, "the field of what is socially possible can be shaped at a distance" by historical events that are not aimed at a specific group (Hayward 1998, 18). Power can be exercised without direct interaction: for example, urban African-Americans workers were marginalized "at a distance" by a previous generation of industrial decision-makers, and by the historical legacy of racial discrimination (Hayward 1998, 18) – a notion that may be relevant to address marginalization and social control in the *longue durée* in relation to nascent urbanism and state formation in ancient Italy.

Hayward's analysis relates to J.C. Scott's idea that the powerful and the powerless are equally entangled in the web of roles that are internalized through social interaction, and are often played out without any deliberate intent (Scott 1985; 1992; *cf.* also the *Powercube* 2011). His work defines 'resistance' as a form of power that lies between structure and agency:

> "Most of the political life of subordinate groups is to be found neither in the overt collective defiance of powerholders nor in complete hegemonic compliance, but in the vast territory between these two polar opposites." (Scott 1985, 136)

As Scott (1985; 1992) notes, socially marginalized groups develop covert strategies of resistance, including foot-dragging, slander, elusion, false compliance, thieving, feigned ignorance and sabotage. Scott suggests that by searching for episodes of overt resistance and revolt, we often disregard subtle forms of everyday resistance that may be more effective than open defiance.

This work by Foucault (1991; 1998), Scott (1985; 1992; 2009) and Hayward (1998) urges us towards new ways of looking at the issue of power in ancient societies, including first-millennium BC Italy. Rather than viewing power as an instrument that certain people apply to others who are helpless (although this aspect is addressed in Perego's chapter on ritual violence in Veneto), it may be preferable to think in terms of power as a spectrum. A special emphasis should be put on the less overt or visible end of this spectrum and on how the non-élite or the socially marginalized can develop strategies to actively engage with what Hayward (1998) terms the "norms and boundaries" that make domination possible.

As we have already underlined in the introduction, the funerary record of first-millennium BC Italy offers crucial insights into how past ritual was used by different social agents to construct and defy power at the micro-level of their daily life. In mortuary rites, these ritual practices were linked to the production of specific but culturally variable patterns in the manipulation of material culture and the human body. In this chapter, therefore, we aim to put forwards some food for thought concerning the mechanisms that – through ritual – were linked to the rise of increasingly sophisticated forms of socio-political organization in late prehistoric and proto-historic Italy. In particular, we shall focus on aspects of the relation between agency and structure, and on the identification of innovative theoretical frameworks for Italian archaeology, such as marginality and personhood.

Alternative histories, latent conflict and concealed power

One of the aims of this volume has been to shift the focus of research onto the agency of those who supported the remarkable socio-political developments of the first millennium BC through their labour and social action at the micro-scale, and who also played various different roles in the complex structures of power, domination and exploitation that developed as part of these transformations. As outlined in the introduction, the concept of agency (Dobres and Robb 2000; Gardner 2004) seems to us a helpful tool for achieving this goal, since it involves approaching the material record not exclusively as the reflection of coercive social structures or the norms created by dominant social segments, but also as evidence of people's active role in creating the world in which they lived.

Yet, as we review the chapters, what stands out are the great difficulties involved in seeking to recover the experiences and points of view of the non-élite/socially excluded through the burial record of first-millennium BC Italy. In setting out to recover alternative histories, many of the authors in this book are compelled to examine the marginalized through their absence or their powerlessness. For example, Cuozzo approaches the issue of exclusion from formal burial in Orientalizing central Italy as a ritual means intended to render the vast majority of society 'invisible'. Perego's analysis of ritual violence in Veneto is – among other things – a tale of élite conceit, extreme abuse and victimhood. In the chapter by Zanoni on bone manipulation in *Brandopferplätze*, the fragmented state of the evidence does not help to clarify whether the individuals deposited in these 'places of fire sacrifice' were the victims of the ritual, or its beneficiaries, and who was in charge of these ceremonies.

However, many chapters in this volume invite us to rethink the question of non-élite agency and power, and how we can deal with these issues through the funerary record. Iaia and Perego herself show that it is possible to gain a better view of the non-élites by focusing on the less spectacularly wealthy tombs. Both authors suggest that there are many graves in the cemeteries of the 'proto-urban' settlements of central-northern Italy where secondary élites or even 'middling' social groups might have been buried. Even when discounting the victims of extreme social exclusion or ritual violence that are a major focus of Perego's chapter, Venetic cemeteries were relatively rich in inhumation burials that do not display any clear marker of extreme ritual marginalization (*cf.* also Gamba *et al.* 2014; Perego 2014a; 2014b; Perego *et al.* 2015; Saracino *et al.* 2014 with bibliography). Yet, the poor grave assemblages and 'marginal' locations of some of these burials seem to speak of diversity and – potentially – social exclusion: were these people forced to adopt inhumation by their lack of means? Were they pushed to adopt a less prestigious funerary rite by the more powerful individuals choosing cremation rites for themselves and their families? Or was inhumation deliberately selected by some individuals, as *social agents*, to underline some 'diversity' existing between them and those adopting cremation? As shown in Figure 12.6 (*cf.* Perego this volume; Voltolini 2013), the elderly woman buried around 650 BC in the Emo Capodilista cemetery of Padua was accompanied by a grave assemblage that did not differ dramatically from those found in contemporaneous cremation tombs of good standing. Among her grave goods were some ceramic vessels that were possibly used in the framework of ritualized drinking practices – a burial custom that in many parts of ancient Italy was not confined to the highest echelons of society.

Indeed, in his chapter Iaia argues that 'alternative' social actors such as sub-élite groups, or even (potentially) non-élite women from central Italy were able to elaborate their own drinking etiquette, which involved the use of vessels that were different from those found in the tombs of the highest élite. In expanding upon ideas of agency and non-élite identity, Zamboni shows that not all the people living in mid-first millennium BC Italy were prone to adopt the widespread 'rhetoric' of the funerary ritual banquet (or ritual drinking) in their expression of rank and status in burial. Rather, the social agents of sixth-century BC western Emilia created their own narrative of death – one so elusive and localized that Italian scholars have long tried to pigeonhole the relatively simple graves from this area into rigid and aprioristic ethnic categories (attempts that Zamboni carefully debunks in his chapter; on the complexity of ethnic categories in proto-historic Italy *cf.* also Rajala's chapter).

The work of these authors is an important reminder that the powerful are not the sole producers and consumers of material culture – even when the latter is traditionally associated with supposedly 'elitist' practices such as Iron Age and Orientalizing wine consumption. Rather, innovation, creativity and self-assertion are a prerogative of both high-status and low-status social strata. The struggle to engage creatively with the material world is maintained even when individuals face extreme abuse, poverty and annihilation. For example, in commenting upon the use of material culture by inmates at Auschwitz, Myers (2007, 61–2) notes:

"... the high status of the prisoner's bowl and spoon demonstrates the primacy of material objects in the camps. Without a bowl, a prisoner had no way to receive his daily ration... The bowl and the spoon were critical first acquisitions but all prisoners were wise to make further use of exchange on the camp black market. Ubiquitous in the camps, the black market provided other aids in the struggle for survival ... A scrap of paper, cloth, metal, wire, or string, if not of immediate use to the owner, was useful to another, and hence held trade value. (...) Every inmate motivated to survive scavenged, traded and stole; but the most industrious put any special skills to use and actually produced saleable goods (...) Whenever and wherever possible, these Auschwitz artisans used scavenged and stolen materials to fashion useful tools and other goods both to use for themselves and to sell on the camp black market."

Perego and especially Scopacasa show that another way to recover alternative histories is to focus on the frailty of élite or sub-élite power in phases of dramatic socio-political change. In her chapter, Perego discusses how the frantic reaction of powerful Venetic individuals or groups to social change or uncertainty may have resulted in increased ritual violence, which in turn rendered the victims of such abuse visible in the archaeological record. Significantly, these events took place in a period that in Veneto was also characterized by environmental instability and extensive flooding, documented in the stratigraphic sequences of major Venetic settlements such as Este and Padua (e.g. Balista 1998).[1] Scopacasa discusses instead how élites in Samnium attempted to assert their continued pre-eminence at a time of accelerated socio-political transformation, by restricting access to burial in long-standing cemeteries in the fourth and third centuries BC. During that time, some exceptionally powerful élites seem to have developed altogether new forms of self-legitimization that relied more on Hellenistic forms of euergetism, probably in response to growing pressure from non-élite social segments, which were apparently becoming more self-reliant owing to economic growth throughout the region.

Other chapters in this volume indicate that the study of élite practices and beliefs can provide an understanding of the frailties and weaknesses of the political systems that supported these élites, and of the pressures from other social segments that the most powerful (or – at least – the most archaeologically visible) social strata had to deal with on a constant basis. A case in point is Morris's discussion of the so-called 'princely burial phenomenon' (d'Agostino 1977; Fulminante 2003; cf. also Cuozzo, Rajala this volume), even though his primary focus is on tracing the social networks through which the cultural innovations associated with 'princely' tombs spread throughout ancient Campania. Among the various cultural, political and social implications of this phenomenon, one that stands out is the fact that such extreme degrees of ostentation may have come as a response to mounting pressure on the élite groups that were able to amass and give away in burial the amount of wealth needed to create these outstanding graves. This would explain why these Campanian élites felt compelled to try to legitimize their power and standing through what appears to be such an overstated rhetoric of prestige (for a similar argument regarding the

Hallstatt burials of central Europe *cf.* Dietler 1995). It is not always clear whether such mounting pressure came from competing individuals and families pushing their way to the top, or instead from the disenfranchised sectors who bore the brunt of the burgeoning political systems. That such confrontations did occur is confirmed by historically documented episodes in neighbouring areas of ancient Italy, such as the sedition of the plebs in Early Republican Rome (*cf.* Drummond 2008[1990]). It was most likely a combination of intra-élite competition and popular challenges to élite authority that shaped the funerary patterns discussed in this book.

Intense competition within the ranks of the élites is also something that looms large in many of the chapters focusing on 'aristocratic' burial. In her chapter, Cuozzo considers the different means that the élite groups of Etruria and Campania used to reassert their power in times of change; these practices ranged from the creation of 'princely' burial rituals to the adoption of very sophisticated – and highly diversified – forms of manipulation of the dead body. In Di Lorenzo and colleagues' chapter on child burial at Verucchio, competition among the local aristocracies is suggested by the deep concern that these families put into burying their children with all the trappings of high social status. Such burials were probably geared towards reaffirming the élite families' continuing power and authority, so as to deny the break in the descent line caused by premature death. In this volume, a similar phenomenon is also addressed by Cuozzo in discussing Tomb 5 at Monte Michele. A similar dynamic might also explain the exuberant richness of some child graves in Veneto, during the crucial period of both instability and growth examined by Perego (*cf.* for example the case of Este Benvenuti Tomb 126: Chieco Bianchi and Calzavara Capuis 2006). Overall, the aristocratic families of Verucchio seem to have used funerals as a key means of emphasizing their social standing and power, in order to maintain a dynamic equilibrium between themselves. Their strategy to 'enforce' expected social roles on children underscores the central importance of sub-adults in the self-legitimizing rhetoric of the highest echelons of Verucchio's society. As we shall discuss below, this means that we cannot fully understand how the political systems of first-millennium BC Italy worked without taking into account how sub-adults (and women) fit into the picture, even though in many cases these individuals might have been formally barred from direct participation in decision-making processes.

The chapters on Verucchio (Di Lorenzo *et al.*), Pontecagnano (Cuozzo; Morris), Tarquinia (Iaia; Shipley) and Chiusi (O'Donoghue) remind us of the delicate balance that needed to be maintained among leading families for the political community to be able to function. Whilst funerary ostentation was to some extent an element of competition between élite families, it also afforded a common language for the different 'aristocratic' factions to negotiate their position in relation to each other. Bearing in mind differences in historical context, the funerary dynamics explored in this volume are generally consistent with what the historical record tells us about the emergence of the Republican State in late sixth-century BC Rome. In a recent discussion of this process, N. Terrenato

(2011) argues that the development of formal and collegiate magistracies in the Early Republic (late sixth–fifth centuries BC) was originally a strategy meant to alleviate the constant vying for power and prestige among aristocratic families. The creation of yearly magistracies would have ensured that all élite families had an equal share of power, hence decreasing the need for violent competition, which nevertheless remained a real threat to the political system. Although we have no such historical evidence for most of the communities discussed in this volume, the above-mentioned chapters demonstrate how the funerary record can be used to shed light on potential dynamics of intra-élite negotiation and accommodation which sometimes may have resulted in archaeologically visible abuse and ritual violence (for different perspectives *cf.* Perego, Cuozzo this volume).

Gender and burial

When it comes to addressing the rise of socio-political complexity in view of the experiences of women and children, we face a particular set of challenges.[2] On the one hand, these demographic segments are often well represented in the Italian mortuary record, albeit frequently in contexts that tend to be élite-exclusive or élite-dominated (*cf.* Cuozzo, Morris and Di Lorenzo *et al.* this volume). On the other hand, the theoretical approaches to agency and power discussed in the previous paragraphs, invite us to reflect further on the roles and identities of women and children (as well as men) in ancient Italy. By approaching these individuals – especially the women – as social agents in their own right, and not as inanimate cogs in the grand machinery of state formation, authors such as Cuozzo, Iaia, Faustoferri and Morris offer more nuanced insights into power dynamics across a broader social spectrum. The conclusions reached in their chapters can help to cast new light on the processes that we have become accustomed to describe in terms of large-scale and macro-level developments, such as urbanization, intercontinental trade and the formation of city-states and ethnic groups.

Yet the funerary record is ambiguous, and we must always consider the possibility that the burials of women and children found in the cemeteries of first-millennium BC Italy are not indicative of these people's agency in life. Obviously, this is not a new argument. Put simply, certain women may have been buried lavishly in order to underscore the power and prestige of their male counterparts or families (for a critical discussion of this viewpoint *cf.* Arnold 1999; Scopacasa 2014).

However, additional reflections on this issue are both possible and desirable. A first consideration is that women living in past societies were certainly able to harness power and independence on their own, sometimes in unexpected and unpredictable ways. For example, historian M. Pellegrino Sutcliffe (2015) recounts the story of a female miner and soldier, who gained some notoriety in both Italy and the UK for her exploits during Italy's unification process (*c.* 1815–1871):

"A soldier named Mariotti, of the 11th Battalion of the Italian Bersaglieri, though confined to the room by illness, refused to be carried to the hospital. Ultimately, on being forcibly removed thither, the soldier was discovered to be a woman. She joined the army during the war of 1866, to enable her brother to remain with his wife and six children. She had previously, being very strong, worked in the mines. At Custozza (*sic*) she won a medal of bravery. The king has now conferred on her a decoration and sent her home with a pension of 300 lire."[3]

While bearing in mind differences in time and context, the story of Mariotti invites us the re-consider the issue of past women's agency. An increasing focus on 'powerful' or socially active proto-historic Italian women is indeed notable in the literature (e.g. Gangemi *et al.* 2015; von Eles 2007; Saltini Semerari 2009; *cf.* also Morris, Iaia, Cuozzo and Faustoferri this volume).[4] However, many studies in this frame tend to focus on the most archaeologically visible subjects, or on those belonging to the highest ranks of society (i.e. the 'princess', the 'priestess', the banqueter and the weaver of 'noble' extraction).[5] By contrast, a stronger emphasis on alternative social agents, such as disabled, diseased, non-élite and socially marginal female individuals would be desirable in order to explore the full range of power interactions that developed in past societies (*cf.* the discussion above about Hayward 1998, Foucault 1991; 1998 and Scott 1985; 1992; 2009; Iaia this volume). As noted by some scholars (e.g. Whitehouse 2015), new perspectives on gender in Italian late prehistory are possible thanks to bioarchaeology, a discipline that also offers crucial opportunities for studying past violence, disease, disability and social exclusion (e.g. Agarwal and Glencross 2001; Gowland and Knüsel 2006; Martin *et al.* 2013; Waldron 2009; *cf.* Perego, Zanoni this volume).

Another reflection, emerging with special clarity from the chapters by Di Lorenzo and colleagues, Rajala, Cuozzo, Iaia and Shipley, relates to the symbolic and ritual value of both human remains and grave goods. Studying this connection can offer important insights into the relation between individual agents and social structure, and has enabled many contributors (chiefly Iaia, Morris, O'Donoghue and Cuozzo, but also Faustoferri and Di Lorenzo *et al.*) to explore how the material culture linked to different genders was used to promote the persistence or the alteration of social systems. Scholarship has long focused on human-thing interaction and the role of artefacts (and human remains) in enabling the perpetuation or subversion of identities and power systems (e.g. Appadurai 1986; Chapman 2000; Gell 1998; Gosden and Marshall 1999; Hodder 2012; Joy 2009; on ancient Italy: Perego 2011; Rajala 2014 and Iaia, Rajala, Shipley this volume). The idea of the 'agency' of past objects and dead bodies resides in the meaningfulness that people clearly attributed to them, as envisaged by the practices of ritual manipulation (e.g. re-use, intentional fragmentation) often involved in the management of such substances. As we are accustomed to approach death and the management of cadavers in a much 'cleaner' and impersonal way with respect to many ancient peoples, we might find it impossible to understand the deep, emotional responses that objects and human remains may have aroused in past mourners.

Notably, in many first-millennium BC Italian societies, women's graves tended to be more numerous and even richer in grave goods than men's graves (for different regional cases *cf.* for example Perego 2011; Saltini Semerari 2015). Therefore, women's burials would have offered crucial opportunities for ritual manipulation, especially when these graves were re-used by the mourners. In Veneto, for example, the objects and bodies involved in funerary practices of bone mingling and grave-good fragmentation were mainly those of women and children (e.g. Perego 2011, 31–5). Therefore, if human remains and grave goods had any significance as mementoes of individuals, recipients of personal histories, and instruments for the negotiation of social and family membership, their meaningfulness in first-millennium BC Italy was often strongly related to women and even children (*cf.* Di Lorenzo *et al.* this volume). As such, even individuals who were potentially barred from formal decision-making were not inconsequential in history: rather, their bodies and possessions were at the core of discourses about power, identity and social memory. Even more importantly, dealing with the agency of inanimate beings draws our attention to the influences they had in stimulating powerful emotional responses at the funeral. Even when these tombs were arranged by men, with no room for female agency, these 'female' grave goods must have meant something in terms of the 'impact' they had on the mourners, and the forms of engagement the living built with the dead.

A third reflection involves the issue of men's agency. If the "dead do not bury themselves", this is true also of high-ranking males; since the funerary record is itself an ideological construct (Parker Pearson 1999), the burials of adult men were just as much the object of manipulation as those of women and children. That being the case, how sure can we be that prestige markers buried with men were personal possessions, rather than symbols of family status or power (*cf.* Saltini Semerari 2015, 139)? It is also worth recalling cases in northern Europe of males that were either too young or too old to have used the weapons they were buried with: such cases indicate that the 'masculine identity' of these individuals was also an ideological construct (Harke 1990). Similarly, Di Lorenzo and co-authors argue that the construction of funerary identities at Verucchio was so complex, that it is difficult to discriminate not only between the actual role of the deceased in life and the identity they were given in death – but also between all the different layers of identities articulated through the careful positioning of different objects in the grave.

Yet, when we speak of symbols of power, wealth and prestige in male graves, we seem to be more disposed to see these artefacts as indicative of the deceased person's actual power in life. By contrast, when it comes to women, there is a tendency to think about the use of female graves and female bodies as male tokens. While this is perfectly possible, it is important to be aware of our interpretative bias. To escape this bias, we must reckon with the possibility that even élite men – even when apparently in full possession of power and authority – might themselves have been smaller players within the broader 'structure' in agency theory terms – that is, the web of relations in which these people's power developed, was legitimized, accepted and even exploited by others. To what extent can we really see the adult men whose graves we come to study as symbols of warriorhood, power and prestige as 'real' social agents, and not just as the products of funerary ideology, their society and *our own assumptions* about what past masculine ideology should have been?

In recent gender research, some scholars working on masculinity have indeed discussed how archaeology might promote the construction of static and monolithic notions of maleness. For example, Alberti (2006, 401) has noted:

> "'Men' ... have always been visible [in the archaeological record] but their gender has been 'unmarked' ... Their presence has been assumed – but assumed on the basis of a 'neutral' body, unmarked by gender, race or any other category of identity ... The genderless man comes to stand for society as a whole."

As O'Donoghue and Faustoferri show in this volume, the proto-historic Italian men we discuss are often as constructed as the 'submissive' women or the elegant wives of the 'princes', adorned with jewels, that some scholars have conceptualized: we have then the 'prince' himself, the 'chief', the 'powerful warrior', and so on (*cf.* the introduction for further analysis and bibliography). By contrast, many crucial dimensions in a man's life (e.g. fatherhood, spousal relations) are often glossed over by scholars, even when references to such aspects of male identity are visible – and even strongly underlined by the mourners – in the funerary record. A case in point is bone mingling, namely a funerary ritual that involved burying the cremated remains of different dead individuals in the same cinerary urn. Very well attested in both Veneto (Bianchin Citton *et al.* 1998; Gamba *et al.* 2014; Perego this volume; 2012a; 2012b) and Verucchio (Di Lorenzo *et al.* this volume), bone-mingling rituals were often adopted to emphasize close family ties, including spousal and father–child relations (*cf.* especially the Venetic case: Perego 2012a; 2012b). Yet, while studies of proto-historic Italian women as 'wives' and 'mothers' are widespread (e.g. Bartoloni and Pitzalis 2012; also Caporusso 2007), a focus on men as 'husbands', 'fathers' and so on is often poor or absent.[6] At this point in the development of the field, it is even possible that we can 'see' women better than men, thanks to all the work done in gender archaeology.

Personhood, marginality and extreme social exclusion

An increasing attention to anomalous funerary rites that might be indicative of social exclusion and social abnormality is evident in late prehistoric and proto-historic Italian archaeology (e.g. Bartoloni and Benedettini 2007/2008; Belcastro and Ortalli 2010; Saracino 2009; Zanoni 2011). However, still scanty is research directly focusing on *extreme* social marginality and the construction of suitable theoretical and methodological frameworks for the identification of socially marginal individuals in the archaeological record (*cf.* however Perego 2014a, 2014b; Perego *et al.* 2015; Saracino and Zanoni 2014; Saracino *et al.* 2014).[7]

In spite of the overbearing presence of élite and dominant social segments in analyses of the funerary record of proto-historic Italy, this volume has attempted to draw attention to some key instances offering more direct access into the world and experiences of those who were excluded from positions of power and influence.

An example is Perego's chapter on anomalous burials and the abuse of human beings by the social segments who controlled the Venetic cemeteries and ritual sites *c.* 800–500 BC. Her chapter is a discussion of how people might have been manipulated as 'symbolic capital' by the élites, and of how power over people and their bodies was something that the Venetic dominant groups displayed to the arguably extreme degree of human sacrifice. Here we are perhaps shown one of the grimmer aspects of social marginalization in Iron Age Italy, where the people who were the object of anomalous burial practices might have been stripped of their humanity and regarded as 'non-persons' so that the ruling segments could legitimize their authority. It seems significant – if not ironic – that the non-élite and marginal individuals we look for should owe one of their clearest manifestations in the archaeological record to practices that may have served to deprive them of their value as human beings.

Some of Perego's conclusions about abnormal burial in Veneto might be applicable to the ritual sites that Zanoni examines, many of which feature burnt human remains. One is tempted to speculate that the 'adolescents' and 'young adults' whose bones tended to be deposited in *Brandopferplätze* might, in some cases at least, have been the victims of practices of abuse (or re-use of human remains for ritual purposes) similar to the ones noted in Veneto. For the areas that Zanoni considers, such as Trentino–South Tyrol, it is more difficult to draw conclusions because of the fragmentary nature of the evidence. However, Zanoni's chapter provides us with important information on a long-lived series of ritual phenomena in what remains a poorly understood part of ancient Italy. Her work raises questions for future research on both *Brandopferplätze* and the socio-political development of this secluded corner of ancient Italy, which was nevertheless important for its routes, local resources and trade links (Bellintani 2015). In the end, who did select the individuals deposited in *Brandopferplätze*? Apart from age, did more subtle forms of social classification determine the selection of the individuals found in these ritual sites, even among the age classes discussed by Zanoni? Was human sacrifice practiced in *Brandopferplätze* or were they just the burial sites of people who died elsewhere? Was placement in *Brandopferplätze* a form of reward for individuals deemed to be 'special', albeit potentially anomalous because of their incomplete physical or social development, or was it a form of 'punishment' intended to mark social exclusion? Can we detect variability in the treatment of human remains in *Brandopferplätze* over time? If this was the case, were these changes linked to overall transformations in the socio-political structuring of late prehistoric northern Italy, and evolving social ideas concerning the lifecycle, the body and personhood?

The concept of personhood allows for great flexibility in exploring the dynamics of social exclusion and inclusion, which lie at the heart of the present volume (*cf.* the chapters by Shipley, O'Donoghue and Perego). While numerous approaches to personhood exist in philosophy, anthropology and archaeology,[8] a crucial aspect of this debate focuses on what 'being human' means. In numerous societies, 'persons' are defined as those individuals – generally but not necessarily humans – granted by the group full or partial membership in society (e.g. Conklin and Morgan 1996, 662; Morgan 1997; 2002[1989]; Perego 2012a; this volume). In any given society, prevailing discourses of social classification and normalization promote viable ways of being meaningfully 'human' and sanction possible deviations. Personhood is not automatically granted to all: humans are biological entities that are not necessarily integrated into the social group and can be denied crucial rights and responsibilities in society, including the right to live. Persons are humans – and sometimes other beings – who are socialized into their culture and granted normative social value (Perego 2012a).

The complexity of social practices relating to personhood resonates well with the words by anthropologist L.M. Morgan (1997, 329; 346–7) on foetal and child personhood in modern rural Ecuador:

> "Nascent persons are brought into being slowly, through processes rife with uncertainty and moral ambiguity. Adults are slow to assign individual identity and personhood to the not-yet-born and the newly born. These *criaturas*, as they are often called, bear little resemblance to disembodied, technologized, visualized, personified, and revered U.S. fetuses. These unknown, unknowable *criaturas* may teeter on the cusp of personhood for months before being fully welcomed into a human community ... The trajectory of personhood need not necessarily be linear, because people cannot predict the many influences that bring each person into being... Incipient personhood is understood as openly ambiguous and variable, its character perennially liminal, amorphous, and irresolvable ... A *criatura* said to be formed (and thus *una persona*) by six months' gestation may be said at birth to be 'little more than an animal' until it is baptized."

If we follow this approach, we may note that social dynamics relating to personhood are not only political in nature, or necessarily based on citizenship-like or status-based models of social aggregation. Rather, they also focus on other qualities of people (e.g. physical attributes, age, health status, family links and social connections) which make them valuable to their community or determine their partial or total exclusion from their group. In this regard, therefore, the idea of personhood is an important tool for our exploration of the past: it can indeed offer us a valid theoretical framework for looking beyond those forms of social categorization that are often privileged in scholarly analyses of ancient Italy (e.g. ethnicity or – as mentioned above – citizenship and status).

Multidimensional powers and multiple social actors in state formation

Even fully developed states are relatively delicate structures that rest on a balance between coercion and consent. It is by exploring the everyday context of social interactions that we can gain a fuller appreciation of how this balance is constructed, maintained, contested and ultimately transformed. The idea of power as dynamic and multidimensional also reminds us that power works within the individual, as a sense of self-worth and self-knowledge, as well as within small groups and at the micro-level of everyday life (e.g. Foucault 1991; Hayward 1998; Rabinow 1991; Scott 1985; 1992; *cf.* also the *Powercube* 2011).

Foucault's view of power as social discipline primarily refers to the rise of the modern state (Foucault 1991). He argued that systems of surveillance through institutions such as prisons, schools and mental asylums, originated in modern Europe and greatly enhanced the ability of governments to control their populations, by setting out norms of behaviour that were then internalized by individuals. Foucault stressed how the modern state developed ways of controlling people even at the level of their physical bodies, which were made to behave in certain ways. Although this phenomenon of "bio-power" – as Foucault termed it – is surely an aspect of the modern state, it is not entirely clear that it originated only in modern times and not before. Few would deny that modern states have successfully achieved a kind of soft but extremely deep form of control over people, which was difficult to achieve in previous eras. However, many of the chapters in this volume suggest that the development of subtle forms of management of the person – including their bodies – was also widely achievable in pre-modern societies. Indeed, if power is so widespread and capillary as Foucault himself noticed, then bio-power frameworks of control must work and develop even at the micro-level of the 'small-scale' or 'simple' political negotiations that took place even in less complex societies, and are therefore meaningful for our exploration of the past.

This book has been an attempt to show that archaeology is well equipped to provide a reflection on these issues – especially funerary archaeology. As the foregoing chapters demonstrated, the very complex forms of management of human remains that we can see in first-millennium BC Italy indicate the existence of sophisticated social ideas of the 'person' and their role in society – especially in regard to the expectations about what the 'person' was supposed to be, or needed to become after death. If funerary rituals and the treatment of the corpse are an arena for the negotiation of power (e.g. Parker Pearson 1999; Morgan 2009), the management of the body in first-millennium BC Italy can be seen as a very sophisticated form of bio-power – one that is certainly different from what is achieved by modern political agencies, but was definitely no less real, meaningful, productive, constraining and coercing.

As shown in this volume, funerary rituals may change over time, even over very short periods. This was certainly the case of first-millennium BC Italy. Does this point towards the construction of notions of the person and the body that were continuously shifting and in flux? If we focus on the issues of control and power negotiation, can we detect the development of forms of bio-power and notions of personhood that rapidly evolved in the chaotic process that we call 'state formation'? To what extent, for example, can we see differences in body management and funerary ritual before and after the creation of states and in response to nascent urbanism?

Several chapters in this volume indicate ways to address these issues. Hence, for example, Shipley's suggestion of a growing emphasis on the individual as opposed to the community in the context of mortuary display in tenth–ninth century BC

Tarquinia – which Shipley sees as related to increasing social and political inequality. Shipley's considerations provide food for thought on whether the development of the state and all its attending social, economic and political transformations made the subordinate social sectors increasingly excluded or 'silenced' from the material record (*cf.* also Cuozzo this volume). This would fit well with what we know so far about state formation from a broad anthropological and sociological perspective: namely, that it is a process that strongly relies on increased social stratification, with the ensuing inequality often manifesting itself in the material record in terms of a greater emphasis on the powerful at the expense of the marginalized (for example, through the use of élite cemeteries and monumental ritual complexes) (e.g. Claessen and Skalnik 1978; Gledhill 1988; Johnson and Earle 1987; Terrenato and Haggis 2011).

Yet the picture is not clear-cut, not least because our understanding of state formation and nascent urbanism in ancient Italy is far from thorough. For example, it remains unclear when 'state formation' effectively took place, and what exactly were the thresholds between 'pre-state' and 'state'. The use of the terminology itself (i.e. state, urban, proto-urban and the like) may be misleading and unhelpful in accounting for micro-scalar change, intra-site and inter-site diversity and people's agency. New evidence suggests that the rise of state and urban forms of social organization was a more gradual and faltering process than previously thought, one which may have stretched back, in some of its salient aspects, to the Final Bronze Age (*c.* 1200–1000 BC; on different approaches to this issue *cf.* for example Attema *et al.* 2010; Bietti Sestieri 2008; Fulminante 2014; Guidi 2010; Leonardi 2010).

In Veneto and nearby areas, scholars have come across several relatively large nucleated settlements that originated in the mid- to late (e.g. Fondo Paviani; Fabbrica dei Soci; the Terramare of Emilia) or the late second millennium BC (e.g. Frattesina; Montagnana) (e.g. Bernabò Brea *et al.* 1997; Bianchin Citton *et al.* 1998; Bietti Sestieri 1984; Cardarelli 2010; Cremaschi and Pizzi 2011; De Guio *et al.* 2009; Leonardi 2010; Pearce 1998; Peretto 2010). Often highly diverse in their size, organization and social structuring, these settlements offer crucial insights into socio-cultural variability both at the micro-scale and in the *longue durée*. Their destinies were different, too. Sometimes, it has been possible to identify a succession of micro-phases of crisis and re-growth in some of these sites and their immediate surroundings, which nonetheless prospered again in the Iron Age (e.g. Montagnana/Borgo S. Zeno: Bianchin Citton 1998). In other instances, crisis of entire settlement systems resulted in complex dynamics of micro-scalar collapse, continuity and territorial re-organization in a same area; this is the case, for example, of the so-called 'polity' of the Valli Grandi Veronesi, a Terramare enclave located in Veneto north of the Po River (Betti 2013, 41; Cupitò *et al.* 2012; Dal Corso *et al.* 2012).[9] Finally, sometimes the complete collapse of socio-economic and environmental systems led to the disappearance of whole networks of settlements and to long-term depopulation of the affected areas, such as in the case of the Terramare south of the Po (Betti 2013, 41; Cardarelli 2010, 450; Cremaschi 2010; Cremaschi *et al.* 2006; de Marinis 2010; Frontini 2009).

In conjunction with increasing evidence from other Italian regions (e.g. Attema *et al.* 2010), these data suggest the existence of multiple trajectories towards increased socio-political and technological complexity, even in the same area or region. In these chaotic processes, preceding to rise of urbanism and statehood in the study area, some earlier 'experiments' (such as the Terramare) failed to survive for complex reasons that related to environmental constraints, long-term processes in land management and resource exploitation and, potentially, the 'wrong' choices made by their inhabitants in phases of dramatic change and transformation (e.g. Cardarelli 2010; Cardarelli in Frontini 2009, 192–3).

Even more crucially for the scope of this volume, the funerary evidence available from this area provides valuable insights into the development of social complexity and inequality in late prehistory (e.g. Bietti Sestieri 2011; Cardarelli *et al.* 2015; Perego *et al.* 2015; Salzani 2005). It also sheds light on experimentation with different bodily treatments in death (e.g. Cavazzuti 2011; Cavazzuti and Salvadei 2014; Salzani 2005; 2010a; 2010b) and the rise (or the stiffening) of funerary norms that may have rendered social exclusion and extreme social marginality potentially more visible in the burial record of late prehistoric northern Italy (discussion in Perego 2014b; Perego *et al.* 2015; Saracino and Zanoni 2014; Saracino *et al.* 2014).[10]

A good example is Frattesina di Fratta Polesine, a settlement located close to the Adriatic shore of southern Veneto (Bietti Sestieri 1984; De Guio *et al.* 2009; Leonardi 2010). Placed at a crucial crossroad between the Alps, the Po plain and the Adriatic Sea, in the Final Bronze Age Frattesina developed as a major commercial and productive hub with trade links to the eastern Mediterranean, continental and northern Europe, and central and southern Italy. While the exact 'nature' of the settlement and its social organization remain debated, Frattesina played a crucial role in the late prehistoric central Mediterranean for its glass-making, commercial connections and amber-working (Bellintani 2015).

Although at the end of the second millennium BC Frattesina displayed the hallmarks of a prosperous production center, it failed to develop into an urban settlement and finally disappeared in the early first millennium due to causative factors that remain partly unexplained. The causes of the final crisis may include environmental and climatic instability[11] and a crucial rearrangement in long-distance trade networks (Bellintani 2015). Even before its final disappearance, Frattesina experienced different phases of settlement re-organization and was marred by flooding from the nearby Po di Adria palaeochannel (De Guio *et al.* 2009; Di Anastasio 2010) – evidence that might be further used to explore human-environment interaction, vulnerability and resilience at the micro-scale.

The cemeteries that surrounded Frattesina yielded several hundred cremation graves grouped in clusters that may represent the burial sites of kinship groups and/or social affiliates (*gruppi gentilizio-clientelari* in Cardarelli *et al.* 2015; Salzani 2010a). They also yielded a few dozen inhumation burials, which sometimes display marked evidence of ritual abnormality and – possibly – intentional abuse and ritual marginalization (e.g. prone burial, burial in isolation, potential evidence of 'hasty' interment and violence: Salzani 2010b). Overall, the grave assemblages, spatial locations and varying ritual treatments associated with both inhumation and cremation burials shed lights on the negotiation of status, inequality and social diversity at a key production and commercial site in the late prehistoric Mediterranean (e.g. Bietti Sestieri 2011; Cardarelli *et al.* 2015; Perego 2014b; Salzani and Colonna 2010; Saracino and Zanoni 2014; Saracino *et al.* 2014).

The case of Veneto and nearby areas, therefore, raises additional questions as to whether the long run towards the rise of urban and state realities in ancient Italy was in fact a complex and 'messy' process that often revolved around micro-phases of growth and crisis succeeding one another, even within the same settlement or micro-region. Furthermore, the burial record from this area opens windows into the crucial dynamics of power negotiation that took place in Italy in the second and early first millennia BC – just before the period tackled in this volume. Within this framework, to what extent can we connect these micro-phases of change in both funerary ritual and social structuring, to different forms of agency and power, and attempts at changing the structure of society by different social actors? How did all these processes affect people, especially low-ranking and marginal individuals? Were they always silenced, or were there phases in which their 'voices' emerged more clearly in the archaeological record?

Notions of personhood and identity might have changed abruptly as the state developed, and most certainly with the rise of increasingly complex forms of social structuring, including non-state-like forms of power and organization. However, there is no simple equation that tells us what the funerary correlates of these social dynamics are going to be, nor should we be searching for one. Instead, what the chapters in this volume show is that we need to pay more attention to the diversity and nuances of the funerary record as a means of gaining new insights into the social dynamics behind it. This includes paying increasing consideration to social processes initiated by – or involving – the non-élite and marginal individuals that are often the forgotten protagonists of human history.

Acknowledgements

Elisa Perego and Rafael Scopacasa would like to thank Cristiano Iaia and Silvia Amicone for their insights into many topics discussed in this chapter. Elisa would also like to thank Marcella Pellegrino Sutcliffe, Massimo Saracino, Corinna Riva, Veronica Tamorri, Lorenzo Zamboni, Vera Zanoni and Ruth Whitehouse for discussion about social marginality or gender ideologies in past societies; and Paolo Bellintani for the permission to cite his *Padusa* article, still in press when this chapter was last revised.

Notes

1. Some preliminary considerations on this issue were presented in Perego *et al.* 2014; 2015. This topic is part of the interdisciplinary project *Collapse or survival: Micro-dynamics of crisis, change and socio-political endurance in the first-millennium BC central Mediterranean*, led by the authors of this chapter in collaboration with Silvia Amicone (UCL), and kindly supported by the G.E. Rickman Fund (the British School at Rome) and FAPESP.

2. On similar issues in world archaeology, *cf.* for example Bolger 2013; Baxter 2005a; 2005b; Kamp 2001; Moore and Scott 1997; Sofaer Derevenski 2000. On gender in Italian archaeology: Whitehouse 1998; Perego and Scopacasa this volume, with additional bibliography; recent research on the topic includes Cuozzo 2015; Gleba 2015; Saltini Semerari 2015; Scopacasa 2014; Whitehouse 2015.

3. Citation taken from the quarterly *Englishwoman's Review* (reported in Pellegrino Sutcliffe 2015).

4. For example, a recent exhibition associated with Expo Milano 2015 was entitled *Principesse Etrusche del Tirreno. Femminilità, culto, potere* (note the use of the concept of 'power', in association with 'cult' and 'femininity', to describe the Etruscan 'princesses' mentioned in the exhibition's title).

5. On gendered patterns in ritual drinking and possible cases of alcohol consumption by high-ranking women: Coen 2008; Iaia this volume; Riva 2010; on the social status of weavers and spinners as well as of textile production in ancient Italy: Bietti Sestieri 1992; Gleba 2008; 2015.

6. For example, in a recent edited volume discussing, among other topics, burial in proto-historic Italy (Nizzo 2011), the book session focusing on men is dedicated to "warriors, princes, priests and heroes", while the one dedicated to women speaks of "*mothers, wives*, queens and priestesses" (emphasis added).

7. Research on marginality, slavery and social exclusion in the Roman world and later periods is richer, possibly for the wealth of written sources available: for example, Atkins and Osborne 2006; Bradley and Cartledge 2011.

8. On different approaches to personhood in scholarly debates *cf.* for example Bordo 1993; Battaglia 1983; Conklin and Morgan 1996; Fowler 2004; Knapp and van Dommelen 2008; Lamb 1997; Mauss 1985[1938]; Mines 1998; Morgan 1997; 2002[1989]; 2006; 2009; Thomas 1996; Wagner 1991, and O'Donoghue, Perego, Shipley and the introduction this volume, with additional bibliography.

9. The 'polity' includes the above-mentioned Fondo Paviani and Fabbrica dei Soci; its 'destiny' is also notable for its complex relation to the rise of Frattesina (Betti 2013, 41; Cupitò *et al.* 2012; Dal Corso *et al.* 2012). We want to underline here that our brief discussion of north-east Italy's development in the second millennium BC is intended as an invitation to look more closely at people's agency in times of change; we do not pretend to fully account for issues such as environmental instability, settlement organization etc. in this chapter.

10. In Veneto, the 'deviant' funerary practices attested at some Bronze Age sites, such as Frattesina, may have been a 'prodrome' of the ritual abuse mentioned in Perego's chapter (*cf.* Perego 2014b; Perego *et al.* 2015; Saracino and Zanoni 2014; Saracino *et al.* 2014 for further discussion; *cf.* also Cuozzo, Iaia, Scopacasa, Zanoni, this volume, on exclusion from formal burial in first-millennium BC Italy).

11. This is a complex issue that is impossible to fully explore in this chapter. On environmental, climatic and/or riverine instability in the eastern Po plain, with contributions variously covering the span from the Middle Bronze Age to the early first millennium BC, *cf.* for example Balista 1998; 2009; Cardarelli 2010; Cremaschi 2010; Cremaschi *et al.* 2006; de Marinis 2010; De Guio *et al.* 2009; Di Anastasio 2010; Piovan 2008; Piovan *et al.* 2010.

Bibliography

Agarwal, S.C. and Glencross, B.A. (2011) (eds) *Social Bioarchaeology*. Malden, Wiley Blackwell.

Alberti, B. 2006. Archaeology, men, and masculinities. In S.M. Nelson (ed.) *Handbook of Gender Archaeology*, 401–434. Walnut Creek, Altamira Press.

Appadurai, A. (1986) (ed.) *The Social Life of Things. Commodities in Cultural Perspective*. Cambridge, Cambridge University Press.

Arnold, B. (1999) Drinking the feast: Alcohol and the legitimation of power in Celtic Europe. *Cambridge Archaeological Journal* 9(1), 71–93.

Atkins, M. and Osborne, R. (2006) (eds) *Poverty in the Roman World*. Cambridge, Cambridge University Press.

Attema, P.A.J., Burgers, G.-J. and van Leusen, P.M. (2010) *Regional Pathways to Complexity: Landuse Dynamics in Early Italy from the Bronze Age to the Republican Period* (Amsterdam Archaeological Studies 15). Amsterdam, Amsterdam University Press.

Balista, C. (1998) Le sequenze di deposito alluvionale nella serie archeologica della necropoli. In E. Bianchin Citton, G. Gambacurta and A. Ruta Serafini (eds) *... Presso l'Adige Ridente ... Recenti Rinvenimenti Archeologici da Este a Montagnana. Catalogo della Mostra (Este, Museo Nazionale Atestino, 21 Febbraio 1998–21 Febbraio 1999)*, 29–35. Padova, ADLE.

Balista, C. (2009) Le risposte del sistema paleoidrografico di risorgiva delle Valli Grandi Veronesi Meridionali alle fluttuazioni climatiche tardo-oloceniche e agli impatti antropici legati ai cicli insediativi dell'età del Bronzo, di età romana e di età tardorinascimentale-moderna. *Padusa* 45, 73–131.

Bartoloni, G. and Benedettini, M.G. (2007–2008) (eds) *Sepolti tra i Vivi. Evidenza e Interpretazione di Contesti Funerari in Abitato. Atti del Convegno Internazionale (Roma, 26–29 Aprile 2006)*. Roma, Quasar.

Bartoloni, G. and Pitzalis, F. (2012) Mogli e madri nella nascente aristocrazia tirrenica. In V. Nizzo and L. La Rocca (eds) *Antropologia e Archeologia a Confronto: Rappresentazioni e Pratiche del Sacro. Atti del Convegno. (Roma, Museo Nazionale Preistorico Etnografico "Luigi Pigorini", 20–21 Maggio 2011)*, 137–160. Roma, E.S.S Editorial Service.

Battaglia, D. (1983) Projecting personhood in Melanesia: The dialectics of artefact symbolism on Sabarl Island. *Man* 18(2), 289–304.

Baxter, J.E. (2005a). *The Archaeology of Childhood: Children, Gender, and Material Culture*. Walnut Creek, Altamira Press.

Baxter, J.E. (2005b) (ed.) *Children in Action: Perspectives on the Archaeology of Childhood*. Berkeley, University of California Press.

Belcastro, M.G. and Ortalli, J. (2010) (eds) *Sepolture Anomale. Indagini Archeologiche e Antropologiche dall'Epoca Classica al Medioevo in Emilia Romagna. Giornata di Studi (Castelfranco Emilia, 19 Dicembre 2009)* (Quaderni di Archeologia dell'Emilia Romagna 28). Borgo S. Lorenzo, All'Insegna del Giglio.

Bellintani, P. (2015) Baltic amber, alpine copper and glass beads from the Po plain. Amber trade at the time of Campestrin and Frattesina. *Padusa* (in press).

Bernabò Brea, M., Cardarelli, A. and Cremaschi, M. (1997) (eds) *Le Terramare. La Più Antica Civiltà Padana*. Milano, Electa.

Betto, A. (2013) *Le "Strade" delle Valli Grandi Veronesi Meridionali. Connettività e Management Idraulico nel Quadro di un Paesaggio di Potere*. Unpublished thesis, Università degli Studi di Padova [http://paduaresearch.cab.unipd.it/5855/].

Bianchin Citton, E. (1998) Montagnana tra XIII e VIII sec. a.C.: Un primo bilancio delle ricerche. In E. Bianchin Citton, G. Gambacurta and A. Ruta Serafini (eds) *... Presso l'Adige Ridente... Recenti Rinvenimenti Archeologici da Este a Montagnana. Catalogo della Mostra (Este, Museo Nazionale Atestino, 21 Febbraio 1998-21 Febbraio 1999)*, 429–433. Padova, ADLE.

Bianchin Citton, F., Gambacurta, G. and Ruta Serafini, A. (1998) (eds) *... Presso l'Adige Ridente... Recenti Rinvenimenti Archeologici da Este a Montagnana. Catalogo della Mostra (Este, Museo Nazionale Atestino, 21 Febbraio 1998-21 Febbraio 1999)*. Padova, ADLE.

Bietti Sestieri, A.M. (1984) L'abitato di Frattesina. *Padusa* 20, 413–427.

Bietti Sestieri, A.M. (1992) *The Iron Age Community of Osteria dell'Osa: A Study of Socio-Political Development in Central Tyrrhenian Italy*. Cambridge, Cambridge University Press.

Bietti Sestieri, A.M. (2008) L'età del Bronzo Finale nella penisola italiana. *Padusa* 44, 7–54.

Bietti Sestieri, A.M. (2011) Archeologia della morte fra età del Bronzo ed età del Ferro in Italia. Implicazioni delle scelte relative alla sepoltura in momenti di crisi o di trasformazione politico-organizzativa. In V. Nizzo (ed.) *Dalla Nascita alla Morte: Antropologia e Archeologia a Confronto. Atti dell'Incontro Internazionale di Studi in Onore di Claude Lévi-Strauss (Roma, Museo Nazionale Preistorico Etnografico "Luigi Pigorini", 21 Maggio 2010)*, 397–418. Roma, E.S.S Editorial Service.

Bolger, D. (2013) (ed.) *Blackwell Companion to Gender Prehistory*. Oxford, Blackwell.

Bourdieu, P. (1977) *Outline of a Theory of Practice*. Cambridge, Cambridge University Press.

Bourdieu, P. (1990) *The Logic of Practice*. Cambridge, Polity Press.

Bordo, S. (1993) Are mothers persons? Reproductive rights and the politics of subjectivity. In S. Bordo and L. Heywood (eds) *Unbearable Weight: Feminism, Western Culture and the Body*, 71–97. Berkeley, University of California Press.

Bradley, K. and Cartledge, P. (2011) (eds) *The Cambridge World History of Slavery, Volume 1: The Ancient Mediterranean World*. Cambridge, Cambridge University Press.

Caporusso, D. (2007) *Figlie e Madri, Mogli e Concubine: La Condizione Femminile nel Mondo Antico. Catalogo della Mostra (Milano, Museo Archeologico, 8 Marzo-28 Novembre 2007)*. Milano, Edizioni ET.

Cardarelli, A. (2010) The collapse of the Terramare culture and growth of new economic and social systems during the Bronze Age in Italy. *Scienze dell'Antichità* 15[2009], 449–520.

Cardarelli, A., Cavazzuti, C., Quondam, F., Salvadei, L. and Salzani, L. (2015) Le necropoli delle Narde di Frattesina: Proposta per una lettura delle evidenze demografiche, rituali e sociali a partire dai dati archeologici e antropologici. In G. Leonardi e V. Tinè (eds) *Preistoria e Protostoria del Veneto*. Firenze, Instituto Italiano di Preistoria e Protostoria.

Cavazzuti, C. (2011) *Aspetti Rituali, Sociali e Paleodemografici di Alcune Necropoli Protostoriche a Cremazione dell'Italia Settentrionale*. Unpublished thesis, Università degli Studi di Ferrara.

Cavazzuti, C. and Salvadei, L. (2014) I resti umani cremati della necropoli di Casinalbo. In A. Cardarelli (ed.) *La Necropoli della Terramara di Casinalbo*, 669–707. Borgo S. Lorenzo, All'Insegna del Giglio.

Chapman, J. (2000) *Fragmentation in Archaeology*. London, Routledge.

Chieco Bianchi, A.M. and Calzavara Capuis, L. (2006) (eds) *Este II. La Necropoli di Villa Benvenuti*. Roma, Giorgio Bretschneider Editore.

Claessen, H.J.M. and Skalnik, P. (1978) (eds) *The Early State*. The Hague, Mouton.

Conklin, B.A. and Morgan, L.M. (1996) Babies, bodies and the production of personhood in north America and a native Amazonian society. *Ethos* 24(4), 657–694.

Coen, A. (2008) Il banchetto aristocratico e il ruolo della donna. In M. Silvestrini and M. Sabatini (eds) *Potere e Splendore. Gli Antichi Piceni a Matelica. Catalogo della Mostra (Matelica, Palazzo Ottoni, 19 Aprile-31 Ottobre 2008)*, 159–165. Roma, "L'Erma" di Bretschneider.

Cremaschi, M. (2010) Ambiente, clima ed uso del suolo nella crisi della cultura delle terramare. *Scienze dell'Antichità* 15[2009], 521–534.

Cremaschi, M., Pizzi, C. and Valsecchi, V. (2006) Water management and land use in the terramare and a possible climatic co-factor in their abandonment: The case study of the terramara S. Rosa (Northern Italy). *Quaternary International* 151, 87–98.

Cremaschi, M. and Pizzi, C. (2011) Water resources in the Bronze Age villages (terramare) of the north Italian Po plain: Recent investigation at Terramara Santa Rosa di Poviglio. *Antiquity Project Gallery* [http://antiquity.ac.uk/projgall/cremaschi327/].

Cuozzo, M. (2015) Identità di genere, status e dialettica interculturale nelle necropoli della Campania al passaggio tra Prima Età del Ferro e Orientalizzante. In G. Saltini Semerari and G.-J. Burgers (eds) *Early Iron Age Communities of Southern Italy*, 102–117. Roma, Palombi Editore.

Cupitò, M., Dalla Longa, E., Donadel, V. and Leonardi, G. (2012) Resistances to the 12th century BC crisis in the Veneto region: The case studies of Fondo Paviani and Montebello Vicentino. In J. Kneisel, W. Kirleis, M. Dal Corso, N. Taylor and V. Tiedke (eds) *Collapse or Continuity? Environment and Development of Bronze Age Human Landscapes*, 55–70. Bonn, Verlag Dr. Rudolf Habelt GmbH.

d'Agostino, B. (1977) *Tombe Principesche dell'Orientalizzante Antico da Pontecagnano* (Monumenti Antichi 49, Serie Miscellanea 2/1). Roma, Accademia Nazionale dei Lincei.

Dal Corso, M., Marchesini, M., Leonardi, G. and Kirleis, W. (2012) Environmental changes and human impact during the Bronze Age in Northern Italy: On-site palynological investigation at Fondo Paviani, Verona. In J. Kneisel, W. Kirleis, M. Dal Corso, N. Taylor and V. Tiedke (eds) *Collapse or Continuity? Environment and Development of Bronze Age Human Landscapes*, 71–83. Bonn, Verlag Dr. Rudolf Habelt GmbH.

De Guio, A., Baldo, M., Balista, C., Bellintani, P. and Betto, A. (2009) Tele-Frattesina: Alla ricerca spettrale della complessità. *Padusa* 45, 133–168.

de Marinis, R.C. (2010) Continuity and discontinuity in Northern Italy from the Recent to the Final Bronze Age: A view from North-Western Italy. *Scienze dell'Antichità* 15[2009], 535–545.

Di Anastasio, G. (2010) La serie stratigrafica: Osservazioni geoarchaeologiche. In L. Salzani and C. Colonna (eds) *La Fragilità dell'Urna. I Recenti Scavi a Narde, Necropoli di Frattesina (XII-IX sec. a.C.). Catalogo della Mostra (Museo dei Grandi Fiumi, Rovigo, 5 Ottobre 2007-30 Marzo 2008)*, 35–49. Rovigo, Museo dei Grandi Fiumi.

Dietler, M. (1995) Early "Celtic" socio-political relations: Ideological representation and social competition in dynamic comparative perspective. In B. Arnold and D. Blair Gibson (eds) *Celtic Chiefdom, Celtic State. The Evolution of Complex Social Systems in Prehistoric Europe*, 64–72. Cambridge, Cambridge University Press.

Dobres, M.-A. and Robb, J. (2000) (eds) *Agency in Archaeology*. London, Routledge.

Drummond, A. (2008[1990]) Rome in the fifth century II: The citizen community. In F.W. Walbank, A.E. Astin, M.W. Frederiksen and R.M. Ogilvie (eds) *The Cambridge Ancient History Volume 7, Part 2. The Rise of Rome to 220 BC*, 172–242. Cambridge, Cambridge University Press (online edition).

Eles, P. von (2007) (ed.) *Le Ore e i Giorni delle Donne. Dalla Quotidianità alla Sacralità tra VIII e VII Secolo a.C.. Catalogo della Mostra (Museo Civico Archeologico di Verucchio, 14 Giugno 2007-6 Gennaio 2008)*. Verucchio, Pazzini Editore.

Foucault, M. (1991) *Discipline and Punish: The Birth of the Prison*. London, Penguin.

Foucault, M. (1998) *The History of Sexuality: The Will to Knowledge*. London, Penguin.

Fowler, C. (2004) *The Archaeology of Personhood. An Anthropological Approach*. London, Routledge.

Frontini, P. (2009) *Contributo allo Studio delle Cause della Fine della Cultura Palafitticolo-terramaricola*. Unpublished thesis, Università degli Studi di Padova [http://paduaresearch.cab.unipd.it/1615/].

Fulminante, F. (2003) *Le Sepolture Principesche nel Latium Vetus. Tra la Fine della Prima Età del Ferro e l'Inizio dell'Età Orientalizzante*. Roma, "L'Erma" di Bretschneider.

Fulminante, F. (2014) *The Urbanization of Latium Vetus: From the Bronze Age to the Archaic Era*. Cambridge, Cambridge University Press.

Gamba, M., Gambacurta, G., Ruta Serafini, A., Tiné, V. and Veronese, F. (2013) (eds) *Venetkens. Viaggio nelle Terra dei Veneti Antichi. Catalogo della Mostra (Padova, Palazzo della Ragione, 6 Aprile-17 Novembre 2013)*. Venezia, Marsilio.

Gamba, M., Gambacurta, G. and Ruta Serafini, A. (2014) (eds) *La Prima Padova. Le Necropoli di Palazzo Capodilista-Tabacchi e di Via Tiepolo-Via San Massimo tra il IX e l'VIII a.C.*. Padova, La Tipografica.

Gangemi, G., Bassetti, M. and Voltolini, D. (2015) (eds) *Le Signore dell'Alpago: La Necropoli Preromana di "Pian de la Gnela". Pieve di Alpago (Belluno)*. Treviso, Canova.

Gardner, A. (2004) (ed.) *Agency Uncovered: Archaeological Perspectives on Social Agency, Power, and Being Human*. Walnut Creek, Left Coast Press.

Gaventa, J. (2003) *Power after Lukes: A Review of the Literature*. Brighton, Institute of Development Studies.

Gaventa, J. (2006) Finding the spaces for change; A power analysis. *IDS Bulletin* 37(5), 23–33.

Gell, A. (1998) *Art and Agency*. Oxford, Clarendon Press.

Giddens, A. (1984) *The Constitution of Society. Outline of the Theory of Structuration*. Cambridge, Polity Press.

Gleba, M. (2008) *Textile Production in Pre-Roman Italy*. Oxford, Oxbow Books.

Gleba, M. (2015) Women and textile production in Early Iron Age Southern Italy. In G. Saltini Semerari and G.-J. Burgers (eds) *Early Iron Age Communities of Southern Italy*, 103–117. Roma, Palombi Editore.

Gledhill, J. (1988) Introduction: The comparative study of social and political transitions. In J. Gledhill, B. Bender and M.T. Larsen (eds) *State and Society: The Emergence and Development of Social Hierarchy and Political Centralisation*, 1–29. London, Allen and Unwin.

Gosden, C. and Marshall, Y. (1999) The cultural biography of objects. *World Archaeology* 31 (2), 169–178.

Gowland, R. and Knüsel, C. (2006) *Social Archaeology of Funerary Remains*. Oxford, Oxbow Books.

Guidi, A. (2010) The archaeology of early state in Italy: New data and acquisitions. *Social Evolution and History* 9(2), 12–27.

Harke, H. (1990) Warrior graves? The background of the Anglo-Saxon burial rite. *Past and Present* 126(1), 22–43.

Hayward, C.R. (1998) De-facing power. *Polity* 31(1), 1–22.

Hodder, I. (2012) *Entangled. An Archaeology of the Relationships between Humans and Things*. Chichester, Wiley-Blackwell.

Johnson, A.W. and Earle, T.K. (1987). *The Evolution of Human Societies: From Foraging Group to Agrarian State*. Stanford, Stanford University Press.

Joy, J. (2009) Reinvigorating object biography: Reproducing the drama of object lives. *World Archaeology* 41(4), 540–556.

Kamp, K.A. (2001) Where have all the children gone? The archaeology of childhood. *Journal of Archaeological Method and Theory* 8, 1–34.

Knapp, A.B. and van Dommelen, P. (2008) Past practices: Rethinking individuals and agents in archaeology. *Cambridge Archaeological Journal* 18(1), 15–34.

Lamb, S. (1997) The making and unmaking of persons: Notes on aging and gender in north India. *Ethos* 25(3), 279–302.

Leonardi, G. (2010) Le premesse alla formazione dei centri protourbani del Veneto. *Scienze dell'Antichità* 15[2009], 547–562.

Lukes, S. (2005[1974]) *Power: A Radical View*. London, McMillian.

Martin, D.L., Harrod, R.P. and Pérez, V.R. (2013) *Bioarchaeology: An Integrated Approach to Working with Human Remains*. New York, Springer.

Mauss, M. (1985[1938]) A category of the human mind: The notion of person; the notion of self. In M. Carrithers, S. Collins and S. Lukes (eds) *The Category of the Person*, 1–25. Cambridge, Cambridge University Press.

Mines, M. (1988) Conceptualizing the person: Hierarchical society and individual autonomy in India. *American Anthropologist* 90(3), 568–579.

Myers, A.T. (2007) Portable material culture and death factory Auschwitz. *Papers from the Institute of Archaeology* 18, 57–69.

Moore, J. and Scott, E.C. (1997) (eds) *Invisible People and Processes: Writing Gender and Childhood into European Archaeology*. London–New York, Leicester University Press.

Morgan, L.M. (1997) Imagining the unborn in the Ecuadoran Andes. *Feminist Studies* 23(2), 323–350.

Morgan, L.M. (2002[1989]) When does life begin? A cross-cultural perspective on the personhood of fetuses and young children. In W.A. Haviland, R.J. Gordon and L.A. Vivanco (eds) *Talking About People: Readings in Contemporary Cultural Anthropology*, 35–46. Boston, McGraw-Hill.

Morgan, L.M. (2006) "Life begins when they steal your bicycle": Cross-cultural practices of personhood at the beginnings and ends of life. *Journal of Law, Medicine & Ethics* 34(2), 193–218.

Morgan, L.M. (2009) *Icons of Life: A Cultural History of Human Embryos*. Berkeley, University of California Press.

Navarro, Z. (2006) In search of a cultural interpretation of power: The contribution of Pierre Bourdieu. *IDS Bulletin* 37(6), 11–22.

Nizzo, V. (2011) (ed.) *Dalla Nascita alla Morte: Antropologia e Archeologia a Confronto. Atti dell'Incontro Internazionale di Studi in Onore di Claude Lévi-Strauss (Roma, Museo Nazionale Preistorico Etnografico "Luigi Pigorini", 21 Maggio 2010)*. Roma, E.S.S. Editorial Service System.

Pacific Affairs (2011) *Experiencing the State: Marginalized People and the Politics of Development in Contemporary India. Pacific Affairs Special Issue* 84(1).

Parker Pearson, M. (1999) *The Archaeology of Death and Burial*. Stroud, Sutton.

Pearce, M. (1998) New research on the terramare of northern Italy. *Antiquity* 72, 743–746.

Pellegrino Sutcliffe, M. (2015) Italian women in the making: Re-reading the *Englishwoman's Review* (c. 1871–1889). In N. Carter (ed.) *Britain, Ireland and the Italian Risorgimento*, 179–203. London, Palgrave Macmillan.

Perego, E. (2011) Engendered actions: Agency and ritual in pre-Roman Veneto. In A. Chaniotis (ed.) *Ritual Dynamics in the Ancient Mediterranean: Agency, Emotion, Gender, Reception*, 17–42. Stuttgart, Steinar.

Perego, E. (2012a) *The Construction of Personhood in Veneto (Italy) between the Late Bronze Age and the Early Roman Period*. Unpublished thesis, University College London.

Perego, E. (2012b) Family relationships in late Bronze Age, Iron Age and early Roman Veneto (Italy). Preliminary considerations on the basis of osteological analysis and epigraphy. In R. Lawrence and A. Stromberg (eds) *Families in the Greco-Roman World*, 121–142. London, Continuum.

Perego, E. (2014a) Anomalous mortuary behaviour and social exclusion in Iron Age Italy: A case study from the Veneto region. *Journal of Mediterranean Archaeology* 27(2), 161–185.

Perego, E. (2014b) Final Bronze Age and social change in Veneto: Group membership, ethnicity and marginality. *Mélanges de l'École française de Rome* 126(2) (online version).

Perego, E., Saracino, M., Zamboni, L. and Zanoni, V. (2015) Practices of ritual marginalisation in protohistoric Veneto: Evidence from the field. In Z.L. Devlin and E.J. Graham (eds) *Death Embodied: Archaeological Approaches to the Treatment of the Corpse*, 129–159. Oxford, Oxbow Books.

Perego, E., Scopacasa, R. and Amicone, S. (2014) Collapse or survival? Micro-dynamics of crisis following disaster events in northern Italy, 1200-400 BC. Poster presented at LAC 2014. Royal Netherlands, Belgian and Swedish Institutes in Rome.

Perego, E., Scopacasa, R. and Amicone, S. (2015) Collapse or survival? Theoretical and methodological approaches to micro-dynamics of crisis in the late prehistoric and early Roman central Mediterranean. Lecture delivered at the CRASIS Annual Meeting – "Crisis! The Identification, Analysis and Commemoration of Crises in the Ancient World". University of Groningen.

Peretto, R. (2010) Villaggi e vie d'acqua. In L. Salzani and C. Colonna (eds) *La Fragilità dell'Urna. I Recenti Scavi a Narde, Necropoli di Frattesina (XII-IX sec. a.C.). Catalogo della Mostra (Museo dei Grandi Fiumi, Rovigo, 5 Ottobre 2007-30 Marzo 2008)*, 13–19. Rovigo, Museo dei Grandi Fiumi.

Piovan, S. (2008) *Evoluzione Paleoidrografica della Pianura Veneta Meridionale e Rapporto Uomo-Ambiente nell'Olocene*. Unpublished thesis, Università degli Studi di Padova [http://paduaresearch.cab.unipd.it/893/1/tesi_10.pdf].

Piovan, S., Mozzi, P. and Stefani, C. (2010) Bronze Age paleohydrography of the southern Venetian plain. *Geoarchaeology* 25(1), 6–35.

Powercube (2011) *Powercube: Understanding Power for Social Change.* Online resource by The Participation, Power and Social Change team at the Institute of Development Studies, University of Sussex [http://www.powercube.net/].

Rabinow, P. (1991) (ed.) *The Foucault Reader: An Introduction to Foucault's Thought.* London, Penguin.

Rajala, U. (2014) Biographies of tombs and the metaphorical representations of the *crustumini*: Remembering the Dead project and the funerary excavations at Cisterna Grande at Crustumerium 2004–2008. In A.J. Nijboer, S.L. Willemsen, P.A.J. Attema and J.F. Seubers (eds) *Research into Pre-Roman Burial Grounds in Italy* (Caeculus: Papers in Mediterranean Archaeology and Greek & Roman Studies), 63–81. Leuven, Peeters.

Riva, C. (2010) *The Urbanisation of Etruria: Funerary Ritual and Social Change, 700-600 BC.* Cambridge, Cambridge University Press.

Saltini Semerari, G. (2009) Heroic status for women in Basilicata: The adoption and adaptation of Greek ideology in Southern Italy. *Accordia Research Papers* 11, 119–135.

Saltini Semerari, G. (2015) Towards a gendered Basilicata. In G. Saltini Semerari and G.-J. Burgers (eds) *Early Iron Age Communities of Southern Italy*, 91–101. Roma, Palombi Editore.

Salzani, L (2005) (ed.) *La Necropoli dell'Età del Bronzo all'Olmo di Nogara.* Verona, Museo Civico di Storia Naturale.

Salzani, L. (2010a) La necropoli di Narde a Fratta Polesine. Ricerche nell'area sepolcrale di Narde II. In L. Salzani and C. Colonna (eds) *La Fragilità dell'Urna. I Recenti Scavi a Narde, Necropoli di Frattesina (XII-IX sec. a.C.). Catalogo della Mostra (Museo dei Grandi Fiumi, Rovigo, 5 Ottobre 2007-30 Marzo 2008)*, 21–33. Rovigo, Museo dei Grandi Fiumi.

Salzani, L. (2010b) Considerazioni. In L. Salzani and C. Colonna (eds) *La Fragilità dell'Urna. I Recenti Scavi a Narde, Necropoli di Frattesina (XII-IX sec. a.C.). Catalogo della Mostra (Museo dei Grandi Fiumi, Rovigo, 5 Ottobre 2007-30 Marzo 2008)*, 295–304. Rovigo, Museo dei Grandi Fiumi.

Salzani, L. and Colonna, C. (2010) (eds) *La Fragilità dell'Urna. I Recenti Scavi a Narde, Necropoli di Frattesina (XII-IX sec. a.C.). Catalogo della Mostra (Museo dei Grandi Fiumi, Rovigo, 5 Ottobre 2007-30 Marzo 2008).* Rovigo, Museo dei Grandi Fiumi.

Saracino, M. (2009) Sepolture atipiche durante il Bronzo Finale e la seconda Età del Ferro in Veneto. *Padusa* 45, 65–72.

Saracino, M., Zamboni, L., Zanoni, V. and Perego, E. (2014) Investigating social exclusion in late prehistoric Italy: Preliminary results of the "IN or OUT" Project (Phase 1). *Papers from the Institute of Archaeology* 12(1), 1–12.

Saracino, M. and Zanoni, V. (2014) The marginal people of the Iron Age in north-eastern Italy: A comparative study. i.e. The Iron age written by the losers. *Revue Archéologique de l'Est (36e Supplément)*, 535–550.

Scopacasa, R. (2014) Gender and ritual in ancient Italy: A quantitative approach to grave goods and skeletal evidence in pre-Roman Samnium. *American Journal of Archaeology* 118(2), 241–266.

Scott, J.C. (1985) *Weapons of the Weak: Everyday Forms of Resistance.* New Haven–London, Yale University Press.

Scott, J.C. (1992) *Domination and the Arts of Resistance: Hidden Transcripts.* New Haven–London, Yale University Press.

Scott, J.C. (2009) *The Art of Not Being Governed: An Anarchist History of Upland Southeast Asia.* New Haven–London, Yale University Press.

Sofaer Derevenski, J. (2000) (ed.) *Children and Material Culture.* London–New York, Routledge.

Tamura, E.H. (2008) (ed.) *The History of Discrimination in U.S. Education. Marginality, Agency, and Power.* London, Palgrave McMillan UK.

Terrenato, N. (2011) The versatile clans: Archaic Rome and the nature of early city states in central Italy. In N. Terrenato and D. Haggis (eds) *State Formation in Italy and Greece: Questioning the Neoevolutionist Paradigm*, 231–244. Oxford, Oxbow Books.

Terrenato, N. and Haggis, D. 2011 (eds) *State Formation in Italy and Greece. Questioning the Neoevolutionist Paradigm.* Oxford, Oxbow Books.

Thomas, J. (1996) *Time, Culture and Identity: An Interpretative Archaeology.* London, Routledge.

VeneKlasen, L. and Miller, V. (2002) *A New Weave of Power, People and Politics: The Action Guide for Advocacy and Citizen Participation.* Oklahoma City, World Neighbors.

Voltolini, D. (2013) Tomba Emo 468. In M. Gamba, G. Gambacurta, A. Ruta Serafini, V. Tiné and F. Veronese (eds) Venetkens. *Viaggio nella Terra dei Veneti Antichi. Catalogo della Mostra (Padova, Palazzo della Ragione, 6 Aprile–17 Novembre 2013)*, 351. Venezia, Marsilio.

Wagner, R. (1991) The fractal person. In M. Godelier and M. Strathern (eds) *Big Men and Great Men: Personifications of Power in Melanesia*, 159–173 Cambridge, Cambridge University Press.

Waldron, T. (2009) *Paleopathology.* Cambridge, Cambridge University Press.

Whitehouse, R.D. (1998) (ed.) *Gender and Italian Archaeology: Challenging the Stereotypes.* London, Accordia Research Institute and Institute of Archaeology, University College London.

Whitehouse, R.D. (2015) Investigating gender in the Italian Iron Age. In G. Saltini Semerari and G.-J. Burgers (eds) *Early Iron Age Communities of Southern Italy*, 133–147. Roma, Palombi Editore.

Winter, W.S. (2004) *Winter Time: Memoirs of a German who Survived Auschwitz.* Hatfield (UK), University of Hertfordshire Press.

Zanoni, V. (2011) *Out of Place. Human Skeletal Remains from Non-Funerary Contexts: Northern Italy during the 1st Millennium BC* (BAR S2306). Oxford, Archaeopress.

INDEX